Mc Graw Hill

学术英语能力系列

华研外语
TOPWAYENGLISH

WRITING MATTERS

A Handbook for Writing and Research

美国大学写作与研究

[美]丽贝卡·摩尔·霍华德 著

世界图书出版公司

广州·上海·西安·北京

U0652499

Preface 前言

对国内英语及相关专业学生以及需要发表英文论文的职场人士来说，如何撰写英语学术论文是一堂必修课，这是求学和职场晋升中绕不开的难题。而对于有志于留学的学生来说，无论所学是哪个专业，用英语做学术研究与撰写论文的能力就更为重要了。但对于非英语母语学习者来说，撰写英语学术论文包括以下几大难题：缺乏批判性思维训练，不知如何选题；不知道如何查找文献，筛选有效信息；不懂论文格式规范；缺乏学术英语基础，用词口语化；缺少英语语言能力，语法硬伤多等等。

针对非英语母语学习者的这些问题，《美国大学写作与研究》（*Writing Matters: A Handbook for Writing and Research*）提出了相应的解决方案。本书引进自美国知名教育出版社，是一本百科全书式的学术论文写作指南。全书分为12个部分、61章，分别针对论文写作流程、选题、规划布局、搜集资料、各类文献引用格式、语言风格、语法知识、标点符号等进行讲解。在知识点讲解后，用"专业范文"（Professional Model）及"学生范文"（Student Model）作为实例供参考对比。本书既可作为工具书查阅，也可作为课堂教学和自学教材。

- 第一部分介绍论文写作者的责任，指导如何避免"剽窃"。
- 第二部分介绍论文写作的基本流程，以及各个流程要注意的问题。
- 第三部分指导如何对论文进行规划布局，介绍如何在论文中使用图片、表格、多媒体等元素为论文增色。
- 第四部分比较了不同学科的学术论文特点，重点讲述了文学类学术论文的写作特点。
- 第五部分指导学术论文的选题和搜集、筛选以及引用资料等注意事项。
- 第六至八部分分别介绍MLA、APA、Chicago Style和CSE Style这四种文献引用格式的具体规范。
- 第九至十二部分针对非英语母语学习者而设，分别就论文写作中的语言行文风格、措辞语法错误、标点符号细节语言问题给出建议。

本书还具有以下特色

一、双范文指导

二、5大特色版块

负责任地写作：提示如何避免"剽窃"

Writing Responsibly — Taking Yourself Seriously as a Writer

Many students enter writing classes thinking of themselves as "bad writers." This belief can be a self-fulfilling prophecy: Students fail to engage because they already believe they are doomed to fail. You can escape from this vicious circle by remembering that writing is not an inborn talent, but rather a skill to be learned. Instead of thinking of yourself as a bad writer, think of yourself as a writer-in-progress, someone who has something to say and who is learning how to say it effectively. If you speak or have studied another language, think of yourself as someone who is learning to draw on that experience.

to SELF

快速查阅：重要概念、技巧、策略的归纳总结

Quick Reference — Analyzing the Purpose of an Assignment

If the assignment asks you to . . .	The purpose is . . .	The approach is . . .
describe, explain	informative (expository)	to put into words what something looks, sounds, feels, smells, or tastes like; to discuss how something functions
assess, evaluate, argue	persuasive	to make a judgment based on evidence or offer an interpretation based on close reading, and to explain why
analyze, consider, discuss	informative or persuasive	to break a topic, reading assignment, or issue into its component parts and explain how it works; to reflect critically on the pros and cons of an issue, offer an interpretation based on a close reading, and sometimes explain why you have reached this conclusion

---

自我评测：

简易检查清单，方便自检和修订论文

Self Assessment

As you revise your argument, consider the following issues. If your answer to any of these questions is no, revise as necessary.

□ **Claim.** Do you take a position based on an opinion or belief on which reasonable people could disagree? Have you modified the claim to avoid making it stronger than you can effectively support?

□ **Evidence.** Do you supply evidence in support of your claim? Do you use rational appeals that are appropriate to your topic, purpose, and audience? Where appropriate, do you make emotional appeals that are supported by evidence and use visuals to support your claim?

□ **Counterevidence.** Have you acknowledged alternative interpretations of your evidence? Have you explained why your position is the most reasonable despite these objections?

□ **Organization.** Have you followed an appropriate model of argument, such as classical, Rogerian, or Toulmin? Is the organizational structure appropriate to your overall aim—persuasion or exploration?

□ **Ethos.** Have you established your credibility by avoiding fallacies and providing evidence from reliable sources, treating those with whom you disagree respectfully, and revising, editing, and proofreading with care?

技术帮助：提醒在使用网络技术写作时要注意的问题

Tech — Grammar Checkers and Verb Problems

Grammar checkers in word processing programs will spot some errors that involve irregular or missing verbs, verb endings, and the subjunctive mood, but they will miss other errors and may suggest incorrect solutions. You must look for verb errors yourself and carefully evaluate any suggestions from a grammar checker.

EFL提示：针对非英语母语学习者的语言提示

Modal Verbs English modal verbs have a range of meanings and unusual grammatical characteristics that you may find challenging. For example, they do not change form to indicate number or tense.

▶ In a close election, one vote ~~cans~~ make a difference.
    can

三、人性化的查阅指引

...se to your purpose, audience, context, and medium; ...end you may ignore the conventions of punctuation ...for example, but you would not do so when writing

...focuses on print literacy because it remains cen-...resses digital, visual, oral, and information literacies ...become impossible to separate from one another ...al print literacy. As a reader, you must be able not ...ritten language but also to interpret visuals, drawing ...ertisements, for example, and subjecting them to ...l shopper. As a writer, you may incorporate graphics ...nomics and psychology, contribute to class blogs or ...entations using Prezi. As both a reader and a writer, ...ed to manage all the information you receive and ...ultiliterate *means* being information literate.

▶ **More about**
Writing business documents, 56–59
Creating PowerPoints, 64–65
Creating websites, 59–60
Writing in literature, 88–98
Reading critically, 7–13
Interpreting visuals, 11
Incorporating visuals, 54–55
Searching online databases, 109–11
Searching library catalogs, 112–13
Searching the Internet, 106–08

侧栏导航

页眉导航

The Writer's Responsibilities 写作者的责任   2c   5

Writing Responsibly — Your Responsibilities as a Writer

When you write, you have four areas of responsibility:
1. To your audience   3. To other writers
2. To your topic   4. To yourself

引进版主要修订

本书在引进时对内容主要做了以下修订：

● 书中各级标题增加中文翻译，侧栏中关键词增加中文释义。

● 删减或替换原版的部分图片。

Contents 目 录

A Menu of Resources 资源总览

▶ EFL Notes 对非英语母语学习者的提示

▶ Self-Assessment 自我评测

▶ Tech 技术帮助

1
Writing 负责任地写作
Responsibly
Tools for the Information Age 信息化时代的工具

*Use part 1 to learn, practice, and master these **writer's responsibilities:***

❏ **To Audience**

Focus on a topic readers will find engaging, provide persuasive reasons and evidence, choose reliable sources, fulfill readers' expectations of the genre, avoid bias and treat others with respect, and use language clearly, correctly, logically, and with flair.

❏ **To Topic**

Support your claims with logical reasons and solid evidence from relevant and reliable sources and consider alternative viewpoints and evidence, even when they undermine your claims.

❏ **To Other Writers**

Acknowledge borrowed words and ideas, and represent the ideas of others fairly and accurately.

❏ **To Yourself**

Select a topic you find engaging, synthesize information from sources to produce fresh ideas, and create a persona that reflects your best self.

Writing Today 当下的写作

"I just can't write." We've all heard the lament; most of us have uttered it at least once. Some mistakenly believe that just as some people have an "ear" for music, so others have an inborn "gift" for writing. In truth, though, no one is a born writer. There are no three-year-old children who are amazing writers. Expert writing comes from training—it is not a "gift." Writing is a skill that is learned and practiced.

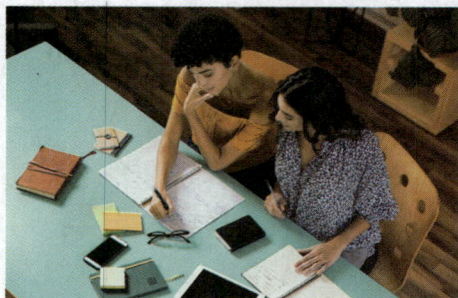

Successful writing holds out the promise of self-expression, even self-discovery. It is also a valuable asset in the workplace: A report from the National Commission on Writing revealed that U.S. corporations expect their salaried employees to be able to write clearly, correctly, and logically. Eighty percent of finance, insurance, and real estate employers take writing skills into consideration when making their hiring decisions.

Whether texting a friend or composing a paper for a college course, we write to develop and evaluate beliefs and ideas, to move others, to express ourselves, and to explore possibilities. For all these reasons and more, writing matters.

1a The Expanding Definition of Literacy 广义的读写能力

Long before Johannes Gutenberg introduced the printing press in the fifteenth century, a *page* was seen as a sheet of paper covered with text, and *literacy* meant the ability to read and write a text, whether written on the page or carved in stone. With the spread of literacy has come the spread of information, which has led to improvements in health and productivity. The ability to read is needed to understand the safety warnings on medication inserts and to check the ingredients on a jar of baby food. The ability to write is needed to craft and convey documents ranging from emergency plans to instructions for assembling shelving from Ikea. More importantly, the spread of literacy has strengthened our democratic institutions. Without news reports and a wide audience to read them, the decisions of politicians could go unchallenged, and voters would have little idea of a candidate's positions. These are just a few of the many reasons our society values print literacy.

But just as the Internet revolution changes our understanding of what a page is, it also expands our concept of literacy (Figure 1.1). Today, a page can be a sheet of paper, but it can also be a website on a screen or an email on a smartphone. It can include not only words, but also images and sound files, links to other web pages, and animations.

FIGURE 1.1 The media revolution In the fifteenth century, few could read (or had access to) the Gutenberg Bible. Today, readers can view its pages on their phones, but to do so they must be multiliterate: Not only must they be able to read and write, but they must also know how to access multiple media online.

1b Multiliteracies and Print Literacy
多模态读写能力与纸媒读写能力

Like most people reading this book, you are probably already multi-literate: You "code shift," switching from medium to medium easily, because the "literacies" required for each medium are not entirely separate. Whether penning a thank-you note, searching a library database, composing a college paper, or texting your best friend, you adjust your message in response to your purpose, audience, context, and medium: When texting a friend you may ignore the conventions of punctuation and capitalization, for example, but you would not do so when writing a résumé.

This handbook focuses on print literacy because it remains central, yet it also addresses digital, visual, oral, and information literacies because they have become impossible to separate from one another and from traditional print literacy. As a reader, you must be able not only to decipher written language but also to interpret visuals, drawing meaning from advertisements, for example, and subjecting them to the scrutiny of a careful shopper. As a writer, you may incorporate graphics into papers in economics and psychology, contribute to class blogs or Twitter discussions, search online databases and electronic library catalogs, or create presentations using Prezi. As both a reader and a writer, you will be expected to manage all the information you receive and transmit. Being multiliterate *means* being information literate.

> **More about**
> Writing business
>   documents,
>   55-58
> Creating Power-
>   Points, 63–64
> Creating websites,
>   58–59
> Writing in litera-
>   ture, 87–97
> Reading critically,
>   9–15
> Interpreting
>   visuals, 13
> Incorporating
>   visuals, 53–54
> Searching online
>   databases,
>   108–10
> Searching library
>   catalogs, 110–11
> Searching the
>   Internet, 106–07

2 The Writer's Responsibilities 写作者的责任

Your opportunities to express and even create yourself in words come with responsibilities. Like the palm fronds being woven into a basket in the photograph, your responsibilities as a writer are intertwined and difficult to tease apart. They include the responsibilities you have to your readers, to the topics you address, to the other writers from whom you borrow and to whom you respond, and perhaps especially to yourself as a writer with ideas and ideals to express.

2a Understanding Your Responsibilities to Your Audience 明白你对受众的责任

Audience members make a commitment to you by spending their time reading your work. To help them feel that this commitment was worthwhile, you can do the following:

◆ Choose a topic that your audience will find interesting and about which you have something you want to say.

◆ Make a claim that will help your audience follow your thoughts.

◆ Support your claim with thoughtful, logical, even creative evidence drawn from sources that you have evaluated carefully for relevance and reliability.

◆ Write clearly so that your audience (even if that audience is your composition teacher) does not have to struggle to understand. To write clearly, build a logical structure; use transitional techniques to guide readers; and correct errors of grammar, punctuation, and spelling.

◆ Write appropriately by using a tone and vocabulary that are right for your *rhetorical situation*—your topic, audience, context, and genre.

◆ Write engagingly by varying sentence structures and word choices, avoiding wordiness, and using repetition only for special effect.

Most writers cannot accomplish all this in a first draft. They must revise thoughtfully and edit and proofread carefully to fulfill their responsibilities to their readers.

Writing Responsibly — Your Responsibilities as a Writer

When you write, you have four areas of responsibility:

1. To your audience
2. To your topic
3. To other writers
4. To yourself

2b Understanding Your Responsibilities to Your Topic
明白你对话题的责任

You treat your topic responsibly when you explore it thoroughly and creatively; rely on trustworthy sources; and offer supporting evidence that is accurate, relevant, and reliable. You treat your topic responsibly when you provide enough evidence to persuade readers of your claims and when you acknowledge evidence even when it does not support your position. In a college writing project, not fulfilling your responsibilities to your topic might lead to a bad grade. In the workplace, it could have great financial, even life-and-death consequences: The Merck pharmaceutical company, for example, was accused of suppressing evidence that its drug Vioxx could cause heart attacks and strokes. As a result, Merck faced a host of lawsuits, trials, and out-of-court settlements.

2c Understanding Your Responsibilities to Other Writers 明白对其他写作人的责任

You have important responsibilities to other writers whose work you may be using.

1. Acknowledge your sources 标明引用来源

Writing circulates easily today, and vast quantities of it are available online, readily accessible through search engines such as Google and databases such as JSTOR. It may seem natural, then, simply to copy the information you need from a website and paste it into your own text, as you might if you were collecting information about a disease you are facing or a concert you hope to attend. But when you provide readers with information, ideas, language, or images that others have collected or created, you have a responsibility to *acknowledge* those sources. Such acknowledgment gives credit to those who contributed to your thinking, and it allows your audience to read your sources for themselves. Acknowledging your sources also protects you from charges of plagiarism, and it builds your authority and credibility as a writer by establishing that you have reviewed key sources on a topic and taken other writers' views into consideration.

To acknowledge sources in academic writing, you must do *all three* of the following:

More about
When to quote, paraphrase, or summarize, 124–28
Using quotation marks, 448–53
Formatting block quotations, 165, 200, 449
Adjusting quotations using brackets and ellipses, 457–58, 460–61
Citing and documenting sources, 157–284
Avoiding plagiarism and patchwriting, 123–28, 136–55
Common knowledge, 123

Reference   Your College's Plagiarism Policy

Most colleges publish their plagiarism policies in their student handbook, which is often available online. **Find your plagiarism policy** by searching the student handbook's table of contents or index. Or search your college's website, using key terms such as *plagiarism, cheating policy, academic honesty,* or *academic integrity.* Before writing a research project, **read your school's plagiarism policy** carefully. If you are unsure what the policy means, talk with your adviser or instructor. In addition to the general policy for your college, **read your course syllabi** carefully to see which specific guidelines your instructors may provide there.

1. When quoting, copy accurately and use quotation marks or block indention to signal the beginning and end of the copied passage; when paraphrasing or summarizing, put the ideas fully into your own words and sentences.
2. Include an in-text citation to the source, whether you are quoting, paraphrasing, or summarizing.
3. Document the source, providing enough information for your readers to locate the source and to identify the type of source you used. This documentation usually appears in a bibliography (often called a list of works cited or a reference list) at the end of college research projects.

Writing Responsibly around the World Concepts of plagiarism vary from one culture to another. Where one may see cooperation, another may see plagiarism. Even if borrowing ideas and language without acknowledgment is a familiar custom for you, writers in the United States (especially in academic contexts) must explicitly acknowledge all ideas and information borrowed from another source.

2. Treat other writers fairly 公平对待其他写作者

Your responsibility to other writers does not end with the need to acknowledge your use of their ideas or language. You must also represent *accurately* and *fairly* what your sources say: Quoting selectively to distort meaning or taking a comment out of context is irresponsible. So is treating other writers with scorn.

It is perfectly acceptable to criticize the ideas of others. In fact, examining ideas under the bright light of careful scrutiny is central to higher education. But treating the people who developed the ideas with derision is not. Avoid *ad hominem* (personal) attacks, and focus your attention on other writers' ideas and their expression of them.

> **More about**
> Bias, 306–08
> *Ad hominem*, 81

2d Understanding Your Responsibilities to Yourself
明白对自己的责任

You have a responsibility to yourself as a writer. Writers represent themselves on paper and screen through the words and images (and

Writing **Responsibly** | Taking Yourself Seriously as a Writer

Many students enter writing classes thinking of themselves as "bad writers." This belief can be a self-fulfilling prophecy: Students fail to engage because they already believe they are doomed to fail. You can escape from this vicious circle by remembering that writing is not an inborn talent, but rather a skill to be learned. Instead of thinking of yourself as a bad writer, think of yourself as a writer-in-progress, someone who has something to say and who is learning how to say it effectively. If you speak or have studied another language, think of yourself as someone who is learning to draw on that experience.

to SELF

> **More about**
> Synthesis,
>   13–14, 133
> Common sentence
>   problems, tutorial
>   in part 10
> Style, 286–323
> Sentence gram-
>   mar, 331–404
> Punctuation and
>   mechanics,
>   433–80

even sounds) they create and borrow, so submitting as your own a paper that someone else has written is a form of impersonation—it does not represent you. Make sure that the writing "avatar," or *persona,* you create is the best representation of yourself it can be. Encourage readers to view you with respect by treating others—not only other writers but also other people and groups—without bias. Earn your audience's respect by synthesizing information from sources to produce new and compelling ideas and by using language clearly, correctly, logically, and with flair.

If you graduate from college having learned to be an effective writer, you will have learned something employers value highly. More importantly, though, you will have fulfilled a key responsibility to yourself.

2

Writing 关注写作流程

Matters

Planning, Writing, Editing 规划、写作、编辑

Use part 2 to learn, practice, and master these **writer's responsibilities:**

❏ **To Audience**

Choose language that readers will find appropriate and compelling; craft paragraphs and writing projects that readers will find relevant, unified, and coherent; integrate source material fully; and revise, edit, and proofread to provide readers with a worthwhile reading experience.

❏ **To Topic**

Fully engage with texts so that you can put source material in context and respond creatively, devise thesis statements that encourage insight into your topic, develop solid reasons of your own, and provide evidence from sources to support your ideas.

❏ **To Other Writers**

Understand fully what you have read in other sources and represent the ideas of other writers accurately.

❏ **To Yourself**

Get as much as you can from your reading, consider your writing situation and assignment so you can meet your goals, choose a topic that engages your interest, and manage your time to create a text that is a reflection of your best self.

3 Reading Critically 批判性阅读

When you read critically, you peel back a text to uncover its meaning. You begin with comprehension, just getting the gist of a text. Next comes reflection, when you annotate and analyze the text. As you prepare to write, you explore not only what is written but also what is left unstated, and you draw on your own experience and other texts to hone your evaluation. The process of peeling back a text, as you would the layers of an onion, is what drives and deepens the intellectual process.

3a Comprehending the Text 理解文本

Most of the texts you read in college were written to inform or educate you about an issue or topic. They may also have a secondary purpose: to persuade you to accept a position on that issue or topic. Because most college-level reading assignments attempt to engage you in the complexities of an issue, you should read the text several times. In your first reading, focus on getting the gist of, or *comprehending*, the text:

- Preview the text by noting the title, subtitle, and headings; reading the abstract (or *summary*), introduction, and conclusion; noting the key terms, usually indicated in italic or boldface type; and scanning illustrations and captions.

> **More about**
> Summarizing,
> 126–28
> Drafting a thesis,
> 23–24, 131–32

- Read the text, circling words or phrases to look up later, determining the author's main claim, or *thesis,* and identifying key supporting evidence.
- Summarize the text by restating the thesis and major supporting points accurately in your own words and sentences.

3b Reflecting on the Text 对文本进行思考

For many readers, the first step in coming to terms with a text is to *annotate* it—that is, to read it with a pencil in hand, making notes and adding responses directly on the page. For others, taking notes in a notebook or computer or discussing the text with a classmate or friend works best. Whatever techniques work for you, focus on the following when rereading a text:

- Look up unfamiliar words.
- Underline the most important, interesting, or difficult concepts, and return to these passages to consider their significance.

Writing Responsibly) **Engaging with What You Read**

When conducting research, you have a responsibility to engage with the texts you read. If you are struggling, begin by determining which barrier is keeping you from making a connection with the text: Is the language too challenging? Is the topic unfamiliar or too familiar? Is your concentration poor because you did not eat lunch? Then try to overcome the barrier: Use a dictionary to acquaint yourself with the unfamiliar vocabulary; consider the material as a primer or a recapituation of an important topic; eat a sandwich.

to TOPIC

Tech   **Annotating Online Texts**

As you conduct research, take notes on what you learn. Then use Track Changes or footnoting options to comment and the highlighting function to mark key ideas.

> *More about*
> Tone, 17–18, 74,
> 309–10
> Bias, 306–08

■ Note the writer's attitude, or *tone*—sarcastic, sincere, witty, shrill—and circle the words and phrases that convey it.

■ Consider what surprised or impressed you, whether the logic was sound, and what challenged your own assumptions. Note specifics in the text that prompted your reaction.

The annotations to the following newspaper article reflect one student's thoughts, insights, and struggles with the text. Michael Wedd's annotations define vocabulary, note reflections, and make connections.

Professional Model 专业范文 **Newspaper Article**

Tiny Bat Pits Green against Green

By MARIA GLOD
The Washington Post, October 22, 2009

GREENBRIER COUNTY, W.VA.—Workers atop mountain ridges are putting together 389-foot windmills with massive blades that will turn Appalachian breezes into energy. Retiree David Cowan is fighting to stop them.

Because of the bats.

Cowan, 72, a longtime caving fanatic who grew to love bats as he slithered through tunnels from Maine to Maui, is asking a federal judge in Maryland to halt construction of the Beech Ridge wind farm. The lawsuit pits Chicago-based Invenergy, a company that produces "green" energy, against environmentalists who say the cost to nature is too great.

The rare green vs. green case went to trial Wednesday in U.S. District Court in Greenbelt.

It is the first court challenge to wind power under the Endangered Species Act, lawyers on both sides say. With President Obama's goal of doubling renewable energy production by 2012, wind and solar farms are expanding rapidly. That has sparked battles to reach a balance between the benefits of clean energy and the impact on birds, bats, and even the water supply.

At the heart of the Beech Ridge case is the Indiana bat, a brownish-gray creature that weighs about as much as three pennies and, wings outstretched, measures about eight inches. A 2005 estimate concluded that there were 457,000 of them,

Annotations (margin notes):

How out of date is this material? Research what's happened since 2009.

Standard size for windmills?

Main claim

Why Maryland if the area in question is in West Virginia?

Rare? My instructor passed out 2 news articles about similar cases from other newspapers.

What is the Endangered Species Act? I will have to look it up!

Bats are dying regardless of windmills.

half the number in 1967, when they were first listed as endangered.

"Any kind of energy development is going to have environmental impacts that are going to concern somebody," said John D. Echeverria, a Vermont Law School professor who specializes in environmental law and isn't involved in the suit. "This has been an issue for the environmental community. They are enthusiastic; at the same time, they realize there are these adverse impacts."

adverse—unfavorable

Indiana bats hibernate in limestone caves within several miles of the wind farm, which would provide energy to tens of thousands of households. The question before the judge: Would the bats fly in the path of the 122 turbines that will be built along a 23-mile stretch of mountaintop?

Eric R. Glitzenstein, an attorney for the plaintiffs, said in his opening statement that both sides agree the windmills will kill more than 130,000 bats of all types over the next 20 years.

How many bats of all types will die of natural causes over the next 20 years? Some context would be helpful.

"The question comes down to whether there is some reason to think Indiana bats will escape that fate," he said. "The position of the defendants is, 'Let's roll the dice and see what happens.' We believe that the rolling-the-dice approach to the Endangered Species Act is not in keeping with what Congress had in mind."

This is the plaintiffs' argument.

Cowan and other plaintiffs, including the D.C.-based Animal Welfare Institute, support wind power as one way to mitigate climate change. But they say this setting, a lush rural area where coal and timber industries once dominated, is the wrong one.

mitigate—to make less harsh or hostile

They say Indiana bats are likely to fly near the turbines in the fall as they migrate to caves from forests, where they spend spring and summer. Some biologists who analyzed recordings at the site say they are nearly certain that Indiana bats made some of the calls.

Which biologists? How many of the calls are from Indiana bats? Sentence seems vague.

Any deaths would be a blow to a species that has been slow to rebound from the damage caused by pollution and human disturbance of their caves, partly because females have only one baby each year, the plaintiffs say.

Invenergy argues there is no sign that Indiana bats go to the ridge. When a consultant put up nets at or near the site in summer 2005 and 2006 to search for bats, no Indiana bats were captured. Some bat experts say that the females prefer lower areas when they have their young and that the ridge is too high. The company also stresses that there is no confirmed killing of an Indiana bat at any wind farm nationwide.

The "consultant" was paid by Invenergy and therefore could be biased.

Does that mean that other types of bats were captured?

"A $300 million, environmentally friendly, clean, renewable energy project waiting to serve 50,000 households is in limbo over a rare bat nobody has ever seen on the project site," Clifford J. Zatz, a lawyer at Crowell & Moring, which represents the wind farm, said in court.

Argument of the defense. Article reports both sides of the issue.

In an area scarred by mountaintop coal mining, company officials say, the wind farm is a friend to the environment. It also is bringing jobs to the region.

"We're a clean, green energy company," said Joseph Condo, vice president and general counsel. "The project will be able to deliver clean energy for years."

The project has twice survived challenges in the West Virginia Supreme Court, including complaints that it would mar the picturesque view. If the Greenbelt court does not intervene, the first set of 67 turbines is expected to be running next year. The state has required that bat and bird fatalities be tracked for three years. . . .

Brad Tuckwiller, a county commissioner who manages his family's 1,700-acre cattle farm not far from the ridge, is a supporter of the wind farm. When the project was proposed, he visited one of Invenergy's farms in Tennessee.

> *Why now being heard in Maryland? Because it's "the Greenbelt court"? What does "Greenbelt court" mean?*

"I know some of our citizens are upset, but I don't think it's about the bats. I think it's about the viewshed or fear," Tuckwiller said. "If America is going to have energy independence, we have to look at these alternative sources— solar, wind, geothermal—in addition to nuclear and coal."

To Cowan, the risk is too great. The house he and his wife built to be near West Virginia's caves has bat profiles on the windows. The napkin holder on the dining table is decorated with a bat. Their car has a bat bumper sticker.

"I think if the turbines kill one Indiana bat, that ought to end it," he said. "That ought to shut it down."

> *Opinion of a person who is affected by, but not involved in, the lawsuit.*

> *A bit patronizing, maybe?*

Maria Glod, "Tiny Bat Pits Green Against Green," *The Washington Post*, October 22, 2009. Copyright ©2009 The Washington Post. All rights reserved. Used by permission and protected by the Copyright Laws of the United states. The printing, copying, redistribution, or transmission of this Content without express written permission is prohibited.

> **More about**

3c Preparing to Write about the Text 准备写文本

To evaluate a text, you must analyze how it works by considering the following:

- The major claims and whether they are backed by evidence
- The type and quality of the evidence offered to support the claims
- The presence or absence of counterevidence
- The sources the author draws on (if any) and their reliability
- The organizational or rhetorical patterns (such as comparison-contrast or cause-effect) and their possible effects on the audience
- The rhetorical appeals used in the text: *logos* (rational, logical claims or evidence), *ethos* (showing the expertise or credibility of the author or the sources), or *pathos* (drawing on the audience's emotions or sympathy)
- The logical pattern, which provides information about the author's purpose. Exploratory arguments are likely to use **inductive logic,** citing particular examples and then drawing a general conclusion. Persuasive arguments are likely to use **deductive logic,** offering

generally accepted truths from which conclusions can be drawn about specific instances.

- The style or tone and what that reflects about the author's purpose or attitudes

After analyzing the text, *interpret* it by considering its significance or meaning and drawing conclusions about what may be below the surface. Use the following questions to help guide your interpretation:

- What assumptions does the writer make about the subject or audience? Why are such assumptions significant?

- What does the text omit (evidence, opposing views), and what might these omissions indicate?

- What conclusions can you draw about the author's attitude from the tone? Which motives can you infer from the author's background or previous publications?

- Who published this text or sponsored the research, and how might these sponsors influence the way the information, arguments, or evidence is presented?

- In what context was the text written—place, time, cultural environment—and how might this context have influenced the writer?

Writing Responsibly **Drawing Conclusions**

A conclusion is only as good as what it is based on. Conclusions based on facts are fair; those based on personal values and beliefs or on a faulty understanding of the text are apt to be one-sided and unfair. Aim for the former and avoid the latter.

to TOPIC

More about
Identifying bias and vested interests, 115–18
Interpreting, 87–90
Synthesizing, 133

Self Assessment   **Evaluating Visuals**

When evaluating visuals, consider the following questions. Return to these questions as you evaluate your draft and revise as needed.

Analysis

- What does the image depict in the foreground and background? When was the work created? Who produced or sponsored it? How do accompanying words (if any) affect your understanding?
- What is the artist's purpose, or goal?
- Who is the intended audience?
- What is the artist's attitude toward the subject?
- What values does the image assume or promote? Do they challenge or reinforce the values of the intended audience?
- Is something missing? Has the visual been cropped, for example, to elimi-

nate background? If so, how does this affect your understanding?

Synthesis

- What do you know about the time or place in which the image was created, and how does this affect your understanding?
- How is this image similar to or different from others that you know? Have you read or studied anything that could help you understand this visual?
- What knowledge or personal experiences do you have that might deepen your understanding?

Critique

- What, based on your analysis, were the artist's aims?
- Were the artist's aims achieved? Why or why not?

Writing **Responsibly** Understanding *Criticism*

In everyday speech, the word *criticism* is often used simply to mean "finding fault." But in academic disciplines, *criticism* means "evaluating a work's merits based on a careful and fair analysis." The ideal critic approaches a text skeptically yet with an open mind and provides evidence for the judgments she makes. You may be used to thinking about published texts as absolutely authoritative sources of information, but it is important for you to realize that *all* texts present only partial views that can always be challenged.

to AUDIENCE

College assignments often ask you to *synthesize*—to connect what you have read to ideas you have discussed in class or read about in other texts. To synthesize, ask yourself the following questions:

- What outside forces (historical events, socioeconomic forces, cultural shifts) might influence or underlie the text?
- What else have you read or experienced that this text may explain, illustrate, clarify, complicate, or contradict?
- What claims could these texts, taken together, provide evidence for?
- How is your understanding of a topic enhanced or your thinking changed by putting these texts together? What might others gain by seeing these texts together?
- What expertise or life experience does the writer bring to the topic?

A *critique* is a well-informed evaluation. It may be positive, negative, or a bit of both. A movie review, for example, is a critique; it provides readers with an evaluation, supported by evidence from the film, to help them decide whether to see it. As you prepare to critique a text, consider the following issues:

- What are the author's goals? Does she or he achieve them? Are they worth achieving?
- What are the writer's claims? Are you persuaded by them? Why or why not?
- How credible is the evidence? Is the evidence verifiable and relevant? Is the author's reasoning sound?

> **More about**
> Claims, 23–24,
>   73–75
> Evidence, 40,
>   75–76, 91
> Authority, 75
> Relevance, 114
> Reliability, 115–18
> Audience, 17, 100

Student Model 学生范文 **Critique of an Advertisement**

Michael Wedd uses analysis, interpretation, and synthesis as well as critique in his assessment of an advertisement designed to encourage energy conservation. As you read, consider whether Wedd fulfills his responsibility to his topic by analyzing the visual thoroughly and by supplying accurate and persuasive evidence to support his claim.

Michael Wedd

Professor Locke

English 102

18 Sept. 2016

Critique of an Advertisement

The explicit claim of the Keep America Beautiful ad from 1971 (Fig. 1) is that "Pollution hurts all of us," so everyone should "get involved" in helping to lessen it. The bold white letters set against the black background give the message force and a sense of urgency, and the photograph of a Native American shedding a tear for the degeneration of the land adds an emotional appeal.

Fig. 1. Advertisement for the Keep America Beautiful Campaign, 1971 ("Historic Campaigns," *Ad Council.* Advertising Council, n.d., www.adcouncil.org/Our-Campaigns/The-Classics /Pollution-Keep-America-Beautiful-Iron-Eyes-Cody.)

The implied connection between the Native American and his concern about pollution is implicitly contrasted with the attitude of most Americans, those people who have not yet gotten involved in the fight against pollution. (The television spot we saw in class makes this contrast explicit; it shows the Native American in traditional Indian dress weeping over pollution, while a white American man on a car-choked highway throws garbage out his car window.) Aldo Hendricks, my environmental studies teacher, called this ad a major influence in heightening awareness and generating support for the environmental movement.

By today's standards, the use of a Native American, wearing a feather in his long pigtails, seems stereotypical, and the assumption that Native Americans have a closer connection to the Earth also seems like bias (even though it is a positive bias). Despite this depiction, however, the ad is still powerful. The tear shed by Iron Eyes Cody reinforces the personal responsibility we each have to protect our environment.

4 Planning and Drafting Your Project
规划与初稿撰写

Before producing a new line of clothing or an automobile, designers sketch the product, planning and arranging the shapes before dressing them in colors and textures. Writers, too, begin with a plan. They take into account the writing situation (purpose, audience, topic, context, and genre), then sketch their ideas in words and arrange them in sentences and paragraphs. Both designers and writers sometimes erase initial ideas and revise early efforts. For both, until that first sketch is penned, the finished work is merely an idea.

4a Analyzing Your Writing Situation 分析写作情景

A first step in planning a writing project is to consider your *writing situation* (or *rhetorical situation*):

- What is your *purpose?* What might you accomplish with the text?
- Who is your *audience?* Who will be reading the text you produce, and why?
- What *topics* might interest them, and why? What information about the topic might the audience be expected already to know, and what might you need to explain?
- What *tone* is appropriate to your purpose and audience?
- What is the *context* (academic, business, personal) of your writing project, and what *genre* (or type) of writing will you produce (research report, résumé, Facebook status update)? How will your context and genre affect the way you write this project?

1. Purpose 目的

Student Models
Informative writing projects:
First Draft: "Issues with Alternative Energy," Michael Wedd, 26–28
"The Power of Wardrobe," Heather DeGroot, 246–54

Writers write for a variety of reasons, or *purposes*: to entertain, inform, or persuade an audience; or for the writer's own self-expression or learning.

To entertain. Entertaining your readers (by providing them with an engaging reading experience) is a goal that all writers share, but it is unlikely to be your primary purpose in academic or workplace writing.

To express feelings or beliefs. In *expressive* writing, an experience is often conveyed through *description*, and the language is richly evocative.

To inform. An *informative* (or *expository*) text may explain a concept, describe a sequence of events or a process, or analyze a relationship. Scientific, technical, journalistic, and business writing are typically informative.

Writing **Responsibly** | **Seeing and Showing the Whole Picture**

As a writer, you have a responsibility to look beyond your own experiences, beliefs, and self-interest. As you explore an issue, give thorough, respectful attention to interpretations that contradict or conflict with yours. Figure out what motivates the supporters of opposing positions. Consider whether your own opinion should be revised. Then, as you write, no matter which position you support in your text, let your audience see all the viewpoints and the reasons for them.

to AUDIENCE

To persuade or argue. Texts that try to convince readers to adopt beliefs or opinions or to take action have a *persuasive* (or *argumentative*) purpose.

To learn. As writers struggle to find the words to express a complex thought, they are actually struggling to understand the topic. Many college writing assignments are designed not only to have you practice your writing techniques but also to help you grasp the material you are writing about.

> **More about**
> Analyzing and crafting arguments, 73–86

2. Audience 受众

A text is seldom written for the writer alone. Rather, it is intended for an *audience.* Before putting fingers to keyboard, consider the characteristics of your audience, such as age and gender, occupation and interests, educational background, abilities, sexualities and identities, political or cultural affiliations, and ethnic or religious background. Then consider what will make your writing most effective for this audience:

- What information will your audience need to understand and appreciate what you are saying?
- What kinds of language, examples or evidence will be most effective?

> **Student Models**
> Persuasive writing projects:
> "Rethinking Alternative Energy," Michael Wedd, 45–49
> "Why Students Cheat," Tom Hackman, 81–86
> "My View on a Long-Lost but Timeless Poem," Jewel Andrews, 93–97
> "Holy Underground Comics, Batman!" Lydia Nichols, 202–11

3. Topic 主题

Frequently in college writing, a *topic,* or subject, will be assigned. When you are expected to devise your own topic, however, consider not only what will sustain your interest, but also what you have special insight into and what your reader will find intriguing and relevant.

4. Tone 语气

When you speak, your tone of voice, gestures, facial expressions, and body language all convey your attitude. Are you patient, annoyed, angry, pleasantly surprised? Writers also convey their attitude toward their readers and their subject through their *tone.* In writing, tone is conveyed primarily through *level of formality* and the *connotation* (emotional resonance) of the words you choose. To write at a formal level, use standard American English; avoid regionalisms (such as

> **More about**
> Level of diction, 293–98
> Connotation and denotation, 309–10, 313
> Regionalisms, colloquialisms, slang, online shortcuts, 304–05

y'all), colloquial language (such as *what up*), and slang (such as *hot* rather than *good* or *exciting*); and write in complete sentences (*Are you coming?* rather than just *Coming?*).

> **More about**
> Dictionaries for
>   English-language
>   learners, 316
> Writing in college,
>   67–72
> Considering
>   alternative view-
>   points, 76–77
> Business writing,
>   55–58

Recognizing Differences in Connotation A word in your first language may share a literal meaning with a word in another language but have a very different connotation. The word *ambition* ("eagerness for success"), for example, can be positive or negative in English; in Spanish, *ambición* is generally negative. If you are not sure how specific words are used by your prospective readers, consult a cross-language or bilingual dictionary or check with classmates, a writing tutor, or your instructor.

Most instructors will expect you to write at a fairly formal level and to adopt a measured tone. Shrill or sarcastic prose will suggest to your audience that your opinions spring from your heart and not your head. This does not mean that emotional topics are off limits in college writing or that you may not express your beliefs. Rather, you should look at all sides of an issue carefully before drawing a conclusion, and show respect for those with whom you disagree.

5. Context and genre 语境和体裁

The *context* (or setting) in which your text is to be read will affect all your writing decisions. So, too, will the *genre* (or type) of writing you produce. The contexts in which you are likely to write, now and in the future, are academic, business, public, and personal. Like academic writing, business and public writing generally adopt a formal level of diction. In business writing, use words with neutral connotations. In public writing, which ranges from blog posts to press releases and reports, you may sometimes use more impassioned language.

Whether you are writing a business email, a scientific report, a grant proposal, or a letter to the editor, the expectations readers have for this type, or genre, of writing will affect every choice you make, from whether to use the first person (*I*) to how to structure the text. If you are unfamiliar with the context and genre in which you will be writing, read several examples to determine what they have in common.

Writing Responsibly

Choosing an Engaging Topic

When devising a topic, ask yourself the following questions:

1. Is my topic timely or relevant?
2. Do I have something to add?
3. Is it worth reading (and writing) about?

Thinking critically about saturated topics (such as abortion and gun control) is difficult. Instead of articulating your own reasons, you can easily wind up offering a rehash of other people's positions.

The topics about which you can write most interestingly are those on which you have a distinctive perspective. Almost any eighteen-year-old can write passionately about the drinking age, for example, but to justify resuscitating tired topics, you must have something original to add. Whatever topic you choose, you will have your best shot at engaging your readers and doing justice to your topic when you write about something you and your readers find compelling.

to TOPIC

Quick

Reference | **Analyzing the Purpose of an Assignment**

If the assignment asks you to . . .	The purpose is . . .	The approach is . . .
describe, explain	informative (expository)	to put into words what something looks, sounds, feels, smells, or tastes like; to discuss how something functions
assess, evaluate, argue	persuasive	to make a judgment based on evidence or offer an interpretation based on close reading, and to explain why
analyze, consider, discuss	informative or persuasive	to break a topic, reading assignment, or issue into its component parts and explain how it works; to reflect critically on the pros and cons of an issue, offer an interpretation based on a close reading, and sometimes explain why you have reached this conclusion

4b Analyzing the Assignment and Setting a Schedule
分析任务，设定日程

Recognizing the purpose of an assignment is crucial to success. If you are asked to *argue* for or against the goals of the plain speech movement of the 1920s, for example, and, instead, you *describe* those goals, you will probably not get an *A*. When analyzing an assignment, look for words that indicate purpose. (See the Quick Reference above.)

> **More about**
> Argument, 73–86
> Analysis, 12–14,
>   35, 87, 88, 133
> Critique, 14, 133,
>   141–43

The audience for an assignment is, of course, your instructor, and the instructor's goal in assigning the project is to be reassured that you have done the reading, understood the issues, and synthesized information from classroom lectures and discussions with assigned reading. In addition, most instructors want to see that you can express yourself clearly and correctly in writing.

Frequently, an assignment will specify the approach you should take. If you are asked to analyze, your instructor will expect you to break the topic, issue, or text into its component parts and determine how those parts work together. If your instructor asks you to evaluate a text, you will be expected to identify the writer's claims and evidence and to assess their credibility.

Sometimes, an assignment will specify the genre, although the genre may be taken for granted. A biology instructor teaching a laboratory class may assume that you understand that a laboratory report is required. If you are not sure what the genre of the assignment is, or what it requires, ask your instructor.

Finally, writing assignments will generally include a due date. To create a realistic schedule, list the steps in the writing process (from drafting a thesis and generating ideas to revising, editing, proofreading, and formatting) in reverse order on your calendar, working back from the due date. (Remember that writing is not a linear process: You may go back to generate ideas while revising, for example, so leave some extra time.) Be sure to take into consideration your other obligations, such as other assignments and exams, work, rehearsals or team practices, and family and social obligations.

> **More about**
> Scheduling a
>   writing project,
>   99–100
> Online assignment
>   calendar, 101
> Avoiding plagia-
>   rism, 121–30,
>   136–55

4c   **Generating Topics and Ideas** 确定主题与构思

When you are required to come up with a topic on your own, ask your-self these questions:

- What topics are appropriate to the assignment?
- What topics will interest, exasperate, or intrigue me *and* my reader?
- What topics do I have special access to or knowledge about? You can create special knowledge by doing research and by thinking critically about your topic.

> **More about**
> Finding informa-
>   tion, 105–13
> Reading critically,
>   9–15

Invention techniques, like those that follow, can help you devise and develop a topic. No single strategy will work for everyone, and most writers use several methods.

Generating Ideas in English or Your First Language? If English is not your first language, you might find it helpful to keep a journal, freewrite, or brainstorm in English. If you get stuck, try using words and phrases from your first language. But be careful when returning to your notes to translate not merely your *words* but also your *ideas* into English that is appropriate for your readers.

1. Freewrite 自由写作

Freewriting is writing the first thing that enters your head and then con-tinuing to write nonstop for ten to fifteen minutes or for a set number of pages. To be useful, freewriting must be fast and spontaneous. If you find that you cannot resist correcting and revising, turn the brightness down until your screen is very dim or even black. Once the time has elapsed, read through what you wrote and look for usable ideas.

A variation of freewriting is *focused freewriting.* Instead of starting from the first idea to pop into your head, start from something specific: your topic, a quotation, a memory, an image, an idea from your free-writing.

Writing
Responsibly   **Plagiarism and Time Management**

Few writers begin a project with the intention of plagiarizing, but many who buy papers do so because they have not budgeted the time needed to write an effective paper themselves. Even those who write their own essays tend to copy more from their sources when they are pressed for time.

Avoid these dangers by starting work as soon as you receive an assignment, figuring out which steps will be necessary to complete the project well and on time (including multiple drafts), and setting aside chunks of time to work on the pro-ject at a steady pace.

to SELF

2. Brainstorm 头脑风暴

Brainstorming (or *listing*) is writing down everything you can think of on a topic. Brainstorming helps get ideas percolating and provides a record of that percolation. Below is a snippet of brainstorming on the environmental movement, the topic of Michael Wedd's essay.

Student Models
"Rethinking Alterna-
tive Energy," Michael
Wedd, 26–28
(first draft), 45–49
(revised draft)

Student Model Brainstorm
– Types of alternative energy: solar, wind, hydro. – Advantages/disadvantages of each. – Alt energy may benefit consumers; might harm wildlife. – Who is for it, against it. Their different arguments. – Where is alt energy movement strongest, weakest? Why? – Why alternatives to fossil fuels needed. – History of oil exploration and development of alternatives.

3. Cluster 思维导图

Clustering, or *mapping* (Figure 4.1), is a visual method for identifying relationships among ideas. To create a cluster or idea map, write your topic in the middle of the page and circle it. Write other ideas related to your topic around the central idea bubble, and circle each of them. Then draw connecting lines from the word bubbles to the central topic or to the other word bubbles to show how the ideas fit together.

4. Answer the journalists' questions 回答记者的问题（六要素）

The *journalists' questions*—*who, what, where, when, why,* and *how*—not only can help you generate ideas about your topic but also can help you figure out what you need to learn to write your project. When considering a topic, ask yourself questions like those Michael Wedd asked himself (Figure 4.2).

5. Discuss your topics with friends and classmates
和朋友、同学讨论你的课题

Sometimes, just batting ideas around with friends or classmates can help you generate ideas. This can be as casual as a late-night chat with your roommate ("What do you think about... ?") or as formal as a sched-uled brainstorming session with a collaborative writing group. A blog can open up the discussion to others interested in your topic.

6. Use the Internet, the library, and classroom tools
利用网络、图书馆和课堂工具

Surfing the Internet can provide direction and stimulate ideas when you are faced with a new topic. For very current topics, searching a news site or locating a specialized blog can also be useful.

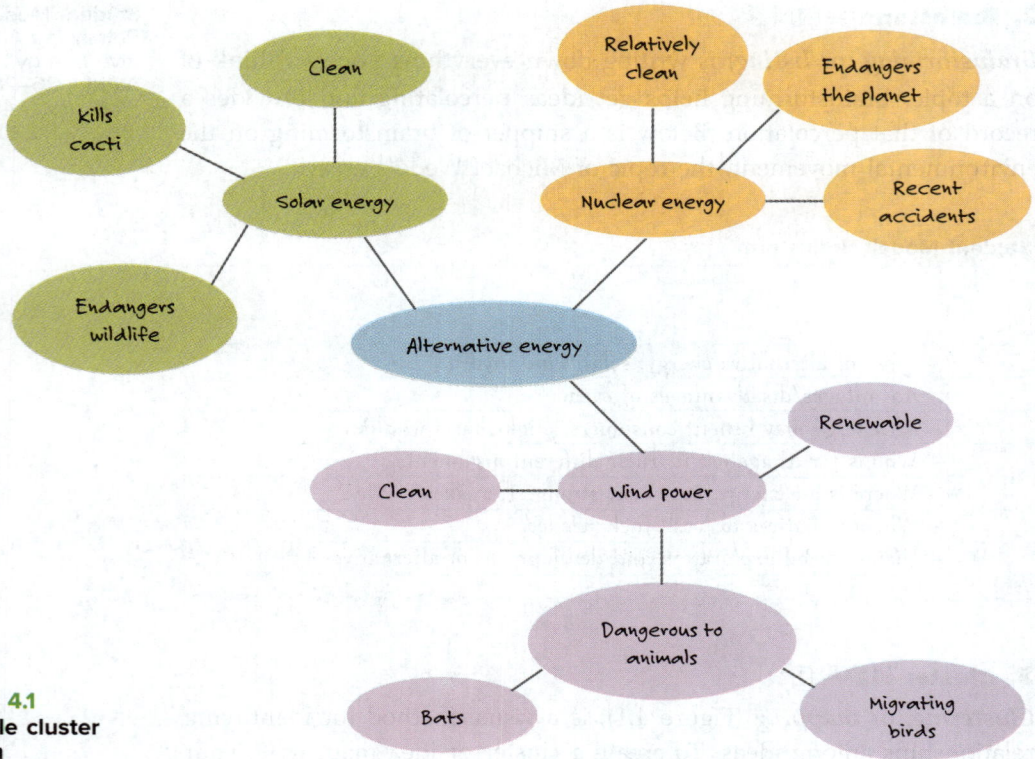

FIGURE 4.1
A sample cluster diagram

Tech   **Brainstorming with Word Clouds**

Your word choices echo the ideas and opinions that resonate most strongly with you. You might process some of your early brainstorming through programs such as Wordle to create "word clouds" of your most frequently used words. The visualization of that information may help you figure out what you are emphasizing, which can help you develop your thesis.

Student Model   **Journalists' Questions**

– Who is affected by the building of wind farms? Who will benefit from their construction?

– What other sources of energy do we have? What impact do they have on the environment? What impact will the wind farms have?

– Where are wind farms being built?

– When will the wind farms go online? When will the courts rule on the challenges to these wind farms?

– Why is there disagreement within the environmental community about whether wind farms should be built?

– How will the issues be resolved? How can animals be protected?

FIGURE 4.2 The journalists' questions

Specialized reference sources can give you a sense of how your topic is usually discussed. Turn to specialized dictionaries or encyclopedias for a more detailed introduction. Searching a library database, like PsycArticles or CQ Electronic Library, can help you devise or narrow a topic.

Because you will often be writing about topics that were introduced in class, look for ideas in your textbook, class notes, and any handouts your instructor has distributed. All can provide context or help you identify a topic that interests you, is relevant, or would benefit from further exploration. Michael Wedd used some articles his instructor had distributed as a jumping-off point for his essay.

More about
Blogs, 107–08
Evaluating online
  sources, 114–20
Reference
  sources, 105–06
Using databases,
  108–10

4d Narrowing Your Topic and Drafting an Effective Thesis
细化论文主题，拟订有效论点

A *thesis* is a brief statement (one or two sentences) of the central claim you will make. To begin drafting possible thesis statements, ask yourself probing questions about your topic and then answer them. Review your answers, looking for ones that identify your topic and make a claim about it. Choose one that will allow you to bring insight to the topic, and use that as your preliminary thesis. Your thesis should do four things:

1. Identify your topic
2. Indicate your purpose (informative or persuasive)
3. Make a claim (or assertion) that you can support—a *claim of fact* (a verifiable issue) for an informative project, or a *claim of judgment* or *value* (a belief or opinion that can be supported by reasons and evidence) for a persuasive project
4. Engage your readers

More about
Generating ideas,
  20–23
Devising a thesis,
  131–33
Purpose, 16–17, 99
Claims, 73–75

Only rarely does a writer accomplish all four of these objectives in the first draft of the thesis. Most writers need to revise the thesis, either before drafting or during revision.

Stating the Main Idea In some contexts and cultures, it is appropriate to imply the main idea rather than state it explicitly. However, readers in the United States, especially in academic and business contexts, will usually expect you to express your thesis clearly and directly, usually at the beginning of your written project.

---

1. Purpose: Informative 目的：信息丰富

The thesis of an informative essay makes a *claim of fact*, an assertion that can be verified. To be engaging, an informative thesis must make a claim of fact that is not yet widely known or accepted by the audience, and it must be specific enough that the writer can explore it in depth:

Student Model
Informative essay:
  26–28, 246–54

DRAFT THESIS

Topic

This paper is about <mark>conflicts within the environmental movement.</mark>

This draft thesis establishes a topic, but it does not make a claim of fact, and it is far too general to explore in depth.

REVISION 1—FOR AN INFORMATIVE PROJECT

Topic

There are <mark>many conflicts within the environmental movement</mark>.

This thesis statement establishes the topic and makes a claim of fact, but the claim is too broad. Because the writer has not specified which conflicts she has in mind, she would potentially have to explain all possible conflicts within the environmental movement to satisfy the promise of the thesis.

REVISION 2—FOR AN INFORMATIVE PROJECT

Topic

Among the <mark>conflicts within the environmental movement</mark> is that between those who want to reduce global warming by replacing fossil fuels with alternatives, like wind energy and solar energy, and those who fear that new energy-generating plants will harm local wildlife.

The thesis statement now narrows the claim—makes it specific—so that it focuses solely on one area of conflict within the environmental movement. It will intrigue readers interested in environmental issues and inform those who know little about the conflicts.

2. Purpose: Argumentative 目的：可论证性

The thesis of an *argumentative* writing project must make a *claim of value* (a belief about the way the world should be) or a *judgment* (an opinion or a provisional decision that is not widely shared). The claim must be one that can be supported with evidence. The revised informative thesis in the preceding example clearly specifies a topic and will probably intrigue readers, but it is not appropriate for an argumentative project because it makes a claim of fact, not a claim of value or judgment:

REVISION 3—FOR AN ARGUMENTATIVE PROJECT

Topic

As serious and time sensitive as the issue of climate change is, <mark>alternative energy</mark> is not a solution if it will be just as harmful to wildlife as conventional energy.

This thesis still specifies the topic, but it now also makes a claim of judgment ("alternative energy is not a solution"). Because it is narrow, focusing on just one issue ("alternative energy [that] is . . . harmful to wildlife"), it can be explained in a brief essay. Because it demonstrates the importance of the topic ("As serious and time sensitive as the issue of climate change is"), it is likely to interest readers.

When drafting your thesis statement, make sure that it focuses on a claim you can support and that it will interest your reader. When revising your thesis statement, make sure that the reasons and evidence you provide support your claim directly. If they do not, either replace the irrelevant reasons and evidence, or revise your thesis so that the support you offer is pertinent.

4e Organizing Your Ideas 整理思路

Outlines, whether formal or informal, not only guide you as you draft your essay, but also allow you to experiment with ways of sequencing your supporting paragraphs. The type of outline you choose depends entirely on your own preferences, the complexity of your essay, and your instructor's expectations. For a brief writing project, an *informal outline* may be all you need. An informal (or *scratch*) outline is simply a list of your ideas in the order you want to present them. You can jot down your ideas in words, phrases, complete sentences, even pictures—whatever you need to jog your memory about what to put next. Here is a sample informal outline for Michael Wedd's draft essay on conflicts within the environmental movement.

Student Model Informal (or Scratch) Outline

Intro
Green/environmental movement: brief explanation
Growing importance and awareness in recent years → conflict within the movement about how to handle these issues
Thesis: A major goal of the green movement is to find fossil fuel alternatives, but some members are concerned that wind, solar, and nuclear power sites will also harm the environment.

Body
Benefits/importance of alternative energy; types of alternative fuels being proposed: wind, solar, nuclear
Problems with alternative energy sources: harmful to animals, their habitats, and safety for humans

Conclusion
Conflicts might be inevitable, but we have to move forward, find creative compromises, use less energy

A *formal outline* is helpful when drafting longer, more complex writing projects. In a formal outline, roman numeral headings indicate your main ideas and capital letters and arabic numbers indicate your supporting points. Each point in your outline must support the idea at the level above it and must be supported by the points in the level below it.

A *topic outline* uses words and phrases to indicate the ideas to be discussed. A *sentence outline* uses complete sentences. Some writers prefer a topic outline because it is easier to construct. Others prefer a sentence outline because it provides a starting point for drafting. Compare a section of a topic outline with a section of a sentence outline for a later draft of Michael Wedd's essay.

Student Models   Topic Outline and Sentence Outline

Thesis: A major goal of the green movement is to find fossil fuel alternatives, but some members are concerned that wind, solar, and nuclear power sites will also harm the environment.

Topic Outline

I. Changing perspectives on alternative energy to include risks as well as benefits

   A. Benefits of alternative fuels

      1. Fewer greenhouse gas emissions/less warming

      2. Sustainable renewable energy sources: the sun, wind, and water

   B. Drawbacks

      1. Bad for environment: scenery, humans

      2. Destruction of animal habitats, extinction

      3. Future problems unknown without tests

Sentence Outline

I. The issue of global warming is urgent and serious, but we ought to consider the costs of alternative energy production that we deploy.

   A. There are numerous potential benefits of using alternative fuel sources.

      1. Alternative energy produces fewer carbon dioxide and other greenhouse gas emissions, improving air quality and slowing the rate of global warming.

      2. Renewable energy sources, including the sun, wind, and water, are sustainable; they cannot be depleted and therefore can be used for the foreseeable future.

   B. Although there are many advantages to alternative fuel sources, there are drawbacks as well.

      1. New structures can have negative consequences on their surroundings, ranging from ruining picturesque views to endangering human health.

      2. Animal habitats may be destroyed, leading to extinction of species.

      3. The long-term effects of building new facilities are still largely unknown and could present even greater problems in the future.

4f Drafting Your Writing Project 撰写初稿

> **More about**
> Topic sentences, 29
> Developing paragraphs, 29–39

When the moment comes to combine words and sentences into paragraphs and paragraphs into a writing project, set aside some time and find a place where you can concentrate. Begin drafting by reviewing the writing you have done while generating ideas, drafting your thesis, and creating an outline. Even in the best circumstances, you may encounter writer's block, but by using the appropriate techniques—write what you can, in parts rather than all at once; take breaks; avoid perfection—you should be able to get past it.

Tech   Protecting Your Work

Because terrible things happen to computer files all the time, it is important to **save early and often,** and to **save your file in multiple locations:** Burn it to a disc, save it on a flash drive, or send a copy to your email account. Remember to date each version of a file so you know which is the most recent.

Your project should explain *why* you believe that your thesis statement is true and why your readers should agree with you. The topic sentence (or main idea) in each supporting paragraph will form the backbone of your essay, and the reasons and evidence you supply will be the flesh that covers the skeleton. Some kinds of evidence you can draw on to convince your readers include facts and statistics, expert opinion, examples and anecdotes, observations and case studies, and passages from the text you are studying. The chapter that follows describes how to write well-developed and compelling paragraphs for the introduction, conclusion, and body of your writing project.

Student Models
Development of "Rethinking Alternative Energy"
Brainstorming, 21
Clustering, 22
Journalists' questions, 22
Draft thesis, 24
Revised thesis, 24
Outlines, 25, 26
Final draft, 26–28

Student Model   First Draft

Read the first draft of Michael Wedd's essay on conflict within the environmental movement. Note that he does not worry about polished writing or perfect grammar and spelling. He knows he can make changes as he revises. For now, his focus is on getting his ideas down in a logical order and supporting his thesis. Consider what he will need to do as he revises to fulfill his writer's responsibilities.

Michael Wedd
Professor Dunn
English 102
19 Sept. 2016

Issues with Alternative Energy

The rise of Alternative Energy Industries has been challenging, controversial,
and turbulent these days. With the availability of many forms of alternative
energy systems globally (wind, solar, nuclearetc.), it is worth pausing for a
minute to ask some questions. People are talking at many levels of society
about both the costs and the benefits of alternative energy. The problematic
relationships between Alternative Energy Industries and the things they
claim to be protecting are emerging as a key focus of these debates.

Environmentalists are conflicted when it comes to alternative energy.
Most agree that fossil-fuel-based power plants are damaging the climate and
making life harder for many of the worlds species. One of the primary benefits
of alternative energy sources is that they are in practically limitless supply. They
are producing energy all the time anyways. Obvious benefits aside, the structures
needed to produce these forms of alternative energy can have bad affects on
their surrounding environments (Pulitzer, Cherry, DW, McCurry). The issue
of global warming is urgent and serious and we ought to consider the costs
of alternative energy production that we deploy. Alternative energy might be
putting the environment in danger. Maybe its time to question the way we as a
society use these alternatives.

Wind energy seems to be a harmless, passive, and effective way of
producing energy, but upon closer inspection it also has its drawbacks. Wind
turbines are killing birds and other airborne creatures at fast rate. A report by
The American Bird Conservancy states that "[t]he United States now has 48,000
wind turbines installed from coast to coast, with many more planned. Those
turbines killed nearly 600,000 birds in 2012, from Golden Eagles to migratory
songbirds" ("Bird Strikes"). These wind turbines reach hundreds of feet into the

First draft, so not concerned with spelling, style, grammar, or title

Thesis statement makes a claim of fact, appropriate if purpose is informative but not if purpose is persuasive.

Facts and specifics needed to better support writer's points

Sources cited even in first draft

Topic sentence introduces first example and prepares reader for discussion about problems with wind energy.

air and threaten birds. By 2030, "a ten-fold increase in turbines is expected to boost annual bird mortality to 1.4 to 2 million."

Solar energy is another alternative that at first seems benign but is actually putting airborne wildlife in grave danger. At the $2.2 billion-dollar Ivanpah solar facility in the CA desert, which is part of the largest solar energy complex in the world, birds are being burn mid-flight and plummeting to earth like meteorites. A report by the Pulitzer Center states that "[u]nsuspecting birds fly through Ivanpah's airspace, where the superheated air between the heliostats and the towers can reach temperatures as high as 900 degrees Fahrenheit. flesh catches fire as the birds are ignited in midair" (Pulitzer). The way we are generating solar electricity is producing high risks for a number of animals.

The most controversial of these alternative energy sources is the atom. Japan's 2011 Fukushima nuclear meltdown is still recent. Naoto Kan believes that the Japanese gov. isn't taking the dangers of nuclear power seriously enough after the recent meltdown. He was quoted in *Deutche Welle* saying, "Unfortunately, I have the impression that neither the Japanese public nor the experts have learned the right lessons from the disaster" (DW). We must carefully consider the dangers of nuclear power before embracing it as the clean energy of the future.

People acknowledge how important it is to check global warming and diversify our energy portfolio, but it is crucial that we also protect the flora and fauna with which we share this planet. It's not enough to be environmentally conscious about the sources from which we draw our energy; we also need to be careful about how we harvest from them. The solution to this will have to include ideas for not only increasing renewable energy production safely but also of reducing global consumption equilaterally.

Works Cited

Bird Strikes. American Bird Conservancy.

"The Fall Of Icarus: Ivanpah's Solar Controversy." *Pulitzer Center*.

"Former Japanese PM Naoto kan: 'Fukushima radically changed my Perspective' Asia *DW.COM* 25.02.2015. DW.COM.

Mccurry, Justin. "Japan Restarts First Nuclear Reactor since Fukushima Disaster." The *Guardian* August 11th, 2015. *The Guardian*.

5 Crafting and Connecting Paragraphs
段落撰写与衔接

American landscape architect Frederick Law Olmsted understood that an alluring landscape consists of more than just individual trees, flowers, and lawns. When called upon to design New York City's Central Park, he wanted both a functional and a beautiful park. To satisfy these goals, Olmsted created a deceptively natural-looking oasis of bridges, paths, and ponds that turned the park in Manhattan into an essential part of the city. Similarly, a writing project will be most effective—and a pleasure to read—when each paragraph is essential to the whole. When is a paragraph essential? It is essential when it is relevant, unified, coherent, well developed, interesting, and carefully connected to the paragraphs that come before and after it.

5a Writing Relevant Paragraphs 撰写的段落要切题

A *relevant* paragraph not only describes the general topic of your project but also contributes to the reader's understanding of or belief in the main claim of the project (the *thesis*). Compare this paragraph to the essay's thesis:

Second, by calling hip-hop a "lethal genre," Staples places it into a category separate from other works of art that are not as "virulent." Yes, many hip-hop lyrics are violent, but that does not distinguish these songs from many other artistic works. Edgar Allan Poe, considered one of America's greatest writers, wrote numerous stories about murder and death, including "The Tell-Tale Heart," whose narrator is a confessed killer. *The Talented Mr. Ripley*, a novel by Patricia Highsmith, and the movie based on this novel, make Tom Ripley, an unrepentant murderer, a sympathetic character. Sculptor Kiki Smith depicts mutilated or deformed bodies in her art; instead of being criticized, she is considered one of today's most important sculptors. No one would claim, I think, that Kiki Smith influences her viewers to commit mayhem. Clearly, hip-hop artists are not alone in depicting horrible people and events; they should not be singled out for doing so, and it should not be assumed that their audience will blindly follow suit.
—Alea Wratten, SUNY–Geneseo, "Reflecting on Brant Staples's Editorial 'How Hip-Hop Music Lost Its Way and Betrayed Its Fans'"

Thesis: . . . [Staples's] argument fails to be persuasive for several reasons: He doesn't account for the influence that positive role models have, he ignores the fact that art frequently depicts violence without dire consequences to its consumers, and he overlooks the broad spectrum of hip-hop to focus on only a single strand.

Topic Sentence

Concession/rebuttal

Example 1

Example 2

Example 3

Concluding Sentence (also recalls thesis)

5b Writing Unified Paragraphs 撰写的段落要一致

Paragraphs are *unified* when they focus on a single main idea. Unifying a paragraph is easiest when it includes a *topic sentence*, a single sentence (sometimes two) that clearly states the main idea of the paragraph. The following paragraph would be more unified if its writer pruned the sentences that do not relate to working on an organic farm in Costa Rica.

Topic sentence	Last summer, I traveled to Costa Rica to work on an organic farm. I had always
Relevant	wanted to experience Central America, and this was a perfect opportunity to truly get to know the land. Thailand and Cambodia also fascinate me. I worked eight hours each day on the farm, helping to care for the animals and learning how to raise organic vegetables. After a day outside, I would help my host family prepare dinner, with food fresh from the land. Breakfast is actually
Irrelevant	my favorite meal because I like to eat eggs and hash browns. As I ate, I knew that I had played a part in the food I was eating. Though I stayed in Costa Rica only for the summer, I came back with much higher expectations for my food. I think I'm going to go back to Costa Rica next summer to work with a nonprofit to build houses in San Jose.

Topic sentences typically appear at the beginning of a paragraph so that readers can see immediately the relationship between the main idea and the supporting reasons and evidence that follow.

Topic sentence	Environmentalists paint a bleak picture of aquaculture. The David Suzuki Foundation, for example, maintains that fish waste contained in the fishery pens kills organisms living in the seabed. Yvon Gesinghaus, a manager of a tribal council in British Columbia, Canada, also notes that the scummy foam from the farms collects on the beaches, smothering the clams that provide the natives with food and money. George K. Iwama, Biksham Gujja, and Andrea Finger-Stich point to the destruction of coastal habitats in Africa and Southeast Asia to make room for shrimp ponds.

—Adrianne Anderson, Texas Christian University

Occasionally, writers may place the topic sentence at the end of a paragraph to draw a conclusion based on the evidence presented and to enhance dramatic effect or in the middle of the paragraph, where the topic sentence acts as a linchpin. Some paragraphs (especially descriptive and narrative ones) may even leave the main idea unstated if it is clearly conveyed by the details and the word choices.

5c Writing Coherent Paragraphs 撰写的段落要连贯

A paragraph is *coherent* when readers can understand the relationships among the sentences without having to pause or ponder. Readers are most likely to find a paragraph coherent when writers use transitional strategies to link sentences.

Transitional words and phrases alert readers to the significance of what the writer is saying and point to the relationships among ideas. The paragraph below uses transitional words and phrases indicating contrast, cause and effect, emphasis, and time to guide readers through a comparison of two books.

Contrast	Baron's book, which is written in the relentlessly melodramatic style of *Jaws*, describes cougars spreading inexorably eastward. By contrast, Elizabeth Marshall Thomas, in *The Tribe of Tiger: Cats and Their Culture*, argues that cougars were never fully exterminated in the East and instead survived in remote areas by being especially stealthy around humans. The difference
Cause-effect	is significant. If you accept Marshall Thomas's argument, then the Eastern

Seaboard sounds a great deal like pre–cougar-resurgence Colorado. Indeed, the herds of deer plaguing the-unbroken strip of Eastern suburbs makes a replay of the Boulder situation likely—but on a far larger scale. Already, bears and coyotes are invading the Eastern suburbs. Can cougars and wolves be far behind?

—Peter Canby, "The Cat Came Back," *Harper's*

> Emphasis
>
> Time

Quick Reference | Sample Transitional Words and Phrases

To add to an idea: *again, also, and, and then, besides, further, furthermore, in addition, incidentally, likewise, moreover, next, still, too*

To indicate cause or effect: *accordingly, as a result, because, consequently, hence, since, then, therefore, thus*

To indicate chronology (time sequence): *after, afterward, as long as, as soon as, at last, before, earlier, finally, first, formerly, immediately, in the first place, in the interval, in the meantime, in the next place, in the last place, later, latter, meanwhile, next, now, often, once, previously, second, shortly, simultaneously, since, sometime later, subsequently, suddenly, then, third, today, tomorrow, until, until now, when, years ago, yesterday*

To conclude: *all in all, finally, in brief, in conclusion, in other words, in short, in sum, in summary, that is, to summarize*

To compare: *alike, also, in the same way, like, likewise, resembling, similarly*

To concede: *certainly, granted, of course*

To contrast: *after all, although, and yet, but, conversely, despite, difference, dissimilar, even so, even though, granted, however, in contrast, in spite of, instead, nevertheless, nonetheless, notwithstanding, on the contrary, on the other hand, otherwise, regardless, still, though, unlike, while this may be true, yet*

To emphasize: *after all, certainly, clearly, even, indeed, in fact, in other words, in truth, it is true, moreover, of course, undoubtedly*

To offer an example: *as an example, for example, for instance, in other words, namely, specifically, that is, thus, to exemplify, to illustrate*

To indicate spatial relationships: *above, adjacent to, against, alongside, around, at a distance from, behind, below, beside, beyond, encircling, far off, farther along, forward, here, in front of, inside, nearly, near the back, near the end, next to, on, over, surrounding, there, through, to the left, to the right, to the north, to the south, up front*

Writing Responsibly | Guiding the Reader

As a writer, you have a responsibility to guide your reader from point to point, highlighting the relationships among your words, sentences, and paragraphs. Do not leave readers to puzzle out the relationships among your ideas for themselves. Few academic readers in the United States will think explicit claims and transitions insult their intelligence.

to AUDIENCE

The Quick Reference box on the previous page lists other types of transitional words and phrases. The number of possibilities is great, so choose transitions that convey the relationship you are trying to express and vary your selection.

Repetition of keywords and sentence structures, when used judiciously, can also knit sentences together into a unified paragraph, as can replacing keywords with pronouns, synonyms (words that mean the same thing), and equivalent expressions. The paragraph below provides an example of how these strategies can be used effectively:

Repeated structure	The first law of gossip is that you never know how many people are talking about you behind your back. The second law is thank God. The third—and most important—law is that as gossip spreads from friends to acquaintances to people you've never met, it grows more garbled, vivid, and definitive. Out of stray factoids and hesitant impressions emerges a hard mass of what everyone knows to be true. Imagination supplies the missing pieces, and repetition turns these pieces into facts; gossip achieves its shape and amplitude only in the continual retelling. The best stories about us are told by perfect strangers.
Keyword	
Pronouns	
Equivalent expressions	

—Tad Friend, "The Harriet-the-Spy Club," *The New Yorker*

5d Developing Paragraphs Using Patterns of Organization
采用组织模式展开段落

To be effective, a writing project must offer enough "meat" to satisfy readers. How much is enough? There are no hard-and-fast rules, but you should provide enough support to explain your ideas fully. Consider the paragraph below:

Topic sentence	One of the most important . . . features of American life in the late twentieth century was the aging of the American population. After decades of steady growth, the nation's birth rate began to decline in the 1970s and remained low through the 1980s and 1990s. In 1970, there were 18.4 births for every 1,000 people in the population. By 1996, the rate had dropped to 14.8 births.

Left as is, the paragraph above would be inadequately developed: The topic sentence discusses the aging of the population, but the supporting sentences discuss only the birth rate—a factor in the aging of a population, but not the whole story.

Now consider the complete paragraph:

Topic sentence	One of the most important . . . features of American life in the late twentieth century was the aging of the American population. After decades of steady growth, the nation's birth rate began to decline in the 1970s and remained low through the 1980s and 1990s. In 1970, there were 18.4 births for every 1,000 people in the population. By 1996, the rate had dropped to 14.8 births. The declining birth rate and a significant rise in life expectancy produced a substantial increase in the proportion of elderly citizens. Almost 13 percent of the population was more than sixty-five years old in 2000, as compared with 8 percent in 1970. The median age in 2000 was 35.3, the highest in the nation's history. In 1970, it was 28.0.
Compares birth rates	
Compares life expectancies	
Compares median ages	

—Alan Brinkley, *American History: A Survey*

Here, the writer compares the population in 1970 with the population in later periods on not one but three traits—birth rate, life expectancy, and median age—and he provides concrete evidence (facts and statistics) to convince readers that the population was aging. Some other kinds of evidence you can draw on to support your claims include expert opinion, examples, observations, case studies, anecdotes, passages from a text you are studying, and your own analysis.

Patterns of organization, such as comparison-contrast (as in the example paragraph above), description, narration, and exemplification, can help you flesh out your paragraphs (and your writing projects) fully. They lend a structure to your paragraphs, and they suggest the types of evidence that will be most effective.

1. Use comparison-contrast: Show similarities and differences 运用比较与对比：说明相似性与差异性

A paragraph that is developed using comparison-contrast points out similarities or differences (sometimes both) of two or more items. The example paragraph above, for instance, compares the US population in 1970 with the US population in later periods. Note that this paragraph compares the US population on each of three traits, using facts and statistics to support its claims. The paragraph uses the *alternating pattern* of organization, switching back and forth between 1970 and the last decade of the twentieth century.

Another option for organizing comparison-contrast paragraphs is to discuss all the traits of the first item before moving on to all the traits of the second item. The paragraph below follows the *block pattern* of organization.

> Europeans interpreted the simplicity of Indian dress in two different ways. Some saw the lack of clothing as evidence of "barbarism." André Thevet, a shocked French visitor to Brazil in 1557, voiced this point of view when he attributed nakedness to simple lust. If the Indians could weave hammocks, he sniffed, why not shirts? But other Europeans viewed unashamed nakedness as the Indians' badge of innocence. As remnants of a bygone "golden age," they believed, Indians needed clothing no more than government, laws, regular employment, or other corruptions of civilization.

Topic sentence
First item of comparison
Second item of comparison

—James West Davidson et al., *Nation of Nations*, 5th ed.

This paragraph uses examples as support. In general, the block pattern works best with fewer points of comparison.

2. Use description with details 使用细节描述

When describing, include details that appeal to the senses (sight, sound, taste, smell, touch) and organize them spatially (from left to right, top to bottom, near to middle to far) to mimic how we normally take in a scene. Spatially organized paragraphs rely on indications of place or location to guide the reader by the mind's eye (or ear or nose).

> A few moments later French announces, "Bottom contact on sonar." The seafloor rolls out like a soft, beige carpet. Robison points to tiny purple jellies floating just above the floor. Beyond them, lying on the floor itself, are several

Sensory description
Indications of place or location

bumpy sea cucumbers, sea stars with skinny legs, pink anemones, and tube worms, which quickly retract their feathery feeding arms at *Tiburon's* approach. A single rattail fish hangs inches above the bottom, shoving its snout into the sediments in search of a meal.

—Virginia Morell, "OK, There It Is—Our Mystery Mollusk," *National Geographic*

3. Tell a story or describe a process 讲故事或描述过程

A paragraph that tells a story or describes a process unrolls over time. Include each step or key moment, and describe it in enough detail that readers can envision it.

Step 1
Step 2
Step 3
Step 4
Step 5
Step 6
Step 7

The very first trick ever performed by Houdini on the professional stage was a simple but effective illusion known generally as the "Substitution Trunk," though he preferred to call it "Metamorphosis." Houdini and his partner would bring a large trunk onto the stage. It was opened and a sack or bag produced from inside it. Houdini, bound and handcuffed, would get into the sack, which was then sealed or tied around the neck. The trunk was closed over the bag and its occupant. It was locked, strapped, and chained. Then a screen was drawn around it. The partner (after they married, this was always Mrs. Houdini) stepped behind the screen which, next moment, was thrown aside—by Houdini himself. The partner had meanwhile disappeared. A committee of the audience was called onstage to verify that the ties, straps, etc. around the trunk had not been tampered with. These were then laboriously loosened; the trunk was opened and there, inside the securely fastened bag, was—Mrs. Houdini!

4. Exemplify: Explain through example 举例说明：通过例子进行解释

Exemplification works by providing examples to make a general point specific:

For many years I believed that women had only one thing to learn from men: how to get the attention of a waiter by some means short of kicking over the table and shrieking. Never in my life have I gotten the attention of a waiter, unless it was an off-duty waiter whose car I'd accidentally scraped in a parking lot somewhere. Men, however, can summon a maître d' just by thinking the word "coffee," and this is a power women would be well-advised to study. What else would we possibly want to learn from them? How to interrupt someone in midsentence as if you were performing an act of conversational euthanasia? How to drop a pair of socks three feet from an open hamper and keep right on walking? How to make those weird guttural gargling sounds in the bathroom?

Example 1
Example 2
Example 3

—Barbara Ehrenreich, "What I've Learned from Men: Lessons for a Full-Grown Feminist," *Ms.*

5. Give reasons and consequences 说明原因和结果

A cause-and-effect paragraph explains why something happened or what its consequences are:

Causes
Effects

Here is a modest suggestion for what Twitter can do to fix one of the problems that most annoy me and I imagine many other users: the problem of crackpot, abusive tweets. The paradox of Twitter is that the more followers you have (I currently have over 20,000), the more abusive tweets you are likely to get calling you various scatological names or passing along insane conspiracy theories. Some of this is bearable, but after a while you want to take a hot bath and never go back into the cesspool again. I'm not suggesting that these offensive tweets comprise the bulk of what's on Twitter—far from it. I would have stopped using it long ago if that were true. But it's more of a chore than it should be to find the good stuff in your feed among all the abusive attacks that are out there.

—Max Boot, "Abusing Anonymity," *Commentary*

6. Analyze by dividing a whole into its parts 分点分析

Analysis divides a single entity into its component parts:

The central United States is divided into two geographical zones: the Great Plains in the west and the prairie in the east. Though both are more or less flat, the Great Plains—extending south from eastern Montana and western North Dakota to eastern New Mexico and western Texas—are the drier of the two regions and are distinguished by short grasses, while the more populous prairie to the east (surrounding Omaha, St. Louis, and Fort Leavenworth) is tall-grass country. The Great Plains are the "West"; the prairie, the "Midwest."

—Robert D. Kaplan, *An Empire of Wilderness*

| United States |
| Great Plains |
| Prairie |

7. Define a word by explaining its meaning or concept
下定义：解释含义或概念

Like the definition in a dictionary, a definition in an essay explains the meaning of a word or concept by grouping it into a class and then providing the distinguishing characteristics that set it apart from other members of that class:

Term to Be Defined	Class	Distinguishing Characteristics
Argument is	a way to discover truth	by examining all sides of the issue.

Extended definitions (definitions that run to a paragraph or more) analyze in detail what a term does or does not mean. They go beyond a dictionary, often using anecdotes, examples, or reasons for using the word in this particular way:

The international movement known as *theater of the absurd* so vividly captured the anguish of modern society that late twentieth-century critics called it "the true theater of our time." Abandoning classical theater from Sophocles and Shakespeare through Ibsen and Miller, absurdist playwrights rejected traditional dramatic structure (in which action moves from conflict to resolution), along with traditional modes of character development. The absurdist play, which drew stylistic inspiration from dada performance art and surrealist film, usually lacks dramatic progression, direction, and resolution. Its characters undergo little or no change, dialogue contradicts actions, and events follow no logical order. Dramatic action, leavened with gallows humor, may consist of irrational and grotesque situations that remain unresolved at the end of the performance—as is often the case in real life.

—Gloria Fiero, *The Humanistic Tradition*, 5th ed.

| Term to be defined |
| Class |
| Distinguishing characteristics |

5e Writing Introductory Paragraphs 撰写引言段

Introductory paragraphs shape readers' attitudes toward the rest of the text, so they are an important part of the writing project. Yet writers

Student Models
Introductions: 27, 38, 46, 82, 94, 203, 248–49

often have a hard time producing these paragraphs. Many find it helpful to draft the body of the project before tackling the introduction.

Whether you write it first or last, the introduction should prepare the reader for what follows. In many cases, this means including the thesis in the introduction, often at the end of the introductory section or paragraph.

Regardless of where you place your thesis, your introduction should identify and convey your stance toward your topic, establish your purpose, and engage readers to make them want to read on. Some strategies for writing an effective introduction include the following:

- Begin with a vivid quotation, a compelling question, or some interesting data.
- Start with an engaging—and relevant—anecdote.
- Offer a surprising but apt definition of a key term.
- Provide background information readers will need.
- State a commonly held belief and then challenge it.
- Explain what interesting, important, conflicting, difficult, or misunderstood territory the project will explore.

In the introductory paragraph that follows, the writer uses several effective strategies: She begins with a question that challenges the audience to examine some common assumptions about the topic, she provides background information that her readers may lack, and she concludes with a thesis statement that explains why reading her text should be important to the audience.

Opening question	Many people enjoy sitting down to a nice seafood dinner, but how many of those people actually stop to think about where the fish on their plate came from?
Answer that provides background information	With many species of wild fish disappearing because of overfishing, increasingly the answer will be a fish farm. But while fish farming can help to supply the demand, it can threaten the environment and cause problems with wild fish. It can also threaten the health of consumers by increasing the risk of disease and increasing the quantity of antibiotics consumed.
Thesis	In fact, as a careful and conscientious consumer, you would do well to learn the risks involved in buying and eating farm-raised fish before one winds up on your dinner plate.

—Adrianne Anderson, Texas Christian University

Brief essays may require only a one-paragraph introduction, but longer projects often need more. A text of twenty pages may have an introduction that runs several paragraphs, and introductions to books are generally the length of a short chapter. There are no firm rules about the length of the introduction, but it should be in proportion to the project's length.

Avoid Praising the Reader in Your Introduction In some contexts and cultures, writers attempt to win the approval of readers by overtly praising their taste, character, or intelligence. Generally, however, this is considered inappropriate for a college project, and academic and professional writers in the United States avoid referring directly to the reader and occasionally will actually challenge the reader's beliefs.

5f Writing Concluding Paragraphs 撰写结论段

Student Models
Conclusions: 28, 39,
  48–49, 85, 96, 210,
  251–52

As with the introduction, the conclusion is a part of the essay that readers are likely to remember. In fact, because it is the last thing the audience will read, it is what they will probably remember best. Thus, it demands a writer's best work.

Conclusions often start out specific, with a restatement of the thesis (in different words), and then broaden out. The purposes of the conclusion are twofold: to provide readers with a sense of closure and to provide them with a sense that reading the text was worthwhile. Some ways to achieve closure and to convey the importance of the essay include the following:

- Recur to the anecdote, question, or quotation with which the project began.
- Summarize your findings (especially in long or technical projects).
- Discuss how what you have learned has changed your thinking.
- Suggest a possible solution (or solutions) to the problems raised in the text.
- Indicate additional research that needs to be conducted or what the reader can do to help solve the problem.
- Leave the reader with a vivid and pertinent image, quotation, or anecdote.

The concluding paragraph below provides an example of an effective conclusion.

> The farmers of nineteenth-century America could afford to do here what they had not dared to do in the Old World: hope. This hope—for greater economic security, for more opportunity for themselves, their children, and their grandchildren—is the optimism and idealism that has carried our country forward and that, indeed, still carries us forward. Although the American dream has evolved across the centuries, it survives today and is a cornerstone of American philosophy. It is what underlies our Constitution and our laws, and it is a testimony to the vision of the farmers who founded this nation.
>
> —Leonard Lin, University of Southern California,
> "The Middle Class Farmers and the American Philosophy"

Makes reader feel time reading was well spent by showing importance of American dream

Restates thesis (American dream = hope for greater security, opportunity)

Achieves closure by recurring to introduction with mention of American dream

5g Connecting Paragraphs 段落衔接

Readers need to know not only how sentences connect to one another but also how paragraphs are connected. You can link paragraphs using the same techniques you use to link sentences:

- Providing transitional expressions (and sentences)
- Repeating words and phrases strategically
- Using pronouns, synonyms, and equivalent expressions to refer back to words and ideas introduced earlier
- Creating parallel sentence structures

You can also create coherence among paragraphs by referring back to the writing project's main idea.

The following speech by President-elect John F. Kennedy, delivered on January 9, 1961, to the General Court of the Commonwealth of Massachusetts, uses all of these strategies to create a cohesive—and powerful—text.

The City Upon a Hill

By JOHN F. KENNEDY

I have welcomed this opportunity to address this historic body, and, through you, the people of Massachusetts to whom I am so deeply indebted for a life-time of friendship and trust.

Words chosen to emphasize the speaker's bond with his audience

For fourteen years I have placed my confidence in the citizens of Massachusetts—and they have generously responded by placing their confidence in me.

Now, on the Friday after next, I am to assume new and broader responsibilities. But I am not here to bid farewell to Massachusetts.

For forty-three years—whether I was in London, Washington, the South Pacific, or elsewhere—this has been my home; and, God willing, wherever I serve this shall remain my home.

It was here my grandparents were born—it is here I hope my grandchildren will be born.

Evidence for the claim that follows: Massachusetts is a model for the world

I speak neither from false provincial pride nor artful political flattery. For no man about to enter high office in this country can ever be unmindful of the contribution this state has made to our national greatness.

Its leaders have shaped our destiny long before the great republic was born. Its principles have guided our footsteps in times of crisis as well as in times of calm. Its democratic institutions—including this historic body—have served as beacon lights for other nations as well as our sister states.

For what Pericles said to the Athenians has long been true of this commonwealth: "We do not imitate—for we are a model to others."

And so it is that I carry with me from this state to that high and lonely office to which I now succeed more than fond memories of firm friendships. The enduring qualities of Massachusetts—the common threads woven by the Pilgrim and the Puritan, the fisherman and the farmer, the Yankee and the immigrant—will not be and could not be forgotten in this nation's executive mansion.

thesis

The are an indelible part of my life, my convictions, my view of the past, and my hopes for the future.

Allow me to illustrate: During the last sixty days, I have been at the task of constructing an administration. It has been a long and deliberate process. Some have counseled greater speed. Others have counseled more expedient tests.

Example supports his claim

But I have been guided by the standard John Winthrop set before his shipmates on the flagship Arabella three hundred and thirty-one years ago, as they, too, faced the task of building a new government on a perilous frontier.

"We must always consider," he said, "that we shall be as a city upon a hill—the eyes of all people are upon us."

Central motif: the city on a hill

Today the eyes of all people are truly upon us—and our governments, in every branch, at every level, national, state and local, must be as a city upon a hill—constructed and inhabited by men aware of their great trust and their great responsibilities.

For we are setting out upon a voyage in 1961 no less hazardous than that undertaken by the Arabella in 1630. We are committing ourselves to tasks of statecraft no less awesome than that of governing the Massachusetts Bay Colony, beset as it was then by terror without and disorder within.

History will not judge our endeavors—and a government cannot be selected—merely on the basis of color or creed or even party affiliation. Neither will competence and loyalty and stature, while essential to the utmost, suffice in times such as these.

For of those to whom much is given, much is required. And when at some future date the high court of history sits in judgment on each one of us—recording whether in our brief span of service we fulfilled our responsibilities to the state—our success or failure, in whatever office we may hold, will be measured by the answers to four questions:

> *Sets up key terms that will dominate his conclusion*

First, were we truly men of courage—with the courage to stand up to one's enemies—and the courage to stand up, when necessary, to one's associates—the courage to resist public pressure, as well as private greed?

> *Transitional words clarify and emphasize his statements*

Secondly, were we truly men of judgment—with perceptive judgment of the future as well as the past—of our own mistakes as well as the mistakes of others—with enough wisdom to know that we did not know, and enough candor to admit it?

Third, were we truly men of integrity—men who never ran out on either the principles in which they believed or the people who believed in them—men who believed in us—men whom neither financial gain nor political ambition could ever divert from the fulfillment of our sacred trust?

Finally, were we truly men of dedication—with an honor mortgaged to no single individual or group, and compromised by no private obligation or aim, but devoted solely to serving the public good and the national interest.

Courage—judgment—integrity—dedication—these are the historic qualities of the Bay Colony and the Bay State—the qualities which this state has consistently sent to this chamber on Beacon Hill here in Boston and to Capitol Hill back in Washington.

> *Repeats his key terms to explain his main claim*

And these are the qualities which, with God's help, this son of Massachusetts hopes will characterize our government's conduct in the four stormy years that lie ahead. Humbly I ask His help in that undertaking—but aware that on earth His will is worked by men. I ask for your help and your prayers, as I embark on this new and solemn journey.

Text Credits

p. 31 Canby, Peter, "The Cat Came Back," *Harper's Magazine*, March 2005. Copyright © 2005 by Peter Canby for *Harper's Magazine*. Reprinted by permission of International Creative Management, Inc. **p. 32** Friend, Tad, "The Harriet-the-Spy Club," *The New Yorker*, July 31, 2000. Reprinted by permission of International Creative Management, Inc. Copyright © 2000 by Tad Friend for *The New Yorker*. **p. 32, bottom** Source: Brinkley, Alan, *American History: A Survey*, 13th Edition. New York: McGraw-Hill Education, 2008. **p. 33, top** Source: Davidson, James West et al., *Nation of Nations: A Narrative History of the American Republic*, 5th Edition. New York: McGraw-Hill Education, 2007. **pp. 33-34** Morell, Virginia, "OK, There It Is—Our Mystery Mollusk," from "Monterey Menagerie," *National Geographic*, June 2004. Copyright © 2004 by Virginia Morell. Reprinted by permission of the author. **p. 34,** Ehrenreich, Barbara, "What I've Learned from Men: Lessons for a Full-Grown Feminist," published in *Ms. Magazine*, 1985. Copyright © 1985 by Barbara Ehrenreich. Reprinted by permission of International Creative Management. **pp. 34-35, middle** Boot, Max, "Abusing Anonymity," *Commentary*, February 23, 2016. Copyright © 2016 Commentary, Inc. Used with permission. **p. 35, middle** Source: Kaplan, Robert D., *An Empire of Wilderness: Travels Into America's Future*. Copyright © 1998 by Robert D. Kaplan. New York: Random House, Inc. 1998. **p. 35, bottom** Source: Fiero, Gloria, *The Humanistic Tradition*, 5th Edition. New York: McGraw-Hill Education, 2005. **pp. 38-39** Source: Kennedy, John F., "City Upon a Hill" speech delivered to a Joint Convention of the General Court of the Commonwealth of Massachusetts, The State House, Boston, January 9, 1961.

6 Revising, Editing, and Proofreading
修改、编辑与校对

As writers revise, they chisel meaning from their first words and sentences, they erase and redraw parts of the broad outline, they carve out details from generalities, and they sand down rough edges. Only through revising, editing, and proofreading carefully can a writer transform a rough-hewn draft (like a sculpture emerging from stone) into a polished work.

6a Revising Globally: Analyzing Your Own Work 全篇修改：分析论文

Revising globally means looking at the big picture to address issues like thesis, evidence, audience, context, genre, and ethical responsibilities. The first step toward assessing these aspects of your writing is to take a step backward to gain the distance needed for being objective about your own work. The second is to dive in, adjusting thesis and evidence, making changes to address your audience more effectively, and organizing your ideas more logically. You may find it possible to revise for thesis, evidence, audience, and organization simultaneously, but most writers focus on one issue at a time.

1. Thesis and introduction 论题与引言

> **More about**
> Drafting and revising a thesis, 23–24, 131–32

Because writers often discover and develop their ideas as they draft, the draft thesis may no longer capture the project's main idea. (Often, the true thesis appears in the conclusion of the first draft.) This might mean you should adjust your evidence to match your thesis. More frequently it means that you should revise your thesis to match the evidence offered in your draft. Check your draft, too, to be sure that the introduction indicates your purpose—your reasons for writing—and your attitude toward your material.

2. Evidence and counterevidence 正反两方证据

> **More about**
> Effective arguments: classical, Rogerian, Toulmin models, 77–79

In rereading your text, you may have had concerns about the evidence you offered in support of your thesis. Perhaps you noticed something weak, irrelevant, or overly general, or you discovered that you just did not supply enough evidence. If you need more or better evidence, go back to the idea-generating stage or return to the library to do additional research. Perhaps your draft talked only about the reasons for believing your thesis, while ignoring conflicting information and alter-

Writing
Responsibly | The Big Picture

A useful way to think about revising is to focus on your responsibilities to your audience, your topic, other writers, and yourself:

- Have you provided your audience with a worthwhile reading experience?
- Have you explored your topic fully and creatively?
- Have you represented borrowed ideas accurately and acknowledged all your sources, whether you have quoted, summarized, or paraphrased?
- Have you developed a stance that readers will find credible, represented your ideas clearly and powerfully, and written in a voice that is a reflection of your best self?

to SELF

native interpretations. An effective argument shows both evidence and counterevidence and explains why the writer believes the evidence is more valid or useful than the counterevidence.

3. Audience 读者

After rereading your text, consider how your readers will react. Have you won them over? Think about your introduction: Does it make your audience want to keep reading? Next, consider the evidence in your body paragraphs. Will it persuade the people who will be reading your project? Is the language appropriate to those people? Finally, review your conclusion. Does it provide readers with a feeling of closure?

More about
Audience, 17
Introduction, 35–36
Development, 26, 32–35
Connotation, 17–18, 309–10
Level of formality, 17–18
Conclusions, 37

4. Organization 组织结构

Rereading your text may have alerted you to problems with organization. When revising, make sure that all the paragraphs support the thesis and that all the details in each paragraph support the paragraph's main idea. Make sure, too, that your ideas are presented in a logical order, with smooth transitional words and phrases, and that no steps are missing.

More about
Unity, 29
Coherence, 30–32

6b Reconsidering Your Title 重审标题

Once you have revised your draft globally, revisit your title. It should prepare the audience for what they will read in your text. For most college projects, your title should accurately reflect not only the topic but also your approach to it:

- The Power of Wardrobe: An Analysis of Male Stereotype Influences

Topic

Approach

Some writers use a clever turn of phrase, a quotation, or a question to intrigue their readers and draw them into the project:

Clever phrase

Descriptive phrase

- Holy Underground Comics, Batman! <u>Moving Away from the Mainstream</u>

However, this may not be appropriate in all disciplines.

6c Gaining Insight from Peers 求助同辈，深化论点

Writers frequently feel a sense of "ownership" that helps them produce an authentic voice and a commitment to the ideas they express. This sense of ownership, however, can sometimes hold a writer back from making the kinds of changes needed for the success of a writing project. Outlining your draft to check its organization, or allowing time between drafts, can help you gain the distance you need. You can also gain perspective by having a friend read your draft aloud to you or by asking readers for feedback in peer review.

1. The writer's role 写作者的任务

When it is your turn to get feedback, adopt an engaged and receptive stance:

- **Talk.** Explain what you are trying to accomplish and what you would like help with.
- **Listen.** Listen instead of arguing or defending. If readers seem confused or careless, figure out how you can revise the text so that even a confused or careless reader can understand what you are trying to say.
- **Question.** Ask readers to point to specific passages to support their claims or to explain points you find unclear.
- **Write.** Take notes as group members talk so that you have a record when it is time to revise.
- **Evaluate.** Be open to advice, but consider whether there may be a better way of solving a problem.

Peer Review with Multilingual Students Many students are nervous about working in peer groups, but participation can reduce people's fears by showing that everyone makes mistakes and benefits from their experience with diversity. Group work helps non-native speakers of English become more familiar with the rules and idiosyncrasies of English—resolving difficult issues of idiom and word choice, for example—and more trustful of native speakers' natural abilities with their language.

Native English-speaking students may also be hesitant to work in groups with peers from different language backgrounds. However, workplaces, like col-

▶ *More about*
Mastering idioms, 313
Effective word choice,
    309–14

lege, are increasingly diverse. Enhancing the generally excellent practice of peer response, it may be especially useful for native English speakers to hear from multilingual peers whose diverse experiences with language may provide insightful perspectives on topic, organization, word choice, grammar, and style.

2. The reviewer's role 审稿人的任务

When giving feedback to a classmate, keep the following guidelines in mind:

- **Stay positive.** Tell the writer what is working well, along with what could be improved.

- **Respond to the writer.** Listen to the writer's concerns, whether conducting the session face-to-face or electronically.

- **Look at the big picture, but be specific.** Start by stating what you take to be the writing project's main idea. Support general comments by pointing to specific passages in the text and explaining as best you can why they do not work for you.

- **Be a reader and a fellow writer—not a teacher, editor, or critic.** Remember that your job is not to judge the text or to rewrite it, but rather to help the writer recognize and resolve issues.

NOTE Many colleges and universities sponsor writing centers that offer free tutoring. When planning your schedule, include time to take advantage of these services.

6d Revising Locally: Editing Your Words and Sentences
局部修改：字斟句酌

Your writing is a reflection of you—your ideas and your attitude toward your topic and audience. Revising locally means making sure that your individual words and sentences reflect your meaning and create a *persona* that is appropriate for your writing situation.

1. Words 字词

First, be sure that each word reflects your intended meaning, that it has the right *denotation.* If readers have to guess your intent, they may not guess correctly, and they may be annoyed at having to figure it out. Also consider the emotional associations, or *connotations,* that words carry. These indicate the writer's attitude. Compare *freedom fighter* with *terrorist.* Both refer to people who use violence to achieve political ends. The connotative difference, however, is enormous.

> **persona** 外表，形象
> The apparent personality of the writer as conveyed through tone and style

> **More about**
> Denotation, 309–10
> Connotation, 18, 309–10

More about
Levels of for-
mality, 17–18,
287–88
Biased language,
306–08
General and spe-
cific language,
310–11

Next, consider the level of formality that is appropriate to your writing situation. A text message to a friend may be filled with slang and
acronyms, but this informality is rarely appropriate in academic or professional writing. Writers who intend to sound sophisticated by trotting
out a word like *progenitor* to mean *parent* may instead make themselves
sound pompous. All writing benefits from avoiding biased language—
language that unfairly or offensively characterizes groups or individuals.

Finally, consider whether you have combined general, abstract language with specific, concrete words. Explaining broad issues requires
abstract language, but specific words will make your writing more compelling.

2. Sentences 句子

When revising, ask yourself these three questions about your sentences:

1. Are they grammatically correct?
2. Are they varied, and do they emphasize the most important
   information?
3. Are they as concise as they can be without losing meaning or
   affecting style?

More about
Common sen-
tence problems,
tutorial in part
10
Sentence prob-
lems, 331–404
Variety, 293–303
Emphasis, 300–
03, 303–06
Writing concisely,
286–89

NOTE Instructors often use symbols to indicate the most common mistakes. A list of commonly used editing symbols appears at the end of
this book.

Compare the first paragraph in the revised version of Michael Wedd's
writing project (page 46) with the version that appears on page 27. How
do the changes Michael made improve the reading experience?

6e   Proofreading Your Project Carefully 细心校对

When revising, you concentrate on your ideas and how you express them;
when proofreading, you concentrate on correcting errors. An effective
way to achieve the distance you need to proofread effectively is to print
out your draft and read the hard copy line by line from the bottom up.
Mark each correction on the printout as you read; enter them one by

Writing
Responsibly   Beware the Spelling Checker!

While spelling checkers and autocorrect can be very helpful in catching
typos, they cannot always distinguish between homonyms (*they're, their*) or
other frequently confused words (*lay, lie; affect, effect*). They may even lead
you astray, suggesting words that are close to the word you mistyped (*defi-
ant* for the misspelled *definate*) but worlds away from the word you intended
(*definite*). As a writer, you have a responsibility not to leave your reader
guessing. Do not completely rely on automated spelling correction; also use
a dictionary to double-check the program's suggestions, check usage in the
usage glossary in this book, and proofread your text carefully. Only you can
know what you *meant* to say!

to SELF

Self Assessment   A Checklist for Proofreading

Before you submit your text to your instructor, check your work. If you did not do the following, revise as needed.

Spelling
- ☐ Spell-check your project.
- ☐ Read through the text carefully, looking for misused words.
- ☐ Check specifically for words you frequently confuse or misspell.

Punctuation
- ☐ Check sentence punctuation, especially use of the comma and the apostrophe.
- ☐ Make sure that all quotations have quotation marks or block indentation, that you provided end punctuation for all your sentences, and that end punctuation and in-text citations are correctly placed.

- ☐ Check specifically for errors you regularly make (for example, comma splices or fused sentences).

Other Errors
- ☐ Check to make sure that remnants of previous corrections—an extra word, letter, or punctuation mark—do not remain.
- ☐ Check that you have included all in-text citations where needed (for summaries, paraphrases, quotations, or ideas you have borrowed) for a research project.
- ☐ Check that all in-text citations are included in the references list or list of works cited, and make sure that documentation formatting is correct and consistent.

one, and then check to make sure that you have made each correction without introducing additional errors. Another option for proofreading is to work in teams: One person reads the text (including punctuation marks) out loud, while the other person marks errors on the printout.

A proofreading checklist appears in the Self-Assessment box above. Adjust it to your own needs by adding the errors you make most frequently.

> **More about**
> Using a dictionary, 315–18
> Usage glossary, 318–23

Proofreading If you have difficulty proofreading a project, try reading it aloud; whatever your background and culture, you will find this helps you recognize errors. If you are a non-native speaker of English, ask your instructor if you can have a friend or classmate help you proofread. A visit to the writing center may help, too.

Student Model 学生范文 Final Draft

You have seen the essay by Michael Wedd (Columbia College) as it developed, from freewriting and brainstorming to drafting a thesis statement, outline, and first draft. Now consider his final draft. Notice how he has revised his thesis—his purpose has changed from informative to persuasive. He has also worked to provide a better reading experience for his audience by making his introduction and conclusion more compelling. Notice, too, how he has developed his ideas more fully and provided additional reasons to support his claims. Has he now successfully fulfilled his responsibilities to his audience, topic, other writers, and himself? Why or why not?

> **Student Models**
> Development of "Rethinking Alternative Energy"
> Brainstorming, 21
> Clustering, 22
> Journalists' questions, 22
> Draft thesis, 24
> Revised thesis, 24
> Outlines, 25, 26
> First draft, 26–28

Header (last name and page number) appears on all pages

Identifying information

Michael Wedd

Professor Dunn

English 102

5 Oct. 2016

Rethinking Alternative Energy

Descriptive title (centered)

The rise of alternative energy industries has been challenging, controversial, and turbulent. With the availability of many forms of alternative energy systems globally, it is worth pausing for a minute to ask some questions. Conversations are taking place at many levels of government and society about both the costs and the benefits of alternative energy. The problematic relationships between alternative energy industries and the environment they claim to be protecting are emerging as a key focus of these debates.

Environmentalists are conflicted when it comes to alternative energy. Most agree that fossil-fuel-based power plants are damaging the climate and making life harder for many of the world's species. Which forms present the best alternative to fossil-fuels, though, remains a difficult question. One of the primary benefits of energy sources such as the wind, sun, and water is that they are in practically limitless supply. They are producing harvestable energy every day. Despite the clear benefits of these sources, some environmental activists, government regulators, and members of the general public are concerned about the risks. The structures needed to produce these forms of alternative energy can have grave effects on their surrounding environments, ecosystems, wildlife, and in the case of nuclear power plants, on human beings, too (Cherry; Deverakonda; "Former Japanese"; McCurry). Despite how serious and pressing the issue of global warming is, we must be careful to consider not only the benefits but also the costs of the forms of alternative energy production that we deploy. If alternative energy ends up putting the environment—and in some cases humanity directly—in jeopardy, then we need to rethink the ways in which we use it.

Introduction

Thesis statement

Wind energy seems to be a harmless, passive, and effective way of producing energy, but upon closer inspection it also has its drawbacks. Wind turbines are killing birds, bats, and other airborne creatures at an alarming

Topic sentence

counterevidence

evidence

and quickening rate. The American Bird Conservancy (ABC), a group whose mission is to protect bird species and their habitats throughout the Americas, targets wind turbines as a growing threat to birds. An ABC report states that "[t]he United States now has 48,000 wind turbines installed from coast to coast, with many more planned. Those turbines killed nearly 600,000 birds in 2012, from Golden Eagles to migratory songbirds" ("Bird Strikes"). These wind turbines, which are being built increasingly larger to increase their productivity, reach hundreds of feet into the air and threaten birds, some of which are endangered. The group predicts that by 2030, "a ten-fold increase in turbines is expected to boost annual bird mortality to 1.4 to 2 million." Wind turbines put bats at great risk, too. Steven Cherry, a reporter with The Iowa Center for Public Affairs Journalism—a state-wide political watchdog group—highlighted some of these risks in a recent article. He explains, "Wind turbine blades catch the [bats] in a vortex wake that ruptures their lungs, causing them to drown in their blood, experts have found" (Cherry). He lists the Northern long-eared bat, which is an endangered species, as a common casualty. Wind turbines should not be marketed as a safe, "clean" form of alternative energy while their blades are being bloodied by hundreds of thousands of airborne creatures annually in the United States alone.

Solar energy is another alternative that at first seems benign but is actually putting airborne wildlife in grave danger. At the $2.2 billion-dollar Ivanpah solar facility in the California desert, which is part of the largest solar energy complex in the world, birds are being scorched mid-flight and plummeting to earth like meteorites. A report by the *Pulitzer Center* states that "[u]nsuspecting birds fly through Ivanpah's airspace, where the superheated air between the heliostats [mirrors] and the [boiling] towers can reach temperatures as high as 900 degrees Fahrenheit. Flesh catches fire as the birds are ignited in midair" (Deverakonda). Researchers with the U.S. Fish & Wildlife Service, who visited Ivanpah in 2012, were quoted as referring to the complex as a "mega-trap" for a number of wildlife species (Deverakonda). Solar energy is one of the most abundant and seemingly limitless sources of

counterevidence

Transition

Topic sentence

harvestable energy in our solar system, but the ways in which we are capturing it are producing high risks for a number of animal species.

evidence

Topic sentence

The most controversial of these alternative energy sources is the atom. Nuclear energy accounts for significant portions of the world's alternative energy portfolio, but recent events cast a dark shadow on the industry. Japan's 2011 Fukushima nuclear meltdown is still in recent memory. Its physical effects are predicted to reach decades into the future, and its psycho-social effects could last much longer. Japan's powerful nuclear lobby is attempting to rekindle their reactors, though, despite the long shadow cast by Fukushima's triple-meltdown. *The Guardian* reports that "Japan's revamped Nuclear Regulation Authority (NRA) said the new safety checks meant there would be no repeat of the Fukushima catastrophe" (McCurry). Naoto Kan, former prime minister of Japan, believes that the Japanese government is not taking the dangers of nuclear power seriously enough, though. He was quoted in *Deutche Welle*, a German broadcasting service, saying, "[u]nfortunately, I have the impression that neither the Japanese public nor the experts have learned the right lessons from the disaster. If the accident had been a bit more severe, we would have had to evacuate . . . [an area of] 250 kilometers for a long period of time" ("Former Japanese"). Nuclear energy holds potential as an alternative source, but with the aftershocks of both the Chernobyl crisis of the 1970s and 1980s and the more recent Fukushima disaster still affecting people and whole ecosystems today, we must carefully consider the dangers of nuclear power before embracing it as the clean energy of the future.

Restates thesis more specifically

Transition

Clearly, environmentally conscious citizens acknowledge how important it is to check global warming and diversify our energy portfolio, but it is crucial that we also protect the flora and fauna with which we share this planet. It is not enough to be environmentally conscious about the sources from which we draw our energy; we must also consider the ways in which we harvest from those sources, and the tangible effects that alternative energy infrastructure can have on its surroundings. Instead of merely replacing fossil-fuel sources with renewable ones, it is also important that we ask whether it is possible to scale back energy consumption as well. It will be a long time before alternative energy production can meet the accelerating global demand. The solution to this problem will have to include ways of not only increasing renewable energy production safely but also of reducing global consumption substantially.

Concludes by emphasizing importance of issue

————————————[new page]————————————

List of works cited follows MLA style.

Works Cited

"Bird Strikes." *American Bird Conservancy*, 2016, abcbirds.org/.

Cherry, Steven. "Wind Energy Industry Spun into Bat Preservation Effort." *The Iowa Center for Public Affairs Journalism*, 30 June 2015, iow-awatch.org/2015/06/30/wind-energy-industry-spun-into-in-bat-preserva-tion-effort/.

Deverakonda, Akshay. "The Fall of Icarus: Ivanpah's Solar Controversy." *Pulitzer Center on Crisis Reporting*, 5 Mar. 2015, pulitzercenter.org/reporting/united-states-california-ivanpah-solar-electric-generating-system-birds-controversy-sharp-seminar.

"Former Japanese PM Naoto Kan: 'Fukushima Radically Changed My Perspective.'" *Deutsche Welle*, 25 Feb. 2015, www.dw.com/en/former-japanese-pm-naoto-kan-fukushima-radically-changed-my-perspective/a-18275921.

McCurry, Justin. "Japan Restarts First Nuclear Reactor since Fukushima Disaster." *The Guardian*, 11 Aug. 2015. www.theguardian.com/environment/2015/aug/11/japan-restarts-first-nuclear-reactor-fukushima-disaster.

3

Design 关注论文设计

Matters

Designing in Multiple Media 多媒体设计

*Use part 3 to learn, practice, and master these **writer's responsibilities:***

❑ **To Audience**

Guide readers by using the principles of design, fulfilling readers' design expectations by formatting in accordance with academic expectations, and using language and presentation techniques that will help you connect with your audience.

❑ **To Topic**

Use design to create an impression that is appropriate to your topic, use associations and color combinations that are appropriate, and use visuals and multimedia to aid understanding (when they are appropriate to your context and genre).

❑ **To Other Writers**

Treat sources with respect and acknowledge your sources, including when you are making a presentation.

❑ **To Yourself**

Show pride and commitment by using design to reject and reinforce what you want to express, adopting positions you believe in, and preparing fully for all projects and presentations.

7 Designing Printed and Electronic Documents
纸稿与电子稿的设计

The early Peruvians wove this design to represent and honor their sun god. They used proximity (to connect the head and tail to the figure's torso), alignment and repetition (of lines and shapes, to create a background against which the figure stands out), and contrast (of white outline against brown background) to define the figure and attract the eye. According to renowned designer Robin Williams, these four principles—proximity, alignment, repetition, and contrast—are the pillars on which effective design rests.

7a Planning Your Design Project 制订设计计划

To figure out the best way to apply the four principles of design, begin with a careful consideration of your rhetorical situation:

- **Topic.** What is your topic, and how can you reflect that topic through your design?
- **Audience.** Who will your audience be, what kind of expectations do readers bring with them, and what kind of relationship do you have (or want to have) with them?
- **Purpose.** Is your purpose to inform, to persuade, to express yourself, or to entertain, and how should this be reflected in your design?
- **Context.** In what context (academic, business, public) or setting (over the Internet, in person) will your project be received, and how might this affect its design?
- **Genre.** What genre (résumé, business letter, essay, lab report) will best fulfill your purpose, and what design conventions are associated with this genre?
- **Circulation.** Will this document be distributed in print or digitally? If digitally, in what sort of media? Should it operate on a variety of electronic devices? Consider audience and context as you make these decisions.

> **More about**
> Purpose, 16–17, 23–24, 99
> Audience, 17, 100
> Topic, 17, 20–24, 100–01
> Context and genre, 18

Then determine how the pieces of information you want to convey relate to one another, and organize them accordingly. Ask yourself the following questions:

- What information is most and least important?
- Does some of the information support a broader claim or provide evidence for this claim?
- How might you convey or reinforce your ideas visually?

> **More about**
> Organizing, 25–26, 132–33

7b Laying Out and Formatting Your Document 布局与版式设计

Once you have assessed your writing situation and organized your project, you are ready to begin designing it.

1. Create an overall impression 确定整体基调

Start by considering the overall impression you want to give the reader: Should the design be conservative or trendy, serious or playful? Let your

> **More about**
> Formatting college projects, 55
> Formatting business projects, 55–58

own sense of style and the nature of your project guide you in your choice of colors, fonts, and visuals.

2. Plan the layout 规划布局

Next consider the overall *layout*, the visual arrangement of text and images. An effective layout should use proximity, alignment, repetition, and contrast to make the relationships among the elements clear. Keep your layout simple, and use it to direct the reader's eye to the most important pieces of information.

3. Format the document 版式设计

Create a cohesive and attractive design by using the following elements:

> **More about**
> Using italics and underlining, 466–68

Fonts Word processors give writers a wide range of fonts (or typefaces) to choose from. Serif fonts (fonts with a little tail on the ends of letters, like Cambria and Times New Roman) are easier to read when printed on paper, while sans serif fonts (such as Arial and Calibri) are easier to read on screen and are preferred for web publishing.

In addition to selecting the font family, you can set your font in a variety of styles, including **boldface**, *italics*, underlining, or color. Use color or **boldface** for emphasis and contrast, but do so consistently and sparingly: The more they are used, the less attention they will call to themselves. Because *italics* and underlining often have specific meaning, avoid using them except when necessary. Apply the core design principles of repetition and contrast to your font choices: Repeat the same font for consistency and use a different font to produce contrast.

When choosing a font size, make sure it will be easy to read (especially if you are using it for the body of your project). Generally, a 10- or 12-point type will be legible to most readers, but print out a page of text to check the font size: 10-point type in one font may look larger than 12-point type in another font.

The font you choose can also add contrast, or it can group items through repetition: If most of your text is in a serif font, a sans serif font (or the same font in bold or a different color) can call attention to a heading.

Writing
Responsibly **Selecting Fonts with Readers in Mind**

Not all readers have perfect vision. If your audience might include members over forty (or under twelve), use a font size of at least 12 points to make the reading experience easier and more pleasant. If your audience might include visually impaired people, increase your font size even more.

to AUDIENCE

Writing
Responsibly **Establishing a Consistent Font**

When you copy material from a source, you have the responsibility of citing the source, indicating that it is a direct quotation, and providing full information about the source in a bibliography. When you cut and paste your direct copy from an electronic source, you also have the responsibility of converting its font to the one you are using for your main text. Otherwise, when the font suddenly shifts from black to blue, or from Times to Arial, the audience may be distracted from your message.

to OTHER WRITERS

> **More about**
> Using information responsibly, 122–30

NOTE For college writing, check the style guide for your discipline to determine the most appropriate font and style.

White space The portion of a page or screen with no text or images, the *white space*, does not literally have to be white. Margins provide white space, as does the extra space before a paragraph and around a heading. Extra white space can group elements into a section or lend emphasis through contrast. Ample white space makes a page inviting and easy to read; without it, a page looks crowded, and the eye has difficulty knowing where to focus.

Headings The principles of repetition and contrast are crucial with headings:

- Set all headings of the same level in the same font, style, and color, and align them in the same way on the page or screen:

   First-level heading (title)

   Second-level heading (major section)

   Third-level heading (subsection)
- Use the same grammatical structure for all headings of the same level. For example, use all *-ing* phrases (*Containing the Economic Downturn, Bailing Out Wall Street*) or all *noun* phrases (*Economic Downturn Ahead, Wall Street Bailout*).

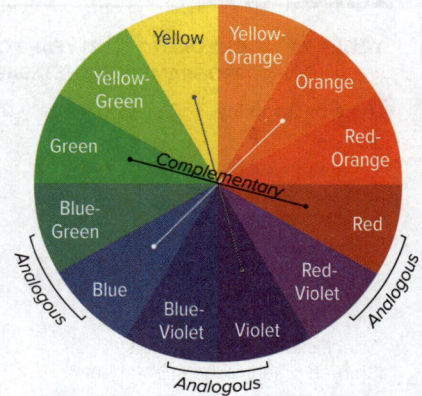

FIGURE 7.1 The color wheel. Colors opposite each other on the color wheel are complementary; colors adjacent to each other are analogous.

Lists Another strategy for grouping related items (and for adding white space) is to use lists. Keep lists succinct to allow readers to skim them for information. They can be particularly effective in web pages.

Color Color, through contrast, calls the reader's attention to what is important in the text, but use color judiciously:

- Use a limited color palette to avoid a hodgepodge effect.
- Use analogous colors, those adjacent to each other on a color wheel (Figure 7.1), to create a softer, more harmonious look; use complementary colors, those opposite each other on the color wheel, to contrast with each other and make the other color look brighter.
- Make sure that color combinations are readable, that they contrast sufficiently with their background.
- Consider the associations colors and combinations of colors carry: pastels for new babies, bright yellow and black for warnings, green for nature. Consider your audience carefully as you choose colors; their associations vary from one culture to another. White, for example, is the color for weddings in the United States; in China, the "wedding color" is red.
- Repeat colors to group items of the same type.

> *More about*
> Parallelism, 290–93

7c Adding Visuals 添加视觉资料

To be effective, images must expand your readers' understanding of your text, and they must be appropriate to your writing situation. When including visuals, be sure to place them as soon as possible after the text discussion that refers to them. Make sure, too, that you choose the visual that is most appropriate to the information you are conveying. (See the Quick Reference box on the next page.)

> *More about*
> Visuals in academic writing, 69

Reference   Matching Your Evidence to the Correct Type of Visual

TABLE 7.1   CHILDREN 3 TO 21 YEARS OLD SERVED IN FEDERALLY SUPPORTED PROGRAMS FOR THE DISABLED, BY TYPE OF DISABILITY (2006–09)

Type of Disability	2005–06	2006–07	2007–08	2008–09
Autism	3.3	3.9	4.5	5.2
Developmental delay	5.1	5.0	5.4	5.5
Emotional disturbance	7.1	6.9	6.7	6.5
Hearing impairments	1.2	1.2	1.2	1.2
Intellectual disability	8.3	8.0	7.6	7.4
Multiple disabilities	2.1	2.1	2.1	2.0
Orthopedic impairments	1.1	1.0	1.0	1.1
Other health impairments	8.5	9.1	9.7	10.2
Specific learning disabilities	40.7	39.9	39.0	38.2
Speech or language impairments	21.9	22.1	22.0	22.0
Visual impairments	0.4	0.4	0.4	0.4
Traumatic brain injury	0.4	0.4	0.4	0.4

Source: US Department of Education, Institute of Education Sciences, National Center for Education Statistics, *Digest of Education Statistics,* 2010.

Tables. Use tables to display large amounts of data, data that include decimals, or data on multiple variables that are difficult to convey in a graph.

Pie charts. Use pie charts to convey significant divisions in a single entity that add up to 100 percent.

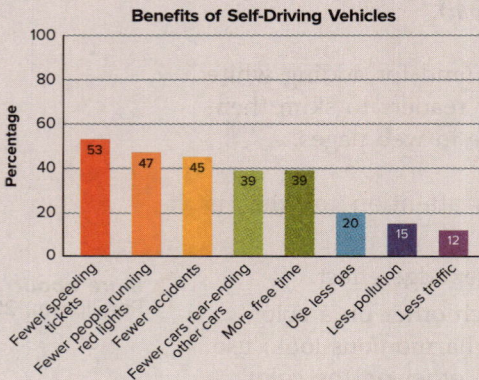

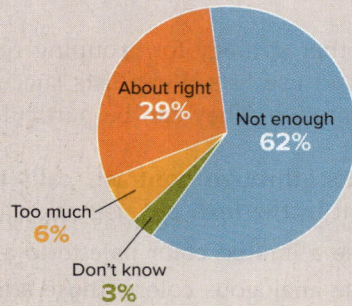

Bar graphs. Use bar graphs to compare two or more variables.
Source: Data from Nielsen's Youth Viewpoint on Self-Driving Cars study conducted by the Harris Poll, Oct. 2015

Americans' Opinion about Government Aid to the Middle Class
Source: Data from Pew Research Center, Dec. 8–13, 2015 http://www.pewresearch.org

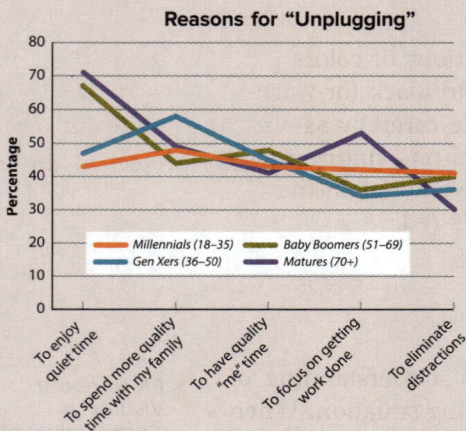

Line graphs. Use line graphs to show changes among variables over time.
Source: Data from the Harris Poll, Jan. 2016 http://www.harrisinteractive.com

Photographs and other images. Use photographs and other images, such as movie stills and screenshots, to provide an example or other reference point or to depict a process.

8 Designing in Context: Academic and Business Documents 设计要基于语境：学术文本与商务文本

If you were meeting friends for a casual dinner or to see a band, many outfits might be appropriate, but few would be right for the world of business, where your appearance can be a strike against you. Just as an outfit sends a message to a potential employer about whether you would be a good fit, the texts you write also represent you. To be successful, your words must be tailored to the context in which they are going to be read. Such tailoring allows readers to focus on the ideas, not on the appearance of your writing project.

8a Formatting (and Writing) Academic Texts
学术文本的版式设计（与撰写）

As with any other type of writing, writing in an academic context requires that you consider the expectations of your reader. Because your reader (usually, your instructor) will be focusing mainly on your content—your ideas and how you express them—keep formatting simple, and focus on presenting your text clearly, using a standard font (such as Times New Roman or Arial) in 10- or 12-point type and leaving 1- to 1.5-inch margins. Include identifying information on the first page or on a title page and in a header that appears on each page (in case pages get separated). Double-space the text to provide a comfortable reading experience.

> **More about**
> MLA format,
>   157–211 (part 6)
> APA format,
>   213–54 (part 7)

In most academic areas, a style guide, such as the *MLA Handbook* for courses in literature and language or the *Publication Manual of the American Psychological Association* for courses in psychology and other social sciences, will provide formatting standards. Sample pages from an MLA-style project appear in Figure 8.1.

For a sample research report, and a discussion of the formatting requirements of APA style, see Heather DeGroot's project at the end of part 7.

8b Formatting (and Writing) Business Texts
商务文本的版式设计（与撰写）

Regardless of what you do after college, you will need to know how to write business letters and email messages, résumés, and letters of application. All these business communications share an emphasis on getting to the point quickly and conveying information clearly, directly, and concisely.

Student Models 学生范文 MLA-Style Writing Project and Works Cited

Tom Hackman
Professor Howard
Writing 109
28 November 2016

Heading includes writer's name, instructor's name, course number, and date at top left of first page

Date in day month year order

Why Students Cheat: The Complexities and Oversimplications of Plagiarism

Title centered

The system of American higher education is founded on principles of honesty and academic integrity. For this reason, nearly all those invested in this system—students, instructors, and administrators—recognize that plagiarism cannot be tolerated. They also agree that a lot of plagiarism is occurring. A survey published in *Who's Who Among American High School Students* (reported by Newberger) indicated that 15% of top-ranked high schoolers plagiarize. Practices among higher education students are not much better. According to research by Donald L. McCabe, a professor at Rutgers University who has done extensive work on cheating, 70% of college students admitted to committing forms of plagiarism in the previous year (38). A 2006 study by Hard et al. showed that plagiarism was common among the 421 students who participated in their research. Figure 1 illustrates the various forms this plagiarism took.

Text double-spaced throughout

- 60.6% Copied text from a source without using quotation marks or giving proper acknowledgment
- 39.4% Copied information from websites without acknowledgment
- 35.1% Used unauthorized materials or fabricated data (e.g., falsified data in a research paper or lab report)
- 8.2% Bought a paper and submitted it as student's own work

Fig. 1. Common types of plagiarism and the percentage of students who commit them. (Data and categories from Hard et al. 1069)

Figure caption below figure, includes figure number, title, and source

Birchard, Karen. "Canada's Simon Fraser U. Suspends 44 Students in Plagiarism Scandal." *The Chronicle of Higher Education*, vol. 53, no. 8, 24 Oct. 2002, p. 46. *EbscoHost*, chronicle.com/article/Canadas-Simon-Fraser-U/116779.

Hard, Stephen F., et al. "Faculty and College Student Beliefs about the Frequency of Student Academic Misconduct." *The Journal of Higher Education*, vol. 77, no. 6, Nov.Dec. 2006, pp. 1058–80.

Hunt, Russell. "Four Reasons to Be Happy about Internet Plagiarism." *Teaching Perspectives*, Dec. 2002, stu.ca/~hunt/4reasons.htm.

Li, Yongyan. "Text-Based Plagiarism in Scientific Writing: What Chinese Supervisors Think about Copying and How to Reduce It in Students' Writing." *Science and Engineering Ethics*, vol. 19, no. 2, June 2013, pp. 569–83.

Marsden, Rhodri. "The Big Steal: Rise of the Plagiarist in the Digital Age." *The Guardian*, 21 Mar. 2014, www.theguardian.com/technology/2014/mar/21/rise-plagiarism-internet-shia-labeouf.

McCabe, Donald L. "Cheating: Why Students Do It and How We Can Help Them Stop." *American Educator*, Winter 2001, pp. 38–43.

Newberger, Eli H. "Why Do Students Cheat?" *School for Champions*. School for Champions, 6 Dec 2003, school-for-champions.com/character/newberger_cheat¬ing2.htm#.VvI8THpxBqs.

Pecorari, Diane, and Bojana Petric. "Plagiarism in Second-Language Writing." *Language Teaching*, vol. 47, no. 3, July 2014, pp. 269–302.

Tran, Nam. "Plagiarism Policies Lead to Confusion among Students." *The Daily Nebraskan*, 9 Oct. 2015, dailynebraskan.com/news/plagiarism-policies-lead-to-confusion-among-students/article_2c875fa2-6e2c-11e5-ad00-cfbdd1242e21.html.

Heading centered, double-space between heading and first entry

List of works cited double-spaced

FIGURE 8.1 The first page of an MLA-style writing project (*left*) and an MLA-style list of works cited

> **More about**
> Abbreviating titles, 469

1. Business letters and email messages 商务信函与邮件信息

Readers of business letters (Figure 8.2, p. 57) and email messages expect you to state your purpose in your first paragraph, keep your paragraphs short, and be clear and specific so that they can skim your communications and grasp the main points immediately. Adopt a positive and somewhat formal tone. (IM abbreviations such as IMO, for "in my opinion," are out of place in business communications.)

Business letters should include a date, a return address (unless you are using letterhead stationery), the address of the recipient (or *inside address*), and a formal salutation ("Dear Ms. Grayson:") and closing ("Sincerely," "Yours truly," "Best wishes,"). Include a formal salutation and closing only in the most formal emails. Business email should include a subject line that accurately summarizes the content of the message. Include in the To line only those recipients who need to take action on the message; include in the cc (or "carbon copy") line anyone who must be kept informed but from whom you do not need a reply.

Both business letters and email messages usually use *block style*, in which all text aligns with the left-hand margin. Instead of indenting paragraphs, an extra line of space is inserted between them.

Creating Task-Oriented Email In formal settings in the United States, email messages are task oriented, and they frequently dispense with formalities and personal touches. In some cultures such messages would be considered rude, but members of some professional communities in the United States view them as efficient and time-saving.

2. Résumés and cover letters 简历和求职信

A *résumé* (Figure 8.3) is a brief document that summarizes your work and educational experience for a prospective employer. A résumé is usually accompanied by an *application* or a *cover letter* (Figure 8.4), which is essentially a sales letter—an opportunity to sell yourself to prospective employers. In drafting your résumé and cover letter, keep your audience and purpose in mind: What will your readers want to know? What will persuade them to put your application at the top of the pile?

Your résumé should indicate the position for which you are applying, a listing of the degrees you hold (college and above) and when you received them, and any honors or certifications you have attained. Especially for those new to the workforce, the résumé should focus on the skills you have acquired from any work experience. For example, you might explain that you "maintained good customer relations" and "presented a positive corporate image" in your job at a fast-food restaurant. Be sure to list your employers in reverse chronological order (most recent first). Include any specific skills (such as proficiency in Excel or Dreamweaver or fluency in another language), and include references or indicate that they are

Student Model 学生范文 **Business Letter**

October 10, 2017

4 line spaces

Ms. Lauren Grayson   Inside address
6243 North Sheridan Road
Chicago, IL 60610

Dear Ms. Grayson: Salutation

I am responding to your letter of September 28 about the difficulties you had in trying to purchase a gift certificate for your friends, the Websters. First let me say that I apologize and can assure you that the employee you spoke to on the phone apologizes as well.

We do offer our guests the option of purchasing gift certificates via fax. The only things we require are faxed copies of identification and a credit card, and a filled-out gift certificate form—all of which you supplied. It is also our policy to keep guest information confidential at all times. In this instance, however, it is clear that we failed to execute our procedures.

I have spoken to the employee involved and explained the importance of our system and guest satisfaction. I am enclosing a $75 gift certificate as a token of my apology.

Furthermore, I have sent a $75 gift certificate to the Websters, in the hope that they also accept our apologies and understand how important our guests are to us here at Rebecca's.

Please feel free to contact me personally if you ever need anything in the future. I will do my best to help you in any way I can.

Sincerely,   Closing

4 line spaces   *Christopher Juarez*

Christopher Juarez   Signature
General Manager

Enc.   Enclosure indicated

FIGURE 8.2 Block-style business letter

> **More about**
> Document design,
> 51–54

Writing Responsibly   Maintaining Confidentiality in Email

You may have noticed the bcc (or "blind carbon copy") option in the header of your email messages. Any recipient you list in this line will receive a copy of your message but will not be identified to other recipients. Sending blind copies to keep the email addresses of recipients private is ethical, but blind-copying a recipient to deceive your correspondent into believing a message is confidential is not. So your readers will not mistakenly believe they are the only recipient of a message, mention in the body of the message that it is being shared with others. If you wish to forward another's email, first obtain permission.

to SELF

Student Models 学生范文 **Résumé and Cover Letter**

FIGURE 8.3 Résumé

Name and contact information set off from rest of résumé

Sonja Jacques
7716 W. Birchwood Street
Chicago, IL 60648
(312) 555–1212
sonjaja@gmail.com

OBJECTIVE: To obtain an assistant to curator position at a museum

Education first, as typical for recent graduate

EDUCATION: B.S., University of Illinois, Chicago Circle, June 2017.
History major; International studies minor
GPA: 3.8 (on a 4-point scale)

Summer studies in Museum Curatorship, James Cook University, North Queensland, Australia, 2015.
Courses in artifact preservation, program management, museum funding.

EMPLOYMENT: Workstudy employee, UIC University Library, fall 2015–spring 2017.
Trained workstudy employees in library policies; shelved returned books.

Intern, Smithsonian Institution, Washington, DC, summer 2016.
Conducted museum tours for school groups; catalogued textual archives; assisted researchers.

Sales clerk, Moheiser's, Park Ridge, IL, summer 2012–spring 2014.
Organized inventory; waited on customers; learned apparel business.

SPECIAL SKILLS AND HONORS: Fluent in French.
Tutored seventh-graders in French, Ebinger School, Chicago, IL, 2014–2016.
Experience with Microsoft Word, PageMaker, and Internet research.
President, Phi Kappa Phi Honor Society, UIC chapter, 2017.
Dean's list, 2016–2017.

REFERENCES: Available on request.

FIGURE 8.4 Cover letter

7716 W. Birchwood Street
Chicago, IL 60648

July 1, 2017

Modified block style: Return address and date align right of center

Mr. Aaron Gieseke
Recruitment, Human Resources
Museum of Science and Industry
57th Street and Lake Shore Drive
Chicago, IL 60637

Addresses specific person formally

Dear Mr. Gieseke:

I am applying for the entry-level position of assistant to the curator, which you advertised in the June 30 issue of the *Chicago Tribune*. Since childhood, I have been delighted by the museum's extraordinary exhibits, from Colleen Moore's Fairy Castle to the walk-through heart and chick hatchery. I would welcome the opportunity to put my skills and knowledge to work at your renowned institution.

Mentions specific job and shows familiarity with museum

Two years ago, I was fortunate to take several in-depth courses in museum curatorship at James Cook University. With European curators as teachers, I came to understand the many facets of running a museum, including preserving artifacts and tapping sources of funding. I also learned about the myriad jobs that go on behind the scenes and decided that museum life was where I wanted to be in my professional life.

Highlights educational ties to job

This decision was reinforced many times over while I was an intern at the Smithsonian last summer. I especially enjoyed working with researchers on new interactive exhibits and using my French language skills with international visitors. Inasmuch as the Museum of Science and Industry was the first to initiate interactive exhibits and welcomes thousands of overseas travelers each year, I believe my qualifications are ideal for the job.

Links work experience to job and shows knowledge of museum

My résumé is enclosed. I would be delighted to meet with you for an interview at any time. You may phone me at (312) 555–1212 or email me at sonjaja@gmail.com. I look forward to hearing from you.

Asks for interview and gives contact information

Sincerely,

Sonja Jacques

Sonja Jacques

Modified block style: Closing and signature align with return address

Enc.

available on request. Limit your résumé to one page unless your work experience is extensive. Figure 8.3 shows the sections included in most résumés.

Address your cover letter to a specific person, even if you have to phone the company to determine who that is. Start your letter by mentioning the specific job for which you are applying. In subsequent paragraphs, explain what qualifies you for the job, pointing out items on your résumé that are a good fit for this position but not just repeating the résumé. Conclude your letter by asking for an interview and providing information about how you can be reached. Throughout your résumé and cover letter, you need to walk a fine line: Do not be too modest about your accomplishments, but do not exaggerate your qualifications, either.

8c Creating Websites and Web Pages 创建网站和网页

"Writing for the web" can involve a wide range of social media work, such as maintaining a Twitter feed or Facebook page. Or it can mean creating a *website,* a collection of files located at a single address, or URL, on the World Wide Web.

Every website begins with a *home page,* the page designed to introduce visitors to the site. Many writers turn to a blogging platform such as WordPress to host not only a traditional blog but also websites. However you create your website, the home page should include the website's title, the date the site was created or last updated, contact information, a copyright or Creative Commons notice, and clear navigation to site content, through either navigation bars or a site map.

Reference   Consider Your Rhetorical Situation When Creating a Website

Purpose and Focus

Readers scan websites quickly, so keep your sentences brief and clear and your focus tight. Images, sound files, and design should reflect your purpose and capture readers' attention.

Context and Audience

Consider any restrictions of your host (site sponsor) as you plan your site. Consider, too, the needs and expectations of your readers, but remember that unintended readers may

also see what you post on the open web, so avoid language or content that you or others might find embarrassing or offensive.

Genre

If the information you are providing will remain current for a long time, create a website that you update once or twice a year; if your site requires daily or weekly updates, create a *blog*; if you want readers to contribute to the site's content, create a *wiki*.

Unlike print documents in which reading traditionally proceeds *linearly* (the document is arranged so that all readers begin at page 1 and read through to the end), most websites are *networked* (users may enter the site at any page and follow their own path through it). A site that includes a home page and a handful of *web pages*—documents that, like the home page itself, may include text, audio, still images, and database files—with loosely related content may work best with a hub-and-spoke structure, where each page links back to the home page (Figure 8.5). If your website will offer a series of pages with related content, a hierarchical arrangement, with links from the home page to lower-level pages and from page to page, may be more useful (Figure 8.6).

Since users frequently move from page to page in search of information, make navigation easy by providing links within a web page and *menus* at the top or side of the page. Include a link to the site's home page on every web page.

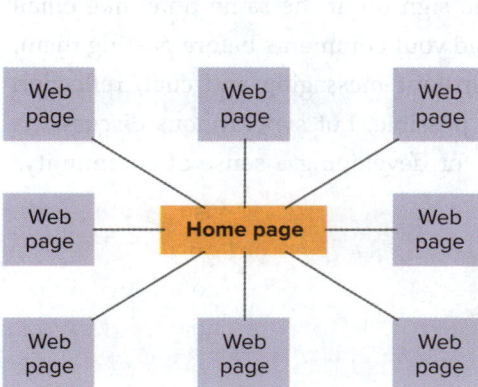

FIGURE 8.5 A hub-and-spoke structure

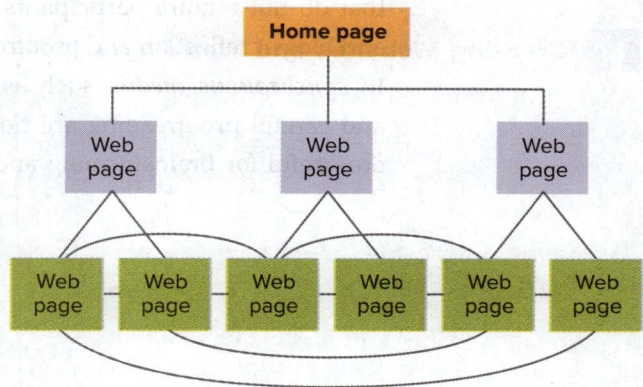

FIGURE 8.6 A hierarchical, treelike structure, with additional links

❯ **More about**
Ad hominem and
other logical
fallacies, 79–81

Writing
Responsibly | Flaming

The quick interactivity and the anonymity of online media present a special challenge: keeping your temper. **Flaming**—writing a scathing response to someone with whom you disagree—is a great temptation, but it shuts down reasoned discussion, instead encouraging *ad hominem* (personal) attack. Flaming may impart a sense of power for your having found a biting way to put down an opponent, but it also minimizes the likelihood of anyone's listening to or being influenced by you.

to OTHER WRITERS

8d   Writing Responsibly in Social Media
在社交媒体上负责任地写作

Online communication is woven deeply into the fabric of contemporary life: Email, texting, wikis, blogs, and an array of social apps, from Twitter to Snapchat, are found in classrooms, professional settings, and homes alike. The very familiarity of these media can lull writers into making errors that they later regret. Writers must always adapt their style and tone to their *rhetorical situation*; now the medium and the app are part of a writer's rhetorical situation, too. As writers seamlessly move from the Yik Yak app to the Mail app, for example, the style and tone of what they write must also make the instantaneous change. Think about your purpose, and tailor your writing style and tone to your intended audience.

When participating in online discussions, focus on responding directly to the comments of other participants and summarizing the discussion before moving on. Your online voice can be casual, but strive to keep your comments clear and to maintain a voice that is friendly and polite, even when you disagree.

When participating in a discussion in *asynchronous media* (media that do not require participants to sign on at the same time, like email and blogs), reflect on and proofread your comments before posting them. In *synchronous media*, such as instant messaging and chat, reflection and careful proofreading are not possible, but synchronous discussions are useful for brainstorming and for developing a sense of community.

9 Designing a Multimedia Presentation
多媒体演示设计

Al Gore's presentation on global warming, captured in the classic documentary *An Inconvenient Truth,* has been seen by millions of viewers worldwide. Very few of us ever have an opportunity to reach such a large audience on a topic of global importance. Still, we are often called upon to present our ideas at school, at work, and in our communities. If we can present them clearly and compellingly, using multiple media when they will help us reach listeners, we, too, can effect change.

9a Identifying Your Writing Situation 确定写作情景

As with any writing project, begin planning a presentation by considering your *purpose, audience, topic, context,* and *genre.* In an academic or a business context, your primary *purpose* is likely to be the same as for a written text: to present information or to persuade others to accept your position or to take action. Even more so than a written text, an oral presentation is likely also to have a secondary purpose: to engage the imagination or emotions of the audience so that members can more readily identify with and remember the key points.

When addressing classmates or colleagues, you will probably have a sense of the needs and expectations of your *audience.* When addressing an unfamiliar group, ask yourself why the group has assembled and which topics they would be interested in. It may be useful to ask the event organizers about audience characteristics and interests.

The *context,* or setting, in which you deliver your presentation will affect the kinds of equipment you will need, the types of multimedia aids you create, and the relationship you can establish with your audience. When addressing a small group in a college classroom, for example, you will probably not need any special equipment, whereas in larger settings you may need a projector, a sound system, and special lighting.

Finally, consider the *genre* of your presentation. As a college student, you are most likely to be asked to contribute to or lead a class discussion, or to give a presentation online or in person to a class, student group, or social service organization. In business, you may be asked to train colleagues or make a sales pitch to potential customers in person or online.

Contributing to Class Discussion In US schools, active participation in class is an important part of the learning experience, and it often plays

> **More about**
> Purpose, 16–17,
>   23–24, 99–100
> Audience, 17, 41,
>   100
> Topic, 17, 20–24,
>   100–01
> Context and
>   genre, 18

a role in instructors' grades. If you are uncomfortable with the idea of speaking in class, let your instructor know. If students in your class seem uncomfortable when they speak, remember that you are responsible for being an effective listener as well as a speaker. That means listening patiently and respectfully at all times.

9b Devising a Topic and Thesis 主题与论文构思

▶ **More about**
Devising a topic,
20–23, 100–01
Crafting a thesis,
23–24, 101–02

A presentation, like a written text, begins with an appropriate topic and a well-focused thesis. Your topic and approach should engage you and your audience and offer special insight. Craft a thesis that conveys your purpose and that will engage and guide your audience.

9c Organizing the Presentation 组织演讲

It is more difficult for people to understand and remember ideas they have heard than ideas they have read. Organize your talk to help your audience hold your main points in memory while the presentation unfolds.

1. Introduction 引言

▶ **More about**
Introductions,
35–36

Use your introduction (10–15 percent of your presentation) to develop a rapport with your audience and to establish the key points of your presentation. Your introduction should specify your topic and approach, convey why it should matter to your audience, engage your audience, establish your credentials, and provide a brief overview of your main points.

2. Body 主体

▶ **More about**
Organizing,
25–26, 41,
132–33
Explaining and
supporting ideas,
26, 32–35,
40–41, 91,
133–35
Finding informa-
tion, 105–13
Transitions, 30–32
Adding visuals,
53–54

The body (75–85 percent of your presentation) should explain the points that you previewed in your introduction. For each claim you make, supply appropriate, relevant evidence, such as specific examples drawn from your reading or your experience. Facts and statistics can be very effective as long as you do not burden your audience with more numbers than it can process. Use transitions such as "first," "second," and "third" to guide your audience, and provide a brief summary of the main points you made earlier ("As I explained a few minutes ago . . .") and a preview of the points you are about to discuss ("Next I will show how . . ."). Presenting statistics in graphs or charts can also help.

3. Conclusion 结论

▶ **More about**
Conclusions, 37

Keep your conclusion brief (5–10 percent of your presentation). Use it to reinforce the main point of the presentation: Repeat the main idea and key points, end with a brief but powerful statement, or return to the opening anecdote, example, or statistic.

9d Rehearsing the Presentation 演讲排练

For an oral presentation, you may speak off-the-cuff or read a presentation aloud, but speaking from notes will usually be the most effective means of delivery. The notes will keep you organized and prevent you from forgetting important points while allowing you to make eye contact with the audience.

1. Prepare a speaking outline 准备演讲提纲

When speaking from notes, create a speaking outline by jotting notes on a topic outline about where to pause, when to increase the urgency in your voice, and when to advance to the next slide or visual aid. Add content notes, too, but keep them brief, including only as much information as you need to remind yourself of the point you want to make.

> **More about**
> Topic outlines,
> 25–26, 133

2. Use language effectively 有效使用语言

Well-chosen language can help listeners understand and remember your main points. When you can, use familiar, concrete words; support abstract words with concrete examples and vivid figures of speech such as metaphors and similes; keep your sentences concise; and use parallelism and repetition to emphasize your points.

> **More about**
> Abstract versus
> concrete lan-
> guage, 310–11
> Eliminating wordi-
> ness, 286–89
> Figures of speech,
> 311–12
> Parallelism, 290–
> 93
> Repetition (inten-
> tional), 302

3. Use visual, audio, and multimedia aids 使用视听和多媒体辅助工具

When using visual, audio, or multimedia aids during a presentation, make sure the aids are relevant, that you explain them clearly and succinctly, and that you do not provide so many that the audience pays attention to them rather than to you. Be sure, too, that you speak to your audience, not to your visual aids.

Presentation software such as Microsoft PowerPoint, Google Slides, or Apple Keynote usefully projects visual, audio, and multimedia aids. However, overuse of presentation software or poor preparation of slides can cause "death by PowerPoint." (For advice on effective use of presentation software, see the Self-Assessment box on the next page.)

> **More about**
> Visual design,
> 51–54
> Using visuals
> appropriately,
> 53–54

Quick Reference Overcoming Presentation Anxiety

If you get anxious before making a presentation, you are in good company. The following tips may help you get through your presentation with a minimum of nerves.

- Envision your success: Picture yourself calm and relaxed at the podium; imagine your sense of accomplishment at the end of the presentation.
- Take several slow, deep breaths, or tighten and relax your muscles just before you take the podium.

- Ignore your racing heart or clammy hands. Instead, use the adrenaline surge to add energy to your presentation.
- Focus on your message: Get excited about what you have to say, and you will bring the audience with you.
- Accept the fact that you may stumble, and be prepared to go on.

Self Assessment — Using Presentation Software Effectively

When preparing a presentation, reflect on your work. If you answer no to any of the following questions, revise as necessary.

- **Did you review your outline to determine where slides would enhance your presentation?** Do not overwhelm your presentation by creating a slide for every moment.

- **Did you begin with a title slide?** This slide should include the title of your presentation, your name, and any other useful identifying information, such as your college or business affiliation and your Twitter handle.

- **Did you keep text brief, design uniform, and contents varied?** The audience should be listening to you, not reading your slides. To make slides easy to absorb, maintain a consistent design and keep text brief. To enhance interest, vary the other components (images, information graphics, video clips).

- **Did you add blank slides?** Go to a blank slide when no illustration is relevant.

- **Did you check that slides are visually pleasing?** Keep slides uncluttered and balanced; limit your use of animations (the way text or images enter a slide).

- **Did you proofread your slides?** Correct all misspellings and mistakes of grammar, punctuation, and mechanics.

- **Did you learn your software's commands?** Keystroke commands allow you to advance or return to slides, use the animation effects, and end the slide show.

- **Did you practice your presentation with your slides in advance?** Use animations to bring information forward, and do not leave slides up after you have moved on to the next topic.

- **Did you check your equipment in advance?** Make sure that cords are long enough, that you can lower the lights and cover windows, and so forth.

- **Did you practice giving your presentation without your slides?** Murphy's law—whenever something *can* go wrong, it *will* go wrong—applies to presentation software. If the power fails or your computer dies, you should still be able to go on with the show.

Writing
Responsibly
Remembering the Speaker's Responsibilities

In addition to your responsibilities as a writer, keep these additional responsibilities as a speaker in mind:

- Know your material and your purpose. For an informative speech, be sure your information is current and your examples pertinent. For a persuasive speech, adopt a position that you believe in, one for which you can offer compelling, concrete evidence.
- Acknowledge counterevidence and alternative interpretations. Do not alter quotations unfairly or misuse statistics. Avoid words and images that manipulate your audience or that rely on logical fallacies.
- Since your audience will not have access to your written text, acknowledge sources with signal phrases such as "Alison Ling's research shows . . ." and be prepared to provide a list of works cited if requested.
- Respect the time and attention of your audience by practicing your presentation until you can deliver it with confidence and grace and without overreliance on notes.

to AUDIENCE

4. Rehearse 排练

Practice your presentation out loud in front of a mirror, a group of friends or family, or a video camera. Plan at least two or three practice sessions to become comfortable with the content of your presentation and to polish your delivery.

> **More about**
> Logical fallacies,
> 79–81

Adjusting Your Gestures to Appeal to a Multicultural Audience Gestures vary from culture to culture. As you prepare to give formal presentations, pay attention to the gestures commonly made by classmates or other peers who represent your prospective audience. How do they differ from gestures you are accustomed to? Are you aware of any gestures you should not use while speaking to a multicultural audience?

9e Connecting with the Audience 与观众沟通

When the time comes to make your presentation, approach the podium and wait for your audience to settle down. Then introduce yourself, thank the audience for attending, and smile. As you speak, look out at the audience, turning to the left, the right, and the center, so all members of the audience feel included. Speak slowly and clearly. Pause between sections of your presentation, and vary the tone of your voice. If you sense that you are losing your audience, slow your pace, increase your volume, or step closer to the audience. To avoid ableism, assume that some members of your audience have impaired hearing or vision. Speak loudly and clearly; make your graphics large; and do not choose a background design that interferes with readability.

4

Genre 关注论文类型
Matters
Writing in College 大学写作

Use part 4 to learn, practice, and master these writer's responsibilities:

❏ **To Audience**

Adjust your approach, your language, your citation style, and your use of visuals in response to the expectations of academic readers; reason logically, and appeal to the intellect and (when appropriate) the emotions of the audience.

❏ **To Topic**

Choose topics that are appropriate to your discipline, that are debatable when writing an argument, and that go beyond summary when analyzing literature.

❏ **To Other Writers**

Treat alternative viewpoints fairly and opponents with respect, and cite and document sources fully, using the style guide that is appropriate to the discipline in which you are writing.

❏ **To Yourself**

Establish your credibility by adopting a reasonable tone, using sound logic, and treating opposing views fairly; take the time to think deeply about your topic and to write about it creatively and thoughtfully.

10

Writing in College: Comparing the Disciplines 大学写作：学科比较

Academic studies are classified into groups, or *disciplines*: communities of scholars who share a subject, approaches, and resources (types of evidence) for answering questions. The traditional disciplines are the humanities, the social sciences, and the natural sciences. Just as we eat from all four food groups (meat and beans, fruits and vegetables, dairy, grains) to maintain a balanced diet, so do many colleges require students to taste each of the disciplines to achieve a balanced education. Whether you focus on a single discipline or take a bite from them all, understanding the academic approach and tools of each discipline is crucial to college success.

10a Adopting an Academic Approach 采用学术方法

The disciplines differ in what counts as good evidence. A biologist, for example, is likely to test claims by producing laboratory data, a sociologist might administer a survey, and a literature scholar might read a novel or poem closely. The disciplines also vary according to the types of sources they use, the ways they use language, the way they cite and document their sources, the way they use visuals, and the kinds of questions they ask on exams. One thing they all require, however, is that students adopt an analytical approach to the subject matter and that they fulfill their responsibilities by doing the following when writing:

> *More about*
> Analysis, 12–14,
> 35, 88, 130, 133

- Crafting a thesis that represents the writer's own insights or a synthesis of sources
- Presenting an unbiased assessment of evidence
- Depicting honestly any shortcomings in their research or alternatives to their claims
- Representing and citing ideas, information, and images accurately

Writing Responsibly | Writing Responsibly across the Disciplines

Most disciplines have not only their own subjects and approaches, but also specific ethical expectations for researchers and writers. As you learn the research methods of a discipline, take the time to locate its ethical code and learn what that discipline most values in its writing and research.

to TOPIC

More about
Specialized reference works, 105
Scholarly versus popular sources, 115–18
Finding articles, 108–10
Primary versus secondary sources, 89–90, 111–13

10b **Using the Sources of the Discipline** 利用学科资源

Researchers may use discipline-specific reference works to begin their study of a topic, but they continue their research with *scholarly sources*—peer-reviewed journal articles and books by experts, often published by university presses. To find scholarly articles, use discipline-specific databases, such as the MLA International Bibliography (for literature) or PsycArticles (for psychology). A librarian can help you determine which databases are most appropriate for your discipline.

For researchers, the scholarly books and articles they use are *secondary sources*. These sources describe, evaluate, or interpret primary sources, and they *synthesize* information from primary and secondary sources. Academic researchers also rely on *primary sources*. In the humanities, those may be works of literature, art, or film, or they may be historical documents or speeches. In the natural sciences and social sciences, primary data come from observational studies, surveys, interviews, and laboratory or field experiments.

Academic Expectations in the United States Academic expectations vary from culture to culture. In some cultures, students are expected to memorize and report the information the instructor conveys in class. In the United States, most instructors also expect students to express their own ideas and to think critically about what they are learning. If you find this difficult, you are not alone. Most college students, regardless of their national origin or native language, find these expectations challenging.

10c **Using the Language of the Discipline** 使用学科语言

Each time you enter an academic discipline, you enter a new language group. Courses may be taught in English, but the vocabulary is specialized. Consider, for example, the following passage from an article in a linguistics journal:

> My corpus data largely supports these arguments, although there are also early instances of YOU that do not occur in ambiguous contexts. . . . In accusative plus infinitive constructions with verbs such as *pray,* there is a great deal of variation in the choice of the pronoun form. . . . Variation between the two pronoun forms was quite prolonged in optative sentences . . . (58).
>
> —Helena Raumolin-Brunberg, "The Diffusion of Subject YOU: A Case Study in Historical Sociolinguistics," *Language Variation and Change,* Vol. 17, No. 1, March 2005, pp. 55–73.

More about
Specialized encyclopedias and dictionaries, 105, 315–16

Corpus data? Accusative constructions? Optative sentences? What does it all mean? To understand this paragraph, readers have to learn specialized vocabulary. Fortunately, most instructors (and textbook authors) explain specialized vocabulary as they introduce new words and concepts. If they do not, ask your instructor for an explanation or consult a specialized encyclopedia or dictionary. (Some may be available online through your college library.) Remember that every reader of articles like this—even your instructor—once had to master this vocabulary.

Not only must you learn a new vocabulary, but you must also learn the language group's expectations:

- Do writers use the past tense, the present tense, or a combination? In literature and the humanities, most writers use the present tense to discuss the work and the past or present tense to discuss actual events. In the natural sciences and social sciences, writers use the past tense to discuss the research they have conducted; they use the present tense to discuss their conclusions.
- Is it acceptable to write in the first person (*I*) or must you use the third person (*she, he, it*)? In most disciplines, writers tend to use the third person, unless they are emphasizing their own experience.
- Should you use the active voice, the passive voice, or a combination? In the humanities, writers tend to use the active voice (*Shelley uses symbolism and rhythm . . .*). In the natural sciences and social sciences, writers often use the passive voice to describe how research was conducted (*The participants were randomly assigned to one of three groups . . .*).

> **More about**
> Writing about
> literature, 87–97
> First person
> versus third per-
> son, 358–59
> Active versus pas-
> sive voice, 288–
> 89, 302–03,
> 340–41

To learn the expectations of your new language communities, read assigned texts and listen to lectures, paying close attention to how language is used.

10d Citing and Documenting Information Borrowed from Sources 引用和记录原始资料

Every discipline expects writers to acknowledge borrowed ideas and information, and each discipline has its own style manual to guide this process. In literature and language, the most commonly used style guide is the *MLA Handbook,* 8th ed. Writers in the other humanities tend to use the *Chicago Manual of Style.* The most commonly used style guide in the social sciences is the *Publication Manual of the American Psychological Association.* In the natural sciences, writers tend to use *Scientific Style and Format: The CSE Manual for Authors, Editors, and Publishers.* Models for citing sources in the text and providing bibliographical information in the list of references or works cited appear in parts 6, 7, and 8. Always use the latest edition of these texts.

> **More about**
> MLA style, 157–211
> APA style, 213–54
> *Chicago* style,
> 256–71
> CSE style, 272–84

10e Using Visuals in the Disciplines 在学科写作中使用视觉资料

When considering the use of visuals as supporting evidence for your project, think carefully about the needs of your subject and the expectations of your audience. Although writers in some academic disciplines (such as anthropology, biology, geology, and history) regularly use information graphics (tables, graphs) and other visuals (photographs and schematic drawings) to explain and support their ideas, others (such as those writing in English literature and philosophy) rarely do so, unless the subject of the project is visual (as when writing about a film or a work of art).

> **More about**
> Using visuals,
> 53–54

10f **Preparing for and Taking Examinations** 准备和参加考试

Writing appropriately for the disciplines also requires flexibility in test-taking strategies as you move from a short-answer exam in your management class to an essay exam in anthropology.

Prepare for the Exam 准备考试

> **More about**
> Reading critically,
>   9–15, 87–90
> Taking notes,
>   123–30
> Synthesis, 13–14,
>   133

The most successful preparations begin long before the exam, as you stay on schedule with assigned readings, take notes and listen attentively in class, and work on assignments throughout the term. As you take notes, focus on the major points; do not try to write down every detail. Pay special attention to ideas in the text or lecture that strike you as crucial or interesting, and connect them to ideas you are learning in other classes.

Before the exam, identify essential terms, concepts, issues, and patterns that have arisen repeatedly. Then draft—and answer—possible questions based on them.

Approach the Exam Strategically 有策略性地应对考试

When you take the exam, look it over before beginning to write. Determine how many points are assigned to each question, and set a time limit for answering each part.

Quick **Reference**   **Common Verbs on Essay Exams**

What is the question?	What am I supposed to do?
1. **Analyze** the architectural style of Frank Lloyd Wright.	1. **Identify** the elements of his style, and then **critically examine** those elements and the style as a whole.
2. **Compare and contrast** the major economic problems of the North and South during the Civil War.	2. State the economic problems and explain how they were **similar and different** in the North and South.
3. **Define** the terms *denotation* and *connotation,* and discuss these terms in regard to the word *brother.*	3. Give the **main characteristics** of the terms. **Show that you understand** the definitions by applying them to *brother.*
4. **Describe** how bees build a hive.	4. Create, in words, a **step-by-step picture** of what bees do.
5. **Evaluate** John F. Kennedy's performance as commander in chief during the Cuban missile crisis.	5. State **what you think** of Kennedy's performance, and give specific **reasons** and concrete **evidence** for your opinion(s).
6. **Illustrate** the effects of global warming on mammals of the Arctic, including the walrus and the polar bear.	6. Give specific **examples** of the effects on the animals named and at least one additional animal.
7. **List** and **explain** the four main causes of an economic recession.	7. **Jot down** the causes and **tell clearly** how each results in a recession.
8. **Summarize** Carl Rogers's humanist approach to psychology.	8. Give the **main points** of his approach, and keep your answer **concise.**

Next, analyze each question. Consider what it asks you to do: *Compare* is quite different from *define* or *summarize,* so pay close attention to verbs, and do what they tell you. (See the Quick Reference box on the previous page for analyses of sample essay questions.)

Then, write an outline and *thesis statement* that responds directly to the question. As you write your answer, incorporate evidence and connect it back to your thesis. Devote most of your time to supporting your thesis, but try to wrap up your answer with a concluding statement or paragraph.

Finally, check your work: Does your thesis answer all parts of the question precisely and fully? Did you support all of your major points sufficiently? Did you include any irrelevant material? Did you make any mistakes of grammar or spelling? Are any words illegible?

> **More about**
> Analysis, 12–14,
>   35, 88, 130, 133
> Comparison-
>   contrast, 33
> Definition, 35
> Summary, 9,
>   126–28
> Outlining, 25–26,
>   132–33
> Thesis statements,
>   23–24, 90–91,
>   131–32
> Proofreading,
>   44–45

Student Model 学生范文 **Effective Essay Exam Response**

The sample answer on page 72 responds directly to the exam question by comparing *The Big Lebowski* and *The Big Sleep* and by including the core concept "film noir" in the answer. Notice that this writer fulfills his responsibility to his reader (and to himself) by demonstrating that he understands the issues discussed in class and can synthesize information from films he has seen to support his claims.

Essay Exam Question

Identify and compare/contrast the films from which the stills below are taken. Be sure to include in your discussion at least one of the core concepts we have discussed in class, such as genre, dialog, and film noir.

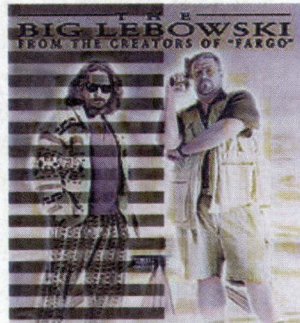

Thesis: Big Lebowski is a variation on film noir, main difference is kind of hero

Thesis answers question

Core concept discussed in class

Though The Big Lebowski is generally considered a parody of film noir detective stories such as The Big Sleep, this 1998 cult classic might also be categorized as a contemporary variation on the style. As the still photos show, the differences are obvious: Gonzo comedy aside, Lebowski chiefly differs in the nature and quality of its hero. Instead of the occasionally superhuman wit and capability of Philip Marlowe, we have The Dude, called by the film's narrator "one of the laziest people on the planet Earth." However, though The Dude's ineptitude is largely played for laughs, much of the humor derives from discomfort and even dread; his insufficiency as a hero only heightens the sense of alienation.

Emphasizes contrast between heroes

At the beginning of The Big Sleep, Marlowe is made to sit in an orchid hothouse, where he proceeds to grow more physically uncomfortable with every passing moment, but he is able to speak his client's language, anticipate his interests and needs, and ultimately earn the general's quiet admiration. The Dude, in contrast, is so out of his depth that he seems incapable of scoring a single point against anyone he meets. When The Dude finds himself in a shadow-drenched room, the viewer may not feel an immediate sense of dread, but it does seem clear that the protagonist has little hope of prevailing. In a particularly revealing scene, The Dude's "client" taunts him with the failure of his generation's ideals, and our hero has no real answer.

Supports claims with details about heroes from these films

These two scenes reveal the core of the typical noir hero: the individual who loses, over and over again, and who is compelled to absorb these defeats and continue on, often with a diminished sense of self. The hero responds by creating a persona to act as surrogate for this loss—one as the hard-boiled detective (Marlowe), and the other as the hyper-passive Dude.

Conclusion compares/contrasts heroes

Returns to key concept and how these heroes display it

11 Analyzing and Crafting Arguments
分析和构思论点

Our culture often confuses *arguing* with *fighting*. While arguments can indeed lead to fights, they usually do not. We are also accustomed to hearing about "both sides" of an argument, which is a misleading concept: arguments are discussions that usually have *many* sides, many points of view, many pros and cons that cannot easily be weighed against each other. This chapter introduces several different forms of argument, ranging from exploration to persuasion, that are appropriate in academic and professional settings, and it explains how you can enter into argument as a critical thinker, not just a fighter.

11a Persuading and Exploring 说服与探究

Arguments may be *persuasive* or *exploratory*. Classical and Toulmin arguments are thesis driven and claim based, seeking to persuade the audience. Rogerian arguments are thesis seeking and inquiry based; they explore a complex problem and look for the best course of action.

A persuasive argument articulates and advocates for a *claim of judgment*. It is most effective when it provides compelling explanations and evidence in support of the claim and when the writer's tone is reasonable.

An exploratory argument begins by examining the evidence, which it then uses to arrive at a well-founded recommendation for the best course of action. This recommendation is expressed in the thesis.

Exploratory versus Persuasive Approaches to Argument For personal or cultural reasons, you may be more comfortable seeking consensus than asserting an opinion. Seek help in formulating an argument, or if you want to take an exploratory approach, check with your instructor to be sure this is acceptable.

11b Making Claims 做陈述

Most texts—speeches, websites, journal or magazine articles—have a main point or thesis that makes a claim. Informative (or expository) writing projects make claims of fact; persuasive and exploratory writing projects make claims of judgment or value.

> **More about**
Purpose, 16–17, 99

1. A claim of fact can be verified 事实性陈述可被验证

Claims of fact are statements that are either true or false:

TRUE	Susan B. Anthony and Martha Carey Thomas worked for women's voting rights in the United States.
FALSE	Denmark became a constitutional monarchy in 1848. [No, Denmark became a constitutional monarchy in 1849.]

Because they are either true or false, claims of fact are not debatable. They cannot be the central claim in a persuasive or exploratory writing project. When writing or revising an argument, make sure you have taken a position on which reasonable people could disagree.

2. A claim of value is based on moral or religious beliefs
价值性陈述基于道德或宗教信仰

Claims of value are statements of fundamental moral or religious principles that individuals or groups hold to be inarguably true:

> All people should be treated fairly under the law.

> Stealing is unjustifiable.

▶ **More about**
Warrants, 77

People tend to defend firmly held beliefs with great passion, and claims of value, like the statements above, are frequently at the heart of arguments. However, since claims of value rest on shared assumptions, they can be difficult to support with objective evidence. As you craft your own argument or read the arguments of other writers, carefully assess the relationship between claims of value and the assumptions (or warrants) underlying them. Will readers who do not share your beliefs be persuaded to accept your claim?

3. A claim of judgment reflects a reasoned opinion
判断性陈述反映合理意见

Claims of judgment are opinions based on available information:

> The healthiest diet is low in carbohydrates.

> The Adam Ezra Group is destined to have a number-one hit song.

Supplied with identical facts, not everyone will hold the same opinion, so claims of judgment are debatable. Because holders of an opinion regard it as the most plausible answer *for now,* based on an evaluation of the available facts, they can be persuaded to change their minds. When opinions are not provisional or temporary, they become *prejudices*:

> Women are too emotional to be president.

> Blondes are dumb.

Writing
Responsibly The Well-Tempered Tone

▶ **More about**
Ethos (credibility), 75

In public discourse, especially in public blogs, an insult or clever put-down is often used to trump an opponent. Sarcasm also thrives: Some bloggers take a sarcastic tone toward whatever they oppose. However, if you want your argument (and yourself) to be taken seriously—especially in academic and business circles—and if you want to persuade people who do not already agree with you, establishing a fair, even-tempered tone and avoiding sarcasm are crucial. Use logic and sound evidence, not snide comments, to make your point.

to SELF

Writing Responsibly

Preparing Oral Arguments

When you write formal arguments for college courses, rational appeals are usually more appropriate to your context and genre. In contrast, when you deliver a speech, presentation, or other form of oral argument, supplement logical appeals with vivid emotional appeals that your audience will remember. Be sure to support emotional appeals with logical evidence: After telling a moving story about an individual, use statistics to show how the issue affects others. Without logical evidence, an emotional appeal merely manipulates your audience.

to AUDIENCE

11c Choosing Evidence Rhetorically 根据修辞学选择论据

An argument will be only as persuasive as the explanations and evidence, or *grounds*, that support the claim. Support can appeal to your readers' intellect, it can draw on the authority of a figure they respect, or it can appeal to their emotions. Each of these is a *rhetorical appeal*. The ancient Greeks called these appeals *logos, ethos,* and *pathos.* Each has a place in responsible writing. As you develop your evidence, you have a responsibility, to your audience and yourself, to make rhetorical appeals that your audience will find appropriate and persuasive.

> *More about*
> Evaluating
> reliability,
> 115–20

1. Appeal to your readers' intellect (logos)
诉诸于读者的理性（晓之以理）

Logos refers to evidence that is rational and relevant; it appeals to readers by engaging their logical powers. Academic writing relies heavily on reasoned support and concrete evidence (facts, statistics, examples) for its persuasive power.

Visuals can also provide concrete evidence. This evidence may be displayed in a graph, chart, or map.

2. Appeal to your readers by establishing your credibility (ethos)
建立可信度，说服读者（道之以信）

Establishing a credible *ethos*—good character, sound knowledge, or good reputation—encourages readers to have confidence in what you say. Maxine Paetro, for example, establishes her credentials before she expresses her judgments:

> As the executive recruiter for several major ad agencies, I've eyeballed more than 40,000 cover letters. Some were winners. Some should have been deleted before ever seeing the light of print.
>
> —Maxine Paetro, "Mission: Employable," *Mademoiselle*

Background

Experience

3. Appeal to your readers' emotions (pathos)
诉诸于读者的情感（动之以情）

Using *pathos* to support a claim means stirring the audience's emotions in an effort to elicit sympathy and, thus, agreement. Pathos often relies

> *More about*
> Making a presentation, 61–65
> Tone, 17–18, 74,
> 305–06, 309–10

Writing
Responsibly **Establishing Yourself as a Responsible Writer**

As a writer, you can establish your ethos not only by offering your credentials, but also by providing readers with sound and sufficient evidence drawn from recognized authorities on the topic, thereby demonstrating your grasp of the material. By adopting a reasonable tone and treating alternative views fairly, you demonstrate that you are a sensible person. By editing your prose carefully, you establish your respect for your readers.

to SELF

FIGURE 11.1 Loss of sea ice poses a threat to the polar bear This photograph makes an emotional appeal—we fear for the safety and well-being of the polar bear—but it would be out of place without statistics that show, for example, a clear relationship between dropping polar bear populations and reduced ice coverage caused by global warming.

on examples, stories, or anecdotes to persuade readers. It also uses a tone that stimulates readers' feelings. Visuals that appeal to the readers' emotions or beliefs (Figure 11.1) make an emotional (or *pathetic*) appeal. Use pathos cautiously: Arguments that appeal solely to readers' emotions can be manipulative, even unethical, unless they are backed by strong logical evidence. In addition, many academic disciplines respect only logos and ethos as rhetorical appeals.

Logos and Ethos in the United States In academic and business writing in the United States, argument relies primarily on rational appeals. Mentioning highly revered traditional authorities or sources (such as important political figures or religious works) is not considered a sufficient form of support. Instead, evaluate the arguments and supporting evidence of these authorities, and include their work as support only if it directly contributes to your argument.

11d Considering Alternative Viewpoints 考量其他观点

More about
Finding information, 105–13

To understand an issue in all its complexity, you must consider alternative viewpoints. When writing an argument, consider *counterevidence*: the doubts you or other reasonable people might have or the objections that opponents might raise. Ask friends or colleagues to help you brainstorm alternative positions or search for alternative voices in printed and online sources. When assessing an argument, consider whether the writer has taken alternative viewpoints into consideration and how well the writer responds to critics' concerns.

Responses to alternative viewpoints can take several approaches:

- They can provide counterevidence that refutes the opposition.

  To reject all hip-hop because gangsta rap espouses violence is unfair to performers like Kanye West and Lauren Hill, who offer a positive message to listeners.

Counterevidence

- They can acknowledge alternative views and explain why the writer's position is still the most reasonable *despite* this counterevidence.

  Clearly, some of the most popular hip-hop songs do revolve around violent or sexist themes. Still, it is important to remember that these themes draw attention to conditions in the communities out of which hip-hop developed.

Acknowledgment of alternative views

Support despite counterevidence

- They can make concessions, using qualifiers such as *some* or *usually*.

  The lyrics of some rap songs are violent, but most listeners are mature enough to realize that these are works of art, not strategies for living in society.

  —Alea Wratten, SUNY–Geneseo, "Reflecting on Brent Staples Editorial 'How Hip Hop Music Lost Its Way and Betrayed Its Fans'"

Qualifiers

11e Discovering Assumptions and Common Ground
发现假设，达成共识

To persuade an audience of the truth of a claim, the writer must persuade readers to accept certain common assumptions, or **warrants**. When W. E. B. DuBois said in 1903, "The problem of the twentieth century is the problem of the color-line—the relation of the darker to the lighter races of men in Asia and Africa, in America and the islands of the sea," he may have assumed that his statement would lead to social change. That would depend, however, on whether his audience *wanted* equality between the races. DuBois knew that some of the audience did not agree with that principle, so his book, *The Souls of Black Folk*, offers evidence in support of the need for change.

As you read and write arguments, consider carefully the assumptions that underlie the claims being made: On what common ground must both reader and writer stand before they can discuss a topic productively? What must both writer and audience agree is true without argument or evidence? What information should you share that might help move your audience to endorse your principles?

11f Organizing Arguments: Classical, Rogerian, and Toulmin
Models 组织论点：古典、罗氏与图尔敏论证模型

As with any writing, an argument is most effective when it is carefully organized. The following are three widely used models for organizing arguments. Each one serves certain purposes of argument; organize your argument with your purpose and audience foremost in your mind.

> *More about*
> Organization,
> 25–26, 132–33
> Purpose, 16–17,
> 23–24, 99
> Audience, 17, 41,
> 100

1. The classical model 古典论证模型

The *classical model* of argumentation derives from the work of ancient Greek and Roman orators. It is well suited to persuasive arguments and is composed of five parts, usually presented in this order:

1. **Introduction.** Acquaint readers with your topic, give them a sense of why it is important and why you are qualified to address it, suggest the purpose of your argument, and state your main claim (or thesis) in one or two sentences.
2. **Background.** Provide whatever information your audience will need to understand and appreciate your position. You might include a brief review of major sources or a chronology of relevant events.
3. **Evidence.** This is the heart of your argument, and it should be the longest section in your project—at least 50 percent of the whole. In it, explain to readers why you believe what you do. Support your argument with *logos*, *ethos*, or *pathos* depending on rhetorical considerations such as your purpose, your audience, and the genre in which you are writing.
4. **Counterevidence.** Concede facts that undermine your position and refute counterevidence with which you disagree, but treat alternative viewpoints fairly and opponents with respect.
5. **Conclusion.** Leave readers with a strong sense of why they should agree with you by suggesting solutions, calling for action, or re-emphasizing the value of your position.

2. The Rogerian model 罗氏论证模型

The *Rogerian model* builds common ground on complex issues, rather than seeking to "win" an argument. It was developed by Carl Rogers, a twentieth-century psychologist who hoped this method would make discussion more productive. The Rogerian model is composed of the same five parts as the classical model, but in a different order:

1. **Introduction**
2. **Background**
3. **Counterevidence**
4. **Explanations and evidence**
5. **Conclusion**

In a Rogerian argument, the counterevidence appears before the evidence because the presentation of counterevidence helps establish the complexity of the issue. Instead of refuting the counterevidence, the writer explores its legitimacy first and then explains why he or she nevertheless believes the thesis. Tom Hackman's essay at the end of this chapter follows the Rogerian model.

Writing Responsibly — Visual Claims and Visual Fallacies

In academic writing, you might use a visual to *support* a claim, but you should be cautious about using a visual to *make* a claim. Visual claims are effective sales tools (they are common in advertisements), but they are likely to commit a visual fallacy, such as *hasty generalization*—drawing a conclusion based on too little evidence. (Is it reasonable to assume that *all* women using a certain brand of soap or shampoo will look like a movie star simply because one celebrity claims to use the product?) As this vintage ad indicates, such consumer-manipulating arguments are not new.

to TOPIC

3. The Toulmin model 图尔敏论证模型

The *Toulmin model* for arguments, developed by philosopher Stephen Toulmin, includes five parts, but the parts are somewhat different from those of classical and Rogerian argument:

1. **Claim:** your thesis, the central argument
2. **Grounds:** the reasons you believe the claim and the evidence supporting your claim
3. **Warrants:** any assumptions that explain how the grounds support the claim
4. **Backing:** supporting evidence for the warrants, which require their own supporting evidence because they are themselves claims
5. **Rebuttal:** counterevidence and your response to it

Like classical argument, the Toulmin model is persuasive. Also like classical argument, it presents the main claim and evidence before counterevidence. One distinctive feature of Toulmin argument is that it places counterevidence last, and it also refutes the counterevidence, leaving less doubt that the main claim is the best perspective. It also recognizes that assumptions underlie all claims and brings those assumptions to the surface, making the search for common ground easier (or at least clarifying the terms of the discussion).

11g Avoiding Logical Fallacies 避免逻辑谬误

When assessing an argument or writing one, keep an eye out for logical *fallacies*. Familiarizing yourself with logical fallacies will help you avoid them as you write your own argument, and it will help you evaluate the trustworthiness of the sources you consult. Because inductive arguments depend on examples and the conclusions you draw from them, fallacies like the following can creep in:

- **Hasty generalization (jumping to conclusions).** *Look at her, running that stop sign! She's a terrible driver!*

  A hasty generalization occurs when a general conclusion is based on insufficient evidence: Since even the best drivers occasionally make mistakes, this one piece of evidence is not enough to incriminate this driver.

- **Sweeping generalization.** *She's a typical woman driver—terrible!*

  A sweeping generalization applies a claim to *all* cases when it actually applies to only a few or maybe to none. Stereotypes are often based on sweeping generalizations.

- **False analogy.** *Bob's victories over his enemies during the war will ensure his victory over his political opponents in this election.*

  A false analogy draws a connection between two items or events that have few or no relevant common characteristics. This false analogy does not explain why previous military victories would guarantee a political victory. Is the political process really like a military campaign? Are opposition candidates really like enemy soldiers?

- **Bandwagon appeal.** *"Mom and Dad, I really need an iPhone. All my friends have one!"*

  The bandwagon appeal implies that the majority opinion is the right opinion and invites you to climb aboard. Some bandwagon appeals may be based on poll results, lending them the impression of reliability. Poll results, however, merely report what the majority of respondents *believe* to be true. Many Americans in 1860 might have believed that holding other people in slavery was perfectly acceptable, which goes to show that the majority can be wrong.

The power of deductive arguments depends on the strength of your premises and the relationship between your premises and your conclusion, so watch out for arguments based on dubious, hidden, or missing premises or conclusions that do not follow from the premises:

- **Begging the question (circular reasoning).** *You must believe me because I never lie.*

  An argument that begs the question uses the conclusion (in a disguised form) as one of the premises in the argument. In this example, the second half of the sentence repeats the conclusion rather than offering a premise from which the conclusion can be derived.

- **Non sequitur (irrelevant argument).** *You can solve a lot of problems with money, so the rich must be much happier than we are.*

  A non sequitur (which means "it does not follow" in Latin) draws a conclusion from a premise that does not follow logically. The conclusion in the statement above equates money with happiness, but anyone with money will tell you that the two do not necessarily go hand in hand.

- ***Post hoc, ergo propter hoc* (false cause).** *This ring must be lucky: I wore it for the first time today, and I pitched a perfect game.*

  Post hoc, ergo propter hoc means "after this, therefore, because of this" in Latin. In a *post hoc* fallacy, the speaker wrongly assumes

Self

Assessment

As you revise your argument, consider the following issues. If your answer to any of these questions is no, revise as necessary.

☐ **Claim.** Do you take a position based on an opinion or belief on which reasonable people could disagree? Have you modified the claim to avoid making it stronger than you can effectively support?

☐ **Evidence.** Do you supply evidence in support of your claim? Do you use rational appeals that are appropriate to your topic, purpose, and audience? Where appropriate, do you make emotional appeals that are supported by evidence and use visuals to support your claim?

☐ **Counterevidence.** Have you acknowledged alternative interpretations of your evidence? Have you explained why your position is the most reasonable despite these objections?

☐ **Organization.** Have you followed an appropriate model of argument, such as classical, Rogerian, or Toulmin? Is the organizational structure appropriate to your overall aim—persuasion or exploration?

☐ **Ethos.** Have you established your credibility by avoiding fallacies and providing evidence from reliable sources, treating those with whom you disagree respectfully, and revising, editing, and proofreading with care?

that the first event caused the second: Just because the player wore a ring while pitching a perfect game does not mean that the ring is "lucky."

- **Either-or fallacy (false dilemma).** *You're either for us or against us!*

The either-or fallacy allows, misleadingly, for only two choices or sides in an argument, never acknowledging compromise or complexity.

- **Ad hominem (personal attack).** *His views on the campus parking problem are ridiculous! What would you expect from a member of a frat that has its own parking lot?*

An ad hominem (personal attack) attempts to undermine an opposing viewpoint by criticizing the motives or character of the individual holding the position, without connecting character flaws to the issues in question. (*Ad hominem* means "to the man" in Latin.)

Student Model 学生范文 Exploratory Essay

In the following essay, Tom Hackman, a student at Syracuse University, argues that universities should take differences in motivation into consideration when devising their plagiarism policies. As you read, consider whether Hackman demonstrates responsibility by treating those who disagree with him fairly and by supplying enough evidence to be persuasive.

Tom Hackman

Professor Howard

Writing 109

28 November 2016

Why Students Cheat: The Complexities and Oversimplifications of Plagiarism

Introduction: Explains why topic matters

Background: Describes extent and severity of plagiarism

The system of American higher education is founded on principles of honesty and academic integrity. For this reason, nearly all those invested in this system—students, instructors, and administrators—recognize that plagiarism cannot be tolerated. They also agree that a lot of plagiarism is occurring. A survey published in *Who's Who Among American High School Students* (reported by Newberger) indicated that 15% of top-ranked high schoolers plagiarize. Practices among higher education students are not much better. According to research by Donald L. McCabe, a professor at Rutgers University who has done extensive work on cheating, 70% of college students "copied almost word for word from a source and submitted it as their own work" (41). A 2006 study by Hard et al. showed that plagiarism was common among the 421 students who participated in their research. Fig. 1 illustrates the various forms this plagiarism took.

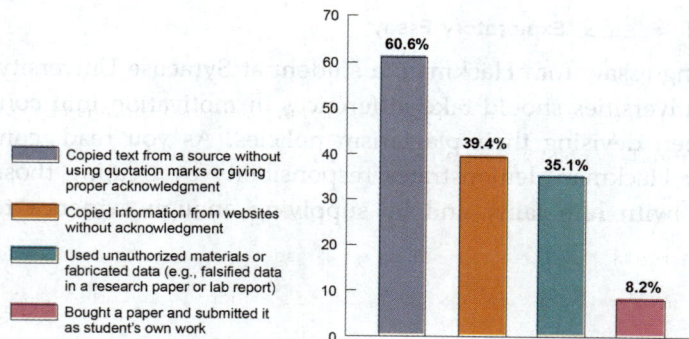

Copied text from a source without using quotation marks or giving proper acknowledgment

Copied information from websites without acknowledgment

Used unauthorized materials or fabricated data (e.g., falsified data in a research paper or lab report)

Bought a paper and submitted it as student's own work

60.6% 39.4% 35.1% 8.2%

Fig. 1. Common types of plagiarism and the percentage of students who commit them. (Data and categories from Hard et al. 1069.)

There is a commonly held myth about how most plagiarism occurs. Late at night, a student sits staring at a computer screen. A paper is due the following morning, and research needs to be done, notes need to be taken, and, in the end, an essay needs to be written and edited. Instead of completing this immense task, though, the student succumbs to the temptations of plagiarism—"cutting and pasting" from sources, downloading an essay from the Internet, or simply buying a paper from another student. In this myth, students are too apathetic and slothful to complete their assignments on their own; instead, they cheat.

> **Counter-evidence: Describes alternative perspectives**

Undeniably, some plagiarism occurs because students find it easier than simply doing the work required. The mind of a plagiarist, however, cannot be fit so easily into a single stereotype. The argument that laziness is the main cause of plagiarism is at best incomplete, and moreover it seems fed by unfair stereotypes of modern students as bored by academic rigor, more interested in video games or their Facebook page than the hard work of learning.

> **Acknowledges the legitimacy of the counterevidence**

In fact, some plagiarism grows from the opposite of these characteristics. High-achieving students, for example, fear what a bad grade will do to their otherwise stellar GPA. Such students treat the attainment of impressive marks as a necessity and will betray the very academic system they revere in order to sustain their average.

> **Evidence: Expert opinions, examples**

Other students plagiarize more from lack of interest in a particular course than general idleness. Students who view writing papers as hoops they must jump through to graduate, for instance, are more likely simply to download a paper from an online "paper mill" than write one themselves. For them, a college writing class is something to be endured, rather than an opportunity for learning. Russell Hunt, a professor at St. Thomas University in Canada, explains this attitude in point 2 of his article:

> **Quotes authority to support claim; notes the author's credentials**

> If I wanted to learn how to play the guitar, or improve my golf swing, or write HTML, "cheating" would be the last thing that would ever occur to me. It would be utterly irrelevant to the situation. On the other hand, if I wanted a certificate saying that I could pick a jig, play a round in under 80, or produce a slick webpage (and never actually expected to perform the activity in question), I might well consider cheating. . . .

Students draw a distinction between their interests and their academic assignments. They rationalize their plagiarism as a way to escape an "unfair" academic obligation. Websites such as essaytown.com, which will write a paper to order, cater to students like these, who consider at least some aspects of academia essentially useless.

Many other instances of plagiarism are committed by students with honest intentions but who are ignorant of citation methods. Writing for his college newspaper, Nam Tran describes widespread confusion among college students about what constitutes plagiarism. Even students who recognize the importance of citation may not know how to cite their sources correctly. A student who omits the source of a paraphrase in a paper would probably be surprised to learn that he or she is often considered as guilty of plagiarism as the student who downloads an essay.

The Internet has compounded confusion with regard to citation. The Internet is a place of free exchange where information moves from computer to computer with the click of a mouse. In this environment, ownership and citation become hazy. And as Rhodri Marsden, who writes about technology and the arts for *The Guardian*, notes, the more information becomes available on the Internet, the more material is available for easy plagiarizing. Many students find it is easy and "natural" to take text from an online source—for instance, by highlighting the text, copying it, and pasting it into a word processing document. Because it can be difficult to keep track of everything they have read, the chances of accidental plagiarism (forgetting to cite the copied text) increase. So, too, does the likelihood of "patchwriting," which researchers Pecorari and Petric define as substituting synonyms or moving sentences around, but not fully putting the borrowed text into the writer's own words. While patchwriting can be done deliberately, Pecorari and Petric identify a subset of patchwriters who don't realize they're doing anything wrong (278). Li's research supports the existence of this subset; the Chinese senior professors in that study actively discouraged plagiarism, but some of their doctoral students thought patchwriting was acceptable. Finally, some students will also be tempted to commit intentional plagiarism, choosing to leave a block of copied text uncited.

Provides example that illustrates claim

Evidence: Quotes authority and provides author's credentials

Paraphrases authority to corroborate claim

Despite the many varieties and causes of plagiarism, college instructors and administrators too often treat the issue simply as a crime committed by the laziest of pupils. Birchard quotes a dean of Canada's Simon Fraser University, who voices a typical view: "We have a zero tolerance policy for cheating.... And we hope the severity of the penalties sends a strong message to other students who might be tempted to cheat or cut academic corners." Granted, there is ultimately no excuse for plagiarism, and any honest student should share the goal of eliminating it from academic life. Yet a less simplistic response to plagiarism would ultimately be more productive than the widespread law-and-order mentality that now exists.

The motivations behind plagiarism, and the situations that give rise to it, are varied. Importantly, much plagiarism occurs without the guilty student understanding that what he or she is doing represents academic dishonesty. Effectively combating plagiarism, in all its forms, requires a fuller understanding of how and why students break the rules. Academic policy writers must realize that plagiarism is not a single offense but a general term for a lack of citation, and plagiarism must be recognized as dynamic behavior, with many motivations, including social expectations, desires for high GPAs, disregard for the value of learning or intellectual property, and unawareness of citation standards. A regular user of a paper mill website has far different attitudes than a nonciting Chinese exchange student (or professor). The various categories of plagiarism threaten academia to varying extents and therefore demand a flexible response based upon the specifics of each incident. Only through this approach will plagiarism, in all its forms, be reduced.

Counterevidence

Conclusion: Shows complexity of the issue; states thesis

Returns to thesis

Works Cited

Birchard, Karen. "Canada's Simon Fraser U. Suspends 44 Students in Plagiarism
Scandal." *The Chronicle of Higher Education*, vol. 53, no. 8, 24 Oct. 2002, p. 46.
EbscoHost, chronicle.com/article/Canadas-Simon-Fraser-U/116779.

Hard, Stephen F., et al. "Faculty and College Student Beliefs about the Frequency of
Student Academic Misconduct." *The Journal of Higher Education*, vol. 77, no. 6,
Nov.–Dec. 2006, pp. 1058–80.

Hunt, Russell. "Four Reasons to Be Happy about Internet Plagiarism." *Teaching
Perspectives*, Dec. 2002, stu.ca/~hunt/4reasons.htm.

Li, Yongyan. "Text-Based Plagiarism in Scientific Writing: What Chinese Supervisors
Think about Copying and How to Reduce It in Students' Writing." *Science and
Engineering Ethics*, vol. 19.2, June 2013, pp. 569–83.

Marsden, Rhodri. "The Big Steal: Rise of the Plagiarist in the Digital Age." *The
Guardian*, 21 Mar. 2014, www.theguardian.com/technology/2014/mar/21/rise-
plagiarism-internet-shia-labeouf.

McCabe, Donald L. "Cheating: Why Students Do It and How We Can Help Them Stop."
American Educator, Winter 2001, pp. 38–43.

Newberger, Eli H. "Why Do Students Cheat?" *School for Champions*. School for
Champions, 6 Dec 2003. school-for-champions.com/character/newberger_cheating2.
htm#.Vvl8THpxBqs.

Pecorari, Diane, and Bojana Petric. "Plagiarism in Second-Language Writing." *Language
Teaching*, vol. 47.3, July 2014, pp. 269–302.

Tran, Nam. "Plagiarism Policies Lead to Confusion among Students." *The Daily
Nebraskan*, 9 Oct. 2015, dailynebraskan.com/news/plagiarism-policies-lead-to-
confusion-among-students/article_2c875fa2-6e2c-11e5-ad00-cfbdd1242e21.html.

12 **Writing about Literature** 文学写作

There is rarely one right way to interpret or appreciate literature. Instead, novels, poems, and plays offer readers multiple doors to understanding. At first glance, these doors may seem confusing, but they actually offer rewarding opportunities to explore the many ways of being human.

12a Reading and Analyzing Works of Literature (Novels, Poetry, Plays) 阅读和分析文学作品（小说、诗歌、戏剧）

Whether focused solely on the text or on its social, historical, or cultural contexts, writing about literature is an act of interpretation. While those who study literature produce multiple meanings, each interpretation must be based on a careful analysis of the text and use evidence from the text to persuade others to accept the writer's position.

1. Read actively and reflectively 主动性与反思性阅读

Understanding works of literature is not merely a matter of extracting information, but it does begin with reading to gain a basic understanding of the text. Begin by writing a summary: What is the main point of the work? In literature, this is the *theme*. A summary will help you get to the heart of the matter, but keep in mind that literary analysis must do more than summarize what the text says.

Next, annotate or make notes about the work. Some of your notes may provide perspectives on the work that you can use later when writing. The notes in Figure 12.1, for example, show the beginnings of themes that Jewel Andrews explores in her analysis of Percy Bysshe Shelley's "Poetical Essay on the Existing State of Things."

> **More about**
> Summary, 9,
>   124–28
> Annotation, 9–12

> **Student Model**
> "My View on a Long-Lost But Timeless Poem: Shelley's 'Poetical Essay on the Existing State of Things,'" Jewel Andrews, 93–97

Writing Responsibly   Reading with Study Guides

SparkNotes and similar study guides, long a staple of college bookstores and now available online, may tempt struggling students to substitute the guide for the text itself. Do not succumb! You not only deprive yourself of a learning experience, but you may also find that the study guide leaves you unprepared for the sophisticated level of understanding your instructor expects. If you are having difficulty making sense of a text, discuss the work with classmates, read essays about or reviews of the work at your college library, watch a reading or a performance of the work, or seek advice from your instructor.

to SELF

Finally, allow yourself to enjoy what you are reading. If you make an effort to appreciate the language, note insights, or make connections to something in your own experience, you will get more out of your reading.

▶ *More about*
Analysis, 12–14,
35, 130, 133

2. Analyze the text 分析文本

Understanding a work of literature involves analysis, dividing the work into its component parts to see how they work together. The Quick Reference box below lists some of the elements that a literary analysis should take into consideration. Usually you will need to study the text

Student Model 学生范文 **Textual Analysis**

Poetical Essay on the Existing State of Things

By Percy Bysshe Shelley

DESTRUCTION marks thee! o'er the blood-stain'd heath

Is faintly borne the stifled wail of death;

Millions to fight compell'd, to fight or die

In mangled heaps on War's red altar lie.

The sternly wise, the mildly good, have sped

To the unfruitful mansions of the dead.

Whilst fell Ambition o'er the wasted plain

Triumphant guides his car—the ensanguin'd rein

Glory directs; fierce brooding o'er the scene,

With hatred glance, with dire unbending mien,

Fell Despotism sits by the red glare

Of Discord's torch, kindling the flames of war.

For thee then does the Muse her sweetest lay

Pour 'mid the shrieks of war, 'mid dire dismay;

For thee does Fame's obstrep'rous clarion rise,

Does Praise's voice raise meanness to the skies.

Are we then sunk so deep in darkest gloom,

That selfish pride can virtue's garb assume?

Does real greatness in false splendour live?

When narrow views the futile mind deceive,

When thirst of wealth, or frantic rage for fame,

When legal murders swell the lists of pride;

When glory's views the titled idiot guide,

Then will oppression's iron influence show

The great man's comfort as the poor man's woe.

Notes (handwritten):

- Why "essay" and not "poem"?
- Thought-provoking: "the sternly wise, the mildly good"
- Lots of use of the word "red" (= blood)
- Dramatic phrase! "Unfruitful mansions of the dead"
- "car" probably means "chariot"?
- Did regular people really talk like this in Shelley's time, or is he playing with words for rhythm and rhyme?
- Abbreviates words, often by removing syllables. To keep a tight rhythm?
- Lots of unnatural-sounding word order to make it rhyme.
- "legal murders" and "titled idiot"—great phrasing!

FIGURE 12.1 Notes from a close reading of the poem "Poetical Essay on the Existing State of Things" by Percy Bysshe Shelley

again (and again) to identify the elements from which it is constructed and to determine how these parts work together.

3. Adopt a critical framework 采用批判性框架

In introductory classes in literature, students are often expected to take a *formalist approach*, looking closely at the work itself (the primary source) to understand how it functions. Other critical approaches are outlined in the Quick Reference box on this page.

Before adopting a critical approach, consider the issues you have discussed in class or in other classes you are taking. A psychology class, for example, may provide a theory that will help you explain the behavior of a character; an economics class may help you understand the market forces affecting the plot; a women's studies class may provide methods of interpretation that will give you new perspectives on historical events.

Secondary sources—works about the author, period, text, or critical framework—may provide you with needed background about the primary source you are studying. Use secondary sources to develop and support, not substitute for, your own interpretation. To find secondary sources,

> **More about**
> Synthesis, 13–14,
>   131, 133
> Searching a library
>   catalog, 110–11
> Searching a peri-
>   odical database,
>   108–10

Quick

Reference   Elements of Literature

When writing about a work of literature, consider the following elements and ask yourself these questions:

Genre. Into which broad category, or genre (fiction, poetry, drama), does the work fit? Into which narrower category (mystery, sci-fi; sonnet, ode; comedy, tragedy) does the work belong? What expectations are set up by the genre, and how does the work adhere to or violate these expectations?

Plot. What happens? Does the plot unfold chronologically (from start to finish), or does the text use flashbacks or flash-forwards? Does the plot proceed as expected, or is there a surprise?

Setting. Where and when does the action occur? Is the setting identifiable? If not, what hints does the text give about the where and when? Are time and place consistent, or do elements from other times or places intrude?

Character. Who is the *protagonist,* or main character? Who are the supporting characters? How believable are the characters? Do they represent types or individuals?

Point of view. Who is telling the story—one of the characters or a separate narrator? Which

point of view does the narrator take—first person (*I*), second person (*you*), or third person (*she, he, it*)? Does the narrator have special insight into the characters or recount events as an outsider?

Language/style. Which level of diction (formal, informal, colloquial, dialect) does the text use, and why? How are words put together? Does the text contain long, complex sentences or short, direct ones? Does the text contain figurative language (such as metaphor and simile), or is the writing more literal?

Theme. What is the main point? If you were to tell the story as a fable, what would its moral be?

Symbol. Do any of the characters, events, or objects represent something more than their literal meaning?

Irony. Is there a contrast between what is said and what is meant, between what the characters know and what the reader knows?

Allusion. Does the work contain references to literary and cultural classics or sacred texts?

Quick

Reference   Critical Approaches

Biographical approach. Focus on the author's life to understand the work. Does the work reflect the trajectory of the author's own life or perhaps depict a working out in literature of something the author was unable to work out in reality?

Feminist approach. Focus on the power relations between men and women (or elements in the work that take on gender traits). Does the work reinforce traditional power relations or challenge them?

New historicist approach. Focus on the social-historical moment in which the work was created. How does the work reflect that historical moment?

Postcolonial approach. Focus on the power relations between colonizing and colonized peoples (or on elements in the work that reflect colonial power dynamics). Does the work reinforce or challenge those power relations?

Queer approach. Focus on the power relations between "normal" and "deviant." How differently can a text be read when the reader rejects this dichotomy?

Reader response approach. Focus not on the author's intentions or the text's meaning but on the experience of the individual reader. How does the individual reader construct meaning in the act of reading the work of literature?

search your library's catalog and specialized databases such as the MLA International Bibliography, the Book Review Digest, and Literature Criticism Online.

> **More about**
> Devising a thesis,
> 23–24, 101–02,
> 131–32

12b Devising a Literary Thesis 文学论文构思

Narrow your focus to an idea you can develop fully in the assigned length. To devise a topic in literature, ask yourself questions about the elements of the work:

- What are the central conflicts among or within characters?

- Which aspects of the plot puzzled or surprised you, and why?

- How might the setting (time and place) have influenced the behavior of the characters?

- Did the writer use language in a distinctive (or difficult or obscure) way, and why?

- Which images recurred or were especially powerful, and why?

- What other works did you think about as you were reading this one, and why?

Then answer one of your questions. Your answer can be your *working thesis*.

As you draft your paper, you should analyze or interpret (not merely summarize) the text, as these contrasting examples demonstrate:

SUMMARY THESIS   In this poem, Shelley invokes the suffering and tragedy of war.

INTERPRETIVE/
ANALYTICAL THESIS

In this poem, Shelley uses symbolism and rhythm to denounce the actions of his government and evoke the devastating toll of war.

To support the first thesis, the writer could merely report the poem's main point. To support the second thesis, however, the writer must analyze the poem's symbolism and rhythm and then use that analysis to explain her interpretation of the poem's central conflict.

12c Supporting Your Claims with Evidence from the Text
从文本中找论据，支撑你的论点

As with any writing project, you can use idea-generating techniques like brainstorming, freewriting, and clustering to figure out what your thesis is and why you believe it. Then turn back to the text: Which details from the work illustrate or support your reasons? These details are the *evidence* your readers will need. Although your paper may draw on secondary sources (works about the author, text, or period), your main source of supporting evidence is from your analysis of, interpretation of, or response to the novel, poem, or play itself.

> **More about**
> Idea-generating techniques, 20–23

Consider this passage from Jewel Andrews's essay:

> The 172-line "Poetical Essay" is full of the poet's outrage at the state of the world. A first reading of the poem suggests that he is writing about the brutality and tragedy of war in general, but a closer read plus research on Shelley and his writing makes it clear he's taking aim at Britain's involvement in the Napoleonic Wars against the French, and at the imprisonment of an Irish journalist critical of British military operations. Shelley sets the tone right away: "Millions to fight compell'd, to fight or die / In mangled heaps on War's red altar lie" (lines 3–4) and, in a takedown of the privileged ruling class into which he was born, he taunts: "When glory's views the titled idiot guide" (24). The lines "Ye cold advisers of yet colder kings, / To whose fell breast no passion virtue brings" (37–38) make it clear whose side he is on.

> Topic sentence: States claim

> Evidence: Uses quotations and summary from the poem and explains their relevance

Andrews argues that Shelley uses powerful symbolism to depict the barbarity of war and the cold arrogance of the aristocracy, and she offers concrete evidence from the text—some quoted, some summarized—to support her claim. Note that Andrews does not merely drop the evidence from the poem into her essay but instead explains its relevance.

> **More about**
> Incorporating evidence, 26, 40–41, 134–35

12d Using the Appropriate Tense, Point of View, and Voice
使用适当的时态、视角和语态

Each discipline uses language distinctively. Some of the conventions for writing about literature are discussed here.

1. Use past and present tense correctly 正确使用过去时和现在时

In literature, writers use the present tense when writing about the work being studied (the events, characters, and setting) or the ideas of other

> **More about**
> Tense, 374–78

scholars, and they use the present or past tense (as appropriate) when discussing actual events, such as the author's death or a historical or cultural event from the time that the work was published.

Present Tense

These witches and ghosts are real, and often present, for Haun's characters, and "witch doctors" have busy practices fending them off.

—Lisa Alther, "The Shadow Side of Appalachia:
Mildred Haun's Haunting Fiction"

Past Tense

Margaret Lindsey, defamed as a sorceress (incantatrix) by three men in 1435, successfully purged herself with the help of five women; her accusers were warned against making further slanders under pain of excommunication.

—Kathleen Kamerick, "Shaping Superstition in Late Medieval England"

> **More about**
> Person, 358–59

2. Use first and third person correctly 正确使用第一人称和第三人称

In literary studies, the emphasis is on the work of literature, so writers use the third person whenever reasonable. Compare these two versions of a sentence from Jewel Andrews's essay on Shelley's poem "Poetical Essay on the Existing State of Things":

First Person	Third Person
When I first read the poem, I thought Shelley was writing about the brutality and tragedy of war in general, but a closer look made it clear to me he's taking aim at Britain's involvement in the Napoleonic Wars against the French.	A first reading of the poem suggests that he is writing about the brutality and tragedy of war in general, but a closer read . . . makes it clear he's taking aim at Britain's involvement in the Napoleonic Wars against the French.

The version in the third person shifts the emphasis from the writer to the poem and is thus less personal and more persuasive. (Notice also that it shifts to the present tense.)

> **More about**
> Active versus passive voice, 288–89, 302–03, 340–41

3. Use the active voice 使用主动语态

In literature, writers typically use the active voice:

ACTIVE   Janie's relationship with her third husband, Tea Cake, plays a key role in transforming her concept of racial identity.

Uses present tense to discuss the work studied

Uses past tense to discuss earlier events

PASSIVE　　A key role in transforming her concept of racial identity was played by Janie's relationship with her third husband, Tea Cake.

Use the passive voice only when the "who" is unknown or when you want to emphasize the action rather than the actor.

4. Use the author's full name at first mention and surname only thereafter 第一次提及时用作者的全名，之后仅用作者的姓氏

In writing about literature, provide the author's complete name (*Percy Bysshe Shelley*) the first time it is mentioned and thereafter use the surname (*Shelley*) only, unless this will cause confusion. (When writing about the Brontë sisters, for example, you may need to specify whether you are discussing Charlotte, Emily, or Anne.)

5. Include the work's title in your title 论文标题中须包含文学作品的标题

When writing about a work of literature, provide the title of the work in the title and first paragraph of your project.

> **More about**
> Capitalizing titles, 465
> Quotation marks versus italics for titles, 450–61, 465

12e Citing and Documenting Sources in MLA Style 采用MLA格式引用和标记文献来源

Whenever you quote, paraphrase, summarize, or borrow ideas or information from a work, you must cite your source in the text and document it in your list of works cited. Writers in literature usually follow the *MLA Handbook,* 8th ed.

> **More about**
> Citing and documenting sources in MLA style, 157–211

Student Model 学生范文 Explication

The essay that begins on the next page was written by Jewel Andrews. Andrews draws evidence from a close reading of the poem "Poetical Essay on the Existing State of Things" (see Figure 12.1) to support her claim that the poet Percy Bysshe Shelley uses symbolism and rhythm to persuade readers to accept his view of war. To build her case, Andrews also draws on other primary and secondary sources, including videos, podcasts, and interactive media relating to the poet and artifacts and historical documents that belonged to Shelley.

Text Credits
p. 92 *Appalachian Heritage, 36*(2), Spring 2008, pp. 30–38. *Magic, Ritual, and Witchcraft, 3*(1), Summer 2008.

Jewel Andrews

Professor Sewell

English 110

5 May 2016

Title: Includes author's name and title of poem

My View on a Long-Lost but Timeless Poem:

Shelley's "Poetical Essay on the Existing State of Things"

Ask someone today to describe the work of nineteenth-century English

poet Percy Bysshe Shelley and you might hear "sentimental" or, worse, "corny."

Names author, poem, in first ¶

To our twenty-first-century ears, his elaborate verse can sound overripe. But

Shelley (1792–1822), one of the greatest Romantic poets of his or any era, was

far from mushy: Born a wealthy aristocrat, his radical political and social views

made him an outcast in his own country, and he fled to Italy with his wife, Mary

Introduction: Provides background on Shelley, places poem in context

Shelley (who later wrote *Frankenstein*). Shelley's political poetry expressed his

passionate views on war, poverty, imperialism, and the failure of governments. In

his "lost" poem "Poetical Essay on the Existing State of Things"—rediscovered in

2006 and made available to the public in 2015, roughly 200 years after he wrote

Topic sentence (begins first half of body)

it at age 18[1]—Shelley uses symbolism and rhythm to denounce the actions of

his government, ridicule those in power, and evoke the devastating toll of war.

Thesis: Calls for analysis and interpretation

The 172-line "Poetical Essay" is full of the poet's outrage at the state of

the world. A first reading of the poem suggests that he is writing about the

brutality and tragedy of war in general, but a closer read plus research on

Shelley and his writing makes it clear he's taking aim at Britain's involvement

in the Napoleonic Wars against the French, and at its imprisonment of an Irish

journalist critical of British military operations (*The Economist*). Shelley sets

the tone right away: "Millions to fight compell'd, to fight or die / In mangled heaps on War's red altar lie" (lines 3–4) and, in a takedown of the privileged ruling class into which he was born, he taunts: "When glory's views the titled idiot guide" (24). The lines "Ye cold advisers of yet colder kings, / To whose fell breast no passion virtue brings" (37–38) make it clear whose side he is on.

Uses quotation and summary as evidence, and explains relevance

Topic sentence

Shelley employs the color red throughout to symbolize blood and death: "War's red altar lie" (4), "Fell Despotism sits by the red glare" (11), and "To snatch at fame, to reap red murder's spoil" (43). Similarly, he uses words and phrases like "shrieks of war," "legal murders," and "tenfold grief" to bring to life fearful images of suffering and misery.

Topic sentence

As well as the blood and death symbolism, Shelley conjures up vivid pictures of social tyranny: "Then will oppression's iron influence show / The great man's comfort as the poor man's woe" (25–26) and "Must starving wretches torment, misery bear?" (48). The potent phrase "Oppression's iron influence" is paired with "great man's comfort" to depict the power and privilege of the ruling classes, while the "starving wretches" who must "bear" their "torment" and "misery" summon up the powerlessness of the poor and downtrodden.

Explains signifi- cance of symbol

Topic sentence (begins second half of essay)

In addition to symbolism, Shelley employs rhythm and rhyme to convey a sense of anger and urgency. When read aloud, the tight rhythmic pattern of the couplets is obvious. For example, lines 51–52 ("Yet shall the vices of the great pass on, / Vices as glaring as the noon-day sun") and 103–104 ("Though hot with gore from India's wasted plains, / Some Chief, in triumph, guides the tightened reins") have an almost chanting, marching cadence, a beat that reinforces the theme of the battlefield. The poet's reference to India indicates his strong anti-colonial feelings at a time when the British Empire's global reach was enormous. According to British poet Michael Rosen in an interview in *The Guardian*, Shelley "spends a good few lines on pointing out the oppression of British imperialism in India," in lines like "The fainting Indian, on his native plains / Writhes to superior power's unnumbered pains" (145–146).

Throughout the poem, Shelley uses powerful symbolism and rhythm to articulate his staunch political positions and disgust at the status quo. His words and phrasing are not always easy to understand—after all, he was writing two hundred years ago, when the use of inverted sentences (in which the verb comes before the subject) and archaic words like "meed" (which means "a deserved share or reward") was common. But reading and analyzing the poetry of Percy Bysshe Shelley is well worth the effort; beyond his eloquent phrasing and sharp use of symbolism and meter, this poem, and his other poetical poems such as "The Masque of Anarchy" and "Men of England," are as relevant today as they were when they were written. Let Shelley—who famously said in an essay called "A Defence of Poetry" that "poets are the unacknowledged legislators of the world"—have the last word: "Poetry is a sword of lightning, ever unsheathed, which consumes the scabbard that would contain it."

> Conclusion: Thesis restated, importance of poem's theme reiterated

> Provides closure by circling back to poet

Notes

1. "Poetical Essay" was purchased by the University of Oxford's Bodleian Libraries, which has uploaded a digital copy that can be accessed through its website.

2. The online exhibition "Shelley's Ghost: Reshaping the Image of a Literary Family" is a partnership of the Bodleian Libraries and the New York Public Library.

Works Cited

Flood, Alison. "Lost Shelley Poem Execrating 'Rank Corruption' of Ruling

Class Made Public." *The Guardian*, 10 Nov. 2015, www.theguardian.com/

books/2015/nov/10/lost-shelley-poem-execrating-rruling-class-public-poetical-

essay-on-the-existing-state-of-things.

"Out of the Attic: Fresh Light on the Young Revolutionary." *The Economist*, 14 Nov.

2015, p. 54.

Shelley, Percy Bysshe. "A Defence of Poetry" (1821). *Poetry Foundation*, 13 Oct.

2009, www.poetryfoundation.org/learning/essay/237844.

Works Consulted

Clark, Nick. "Percy Bysshe Shelley Lost Poem to Go Public at University of

Oxford." *The Independent*, 10 Nov. 2015, www.independent.co.uk/arts-en-

tertainment/art/news/poetical-essay-on-the-existing-state-of-things-lost-po-

em-by-percy-bysshe-shelley-to-go-on-display-a6729206.html.

Martyris, Nina. "How Percy Shelley Stirred His Politics into His Teacup." *NPR*, 4

Aug. 2015, www.npr.org/sections/thesalt/2015/08/04/429363868/how-per-

cy-shelley-stirred-his-politics-into-his-tea-cup.

Rich, Adrienne. "Legislators of the World." *The Guardian*, 18 Nov. 2006,

www.theguardian.com/books/2006/nov/18/featuresreviews.guardianreview15.

"Unknown Shelley Poem Discovered." *BBC News*, 13 July 2006, news.bbc.

co.uk/2/hi/entertainment/5177232.stm.

Typically not required, but if your instructor wishes to see works you consulted other than those cited in your project, follow this format.

5

Research 关注资料搜索

Matters

Finding, Evaluating, and Citing Sources 发现、评估和引用文献来源

Use part 5 to learn, practice, and master these writer's responsibilities:

❏ **To Audience**

Understand your assignment, draft a thesis that will focus readers' attention on your main point, contextualize sources so that readers understand why the evidence is relevant and reliable, and organize your project so that readers can follow your logic.

❏ **To Topic**

Answer research questions using relevant and reliable library resources, whether printed or digital; evaluate all sources carefully; use media sources when they are relevant and appropriate; and generate information through field research as needed.

❏ **To Other Writers**

Build a working bibliography to keep track of sources, avoid plagiarism and patchwriting by taking careful notes, and cite sources to show where source information begins and ends.

❏ **To Yourself**

Set a schedule that takes all your responsibilities into account; select a challenging topic that you want to learn about; analyze sources to enhance your understanding; support your own ideas with sources; and revise, edit, proofread, and format your project carefully.

13 Planning a Research Project 规划研究项目

To create a collage, the artist had to devise a plan, gather the right materials, and assemble them to create a unified whole. Yet it took more than just the right materials to produce an intriguing piece of art; it also took an idea that would unify them and engage the viewer. Similarly, when you write a research project, you not only must devise a plan and gather supporting information, but you also must have a vision. The goal of your project should be to present the research in your text in a way that engages and even enlightens the reader. The quality of your *planning*, the first stage of the research process, is crucial to the success of this endeavor.

13a Analyzing the Research Assignment and Setting a Schedule 分析研究任务并制订时间表

Most research projects have one of these purposes:

- **To inform:** to explain an issue, compare proposed solutions, or review the research on a specific topic
- **To persuade:** to argue for a claim or to propose a solution to a problem
- **To inquire:** to explore a complex topic, searching for the best possible solution

The purpose of Lydia Nichols's research project, which appears at the end of part 6 (pp. 202–11), is persuasive; the purpose of Heather DeGroot's research project, which appears at the end of part 7 (pp. 246–54), is informative.

Study your assignment carefully and talk with your instructor to figure out which purpose your project is intended to serve. If your purpose is *to discover and describe the features of your topic* (the merits and risks of nuclear power generation, for example), you should not make an argument on the topic. If you are asked *to explore a topic, take a position, and defend it* (for example, to research nuclear power generation and decide whether it is necessary), you will need to include a description but focus on making an argument. If you are asked *to explore a situation and make a recommendation* (such as on a state initiative to build a nuclear power plant), your research will be inquiry based. Again, you will need to describe the situation, but your focus will be on weighing the pros and cons and then recommending a *provisional* course of action, one based on the best information available but subject to revision as new information comes to light.

Sometimes, college research assignments specify the method of development to use: comparison-contrast, cause-effect, and so on. One of the most frequently used methods of development is *analysis*, in which the writer divides the issue, proposal, or event into its component parts; explains how the parts work together; and discusses the implications.

> **More about**
> Purpose, 16–17, 23–24
> Argument, 76–86
> Methods of development, 32–35, 90
> Interpretation, analysis, synthesis, and critique, 12–14, 35, 88, 130, 133

As a writer, you have a responsibility to shape your project with the needs and expectations of your audience in mind, so consider who that audience will be. For most college assignments, your audience will include your instructor and perhaps your fellow students. Your instructor will want to see not only that you understand the material covered in class, but also that you can interpret it, analyze it, and think creatively and critically about it. Fellow students may need you to define terms or provide background.

To set a realistic schedule, ask yourself not only when your research project is due and how extensive it is to be but also which other responsibilities you have to fulfill, such as other assignments you must complete, tests for which you must study, and family, work, and personal responsibilities you must meet. Then work backward from your due date, filling in dates for the intermediate tasks. Crafting an effective research project usually includes these tasks:

- Devise and narrow a topic.
- Draft research questions and a thesis.
- Develop a working bibliography, reference list, or list of works cited.
- Conduct research.
- Evaluate potential sources and take notes on them.
- Develop an outline.
- Draft the project.
- Revise and edit your draft.
- Proofread and format your draft.

Remember that the writing process is *recursive.* This means that you may complete these tasks in a different order (by drafting, say, before you develop an outline) or that you may need to return to a step along the way. For example, you might decide to revise your thesis, which may lead you to conduct additional research. Leave extra time in your schedule in case you need to return to an earlier stage in the process.

13b **Choosing and Narrowing a Research Topic**
选定研究主题并缩小范围

When the choice is up to you, select a topic that will interest your readers as well as you, ideally one about which you already have some knowl-

Writing
Responsibly | **Using Printed Sources**

With so much information available online, you might think that you no longer need to consult printed materials. However, many classic and scholarly books are not yet available digitally, and your library may not subscribe to the electronic versions of important newspapers, magazines, and scholarly jour-nals. Dedicate yourself to finding the best information available, whether you access it through a search engine like Google or Bing, through an online database like *Academic Search Premier* or *Web of Science*, or through trips to your library's stacks.

to TOPIC

> **Tech**   **Using an Assignment Calculator**
>
> To set a realistic schedule, try using an online assignment calculator. Such tools divide the writing process into steps and suggest a date by which each step should be completed. Check your library's website to see whether a time management calculator is provided, or search for one by typing "assignment calculator" into the search box of a search engine such as Google or Bing.

edge and insight. Idea-generating techniques such as freewriting and brainstorming can help you devise a topic that will be of interest to your readers, and they can help you narrow your topic so that you can write about it specifically and insightfully. For college research projects, conducting preliminary research or reviewing assigned reading or class notes may be the most helpful in choosing and narrowing your topic. You might try putting your general topic into the search box of a library catalog or database to see which topics arise in the results that are returned. A search in the database PsycArticles on "peer influence," for example, generated topics from smoking and group initiation to copycat crime among juvenile offenders.

If you are choosing a topic that you want to investigate further, consider whether the purpose of your assignment is to write an informative, persuasive, or exploratory research project. If you do not know much about your topic, your research will include familiarizing yourself with the basic data and issues surrounding that topic. That approach will work well if your purpose is to inform your audience of what you have learned. If your purpose is to persuade an audience of one position on your topic or to explore the complexities of the topic and make recommendations, however, you will need to conduct additional research. Unless you have been given an information-based assignment or have a lot of free time to devote to this project, you may want to choose a topic with which you are already familiar.

13c Drafting the Thesis with Research Questions
撰写论文初稿——从提出研究问题开始

Once you have chosen a topic and narrowed it to a subtopic that you can explore fully in the assigned length, ask yourself some intriguing questions that you can answer through research. Remember that the best questions will not lead you on a search for facts but rather on an exploration of complex issues for which there is no easy, obviously right answer. Notice that dull questions tend to be overly broad or overly narrow:

> **More about**
> Devising a thesis,
>   23–24, 90–91,
>   131–32
> Taking notes to
>   avoid plagiarism,
>   123–30
> Patchwriting, 122,
>   124–26
> Annotating, 9–12,
>   87–88

Dull Questions	Intriguing Questions
What are the characteristics of superhero comics?	What makes underground comics so much more compelling than superhero comics?
How do teenagers influence one another?	Are men more likely to be influenced by a stereotypically "male" man than by an average or counterstereotypical man?

When you have crafted questions to research, write the answers you expect to find. These answers are the *hypotheses* that your research will test. As you conduct research, your questions and answers will almost certainly change. The *thesis* for your research project will probably come from your answer to one of these questions.

13d Choosing Research Sources 选择研究来源

Your research project must reflect real research, instead of just creating the appearance of it. The sources you choose are key to fulfilling your responsibilities to your reader, your topic, and yourself. When choosing sources, ask yourself these questions:

- Have you visited your library and its academic databases (not just Google) to see what kinds of resources are available?
- Have you consulted, for background, general reference sources that provide basic facts about your topic?
- Have you consulted, for an authoritative overview, specialized reference sources that discuss the debates and issues about your topic?
- Have you found in-depth analyses and arguments written by experts on your topic, and have other experts on the topic reviewed the source before publication?
- Have you located—after finding a journalist, blogger, or website discussing research findings—the research report itself, instead of settling for secondhand information?
- Have you chosen sources that are either up-to-date or classics that established the principles for studying the topic you are researching?
- Have you consulted enough sources to develop a broad understanding of your topic?
- Have you consulted sources that offer a variety of perspectives on your topic, rather than just searching for sources that agree with your hypothesis?
- Have you consulted the best sources, even if they are not available online?
- Have you conducted experiments, observations, surveys, or interviews, when relevant, to develop information of your own?

You may need help to determine whether a source is up-to-date or reliable or to locate sources online or in your library's print collection. When you do, consult a research expert: a reference librarian.

13e Building and Annotating a Working Bibliography 列出并标注参考文献

Start your research by gathering potential sources and reviewing them to discover whether they are relevant and reliable. Then set up a *working bibliography* to record those that might be useful. Annotate each entry so that you can remember why you thought the source was worth examining.

Writing
Responsibly   Avoiding Accidental Plagiarism

The wonderful ease of cutting and pasting from digital sources is matched by the terrible ease of falling into unintentional plagiarism. When taking notes electronically, it is especially important to keep precise records about what you have copied from a source and what you have paraphrased, summarized, or commented on. Consider supplementing your electronic notes with a folder for printouts and photocopies so that you can double-check your draft against your sources.

to SELF

1. Components of a working bibliography 参考文献要素

A working bibliography should include the information you will need for locating and documenting your sources. You will want to note the following information: names (author, editor, publisher), titles (book, article, journal, website), sources (URL, DOI), version (issue, volume), dates (publication, access), and, if required by the documentation style you follow, medium (print, web, DVD, Kindle e-book). See the Quick Reference box below for additional guidance.

As you construct the entries in your working bibliography, follow the documentation style that you will use in your project. Scholars in literature typically use MLA style (part 6), scholars in psychology and other social sciences typically use APA style (part 7), scholars in the humanities (except for literature) typically use *Chicago* style (part 8), and

Quick Reference   Components of a Working Bibliography

To locate and document . . .	include in the working bibliography . . .
a printed book or an article or chapter in a printed book	the call number, the name of the author or editor, the title of the book, the title of the article or chapter (if relevant), the publisher, the place of publication, the date of publication, and the medium of publication (*Print*).
an e-book or an article or chapter in an e-book	all of the above minus the call number, plus the DOI (digital object identifier) or URL (uniform resource locator); include the e-book format (for example, *Kindle e-book, Nook e-book*) as the medium.
a printed article	the name of the author, the title of the article, the title of the journal, the volume and issue number of the journal, the year of publication, the page numbers of the article, and the medium of publication (in this case, *Print*).
an article accessed through a database	all of the above, plus the name of the database, the DOI or, if there is no DOI, the URL for the journal's home page, and the date you last accessed the file. If no page numbers are provided, include paragraph numbers or section name. (The medium will be *Web*.)
an article in an online journal	all of the above. (The medium will be *Web*.)
a web page, wiki entry, or entry in a blog or discussion list	the name of the author, the title of the web page or entry title, the title of the website or blog, the sponsor, and the publication date or the date you last accessed the file. (The medium will be *Web*.)

Student Model
Research essay:
"Holy Underground
Comics, Batman!" Lydia
Nichols, 202–11

Tech | **Citation Management Software**

Citation management software—such as the proprietary Mendeley and Ref-Works and the open source Zotero—can format the entries in your bibliography no matter which documentation style you choose. Your library may make such software available to you for free. Use the documentation chapters in this handbook to test your program for accuracy; not every program performs to perfection, and you are the writer and the person responsible for providing your audience with error-free documentation that does not cause confusion.

▸ *More about*
Documenting books,
tutorials in parts 6
and 7, 157, 213
Documenting articles
in periodicals, tuto-
rials in parts 6 and
7, 158–59, 214–15
Documenting web-
sites and other
sources, tutorials
in parts 6 and 7,
160, 216
Digital object identi-
fier (DOI), 227, 234,
264–65

scholars in the sciences typically use CSE style (part 8). (If you are not sure which documentation style to use, consult your instructor.) Using the appropriate style in the planning stage will save you time later, when you are formatting your finished project.

Saving a copy of an e-file or photocopying a printed document is prudent in case the source becomes unavailable later. Some instructors may also require you to submit copies of your sources with your final project. A PDF generally captures an article as it looked (or would have looked) in print, while an HTML copy provides the text, often without the formatting, page numbers, or illustrations. If both a PDF and an HTML file are available, select the PDF; it will enable you to cite the page numbers of the article and see any illustrations.

2. Annotate the working bibliography 给参考文献加注

In addition to the information needed for documenting and locating a source, an *annotated bibliography* includes a brief summary or evaluation of the source. Below is a sample entry with annotation for an article from Lydia Nichols's research project.

DOI (digital object identifier) A permanent tag that does not change over time or from database to database

> authors   article title
> Fenty, Sean, et al. "Webcomics: The Influence and Continuation of the Comix
>   journal title Volume no. year   URL
> Revolution." *ImageTexT*, vol. 1, no. 2, 2004, www.english.ufl.edu/imagetext/
> archives/v1_2/group/index.shtml.
>
> This article appeared in a peer-reviewed online journal. It provides a definition of underground comics and a good history of the movement. It compares print comics and web comics, concluding that online comics are more experimental than printed comics.

14 Finding Information 查找资料

A simple Internet search can provide ready access to information—some excellent, much unreliable. A simple Internet search will not, however, help you strike a good balance among the types of sources you consult in your research. Searching on the web can easily become an issue of quantity, collecting "enough sources." The inexperienced researcher may tend to choose brief, quickly available online resources that are easy to read but that lead to a shallow project that relies only on general facts or pieces that do not fit together well. Experienced researchers use advanced techniques that yield a good balance between general reference sources, specialized reference sources, popular opinion, and expert insight. And they go beyond the open web to find scholarly resources—the print, electronic, and multimedia gems.

14a Finding Reference Works 找参考书

Unless you are already an expert on your research topic, your search for sources should include both general and specialized reference works such as dictionaries, encyclopedias, biographical sources, bibliographies, almanacs, yearbooks, and atlases. General reference sources, written for newcomers to the topic, can do the following:

- Introduce you to your topic and help you determine whether it will sustain your interest
- Provide an overview and basic facts

Your search should also include specialized, subject-specific reference works written for researchers wanting in-depth understanding of the topic. These sources can offer the following benefits:

- Introduce you to the issues and debates on your topic
- Help you get a sense of subtopics you might want to explore
- Provide lists of reliable sources on the topic
- Introduce and define special terminology, which will help you develop a list of keywords that you can use in further searching for sources

Specialized dictionaries such as the *Blackwell Dictionary of Political Science* or the *Dictionary of American History* can help you develop your list of keywords by introducing and defining the special terminology used in your discipline. Specialized encyclopedias such as the *McGraw-Hill Encyclopedia of Science and Technology* or the *Encyclopedia of Bioethics* can introduce you to the main issues in a debate. Bibliographies can provide a list of reliable sources on your topic, and they often include an abstract, or brief summary, that will help you determine whether a source is relevant to your project. If your library makes *Reference Universe*

> **More about**
> Relevance, 29, 114
> Reliability, 115–18
> Scholarly versus popular sources, 68, 115–17

> **More about**
> Reliability, 115–18

> **More about**
> Searching the library catalog, 110–11
> Selecting a dictionary, 315–16
> Relevance, 29, 114

Writing
Responsibly | Using Wikipedia Responsibly

Wikipedia (www.wikipedia.org) is an online encyclopedia created and revised by users. Its ongoing updates make its entries more up-to-date than those in most other encyclopedias. Most Wikipedia updates, however, are done by a relatively small number of people whose average age is 27, which means most entries are not validated by experts—unlike a source such as the *Encyclopedia Britannica.* Approach Wikipedia with care, and verify the information you find there. Wikipedia is not an authoritative source for most college-level research projects, and its use in your project could subject you to the sort of ridicule that a US presidential candidate encountered when she cited Wikipedia in a campaign ad.

to TOPIC

Quick Reference General Reference Works

American National Biography
CIA World Fact Book
Concise Columbia Electronic Encyclopedia
Oxford Dictionary of National Biography (British)
New Encyclopedia Britannica
Oxford English Dictionary
Webster's Third New International Dictionary
World Almanac and Book of Facts

or *Credo* available, you can search across many of the library's reference works online and the contents of much of its print reference holdings.

You will find reference works listed in your library's catalog. You may also be able to link to electronic reference sources through your library's home page or database portal.

14b Finding Information on the Web 从网上找资料

When most of us want to find out something, we turn to the web. To learn where a movie is playing nearby or when to move the clocks back to standard time, a simple Google search is appropriate. For college research, too, a web search can be a good starting point. Often, however, when researchers limit themselves to a keyword search on the web, they are deluged with more results than they can thoughtfully consider. A Google search using the term *underground comics*—the topic of Lydia Nichols's project at the end of part 6—yielded nearly 2 million hits. Many of these results were unreliable, and most were irrelevant.

There are ways to narrow search results to more relevant websites and web pages. You can group terms using quotation marks or combine terms. A search on *history "underground comics"* reduced the number of hits from almost 2 million to 361,000—still too many but a definite improvement. (See the Quick Reference box on p.108 to learn more about techniques for customizing a search.)

Using a search engine's *advanced search options* can limit results further by pulling up only those sites that are in English, for example, or only those with a specific domain (.edu, .gov, .org, .net, .com). Limiting the search *history "underground comics"* to sites with the domain *.edu* reduced the number of hits to 267 (Figure 14.1).

Quick

Reference　Accessing Government Documents Online

The following websites all provide access to government documents and databases online:

Europa: europa.eu/index_en.htm

FedStats: fedstats.sites.usa.gov

Government Printing Office: www.gpo.gov/fdsys

Library of Congress: www.loc.gov/index.html

National Institutes of Health: www.nih.gov

United Nations: www.un.org

US Census Bureau: www.census.gov

US government: www.usa.gov

Writing **Responsibly**　Going beyond Reference Sources

Because both general and specialized reference works provide background information to orient you to your topic, they are an essential starting point in your research. For a college-level research project, however, reference works are just the beginning; to fulfill your responsibilities to your topic and audience, you must go beyond these sources to find books, articles, and websites that treat your topic in depth.

to TOPIC

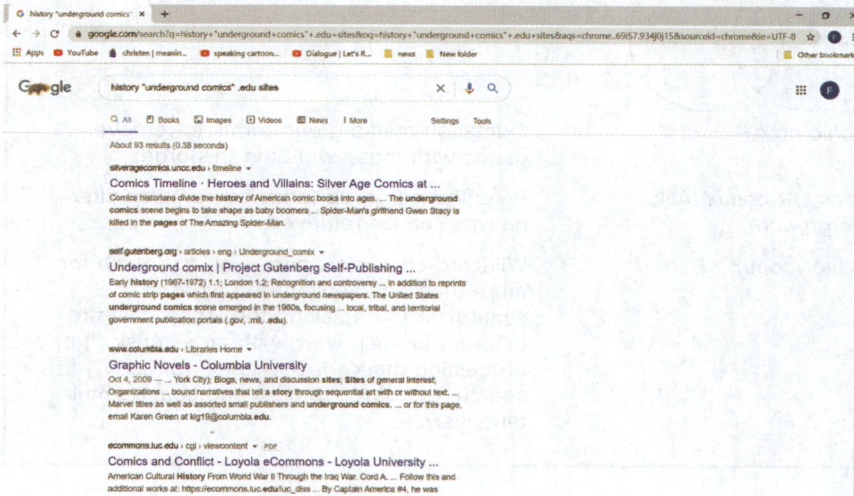

FIGURE 14.1
Narrowing a search by combining terms and limiting the domain to .edu Limiting the search to .edu sites results in no "sponsored" (advertising) sites. Source: google.com

14c Finding Reliable Interactive Media 找可靠的互动媒体

In addition to conventional websites, a variety of other electronic sources, including blogs, discussion lists, and groups on social networking sites like Facebook and Twitter, can be useful if you are researching a popular topic or if your topic is so up-to-the-minute that conventional scholarly sources are not available. To find a blog or discussion list on your topic, add the word *blog, listserv, newsgroup,* or *chat room* to your search term.

News alerts and RSS feeds collect news stories on topics you specify. Registering for alerts at sites such as Google (www.google.com/alerts) will bring daily updates on your chosen topics to your email box. To read RSS feeds, use a website like Feedly or Inoreader to subscribe to site feeds.

> **More about**
> Documenting a blog, 189 (MLA style), 238 (APA style), 268 (*Chicago* style), 282 (CSE style)
> Documenting a discussion list, 189 (MLA style), 237–38 (APA style), 268 (*Chicago* style), 282 (CSE style)
> Reliability, 115–18

Quick

Reference **Customizing a Search**

Most search engines and library databases use Boolean operators to narrow or expand a search.

AND

Comics AND history

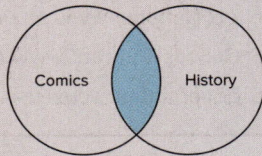

Comics   History

Narrows a search by retrieving items that include *both* terms.

OR

Comics OR history

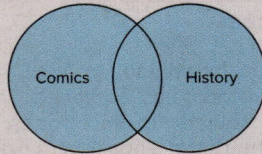

Comics   History

Expands a search by retrieving items that include *either* term.

NOT

Comics NOT history

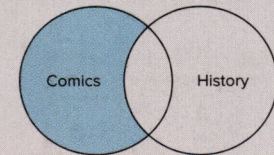

Comics   History

Narrows a search by retrieving items that include one term but not the other.

" "

"graphic novel"

Quotation marks group terms to retrieve pages with these words in this order.

( )

(*comics* OR *comix*) AND (*underground*)

Parentheses group terms so complex alternatives can be retrieved.

* / ?

comi* (or *comi?*)

Wildcard characters allow you to search for more than one version of a word at the same time by replacing the letters that are different in each word with an asterisk (*) or a question mark (?). Use *comi** (or *comi?*) to search for *comic*, *comics*, and *comix* simultaneously.

NOTE Not all blogs, discussion lists, groups, and even news sites are equally authoritative. Evaluate the reliability of such sites carefully, and verify the information you glean from such sources.

14d Finding Articles in Journals and Other Periodicals Using Databases and Indexes 利用数据库和索引找期刊文章

Periodical is the umbrella term for magazines, newspapers, and scholarly journals that are issued at regular intervals—daily, weekly, monthly, quarterly. Articles in periodicals are listed in *databases,* which index them by author, title, subject, and other categories. Search engines such as Google and Bing can point you to articles published online, but their search is not selective. The databases to which your college library subscribes will limit a search to reputable publications, so results are more likely to be reliable. Most allow users to limit a search to articles in scholarly

> **Tech** **HTML versus PDF**
>
> Articles accessed through a database are often available in both HTML and PDF versions. The HTML (often called *full text*) version will download much more quickly, but the PDF (often called *full text PDF*) version may be a duplicate of the article as it appears in the publication, including illustrations and page numbers, which you can then include in your reference list or list of works cited.

journals, which are typically the best sources for college research projects because they provide the most authoritative information and the deepest explanation of academic debates and controversies. Also, many articles you locate through Google will require a fee or subscription for access, whereas the databases available through your college library will typically provide access to articles for free, in either a PDF or HTML file. Databases also provide an *abstract,* or summary, of the articles indexed. (Such abstracts are useful for determining the relevance of articles, but remember that they are no substitute for the articles themselves.)

> *More about*
> Relevance, 29, 114

1. Choose a database 数据库选择

Most college libraries provide a wide variety of databases, including all-purpose databases like *ProQuest Central, Academic Search Premier*, and *Academic OneFile*, which index both popular magazines and scholarly journals. Libraries also typically provide discipline-specific databases, such as *Education Source, PsycArticles*, and *Science Direct*. They may also offer *LexisNexis Academic*, which indexes news reports from around the world. A reference librarian can help you learn which databases available at your library will best suit your research needs. For Heather DeGroot, writing on stereotyping and social influence for her psychology class, *PsycArticles* was a good starting place for her periodicals search. For Lydia Nichols, researching underground comics, a general database such as *ProQuest Central* or *Academic Search Premier* was a good place to start.

> *More about*
> Writing situation,
>   16–19
> Reliability, 115–18

Student Models
Research essays:
"The Power of Ward-
  robe," Heather
  DeGroot, 246–54
"Holy Underground
  Comics, Batman!"
  Lydia Nichols, 202–11

2. Search a database 数据库检索

Searching a database is much like using a search engine such as Google or Bing: You type in a search term and press Enter (or Return). Unlike a search engine, however, the database uses a preset list of subject headings to index articles. If your keywords turn up few relevant articles, try a synonym (*comics* instead of *cartoons*) or ask a librarian for help.

Writing
Responsibly *Really* **Reading** *Real* **Sources**

As you choose your sources, it may seem efficient to select only those that are short and easy to read. Resist this temptation; fulfill your responsibility to your topic by pushing beyond easy, basic information. If you consulted only brief sources, you would be basing your research project only on basic facts and would produce a shallow, less thoughtful paper. Instead, when your source selection is finished, include substantial sources that treat complex questions in complex ways. Reading these sources will be a greater challenge, but the writing you produce from them will be richer and more successful.

to TOPIC

More about
Relevance, 29, 114
Customizing a
search, 108

To make sure the results are relevant, narrow your database search by combining search terms. (See the Quick Reference box on p. 108 for tips on customizing a search.) Typing *comics* in the search box of a database like *Academic Search Premier* generates a list of more than 17,000 items—fewer than with a Google search but still far too many to be helpful. Combining terms using Boolean operators (*comic books AND underground*) narrows the search. The search could be narrowed further by using the database's search options. If narrowing your search by combining terms and using the database's narrowing options is not producing useful results, try running your search on another database. Remember, too, that databases differ from vendor to vendor and are updated frequently, so checking the Help screens or asking a librarian for advice is a good idea.

3. Find copies of articles 找文章副本

Once you have generated a list of articles from your database search, you are ready to retrieve copies of the articles. Some articles you can access directly from the database search page. Not all articles are available electronically, however. To access articles, consult your library's website (or a librarian) for a list of journals your library subscribes to or can obtain through interlibrary loan.

14e Finding Books for In-Depth Information Using Your Library's Catalog 利用图书馆的图书目录找书，获取详细资料

Books provide the most sustained and in-depth treatments of your topic, so they can be very useful sources, especially in the humanities and some social sciences, where up-to-the-minute information is not crucial. To find books on your topic, search your library's online catalog.

More about
Keyword search-
ing, 106–08

Most library catalogs allow users to search for resources by author, title, and subject. Some also allow users to search by call number. Because catalogs differ from library to library, check the Help or Search Tips screen before beginning a search. If your library's catalog allows keyword searching, you may find it useful to conduct a "keyword any-where" search, using your search terms. Most library catalogs include tables of contents for anthologies and edited books, so a keyword search may yield useful results.

As with library databases, library catalogs use preset subject headings to index books. If your keywords turn up only a few relevant books, try a synonym (*comics* instead of *cartoons*) or ask a librarian for help. Once you have located a relevant book, check the subject headings you find in the full record of that book for keywords you can use in a fresh search.

Since books on a topic share the first part of a call number, they are shelved close together. If you are free to wander in your library's stacks, check for other books on your topic shelved close to those you have identified as relevant. If your library catalog allows it, search for other books on your subject by inserting the first part of a relevant book's call number in the catalog's search box. You might also find sources on related topics by checking the results page in an online catalog search on your library's website.

14f Finding Government Information 找政府资料

Although you will usually rely on books and articles in your college research, government documents and datasets can provide you with rich resources, including congressional records, government reports, and legal documents. Local, state, and federal government agencies make thousands of publications available online, free of charge. To locate government documents and datasets, conduct an advanced web search limited to the domain .gov or search databases such as *CQ Press Electronic Library* and *LexisNexis Congressional*. Some useful sites for accessing government publications are listed in the Quick Reference box on page 107.

Quick Reference **Multimedia Resources**

Academy of American Poets
Archive.org
American Rhetoric: The Power of Oratory in the United States
Library of Congress
MIT Open Courseware
National Aeronautics and Space Administration (NASA)
National Park Service
New York Public Library
Perry Castañeda Library Map Collection, University of Texas
Smithsonian Institution

14g Finding Multimedia Sources 找多媒体资料

Besides the video clips you can find on YouTube or the pictures you find on Google Images, you may find appropriate multimedia resources through your library's catalog or online at the sites hosted by the organizations listed in the Quick Reference box on this page. Use them when they are appropriate to your writing situation.

14h Conducting and Reporting Field Research 实地研究与报告

Field research is often part of a research project in which the writer begins by reviewing information from secondary sources (reports of others' research) and then adds to the body of information by conducting primary, firsthand research. The most common types of field research are interviews, observational studies, and surveys.

1. Interviews 访谈

Expertise and the knowledge that comes with experience can often be gained only through an interview. Media such as email, text messaging, video chat, and even the telephone extend your range of possible interviewees. However, face-to-face interviews give you an opportunity to read the other person's body language—facial expressions and bodily gestures—which can provide insight and direction for follow-up questions.

Tech   Online Surveys

A variety of web-based survey tools allow you to conduct surveys online. The following are popular:

- Google Docs
- SurveyGizmo
- SurveyMonkey
- Zoomerang

Each allows users to create and send out a basic survey to a limited number of respondents for free. You might also consider conducting your survey with the help of social media such as Facebook or Twitter.

Researchers may also locate respondents using social networking sites, but be sure that the participants are representative of your target group.

Writing
Responsibly   Reporting Results Fairly

As you integrate the results of your field research into your larger project, explain how you chose your research participants, how many you invited, and how many agreed to participate. Do not, however, name or indirectly identify your participants unless they have agreed to their identity being made public. When you quote from an interview or survey, indicate how typical the quotation is. Did you choose it just because it supports your thesis, or is it typical of the majority of responses?

to AUDIENCE

Interviews will be most useful if you do the following:

- Conduct background research on the topic and on the person whom you are interviewing.
- Develop a number of questions—more than you will probably have time to ask—and list them from most to least important.
- Ask questions that will prompt a thoughtful reply, and avoid simple yes-or-no questions.
- Ask your prepared questions, but also listen for surprises and ask follow-up questions.
- Listen carefully to answers and take good notes or, if permitted, record the interview.
- Reflect on your notes while the interview is still fresh. Jot down your thoughts and any additional questions you would like to ask; then phone or email the interviewee *once* for follow-up. (Multiple follow-up calls are likely to annoy.)
- Send a thank-you note within a day of your interview, and send a copy of your finished project with a note of thanks.

2. Observational studies 观察研究

Observational studies are common in the social sciences, particularly in psychology, sociology, and anthropology. Consider the following before beginning an observational study:

- **Your hypothesis.** What do you expect to learn? Use your tentative answer, or *hypothesis*, to guide your observations. Refine your hypothesis as your observations continue, but start out with a hypothesis to guide your observations and note taking.

- **Your role.** Will you participate in the group or observe from outside? The role you play will influence your perspective and affect your observations. Consider the steps you can take to minimize bias.
- **Your methods.** Establish categories for the observations you expect, and adjust them in response to your observations. Make notes immediately after a research session rather than during it, so your presence will be less obtrusive.

3. Surveys 调查

Surveys are used frequently in politics and marketing, but they are useful in any type of research in which the beliefs, opinions, and behaviors of large groups are relevant. When developing a survey, ask yourself these questions:

- **Your hypothesis.** What do you expect to learn?
- **Your participants.** What group will you reach and how will you contact them? Strive to include a broad and representative range of respondents.
- **Your questions.** What type of questions will you ask, how many questions will you include, and how will you administer the survey? Most questions should be true-false, yes-no, and multiple-choice because these are easier to tabulate, but a few open-ended questions may deepen your sense of the respondents' feelings. Because respondents are not likely to spend more than a few minutes answering questions, surveys should be brief; one to two pages is a reasonable limit.

Most surveys conducted for a college research project cannot meet the high standards of statistical accuracy, but if designed with care, they can provide tentative insights into local situations.

15 **Evaluating Information** 评估资料

In Aesop's fable "The Wolf in Sheep's Clothing," the wolf uses a sheep's skin to lull his intended dinner into a false sense of security. Texts, too,

CLOTHING

"Do you have this in sheep?"

© Marty Bucella/CartoonStock, Ltd.

can be a kind of wolf in sheep's clothing. They can appear to be wonderful resources, full of interesting facts and persuasive arguments while hiding misinformation and faulty reasoning. For this reason, it is crucial that researchers dig below the surface to evaluate their sources carefully for relevance and reliability. Just as a wolf can hide under a sheep's clothing, a book should not be judged by its cover! Evaluating sources includes assessing how *relevant*, or useful, a source is to your research; it includes determining the source's *reliability*—how much you can count on it; and it may include determining whether the source is *fake news*—something that has been invented to convince readers to believe lies or distortions of facts.

More about

Previewing a text, 9
Finding the
  copyright date,
  157–60
  (Documentation
  Matters tutorial in
  part 6)
Primary versus sec-
  ondary sources,
  89–90, 111–13

15a **Evaluating the Relevance of Potential Sources**
评估所有文献来源的相关性

Consider the relevance of each source to your research questions: Does the source offer information that could enrich your understanding of your topic, provide background information or evidence to support your claims, or suggest alternative perspectives? Begin determining a source's relevance by *previewing* it:

- **Check the publication date.** Recently published works are most likely to be of the greatest relevance, as they will probably provide the most up-to-date information. Be alert for classics, though: They contain information or ideas on which researchers still rely.

- **Read the abstract, foreword, introduction, or lead** (first paragraph in a newspaper article). These items usually provide a summary, overview, or key facts discussed in detail in the source.

- **Read the headings and subheadings.** They may provide an outline of the work.

abstract 摘要 A summary of the text's main claims and most important supporting evidence

114

- **Scan figures and illustrations.** These visuals might signal important ideas and explain complex processes.

- **Read the conclusion.** It may summarize the central idea and argument.

- **Consult the index.** It may contain some of the key terms you are using in your research.

15b Evaluating the Reliability of Potential Sources
评估所有文献来源的可靠性

With the exception of fake news, judging the reliability of a source is not a simple, yes-or-no test. Instead, it is a balancing act: You rate a source on a variety of criteria; the more criteria on which you can rate the source highly, the more reliable it is likely to be. Consider these questions during your review of a source:

- **Is the author an expert on the topic?** Look for other works the author has published, see if the author has an academic affiliation, or search the author's name on the web.

- **Is it a scholarly source?** The intended audience of a source significantly affects its reliability. A *scholarly source* is intended for an audience of experts on the topic. Although it may be challenging for you to read, such material will contain the most detailed, insightful information available—so it is well worth your effort to decipher it. Scholarly sources include articles published

---

Quick Reference   **Judging Reliability**

Scholarly work. Was the source published in a scholarly journal or book, or in a popular magazine, newspaper, or book?

Expertise. Is the author an authority on the subject?

Objectivity. Do the tone, logic, quality of the evidence, and coverage of the opposition suggest that the source is unbiased?

Scope. Does the author attempt to test his or her own assumptions and explore alternatives?

Citations. Does the text cite sources, and is it cited in other texts?

Scrutiny. Was the text subjected to scrutiny by someone else before you saw it? For example,

was it selected by the library, reviewed by another scholar, or fact-checked for accuracy?

Presentation. Is the text clearly written, well organized, and carefully edited and proofread?

Domain. Does the main portion of the URL end in .edu or .org, suggesting the sponsor has a noncommercial purpose, or does it end with .com, suggesting the sponsor has a commercial purpose?

Site sponsor or host. Is the site's host identified? Does the host promote a viewpoint or position that might bias the content?

in academic journals and books published by scholarly presses. They usually include citations to other sources and full bibliographic information for those citations, either in notes or in a bibliography.

In contrast, articles in magazines and books published by the *popular press* are geared toward a general audience and are intended to raise enough interest to inspire a large number of people to buy the publication. Often these articles include advertisements that sometimes accompany an "objective" story. Popular sources may be fact-checked, but they are not reviewed by experts.

Between scholarly and popular sources are intellectual periodicals such as *The Chronicle of Higher Education, The New Yorker,* and *Scientific American.* They have all the characteristics of the popular press but are aimed specifically at an educated and well-informed audience. Articles in such periodicals are typically much longer and more detailed than those found in the general popular press. Although they are not peer reviewed and usually do not include citations and a bibliography, their intended audience demands that they be carefully prepared and fact-checked, so they tend to be more reliable than the general popular press.

- **Is the source peer reviewed?** Before they are published, scholarly sources are sent for review to one or more experts in the

Quick Reference   **Typical Characteristics of Scholarly and Popular Sources**

Scholarly
- Articles are written by scholars, specialists, or researchers
- Use technical terminology
- Tend to be long—typically, ten pages or more
- Include citations in the text and a list of references
- Reviewed by other scholars before publication
- Acknowledge any conflicts of interest (such as research support from a pharmaceutical company)
- Generally look serious; unlikely to include color photographs, but may include charts, graphs, and tables
- Published by professional organizations

Popular
- Articles are written by journalists or professional writers
- Avoid technical terminology
- Tend to be brief—as little as one or two pages
- Seldom include citations or a list of references
- Generally fact-checked but not reviewed by a panel of experts
- Unlikely to acknowledge potential conflicts of interest
- Often published on glossy paper with eye-catching color images
- Published by commercial companies

field, who check the accuracy and importance of the content and make recommendations about whether it should be published. On the home page of a peer-reviewed periodical, you should be able to find the words *peer review* or *editorial board*.

- **Does the source seem objective?** Does the source have an objective tone, make reasonable claims supported by logical evidence, include counterevidence, and treat opposing positions with respect? Or does it contain emotionally loaded language, make exaggerated claims, support those claims with faulty logic and questionable or scanty evidence, or omit counterevidence?

- **Is the type of source appropriate to your purpose?** Does the source offer a detailed exploration of the debates surrounding your issue, or does it offer just basic facts or a condensed overview?

- **Does the author or publisher have a vested interest?** Is the author promoting a product or process from which she will benefit financially? Will the author or publisher gain adherents to a political position? Check the author's or publisher's website for advertisements and to see whether a mission statement reveals an agenda.

- **Does the text cite its sources?** Most scholarly articles and books as well as some popular books include a bibliography, and some journal databases list the article's sources in the citation. Reputable newspapers and magazines check a writer's sources, though they often go unnamed, being identified only as a "White House source" or a "source close to the investigation."

> *More about*
> Bias, 306–08
> Tone, 10
> Opinion versus
> belief, 74–75

- **Do other scholars cite the text?** Some journal databases indicate the number of times an article has been cited by other articles indexed by that database. Citation indexes such as *Web of Science, Scopus, Microsoft Academic Search,* and *Google Scholar* also provide this information. If you find very few citations for your source, check the publication date: Sources published within the previous three years may not have been cited yet.

- **How did you find the source?** Sources located through your college library are more likely to be reliable than are sources located through a Google search. A source published solely on the web (unless in a scholarly journal published online) is not likely to have been subjected to the same level of scrutiny as an article published in a peer-reviewed source. Google searches will return such sites, but library databases will not.

> *More about*
> Exploratory argu-
>   ments, 73
> Reasoning logically,
>   12
> Using evidence as
>   support, 75–76
> Citing sources, 157–
>   211 (MLA style,
>   part 6), 213–54
>   (APA style, part 7),
>   256–71
>   (*Chicago* style,
>   part 8), 272–84
>   (CSE style, part 8)

Writing
Responsibly — Keeping an Open, Inquiring Mind

Read sources with an open mind, use reliable sources, avoid exaggerated claims and logical fallacies, and criticize unreasonable or poorly supported conclusions but not the people who hold them. As a researcher, you have a responsibility to avoid bias. Consider all sides of an argument, especially those that challenge the positions you hold. Use difficult sources, too: Do not reject a source because it is written to a more expert audience than you. Find the time to study it carefully and gain at least a provisional understanding of it.

to OTHER WRITERS

- **Is the source well written and edited?** Is the source carefully written, organized, edited, and proofread? Is the page design easy to follow? Are the visuals appropriate to the audience and purpose and free from manipulation or distortion?

15c Evaluating Online Texts: Websites, Blogs, Wikis, and Discussion Forums
评估网络文本：网站、博客、维基百科和论坛

In addition to the reliability tests listed earlier, consider these factors when evaluating websites:

1. URL 网址

Every item on the web has a *URL*, and all URLs end with an extension, or *domain*, that indicates the type of site it is. The most common domains are these:

- **.com** (commercial): sites hosted by businesses
- **.edu** (educational): sites sponsored by colleges and universities
- **.gov** (governmental): sites sponsored by some branch of federal, state, or local government
- **.net** (network): typically sites sponsored by businesses selling Internet infrastructure services (such as Internet providers) but also sometimes chosen by businesses that want to appear technologically sophisticated or organizations that want to indicate that they are part of a network
- **.org** (organization): usually sites sponsored by nonprofit groups (though sometimes the nonprofit status of these groups may be questionable)

2. Sponsor 网站发起人

Sites sponsored by educational, governmental, and nonprofit organizations are likely to be reliable, but your evaluation of a website should never end with its URL. Although businesses usually offer information intended to sell products or services, commercial sites can nevertheless be highly informative. A site ending in .edu may just as easily have been constructed and posted by a student as by an expert.

3. Open versus moderated 开放性与适度性

The reliability of online discussion forums depends in large part on their contributors. Sources to which anyone can contribute should be screened carefully, especially in the case of comments left by readers on an online site. Use what you find there only if you can verify it in reliable sources.

4. Links 链接

An additional step in assessing the reliability of a website is to determine the number and type of sites that link to it. From the Google search page, you can determine the number of times a site has been linked to and review the linked sites. Type "link:" plus the URL in the search box and click Search or hit Return. Popularity alone does not guarantee reliability—the site may just be fun to read or authored by a celebrity—but when coupled with other criteria, it can be an indication of reliability.

15d Detecting Fake News 辨别虚假信息

Researchers working online today must be alert to the possibility of fake news, stories that have been manufactured from lies or that distort the facts. Simply choosing well-respected sources such as *The Los Angeles Times* or *Harper's* magazine is not enough, because a fake news story may be disguised to look as if it comes from a reputable publisher. If an online news source fails any of the following tests, you should reject it:

Writing
Responsibly   Online Plagiarism

The ease with which users can cut and paste information from one site into another means you must be wary of online sites, especially if they are self-sponsored. Unreliable sites frequently copy directly from other, more reliable sites. If you suspect plagiarism, copy a passage and paste it into a search engine's search box. Do any of your hits use the same (or very similar) language? The best way to avoid using material plagiarized from another site is to evaluate sites carefully for reliability.

to SELF

- If the source comes to you through social media, open it up on the web. Explore the website: Is it a full news source, with tabs leading you to a variety of topics, or does it have just a few sensational stories?

- If the source appears to be published by a reliable source like *Time* magazine or *The Washington Post*, open a new tab on your browser, search for that publication, and open its website. Now compare the website URL with the URL of the article you have found. If they are altogether different, the source is fake. If extra characters precede the URL of the source, it is fake. If you can't find your source on the publisher's website, it is fake.

- Evaluate whether the information in the source actually provides evidence for the claim in the headline. If it doesn't, the source is *clickbait*, designed to accumulate "hits" rather than to inform readers.

- Conduct a fact-check. Do other reputable sources offer the same information? Sometimes one publisher has a "scoop" before any of the others, but its advantage won't last for long: News circulates quickly on the web.

Don't rely on a source just because it has been posted or tweeted by someone you respect. Smart people can be deceived by fake news, so you must always verify sources for yourself. Don't let yourself be fooled by a source that says something you want to hear, something you want to be true. For any online news story, explicitly confirm that it is real.

16 Using Information Responsibly: Taking Notes and Avoiding Plagiarism
负责任地使用信息：记笔记和避免抄袭

Plagiarism stories are always in the news cycle. Former star *New York Times* writer Chris Hedges submitted an article to *Harper's* magazine and was rejected for using unattributed quotations from another journalist's research.[1] Harvard historian Doris Kearns Goodwin was accused of plagiarizing portions of her book *The Fitzgeralds and the Kennedys*. She admitted that she had carelessly included some sentences word for word from her sources without putting those sentences in quotation marks. Her publisher was forced to make a financial settlement with the writer whose sentences she lifted, and as was the case for Hedges, Goodwin's credibility was severely undermined.[2]

Plagiarism is of such widespread concern that scholarly research and corporations are devoted to it. A computer science professor at Emory University designs software to determine whether some forms of *patchwriting* (often categorized as a type of plagiarism) are not academic misconduct but rather effective writing techniques.[3] Corporations such as Turnitin.com are devoted to "catching" plagiarism, and instructors, publishers, and colleges pay substantial sums of money for that service. Even Wikipedia employs Turnitin.com to check its entries.[4]

Nor are concerns with plagiarism exclusive to the United States. The Ventures Africa website acknowledges that plagiarism is widespread in Nigeria but asserts that the problem is global.[5] *The Moscow Times* reports that a study in Russia revealed that 21 percent of the graduate theses in Russian universities included significant plagiarism.[6] Among students, scholars, journalists, and writers and publishers worldwide, the issue of plagiarism often arises. Its frequency does not, however, mean that plagiarism is an acceptable practice. Plagiarism is always regarded negatively and is usually penalized. This chapter is designed to help you understand it and keep it out of your own work.

Plagiarism involves the presentation of another person's work—a paper or story, a photograph or graphic, a speech or song, a web page or email message—without indicating that it came from a source. Buying a paper or "borrowing" a sentence (without citation and quotation marks) are both classified as plagiarism.

Sometimes plagiarism may be inadvertent—Kearns Goodwin, for example, claimed that she had copied passages word for word into her notes and then forgot that these passages were not her own.[7] Whether intentional or not, such borrowings are still considered unacceptable.

---

[1]Ketcham, Christopher. "The Troubling Case of Chris Hedges." *New Republic,* 12 June 2014.
[2]Lewis, Mark. "Doris Kearns Goodwin and the Credibility Gap." *Forbes,* 27 Feb. 2002.
[3]Williams, Kimber. "Interdisciplinary Project Analyzes 'Patchwriting' through Math, Computer Science." *Emory News Center,* 13 Oct. 2015.
[4]Schaffhauser, Dian. "Wikipedia Edits Get Student Paper-Style Plagiarism Check." *T/H/E Journal,* 17 Nov. 2015.
[5]Odunmorayo, Emmanuel. "It's about Time We Recognize That Plagiarism Is a Global Problem, Not Peculiar to Nigeria Alone." *Ventures Africa,* 3 Nov. 2015.
[6]"21% of Theses Defended by Russian University Rectors Contain Plagiarism." *Moscow Times,* 23 Nov. 2015.
[7]Kirkpatrick, David. "Historian Says Borrowing Was Wider Than Known," *New York Times,* 23 Feb. 2002.

► *More about*
Patchwriting,
124–26

citation 引用 The acknowledgment of sources in the body of a research project
documentation 文献 记录 Information in a footnote, bibliography, reference list, or list of works cited that allows readers to locate the source cited in the text

► *More about*
Using quotation
  marks, 448–53
Block indention for
  long quotations,
  165, 200 (MLA
  style), 243 (APA
  style)
Citing sources,
  161–76 (MLA style),
  217–26 (APA style),
  256–71
  (*Chicago* style),
  272–73 (CSE style)
Documenting
  sources,
  176–96 (MLA
  style), 226–41
  (APA style), 256–
  70
  (*Chicago* style),
  274–82 (CSE
  style)
Using signal
  phrases,
  137–38,
  161–62, 218

Student plagiarism may not be reported in *The New York Times*, but to many instructors it is even more objectionable than the cases discussed here. After all, when students are given a writing assignment, they are expected to learn something about the topic and about writing itself, and plagiarism prevents this learning.

Also be alert to the possibility of ***patchwriting***, copying and only partially changing the language of a source. The National Council of Writing Program Administrators classifies patchwriting as a misuse of sources. Sometimes, though, instructors and college policies classify it as plagiarism. In either case, patchwriting is not good writing. It is sometimes unintentional, the result of inaccurate note taking, misunderstanding the source, incorrect use of or omission of quotation marks, or incomplete paraphrasing. Whether plagiarism occurs intentionally or unintentionally, however, writers are always held responsible for it. You should make every effort to avoid this practice.

Inform yourself in detail about what your instructor and your college (or your employer) define as ethical writing; although everyone rejects plagiarism, the definition of what constitutes plagiarism can vary subtly from one discipline or profession to another. Still, as you follow the guidelines for writing described in this chapter (and throughout this book), you can be confident that the work you produce will represent its sources responsibly.

Plagiarism and Culture Attitudes toward and definitions of plagiarism vary from one culture to another. Some individualist cultures, like that of the United States, see words and ideas as personal property that can be "stolen" by plagiarists. Some collectivist cultures view information as a shared good. Whether your home culture tends to be individualist or collectivist, when writing for a US academic audience, be especially careful to mark borrowed language as quotation, to provide a citation whenever you borrow language or ideas, and to document sources fully.

16a **Learning What You Do and Do Not Have to Acknowledge**
熟知哪些需标明引用，哪些不需要

The Earth is approximately 93 million miles from the sun on average; US women won the right to vote on August 26, 1920; the Beatles' song "I Want to Hold Your Hand" was that band's first number-one hit in

► *More about*
Citing media
  illustrations, 190–
  95 (MLA style),
  239–40 (APA
  style), 268–69
  (*Chicago* style)

Writing
Responsibly   **Using Illustrations and Avoiding Plagiarism**

The web contains a variety of images, videos, and sound files that you can download to your word processor: A click of the mouse, and they are yours. Or are they? Keep full records of who created them, where you found them, and on what date you downloaded them so that you can cite them fully.

to OTHER WRITERS

Writing Responsibly | Highlighting versus Making Notes

While highlighting is a useful way to signal important information in a source, it is not a substitute for writing your own notes about a text. Highlighting can help you mark what is important, but annotating will push you to engage with the text and save you from leafing through page after highlighted page, looking for a passage that you faintly recall having read. So even though it may seem more time-consuming than highlighting, making notes will actually serve you better in the long run.

to SELF

the United States. Information like this—incontestable facts available in three or more sources—is *common knowledge.* You do not have to cite common knowledge (unless it is included in a quotation). Everything else—surprising facts, interpretations, quotations even from well-known works of literature—must be cited in the text of your research project and documented in a footnote, bibliography, reference list, or list of works cited, regardless of whether you are quoting, paraphrasing, or summarizing from the source.

NOTE What counts as common knowledge can differ from one group of people or one academic discipline to another. If you are unsure whether a fact is common knowledge, err on the side of safety by citing and documenting it.

16b Making Notes That Help You Avoid Plagiarizing
做笔记有助于避免无意识抄袭

Inadvertent plagiarism is a growing problem for researchers today because cutting and pasting material from online sources into notes is so easy. As Doris Kearns Goodwin knows only too well, it is easy to lose track of which material has been borrowed and which material came from which source. The following strategies for maintaining good research notes can help you avoid problems:

- **Keep a working bibliography.** For every source you consult, add a complete entry to your working bibliography.

- **Make a fresh file, blog entry, or notebook selection for notes on each source, and include the author and page number in each note.** Separating notes helps you avoid confusing one source with another.

- **Use columns or different-colored fonts or note cards to distinguish borrowed material from your own ideas.** If done consistently, using one column or color for your own comments and another for quotations, summaries, and paraphrases can provide a useful visual cue for identifying source material and avoiding unintentional plagiarism.

Tech | **Bookmarking and Listing Favorites**

If you will not always be working from a single computer, set up bookmarks on a social bookmarking site like Pinterest or Digg, which allows you to store, tag, and share bookmarks.

> *More about*
> Working bibliography, 102–04

> *More about*
> Annotation, 9–12, 87–88

- **Create a favorites list or bookmark useful web pages.** When taking notes on a computer, bookmarking or creating a favorites list can help you keep track of your sources.
- **Photocopy sources or download PDFs from which you borrow information or ideas.** You will be able to check quotations, paraphrases, and summaries against these copies after you have drafted your research project.

16c Paraphrasing and Summarizing Sources without Patchwriting 改述与总结，拒绝拼凑式写作

Paraphrasing and summarizing force you to understand your sources and to capture their meaning accurately in original words and sentences. They allow you to maintain a consistent voice—yours—throughout the research project. However, paraphrasing and summarizing accurately are difficult. Often, inexperienced writers *patchwrite*: They replace some terms with synonyms, delete a few words, or alter the grammar or sentence structure slightly, but they do not put the passage fully into their own words and sentences. The sections that follow will show you how to paraphrase and summarize without patchwriting.

1. Paraphrase 改述

A *paraphrase* restates someone else's ideas in fresh words and sentences. Paraphrase a source when you want to do the following:

- Understand the logic of complex passages
- Convey the main idea and key supporting points from a source in your own words
- Mention examples and details from the source

Because a paraphrase includes all of the writer's main ideas, it is often as long as, and sometimes even longer than, the original. Like a summary, a paraphrase must not use the same language as the source (except for keywords), and the order of ideas and the sentence structures must be new as well. To paraphrase *without* patchwriting, follow these steps:

1. Read the source until you feel you understand it. Think about the overall meaning of the passage. Figure out whether there are any key terms that must be retained in your paraphrase.
2. Close the text and walk away. Do something else for a few minutes or a few hours.
3. Come back to your desk and write down what you remember. If you cannot remember anything, repeat steps 1 and 2.
4. Check your paraphrase against the source to make sure you have correctly represented what it said. If you have closely followed the language or sentence structure of the source, revise your notes.

> **More about**
> Varying sentence length and structure, 293–94
> Bookending a paraphrase, 138–39
> Using signal phrases, 137–38

Where possible, use synonyms (words with a similar meaning) rather than the words of the source. If no synonym makes sense, then use key terms from the source. Rearrange the ideas of the source so that they make sense in your own text, use different sentence structures from those in the original passage, and omit details that are not relevant to your main point. Introduce the paraphrase with a signal phrase by mentioning the author's name ("MacDonald argues . . . "), and include a page reference (in parentheses) at the end of the borrowed passage; then document the source in your bibliography, reference list, or list of works cited. The following examples show passages that have been paraphrased with and without patchwriting.

Passage from source

With these caveats, we argue more limitedly that digital technology offers new avenues of aesthetic experimentation for comic artists and that the internet has given some comic artists a modest prosperity that they would not have without the internet as a means of distribution. (Sean Fenty et al., "Webcomics: The Influence and Continuation of the Comix Revolution," *ImageTexT*, vol. 1, no. 2, 2004, par. 2. www.english.ufl.edu/imagetext/archives/v1_2/group/.)

Note with patchwriting

Fenty et al. argue that digital technology provides comic artists with an opportunity for artistic experimentation and that some have more success than they would have without the Internet (par. 2).

First author + et al.

Picks up language from source

Uses synonym or word in another form

Paragraph reference (use only when source numbers its paragraphs)

Note without patchwriting

According to Fenty et al., comic artists use the computer to experiment and the Internet to publish their works, allowing them more creative options and earning them more money than they made in the pre-Internet era (par. 2).

Notice that the patchwritten note relies heavily not only on the language but also on the sentence structure of the source. The note without patchwriting captures the main ideas of the passage without borrowing sentence structures or more than a few keywords from the original.

Here is another example:

Passage from source

Until recently, the Church was one of the least studied aspects of the Cuban revolution, almost as if it were a voiceless part of Cuban society, an institution and faith that had little impact on the course of events. (Super, John C. "Interpretations of Church and State in Cuba, 1959–1961." *The Catholic Historical Review*, vol. 89, no. 3, 2003, pp. 511–29.)

Note with patchwriting

Author
Picks up language from source
Uses synonym or word in another form
Page reference

Super 511

According to Super, the Catholic Church until recently was not much studied as an aspect of the Cuban revolution. It was as if the Church was voiceless in Cuban culture, as if it had little influence on events (511).

Note without patchwriting

Super argues that scholarship on the Cuban revolution is only beginning to recognize the influential role of the Church (511).

The revised note still retains key terms from the source: "Cuban revolution" and "Church" appear in both the original passage and the revised note because there can be no synonyms for proper nouns (names). But the passage no longer draws heavily on the source's sentence structure, organization, or word choices.

If you find yourself leaning heavily on the wording of the source, work for greater comprehension of the text by looking up unfamiliar words or thinking about concepts you do not understand. Then turn away from the source, and write from your head rather than the source.

2. Summarize 总结

An effective *summary* briefly captures the major claims (and, if space permits, the key evidence) of a source while omitting the details. A summary is usually at least 50 percent shorter than the material you are summarizing. Summarize a source when you want to do the following:

- Push yourself to a complete understanding of a complex source
- Demonstrate to your reader that you have read and fully engaged with the source
- Help your reader understand a text that is key to your project

To summarize a source, follow these steps:

1. Read the source, underlining key terms and looking up words that you do not know.
2. Annotate the source. Underline or highlight the thesis or main idea of the source, and identify the key supporting ideas. For a longer source, creating an outline may be helpful.
3. Write down—without looking at the source—the thesis or main claim in your own words.

4. Write a one- or two-sentence summary for each group of supporting paragraphs.

5. Combine your restatement of the thesis and your summary of the source's main ideas into a paragraph. Edit to eliminate repetition, and insert transitions to emphasize logical connections among sentences.

6. Check your summary against the source. Have you used fresh words and sentence structures? If not, this may be a sign that you do not yet understand the source. Go back and read the material again, and revise your summary to avoid patchwriting.

7. Record source information.

When you incorporate your summary into your project, cite the original source and include a page reference at the end of the summary. Following is an example of an effective summary of an original source:

> **More about**
> Transitions, 30–32
> Using signal
>   phrases, 137–38
> Citing and docu-
>   menting sources,
>   157–211
> (MLA style), 213–
> 54 (APA style),
> 256–71
> (*Chicago* style),
> 272–84 (CSE
> style)

Student Model 学生范文 **Summary**

Passage from source

Before exploring these connections, however, webcomics must be more clearly defined. Many people are only familar with webcomics through Scott McCloud's explanation of them in *Reinventing Comics*, where he took on the role of a spokesperson for webcomics. While McCloud offered an initial study on webcomics, this paper does not operate within a McCloudian definition of comics, where he expounds upon their potential to revolutionize all comics production. In this paper, the term webcomics must be distinguished from hyperbolic proclamations about the internet as an inevitable site of radical aesthetic evolution and economic revolution for comics. The problems with McCloud's claims about the liberatory and radical properties of the internet have been addressed by others, like Gary Groth in his article for *The Comics Journal*, "McCloud Cuckoo Land." Our argument does not claim that the internet is a superior comic medium, free of those "tiny boxes" and "finite canvases" that seem to trouble McCloud (online). Further, we recognize that the internet has not offered a level playing field, free of corporate domination, "a world," to quote McCloud's *Reinventing Comics*, "in which the path from selling ten comics to selling ten thousand comics to selling ten million comics is as smooth as ice" (188, Panel 1). With these caveats, we argue more limitedly that digital technology offers new avenues of aesthetic experimentation for comic artists and that the internet has given some comic artists a modest prosperity that they would not have without the internet as a means of distribution. (Sean Fenty et al., "Webcomics: The Influence and Continuation of the Comix Revolution," *ImageText*, vol. 1, no. 2, 2004, par. 2. www.english.ufl.edu/imagetext/archives/v1_2/group/.)

Summary

> On the one hand, Scott McCloud claims that the Internet will free underground comic artists from the restrictions of print distribution and make it possible for underground comic artists to reach huge audiences. On the other hand, Fenty, Houp, and Taylor focus on the possibilities for experimentation on the web and argue that the web provides better opportunities to make money publishing underground comics than does print. (Fenty et al., par.2)

Notice that the writer of the summary captures the main idea of the source in her own words and sentence structures. Her summary is about one fourth the length of the original material.

Making Notes in English If you are a non-native writer of English, you may want to save time by copying passages in English into your notes word for word or by copying your own translation of the material into your notes. However, your English language skills will improve more quickly if you make an effort to paraphrase, and you will also be less likely to commit unintentional plagiarism. Remember that writing with sources in US academic and professional settings often means using your sources critically—another reason to avoid simply copying them.

16d Capturing Quotations in Your Notes 笔记要抓住引文关键

A *quotation* is someone else's words transcribed exactly, with quotation marks or block indention to signal that it is from a source. Since readers are interested in what the writer of the research project has to say, you should use quotations sparingly. Quote from a source only for the following reasons:

- To reproduce particularly vivid or engaging language
- To convey a subtle idea or technical passage that might be distorted by a paraphrase or summary
- To lend credibility to your position through an expert's words
- To analyze or highlight the specific language of a source (as when studying a work of literature or a historical document)

If you find that you are quoting frequently but paraphrasing little and summarizing even less, you may not be fully comprehending what you are reading. Slow down. Read the source again, looking up words you do not understand, consulting reference sources that can provide background information, and discussing the source with your instructor, classmates, or friends. Then summarize or paraphrase the source.

Good scholarship requires that you work to understand the whole source, rather than just quoting from the sections that you believe you understand or that you think sound authoritative. Understanding the difficult parts is important, because they may change the meaning of what you thought at first you understood.

The following reading note correctly uses quotation marks to signal material taken word for word from the source, yet it indicates that the writer does not fully understand what she is writing about.

Student Model 学生范文 **Reading Note**

Draft note

> According to Milne, the "free-black community . . . of Five Points" is not reflected in "the areas of Block 160 that were excavated." "All that survived . . . were the remains of their ancestors interred in the mostly forgotten burying ground, a few intriguing and unusual items discarded in the defunct privies and cisterns, and a handful of church addresses." But "it is probable that many members of this community remained in the neighborhood, living 'off-the-grid' . . ." (140).

Authors

Quotations

Page reference

This note is merely a string of quotations, sewn together with a few of the note-taker's own words. Using these notes as is would produce a research project that would similarly be a mosaic of quotations, difficult to read and lacking the researcher's insight and critical judgment. Rereading the source to gain a better understanding of it enabled the writer to summarize with much less quotation. The following revision is also much easier to read:

Revised note

> According to Milne, very few items belonging to members of the African American population in Five Points have been excavated, most likely because members of this community were not part of mainstream society—they were "living 'off the grid'" (140)—not because they had all moved away.

Other chapters in this text discuss the mechanics of using quotation marks and integrating quotations into your text. Consult these sections before you begin your research, as you make notes on sources, and as you draft and revise your text.

> **More about**
> Integrating bor-
>   rowed ideas and
>   words, 144–45
> Using quotation
>   marks, 448–53
> Analysis, interpre-
>   tation, synthesis,
>   and critique,
>   12–14, 89, 133

16e Including Analysis, Interpretation, Synthesis, and Critique in Your Notes 笔记要包含分析、解释、综述和评论

In addition to recording information from sources, the note-taking stage is the time to start analyzing, interpreting, synthesizing, and critiquing what you read. The Self-Assessment box lists questions to ask yourself as you read and take notes on your sources, and the next chapter provides examples of analysis, interpretation, and synthesis in a student's research project.

Self Assessment

When analyzing, interpreting, synthesizing, and critiquing a source, ask yourself the following questions. If the answer is not clear, reread and reevaluate the source, as necessary.

Analysis
- ☐ What is the purpose of the source?
- ☐ Who is the intended audience?
- ☐ What major claims does the source make?
- ☐ What evidence (facts, statistics, examples, expert testimony) does the source use to support these claims?

Interpretation
- ☐ What assumptions does the author make about the subject or audience, and why are such assumptions significant?
- ☐ What does the source omit (evidence, opposing views), and what might these omissions indicate?
- ☐ What conclusions can you draw about the author's attitude from the tone of the source? What motives can you infer from the author's background?
- ☐ Who published this text or sponsored the research, and how might these sponsors have influenced the way the information, arguments, or evidence is presented?
- ☐ In what context was the text written—place, time, cultural environment—and how might this context have influenced the author?
- ☐ What expertise or life experience does the author bring to the subject, and is it relevant to the topic?

Synthesis
- ☐ Do any other sources make a similar (or opposing) claim, reach a similar (or opposing) conclusion, or offer similar (or opposing) evidence?
- ☐ Do any other sources identify similar causes or effects?
- ☐ What else do you know about this topic?
- ☐ How does this source support your claims?

Critique
- ☐ Are the aims of the source worthwhile, and have they been achieved?
- ☐ What claims does the source make? Are you persuaded by them? Why or why not?
- ☐ How credible is the evidence? Is the evidence based on verifiable facts? How relevant is the evidence?
- ☐ How logical is the source? Does the author commit any fallacies?
- ☐ How fairly does the source treat alternative viewpoints?

17 Writing the Research Project
撰写研究项目

Writing a research project is much like entering a conversation. When you first join the conversation, you hang back to learn what the conversation is all about. As you become more comfortable, you overcome your shyness and find your voice. Similarly, when you first start work on a research project, you "listen in" on your sources by summarizing, paraphrasing, and quoting from the experts. As you come to grips with the topic, through analysis, interpretation, synthesis, and critique of your sources, you develop insights that you will share with your partners in the conversation—your readers.

17a Drafting a Thesis Statement Based on Your Research Question 基于研究问题起草论文陈述

You started work on your topic by planning and conducting research. You join in on the discussion that will become your research project by drafting a thesis that states your main claim and serves as the focus of your project. Your thesis should be a one- or two-sentence statement that grows out of your research questions. It should be a statement that you will explain in the body of your research project, using information you have gleaned from sources and your own ideas, and it should convey your *purpose* (typically, for academic and business projects, to persuade or inform). For illustration, read the research question and thesis statement for the student project by Lydia Nichols, which appears at the end of part 6.

Just as a conversation partner may say something that changes your perspective, so you may discover as you draft your project that the counterevidence is overwhelming or that the body of your draft offers a different answer to your research question than the one in your thesis. (Frequently, the true thesis takes shape in the conclusion of the first draft.) If this happens to you, be prepared to revisit your thesis, revising or even replacing it as the evidence necessitates.

Research question: What makes underground comics so much more compelling than superhero comics?

Thesis statement: While far less well known than their superhero counterparts, underground comics offer an innovative and sophisticated alternative to mainstream titles.

> Thesis statement makes purpose clear: uses comparison of comic types to persuade readers that underground comics are more innovative and sophisticated.

131

Quick

Reference   Drafting the Research Project

- **Thesis.** Draft a one- or two-sentence thesis statement that grows out of your research questions and answers. Revise your thesis as you draft your project.
- **Organization.** List and explain the reasons you believe your thesis statement or why you think it is the most reasonable way to address a difficult issue. Sort research notes into separate piles for each of your reasons. Draft an outline that organizes your material so that readers can follow your logic and maintain interest to the end.
- **Analysis, interpretation, synthesis, critique.** Divide ideas into their component parts (analysis), and think about what they mean (interpretation). Then combine ideas from sources with your own ideas to come up with something fresh (synthesis). Decide whether sources have achieved their goals and whether their goals were worthwhile (critique).
- **Evidence and counterevidence.** Incorporate evidence, making sure it is relevant. Use summaries, paraphrases, and a few well-chosen quotations as support. Acknowledge opposing or contradictory evidence, and explain why your position is reasonable despite this. (If your position does *not* seem reasonable in light of counterevidence, revise your thesis.) Make sure you provide enough evidence—and the appropriate types of evidence—to influence your readers.
- **Citation and documentation.** Cite sources in the text, using the style that is appropriate for your discipline (MLA style for literature and languages, APA style for psychology and other social sciences, *Chicago* style for history and other humanities, and CSE style for the sciences). Double-check that you have used quotation marks where needed and that paraphrases have not slipped into patchwriting. Document sources in a list of works cited (MLA), reference list (APA, CSE), or footnotes and bibliography (*Chicago*).

More about
Assessing the writing situation, 16–19
Crafting research questions, 101–02
Devising a thesis, 23–24, 101–02
Organizing, 25–26, 78–79, 132–33
Drafting, 26, 29–39, 134–35
Finding information, 105–13
Acknowledging alternative views, 17, 76–77
Citing and documenting sources, 157–211 (MLA style), 213–54 (APA style), 256–71 (*Chicago* style), 272–84 (CSE style)

Writing Responsibly   Acknowledging Counterevidence

While sorting your notes, be sure to retain *counterevidence*—evidence that *undermines* your claims. If some of your research contradicts or complicates your thesis or supporting reasons, do not suppress it. Instead, revise your thesis or supporting reasons on the basis of this counterevidence, or acknowledge the counterevidence and explain why the reasons for believing your thesis are more convincing than those that challenge it. Your readers will appreciate your presentation of multiple perspectives. to AUDIENCE

17b Organizing Your Notes and Outlining Your Project
整理笔记，列出项目大纲

Start organizing your project by listing the reasons you believe your thesis is true. While these reasons may be derived from your research, they should be *your* reasons, stated in your own words.

Next, review the notes you took while conducting research. Do they provide background information your readers will need? Do they provide evidence for believing your thesis? Separate index cards into piles, or cut and paste notes into separate computer files according to the role they play in your research project.

More about
Generating ideas, 20–23
Making notes, 123–30

> **More about**
> Scratch outlines,
>   25
> Sentence outlines,
>   25–26
> Topic outlines,
>   25–26

Then assess your stock of evidence: If your notes look skimpy, find more supporting evidence, revise your thesis, or delve deeper into your reasons for believing your thesis.

After you have organized your notes, consider writing an outline to help you determine the most effective order for your ideas. Some writers use a scratch (informal) outline, which lists the reasons and major supporting points of the project in order of presentation. A scratch outline is quickest to draft, but it can be too sketchy for a complex project. Others prefer a sentence outline because it aids drafting—each sentence in the outline becomes the topic sentence of a paragraph—and because the formal structure of numerals and letters makes the structure of the draft clear. Still others prefer a topic outline; it is quicker to draft than a sentence outline, but its formal structure (the topic outline, too, uses numbers and letters) makes the structure of the draft clear. Some writers do not use an outline at all, or they create an outline only after they have written a draft, to help them see the structure of their project. A portion of a topic outline for Lydia Nichols's research project appears next.

Student Model
Research project:
"Holy Underground
  Comics, Batman," Lydia
  Nichols, 202–11

Student Model 学生范文 **Topic Outline**

Thesis: While far less well known than their superhero counterparts, underground comics offer an innovative and sophisticated alternative to mainstream titles.

Overall organization: chronological (1930s, 1950s)

I. Success of superhero comics in the late 1930s led to homogenization

   A. Superhero defined

   B. Superman debuted June 1938

   C. Copycat superheroes

II. Further homogenization in the 1950s, with creation of Comics Code Authority (1954)

Uses definitions, facts, examples to support claim

   A. Specific rules of CCA code—letters of the word "crime" cannot be bigger than other letters on the cover

   B. General rules of CCA code

      1. Respect for parents, morality (good triumphs over evil)

      2. Criminals, crimes portrayed negatively

      3. Religion treated respectfully

Student Model
Sentence outline, 26

      4. No profanity

17c Supporting Your Claims with Analysis, Interpretation, Synthesis, and Critique of Sources
对文献进行分析、解释、综述和评论，支撑你的观点

Your goal in a research project is to draw on information from sources to support your own ideas. Use analysis, interpretation, synthesis, and critique of sources to make sense of your claims for the reader. The following paragraphs from Lydia Nichols's essay on underground comics shows how she uses these techniques to support her claim.

Sentence 1: Nichols's claim (topic sentence) offers her interpretation.

Sentences 2, 3, 4, and 5 synthesize information from sources to support her claim.

Sentence 6 provides her own analysis to support her claim.

Sentence 1 continues her own analysis to support her claim.

Illustration provides an example that supports Nichols's claim, and caption offers interpretation of what the reader is seeing there.

In the 1960s, in contrast to mainstream CAA-approved superhero comics, alternatives began to appear. According to Steven Heller, an art director at *The New York Times* and a founder of the Masters in Graphic Arts Program at the School for Visual Arts in New York, Robert Crumb's *Zap* (1968) initiated the "underground comix revolution" (101). Crumb and other like-minded artists did not submit their comics for CAA approval. Though this limited the distribution of their work, it allowed them artistic freedom. From its first issue, *Zap* satirized mainstream, conservative beliefs and did not shy away from sexual or political content (Heller 101–02). Beneath the crude humor of *Zap* and similar comics lay insightful commentary on society and its principles, which many readers found to be a refreshing change from mainstream superhero titles.

Besides *Zap*, other well-known underground titles of the era include *Subvert* and *Weirdo*. Gilbert Shelton's hilariously nonconformist *Fabulous Furry Freak Brothers* and Crumb's most recognizable hero, the sketchy guru *Mr. Natural*, starred in their own, often X-rated, comic books (see fig. 2).

Fig. 2. Examples of late-'60s underground comics. In defiance of the authoritarian standards of the Comic Code Authority and influenced by '50s humor magazine *Mad*, underground artists pushed the boundaries of humor, propriety, and good taste.

17d Supporting Your Claims with Summaries, Paraphrases, and Apt Quotations from Sources
对文献进行总结、改述并适当引用，支撑你的观点

When you are drawing on sources, use quotations sparingly. In most cases, you should put borrowed information and ideas into your own words, using either paraphrase or summary. In the sample paragraphs

---

Quick

Reference   Writing the First Draft

As you begin writing, keep in mind that you are composing a draft—what you write will be revised—so do not worry whether you are saying it "right." A few writers' tricks will help you produce that first draft:

- Keep your thesis statement (and your outline, if you have devised one) in front of you to help you stay focused.
- Start with the sections that are easiest to write, and then fill in the gaps later.
- Begin writing *without* consulting your sources. Add evidence from sources *after* you have sketched out your own ideas.

- When incorporating quotations, paraphrases, or summaries in your draft, note the source of the material (including the page number) so that you will not need to track down this information later and, perhaps, inadvertently commit plagiarism.
- Draft with a notepad next to you or another file open on your computer so that you can jot down ideas that come to you while writing another section.
- Include visuals when they support your points or help your reader understand what you are writing about.

above, Nichols uses a combination of quotation and summary to support her claims. She quotes Heller because the phrase "underground comix revolution" is especially vivid, but she goes on to summarize Heller's ideas to convey his argument concisely.

NOTE When summarizing or paraphrasing, work to avoid patchwriting, and, when quoting, use quotation marks or indent longer quoted passages as a block.

17e Revising, Editing, Proofreading, and Formatting Your Project 研究项目的修改、编辑、校对和版式设计

Once you have composed a first draft, however rough it may be, you can begin the process of shaping and polishing it—the process of *revision*. First, attend to big-picture or global issues, such as clarifying your purpose, making sure your essay is cohesive and unified, and ensuring that your ideas are fully developed. Next, attend to local issues, such as making sure that your word choices reflect your meaning and are at the appropriate level of formality, that you have varied your sentences, and that your prose is concise. This is the time, too, to double-check your in-text citations against your list of works cited or reference list to make sure that you have documented all the sources from which you have borrowed ideas or information (except for common knowledge).

Once revision is complete, edit your text to correct errors of grammar, punctuation, and mechanics. Then proofread carefully, checking not only your spelling and punctuation but also the entries in your list of works cited or references. Finally, double-check that the formatting of your project follows the requirements of your discipline.

More about
Drafting, 26–28, 29–39
Summarizing, 9, 124–27
Paraphrasing, 124–26
Quoting, 128–29
Avoiding patchwriting, 124–27
Quotation marks, 448–53
Incorporating visuals, 53–54, 200–01 (MLA style), 245 (APA style), 270 (*Chicago* style)

Writing Responsibly — Owning the Proofreading Process

While spell-check software can be helpful, it cannot identify words you have misused, such as *it's* (*it is*) for *its* (possessive) or *infer* (*surmise*) for *imply* (*suggest*). Nor will it identify citations that do not appear in your list of works cited. To fulfill your responsibility to yourself and your readers, be sure to proofread your project carefully before submitting it, to check that in-text citations are included in your list of works cited and that all items in that list are referenced in the text of your project, and to check that you have formatted accurately the entries in your list of works cited.

to SELF

18 Citing Expertly 熟练引用

When you research a topic, you explore sources that express a variety of perspectives; you choose those that enhance your understanding of the topic; and then you describe those sources' ideas in ways that will allow readers to understand what the sources have contributed to your point of view.

Source citations are necessary in a researched project, yet simple citations do not help readers see how you are using your sources. For your readers, the clarity of your project comes when you go beyond just naming the source. When you cite expertly, you use accurate signal verbs, show source boundaries, emphasize your own voice, provide context for the source, and accurately integrate altered quotations. Expert citation makes your conversation with sources, like the image or message in a glass paperweight, "transparent": Others can see how your ideas developed and how you are relating to your sources and the information in them.

Citations are an essential part of academic writing. They identify the sources you are using—the other writers with whom you are "talking." At more expert levels of researched writing, *rhetorical citations* accomplish this task and more: They provide helpful information about your sources; they reveal your attitude toward, and judgment of, your sources; and they highlight your own contributions to the "conversation" that takes place between you and your sources.

18a Integrating Source Material Responsibly
负责任地整合文献资料

More about
Using information responsibly, 121–30
In-text citation, 148–49, 157–211 (MLA style, ch. 19), 154–55
Ethos, 75

When writing from sources, your most basic responsibility is to let your audience know whenever your text is drawing on a source. This protects you from charges of plagiarism. It also fulfills a responsibility to your audience, by letting readers know who is speaking in your text. It fulfills a responsibility to yourself, as well: Careful citation increases your writerly *ethos*; it makes you a more credible, respected writer. In MLA style, *in-text citation*—whether through parenthetical references, signal phrases, or a combination of the two—accomplishes all of these goals.

Having a Conversation with Sources You may consider published sources to be authorities, but an important aspect of academic writing is learning how to be critical even of authoritative material. You are free to agree or disagree with any source, but it is important that you use sources to support your claims, rather than simply repeating a source's language and ideas.

1. Use parenthetical citations 文内夹注

You can cite your sources by using the author's last name and relevant page number(s) in a *parenthetical citation.*[1] Place that reference at the end of the material from your source:

---

[1]The terms *parenthetical citation*, *parenthetical note*, and *parenthetical reference* are often interchangeable.

<table>
</table>

Quotation marks indicate the beginning and end of the source's exact words

"His name was Mark Zuckerberg, he was a sophomore, and although Eduardo had spent a fair amount of time at various Epsilon Pi events with him, along with at least one prepunch Phoenix event that Eduardo could remember, he still barely knew the kid" (Mezrich 15).

Source author (last name only)

Mezrich, Ben, The Accidental Billionaires: The Founding of Facebook, A Tale of Sex, Money, Genius and Betrayal (New York: Doubleday, 2009).

Page in source

When paraphrasing or summarizing material, you should also use parenthetical citation to acknowledge that your material comes from a source:

Who wouldn't envy the genius and wealth of the person who invented Facebook? But who wouldn't pity a person who has no close friends? Mark Zuckerberg may have great wealth, but he has few confidantes (Denby 98).

Source author (last name only)

Page in source

2. Use signal phrases 使用信号词

To incorporate borrowed material smoothly into your prose, introduce it with a *signal phrase*. One part of the signal phrase is an identification (usually the name) of the writer from whom you are borrowing. The other part is a verb; choose one that conveys your sense of the writer's intention.

In choosing your signal verb, consider the attitude or position of the writer you are quoting. Is the writer making a claim? Is she or he agreeing or disagreeing or even conceding a point? Or is the writer's position neutral? It is easy to choose a neutral verb, such as *writes, says,* or *comments.* Whenever possible, though, go beyond these neutral verbs to indicate the writer's attitude:

> **More about**
> Verb tense,
> 374–78

Oscar Wilde quipped, "A poet can survive everything but a misprint."

For the Wilde quotation, *quipped* (which means "uttered a witty remark") is clearly appropriate, given the cleverness of the sentence quoted. *Snarled,* in contrast, would not be appropriate: Although Wilde's quip may have an edge to it, few would agree that the comment conveys the anger or viciousness associated with the verb *snarl.*

To maintain your audience's interest, vary the signal words you use while avoiding verbs that might misrepresent the writer's intentions. (A list of signal verbs appears in the Quick Reference box on the next page.) You can also vary your placement of the signal phrase:

Quick Reference — Signal Verbs

Neutral Signal Verbs

analyzes	introduces
comments	notes
compares	observes
concludes	records
contrasts	remarks
describes	reports
discusses	says
explains	shows
focuses on	states
illustrates	thinks
indicates	writes

Writers in literature and the other humanities typically use present tense verbs in signal phrases; writers in the sciences use the present or past tense, depending on the context.

Signal Verbs That Indicate:

Concession	Claim/Argument	
acknowledges	argues	finds
admits	asserts	holds
concedes	believes	maintains
grants	charges	points out
	claims	proposes
	confirms	recommends
	contends	suggests
	demonstrates	

Agreement	Disagreement	
agrees	complains	questions
concurs	contradicts	refutes
confirms	criticizes	rejects
supports	denies	warns
	disagrees	

E. M. Forster asked, "How do I know what I think until I see what I say?"

"How do I know what I think," E. M. Forster asked, "until I see what I say?"

"How do I know what I think until I see what I say?" E. M. Forster asked.

18b Showing Source Boundaries 凸显引文边界

More about
Paraphrasing,
124–26
Summarizing,
124–28
Using quotation
marks, 448–53

When the source material is a quotation, it is easy for the reader to see the boundaries: Quotation marks indicate where the source material begins and ends. When paraphrasing or summarizing, however, where you begin to use source material may not be clear. To solve the problem, you can place a signal phrase at the beginning of the source material and a parenthetical citation at the end. Consider this example:

Signal phrase includes source author (full name on first reference)

Quotation marks indicate the beginning and end of the source's exact words

Page in source

Who wouldn't envy the genius and wealth of the person who invented Facebook? But who wouldn't pity a person who has no close friends? David Denby describes Mark Zuckerberg as having great wealth, but few confidantes. "*The Social Network* is shrewdly perceptive about such things as class, manners, ethics, and the emptying out of self that accompanies a genius's absorption in his work" (98).

Denby, David. "Influencing People: David Fincher and 'The Social Network.'" The New Yorker, October 4, 2010.

In this example, it is clear that the first two sentences are the writer's statement of her own ideas, the third sentence is a paraphrase from the Denby source, and the fourth sentence is a quotation from Denby. Notice that when the author's name is included in the signal phrase, it does not need to be included in the parenthetical citation.

1. Unpaginated source material 未标明页码的文献资料

Many online sources have no page numbers. For an unpaginated source, include only the author's last name in the parenthetical citation:

Source author
(last name only)

"Facebook, which surpassed MySpace in 2008 as the largest social-networking site, now has nearly 500 million members, or 22 percent of all Internet users, who spend more than 500 billion minutes a month on the site" (Rosen).

Rosen, Jeffrey, "The Web Means the End of Forgetting," The New York Times Magazine, July 21, 2010.

When you are paraphrasing or summarizing from an electronic source with no page numbers, you must work subtly with the material to show your audience where the source use begins and ends. Usually you can do this by using the author's name in the parenthetical citation and describing the author in a signal phrase:

Signal phrase
describes
source author

A writer for *The New York Times* explains how damaging Facebook material can be when one searches for a job (Rosen).

Parenthetical
reference
identifies
source author
(last name only)

18c Emphasizing Your Voice 强调你的话语

Just as important as signaling source boundaries is the need to signal your own voice. Your readers want to know clearly when it is *you* talking. In the following example, it is not clear where the student writer stops drawing from the Rosen source and begins to state his own ideas:

> Rosen explains, "Seventy percent of U.S. recruiters report that they have rejected candidates because of information found online, like photos and discussion-board conversations and membership in controversial groups." With 500 million people on Facebook, the dangers are widespread. It is ironic that this phenomenon of personal data revealed to the world was begun by a person who himself had poor social skills.

Signal phrase

Rosen, Jeffrey, "The Web Means the End of Forgetting," The New York Times Magazine, July 21, 2010.

The use of a signal phrase with a parenthetical citation clarifies the boundaries of the information from Rosen:

> A writer for *The New York Times* explains, "Seventy percent of U.S. recruiters report that they have rejected candidates because of information found online, like photos and discussion-board conversations and membership in controversial groups." With 500 million people on Facebook, the dangers are widespread (Rosen). It is ironic that this phenomenon of personal data revealed to the world was begun by a person who himself had poor social skills.

Signal phrase describes source author

Parenthetical reference identifies source author (last name only)

More about
First-person pronouns, 380–87

The final sentence in this passage is an interesting one, and the student writer wants to emphasize that it is his own insight. That could be done with first-person singular phrases such as "I believe" or "in my opinion."

In some genres and writing situations (including many college assignments), first-person singular is inappropriate. Fortunately, there are more sophisticated ways to handle the task. One option is to speak in the first-person plural, subtly drawing the audience into the conversation:

> A writer for *The New York Times* explains, "Seventy percent of U.S. recruiters report that they have rejected candidates because of information found online, like photos and discussion-board conversations and membership in controversial groups." With 500 million people on Facebook, the dangers are widespread (Rosen). We cannot escape the irony that this phenomenon of personal data revealed to the world was begun by a person who himself had poor social skills.

Parenthetical reference shows end of source material

First-person plural suggests shift to student writer's voice

It is even more effective to comment upon the source or its information:

> A writer for *The New York Times* explains, "Seventy percent of U.S. recruiters report that they have rejected candidates because of information found online, like photos and discussion-board conversations and membership in controversial groups." With 500 million people on Facebook, the dangers are widespread (Rosen). Such information suggests an irony: This phenomenon of personal data revealed to the world was begun by a person who himself had poor social skills.

Parenthetical reference shows end of source material

Transition to student writer's interpretation of source material

In this version, the writer's voice is implicitly clear. He uses the adjective *such* to point to the previous material and then provides his interpretation. Demonstrative pronouns (*this, that, these, those*) can also be used as a transition to the student writer talking about the source material.

18d Providing Context 说明语境

Readers appreciate knowing not only when it is your voice they are reading and when it is the voice of your sources, but also *who* your sources are and why you have chosen them. Rhetorical citations provide this information smoothly: Your citations can explain why you chose the source, what kind of source it is, when the source was published, and what its argument was.

1. Explain your choice of sources 解释所选文献

Unless your readers are familiar with your sources, they may have no reason to respect them and thus no reason to believe your claims. You can avoid this problem with rhetorical citations that not only name your source but also indicate why you respect the source, as this writer does:

Source: Wolf, Gary, "The Data-Driven Life." The New York Times Magazine, April 28, 2010.

> Gary Wolf provides a helpful, wide-ranging overview of our motivations for gathering and sharing data about ourselves, offering examples like this: "*Foursquare*, a geo-tracking application with about one million users, keeps a running tally of how many times players 'check in' at every locale, automatically building a detailed diary of movements and habits; many users publish these data widely."

Signal phrase includes student writer's opinion of the source

More about
Evaluating sources,
114–20 (ch. 15)

In this example, the writer establishes that the source can be respected for its thorough treatment of the topic.

The next selection acknowledges the shortcomings of the source while also asserting its usefulness:

> Signal phrase becomes extended explanation of student writer's opinion of the source
>
> Mezrich has made up parts of his story about Zuckerberg's rise, while claiming he is sticking as closely as possible to reality. Yet his fiction is worth reading; it shows how people perceive Harvard and its geniuses: "There was something playful about those eyes—but that was where any sense of natural emotion or readability ended. His narrow face was otherwise devoid of any expression at all. And his posture, his general aura—the way he seemed closed in on himself, even while engaged in a group dynamic, even here, in the safety of his own fraternity—was almost painfully awkward" (15).
>
> Page in source

Source: Mezrich, Ben, The Accidental Billionaires: The Founding of Facebook, A Tale of Sex, Money, Genius and Betrayal (New York: Doubleday, 2009)

2. Identify the type of source 说明文献类型

Is your source a newspaper column? A blog? A scholarly article? The differences between types of sources are important. If you want up-to-the-minute information, a newspaper or blog is likely to have it. If you want carefully researched, accurate information, a scholarly journal article is a good choice. Your readers want to know that you have made appropriate source choices, and you can provide such information in rhetorical citations:

> Signal phrase describes and identifies source author and his credentials
>
> Writing in *The New York Times*, journalist Gary Wolf provides a wide-ranging overview of our motivations for gathering and sharing data about ourselves, offering examples like this: "*Foursquare*, a geo-tracking application with about one million users, keeps a running tally of how many times players 'check in' at every locale, automatically building a detailed diary of movements and habits; many users publish these data widely."

3. Identify the date of publication 注明出版日期

For many topics, the date of publication is important. The number of people who use the Foursquare application, for example, changes constantly. Providing the date on which such information is published helps readers know how fresh the numbers are and how accurate they might still be:

> **Signal phrase includes publication date of time-sensitive information**
>
> In a 2010 article in *The New York Times*, journalist Gary Wolf says, "*Foursquare*, a geo-tracking application with about one million users, keeps a running tally of how many times players 'check in' at every locale, automatically building a detailed diary of movements and habits; many users publish these data widely."
>
> *Wolf, Gary. "The Data-Driven Life." The New York Times Magazine, April 28, 2010.*

4. Identify the larger discussion in the source 引用不可断章取义

For the most successful, persuasive writing from sources, you need to *read* the sources, rather than just pulling sentences from them. That allows you not only to position the quotation, paraphrase, or summary in your text, but also to indicate how it contributed to the source text's discussion. Build a brief source summary into the rhetorical citation:

> **Extended signal phrase includes summary of the source**
>
> In a 2010 article in *The New York Times*, journalist Gary Wolf provides a wide-ranging overview of our motivations for gathering and sharing data about ourselves, offering examples like this: "*Foursquare*, a geo-tracking application with about one million users, keeps a running tally of how many times players 'check in' at every locale, automatically building a detailed diary of movements and habits; many users publish these data widely."

More about
Critical reading,
    9–15
Avoiding plagia-
    rism, 121–30 (ch.
    16)

The phrase "overview of our motivations for gathering and sharing data about ourselves" summarizes the source.

Citation is not only ethical but rhetorical. In addition to protecting you against charges of plagiarism, it creates a sophisticated, readable document that audiences are likely to trust.

18e Integrating Altered Quotations 整合改动的引文

Sometimes you may need to alter a quotation so that it fits into your sentence. In her draft for her project on underground comics, Nichols deletes words from one source's quotation that do not help her make her point. As long as the meaning is not significantly changed, writers may do any of the following to fit quoted material more fluidly into their own sentences:

- Quote short phrases rather than full sentences
- Add or change words for clarity
- Change capitalization
- Change grammar

More about
Using ellipses
    in quotations,
    460–61
Using square
    brackets in quo-
    tations,
    457–58

All added or changed words should be placed in square brackets; deleted words should be replaced with ellipses. The following example shows a responsible alteration of a quotation:

Quotation integrated into student text	Original quotation
Certain portions of the Comic Book Code were incredibly specific and controlling, such as the rule that forbade "[t]he letters of the word 'crime' on a comics magazine . . . [to] be appreciably greater in dimension than the other words contained in the title" (qtd. in "Good Shall Triumph over Evil").	The letters of the word "crime" on a comics magazine shall never be appreciably greater in dimension than the other words contained in the title.

A capital letter was changed to a lowercase letter, double quotation marks were changed to single quotation marks, one word was added and a couple of others were omitted, but the overall meaning of the passage remains the same.

Imagine, however, that the writer had made these changes instead:

Quotation unfairly altered	Original quotation
Certain portions of the code allowed some flexibility. Consider, for example, the rule that allowed "[t]he letters of the word 'crime' on a comics magazine . . . [to] be appreciably greater in dimension than the other words contained in the title" (qtd. in "Good Shall Triumph over Evil").	The letters of the word "crime" on a comics magazine shall never be appreciably greater in dimension than the other words contained in the title.

Clearly this alteration of the quotation is not acceptable, as it changes the meaning of the passage completely.

Self Assessment

As you revise projects that use sources, review your draft with the following questions in mind:

- ☐ Did you cite your sources? Name any from which you are paraphrasing, summarizing, or quoting.
- ☐ Did you use signal verbs? Convey the attitude of your source.
- ☐ Did you use signal phrases and parenthetical citations? Show where each source use begins and ends, even when it is unpaginated.
- ☐ Did you emphasize your own insights? Comment on or analyze the source, rather than just repeat it.
- ☐ Did you provide relevant contextual information? Identify the type of source, its date of publication, and its publisher.
- ☐ Did you reveal your reasoning? Explain why you chose and trusted your sources.

Text Credit

p. 144 Source: Code of the Comics Magazine Association of America, Inc. Adopted October 26, 1954.

Writing **Responsibly** 负责任地写作

Explaining Your Choice of Sources，解释你的资料选择

Make It Your Own! When college writers share their opinion of their sources, their text is more interesting and convincing. Rather than just quoting from your sources, tell *why* you are quoting them, and your writing will be more persuasive.

In much of your college writing, you select and work with sources: You decide how to use sources to help convey your thesis. Your basic responsibility is to acknowledge those sources, cite them correctly, and provide full publication information about them at the end of your project. When you talk *about* your sources—tell what you think of your source and its information—you invite your audience into your thinking processes and portray yourself as an experienced academic writer.

When college writing instructors involved in the Citation Project studied research projects from US colleges, they noticed how few students talked about their sources. Most of the projects just pulled out information—usually a brief quotation—from sources, as if all the sources were alike. The nature of the sources and the student's thoughts about them remained invisible to the audience. The following example, from a project on sexism and sexual violence, shows the drab result:

First draft

> **Student's voice** Hostility toward women can be seen even in the ancient West. Stevenson observes,
> **Quotation** "Livy's underlying message, it would seem, is that Roman men have to regulate public contributions by prominent women, and not accept female advice too easily, without prolonged consideration" (189). **citation**

The material from the Stevenson source is accurately quoted and cited, and the sentences flow. But the passage provokes questions rather than insights. Who are Stevenson and Livy? Where did this source come from? Why did the writer choose it? Why should the writer's audience respect Stevenson's opinions? What else did the source say? What was the context in which the quotation appeared? These are the kinds of questions readers ask, and answering them will bring your text to life:

Revised draft

> **Student's voice** Hostility toward women can be seen even in the ancient West. Tom Stevenson, a classics **Citation**
> **Credentials of author and publisher** scholar at the University of Queensland, writes in the scholarly journal *Classical World* that the Roman historian Livy described women who supported their menfolks' success, which might seem to be a compliment to the women. But notice that the women aren't having their **Summary of the remainder of the source** own successes. Furthermore, all of Livy's women are either described too briefly, or they are flawed. Even as Stevenson provides this analysis, he also cautions against being too simplistic **Counter-evidence**

Revised draft continued

> about Livy's portrayal of women; some of their faults were because their men were flawed. Still, Stevenson concludes, "Livy's underlying message, it would seem, is that Roman men have to regulate public contributions by prominent women, and not accept female advice too easily, without prolonged consideration" (189).

> `Citation`
> `Quotation`

Source: Stevenson, Tom. "Women of Early Rome as *Exempla* in Livy, *Ab Urbe Condita*, Book 1." *Classical World,* vol. 104, no. 2, Winter 2011, pp. 175–89.

Now, not only is the material from the source accurately quoted and cited, but Livy has been identified, and Stevenson's credentials and the authority of the publication have been established, along with a description of his argument.

Sometimes you choose to use a source because you like its argument or presentation of information, even if it may not be particularly scholarly. In these cases, too, you should let your audience know why you have chosen the source:

> `Information about why the writer chose this source`
> `Summary of some information in the source`
> `Citation`

> One good way to understand the treatment of women in contemporary society is to consult news media. They are not reports of research written by experts, but rather are sources that reflect and shape popular opinion. *Time* magazine publishes an article on date rape because it believes this is an issue that readers will or should care about. It also reports on current events. So it is *Time* that reports on a congressional bill intended to reduce sexual violence in colleges. Why is the bill needed? The answer is in the shocking numbers the magazine cites: "One in five college women will be the victim of a sexual assault (and 6% of men)" (Webley).

> `Student's voice`
> `Quotation`

Source: Webley, Kayla. "It's Not Just Yale: Are Colleges Doing Enough to Combat Sexual Violence?" *Time,* 18 Apr. 2011, time.com/time/nation/article/0,8599,2065849,00.html?xid=fblike.

Assessment

self

Review your work with each source. Have you done the following?

☐ Identify the author of the source and his or her credentials. Did you show what makes you trust this person? ▶ *Analyzing and crafting arguments, 73–86*

☐ Identify the publisher of the source and its credentials. Did you show what makes you trust this organization? ▶ *Finding information, 105–13*

☐ Consider the date of publication. Did you provide and comment on the publication date, if it affects your trust in the source?

☐ Summarize the source. Did you indicate how the selection you have drawn from contributed to the argument the source was making? ▶ *Evaluating information, 114–20*

☐ Provide additional discussion. Did you help your audience understand the reasons you chose this source and your selections from it?

Writing Responsibly 负责任地写作
Understanding and Representing the Entire Source
了解和展现整个来源

Make It Your Own! For a research project to be worthwhile, it should represent the overall arguments of its sources—more than just a few sentences—so that readers can understand what the sources were saying and how they fit together.

Each time you write from sources, push yourself to work with them in more substantial ways. Take the time to read each source—the entire source—carefully. Next, **summarize** it, as a way of processing the information: Restate, concisely and in fresh language, the main claims (and the most important supporting evidence) of an entire source. Then when you draft your research project, blend in summaries of your important sources, so that your readers understand how they, too, contribute to your discussion.

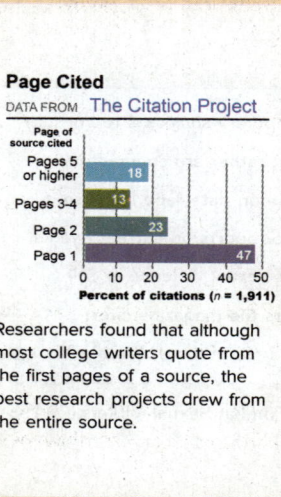

You can also draw from sources by quoting or paraphrasing brief passages. But if you simply paste a quotation into your draft, how much do you or your audience actually understand the source or even the passage you are quoting? **Paraphrasing** is a better alternative, because it pushes you to think about the passage: to know the material well enough to restate it in your own words. Changing just a few words in the passage, however, is not paraphrasing; it is **patchwriting**: a mixture of your words and the source's. This is an error interpreted by many readers as plagiarism.

Page Cited
DATA FROM The Citation Project

Page of source cited	Percent of citations ($n = 1,911$)
Pages 5 or higher	18
Pages 3-4	13
Page 2	23
Page 1	47

0 10 20 30 40 50
Percent of citations ($n = 1,911$)

Researchers found that although most college writers quote from the first pages of a source, the best research projects drew from the entire source.

Because quoting and patchwriting do not require much comprehension and are easy to do, inexperienced college writers rely on them too heavily. Frequently, too, the quotations come from the first few pages of the source—which some students feel is all they have to read. Researchers with the Citation Project found that the majority of college writers' citations came from the first two pages of the source (see chart) and felt the quality of these projects suffered. That is because, in most sources, the first few pages discuss only general findings, while the insightful, detailed examples and evidence that are important to a good analysis or argument are deeper in the text.

When a writer provides only isolated quotations from sources ("dropped quotations"), the result may be uninformative, like this passage from a project about social media and individual identity:

First draft

Student's voice — People value their personal lives and try to separate their private and public selves. Many are aware of being different people in the workplace, in school, on a date. All this may be changing, though. "The fact that the Internet never seems to forget is threatening, at an almost existential level, our ability to control our identities; to preserve the option of reinventing ourselves and starting anew; to overcome our checkered pasts" (Rosen).

Quotation

Parenthetical citation

Notice how, in this draft, readers are given no information about the source; they are presented only with one sentence from it. This causes the reader to wonder: Does the writer understand the source, or has she simply found a "killer quote" that supports her argument? Because the writer provides only the isolated quotation, it is not even clear what her purpose is in including it.

Now consider how this passage is transformed by adding a summary and contextualized quotations:

Revised draft

> **[Student's voice]** People value their personal lives, and many deliberately work to keep their private and public selves separate. Many of us are aware, too, of being different people in the workplace, in school, on the athletic field, on a date. Some value these differences, happy to switch from dedicated intellectual in the classroom to enthusiastic player on the soccer field.
>
> All this may be changing, though. **[Signal phrase providing information about the author]** Writing in *The New York Times*, journalist Jeffrey Rosen **[Summary of the parts of the source relevant to the student's argument]** points out that we may no longer be in control of the multiple identities that were previously taken for granted. In our online lives, what we post on Facebook and Twitter can easily merge with what we post on a school blog, in our comments on a news story, or in our pictures on Flickr. Rosen explains that even in untagged pictures, our faces can be identified through **[Summary of the remainder of the source]** facial-recognition technology. He also describes the privacy-protecting laws that are in development and the companies that offer services to clean up our online reputations. **[Student's voice]** Most central to my research, though, is his explanation for this claim: **[Quotation (no page reference because source is unpaginated)]** "The fact that the Internet never seems to forget is threatening, at an almost existential level, our ability to control our identities; to preserve the option of reinventing ourselves and starting anew; to overcome our checkered pasts."

Source: Rosen, Jeffrey. "The Web Means the End of Forgetting." *The New York Times*, 21 July 2010, www.nytimes.com/2010/07/25/magazine/25privacy-t2.html?pagewanted=all&_r=0.

The writer has shown responsibility to her source, her topic, and her audience. Because she has taken the time to read and understand the source, she is able to summarize it to show what its main claims are. Her audience now knows how the quotation was used in the source and how it supports her argument. With this brief summary, the writer has also explained her ideas clearly and established a "conversation" between herself, her source, and her audience—that is, rather than just "using" sources, she is thinking about them, interacting with them, and giving her audience enough information that they can do the same.

self **Assessment**

Review and revise your work with each source. Have you done the following?

- ☐ Read, understand, and accurately represent the whole source. Did you look for the details deeper in the source?
- ☐ Summarize the main ideas of the source. Did you put the source's ideas in your own words, fairly and accurately? ▶ *Paraphrasing, 124–26*
- ☐ Incorporate your summary into your source analysis. Did you use the best examples and evidence?
- ☐ Locate the most relevant passages. Did you cite from *throughout* the source?
  ▶ *Critical reading, 9–15*

Writing **Responsibly** 负责任地
写作 Choosing and Unpacking Complex Sources
选择和分析复杂的来源

Make It Your Own! Research projects that rely heavily on short, simple sources tend to be simplistic and awkward. If you find, read, and write about lengthy, complex sources, you will produce superior scholarship.

Everyone wants to be efficient, yet college writers trying to save time may inadvertently do themselves and their audience a disservice when they write. While incorporating research into their projects, too many writers choose only short, simple sources that can be read quickly (see chart), and the quality of their writing suffers.

Researchers with the Citation Project were struck by the extent to which the quality of students' research projects was reduced by the shallowness of their sources. More than half of the projects' citations were to a source no longer than five pages, resulting in projects that were simplistic and unimpressive. They lacked the complex information and in-depth opinions that are essential to good research and interesting writing.

Length of Source Cited
DATA FROM **The Citation Project**

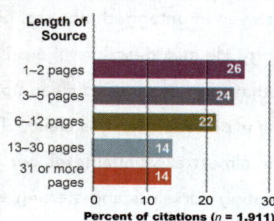

Length of Source	Percent of citations (n = 1,911)
1–2 pages	26
3–5 pages	24
6–12 pages	22
13–30 pages	14
31 or more pages	14

Researchers found that while most college research writers choose short, simple sources, the best writers work from lengthy, complex sources that bring details and insight—and not just basic facts—to the topic.

Writers relying on short sources work with too small a toolbox. Their projects will have very little to say if there is very little to draw on. Sources that are more extensive, in contrast, explore the interesting complexities and important debates about their topic. Such sources give writers—and the writers' audience—things to think about and talk about. They provide essential research material that leads to rich analysis and well-grounded argument.

Simply choosing lengthy sources is not enough, however. You should also "unpack" your sources—share with your audience the complexities and insights of your sources. Note how, in the following example, from an article on unnecessary medical procedures, complexity is lacking when the writer simply drops a quotation into his text and lets it speak for him:

First draft

Student's voice — Every time a person goes to the doctor, he or she should be aware of the risks of unnecessary medical testing. A doctor from San Francisco says, "[M]ost experts agree that overuse needs to be curbed. If it isn't, we could face a future public health problem of rising cancer rates, thanks to our medical overzealousness" (Parikh).

Signal phrase

Parenthetical citation

Quotation

The writer offers a quotation that supports his argument, and he has cited the quotation correctly. He has also provided some information about the writer of the source. However, because this quotation stands alone, readers of this student's project may think that the source made this statement as a simple directive: *Overuse of medical tests should stop*. In fact, the source offered a detailed review of the reasons for the overuse of CT scans, as well as a thoughtful set of recommendations.

Such information deserves to be represented. It is part of your responsibility to your audience and topic to show the whole picture that the source offers. Consider how much more interesting, informative, and persuasive the passage becomes when it provides more information and context:

Revised draft

Student's voice	Every time a person goes to the doctor, he or she should be aware of the risks of unnecessary medical testing.
Signal phrase	San Francisco Bay Area pediatrician Rahul Parikh says that CT scans are a dangerously overused test, putting children in particular risk for cancer due to the radiation levels in the procedure.
Quotation	"[M]ost experts agree that overuse needs to be curbed. If it isn't, we could face a future public health problem of rising cancer rates, thanks to our medical overzealousness," says Parikh.
Signal phrase	He notes, though, that the test is quick and easy. Moreover, television medical shows give people a general awareness of tests like the CT scan, and thus patients may demand it even when it is not medically necessary. Doctors, too, have a reason for overusing the test: It is financially profitable. In addition to recommending that the test be administered less often,
Signal phrase	Parikh advocates adjusting the radiation dose when the CT scan is administered to children.

Summary that clarifies the argument of the source

Summary of the source's complex treatment of the topic

Source: Parikh, Rahul. "How TV Illustrates a Disturbing Medical Trend." *Salon,* 18 Apr. 2011, www.salon.com/2011/04/18/poprx_unncessary_tests/.

Notice that in the first draft, it sounds as if the doctor quoted is talking about all medical testing; the second draft shows that in fact Parikh was talking about a specific test, the CT scan. Choosing extensive sources, paying attention to the complexity of the material, and incorporating that complexity into your project not only increases the sophistication of your own writing; it can also save you from misrepresenting the source.

self

Assessment

Review your work with each source, revising as necessary, to be sure you:

- ☐ Choose lengthy, detailed sources. Did you find material that provides insights and debates on the topic? ▶ *Finding information, 105–113*
- ☐ Discuss the complexities of your sources' treatment of their topic. Did you go beyond simple, basic facts? ▶ *Analyzing, interpreting, synthesizing, and critiquing, 133;*
  "Understanding and Representing the Entire Source," 148–49
- ☐ Explain any material you quote. Did you give background on every source?
  ▶ *Relevance and reliability, 114–18*

Writing **Responsibly** 负责任地 写作
Blending Voices in Your Text 融合文本中的声音

Make It Your Own! Good researched writing is more than collecting the ideas of others; it is instead an exploration of how the sources have helped researchers develop their own ideas. You will produce better work if, as you draft your project, you let your readers see *your* thinking.

Whenever you write from sources, you are blending the voices of your sources with one another and with your own. Although *voice* sometimes refers to the difference between passive and active voice, it also refers to who is talking in the text—the writer or the source.

Your audience wants to know whose voice it is "hearing." When you quote, it knows you are importing the voice of the source. When you **paraphrase** (rewrite the information in fresh language), your audience hears you talking.

But when you **patchwrite** (copy from a source and make minor changes to its language, but not actually paraphrase), you lead your audience to the mistaken belief that it is hearing you when in fact it is neither your voice nor the source's, but rather an inappropriate mixture of the two. To blend voices successfully, you need to avoid patchwriting and show the beginning and end of your use of sources.

Most readers consider it plagiarism when a writer patchwrites. Regardless of whether he or she classifies it as plagiarism, no reader considers patchwriting good writing. The following passage from a source discussing the history of child psychology, followed by a student's first-draft writing from that source, illustrates the issue:

Passage from source

> In the 1910s and later, as child psychology became an academic discipline, teachers increasingly looked to educational researchers rather than librarians as the central experts in children's reading.

Patchwriting

> From the 1910s on, child psychology became a discipline, and teachers more and more thought that educational researchers rather than librarians were the main experts in children's reading (248).

The patchwriting follows the original sentence, deleting a few words and substituting some others, but still dependent on the language and arrangement of the source sentence. Not knowing that this is a blend of two voices—the writer's and the source's—the reader is misled to think this is the student's voice.

Paraphrase

> Child psychology emerged as an academic discipline in the early twentieth century, prompting teachers to look to researchers for expertise about children's reading. Librarians were no longer the primary authority on the topic (248).

The paraphrase appropriately uses keywords from the original, such as *discipline* and *child psychology,* but it otherwise uses fresh language and fresh sentence arrangement to restate the source.

Ground your own writing in paraphrase and summary, include some quotation, and avoid patchwriting altogether. This will allow your voice, rather than those of your sources, to dominate your text. This strategy requires your conscious effort and practice. Writing true paraphrase is an advanced skill that many college writers do not practice (see chart), but those who master this skill write the most successful research projects.

To let your readers know when you are paraphrasing or summarizing, use a signal phrase at the beginning of the source use and a parenthetical citation at the end. If your use of sources is lengthy, you can also occasionally mention the source or the author as you write, just to remind your readers that they are reading your summary or paraphrase of a source:

Students' Use of Sources
DATA FROM The Citation Project

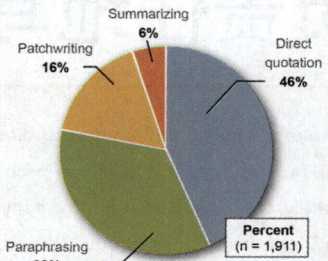

- Summarizing 6%
- Patchwriting 16%
- Direct quotation 46%
- Paraphrasing 32%

Percent (n = 1,911)

Researchers found that while most college research writers use quoting and patchwriting, the best projects were by those who use summary and paraphrase.

Marking where the source use begins and ends

Signal phrase at beginning of source use	McDowell explains that the academic discipline of child psychology, which emerged in the early twentieth century, looked to researchers for expertise about children's reading. Librarians were no longer the leading authorities on the topic. Both librarians and child psychologists were interested in children's reading patterns, but for different reasons. The librarians, McDowell says, wanted to understand what sorts of texts would interest children so they could get them into the library. Child psychologists, in contrast, wanted to understand the children themselves. Both groups collected information about children's reading, but they did it in different ways. The librarians observed children's reading and reported on their observations, while the child psychologists conducted scientific research (248–49).

Paraphrase of a sentence from the source

Signal phrase within the source use

Summary of two pages in the source

Parenthetical citation at end of source use

Source: McDowell, Kathleen. "Toward a History of Children as Readers, 1890–1930." *Book History,* vol. 12, 2009, pp. 240–65.

self | Assessment

Review your work with each source, revising as necessary, to be sure you:

- ☐ Use paraphrase and summary. Did you avoid overreliance on quotations?
  ▶ *Summarizing, 126–28; paraphrasing, 124–26; patchwriting, 122*
- ☐ Paraphrase while avoiding patchwriting. Did you restate source material in fresh language and fresh sentences? ▶ *Taking notes and avoiding plagiarism, 123*
- ☐ Use signal phrases and parenthetical citations. Did you let your audience know where your paraphrase and summary begins and ends? ▶ *Voice, 139–41*

Writing **Responsibly**
负责任地写作 **Acknowledging Indirect Sources** 确认间接来源

Make It Your Own! Confusing direct and indirect sources is a common problem. Fortunately, the procedures for correctly representing indirect sources in your research projects are not hard to learn, and following them will subtly enhance your writing.

When you cite sources, you do not just inform your audience about where you obtained your information; you let your audience know who is speaking in the source. If your source quotes or uses ideas from another writer, that other writer is for you an indirect source:[1] You are not reading that other writer yourself but are reading what he or she said. If you want to use that material from the indirect source, you should acknowledge the indirect source as well as the source that was talking about it. This is a sophisticated technique that takes practice to master; researchers with the Citation Project discovered that citing indirect sources accurately was a challenge for first-year college writers, separating them from experienced writers.

The following example, from a project exploring the Graduate Equivalency Diploma (GED) alternative to traditional high schools, shows how the problem occurs:

Student's first draft

Paraphrase of passage in source	Nontraditional high school students in the GED Options Pathway program shouldn't be labeled "GED kids"; they should be judged on their individual accomplishments. "This is supposed
Quotation from source	to be the land of the free and equal opportunity and all that stuff" (Peterson). *In-text citation*

Peterson, who is cited in the sample above, is the writer of the newspaper story in which the quotation appears. However, Peterson does not speak the sentence in quotation marks. That sentence is being spoken by another source, whom Peterson is quoting in the following passage:

Passage from source

The program does use the Graduate Equivalency Degree, or GED, as a tool. The students all have to pass the test's five sections, but when they complete the program they earn a regular high school diploma. This is an important point for Robbins, and she stresses that her students will get to graduate with their classes.

Quoted passage
"In fact, I'm trying to get everybody to quit calling them those GED kids," she said. "Number one, they've labeled them. That irritates me. This is supposed to be land of the free and equal opportunity and all that stuff. Don't label my kids. Let them prove what they can do. Let the test scores speak."

---
[1] The terms *indirect source* and *indirect quotation* are often used interchangeably.

When you are drawing on material from a source that is quoting, paraphrasing, or summarizing another, your citations should accurately indicate who is speaking and should also indicate where you found the material. This can be accomplished in a parenthetical citation, a signal phrase, or a combination of the two:

Parenthetical citation: Name the speaker, write "qtd. in" (quoted in), then name the source's author

Paraphrase of passage in source	Students in the GED Options Pathway program should not be labeled "GED kids"; they should be judged on their individual accomplishments. "This is supposed to be the land of the free and equal opportunity and all that stuff" (Robbins, qtd. in Peterson).	Parenthetical citation identifies speaker and source
Quotation from source		

Signal phrase: Name both the speaker and the source in your text

Signal phrase identifies source and speaker	Journalist Erica Peterson reports teacher Anastasia Robbins's beliefs: Students in the GED Options Pathway program should not be labeled "GED kids"; they should be judged on their individual accomplishments. "This is supposed to be the land of the free and equal opportunity and all that stuff," says Robbins.	Paraphrase of passage in source
		Quotation

Combination of signal phrase and parenthetical citation:

Signal phrase identifies the speaker	Teacher Anastasia Robbins believes that students in the GED Options Pathway program should not be labeled "GED kids"; they should be judged on their individual accomplishments. "This is supposed to be the land of the free and equal opportunity and all that stuff" (qtd. in Peterson).	Paraphrase of passage in source
Quotation		Parenthetical citation identifies speaker and source

Source: Peterson, Erica. "W.Va. Program Gives High-Risk Students an Option." *West Virginia Gazette,* 24 Apr. 2011, www.wvgazettemail.com/News/201104240499.

Providing the name of the person being quoted (regardless of whether it is a person who was interviewed or another author) is all you need for acknowledging your indirect source; that name should not be in the list of works cited at the end of your project, since you did not read the original article or interview that person. The source you were reading, though, should be both cited in your project and included in your list of works cited.

self **Assessment**

Review your work to be sure that whenever you work from an indirect source, you:

☐ Cite the direct source. Did you name the source in which you found the material and include only the direct source in your list of works cited? ▶ *Direct versus indirect sources, 398–99*

☐ Use parenthetical citation, signal phrases, or a combination of both to acknowledge the name of the speaker in the indirect source and the author of the source in which you found the material. Did you make clear who is speaking? ▶ *Signal phrases, 137–38*

6

Documentation

文献引用格式

Matters

MAL Style 文献引用格式：MLA格式

Use part 6 to learn, practice, and master these writer's responsibilities:

❏ **To Audience**

Cite and document sources so that readers can see where each use of sources begins and ends in your project; format your research project using MLA style, in keeping with readers' expectations.

❏ **To Topic**

Cite and document sources to demonstrate that you have explored your topic fully.

❏ **To Other Writers**

Provide citations for all borrowed ideas and information, whether quoted, paraphrased, or summarized; document all sources cited in the research project in a list of works cited at the end of the project.

❏ **To Yourself**

Use sources to build knowledge, and cite them to show readers where your ideas begin and end; to enhance your ethos, or credibility; and to present your ideas effectively.

Book (Printed)

author   title   publication information

King, Laura A. *Experience Psychology.* McGraw-Hill Education, 2016.

imprint-publisher   publication date

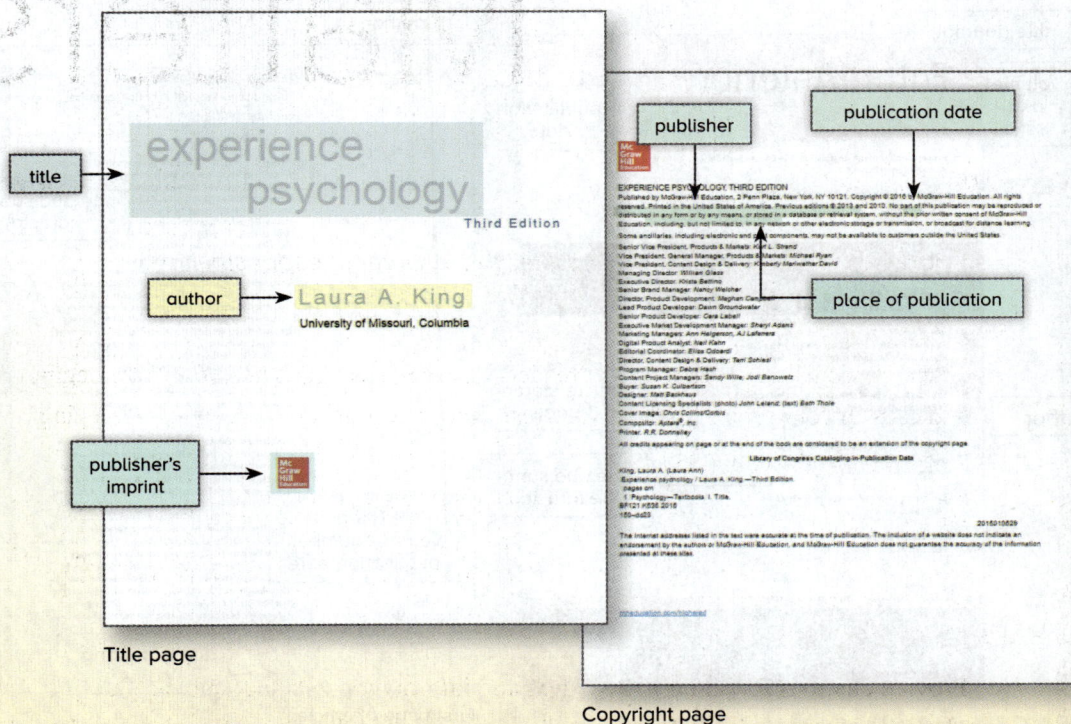

Title page

Copyright page

Look for the information you need to document a printed book on the book's title page and copyright page. (For more about documenting a book, see pp. 176–84.)

Journal Article (Printed)

author | title and subtitle (article)

Chaubal, Mekhala, and Tatum Taylor. "Lessons from 5Pointz: Toward Legal Protection of Collaborative, Evolving Heritage." Future Anterior, vol. 12, no. 1, 2015, pp. 77–97.

vol. | year | pages

title (journal)

volume and issue

FutureAnterior

Journal of Historic Preservation History, Theory, and Criticism GSAPP, Colu...

Volume XII, Number 1, Summer 2015

publication date

Preservation through Replication: The Barnes Foundation
Amanda Reeser Lawrence — 1

Legalizing Architecture: How Congress Defined the Discipline
Sarah M. Hirschman — 17

Origin and Development of a New Tradition: Space, Time, and Architecture in the Translation Zone
Jacob Moore — 33

Public Art and Copyright Law: How the Public Nature of Architecture Changes Copyright Protection
Aura Bertoni and Maria Lillà Montagnani — 47

The Preservation of the Chŏnju Hanok Village: From Material Authenticity to the Themed Replica
Codruta Sîntionean — 57

Lessons from 5Pointz: Toward Legal Protection of Collaborative, Evolving Heritage
Mekhala Chaubal and Tatum Taylor — 77

Book Review: Re-collection: Art, New Media, and Social Memory
Heather Ecker — 98

Exhibition Review: The Mound of Vendôme
Christina E. Crawford — 103

Artist Intervention
Pablo Bronstein

author | **article starting page** | **title and subtitle (article)**

Journal table of contents

author

Mekhala Chaubal and Tatum Taylor

Lessons from 5Pointz
Toward Legal Protection of Collaborative, Evolving Heritage

In November 2013, Jerry Wolkoff hired workers to whitewash the graffiti on the walls of his factory building in Long Island City, Queens. This paint job was a legal act, but so also was the intentional destruction of a historic locus of a community place-making practice that law could safeguard. Occupying the façades of the Neptune Meter building, the 5Pointz Aerosol Art Center drew international attention as a "mecca for graffiti artists"[1] and a "cultural institution."[2] Demonstrating graffiti as a cultural practice of place making, 5Pointz was a *Gesamtkunstwerk* (a synthesized "total artwork") composed of multiple artworks; the ritualistic performance of their composition, interaction, and evolution; and the architectural space where they were curated and created. Neither preservation law nor copyright law could protect the cultural heritage of graffiti in a satisfying way. Based on 5Pointz, we argue that both of these realms of law failed to adequately address the site's essential components: community participation, evolving performance, and integration of cultural practice with architectural space. The loss of 5Pointz illustrates a timely need for dialogue between the fields of heritage and intellectual property law, pursuing a new means of protecting cultural landscapes.[3]

Background of 5Pointz: Development of a Cultural Landscape
The former Neptune Meter building was constructed in 1892 as a factory for the production of water meters, continuing to serve this function until 1972 (Figure 1). Jerry Wolkoff, the current owner, purchased the large industrial complex in 1971 and in the early 1990s began renting studio spaces in the building at a low cost to artists.[3] Around the same time, a group called the Terminators contacted Wolkoff with a proposal. Their goals to establish an outdoor exhibit space for graffiti that would allow artists to legally showcase their work, thereby discouraging them from defacing other structures in Queens. Wolkoff accepted the idea and permitted local aerosol artists to paint the exterior of his building. The site became known as the Phun Phactory and gained repute as a haven for young artists. However, by 1998 the Phun Phactory had attracted criticism from vocal detractors, including members of the police force and the Queens ...

title (journal), volume, number, publication date

Future Anterior
Volume XII, Number 1
Summer 2015

title and subtitle (article)

article starting page

77

First page of article

Look for the information you need to document a journal article on the cover or table of contents of the journal and on the first and last pages of the article. (For more about documenting an article from a printed or online periodical, see pp. 184–88.)

MLA

Journal Article from an Online Database

author   title and subtitle (article)

Joselit, Jenna Weissman. "The Brooklyn Thrill-Kill Gang and the Great Comic Book Scare of the 1950s."

      Journal   Issue ▼

American Jewish History, vol. 100, no. 1, Jan. 2016. *Web of Science*, doi:10.1353/ajh.2016.0015.

         vol.▲   pub. date   database

Database screen: full record of article

Look for the information you need to document an article you accessed through an online database on the search results screen, the full record of the article, or the first and last pages of the article itself. (For more about documenting an article accessed through an online database, see pp. 185–87.)

Short Work on a Website

While access dates are optional, it is helpful to include them in an MLA-style citation if the work has no pub. date.

author   web page title   website title

Wulf, Karin. "The Importance of Academic (History) Writing." *The Scholarly Kitchen,*

pub. date   URL for web page

27 Jan. 2016, scholarlykitchen.sspnet.org/2016/01/27/the-importance-

of-academic-history-writing/.

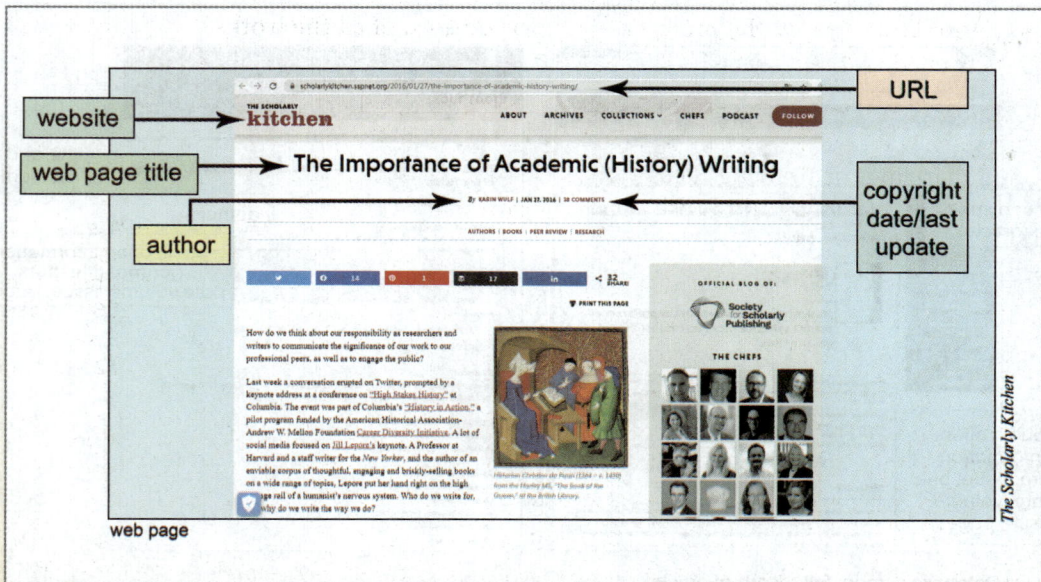

website → THE SCHOLARLY kitchen   ABOUT ARCHIVES COLLECTIONS ˅ CHEFS PODCAST FOLLOW ← URL

web page title → **The Importance of Academic (History) Writing**

author → By KARIN WULF | JAN 27, 2016 | 38 COMMENTS ← copyright date/last update

AUTHORS | BOOKS | PEER REVIEW | RESEARCH

web page

The Scholarly Kitchen

Frequently, the information you need to create a complete entry in the list of works cited is missing or difficult to find on web pages. Look at the top or bottom of the web page or home page or for a link to an "About" or "Contact Us" page. (For more about documenting online sources, see pp. 188–90.)

19 Creating MLA-Style In-Text Citations
MLA格式的文内引用

Developed by the Modern Language Association (MLA), MLA style guidelines are used by many researchers in the humanities—especially in languages and literature—to cite and document sources and to format researched projects in a uniform way. These guidelines are revised every few years, to accommodate writers' needs in a time of ongoing changes in the technologies used for researching and writing from sources. The *MLA Handbook* (8th ed.) requires that writers acknowledge sources in two ways:

- **Citation:** In the body of your project, provide an in-text citation for each source used.
- **Documentation:** At the project's end, provide a list of all the works you cited in the project.

In-text citations appear in the body of your project. They mark each use you make of a source, regardless of whether you are quoting, paraphrasing, summarizing, or drawing ideas from it. They also alert readers to a shift between *your* ideas and those you have borrowed.

> *More about*
> Popular academic
>   styles per
>   discipline, 69
> APA style,
>   213–54 (part 7)
> *Chicago* style,
>   256–71 (part 8)
> CSE style,
>   272–84 (part 8)

19a Using a Signal Phrase and Page Reference or a Parenthetical Citation to Alert Readers to Borrowed Material in Your Research Project 使用信号词、页码索引或文内夹注，提醒读者研究项目中的引用

You can cite a source in your text by using a signal phrase and page reference (in parentheses) or a parenthetical note:

- *Signal phrase.* Include the author's name and an appropriate verb in your sentence before the borrowed material, and put the page number(s) in parentheses after the borrowed material. Often you will use just the author's surname, but you should never use just the author's first name alone.

> *More about*
> Signal verbs, 136–
>   55 (ch. 18)

Writing Responsibly | Citing and Documenting Sources

When you cite and document sources, you demonstrate how thoroughly you have researched your topic and how carefully you have thought about your sources, which encourages your audience to believe you are a credible researcher. In your citations and documentation you acknowledge any material that you have borrowed from a source and you join the conversation on your topic by adding your own interpretation. Accurate entries in the body of your project and list of works cited allow your audience to find and read your sources so that they can evaluate your interpretation and learn more about the subject themselves. Accurate entries also demonstrate the care with which you have written your research project, which further reinforces your credibility, or ethos.

to AUDIENCE

Qualifications of
source author

> While encouraging writers to use figurative language, journalist
> _signal phrase_
> Constance Hale cautions that "a metaphor has the shelf life of a fresh
> _page no._
> vegetable" (224), illustrating the warning with her own lively metaphor.

Using a signal phrase allows you to integrate the borrowed material into your sentence, to put the source in context by adding your own interpretation, and to describe the qualifications of the source author. For these reasons, most summaries, paraphrases, and quotations should be introduced by a signal phrase.

Parenthetical note. Include in parentheses the author's surname plus the page number(s) from which the borrowed material comes:

> While figurative language can make a passage come alive, be aware that met-
> _parenthetical note_
> aphors have "the shelf life of a fresh vegetable" (Hale 224).

Parenthetical notes are useful when you are citing more than one source, when you are establishing facts, or when the author's identity is not relevant to the point you are making.

NOTE The works-cited entry is the same whether you use a signal phrase or a parenthetical note:

> _author_   _title_   _publication info_
> Hale, Constance. _Sin and Syntax._ Broadway, 2001.

> **More about**
> Creating works-
>   cited entries,
>   176–96

> **More about**
> What you do and
>   do not need to
>   cite, 122
> Signal phrases,
>   137–38
> Signal verbs (list),
>   138
> Integrating bor-
>   rowed material
>   into your text,
>   144–45

Quick **Reference** **General Principles of In-Text Citation**

- Cite not only direct quotations but also paraphrases, summaries, and information gathered from a source, whether printed or online.
- In most cases, include the author's surname and a page reference. For one-page and unpaginated sources (such as websites), provide only the author's name.
- Place the name(s) either in a signal phrase or in a parenthetical note. A signal phrase makes it easier to integrate borrowed information or the author's credentials into your own prose. A parenthetical citation is appropriate when establishing facts or citing more than one source for a piece of information.
- For two or more sources by the same author, include the title—either a complete title in the text or an abbreviated title in the parenthetical note.
- Whenever you add a title or abbreviated title, insert a comma between the surname and the title, but not between the title and the page number. In parenthetical citations, do not insert punctuation between the author's surname and the page number.

> **Tech** Page References and Web Pages
>
> Despite the use of the term *web page,* most websites do not have page numbers in the sense that printed books do. Your browser may number the pages when you print a web page from a website, but this numbering appears only on your printed copy. Different computers and printers break pages differently, so your printed page 5 might be someone else's page 4 or 6. For this reason, in-text citations of most web pages include only the author's name. If a website numbers its paragraphs, provide that information in place of a page reference.

19b Including Enough Information to Lead Readers to the Source in Your List of Works Cited
包含足够的信息，引导读者找到引用文献的来源

Whether you are using a signal phrase or a parenthetical note, in-text citations should provide enough information for readers to locate the source in the *list of works cited*. In most cases, providing the author's surname and a page reference is enough. Occasionally, however, you may need to provide more information:

- If you cite more than one source by the same author, mention the title of the work in the text or include a shortened form of the title in the in-text citation. (You may also want to mention the title of the work if it is relevant to the point you are making.)

> Example 6, 168

- If you refer to sources by two different authors who have the same surname, mention the authors' first names in the text, or include the authors' first initials in the in-text citation.

> Example 7, 168

Occasionally, you may need to include less information. For example, you would omit a page number when you are summarizing an entire source, when your source is just one page long, or when your source, such as a web page, is not paginated.

> Example 8, 168
> Example 16a, 173

19c Placing In-Text Citations to Avoid Distracting Readers and to Show Them Where Borrowed Material Starts and Stops
使用文内引用，避免分散读者的注意力并提示引文的起止位置

When you incorporate a quotation, paraphrase, summary, or idea from a source into your own text, carefully consider the placement of the in-text citation, keeping the following goals in mind:

- To make clear exactly which material is drawn from the source
- To avoid distracting your reader

Signal phrase When using a signal phrase, bookend the borrowed information: Insert the author's name *before,* and the page number *after,* the cited material.

Daniels, who has written several books about DC Comics' creations, notes that underground comics artists are not controlled by corporate interests that discourage daring material (165).

More about
Phrases, 342–44
Clauses, 344–45,
    353–54
Sentences, 345–
    46

Signal phrase

Page number

Parenthetical note When using a parenthetical note, place the note at a natural pause—at the end of a phrase, clause, or sentence—after the borrowed material and before any punctuation.

Following a sentence

Common themes of underground comics include sex and sexual identity, politics, and social issues (Daniels 165).

Following a clause

Other common themes of underground comics include sex and sexual identity, politics, and social issues (Daniels 165), as shown in Robert Crumb's *Snarf* comics.

Following a phrase

The themes of underground comics, such as sex and sexual identity, politics, and social issues (Daniels 165), are all demonstrated in Robert Crumb's *Snarf* comics.

Writing Responsibly

Using Signal Phrases to Demonstrate Your Relationship with Sources

More about
Integrating sup-
    porting material,
    136–38
When to use
    signal phrases,
    137–38

As you consider using a source, think about *why* you want to use it. Does it provide a supporting reason or illustration? Does it provide an authoritative voice? Does it make a point that contrasts with your own? Then include a signal phrase that reflects your answer to that question.

Tom Bergin, who covers the oil and gas industry for Reuters, provides one example of the consequences of offshore drilling.

Neurobiologist Catherine Levine agrees with this point of view.

The views of meteorologist John Coleman contrast dramatically with those of the majority of climate scientists.

to TOPIC

Block quotations When the text you are quoting takes up more than four lines of your project, indent the borrowed material as a block by one-half inch from the left margin, and place the parenthetical note one space *after* the closing punctuation mark. Do not use quotation marks when indenting quoted material as a block.

More about
Block quotations,
170–71, 200, 449

Example

> signal phrase
>
> Howard and Kennedy assert that parents and school officials tend to ignore hazing until an incident becomes public knowledge. They describe a concrete incident that demonstrates their claims:
>
> ←— ½" —→ In general, the Bredvik school community (parents, teachers, coaches, and students) condoned or ignored behaviors that could be called "hazing" or "sexual harassment." However, when the incident was formally brought to the attention of the larger, public audience, a conflict erupted in the community over how to frame, understand, and react to the event. (347–48)

19d Adjusting In-Text Citations to Match Your Source 调整文内引用，匹配文献来源

The exact form of an in-text citation depends on the source. Does it have one author, several authors, or no authors? Is the source paginated? Is the source a novel, a story in an anthology, or a PowerPoint presentation? The examples that follow cover the most common source types. (A list of in-text citation examples in MLA style appears on the next page.) For more unusual sources, study the general principles as outlined here and in the *MLA Handbook*, 8th ed. (available in any library), and adapt them to your special circumstances.

1. One author
a. Signal phrase

> Cahill cautions responsible historians against disparaging the Middle Ages. Medieval Europe's reputation as a time of darkness, ignorance, and
>
> page no.
> blind faith is "largely (if not wholly) undeserved" (310).

MLA In-Text Citations Index

1. **One author**
2. Two authors
3. Three or more authors

MLA In-Text Citations Index

b. Parenthetical note

> The Middle Ages are often unjustly characterized as a time of darkness, ignorance, and blind faith (Cahill 310).

2. Two authors Include the surnames of both authors in your signal phrase or parenthetical note; use *and*, not an ampersand (&), in the parenthetical note.

> To write successfully about their families, authors must have motives beyond merely exposing secret histories (Miller and Paola 72).

3. Three or more authors For sources with three or more authors, insert the Latin phrase *et al.* following the first author's surname.

et al. 等人 Abbreviation of the Latin phrase *et alii*, "and others"

NOTE *al.* is an abbreviation, so it requires a period; *et* is a complete word, so it does not. There should be no punctuation between the author's name and *et al.* (Do not italicize this Latin phrase in your citation.)

> 1st author's surname + et al. in signal phrase
> Visonà et al. stress that symbols used in African art are not intended to be iconic
> but instead to suggest a wide variety of meanings. The authors liken this complexity
> to "a telephone line that carries multiple messages simultaneously" (19).

> Symbols used in African art are not intended to be iconic but rather to suggest a
> 1st author + et al.
> complex range of meanings (Visonà et al. 19).

Do the same in your list of works cited.

Example 3, 177

4. Group, government, or corporate author When a government agency, corporation, or other organization is listed as the author, use that organization's name in your in-text citation. The MLA suggests incorporating names into your sentence in a signal phrase to avoid long parenthetical notes.

> government agency as author
> The Federal Emergency Management Agency indicates that Kansas City is
> located in a region of frequent and intense tornado activity (4).

If a parenthetical note makes more sense in the context, use common abbreviations ("US" for *United States,* "Corp." for *Corporation*) to shorten the name where you can.

5. Unnamed author If the author is unnamed and the work is alphabetized by title in the list of works cited, use the title in your in-text citation. Abbreviate long titles in parenthetical citations.

> One nineteenth-century children's book vows that "when examined by the
> microscope, the flea is a pleasant object," and the author's vivid description
> of this sight—a body "curiously adorned with a suit of polished armor, neatly
> jointed, and beset with a great number of sharp pins almost like the quills of a
> title
> porcupine"—may win readers' curiosity, if not their sympathy (*Insects* 8).

❯ Example 4, 177

If you do abbreviate the title, start your abbreviation with the word by which the title will be alphabetized in your list of works cited. Also, only if the author is listed specifically as "Anonymous" should you use that designation.

6. Two or more sources by the same author When you draw on two or more sources by the same author, differentiate between those sources by including titles.

> book title
> In her book *Nickel and Dimed,* social critic Barbara Ehrenreich demonstrates
> that people cannot live on the then-current minimum wage (60). Perhaps, as
> blog entry title
> she notes in her blog entry "'Values' Voters Raise Minimum Wages," they will
> be a little better able to hold their own in the six states (Arizona, Colorado, Mon-
> tana, Missouri, Nevada, Ohio) that have recently raised their minimum wage.

7. Two or more authors with the same surname When you cite sources by two different authors with the same surname, differentiate them by including their first names (the first time you mention them in a signal phrase) or by including their first initials (in a parenthetical reference or subsequent in-text citations).

> Including citations is important not only because they give credit but also because they
> "organize a field of inquiry, create order, and allow for accountability" (S. Rose 243).
> This concern for acknowledging original sources dates back to the early eighteenth
> century: Joseph Addison was one of the first to argue for "the superiority of original to
> imitative composition" (M. Rose 114).

8. Entire source (including a one-page source) Mention an entire source—whether it is a film or a website, a book or an article, a painting or a graphic novel—in your text using the information that begins the entry in your list of works cited.

❯ Example 40b, 191

> The film *The Lady Eve* asks whether love is possible without trust.

9. Selection from an anthology If your source is a selection from an anthology, reader, or other collection, your citation should name the author of the selection—not the editor of the anthology. In the next example, Faulkner is the author of the selection "A Rose for Emily," a story that appears in a literature anthology edited by Robert DiYanni.

Example 10, 180

> Southern fiction often explores the marked curiosity that women of stature
>
> author of selection
> and mystery inspire in their communities. Faulkner's "A Rose for Emily," for
>
> example, describes the title character as "a tradition, a duty, and a care; a sort
>
> of hereditary obligation upon the town . . ." (79).

MLA In-Text Citations Index

  8. Entire source
  9. Selection from an anthology
  10. Multivolume source
  11. Literary source
  12. Sacred text

10. Multivolume source If you use information from more than one volume of a multivolume work, your in-text citation must indicate both the volume and the page from which you are borrowing. (This information can be omitted if you use only one volume of the work, since your works-cited entry will indicate which volume you used.)

Example 15b, 182

> author
> Esteemed journalist Ida Tarbell writes that in 1847 Abraham Lincoln was a
>
> popular man of "simple, sincere friendliness" who was an enthusiastic—though
>
> pg. no. vol. no. ch. no.
> awkward—bowler (210; vol. 1, ch. 13).

Abbreviations for *volume* and *chapter* are used. No abbreviation is needed before the page number.

11. Literary source Because many classics of literature—novels, poems, plays—are published in a number of editions (printed and digital) with pagination that varies widely, your citation should provide your readers with the information they will need to find the passage, regardless of which edition they are reading.

a. Novel Include the chapter number (with the abbreviation *ch.*) after the page number (or location reference for digital books) from your edition.

> Joyce shows his protagonist's dissatisfaction with family, faith, and country
>
> through the adolescent Stephen Dedalus's first dinner at the adult table, an
>
> pg. no. ch. no.
> evening filled with political and religious discord (274; ch. 1).

Use arabic (*2, 9, 103*), not roman (*ii, ix, ciii*), numerals, regardless of what your source uses.

If the novel has chapters grouped into parts or books, include both the part or book number and the chapter number, using the appropriate abbreviation (*pt.* for *part* or *bk.* for *book*).

> Even though New York society declares the Countess Olenska beyond her
>
> prime, Newland Archer sees in her the "mysterious authority of beauty"
>
> (Wharton 58; bk. 1, ch. 8).

b. Play When citing plays, use act, scene, and line numbers (in that order), not page numbers or location numbers (used in digital editions). Do not label the parts. Instead, separate them with periods.

Use arabic (*1, 5, 91*), not roman (*i, v, xci*), numerals for act, scene, and line numbers, and omit spaces after periods between numbers.

> When the ghost of Hamlet's father cries, "Adieu, adieu, adieu! remember me,"
>
> Hamlet wonders if he must "remember" his father through vengeance (1.5.91).

c. Poem For poetry, use line numbers, rather than page or location numbers. With the first reference to line numbers, use the word *line* or *lines;* omit it thereafter.

> 1st ref.
> Shakespeare ends Sonnet 55 with a gesture to his lover (lines 13–14), but
>
> it seems an afterthought to a sonnet that meditates on death: "Like as the
>
> waves make towards the pebbled shore, / So do our minutes hasten to their
>
> later refs.
> end" (1–2).

For long poems that are divided into sections (books, parts, numbered stanzas), provide section information as well, omitting the section type (such as *book* or *part*) and separating the section number from the line number(s) with a period. If you provide more than four lines of the poem, treat the material as you would a block quotation.

More about
Block quotations,
165

Lord Byron's *Don Juan* (1818–1824) begins with a cheeky criticism of heroism,

indicating the poem's irreverent outlook on life that is to come.

> I want a hero: an uncommon want,
>
>   When every year and month sends forth a new one,
>
> Till, after cloying the gazettes with cant,
>
>   The age discovers he is not the true one;
>
> Of such as these I should not care to vaunt,
>
>   I'll therefore take our ancient friend Don Juan—
>
> We all have seen him, in the pantomime,
>
> Sent to the devil somewhat ere his time. (11.1-8)

sec *lines*

Use arabic (*1, 8*), not roman (*i, viii*), numerals, and omit spaces.

12. Sacred text Cite sacred texts (such as the Bhagavad-Gita, the Talmud, the Qur'an, and the Bible) not by page number but by book title (abbreviated in parenthetical notes), chapter number, and verse number(s), and separate each section with a period. Do not italicize book titles or put them in quotation marks, and do not italicize the name of the sacred text, unless you are referring to a specific edition.

sacred text

In the Bible's timeless love poetry, the female speaker concludes her descrip-

tion of her lover with this proclamation: "This is my beloved and this is my

book *ch.verse*

friend, / O daughters of Jerusalem" (Song of Sol. 5.16).

No space

specific edition

The *New Oxford Annotated Bible* offers a moving translation of the timeless love

book

poetry in the Song of Solomon. The female speaker concludes her description

of her lover with this proclamation: "This is my beloved and this is my friend, / O

ch.verse

daughters of Jerusalem" (5.16).

MLA In-Text Citations Index

13. Motion picture, television, or radio broadcast The information you include in an in-text citation for a motion picture or for a television or radio broadcast depends on what you are emphasizing in your project. When you are emphasizing the work itself, use the title; when you are emphasizing the director's work, use the director's name; when you are emphasizing an actor's work, use the actor's name. Start your works-cited entry with whatever you have used in your in-text citation.

▶ Example 40b, 191

> title
> While *The Lady Eve* is full of slapstick humor, it is mainly remembered for its
>
> snappy dialogue, at once witty and suggestive.

> actor's name
> Barbara Stanwyck's portrayal of Jean Harrington is at once sexy and wholesome.

14. Indirect source When you can, avoid quoting from a secondhand source. When you cannot use the original source, mention the name of the person you are quoting in your sentence. In your parenthetical note, include *qtd. in* (for *quoted in*) plus the name of the author of the source in which you found the quotation.

> Handel's stock among opera-goers rose considerably over the course of the
>   author quoted
> twentieth century. In 1912, an English music critic, H. C. Colles, maintained
>
> that "it would be difficult, if not impossible, to make any one of Handel's
>   source of quotation
> operas tolerable to a modern audience" (qtd. in Orrey 62). Today, however,
>
> Handel's operas are performed around the world.

In your list of works cited, include the *indirect* source (*Orrey*), not the source being quoted (*H. C. Colles*).

15. Dictionary or encyclopedia entry In the citation of a dictionary or ency-clopedia entry, omit the page number on which you found the item. For a dictionary entry, place the defined word in quotation marks, followed by the abbreviation *def.* Follow this with the letter or number of the definition you wish to reference.

> Another definition of *honest* is "respectable" ("Honest," def. 6), but what, if
>
> anything, does truth have to do with respectability?

In the parenthetical note for an encyclopedia entry, include the entry's full title in quotation marks.

More about
Parts of a dictionary entry, 316–17

> The study of ethics is not limited to philosophers, as its "all-embracing practical nature" makes it an applicable or even necessary course of study in a wide variety of disciplines, from biology to business ("Ethics").

If you are citing two entries with the same title from different reference sources, add an abbreviated form of the reference work's title to each entry.

> While the word *ethics* is commonly understood to mean "moral principles" ("Ethics," def. 4, *Random House Webster's*), to philosophers it is "the evaluation of human conduct" ("Ethics," *Philosophical Dict.*).

16. Website or other online source Cite electronic sources such as websites, online articles, e-books, and emails as you would print sources, even though many of these sources do not use page numbers.

a. Without page, paragraph, screen, or slide numbers Unless there is another numbering system at work (such as numbered paragraphs, screens, or slides), cite the author without a page reference.

> When first published in 1986, Alan Moore's *Watchmen* revolutionized the comic book. Today, even its harshest critics acknowledge the book's landmark status (Shone).
>
> author only

You may credit your source more elegantly by mentioning the author in a signal phrase and omitting the parenthetical citation altogether.

> signal phrase
> Reading Alan Moore's *Watchmen* in 2005, critic Tom Shone found it "underwhelming," but he admitted that in 1986 the comic book was "unquestionably a landmark work."

b. With paragraph, screen, or slide numbers If an electronic source numbers its paragraphs, screens, or slides, you can reference these numbers as you would pages (with an appropriate identifying abbreviation—*par.* or *pars., screen* or *screens*).

> The Internet has also become an outlet for direct distribution through artist websites, making independent titles not only more accessible to consumers but also more affordable for individual artists to produce and market (Fenty et al. par. 1).

More about
PDF files, 104, 109

Examples 46–50, 194–95

c. In a PDF file Online documents offered as a PDF (portable document format) file include all the elements of the printed document, including the page number. Since pages are fixed, you can and should cite page numbers.

17. Personal communication (email, letter, interview) As with other unpaginated sources, when citing information from a letter, email message, interview, or other personal communication, you should include the author's name in a signal phrase or parenthetical citation. Also indicate the type of source you are citing.

> Many people have asked why teachers cannot do more to prevent school shootings; in an email to this author, one instructor responds: "As creative writing teachers untrained in psychology, can we really determine from a student's poetry whether he or she is emotionally disturbed—even a threat to others?" (Fox).

source type ... *author of email*

18. Table, chart, or figure If a copy of the visual you are discussing is *not* included in your project, include relevant information in the text (artist's name or table title, for example), and include an entry in your list of works cited.

> There is no experience quite like standing in front of a full-size painting by Jackson Pollock. His paintings have an irresistible sense of movement to them, the particular quality of which is unique to his work. This is especially evident in *One (Number 31, 1950)*, which once hung on the fourth floor of New York's Museum of Modern Art.

If a copy of the visual *is* included in your project, reference it in your text and include the source information in a table's source note (Figure 19.1) or in a figure's caption (see the figure caption on page 205 in the project at the end of chapter 22).

19. Government document Because government documents are alphabetized in the list of works cited by the name of the nation that produced them, mention the country as well as the agency in your text.

TABLE 1 THE DEMISE OF THE THREE-DECKER NOVEL

Year	No. of three-deckers published
1894	184
1895	52
1896	—
1897	4
1898	0

Source: Information from John Feather, *A History of British Publishing.* Crown Helm, 1988, p. 125.

FIGURE 19.1 Table in MLA style

> Example 51, 195

Just as the nation was entering World War II, the United States War Department published a book outlining what it had learned about reading aerial photographs.

20. Legal source Laws, acts, and legal cases are typically referred to by name either in your sentence or in a parenthetical citation. Laws and acts are neither italicized nor enclosed in quotation marks.

> Example 52, 195

In 2008 the US Congress passed the Combat Bonus Act.

Legal cases are italicized in your text, but not in the list of works cited.

In 1963 the Supreme Court ruled that poor defendants should receive legal representation, even if they could not pay for it themselves (*Gideon v. Wainwright*).

21. Multiple sources in one sentence When you use different information from multiple sources within a single sentence, give separate citations in the appropriate place.

Other common themes of underground comics include sex and sexual identity, politics, and social issues (Daniels 165), as shown in Crumb's work, which is well known for its satirical approach to countercultural topics (Heller 101–02).

22. Multiple sources in one citation When you draw information from more than one source, follow the borrowed material with a list of all relevant sources, separated by semicolons.

Jamestown was once described as a failed colony populated by failed colonists, but new findings suggest that the colonists were resourceful survivors (Howard; Lepore 43).

Entire source—no page reference

20 Preparing an MLA-Style List of Works Cited 准备MLA格式的参考文献列表

The list of works cited, which comes at the end of your research project, includes information about the sources you have cited in your text. (A bibliography that includes sources you read but did not cite in your research project is called a *list of works consulted*.) Your list of works cited provides readers with the information they need to locate the material you used in your project. The format of each entry depends in part on the type of source it is. (See the Quick Reference box on pp. 178–79 for a list of MLA-style examples included in this chapter.)

> Annotated visual of where to find author, title, and publication information, tutorial in part 6

Books—Printed and Electronic 书籍——纸质版与电子版

In a printed book, most or all of the information you need to create an entry in the list of works cited appears on the title and copyright pages, which are located at the beginning of the book. In an online or e-book, print and electronic publication information often appears at the top or bottom of the first page or screen or is available through a link.

1. One author

a. Printed The basic entry for a printed book looks like this:

Author's surname, First name. *Title: Subtitle.* Publisher (shortened), date of publication.

Here is an example of an actual entry in the list of works cited:

author   title   publication information
Morrison, Toni. *Home.* Knopf, 2012.
       pub. date

b. Database Some books are available in online, full-text archives, or databases, such as *Bartleby.com.* When you are documenting a book you accessed through a database, add the name of the database and include the complete URL for that book within the database.

> Wharton, Edith. *The Age of Innocence.* D. Appleton, 1920.
>
> database
> *Bartleby.com,* www.bartleby.com/1005/.
> URL

c. E-book The citation for an electronic version of a book is the same as for a printed book except for the inclusion of the specific type of the e-book version you read: Nook ed., Microsoft Reader ed., Kindle file, and so on.

> Morrison, Toni. *Home.* Kindle ed., Knopf, 2012.

2. Two authors List authors in the order in which they appear on the title page. Only the first author should be listed with surname first.

> author 1   author 2
> Zimmerman, Julie, and Olaf F. Larson. *Opening Windows onto Hidden Lives: Women, Country*
>
>   *Life, and Early Rural Sociological Research.* West Virginia UP, 2010.
> author 1   author 2
> Anderson, Poul, and Karen Anderson. *Innocent at Large.* Project Gutenberg, 3 Apr. 2016,
>
>   www.gutenberg.org/files/51650/51650-h/51650-h.htm.

3. Three or more authors Either list all the authors, or just list the first and add *et al.* Whichever you choose, do the same in your in-text citation.

> Andersen, Thomas Hestbaek, et al. *Social Semiotics: Key Figures, New Directions.*
>
>   Routledge, 2015.
>
> Collinson, Diané, et al. *Fifty Eastern Thinkers.* Routledge, 2000, routledgeonline.com:80/
>
>   religion/Book.aspx?id=w035&SiteId=ROL.

4. Unnamed (anonymous) author Start the entry with the title.

> title
> *Terrorist Hunter: The Extraordinary Story of a Woman Who Went Undercover*
>
>   *to Infiltrate the Radical Islamic Groups Operating in America.*
>
>   Ecco-HarperCollins, 2003.

Alphabetize the entry in your list of works cited using the first significant word of the title (not an article such as *a, an,* or *the*). Only if the author is listed specifically as "Anonymous" should you use that designation in the works-cited entry (and in your text).

> Anonymous. *Go Ask Alice.* Prentice, 1971.

MLA Works-Cited Entries

1. One author
2. Two authors
3. Three or more authors
4. Unnamed (anonymous) author
5. Author using a pen name
6. Two or more works by the same author

▶ **More about** *et al.,* 166–67

▶ Example 3, 166

MLA Works-Cited Entries

5. Author using a pen name (pseudonym) If the author is using a pen name (or *pseudonym*), document the source using the author's pen name and insert the author's actual name in brackets following the pseudonym.

Keene, Carolyn [Edward Stratemeyer]. *The Secret of the Old Clock.* Grosset, 1930.

6. Two or more works by the same author Alphabetize the entries by the first important word in each title. Supply the author's name only with the first entry. For subsequent works, replace the author's name with three hyphens.

Ritter, Kelly. *Before Shaughnessy: Basic Writing at Yale and Harvard, 1920–1960.* Southern Illinois UP, 2009.

---. *Reframing the Subject: Instructional Film and Class-Conscious Literacies.* U of Pittsburgh P, 2015.

7. Group or corporate author Treat the sponsoring organization as the author.

corporate author

Blackfoot Gallery Committee. *The Story of the Blackfoot People: Niitsitapiisinni.*

Firefly, 2002.

8. Edited book or anthology When citing the book as a whole, treat the editor as the author and insert the word *editor* (or *editors* if there is more than one editor) after the name. For more than two editors, use the first editor's name (surname first), followed by a comma and the words *et al., editors*.

Hage, Erik, editor. *The Melville–Hawthorne Connection: A Study of the Literary*

Friendship. McFarland, 2014.

Callahan, Vicki, and Virginia Kuhn, editors. *Future Texts: Subversive Performance*

and Feminist Bodies. Parlor, 2016.

MLA Works-Cited Entries

5. Author using a pen name
6. Two or more works by the same author
7. Group or corporate author
8. Edited book or anthology
9. Author and editor or translator

Sarto, Guida, et al., editors. *The Cambridge Companion to Boccaccio.*

Cambridge UP, 2015. University Publishing Online, dx.doi.org/10.1017/

CCO9781139013987.

9. Author and editor or translator List the author first. After the title, include the words *Edited by* or *Translated by* (as appropriate) before the editor's or translator's name. If the book was accessed online, add the information shown in item 1b–c.

Larsson, Asa. *Sun Storm.* Translated by Marlaine Delargy. Delacorte, 2006.

10. One or more selections from an edited book or anthology (printed or online) If your source is a selection (such as a chapter, story, poem, or image) in an edited book or anthology, think of that book or anthology as a container, and provide full information about both your source and its container. Start your entry with the selection's author and title.

author · title (selection)

Faulkner, William. "A Rose for Emily." *Literature: Reading Fiction, Poetry, and Drama,*

pages (selection)

edited by Robert DiYanni, 6th ed. McGraw-Hill, 2007, pp. 79–84.

When documenting a longer work, such as a novel or a play, that is included in the anthology or collection, italicize the work's title.

title (selection)

Ives, David. *Sure Thing. Literature: Reading Fiction, Poetry, and Drama.* . . .

> Example 8, 179

If you are citing more than one selection in the anthology or collection, include an entry for the collection as a whole.

DiYanni, Robert D., editor. *Literature: Reading Fiction, Poetry, and Drama,*

6th ed., McGraw-Hill, 2009.

Then, for each selection you use from the anthology, include only the author and title of the selection, the surname of the anthology's editor, and the page numbers of the selection.

Faulkner, William. "A Rose for Emily." DiYanni, pp. 79–84.

> Example 24a–c, 185

For a scholarly article included in an edited book, include the article's original publication information first, *Reprinted in,* and then the publication information for the anthology.

original publication info

Stock, A. G. "Yeats and Achebe." *Journal of Commonwealth Literature* vol. 5,

reprint publication info

no. 3, 1970, pp. 105–11. Reprinted in *Things Fall Apart,* by Chinua Achebe.

Edited by Francis Abiola Irele. Norton, 2008, pp. 271–77.

If the book was accessed online, add the information shown in item 1b–c.

11. Edition other than the first Insert the edition number (*2nd ed., 3rd ed.*) or edition name (*Rev. ed.* for "revised edition") before the publication information. The edition number or name should appear on the title page.

> Feather, John. *The Information Society: A Study of Continuity and Change,* 6th ed.
>
> Facet, 2013.

12. Imprint (division) of a larger publishing company Name only the main publisher.

> Betcherman, Lita-Rose. *Court Lady and Country Wife: Two Noble Sisters in*
> *Seventeenth-Century England.* publisher HarperCollins, 2005.

13. Introduction, preface, foreword, or afterword Begin with the name of the person who wrote this section of the text. Then provide a descriptive label (such as *Introduction* or *Preface*), the title of the book, and the name of the book's author. (If the author of the section and the book are the same, use only the author's surname after the title.) Include the page numbers for the section.

> author · label · title of book
> Howard, Rebecca Moore. Foreword. *Authorship Contested: Cultural Challenges*
> editors of book
> *to the Authentic, Autonomous Author,* edited by Amy E. Robillard and Ron
> pages (foreword)
> Fortune. Routledge, 2016, pp. xii–xiii.

If this section has a title, include it before the descriptive label.

> afterword's title
> Burton, Larry W. "Countering the Naysayers: Independent Writing Programs as
> label
> Successful Experiments in American Education." Afterword. *A Field of*
> *Dreams: Independent Writing Programs and the Future of Composition*
> *Studies,* edited by Peggy O'Neill et al. Utah State UP, 2002, pp. 295–300.

14. Entry in a reference work Format an entry in a dictionary or encyclopedia as you would a selection from an edited book or anthology. For signed articles, include the author's name. (Articles in reference works often carry the author's initials only, so you may need to cross-reference the initials with a list of contributors in the front or back of the book.) If an article is unsigned, begin with its title.

a. Printed For familiar reference works, omit publication information other than the edition and year of publication. If the entries are arranged alphabetically, omit a page reference.

> "Culture." *Oxford English Dictionary,* Compact 2nd ed. 1991.
>
> Green, Michael. "Cultural Studies." *A Dictionary of Cultural and Critical Theory.*
>
> Blackwell, 1996.

b. Online For online reference works, include the full URL of the site you referenced.

> "Culture." *Merriam-Webster Online Dictionary*, 2016, www.merriam-webster.com/
> dictionary/culture.

c. CD or DVD Although CDs have largely been replaced by the Internet, you may still need to use them. If the CD or DVD is published in versions rather than editions, include the version number before the publication information. Including the medium (CD, DVD) is not necessary, but if your source contains multiple discs, include the disc number you used (such as disc 1) after the publication date.

> Cooley, Marianne. "Alphabet." *World Book Multimedia Encyclopedia*,
>   version
>   Version 6.0.2. World Book, 2002.

Example 10, 169

15. Multivolume work

a. Multiple volumes Indicate the span of years in which the volumes were published, as well as the total number of volumes, followed by the abbreviation *vols.* Specify the volume from which you borrowed a particular passage or idea in your in-text citation.

> Tarbell, Ida M. *The Life of Abraham Lincoln*. Lincoln Memorial Assn., pub. dates 1895–1900,
>   no. of vols.
>   2 vols.

b. One volume

If you used only one volume, include the number of the volume you used before the publication information, and give only the publication date of that volume.

> Tarbell, Ida M. *The Life of Abraham Lincoln*, vol. used Vol. 1. Lincoln Memorial Assn., pub. date 1895.

16. Book in a series
If the book you are citing is part of a series, the series title will usually be noted on the book's title page or on the page before the title page. Insert the series title (with no quotation marks or italics) after the publication date. If books in the series are numbered, include the number following the series title.

> Todorov, Tzvetan. *Mikhail Bakhtin: The Dialogical Principle*. Translated by Wlad
>   Godzich. U of Minnesota P, 1995. series title Theory and History of Literature no. 13.

17. Republished book
If a book has been republished, its original date of publication will appear on the book's copyright page. If the original publication date may be of interest to your readers, include it before publication information for the version you consulted. If the book was edited or an introduction was added, include that information before the republication information.

> Burroughs, William S. *Naked Lunch*. orig. pub. date 1959. editors Edited by James Grauerholz and Barry
>   repub. info
>   Miles, Grove, 2001.

18. Title within a title Omit italics from any title that would normally be italicized when it falls within the main title of a book.

> book title · · · · · · · · · · · · · · · title within title
> Birmingham, Kevin. *The Most Dangerous Book: The Battle for* Ulysses. Penguin
>
> Books, 2014.

If the title within the title would normally appear in quotation marks, retain the quotation marks and italicize both titles.

19. Sacred text Italicize the title of the edition you are using. Editors' and translators' names follow the title.

> *The New Oxford Annotated Bible.* New Revised Standard Version, edited by
>
> Michael D. Coogan et al., 3rd ed. Oxford UP, 2010.
>
> *The Holy Qur'an.* Edited and translated by Abdullah Yusuf Ali, 10th ed. Amana, 1997.

20. Missing publication information Certain sources may not include page numbers, date of publication, or publisher. Provide as much information about your source as you are able to locate. The following source does not contain printed page numbers or a publication date. Therefore, these items are not included in the citation.

> Barrett, Edgar, editor. *Football West Virginia 1960.* West Virginia.

21. Pamphlet, brochure, or press release Follow the format for book entries. For a press release, include the day, month, and year of publication, if available.

> Worcester Police Department. *Preparations Underway for St. Patrick's Day Parade.*
>
> City of Worcester, MA, 10 Mar. 2016, www.worcesterma.gov/wpd-press
>
> -releases/-preparations-underway-for-st.-patrick-s-parade#
>
> idIPWSypnuVJtYkjrIA9vDrQ.

If the item was emailed or published online, document it as you would a book published online.

22. Conference proceedings Include the title of the conference, the sponsoring organization (if its name is not cited in the conference title), and the date and location of the conference, if that information is not already included in the publication's title.

> · sponsor
> Bizzell, Patricia, editor. *Proceedings of the Rhetoric Society of America:*
> · · · · · · title (conference) · · · · · · · · · · · · · · date
> *Rhetorical Agendas: Political, Ethical, Spiritual.* 28–31 May 2004,
> · · · location
> U of Texas—Austin. Erlbaum, 2005.

For a paper delivered at a conference, include the word *Lecture* at the very end of the citation.

Example 1, 176

Example 45, 193

23. Dissertation Include the word *Dissertation,* the school to which the dissertation was submitted (abbreviate *University* to *U*), and the year it was submitted. For published dissertations, italicize the title.

> Brackins, Genevieve. *Mothering Amidst and Beyond Hegemony in Margaret Atwood's The Handmaid's Tale and Toni Morrison's Beloved.* Dissertation, Florida State U, 2014. *ProQuest,* fsu.digital.flvc.org/islandora/object/fsu%3A253602.

For unpublished dissertations, put the title in quotation marks.

> Brommer, Stephanie. "We Walk with Them: South Asian Women's Organizations in Northern California Confront Domestic Abuse." Dissertation, U of California—Santa Barbara, 2004.

Periodicals—Printed and Electronic 期刊——纸质版与电子版

Newspapers, magazines, and scholarly journals are types of *periodicals* that publish collections of texts such as stories, articles, poems, and images at regular intervals—daily, monthly, or at set intervals during the year. Most researchers today find articles in periodicals by searching their library's **databases**, online indexes that provide citation information as well as an abstract (or summary) and sometimes an electronic copy of the article itself, in either PDF or HTML format. (A PDF file shows the article more or less as it would have appeared in print; an HTML file includes the text of the article but not the illustrations or formatting of the print version.) As you construct your works-cited entry for a selection in a periodical, think of that periodical as the selection's *container,* and provide full information about both the selection and the container. Include not only the title of the article (in quotation marks) but also the title of the periodical (in italics). The other publication information you include depends on the type of periodical you are documenting.

> Annotated visual of where to find author, title, publication, and other information, tutorial in part 6

24. Article in a scholarly journal The information you need to create an entry for a printed journal article is found on the cover or in the table of contents of the journal and on the first and last pages of the article. For articles downloaded from a database, the information you need appears on the screen listing the articles that fit your search terms, on the first and last pages of the file you download, or in the full record for the article you select. For articles that appear in journals published solely online, you may find the information you need on the website's home page, in the journal's table of contents, or on the first screen of the article. Access dates for database and online articles should come from your notes.

a. Printed The basic entry for an article in a printed journal looks like this:

Surname, First name. "Article Title." *Journal Title*, vol. #, (issue) no. #, year, pp.

Here is an example of an actual entry:

author   article title
Weaver, Karen. "Trophies, Treasure, and Turmoil: College Athletics at a Tipping
        journal title   issue   pages
Point." *Change*, vol. 47, no. 1, 2015, pp. 36–45.
                    vol.   year

b. Accessed through a database When you document an article from a scholarly journal that you accessed through an online database, add the name of the database (in italics) and add the full URL or DOI for the article.

Weaver, Karen. "Trophies, Treasure, and Turmoil: College Athletics at a Tipping

Point." *Change*, vol. 47, no. 1, 2015, pp. 36–45. Taylor & Francis Current

Content Access, doi:10.1080/00091383.

c. Online To document an online journal article, follow the model for a printed journal article. After the publication information, add a comma and provide a complete URL or DOI for the article. (The parts that are different from a printed journal article are highlighted.)

Woolums, Viola. "Gendered Avatar Identity." *Kairos*, vol. 16, no. 1, 2001, kairos

.technorhetoric.net/16.1/topoi/woolums/.

25. Article in a magazine (weekly, monthly)

a. Printed Provide the issue's publication date (month and year or day, month, and year) and the page range for the article, but not the magazine's volume or issue number, even when they are available.

Fuller, Alexandra. "Her Heart Inform Her Tongue: Language Lost and
                                    pub. date   pgs.
        Found." *Harper's Magazine*, Jan. 2012, pp. 60–64.

Gladwell, Malcolm. "Thresholds of Violence." *The New Yorker*, 19 Oct. 2015, pp.

30–37.

If the article appears on nonconsecutive pages (for example, the first part appears on p. 2 but the rest of the article is continued on p. 10), include a plus sign after the first page number (2+).

b. Accessed through a database

Fuller, Alexandra. "Her Heart Inform Her Tongue: Language Lost and
                                            database
        Found." *Harper's Magazine*, Jan. 2012, pp. 60–64. EBSCOhost,

www.ebsco.com/ezproxy/fuller_01/12.

c. Online
                                website
Carr, Nicholas. "Is Google Making Us Stupid?" *The Atlantic*, July/Aug. 2008,

www.theatlantic.com/magazine/archive/2008/07/is-google-making-us-

stupid/306868/.

Thomas, June. "Is Social Acceptance Killing Queer Cinema?" *Slate*, 27 Nov. 2015, www
.slate.com/blogs/outward/2015/11/27/gay_movies_two_hollywood_
reporter_cities_think_2015_s_queer_films_are_terrible.html.

website

26. Article in a newspaper The information you need to create an entry for a printed newspaper article is found on the masthead of the newspaper (at the top of the first page) and on the first and last pages of the article. For newspaper articles downloaded from a database, the information you need appears on the screen listing the articles that fit your search terms or on the first and last pages of the article itself. Articles that appear in online versions of the newspaper usually contain all the information you need at the top of the first screen. Use conventional capitalization of titles even when your original source does not.

> **More about**
> Title capitalization,
> 465

a. Printed For an article in a daily newspaper, include the date (day, month, year). If the paper paginates sections separately, include the section number, letter, or name immediately before the page number.

Richtel, Matt, and Julie Bosman. "To Serve the Young, E-Book Fans
Prefer Print." *The New York Times*, 21 Nov. 2011, p. B1.

date   sec. & pg.

MLA Works-Cited
Entries

24. Article in a
    scholarly journal
25. **Article in a**
    magazine
26. **Article in a**
    newspaper
27. Article on micro-
    form
28. Review (printed
    or online)

If the section number or letter is not part of the page number, add the abbreviation *sec.* and the section name, number, or letter. If the section is named, add the section name before the abbreviation *sec.* If no author is listed, begin the entry with the title of the article. If the article continues on a nonconsecutive page, add a plus sign after the first page number (*A20+*). If the newspaper's masthead specifies an edition (such as late edition or national edition), include that information after the date.

Keller, Julia. "Viral Villainy." *Chicago Tribune*, 22 Mar. 2009, final ed., sec. 6,
pp. 1+.

section

nonconsecutive pg.

edition

If the name of the city in which the newspaper is published does not appear in the newspaper's title, include it in brackets after the title.

Speciale, Samuel. "Majority of Students Apply to Only One College, Federal Study
Says." *Gazette-Mail* [Charleston], 26 Nov. 2015, p. B1.

For well-known national newspapers (such as *The Christian Science Monitor, USA Today,* and *The Wall Street Journal*), no city or state is needed. If you are unsure whether the newspaper is well known, consult your instructor or a reference librarian.

b. Accessed through a database For a newspaper article accessed through a database, add the database name and include the full URL or DOI for the article.

> Maiman, Bruce. "In Praise of Common Courtesy." *The Sacramento Bee*, 15 Apr.
> database
> 2014, p. 11A. Access World News, sacbee.com/opinion/op-ed/bruce-
> maiman.

c. Online For an online newspaper article, include the full URL or DOI.

> website
> Netburn, Deborah. "Theaters Set Aside Tweet Seats for Twitter Users." *Los Angeles*
> *Times*, 6 Dec. 2011, latimesblogs.latimes.com/technology/2011/12/
> theaters-tweet-seats-twitter.html.

27. Article on microform Many libraries still store some back issues of periodicals on microform—that is, as a photograph of a periodical printed on plastic and viewed through a special microform reader. Your entry for an article on microform is the same as for a printed article.

If your source is preserved on microform in a reference source such as NewsBank, add the title of the reference source and any access numbers (such as fiche and grid numbers) following the publication information.

❯ Example 24a, 185
Example 25a, 185
Example 26a, 186

❯ Example 24a–c, 185
Example 25a–c, 185–86
Example 26a–c, 186–87

28. Review (printed or online) Begin with the reviewer's name (if provided), followed by the title of the review (if any) and the label *Review of*. Then include the title and author of the work being reviewed. Finally, include the title of the periodical and its publication information. If the review was accessed online, add information as shown in item 24b–c, 25b–c, or 26b–c.

> reviewer   title (review)   title (book)
> Grover, Jan. "Unreliable Narrator." Review of *Love Works Like This: Opening*
>   author
> *One's Life to a Child*, by Lauren Slater. *Women's Review of Books*,
> vol. 19, nos. 10–11, 2002, p. 40.

29. Editorial (printed or online) Often editorials are unsigned. When that is the case, begin with the title of the editorial (if any). Then insert the label *Editorial* and follow with the periodical's publication information.

> editorial title   label
> "Making Tax Season Worse." Editorial. *Columbus Dispatch*, 28 Feb. 2015, p. 11A.

If the editorial was accessed online, add information as shown in item 24b–c, 25b–c, or 26b–c.

MLA Works-Cited Entries

24. Article in a scholarly journal
25. Article in a magazine
26. Article in a newspaper
27. Article on microform
28. Review
29. Editorial
30. Letter to the editor
31. Website

Example 24a–c, 185
Example 25a–c, 185–86
Example 26a–c, 186–87

30. Letter to the editor (printed or online) Begin with the author's name, followed by the label *Letter to the editor* and the periodical's publication information.

letter author   label
Park, John. Letter to the editor. *Time*, 5 Dec. 2011, p. 9.

If the letter to the editor has a title, add it (in quotation marks) after the author's name. If the letter to the editor was accessed online, add information as shown in item 24b–c, 25b–c, or 26b–c.

Other Electronic Sources 其他电子资源

Annotated visual of where to find author, title, and publication information, tutorial in part 6

While it is usually easy to find the information you need to create a complete entry for a book or an article in a periodical, websites can be a bit trickier. Most of the information you need will appear on the site's home page, usually at the bottom or top of the page, or on the web page you are documenting. Sometimes you may need to look further: Click on links such as "About us" or "More information." Frequently, websites do not provide complete information, so include as much as you can.

31. Website The basic entry for a website looks like this:

Author's surname, First name. *Website title*. Publisher, Publication date, URL.

Here is an example of an actual entry:

editor   title (website)
McGann, Jerome J., ed. *The Complete Writings and Pictures of Dante Gabriel Rossetti:*

A Hypermedia Archive. Institute for Advanced Technology in the Humanities,
publisher
U of Virginia, and Networked Infrastructure for Nineteenth-Century
publication date   URL
Electronic Scholarship, 2008, www.rossettiarchive.org/index.html.

If no author or editor is listed, begin with the website's title.

32. Web page or short work on a website If your source is part of a larger website, think of the larger site as a *container,* and provide full information about both your source and its container. Add the title of the web page to the entry for a website.

page title
Callaghan, Jennefer. "Adorno, Theodor." *Postcolonial Studies @ Emory.*

Dept. of English, Emory U, Oct. 2012, scholarblogs.emory.edu/

postcolonialstudies/6/01/65/.

33. Home page (academic)
a. Course

title (page)
"Philosophy of the Program: The Basics Underscoring the Approach to Composition
title (website)   publisher
Classes at Labette Community College." *Department of English*, Labette Community

College, 2014, www.labette.edu/english/philosophy.html.

b. Department

English Dept. U of California—Santa Barbara. 2013, www.english.ucsb.edu/.

34. Discussion list posting
Treat the subject line (or *thread*) as the title, and include the name of the list, the sponsoring group, and the date of the posting.

subj. line   list name
Ballard, Donna Kim. "Punctuation Question." *Writing Program Administration*

Discussion List, 19 Jun. 2014.

35. Article on a wiki
Usually wikis are written and edited collaboratively, so there is no author to cite. Instead, begin the entry with the article title.

Quigley, Nina, and Madeline Moore. "History of Sweatshop Protests at SU,

2000–2001." *SyrGuide*, 11 June 2014, syrguide.com/guide/2014

/06/11/history-of-sweatshop-protests-at-su-2000-2001/.

36. Blog
a. Blog

title (blog)   sponsor   date of publication   URL
Browsings. Harper's Magazine, 28 Nov. 2015, harpers.org/blog/2015/11/.

b. Blog posting

author (post)   title (post)
Luther, Jason. "Our Failed Writing Center: A Response." *Taxomania!*,
date (post)
11 Nov. 2011, taxomania.org/blog/our-failed-writing-center-a-response/.

c. Comment on a blog posting

author   title of entry commented on
Danderson, Mark. "Some Tough Love for Authors." *The Scholarly Kitchen*. Society for
date (comment)
Scholarly Publishing, 25 Oct. 2011, 3:12 p.m., scholarlykitchen.sspnet

.org/2011/10/25/some-tough-love-for-authors/#comments.

If the comment's author uses a screen name, use that; if the actual name is available and of interest to readers, provide that as well, following the screen name, in square brackets. Also, if there is a time stamp included with the comment, include that as part of your citation.

37. Pseudonym or Online Username If the author/speaker uses a different name than the writer's actual name, use the pseudonym or online username.

> @NASA. "Behemoth Black Hole Found in an Unlikely Place: The Center of a Galaxy in Cosmic Backwater." Twitter, 7 Apr. 2016, 3:30 p.m., twitter.com/NASA/status/717851257403211778.

38. App (for an e-device)

Minecraft Pocket Edition. Version 0.14.0, Mojang AB. Accessed 8 Apr. 2016.

39. Video game (for devices such as Xbox and Wii)

game — publisher
Rock Band 2. Wii. Nintendo, 2008.
platform — release date

Audio and Visual Sources 视听资源

The information you need to create an entry for most audio and visual sources will appear on the cover, label, or program of the work or in the credits at the end of a film. The person you list in the "author" position—the director, performer, artist, or composer—will vary depending on what you have emphasized in your research project. If you are writing about a director's body of work, put the director's name first; if you are writing about a performance, put the performer's name first. If it is the work itself that you are writing about, put the title of the work first. (This decision should be mirrored in your in-text citation.) However you choose to organize the entry, indicate the role of those whom you list, using phrases such as *performance by, directed by,* and *conducted by.*

As with any other entry, italicize the titles of complete or longer works (such as albums, films, operas, and original works of art) and place quotation marks around the titles of shorter works or works published as part of a larger whole (such as songs on a CD or a single episode of a television show). Publication information includes the name of the distributor, production company, or network, as well as the date on which the audio or visual was created, recorded, or broadcast. If you found the audio or visual source online and there is no date of publication, also include the date on which you accessed it.

40. Motion picture

a. Film

title — director — distributor — release date
Good Deeds. Directed by Tyler Perry. Lionsgate, 2012.

If other artists besides the director are relevant to your project, list them between the director and the distributor.

> performers
>
> *Good Deeds.* Directed by Tyler Perry, performances by Perry and Thandie
>
> Newton. Lionsgate, 2012. Film.

If your project stresses the director, performer, or other contributor, place that information at the beginning of the citation.

> Perry, Tyler, director. *Good Deeds.* Performances by Perry and Thandie Newton,
>
> Lionsgate, 2012.

b. Video or DVD Include the original release date, when relevant, before the distributor.

> *The Lady Eve.* Directed by Preston Sturges, performances by Barbara Stanwyck
>
>   orig. release   distributor
>
> and Henry Fonda. 1941. Universal Home Entertainment, 2006.

c. Internet download Include the source you used to download the video, as well as the film's URL.

> *Juno.* Screenplay by Diablo Cody, directed by Jason Reitman, performances by Ellen
>
> Page and Jason Bateman. Fox Searchlight, 2007. *iTunes,* www.itunes.com/.

d. Online video clip Cite a video clip on YouTube or a similar site as you would a web page. If the name of the uploader appears, include it after the website (*uploaded by*). Since these types of videos are not always stable, you may want to include the date you accessed the material.

> performer   video clip title   website
>
> OK Go. "This Too Shall Pass—Rube Goldberg Machine Version." *YouTube,*
>
>   date posted
>
> 2 Mar. 2010, www.youtube.com/watch?v=qybUFny7y8w.
>
>   date accessed
>
> Accessed 8 Apr. 2016.

e. DVD extras Add the title of the extra (in quotation marks).

>   DVD extra
>
> "The Making of *Winter's Bone.*" *Winter's Bone.* Directed by Debra Granik,
>
> performances by Jennifer Lawrence and John Hawkes. Lionsgate, 2010.

41. Television or radio broadcast If your source is an episode in a series, think of that series as a *container*, and provide full information about both your source and its container. Start your entry with the title of the series or episode. Follow that with a list of the relevant contributors and include the network on which the series or episode aired. Because the director may change from episode to episode,

---

other contributors, such as the creator or producer, may be more relevant. Include the date of the program. If your project emphasizes an individual, begin with that person's name.

a. Series

series title

How I Met Your Mother. Created by Carter Bays and Craig Thomas, produced by

network

Bays et al., performances by Josh Radnor and Alyson Hannigan. CBS,

broadcast dates

19 Sept. 2009–31 Mar. 2014.

b. Episode

"There Will Be a Future." *Narcos,* performance by Wagner Moura, season 1,

episode 5. *Netflix,* www.netflix.com/watch/80025317?trackId=14170104&

tctx=0%2C4%2C316dcd53-46a2-4312-bf21-cdfc24d01eb6-43631335.

c. Single program

Persuasion. By Jane Austen. Adapted by Simon Burke, performances by Julia Davis

and Rupert Penry-Jones, PBS, 13 Jan. 2008.

d. Podcast For a podcast, add the full URL for the file.

"The Giant Pool of Money." *This American Life,* narrated by Ira Glass, Natl. Public

Radio, 9 May 2008, www.thisamericanlife.org/radio-archives/episode/355/

the-giant-pool-of-money.

42. Musical or other audio recording Begin with whichever part of the entry is more relevant to your project—the name of the composer or performer, or the title of the CD or song. Place the title of shorter works, such as a song, in quotation marks. Italicize the titles of longer works, such as the title of an opera, but not the titles of symphonies identified only by form, number, and key, such as Brahms's Symphony no. 1.

a. CD, LP, audiobook

Adamo, Mark. *Little Women.* Performance by Stephanie Novacek et al., conducted

prod. co. & release date

by Patrick Summers, Ondine, 2001.

Brahms, Johannes. Symphony no. 1. Performance by Chicago Symphony Orchestra,

conducted by Georg Solti, Decca, 1992.

b. Song or selection from a CD or LP or a chapter from an audiobook

Vetiver. "Last Hurrah." *Complete Strangers,* Easy Sound Recording Company, 2015.

c. Compressed music file (MP3, MP4)

Beyoncé. "Formation." *Tangerine*, Parkwood/Columbia, 2016, listen.tidal.com/
artist/1566.

d. Online sound file or clip For a sound recording accessed online, combine the format for a web page with the format for a sound recording.

Example 32, 188

"The General Prologue, The Knight's Portrait, II, 43–78." *The Riverside Chaucer*,
3rd ed., 2000. *Baragona's Literary Resources*, alanbaragona.wordpress.com/
the-criyng-and-the-soun/the-general-prologue-the-knights-portrait-ii-43-
78-baragona/.

43. Live performance The entry for a performance is similar to that for a film. Include the venue and city of the performance and the date of the performance you attended. If your project emphasizes the composer, writer, or performer, begin the entry with that information. If the performance is untitled, include a descriptive label.

a. Ensemble

The Importance of Being Earnest. By Oscar Wilde, directed by Jerry Chipman,
performance by Brian Everson et al., Theatre Memphis, 27 Jan. 2012,
[group] [perf. date]
Lohrey Stage, Memphis.

b. Individual

[performer] [label]
Hartig, Caroline. Clarinet recital, 18 Nov. 2011, Brigham Young U, Provo.

44. Musical composition To document a musical composition itself rather than a specific performance, recording, or published version of it, include only the composer and the title of the work (in italics unless the composition is identified only by form, number, and key).

[composer] [untitled symphony]
Schumann, Robert. Symphony no. 1 in B-flat major, op. 38.

45. Lecture, speech, or debate Treat the speaker as the author; place the title in quotation marks (if there is one); and indicate the occasion and sponsoring organization (if relevant), location, date, and mode of delivery (such as *Lecture* or *Address*). If the lecture, speech, or debate is untitled, replace the title with a brief descriptive label.

[speaker] [title] [sponsor] [location]
Capri, Frank. "The Peace Movement of the 1960s." 92nd Street Y, New York.
[date]
14 Mar. 2010. Lecture.

Example 18, 174

46. Table For a table included in your project, place source information in a note below the table. For a table that you are discussing but that does not appear in your project, include an entry in your list of works cited following the model below.

         author   title   label   website

United States Senate. "Senate Salaries since 1789." Table. *US Senate*, 7 June 2012,

    www.senate.gov/artandhistory/history/common/briefing/senate_salaries.htm.

Example 18, 174

47. Work of art For a work of art included in your project, place source information in the figure caption. For a work that you discuss but that does not appear in your project, include an entry in your list of works cited following the models below.

a. Original work

                           date of

    artist   title   production   location

Pollack, Jackson. *One (Number 31)*. 1950. Museum of Modern Art, New York.

b. Reproduction of a work of art

    Lichtenstein, Roy. *Whaam!* 1963. Acrylic on canvas. *Responding to Art: Form, Content, and Context.*

    By Robert Bersson, McGraw-Hill, 2004.

48. Comic or cartoon For a cartoon reproduced in your project, provide source information in the caption. For cartoons that you discuss without providing a copy of the image in your project, include an entry in your list of works cited following the models below.

a. Cartoon or comic strip

    artist   title   publication information

Thaves, Bob. "Frank and Ernest." *Evening Sun* [Norwich], 26 Nov. 2015, p. 14.

b. Comic book or graphic novel

          authors   title

Pekar, Harvey, and Joyce Brabner. *Our Cancer Year*, illustrated by Frank

          pub. info

Stack, Running Press, 1994.

49. Map or chart For a map or chart reproduced in your project, provide source information in the caption. For a map or chart discussed but not included in your project, include an entry in your list of works cited following the model below.

Example 18, 174

"The Invasion of Sicily: Allied Advance to Messina (23 July–17 August 1943)."

The West Point Atlas of American Wars, vol. 2, edited by Vincent J.

Esposito. Praeger, 1959, p. 247.

50. Advertisement For an advertisement reproduced in your project, provide source information in the caption. For an advertisement discussed but not included in your project, include an entry in your list of works cited following the models below.

> Earthlink Cable Internet. Advertisement. *Metro*, 17 Apr. 2007, p. 11.
>
> Infiniti. Advertisement. *Yahoo.com*. Accessed 20 Apr. 2016.
>
> Domino's Pizza. Advertisement. *Comedy Central*, 2 Aug. 2006.

Miscellaneous Sources—Printed and Electronic
其他来源——纸质版与电子版

51. Government document If no author is listed, use the name of the governing nation and the government department and agency (if any) that produced the document, as you would for a work with a corporate author.

Example 7, 179
Example 19, 175

> United States, War Department. *Advanced Map and Aerial Photograph*
>
> *Reading*. Government Printing Office, 1941.

For congressional documents, include the number and session of Congress and the number and type of document.

a. Printed

> United States, Congress, House. *Combat Bonus Act*. Government Publishing
>
> Office, 2008. 110th Congress, 2nd session, House Report 6760.

b. Online

> United States, Congress, House. *Combat Bonus Act*. Library of Congress, 31 July
>
> 2008, www.congress.gov/bill/110th-congress/house-bill/6760.

52. Legal source

> United States, Supreme Court. *Gideon vs. Wainwright*. 1963. *FindLaw*, caselaw.findlaw.com/
>
> us-supreme-court/372/335.html.

53. Letter (published)

a. Single letter Cite a single letter as you would a selection from an edited book or anthology but add the recipient's name, the date the letter was written, and the letter number (if there is one).

Example 10, 180

> Brooks, Phillips. "To Agnes." 24 Sept. 1882. *Children's Letters: A Collection of*
>
> *Letters Written to Children by Famous Men and Women*, edited by Elizabeth
>
> Colson and Anna Gansevoort Chittenden, Hinds, 1905, pp. 3–4.

b. Collection of letters Cite as you would an edited book or anthology.

Example 8, 179

Examples 24–26,
184–87
Example
41, 191–92

MLA Works-Cited
Entries

53. Letter
(published)
54. Interview
55. Personal
correspondence
56. Diary or journal

54. Interview Treat a published interview as you would an article in a periodical. Treat an interview broadcast on radio or television or podcasted as you would a broadcast. For an unpublished interview you conducted, include the name of the person interviewed, the label *Personal interview, Telephone interview,* or *Email interview,* and the date on which the interview took place.

person interviewed   label   date
Harberg, Amanda. Personal interview. 11 Feb. 2016.

55. Personal correspondence To document personal correspondence, such as a letter, include a descriptive label such as *Letter to the author.*

a. Letter

letter writer   label   date written
Gould, Stephen Jay. Letter to the author. 13 Nov. 1986.

b. Email

email   author   subject line
Elbow, Peter. "Re: bibliography about resistance." Received by Rebecca Howard,
date sent
12 Apr. 2016.

c. Memorandum Very few institutions send out printed memos anymore, but if you need to document one, treat it as you would an email message.

d. Instant message (IM)

Grimm, Laura. Message to the author. 14 June 2012.

Example 10, 180

56. Diary or journal

a. Single entry, published Treat an entry in a published diary or journal like an article in an edited book or anthology, but include a descriptive label (*Diary entry*) and the date of composition after the entry title.

b. Single entry, unpublished

author   title
Zook, Aaron. "Sketches for *Aesop's Foibles* (new musical)."
label   entry date
Journal entry. 1 May 2016.

Example 8, 179

c. Diary or journal, published Treat a complete diary or journal as you would an edited book or anthology.

21 Using MLA Style for Informational Notes 参考文献注释采用MLA格式

In addition to in-text citations, MLA style allows researchers to include informational notes to provide relevant, but potentially distracting, content or to provide bibliographic information about one or more sources. MLA style recommends using a list of endnotes at the end of the project. To identify informational notes in the text, include a superscript (above-the-line) arabic number that corresponds to the note number in the list of endnotes. Include an entry for each source in your list of works cited.

> Beneath the crude humor of *Zap* and similar comics lay insightful commentary on society and its principles, which many readers found to be a refreshing change from mainstream superhero titles.[1] . . . Comics like Tomine's provide a subject or situation that readers can identify with more easily than, say, Super-man's battles with Brainiac.[2]

Notes Heading (centered), new page

1/2" [1]. According to Schnakenberg, more than two million copies of *Zap* comics were in print by 1999.

[2]. For an intriguing argument that the world of classic comic book superheroes is not so different from our own—including a discussion of how comics before World War II commented on then current events—see Wright 1–28.

Use *content notes* to provide information that clarifies or justifies a point in your text, but avoid notes that include interesting digressions that could distract your readers. You can also use content notes to acknowledge the contributions of others (tutors, classmates, and so on) to the preparation of your project.

Bibliographic notes can add information about a source or point readers to other sources on the topic. If several sources provide the same information, cite the most valuable source in your text, and list the others in a bibliographic note. Then include the full citation of all these sources in your list of works cited.

22 Formatting a Paper in MLA Style
论文版式采用MLA格式

The care with which you cite and document your sources reflects the care you have taken in writing your research project. Continue that care by formatting your project in the way your readers expect. For most writing projects in literature and composition, follow the MLA's formatting guidelines.

22a Margins and Spacing 边距和间距

Student Model
Research project, MLA style, 202–11

Set one-inch margins at the top, bottom, and sides of your paper. Double-space the entire paper, including long quotations, the list of works cited, and any endnotes. Indent the first line of each paragraph by one-half inch, and do not add an extra space between paragraphs. Use a hanging indent for each entry in the list of works cited: The first line should be flush with the left margin with subsequent lines indented one-half inch. (For more on creating a hanging indent in a word processing program, see the Tech box on the next page.)

22b Typeface 字体

> **More about**
> Choosing a typeface and type size, 52–53

Choose a standard typeface, such as Times New Roman or Arial, in an easily readable size (usually 12 points).

22c Header 页眉

MLA style requires that each page of your project include a header, consisting of your surname and the page number. Place the header in the upper right-hand corner, one-half inch from the upper edge and one inch from the right edge of the page.

Tech Creating a Header

Most word processing software allows you to insert a header. In Microsoft Word, select "Header" from the Insert tab. Any information you type into the header space will then appear at the top of every page of your manuscript. You can also choose to insert page numbers to paginate your project automatically.

Tech   Indentation

The major style guides (MLA, APA, *Chicago*, CSE) were initially written before the widespread use of personal computers, when most writers still worked on typewriters. To create a paragraph or hanging indent on a typewriter, the typist would hit the space bar five times or set a tab. Now, just about everyone creates writing projects on a computer, where paragraphs and hanging indents are created using the Ruler or Paragraph Dialog box.

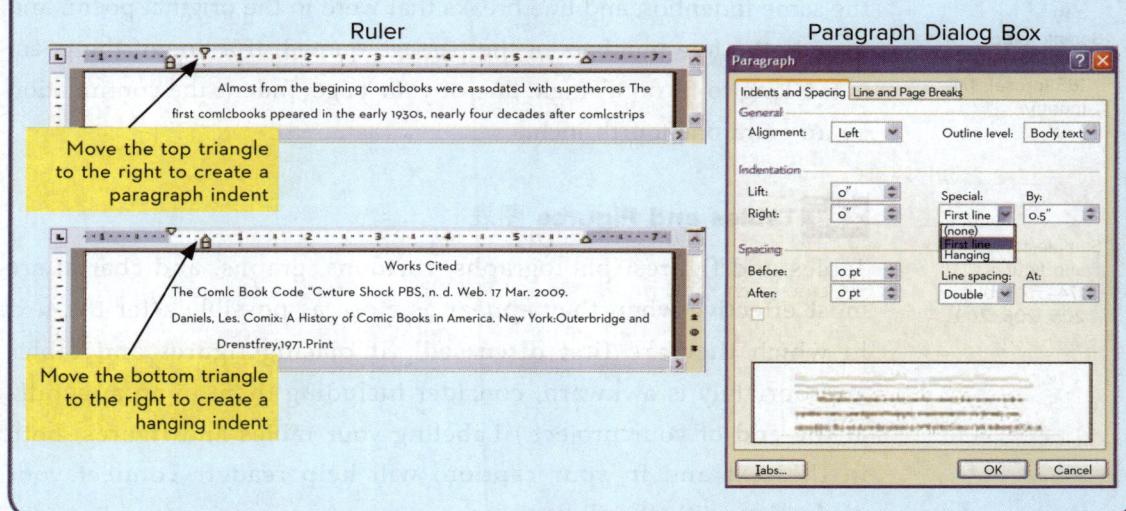

Ruler

Almost from the begining comlcbooks were assodated with supetheroes The first comlcbooks ppeared in the early 1930s, nearly four decades after comlcstrips

Move the top triangle to the right to create a paragraph indent

Works Cited
The Comlc Book Code "Cwture Shock PBS, n. d. Web. 17 Mar. 2009.
Daniels, Les. Comix: A History of Comic Books in America. New York:Outerbridge and Drenstfrey,1971.Print

Move the bottom triangle to the right to create a hanging indent

Paragraph Dialog Box

Paragraph

Indents and Spacing | Line and Page Breaks
General
Alignment: Left   Outline level: Body text
Indentation
Lift: 0"   Special: By:
Right: 0"   First line   0.5"
          (none)
          First line
          Hanging
Spacing
Before: 0 pt   Line spacing: At:
After: 0 pt   Double
☐

Tabs...   OK   Cancel

22d Identifying Information 识别信息

No title page is required in MLA style. Instead, include the following identifying information in the upper left-hand corner of the first page of your research project, one inch from the top and left edges of the paper:

- Your name
- Your instructor's name
- The number of the course in which you are submitting the paper
- The date

If your instructor requires a title page, ask for formatting instructions or follow the model on page 247.

22e Title 标题

Center the title of your project and insert it two lines below the date. Do not put quotation marks around your title or italicize it. Drop down two more lines before beginning to type the first paragraph of your research project.

> **More about**
> Crafting a title, 41

22f Long Quotations 大段引文

Set quotations of prose longer than four lines of your text as a block: Omit the quotation marks, and indent the entire quotation one-half inch from the left margin of your text. When quoting four or more lines of poetry, indent all the lines one-half inch from the left margin; keep the same indention and line breaks that were in the original poem, and include the line numbers of the passage quoted. If a line of the poem is too long to fit on a single line of your page, indent the continuation by an extra one-fourth inch.

▶ **More about**
Block quotations, 165, 170–71, 449
Sample block quotations, 165 (prose), 171 (poetry)

22g Tables and Figures 图表

▶ Sample tables and figures, 174–75 (table); 205, 206, 209

Tables and figures (photographs, cartoons, graphs, and charts) are most effective when they appear as close as possible after the text in which they are first discussed. (If placing figures and tables appropriately is awkward, consider including them in an appendix at the end of your project.) Labeling your tables and figures, both in the text and in your caption, will help readers connect your discussion with the illustration:

- Refer to the visual in your text using the word *table* or the abbreviation *fig.*, and number tables and figures in a separate sequence using arabic numerals (table 1, table 2; fig. 1, fig. 2). MLA style uses lowercase for in-text references to tables and figures unless they begin a sentence: "Table 1 presents 2010 data, and table 2 presents 2012 data."

- Accompany each illustration with the word *Table* or the abbreviation *Fig.*, the appropriate number, and a brief, explanatory title. Customarily, table numbers and titles appear above the table, and figure numbers and titles appear below the figure. Generally, they use the same margins as the rest of the paper.

- If additional information is needed, provide an explanatory caption after the number and title. (Remember that your text

Writing Responsibly   Of Deadlines and Paperclips

Instructors expect students to turn in thoughtful, carefully proofread, and neatly formatted papers on time—usually in class on the due date. Another expectation is that the writer will clip or staple the pages of the paper *before* it is submitted. Do justice to yourself by being fully prepared.

to SELF

should explain what the figure or table demonstrates. That information should not be repeated in the caption.)

- If you borrow the illustration or borrow information needed to create the illustration, cite your source. Any photographs or drawings you create yourself should identify the subject but do not need a citation. Citations usually appear below the table in a source note or in the figure caption. If you document the illustration in a figure caption or source note, you do not need to include an entry in your list of works cited.

22h Printing and Binding 打印装订

If you are submitting a hard copy of your project, print it using a high-quality printer (make sure it has plenty of ink), on opaque 8½ × 11–inch white paper. Most instructors do not want you to enclose your project in a binder. Unless your instructor tells you otherwise, staple or paperclip the pages together in the upper left-hand corner.

22i Portfolios 文件夹打包

Many instructors ask students to submit the final draft of the research project in a portfolio, which may include an outline, preliminary notes and drafts, a working or annotated bibliography, and a personal statement describing their writing process and what they have learned from the experience (Figure 22.1).

More about
Outlining, 25–26,
    132–33
Note taking, 9–12,
    123–30
Writing a first
    draft, 26
Working or anno-
    tated bibliogra-
    phy, 102–04

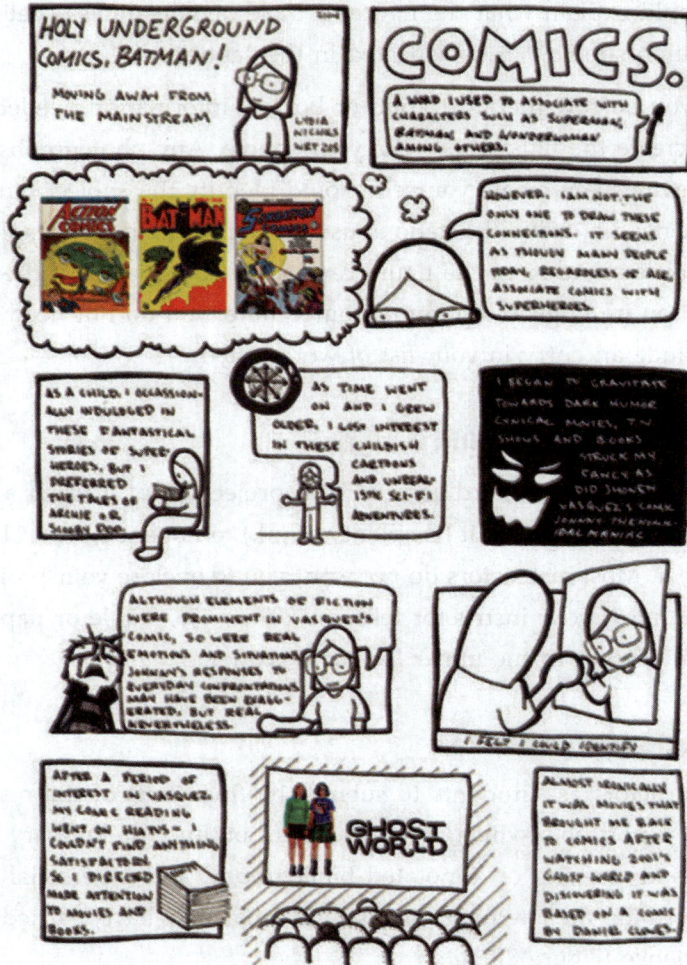

FIGURE 22.1 Page 1 of Lydia Nichols's personal statement Nichols created a visual personal statement to explain how her interest in underground comics developed.

Student Model 学生范文 **Research Project: MLA Style**

In the sample student research project that follows, Lydia Nichols fulfills her responsibilities to topic and audience. She uses comparison-contrast to support her claim that underground comics are more innovative than their mainstream cousins, and she provides a historical overview to fill in the background her readers lack. Her research draws on a variety of print and online sources, and she uses visuals to support some of her points.

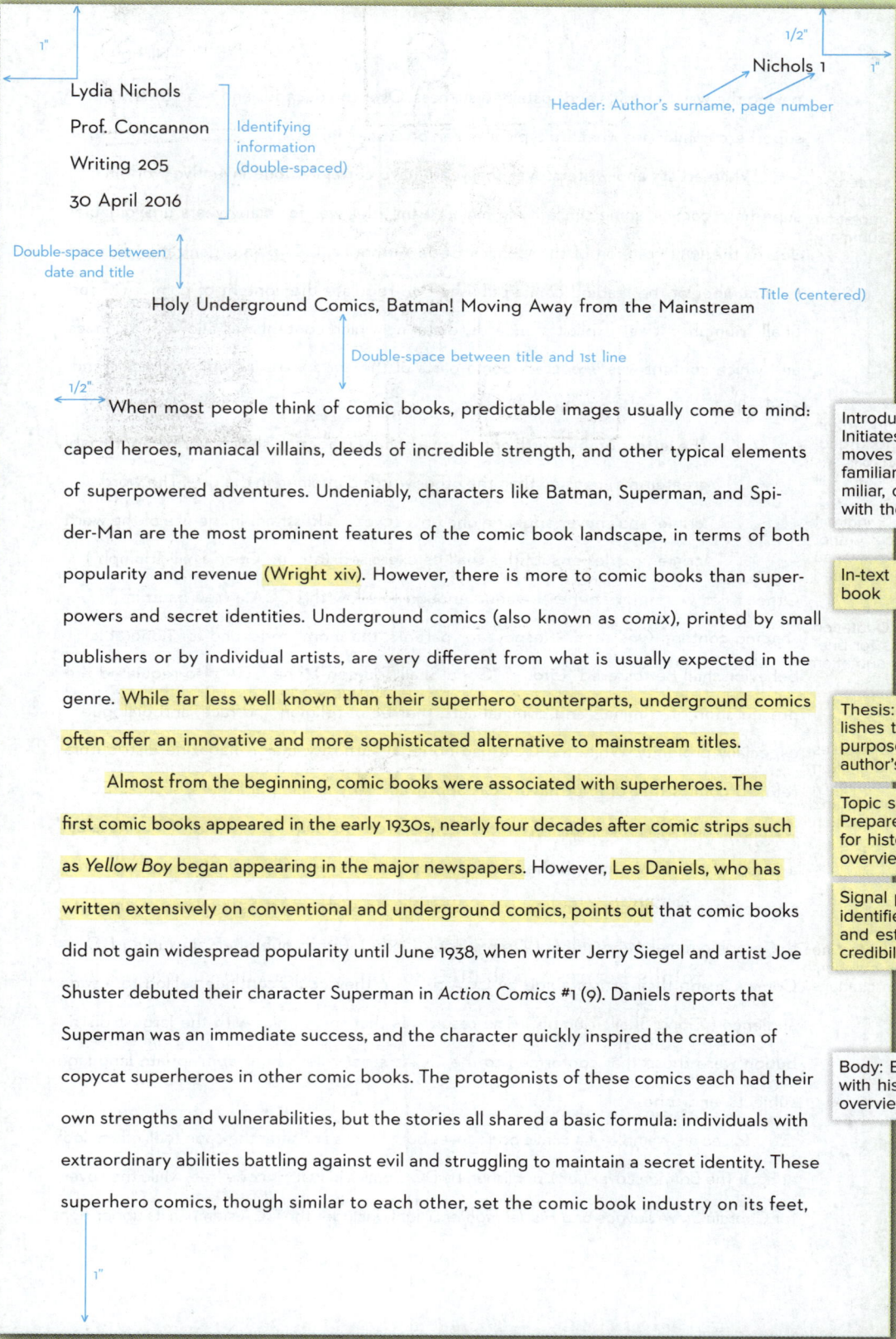

Lydia Nichols

Prof. Concannon

Writing 205

30 April 2016

Identifying information (double-spaced)

1/2"

1"

Header: Author's surname, page number

Double-space between date and title

Holy Underground Comics, Batman! Moving Away from the Mainstream

Title (centered)

Double-space between title and 1st line

1/2"

When most people think of comic books, predictable images usually come to mind: caped heroes, maniacal villains, deeds of incredible strength, and other typical elements of superpowered adventures. Undeniably, characters like Batman, Superman, and Spider-Man are the most prominent features of the comic book landscape, in terms of both popularity and revenue (Wright xiv). However, there is more to comic books than superpowers and secret identities. Underground comics (also known as *comix*), printed by small publishers or by individual artists, are very different from what is usually expected in the genre. While far less well known than their superhero counterparts, underground comics often offer an innovative and more sophisticated alternative to mainstream titles.

Almost from the beginning, comic books were associated with superheroes. The first comic books appeared in the early 1930s, nearly four decades after comic strips such as *Yellow Boy* began appearing in the major newspapers. However, Les Daniels, who has written extensively on conventional and underground comics, points out that comic books did not gain widespread popularity until June 1938, when writer Jerry Siegel and artist Joe Shuster debuted their character Superman in *Action Comics* #1 (9). Daniels reports that Superman was an immediate success, and the character quickly inspired the creation of copycat superheroes in other comic books. The protagonists of these comics each had their own strengths and vulnerabilities, but the stories all shared a basic formula: individuals with extraordinary abilities battling against evil and struggling to maintain a secret identity. These superhero comics, though similar to each other, set the comic book industry on its feet,

Introduction: Initiates contrast, moves from familiar to unfamiliar, concludes with thesis

In-text citation—book

Thesis: Establishes topic, purpose, and author's position

Topic sentence: Prepares reader for historical overview

Signal phrase identifies source and establishes credibility

Body: Begins with historical overview

1"

203

paving the way to profits and sustained success. Over the decades and even today, superhero comics are what are typically seen on store shelves.

[Topic sentence: Claim supported by quotation and summary]

While artists and writers over the years have certainly done inventive work in superhero comics, some similarity in mainstream titles was for many years unavoidable due to the 1954 creation of the Comics Code Authority (CCA), an organization formed by a number of the leading comic publishers to regulate the content of comics ("Good Shall Triumph"). It set explicit standards, dictating which content was allowed in comics and which content was expected. Some parts of the code were incredibly specific and controlling:

[Block indention for long quotation; ellipses mark cut]

[Indirect source: Author unknown, so title used]

> The letters of the word "crime" on a comics magazine shall never be appreciably greater in dimension than the other words contained in the title. The word "crime" shall never appear alone on a cover. . . . Restraint in the use of the word "crime" in titles or subtitles shall be exercised. (qtd. in "Good Shall Triumph")

[Quotation marks for brief quotation]

Other rules were more general—vague enough to allow the CCA a free hand in shaping content. One read, "Respect for parents, the moral code, and for honorable behavior shall be fostered" (qtd. in "Good Shall Triumph"). The CCA also regulated the presentation of criminals and criminal acts, themes of religion and race, and dialogue, especially profanity. While the CCA had no legal authority, major magazine distributors refused comics that did not have CCA approval. Many comic publishers, such as EC Comics (*Vault of Horror, Tales from the Crypt*), were virtually forced out of business as a result of the CCA, though the banned titles would eventually gain the appreciation and respect of collectors and aspiring comic artists such as Art Spiegelman, author of the graphic novel *Maus* (1986) ("Comic Book Code"). Other publishers, including DC Comics, made their artists abide by CCA rules so they could continue selling to a wide audience ("Good Shall Triumph"). The result was that the comics with the largest distribution were those that conformed to the CCA's strict rules about appropriate language, subjects, and tone.

[Paragraph uses combination of summary, paraphrase, and quotation]

[Websites: no page numbers in citations]

To see an example of a comic book cover both before and after the code took effect, look at fig. 1. The *Batman* cover (left), published by DC Comics in 1940, is code free, while the cover for *Captain Steve Savage and His Jet Fighters* (right) includes the CCA stamp in its upper-right

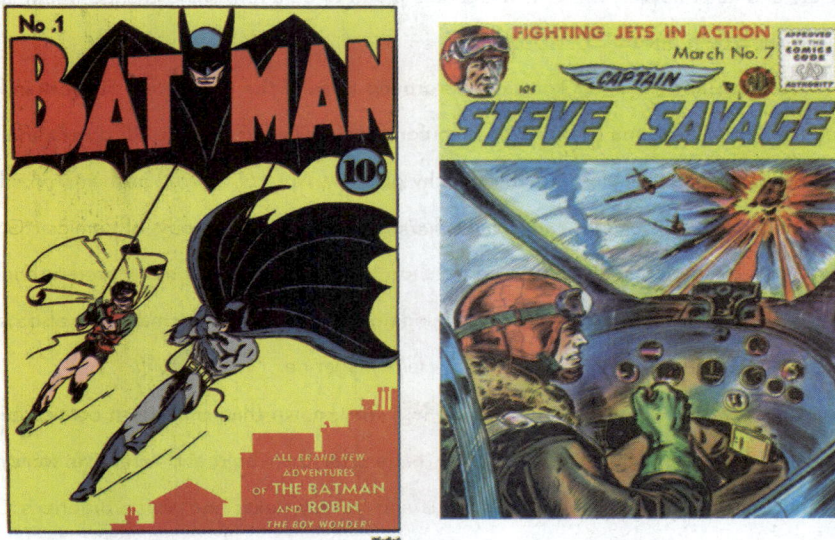

Fig. 1. Batman (with his sidekick, Robin, the Boy Wonder) flies into Gotham in his own comic book (left) in 1940, before the institution of the Comics Code Authority, while Captain Steve Savage (right), ace fighter pilot, shoots down an enemy plane. The CCA stamp ("Approved by the Comics Code Authority") appears in the upper-right corner of the *Captain Steve Savage* comic.

corner. Captain Steve Savage made his first appearance in January 1950, not long after the start of the Korean War—but prior to the CCA's establishment. Issues of the comic book ran without the CCA stamp until 1954, when the CCA took effect; after that, all issues (and reissues—it appears certain covers were recycled) featured the stamp prominently.

In the 1960s, in contrast to mainstream CCA-approved superhero comics, alternatives began to appear. According to Steven Heller, an art director at the *New York Times* and a founder of the Masters in Graphic Arts Program at the School for Visual Arts in New York, Robert Crumb's *Zap* (1968) initiated the "underground comix revolution" (101). Crumb and other like-minded artists did not submit their comics for CCA approval. Though this limited the distribution of their work, it allowed them artistic freedom. From its first issue, *Zap* satirized mainstream, conservative beliefs and did not shy away from sexual or political content (Heller 101–02). Beneath the crude humor of *Zap* and similar comics lay insightful commentary on

Figure number links visual to text discussion

Signal phrase identifies source and establishes credibility

society and its principles, which many readers found to be a refreshing change from mainstream superhero titles.

Topic sentence: Claim supported by visual, analysis; figure number links discussion to visual

Figures analyzed in text

Besides *Zap*, other well-known underground titles of the era include *Subvert* and *Weirdo*. Gilbert Shelton's hilariously nonconformist *Fabulous Furry Freak Brothers* and Crumb's most recognizable hero, the sketchy guru *Mr. Natural*, starred in their own, often X-rated, comic books (see fig. 2). *Comiclopedia*, an online encyclopedia of comic artists maintained by the legendary Dutch comic shop Lambiek, notes that many underground comics were inspired by *Mad* magazine founding father Harvey Kurtzman, who also gave Crumb and Shelton their first break in his *Help!* magazine.

Topic sentence: Claim supported by examples

Underground comics continue to be less well known than superhero comics, but they are better respected among mature readers for their bold and inventive content. Graphic novels, such as Spiegelman's *Maus* and Harvey Pekar and Joyce Brabner's *Our Cancer Year* (1994), have successfully addressed some of the most highly charged and sensitive subjects in modern society.[1] Both of these show the subtlety and wide range

Caption explains how visual supports claim

Fig. 2. Examples of late '60s underground comics. In defiance of the authoritarian standards of the Comics Code Authority and influenced by '50s humor magazine *Mad*, underground artists pushed the boundaries of humor, propriety, and good taste.

of topics that underground comics explore. Daniels notes that underground comics frequently explore themes of sex and sexual identity, politics, and social issues (165), as shown in Crumb's work, which Heller describes as taking a satirical approach to countercultural topics (101–02).

Mainstream superhero comics are set on an epic scale—depicting amazing feats, heroic battles between good and evil, and the like—while underground comics tend to focus on everyday life. Steven Weiner, who reviews graphic novels for *Library Journal*, called Adrian Tomine, for example, "a master of pseudorealistic stories" due to his ability to present an ordinary situation as profoundly interesting and complex (58; see fig. 3). Comics like Tomine's provide a subject or situation that readers can identify with more easily than, say, Superman's battles with Brainiac.[2] The United Nations' World Food Programme (WFP) recognized the broad appeal of the genre when it hired *The New York Times* bestselling graphic novelist Joshua Dysart to travel to Iraq and create a graphic novel highlighting the humanitarian work of the WFP and the people it tries to help. The resulting comic, *Living Level 3*, received worldwide attention when it was serialized in *The Huffington Post* in January 2016.

The quirky perspectives of underground artists would be impossible to include in mainstream comics because the structure for producing and publishing mainstream comics limits the input of the artists working on them. The modern comic book industry is a huge business, selling not only comics but also related merchandise such as T-shirts, toys, and video games, not to mention tickets to comic book–inspired movies. Story decisions involving major characters such as Batman and the Hulk have to be made with profits in mind. Because mainstream comic publishers often change the creative teams working on their titles (Herndon 23) and because teams can include dozens of members (McCloud 180), individual artists can have only so much impact on a particular character or story. Most mainstream comics are the result of work done by many different people.

Topic sentence: Claim supported by example, visual, quotation

Bibliographic note

Citation: Placement clarifies which information comes from which source

In contrast, the individual artist in the underground realm has almost total control in creating his or her comic book. The creative teams working on underground titles are usually very small, and they rarely change (Herndon 23). **Daniels notes** that underground comic artists are not controlled by corporate interests that discourage daring material that might not sell (165, 180). This freedom allows for the uninhibited creativity that distinguishes underground comics from their more commercially oriented counterparts.

Underground artists not only push the envelope in terms of content but also incorporate experimental visual devices, earning critical praise for breaking away from traditional comic layouts in favor of more artistic perspectives. Artists such as Daniel Clowes argue that comic art can be more evocative than film, especially in the use of nonlinear storytelling techniques (Hignite 18). *New York Times* columnist John Hodgman agrees: Discussing a moment of existential crisis in Kevin Huizenga's *Ganges* #1, he writes, "I have never seen any film or read any prose that gets at that frozen moment when we suddenly feel our mortality, when God is seen or denied, as effectively as a comic panel." Artist Chris Ware, in graphic novels like *Jimmy Corrigan: The Smartest Kid on Earth* and *Building Stories*, manipulates the borders and frames in his comics so extensively that even reading his works can feel like an art to be mastered. The demands his comics place on the reader create an interaction between viewer and artist that is unheard of in the pages of superhero titles.

While Ware and Clowes demonstrate how the page can be used to create innovative and complicated layouts, other underground artists excel at creating simple, striking visuals. Unlike mainstream comics, which depict dynamic scenes through loud, flamboyant colors, underground comics often achieve their effects through simplicity. Frequently, they are printed in black and white or with limited colors, with characters rendered in clean, bold lines. The clarity and lack of clutter in such art allows for immediate storytelling (see fig. 3).

Obviously, most underground comics are not intended for young children. Yet because of the childish connotations of the term "comic," most adults overlook the fascinating work that underground comic artists do. The association of comics with

208

©1999 by Adrian Tomine. Used with permission.

Fig. 3. Comic whose characters face realistic challenges—the loss of a loved one, parental guilt—that readers can easily relate to. From Adrian Tomine, *Optic Nerve* #6, Drawn and Quarterly, Feb. 1999, p. 22.

[Source information in caption]

superheroes and children has made reading comics a source of shame for many adults. As Clowes comments, "I think that the average reader is far more open to a well-designed book than a standard comic book. . . . Very few would feel comfortable reading a standard comic book pamphlet" (qtd. in Hignite 17). Artists such as Scott McCloud have changed this

[Establishes credibility]

perception of comic books by offering a broader definition of what a comic is. According to McCloud, comics are "juxtaposed pictorial and other images in a deliberate sequence" (12). This definition includes not only what one might find in the latest Spider-Man comic, but also the experimental work that McCloud and his underground colleagues are creating.

[Signal phrase and parenthetical page reference bookend apt quotation]

McCloud and others have succeeded in bringing underground comics to a wider audience. Since the 1980s, underground comics have been finding their way into gallery and museum exhibitions, where the craftsmanship of the individual comic book artist can be better appreciated (Hignite 18). Major newspapers like *The New York Times* have begun featuring underground comics in their pages, including serialized graphic novels such as *George Sprott (1894-1975)* and *Watergate Sue*. The market for underground comics has also expanded through Internet venues such as *eBay*, where interested readers can find not only new titles but also classic comix otherwise available only in specialty shops. The Internet has also become an outlet for direct distribution through artists' websites, making independent titles not only more accessible to consumers but also more affordable for individual artists to produce and market (Fenty, Houp, and Taylor, par. 1). While underground comics may never sell as well or be as large a part of popular culture as Superman and his ilk, their creators will likely continue to be heroes to anyone seeking courage, creativity, and artistic quality in their comics.

Notes

Heading (centered), new page

1. These are iconic comics; Smith goes so far as to call *Maus* "one of the most important comics in the history of the medium" (509).

2. For an intriguing argument that the world of classic comic book superheroes is not so different from our own—including a discussion of how comics before World War II commented on then current events—see Wright 1-28.

Works Cited

"The Comic Book Code." *Culture Shock,* PBS, 2000, www.pbs.org/wgbh/cultureshock/flashpoints/visualarts/comiccode.html.

"Comics History: Underground Comix and the Underground Press." *Comiclopedia,* Lambiek, 2016, www.lambiek.net/comics/underground.htm.

Daniels, Les. *Comix: A History of Comic Books in America.* Outerbridge, 1971.

Fenty, Sean, et al. "Webcomics: The Influence and Continuation of the Comix Revolution." *ImageTexT,* vol. 1, no. 2, 2004, 22 pars., www.english.ufl.edu/imagetext/archives/v1_2/group/index.shtml.

"'Good Shall Triumph over Evil': The Comic Book Code of 1954." *History Matters: The U.S. History Survey Course on the Web.* American Social History Project/ Center for Media and Learning, CUNY, and the Center for History and New Media, George Mason, 2006, historymatters.gmu.edu/d/6543/.

Heller, Steven. "Zap Comics." *Print,* May/June 2000, pp. 100–05. *Academic OneFile,* www.ebscohost.com/ezproxy/zap_comics/print/2000_0506/.

Herndon, L. Kristin. "Mainstream Culture Is in Trouble, and Superman's Not Gonna Save It. But the Simpsons Might." *Art Papers,* vol. 21, no. 6, 1997, pp. 22–25. *Art Index,* ebscohost.com/tag/SIMPSONS,%20The%20(TV%20program)&offset=400.

Hignite, M. Todd. "Avant-Garde and Comics: Serious Cartooning." *Art Papers,* vol. 26, no. 1, 2002, pp. 17–19.

Hodgman, John. "Comics Chronicle." *The New York Times,* 4 June 2006, www.nytimes .com/2006/06/04/books/review/04hodgman.html.

McCloud, Scott. *Understanding Comics, the Invisible Art.* Harper Perennial, 1994.

Smith, Philip. "Spiegelman Studies Part 2 of 2: *Breakdowns, No Towers* and the Rest of the Canon." *Literature Compass,* vol. 12, no. 10, Oct. 2015, pp. 509–16. *Wiley Online Library,* doi:10.1111/lic3.12263.

Weiner, Stephen. "Beyond Superheroes: Comics Get Serious." *Library Journal,* vol. 7, no. 2, 2002, pp. 55–58. *Academic OneFile,* ebscohost.com/c/articles/5992770/ beyond-superheroes-comics-get-serious.

Wright, Bradford W. *Comic Book Nation: The Transformation of Youth Culture in America.* Johns Hopkins UP, 2001.

211

7

Documentation ＞

文献引用格式

Matters

APA Style　文献引用格式：APA格式

Use part 7 to learn, practice, and master these writer's responsibilities:

❏ **To Audience**

Cite and document sources so that readers can see where each use of sources begins and ends in your project; format your research project using APA style, in keeping with readers' expectations.

❏ **To Topic**

Cite and document sources to demonstrate that you have explored your topic fully.

❏ **To Other Writers**

Provide citations for all borrowed ideas and information, whether quoted, para-phrased, or summarized; document all sources cited in the research project in a reference list at the end of the project.

❏ **To Yourself**

Use sources to build knowledge, and cite them to show readers where your ideas begin and end; to enhance your ethos, or credibility; and to present your ideas effectively.

Book (Printed)

author   title   publication information

King, L. A. (2016). *Experience psychology*. New York, NY: McGraw-Hill Education.

publication date   place of publication   imprint-publisher

title

experience psychology

Third Edition

author → Laura A. King
University of Missouri, Columbia

publisher's imprint

Title page

publisher

publication date

place of publication

Copyright page

Look for the information you need to document a printed book on the book's title page and copyright page. In APA style, if more than one location for the publisher is listed on the title page, use the first. (For more about documenting a book, see pp. 226–33).

Journal Article (Printed)

author · year · title and subtitle (article)

Chaubal, M. & Taylor, T. (2015). Lessons from 5Pointz: Toward legal protection of collaborative, evolving heritage. *Future Anterior, 12*(1), 77–97.

vol. pages

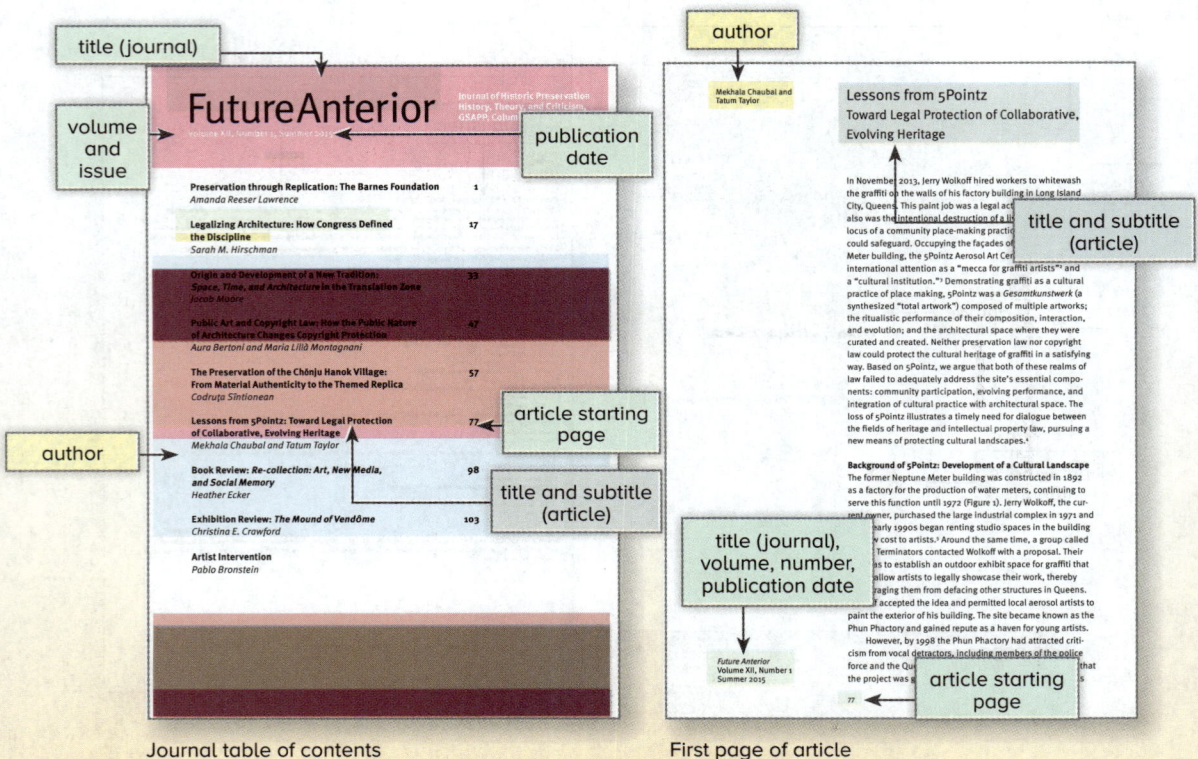

title (journal)

volume and issue

publication date

FutureAnterior
Journal of Historic Preservation History, Theory, and Criticism
GSAPP, Columbia

Volume XII, Number 1, Summer 2015

Preservation through Replication: The Barnes Foundation — 1
Amanda Reeser Lawrence

Legalizing Architecture: How Congress Defined the Discipline — 17
Sarah M. Hirschman

Origin and Development of a New Tradition: Space, Time, and Architecture in the Translation Zone — 33
Jacob Moore

Public Art and Copyright Law: How the Public Nature of Architecture Changes Copyright Protection — 47
Aura Bertoni and Maria Lillà Montagnani

The Preservation of the Chŏnju Hanok Village: From Material Authenticity to the Themed Replica — 57
Codruța Sintionean

Lessons from 5Pointz: Toward Legal Protection of Collaborative, Evolving Heritage — 77
Mekhala Chaubal and Tatum Taylor

Book Review: Re-collection: Art, New Media, and Social Memory — 98
Heather Ecker

Exhibition Review: The Mound of Vendôme — 103
Christina E. Crawford

Artist Intervention
Pablo Bronstein

author

article starting page

title and subtitle (article)

Journal table of contents

author

Mekhala Chaubal and Tatum Taylor

title and subtitle (article)

Lessons from 5Pointz
Toward Legal Protection of Collaborative, Evolving Heritage

In November 2013, Jerry Wolkoff hired workers to whitewash the graffiti on the walls of his factory building in Long Island City, Queens. This paint job was a legal act, but it also was the intentional destruction of a locus of a community place-making practice that preservation could safeguard. Occupying the façades of the Neptune Meter building, the 5Pointz Aerosol Art Center attracted international attention as a "mecca for graffiti artists" and a "cultural institution." Demonstrating graffiti as a cultural practice of place making, 5Pointz was a *Gesamtkunstwerk* (a synthesized "total artwork") composed of multiple artworks; the ritualistic performance of their composition, interaction, and evolution; and the architectural space where they were curated and created. Neither preservation law nor copyright law could protect the cultural heritage of graffiti in a satisfying way. Based on 5Pointz, we argue that both of these realms of law failed to adequately address the site's essential components: community participation, evolving performance, and integration of cultural practice with architectural space. The loss of 5Pointz illustrates a timely need for dialogue between the fields of heritage and intellectual property law, pursuing a new means of protecting cultural landscapes.

Background of 5Pointz: Development of a Cultural Landscape
The former Neptune Meter building was constructed in 1892 as a factory for the production of water meters, continuing to serve this function until 1972 (Figure 1). Jerry Wolkoff, the current owner, purchased the large industrial complex in 1971 and in the early 1990s began renting studio spaces in the building at low cost to artists. Around the same time, a group called the Terminators contacted Wolkoff with a proposal. Their plans to establish an outdoor exhibit space for graffiti that would allow artists to legally showcase their work, thereby discouraging them from defacing other structures in Queens. Wolkoff accepted the idea and permitted local aerosol artists to paint the exterior of his building. The site became known as the Phun Phactory and gained repute as a haven for young artists.

However, by 1998 the Phun Phactory had attracted criticism from vocal detractors, including members of the police force and the Queens that the project was

title and subtitle (article)

title (journal), volume, number, publication date

Future Anterior
Volume XII, Number 1
Summer 2015

77

article starting page

First page of article

Look for the information you need to document a journal article on the cover or table of contents of the journal and on the first and last pages of the article. (For more about documenting an article from a printed or electronic periodical, see pp. 233–37).

Journal Article from an Online Database

author   year   title and subtitle (article)

Joselit, J. W. (2016). The Brooklyn Thrill-Kill Gang and the great comic book scare of the 1950s.

               journal

American Jewish History, 100, 155–56. doi:10.1353/ajh.2016.0015

           vol.↑   pages

Database screen: full record of article

Taylor & Francis Online

Look for the information you need to document an article you accessed through an online database on the search results screen, the full record of the article, or the first and last pages of the article itself. (For more about documenting an article accessed through an online database, see pp. 233–37).

Short Work on a Website

author   pub. date   web page title   retrieval statement
Wulf, K. (2016, January 27). The importance of academic (history) writing. Retrieved
               URL for web page
    from https://scholarlykitchen.sspnet.org/2016/01/27/the-importance-of-academic-history-writing/

Web page

Frequently, the information you need to create a complete entry in the list of works cited is missing or difficult to find on web pages. Look at the top or bottom of the web page or home page or for a link to an "About" or "Contact Us" page. (For more about documenting online sources, see pp. 237–39).

23 Creating APA-Style In-Text Citations
文内引用使用APA格式

Developed by the American Psychological Association, APA style is used by researchers in psychology and many other social science disciplines, such as education, social work, and sociology. The *Publication Manual of the American Psychological Association* (6th ed.) requires that sources be cited in two ways:

- **Citation:** In the body of your project, provide an in-text citation for each source used.
- **Documentation:** At the project's end, provide a reference list.

In-text citations appear in the body of your project. They mark each use you make of a source, regardless of whether you are quoting, paraphrasing, or drawing on an idea. In-text citations should include just enough information for readers to locate the source in your reference list, which appears at the end of the project. They should also alert readers to shifts between *your* ideas and those you have borrowed from a source.

> **More about**
> Popular academic
> documentation
> styles, per
> discipline, 69
> MLA style,
> 157–211 (part 6)
> Chicago style,
> 256–71 (part 8)
> CSE style, 272–84
> (part 8)

23a Placing In-Text Citations So That Readers Know Where Borrowed Material Starts and Stops
使用文内引用，提示读者引文的起止位置

When you incorporate a quotation, paraphrase, summary, or idea from a source into your own prose, carefully consider the placement of the in-text citation, keeping the following goals in mind:

- To make clear exactly which material is drawn from the source
- To avoid distracting your reader

> **More about**
> What you do and
> do not need to
> cite, 122
> Signal phrases,
> 137–38
> Integrating
> borrowed mate-
> rial into your
> text, 144–45

Writing Responsibly · Citing and Documenting Sources

When you cite and document sources, you demonstrate how thoroughly you have researched your topic and how carefully you have thought about your sources, which encourages your audience to believe you are a credible researcher. In your citations and documentation, you acknowledge any material that you have borrowed from a source, and you join the conversation on your topic by adding your own interpretation. Accurate entries in the body of your project and list of references allow your audience to find and read your sources so that they can evaluate your interpretation and learn more about the subject themselves. Accurate entries also demonstrate the care with which you have written your research project, which further reinforces your credibility, or ethos.

to AUDIENCE

Quick

Reference **General Principles of In-Text Citation**

- Cite not only direct quotations but also paraphrases, summaries, and information gathered from a source, whether printed or online.
- Include the author's surname and the year of publication. You may place the name(s) in a signal phrase or in a parenthetical note.
- Place parenthetical citations after the borrowed material; if the author is named in a signal phrase, insert the year of publication in parentheses immediately following the author's name, and include the page reference at the end of the borrowed passage.
- For works with no author, use the first few words of the title in the author position.
- For works with multiple authors, use the word *and* before the last author in a signal phrase; replace the word *and* with an ampersand (&) in a parenthetical citation.
- Include a page or paragraph number when borrowing specific information but not when summarizing an entire source.

You can cite a source in your text in two ways:

- *Signal phrase.* Include the author's name (often just the surname) and an appropriate verb in your sentence, and place the date of publication, in parentheses, immediately following the author's name.

> Psychologist G. H. Edwards (1992) found that subtypes or subcategories of beliefs emerge from within gender categories.

A signal phrase often makes it easier for readers to determine where your ideas end and borrowed material begins. It also allows you to integrate the borrowed material into your sentence and to put the source in context by adding your own interpretation and the qualifications of the source author. For these reasons, most of your summaries, paraphrases, and quotations should be introduced by a signal phrase.

- *Parenthetical note.* In parentheses, provide the author's surname, followed by a comma and the year in which the source was published. Place the note immediately after the borrowed material.

> Subtypes or subcategories of beliefs emerge from within gender categories (Edwards, 1992).

Parenthetical notes are most appropriate when citing more than one source or establishing facts.

NOTE The reference list entry is the same, regardless of whether you use a signal phrase or a parenthetical note:

author   pub. year   title
Edwards, G. H. (1992). The structure and content of the male gender role stereotype: An exploration of subtypes. *Sex Roles, 27*, 553–561.
             publication info

> **More about**
> Creating refer-
> ence list entries,
> 226–41

Provide enough information in your in-text citation for readers to locate the source in the reference list. In most cases, the author's surname and the date of publication are sufficient. Occasionally, you may need to provide more information. When citing works by authors with the same surname, also include the authors' initials.

> Examples 1–2,
> 219–20

> Example 11, 224

While subtypes or subcategories of beliefs may emerge from within gender categories (G. H. Edwards, 1992), broader categories of beliefs emerge from within cultural groups (C. P. Edwards, 1988).

> Example 7, 230

When quoting from a source, include page numbers.

> Example 2, 220

The stereotype effect occurs when "individual members . . . are judged in a direction consistent with group-level expectations . . ." (Biernat, 2003, p. 1019).

23b Adjusting In-Text Citations to Match Your Source
调整文内引用，匹配文献来源

The exact form of an in-text citation depends on the type of source you are citing. The examples that follow cover the most common types. For more unusual sources, study the general principles outlined here and adapt them to your special circumstances or consult the *Publication Manual of the American Psychological Association*, 6th ed. (available in any library).

1. One author, paraphrase or summary The APA does not require that writers include a page reference for summaries and paraphrases, but your instructor may. If your instructor does want you to include a page reference, follow the model for a quotation on page 220.

APA In-Text Citations

1. **One author, paraphrase or summary**
2. One author, quotation
3. Two authors

> Example 2, 220

a. Signal phrase

signal phrase
From her interviews with vegans, Cherry (2015) found that the majority had adopted that lifestyle before the age of 18.

APA In-Text Citations

1. One author, paraphrase or summary
2. One author, quotation
3. Two authors
4. Three to five authors

b. Parenthetical citation

The majority of vegans participating in a sociological study reported having adopted that lifestyle before the age of 18 (Cherry, 2015).

2. One author, quotation If you are borrowing specific language from your source, include the author's name, the year of publication, and a page reference.

NOTE The APA suggests, but does not require, that writers include a page reference for summaries and paraphrases when readers may need help finding the cited passage. Your instructor may require that you always include one, so be sure to ask. If your instructor *does* want you to include a page reference, follow examples 2a–b.

a. Signal phrase In a signal phrase, insert the year of publication immediately after the author's name and a page reference at the end of the cited passage. This not only provides source information but also makes clear which part of your text comes from the source.

Cherry (2015) reports that simply self-identifying as a vegan is not enough to sustain the lifestyle; the 23 vegans interviewed "placed great value on their social networks with other vegans" (p. 67).

b. Parenthetical citation In a parenthetical citation, include all three pieces of information at the end of the passage cited.

Simply self-identifying as a vegan is not enough to sustain the lifestyle; the 23 vegans interviewed "placed great value on their social networks with other vegans" (Cherry, 2015, p. 67).

3. Two authors List two authors by surnames in the order listed by the source; be sure to use this same order in your reference list entry. In a signal phrase, spell out the word *and* between the two surnames; in a parenthetical citation, replace the word *and* with an ampersand (&).

signal phrase (*and* spelled out)
Carpenter and Readman (2006) define physical disability as "the restriction of activity caused by impairments, for example, the loss of a limb, involuntary movements, loss of speech or sight" (p. 131).

Medical doctors define the word *disability* as "an individual problem of
parenthetical citation (ampersand)
disease, incapacity, and impairment" (Carpenter & Readman, 2006, p. 131).

APA In-Text Citations

1. One author, paraphrase or summary
2. **One author, quotation**
3. **Two authors**
4. **Three to five authors**
5. Six or more authors
6. Group or corporate author

4. Three to five authors When a source has three, four, or five authors, list them all in your first in-text citation.

The research of Oller, Pearson, and Cobo-Lewis (2007) suggests that bilingual children may have a smaller vocabulary in each of their languages than monolingual children have in their sole language.

et al. 等人 Abbreviation of the Latin phrase *et alii*, "and others"

In subsequent citations, list only the first author, representing the others with the abbreviation *et al.* In APA style, this abbreviation should not be underlined or italicized.

> The bilingual children in the study were all Spanish-English speakers
>
> (Oller et al., 2007).

NOTE *al.* is an abbreviation, so it requires a period; *et* is a complete word, so it does not. There should be no punctuation between the author's name and *et al.*

5. Six or more authors If the source has six or more authors, use only the surname of the first author plus *et al.* unless confusion will result.

> The study demonstrates that positive stories about honesty, such as "George
>
> Washington and the Cherry Tree," have a positive effect on children's honesty,
>
> whereas negative stories, such as "Pinocchio," do not (Lee et al., 2014).

6. Group or corporate author Provide the full name of the group in your signal phrase or parenthetical note. If you are going to cite this source again in your project, use the group's name in a signal phrase and insert an abbreviation of the name in parentheses. In subsequent in-text references, use only the abbreviation.

> full name
> In 2003 the National Commission on Writing in America's Schools and
> acronym
> Colleges (NCWASC) demanded that "the nation's leaders . . . place writing
>
> squarely in the center of the school agenda, and [that] policymakers at the
>
> state and local levels . . . provide the resources required to improve writing"
>
> (p. 3). The NCWASC also noted that . . .

Alternatively, include the full name in a parenthetical citation, and insert the abbreviation in square brackets afterward.

> If writing is to improve, our society "must place writing squarely in the center
>
> of the school agenda, and policymakers at the state and local levels must
>
> provide the resources required to improve writing" (National Commission on
> full name   abbreviation
> Writing in America's Schools and Colleges [NCWASC], 2003, p. 3).

7. Unnamed (anonymous) author When no author is listed for a source, use the first few words of the reference list entry (usually the title) instead.

More about
Quotation marks
with titles, 450
Italics with titles,
466

> On average, smokers shave about 12 minutes off their life for every
>   title
> cigarette smoked ("A Fistful of Risks," 1996, pp. 82–83).

Set titles of articles or parts of books in quotation marks and titles of books and other longer works in italics.

8. Two or more sources in one citation When the information you are drawing on comes from more than one source, follow the borrowed material with a list of all relevant sources, separated by semicolons. List the sources in alphabetical order, the same order in which they appear in the reference list.

APA In-Text Cita-
tions

5. Six or more
   authors
6. **Group or
   corporate
   author**
7. **Unnamed
   (anonymous)
   author**
8. **Two or more
   sources in one
   citation**
9. **Two or more
   sources by the
   same author in
   one citation**
10. Two or more
    sources by the
    same author in
    the same year

> Introducing domestic animals into the prison environment has beneficial
>
> effects on female inmates (Cooke & Farrington, 2015; Jasperson, 2010).

9. Two or more sources by the same author in one citation When citing two or more sources by the same author in a single citation, name the author once but include all publication years, separating them with commas.

> Wynn's work explores the ability of human infants to perform mathematical
>   pub.   pub.
>   year 1 year 2
> functions, such as addition and subtraction (1992, 2000).

Human infants have shown surprising abilities to perform mathematical

pub.   pub.
year 1   year 2

functions, such as addition and subtraction (Wynn, 1992, 2000).

Example 6, 229

10. Two or more sources by the same author in the same year When your reference list includes two or more publications by the same author in the same year, add a letter following the year (*2006a, 2006b*). Use these year-and-letter designations in your in-text citations and in your reference list.

For history students whose first language is not English, a writing-to-learn

pedagogy has a positive effect on the acquisition of historical reasoning

letter assigned

(Smirnova, 2015b).

11. Two or more authors with the same surname If your reference list includes works by different authors with the same surname, include the authors' initials to differentiate them.

Rehabilitation is a viable option for many juvenile offenders, whose

immaturities and disabilities can, with institutional support and guidance,

first initial + surname

be overcome as the child matures (M. Beyer, 2006).

If a source has more than one author, include initials for the first author only.

12. Reprinted or republished work Include both dates in your in-text citation, with the original date of publication first.

orig. year

Danon-Boileau (2005/2006) takes a cross-disciplinary approach to the study

reprint year

of language disorders in children.

13. Sacred or classical source Cite sacred texts, such as the Bible, the Talmud, or the Qur'an (Koran), in the body of your research project using standard book titles, chapter numbers, and verse numbers, and indicate the version you used.

> In the Song of Solomon, the female speaker concludes her description of
> her lover with this proclamation: "His mouth is sweetness itself, he is all
> delight. / Such is my lover, and such my friend, O daughters of Jerusalem"
> ch.   version
> (5:16, Revised Standard Version).
>   verse

For classical works, cite the year of the translation or version you used: (Plato, trans. 1968).

14. Indirect source When you can, avoid quoting from a secondhand source (source material you have learned about through its mention in another source). When you cannot locate or translate the original source, mention the original author's name in a signal phrase. In your parenthetical note, include *as cited in* followed by the name of the author of the source in which you found the information, and conclude with the year of that source's publication.

> Bonilla-Silva (as cited in Utheim, 2014) locates the origin of US "colorblind racism"
> in the 1960s.

In the reference list, provide only the source you used: For the preceding example, include a reference list entry for Utheim, not Bonilla-Silva.

15. Website or other online source Frequently, the information you need to create a complete in-text citation is missing. Electronic sources may lack fixed page numbers: Page 5 in one browser may be page 4 or 6 in another. Use page numbers only when they are fixed, as in a PDF file. When paragraph numbers are provided, include those (with the abbreviation *para.*) instead of a page number.

❯ *More about*
PDF files, 104, 109

> The Internet has also become an outlet for direct distribution of underground
> comics through artist websites, making independent titles more affordable to
> market (Fenty, Houp, & Taylor, 2004, para. 1).

Examples 26–27, 237

When the source includes neither fixed page numbers nor paragraph numbers, cite the source by author name and publication date only. If the author is unnamed, use the first few words of the title.

> Cell-phone use while driving can impair performance as badly as drinking alcohol does ("Driven to Distraction," 2006, para. 1).

If no date is provided, use *n.d.* for *no date*.

> Barrett (n.d.) unwittingly reveals the sexism prevalent on college campuses in the early 1960s through his account of a football game.

APA In-Text Citations

14. Indirect source
15. Website or other online source
16. Personal communication (email, letter, interview)

16. Personal communication (email, letter, interview) For sources such as personal email messages, interviews, and phone calls that your readers cannot retrieve and read, mention the communication in your text or provide a parenthetical note, but do not include an entry in the reference list.

> The author herself was much more modest about the award (S. Alexievich, personal communication, April 13, 2016).

24 Preparing an APA-Style Reference List
准备APA格式的参考文献列表

The reference list, which comes after the body of your research project, lists the sources you have cited in your text. The format of each entry in the list depends in part on the type of source you are citing, such as a printed book, an article in an electronic journal or accessed through a database, or an audio recording. (See the Quick Reference box on pp. 228 for a list of APA-style reference list examples.)

Books—Printed and Electronic 书籍——纸质版与电子版

In a printed book, the information you need to create a reference list entry appears on the title and copyright pages at the beginning of the book. In an online book or e-book, print and electronic publication information appears at the top or bottom of the first page or is available through a link.

Annotated visual of where to find author, title, and publication information, tutorial in part 7

1. One author

a. Printed The basic entry for a printed book looks like this:

Author's surname, Initial(s). (Year of publication). *Title: Subtitle.* Place of publication (city, state [abbreviated]): Publisher.

Here is an example of an actual citation:

Pollock, J. (2012). *Crime and justice in America: An introduction to criminal justice.* Maryland Heights, MO: Anderson Publishing.

For books, only first word of title and subtitle (plus names) are capitalized.

b. E-book Works published electronically or made accessible online are now frequently tagged with a digital object identifier (DOI). Unlike a URL that may change or stop working, a DOI is a permanent identifier that will not change over time or from database to database. If the e-book you are documenting is tagged with a DOI, use that identifier instead of publication information or URL, and add a description of the source type in brackets after the title. If no DOI has been assigned, replace publication information with the URL from which the electronic file can be obtained. If you accessed the source on a device such as a Kindle or Nook, do not include any URL.

> **More about**
> Digital object identifiers, 103, 104, 227
> URLs, 118, 237–38

Carter, J. (2003). *Nasty people: How to stop being hurt by them without stooping to their level* [Adobe Digital Editions version]. doi:10.1036/0071410228

von Hippel, E. (n.d.). *Democratizing innovation.* Retrieved from http://web.mit.edu /evhippel/www/democ.htm

If no publication date available, use *n.d.*

2. Two authors
When there are two authors, list them in the order in which they appear on the title page.

author 1   author 2
Raskin, H., & Rabiner, D. (2012). *College drinking and drug use.* New York, NY: Guilford.

Use an ampersand (&) between names.

Tech Citing Electronic Sources: DOIs and URLs

Because URLs change and links break, the APA now recommends using a digital object identifier (DOI), a permanent identifying code, whenever available; use a URL, or web address, only when no DOI is available. Most electronic books and articles in academic journals now include a DOI. When your citation ends with a DOI or URL, do *not* add a period after it. Break a DOI or URL (if necessary) only before a slash (except when the slash is part of "http://" in a URL), a dot, or another punctuation mark; do not add a hyphen.

APA Reference List Entries

1. One author
2. Two authors
3. Three to seven authors
4. Eight or more authors

3. Three to seven authors When the book has three to seven authors, list all their names.

> James, J., Burks, W., & Eigenmann, P. (2011). *Food allergy*. Philadelphia, PA:
>
> Saunders.

Use an ampersand (&) between the last two names.

4. Eight or more authors When the book has eight or more authors, list the first six authors followed by three ellipsis points and the last author's name.

> Masters, R., Skrapec, C., Muscat, B., Dussich, J. P., Pincu, L., Way, L. B., . . .
>
> Gerstenfeld, P. (2010). *Criminal justice: Realities and challenges*.
>
> New York, NY: McGraw-Hill.

5. Unnamed (anonymous) author Start the entry with the title followed by the publication date. Alphabetize the entry in the reference list using the first significant word in the title (not an article such as *a, an,* or *the*).

> *And still we conquer! The diary of a Nazi Unteroffizier in the German Africa*
>
> *Corps*. (1968). University, AL: Confederate Publishing.

APA Reference List Entries

1. One author
2. Two authors
3. **Three to seven authors**
4. **Eight or more authors**
5. **Unnamed (anonymous) author**
6. **Two or more books by the same author**
7. Two or more authors with the same surname and first initial

6. Two or more books by the same author For multiple books by the same author (or authors), arrange the entries in order of publication (from least to most recent).

> Benson, T. (2003). *Writing JFK: Presidential rhetoric and the press in the Bay of Pigs*
>
> *crisis*. College Station: Texas A&M University Press.

> Benson, T. (2015). *Posters for peace: Visual rhetoric and civic action*. University
>
> Park: Penn State University Press.

When books were written by the same author(s) in the same year, alphabetize the entries by title and add the letter *a* following the publication date of the first entry, *b* following the publication date of the second entry, and so on.

> Dobrin, S. I. (2011a). *Ecology, writing theory, and new media: Writing ecology*.
>
> New York, NY: Routledge.

> Dobrin, S. I. (2011b). *Postcomposition*. Carbondale: Southern Illinois University
>
> Press.

❯ Example 10, 224

APA Reference List Entries

5. Unnamed (anonymous) author
6. **Two or more books by the same author**
7. **Two or more authors with the same surname and first initial**
8. **Group or corporate author**
9. **Author and editor or translator**
10. Edited book or anthology

Works written by a single author should be listed *before* sources written by that same author plus a coauthor, regardless of publication dates.

Kress, G. (2010). *Multimodality: A social semiotic approach to contemporary communication*. New York, NY: Routledge.

Kress, G., Jewett, C., Ogborn, J., & Tsatsarelis, C. (2015). *Multimodal teaching and learning: The rhetorics of the science classroom*. New York, NY: Bloomsbury.

When citing multiple sources by an author and various coauthors, alphabetize entries by the surname of the second author.

Sternberg, R., Grigorenko, E., & Jarvin, L. (2009). *Teaching for wisdom, intelligence, creativity, and success*. New York, NY: Skyhorse Publishing.

Sternberg, R., & Sternberg, K. (2016). *Cognitive psychology* (7th ed). Belmont, CA: Wadsworth.

7. Two or more authors with the same surname and first initial When your reference list includes sources by two different authors with the same surname and first initial, differentiate them by including their first names in brackets.

Cohen, A. [Andrew]. (1994). *Assessing language ability in the classroom*. Boston, MA: Heinle.

Cohen, A. [Anne]. (1973). *Poor Pearl, poor girl! The murdered girl stereotype in ballad and newspaper*. Austin: University of Texas Press.

> No state abbreviation if state included in name of university press

8. Group or corporate author List the sponsoring organization as the author. Use the full name, and alphabetize it in the reference list according to the name's first significant word (ignoring articles such as *a, an,* or *the*). If the same group or corporation is also listed as the publisher, replace the name of the publisher with the word *Author*.

Fabian Society, Commission on Life Chances and Child Poverty. (2006). *Narrowing the gap: The final report of the Fabian Commission on Life Chances and Child Poverty*. London, UK: Author.

9. Author and editor or translator If the source originally appeared earlier than the edited or translated version, add the date of original publication at the end of the entry. If the work has an editor, use the abbreviation *Ed.* For a translator, use the abbreviation *Trans.*

> Alvtegen, K. (2010). *Shame* (S. Murray, Trans.). New York, NY: Felony and
>
> Mayhem. (Original work published 2006)

10. Edited book or anthology Put the editor's name in the author position.

> Brownell, K., & Gold, M. (Eds.). (2012). *Food and addiction: A comprehensive*
>
> *handbook.* New York, NY: Oxford University Press.

For a book with a single editor, change the abbreviation to *Ed.*

11. Selection from an edited book or anthology Begin with the selection's author, followed by the publication date of the book and the selection's title (with no quotation marks or other formatting). Then insert the word *In,* the editors' names, and the title of the book or anthology (italicized). Next include page numbers for the entire selection (even if you used only part of it). Conclude the entry with the publication information for the book in which the selection appeared.

selection author / selection title / editors
> Smither, N. (2000). Crime scene cleaner. In J. Bowe, M. Bowe, &
>
> selection pg. nos.
> S. Streeter (Eds.), *Gig: Americans talk about their jobs* (pp. 96–103).
>
> New York, NY: Crown.

12. Edition other than the first Insert the edition number (*2nd ed., 3rd ed.*) or edition name (*Rev. ed.* for "revised edition") after the book's title. (The edition number or name usually appears on the title page.)

> Nier, J. A. (2013). *Taking sides: Clashing views in social psychology* (4th ed.).
>
> New York, NY: McGraw-Hill.

13. Introduction, preface, foreword, or afterword The sixth edition of the *Publication Manual of the APA* does not provide an example of an entry for an introduction, preface, foreword, or afterword, but based on other examples, such an entry might look like this:

foreword's author / label / book's author / book's title
> Andretti, M. (2008). Foreword. In D. Daly, *Race to win: How to become a*
>
> pg. nos. (foreword)
> *complete champion* (pp. 2–3). Minneapolis, MN: Quayside-Motorbooks.

Example 11, 231

14. Entry in an encyclopedia or other reference work Format an entry in a reference work as you would a selection from an edited book. For signed articles, include the author's name. (Articles in reference works often carry the author's initials only, so you may need to cross-reference the initials with a list of contributors in the front or back of the book.) If an article is unsigned, begin with its title.

a. Printed

entry author / entry title / entry page nos.

Treffert, D. A. (2000). Savant syndrome. In A. E. Kazdin (Ed.), *Encyclopedia of psychology* (pp. 144–148). New York, NY: Oxford University Press.

b. Online

Kontos, A. (2014). Assimilation. In R. Eklund & G. Tenenbaum (Eds.), *Encyclopedia of sport and exercise psychology*. Retrieved from https://us.sage-pub.com/en-us/nam /encyclopedia-of-sport-and-exercise-psychology/book237359

15. Multivolume work

Tomasello, M. (Ed.). (1998–2003). *The new psychology of language: Cognitive and functional approaches to language structure* (Vols. 1–2). Mahwah, NJ: Erlbaum.

16. Republished book

Huxley, E. (2006). *Red strangers*. New York, NY: Penguin. (Original work published 1939)

Example 13, 224

17. Sacred or classical source No entry in the reference list is needed for a sacred source, such as the Bible, the Talmud, or the Qur'an, or a classical source, such as Plato's *Republic*.

18. Dissertation or thesis Indicate whether the work is a doctoral dissertation or a master's thesis. If the dissertation or thesis was accessed through a database service, include the name of the database from which it was obtained and provide any identifying number. If it was obtained from a university or personal website, include the URL.

a. Published

Pervil, I. (2016). *Ways of thinking about illness representations of cancer* (Doctoral dissertation). Available from ProQuest Dissertations and Theses Global database. (DAI-B 77/03E)

Lillie, A. S. (2008). *MusicBox: Navigating the space of your music* (Master's thesis,

Massachusetts Institute of Technology). Retrieved from http://thesis

.flyingpudding.com/documents/Anita_FINAL_THESIS.pdf

b. Unpublished

Luster, L. (1992). *Schooling, survival and struggle: Black women and the GED*

(Unpublished doctoral dissertation). Stanford University, Stanford, CA.

c. Abstracted in DAI If you used the abstract in the *Dissertation Abstracts International* database, include that information in the entry. Remember, though, that reading the abstract is no substitute for reading the actual source.

Kelley, E. (2008). Parental depression and negative attribution bias in parent

reports of child symptoms. *Dissertation Abstracts International: Section B.*

Sciences and Engineering, 69(7), 4427.

Periodicals—Printed and Electronic 期刊——纸质版与电子版

A periodical is a publication issued at regular intervals—newspapers are generally published every day, magazines every week or month, and scholarly journals four times a year. For periodicals, include not only the title of the article (with no quotation marks or italics) but also the title of the periodical (in italics, all important words capitalized). Other publication information you include depends on the type of periodical you are citing.

19. Article in a scholarly journal The information needed to create a reference list entry for a printed journal article appears on the cover or in the table of contents of the journal and on the first and last pages of the article. For articles downloaded from a database, the information appears on the search results screen, in the full record of the article, or on the first and last pages of the downloaded file. For articles that appear in journals that are published solely online, the needed information may be on the website's home page, in the journal's table of contents, or on the first page of the article.

a. Printed The basic citation for an article in a printed journal looks like this:

Author's surname, Initial(s). (Year of publication). Article title. *Journal Title, vol*

no., pages.

APA Reference List Entries

16. Republished book
17. Sacred or classical source
18. **Dissertation or thesis**
19. **Article in a scholarly journal**
20. Special issue of a journal
21. Article in a magazine

> Annotated visual of where to find author, title, publication, and other information, tutorial in part 7

> *More about* Formatting author information: Examples 1–11, 219–24

Here is an example of an actual citation:

Wright, S. (2011). Invasive species and the loss of beta diversity. *Ethics and the Environment, 16*, 75–98.

If the article is published in a journal that starts each issue with page 1, provide the issue number after the volume number (not italicized, in parentheses).

Sui, C. (2007). Giving indigenous people a voice. *Taiwan Review, 57*(8), 40.

b. Online or accessed through a database More and more, researchers access journal articles electronically, either through online journals or through databases that provide access to articles in PDF or HTML format. Articles accessed electronically now frequently include a digital object identifier (DOI). The DOI is a permanent code that does not change from library to library or from database to database. The DOI makes URLs unnecessary. Whenever a DOI is provided, include it at the end of your reference list entry. The basic citation for an article in an online journal or accessed through an online database that has a DOI is the same as for a printed journal article except that the DOI appears at the end of the citation.

Luo, Y. (2011). Do 10-month-old infants understand others' false beliefs? *Cognition, 121*, 289–298. DOI doi:10.1016/j.cognition.2011.07.011

For an article in an online journal that does *not* provide a DOI, include the phrase *Retrieved from* followed by the URL for the journal's home page.

Janyam, K. (2011). The influence of job satisfaction on mental health of factory workers. *Internet Journal of Mental Health, 7*(1). Retrieved from http:// www.ispub.com /journal/the_internet_journal_of_mental_health/

20. Special issue of a journal

Lowe, B., Souze-Monteiro, D., & Fraser, I. (Eds.). (2015). special issue title Changing food label consumption label behaviors [Special issue]. *Psychology & Marketing, 32*(5).

21. Article in a magazine

a. Printed or accessed through a database Provide the full publication date of the issue (year, month, and day or year and month). If the volume and issue number of the magazine are available, include that information as you would for a journal article.

More about
Digital object identifiers (DOIs), PDFs, 103, 109, 227

Example 19, 233

Greene, K. (2011, December). Our data, ourselves. *Discover*, 42–47.

Goodwin, D. (2015, September). Neuroscience needs hackers. *Scientific American*, 313(3), 24.

b. Online Include the URL for the magazine's home page.

Washington, H. (2015, November). Catching madness. *Psychology Today*. Retrieved from https://www.psychologytoday.com/magazine/archive

If the magazine is available in a printed edition but the article is available only online, include the phrase *Supplemental material* in brackets after the article's title.

Daniller, A. (2007, December). Psychology research done right [Supplemental material]. *GradPSYCH*. Retrieved from http://gradpsych.apags.org

22. Article in a newspaper The information you need to create a reference list entry for a printed newspaper article is found on the masthead of the newspaper (at the top of the first page) and on the first and last pages of the article. For newspaper articles downloaded from a database, the information you need appears on the search results screen, the full record of the article, or the article itself. For articles that appear in online versions of the newspaper, the information you need is usually at the top of the first page of the article.

a. Printed or accessed through a database

author   pub. date   title
Smith, E. (2015, November 17). Preventive side of justice reform.
        newspaper   sec./pg. no.
The Sacramento Bee, p. 1B.

If the title of a newspaper does not include its place of publication, supply the city and state, in square brackets, following the title.

Esch, M. (2011, July 1). New York may ban gas drilling in watersheds, state land. *Evening Sun* [Norwich, NY], pp. 1, 3.

If the pages of the article are not continuous, provide all page numbers.

Apuzzo, M., & Lipton, E. (2015, November 25). Rare alliance on sentencing begins to fray. *The New York Times*, pp. A1, A17.

To cite a newspaper article downloaded from a database, follow the model for a printed newspaper article, but omit the page numbers, and change the comma after the newspaper's title to a period.

APA Reference List Entries

19. Article in a scholarly journal
20. Special issue of a journal
21. Article in a magazine
22. Article in a newspaper
23. Review (printed or online)
24. Letter to the editor (printed or online)

b. Online Follow the format for a printed newspaper article, but omit the page reference and include the words *Retrieved from* and the URL for the newspaper's home page.

> Smyth, J. C., & Thompson, D. (2011, December 10). Public retirement ages come under greater scrutiny. *Denver Post.* Retrieved from http://www. denverpost.com

Examples 19, 21–22, 233–36

23. Review (printed or online) Follow the model for the type of periodical in which the review appeared. In the author position, insert the name of the author of the review; if the review is titled, insert that title in the title position (no italics or quotation marks); and add in brackets the label *Review of the book* (or *Review of the film,* and so forth) followed by the title and author of the reviewed work. End with publication information for the periodical in which the review appeared.

> review author   review title   label
> Oryzysyn, D. (2014, June 10). Writers on death and grief [Review of the book *Dying in character,* by J. Berman]. *Death Studies, 31,* 941-947. doi:10.1080/07481180701603436

Comma between title, author

If the review is untitled, substitute the label *Review of the book,* the book's title, and the book's author in brackets.

> Hurdley, R. (2011, September). [Review of the book *Gripes: The little quarrels of couples,* by J. Kaufmann]. *Cultural Sociology, 5,* 452–453.

Comma between title, author

Examples 19, 21–22, 233–36

24. Letter to the editor (printed or online) Follow the model for the type of periodical in which the letter appeared, and insert the label *Letter to the editor* in brackets following the letter's title.

> letter author   label
> Dennett, D. (2015, March 20). [Letter to the editor]. *Times Literary Supplement, 5842,* p. 6.

If the letter is titled, put that information (no italics or quotation marks) right before the *Letter to the editor* label.

25. Abstract (printed or online) It is always better to read and cite the article itself. However, if you relied only on the abstract, or summary, cite only the abstract to avoid misrepresenting your source and your research.

> Loverock, D. S. (2007). Object superiority as a function of object coherence and task difficulty [Abstract]. *American Journal of Psychology, 120,* 565-591.

Tebeaux, E. (2011). Technical writing and the development of the English para-

graph 1473–1700. *Journal of Technical Writing and Communication, 41,*

219–253. Abstract retrieved from http://www.ebscohost.com

Other Electronic Sources 其他电子资源

While it is usually easy to find the information you need to create a complete citation for a book or an article in a periodical, websites can be a bit trickier. Most of the information you need will appear on the site's home page, usually at the bottom or top of that page, or on the web page you are citing. Sometimes, however, you may need to look further. Click on links with titles such as "About us" or "More information." Frequently, websites do not provide complete information, in which case include as much information in your entry as you can.

> Annotated visual of where to find author, title, and publication information, tutorial in part 7

26. Website In general, when mentioning an entire website in a research project, you do not have to include an entry in your reference list. However, if you quote or paraphrase content from the site or interact with it in a substantial way, include it, following this model:

> Example 15, 225

Author's surname, Initial(s). (Copyright date or date last updated). *Website title.*

Retrieved from + URL

Here is an example of an actual citation:

Gilbert, R. (2001). *Shake your shyness.* Retrieved from http://shakeyourshyness.com

If no author is cited, move the title to the author position. If the web page is untitled, add a description in brackets. If no date is provided, insert *(n.d.)* following the author's name.

> Example 5, 229

27. Web page Provide the title of the page (with no formatting) and the URL for the specific page you are citing.

web page title
American Psychological Association. (2011). Treatment for binge eating.
URL for web page
Retrieved from http://www.apa.org/

28. Discussion list posting Treat the subject line (or *thread*) as the title, and include the label *Discussion list post* (in brackets).

date posted   subj. line   label
Pace, T. (2015, August 24). Genre and workplace writing. [Discussion list post].
URL
Retrieved from https://lists.asu.edu/cgi-bin/wa?A1=ind1508&L=WPA-L#51

Tech Checking URLs and DOIs

DOIs. If your entry includes a DOI, check it before submitting your project by visiting crossref.org and inserting the DOI into the search box.

URLs. Just before submitting your project, test all the URLs. Sometimes web addresses change or content is taken down. If the URL you provided no longer works, search for the work online by title or keyword; you may find it "cached" on the web even though the owner of the original site has taken the work down. Then use the URL for the cached version in your bibliographic entry.

If the name of the list is not included in the URL, add it to the retrieval statement: *Retrieved from Early Childhood Education Discussion List: http://www.dmoz.org/Reference/Education/Early_Childhood*

29. Article on a wiki Cite a wiki article as you would a web page. Because wikis are written and edited collaboratively, there is no author to cite; begin with the article's title. If the date of the most recent update is not noted, include the abbreviation *n.d.* (*no date*) in its place. Always include a retrieval date and direct URL.

retrieval date
Battered person syndrome. (n.d.). Retrieved April 22, 2012, from http://psychol-
URL
ogy.wikia.com

30. Blog Include a screen name if the author's name is not provided.

a. Blog posting

post author   post date   post title   label
Bell, V. (2015, November 7). A medieval attitude to suicide [Web log post].
                                                    URL
Retrieved from http://mindhacks.com/2015/11/07/a-medieval-atti-
tude-to-suicide/

More about
Reliability, 114–20

b. Comment on a blog posting

comment author [avatar]   date posted   subject line (thread title)
Medicinehorse179. (2015, November 17). Re: No more type I/II error confusion
        label   URL
[Web log comment]. Retrieved from http://mindhacks.com/

31. Computer software Provide an entry for computer software only if it is unfamiliar to your readers and it is necessary to a computation you have made.

        title   label
Power Researcher [Computer software]. Atlanta, GA: Uniting Networks.

If the software you are citing is available in more than one version, add a version number in parentheses between the title of the software and the identifying label.

32. Presentation slides The sixth edition of the *Publication Manual of the APA* does not provide an example of an entry for presentation slides, but based on other examples, such an entry might look like the one below:

> label
>
> Stolley, K., & Brizee, A. (2015). Visual rhetoric for student writers [PowerPoint slides]. *Purdue OWL*. Retrieved from https://owl.english.purdue.edu/owl/

Audio and Visual Sources 视听资源

The information you need to create an entry for most audio and visual sources appears on the cover, label, or program of the work or in the credits at the end of a film or television show. As with other citations, italicize the titles of longer works, such as CDs and films, and do not format or add quotation marks to the titles of shorter works, such as single songs or single episodes of television programs.

33. Motion picture

> release title
>
> Grazer, B. (Producer), & Howard, R. (Director). (2001). *A beautiful mind* [Motion
>
> distributor
>
> picture]. United States: Warner Bros.

34. Online video or video blog (vlog)

> label
>
> 25 things psychology tells you about yourself. (2014, December 8). [Video file].
>
> Retrieved from https://www.youtube.com/watch?v=ic9fnTpoYdk

35. Television or radio broadcast

a. Series

> Garcia, R. (Executive producer). (2008–2009). *In treatment* [Television series].
>
> New York, NY: HBO.

b. Episode

> Reingold, J. (Writer), & Barclay, P. (Director). (2009). Mia: Week three
>
> [Television series episode]. In R. Garcia (Executive producer),
>
> *In treatment*. New York, NY: HBO.

c. Podcast

> Vedantam, S. The science of compassion [Audio podcast]. *The Hidden Brain*.
>
> Retrieved from http://www.npr.org/series/423302056/hidden-brain

---

APA Reference List Entries

30. Blog
31. Computer software
32. Presentation slides
33. Motion picture
34. Online video or video blog (vlog)
35. Television or radio broadcast
36. Musical or other audio recording
37. Lecture, speech, conference presentation, or poster session

36. Musical or other audio recording

a. CD, LP, or audiobook

Rockefeller, J. (2014, November 11). *The introvert personality: The advantage of introverts in an extrovert world* [Audio book]. Retrieved from http://www.amazon.com/

b. Selection or song on a CD, LP, or audiobook

writers   © date   performers

Dilly, D., & Wilkin, M. (1959). The long black veil [Recorded by H. Dickens & A. Gerrard]. On *Pioneering women of bluegrass* [CD]. Washington, DC:

recording date

Smithsonian/Folkways Records. (1996).

37. Lecture, speech, conference presentation, or poster session

Guilko, T. (2015, October 4). *From baby boomers to Generation Y: Motivation across the ages.* Paper presented at the British Psychological Society's Division on Occupational Therapy Conference, Oxford, UK.

38. Map

U.S. Census Bureau, Geography Division (Cartographer). (2001). Mean center of population for the United States: 1790 to 2000 [Demographic map]. Retrieved from http://www.census.gov/geo/www/cenpop/meanctr.pdf

Miscellaneous Sources—Printed and Electronic
其他来源——纸质版与电子版

39. Government publication

a. Printed

title

Child Welfare Information Gateway. (2015). *Adoption options: Where do I start?* Washington, DC: U.S. Department of Health and Human Services, Children's Bureau.

> Example 8, 230

If the source includes a publication number, add that information in parentheses after the title.

b. Online

U.S. General Accounting Office. (1993, September 21). *North American Free Trade Agreement: A focus on the substantive issues* (Publication No. GAO/T-GGD-93-44). Retrieved from http://www.gpoaccess.gov/gaoreports/search.html

40. Report (nongovernmental)

Head, A. (2014, July 29). *Trends from the lifelong learning interviews with recent graduates.* Project Information Literacy Progress Report. Retrieved from http://projectinfolit.org/publications

41. Data set

U.S. Department of Justice, Federal Bureau of Investigation. (2007, September). *2006 Crime in the United States* [Data set]. Retrieved from http://www.data.gov/raw/310

42. Fact sheet, brochure, pamphlet

ZGovernment. (2015, February). Agriculture and fisheries [Fact sheet]. Retrieved from http://www.gov.hk/en/about/abouthk/factsheets/

If no author is listed, move the title to the author position. If no publication date is available, insert *n.d.* (for *no date*) in its place.

43. Conference proceedings Cite conference proceedings either as an edited book or as the special issue of a journal, depending on how they were published.

Example 10, 231
Example 20, 234

44. Legal source (printed or online)

case title   *U.S. Reports*   decision
(abbreviated) vol.   no. date
Lynn v. Alabama, 493 U.S. 945 (1989). Retrieved from *Open Jurist* website:
URL
http://openjurist.org/493/us/945/lynn-v-alabama

45. Interview (published or broadcast)

interview subject   broadcast date
Hoffman, B. (2015, November 28). What information do intelligence agencies need to keep US safe? Interview by S. Simon. Retrieved from http://www.npr.org/sections/interviews/

46. Personal communication (email, letter, interview) Cite personal communications that are not available to the public in the body of the research project, but do not include an entry in the reference list.

Example 16, 226

25 Using APA Style for Informational Notes 参考文献注释采用APA格式

In addition to in-text citations, APA style allows researchers to include informational notes. These notes may provide supplementary information, acknowledge any help the writer received, or call attention to possible conflicts of interest.

To add supplementary information, include a superscript (above-the-line) arabic number in the text and at the beginning of the note (either at the bottom of the page for a footnote or in a list of notes at the end of the project).

The participants in each condition were told at the beginning of the experiment that they were participating in a memory-recall task. They were to identify what they could remember from a clip from the movie *Pretty Woman* (Milchan, Reuther, & Marshall, 1990),[1] a stereotypical "chick-flick."

Notes

[1]This romantic comedy starring Julia Roberts and Richard Gere (dir. Garry Marshall) was extremely popular, grossing nearly $464 million worldwide, according to the site Box Office Mojo (http://www.box-officemojo.com/movies/?id=prettywoman.htm). Nevertheless, participants had not seen the film before participating in the experiment.

Sample title page, 247

Add notes to acknowledge help or possible conflicts of interest to the title page, four lines below the date.

26 Formatting a Paper in APA Style
论文版式采用APA格式

The care with which you cite and document your sources reflects the care you have taken in writing your research project. Continue that care by formatting your project in the way your readers expect. For most writing projects in the social sciences, follow the APA's formatting guidelines. The *Publication Manual of the APA* (6th ed.) offers guidance for writers submitting projects for publication in scholarly journals, so not all its formatting requirements are appropriate for student projects. Ask your instructor about making reasonable modifications.

Student Model
Research project (APA style): "The Power of Wardrobe," Heather DeGroot, 246–54

26a Margins and Spacing 边距和间距

- Set margins of at least one inch at the top, bottom, and left- and right-hand sides of your paper.
- Indent the first line of each paragraph half an inch.
- Indent quotations of forty or more words as a block, half an inch from the left margin.
- Double-space the entire paper, including the abstract, title page, block quotations, footnotes, figure captions, and reference list. Set the text so that the right margin is uneven (ragged), and do not hyphenate words at the ends of lines.
- Insert two spaces after punctuation at the end of a sentence.
- Use a hanging indent for each reference list entry: The first line should be flush with the left margin, with subsequent lines indented one-half inch.

More about
Block quotations, 449

Sample reference list, 253

26b Typeface, Header, and Page Number 字体、页眉和页码

Use a standard typeface such as Times New Roman or Arial in a readable size (usually 12 points). Include a header, or *running head,* consisting of the first two or three words of the title (no more than fifty characters) in the upper left-hand corner of the page, one-half inch from the upper edge. Include the page number one-half inch from the top and one inch from the right edge of the page. Use your word processor's header feature to insert the running head and number the pages automatically.

More about
Choosing a typeface and type size, 52–53

Tech　Indention

The major style guides (MLA, APA, *Chicago*, CSE) were initially written before the widespread use of personal computers, when most writers still worked on typewriters. To create a paragraph or hanging indention on a type-writer, the typist would hit the space bar five times or set a tab. Now, just about everyone creates writing projects on a computer, where paragraph and hanging indentions are created using the Ruler or Paragraph Dialog box.

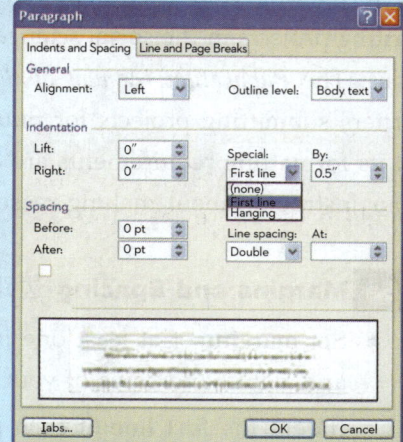

Ruler

Almost from the begining comlcbooks were assodated with supetheroes The first comlcbooks ppeared in the early 1930s, nearly four decades after comlcstrips

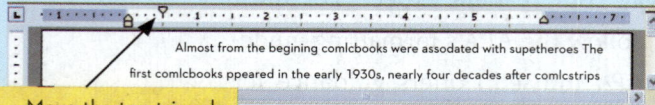

Move the top triangle to the right to create a paragraph indent

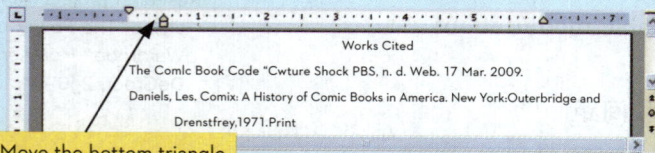

Works Cited

The Comlc Book Code "Cwture Shock PBS, n. d. Web. 17 Mar. 2009.

Daniels, Les. Comix: A History of Comic Books in America. New York:Outerbridge and Drenstfrey,1971.Print

Move the bottom triangle to the right to create a hanging indent

Paragraph Dialog Box

Paragraph

Indents and Spacing | Line and Page Breaks

General
Alignment: Left　Outline level: Body text

Indentation
Lift: 0″　Special: First line　By: 0.5″
Right: 0″　(none)
　First line
　Hanging

Spacing
Before: 0 pt　Line spacing: At:
After: 0 pt　Double

Tabs...　OK　Cancel

More about
Crafting a title, 41
Notes acknowledging help or conflicts, 242, 247

26c　Title Page 标题页

- Insert the title, typed in uppercase and lowercase letters, centered on the top half of the page.

- Insert a blank line and then type your name.

- Papers for submission to a scholarly journal include the author's university or college affiliation; student writers usually include the course number, the name of the instructor to whom the project will be submitted, and the date of submission, with each piece of information being centered on a separate line.

Sample title page, APA style, 247

- If you need to acknowledge help you received—for example, in conducting your research or interpreting your results—include a note on the title page, four lines below the identifying information.

Tech　Creating a Header

Word processing programs, such as Microsoft Word, allow you to insert a header automatically. The directions to create a header vary depending on the type or version of program being used. If you have any questions about creating a header, consult your program's Help directory.

26d Abstract 摘要

The abstract generally includes a one-sentence summary of the most important points in each section of the project:

Sample abstract, APA style, 247

- Introduction—the problem you are investigating
- Methods—the number and characteristics of the participants and your research methods
- Results—your outcomes
- Discussion—the implications of your results. This section concludes your text.

The abstract follows the title page and appears on its own page, headed with the word *Abstract* centered at the top of the page. The abstract should be no more than 150–250 words.

26e Tables and Figures 图表

- Refer to tables and figures in the text using the word *Table* or *Figure* followed by the number of the table or figure in sequence. (The first figure is Figure 1; the first table is Table 1.) Discuss the significance of tables and figures in the text, but do not repeat the information that appears in the table or figure itself.

- Include a caption with each figure. The caption should begin with the word *Figure* and the number assigned in the text (both in italics). The caption, which follows the figure, should describe the figure briefly but not repeat the information in your text. If you borrowed the figure or the data to create the figure, include the source information at the end of your caption.

Sample figure captions, APA style, 254

- Include the word *Table* and the table number (no italics) on one line and, on the next line, the table title (in italics). The table itself should appear below the table number and title. If you borrowed the table or the data to create the table, include source information below the table, preceded by the word *Note* (in italics, followed by a period).

- In research projects submitted for publication, tables should appear, each on a new page, after the reference list or endnotes (if any). Figures (graphs, charts, photographs, maps, and so on) should appear, each on a new page, following the tables. In college research projects, however, your instructor may prefer to see tables and figures in the body of your research project, following their first mention in the text as closely as possible. Check with your instructor before formatting your project.

Sample figures, APA style, 254

26f Reference List 参考文献列表

- Center the heading "References" at the top of the page.
- Use a hanging indent for each reference list entry: The first line should be flush with the left margin, with subsequent lines indented half an inch.
- Alphabetize the entries in the reference list by the surname of the author or, if no author is listed, by the first important word in the title (ignoring *A, An,* or *The*).
- Italicize all titles of books and websites, but do not enclose titles of articles or book chapters in quotation marks.
- Capitalize the first word, the first word following a colon or a dash, and proper nouns in titles of books, articles in periodicals, websites and web pages, films, and so on. Capitalize all major words in journal titles: *Psychology, Public Policy, and Law; Monitor on Psychology.*

> **More about**
> Italics with titles, 466

> **More about**
> Capitalization, 462–65
> Proper nouns, 332

26g Printing, Paper, and Binding 打印、纸张和装订

Print your project using a high-quality printer (make sure it has plenty of ink), on opaque, 8½ 3 11–inch white paper. Most instructors do not want you to enclose your paper in a binder, but if you are in doubt, ask. If it is not submitted in a binder, paperclip or staple the pages together.

Writing Responsibly | **Of Deadlines and Paperclips**

Instructors expect students to turn in thoughtful, carefully proofread, and neatly formatted papers on time—usually in class on the due date. Another expectation is that the writer will clip or staple the pages of the paper *before* the paper is submitted. Do justice to yourself by being fully prepared.

to SELF

Student Model 学生范文 **Research Project: APA Style**

> **More about**
> Writing in college, 67–72

In the sample student research project that follows, Heather DeGroot examines the influence that gender stereotypes can have on behavior. She fulfills her responsibilities to topic and audience by drawing on a variety of relevant and reliable sources to provide the background that her readers will need, by including visuals that help her readers understand her project, and by following the format for an APA-style research project, the format her readers expect. By acknowledging her sources, she fulfills her responsibility to the other writers from whom she has borrowed information. By conducting her primary research with care, by thanking Patrick Brown for the assistance he provided, by acknowledging the limitations of her project, and by revising, editing, and proofreading her project carefully, she demonstrates her own credibility as a researcher and writer.

Running head: Shortened title

The words *Running head*, followed by a colon, may not be needed for college research projects in APA style.

The Power of Wardrobe: Male Stereotype Influences

Heather DeGroot

Psychology 220

Dr. Lawrence

May 2, 2010

Identifying information (double-spaced)

Author Note

I would like to thank Patrick Brown for playing the proctor in each of the three conditions.

Abstract   Heading (centered, 1" from top), new page

This study explores the potential influence of stereotypical appearances on male subjects' stated opinions regarding entertainment perceived as "feminine." Results are based on responses from 26 undergraduate males. Data were analyzed using one-way variance tests and Tukey HSD post hoc tests. The findings show that participants were more likely to give a favorable rating to a "chick-flick" in the presence of a counterstereotypical male ($M = 8.67$, $SD = 1.53$) than in the presence of a stereotypical male ($M = 5.31$, $SD = 1.97$) or control proctor ($M = 5.20$, $SD = 1.99$). Results suggest that participants may have experienced gender role conflict.

Abstract: Summary of problem, methods, results, discussion

The Power of Wardrobe: Male Stereotype Influences   Title (centered)

¶ indent: 1/2"

Stereotypes—expectations placed upon people because of their gender, race, or religion—may be discouraged in their most overt forms, but they continue to flourish in the media. In contemporary American culture, this sort of bias places an exaggerated emphasis on physical appearance. Such attitudes are not isolated features of media programming; rather, they influence many interactions in everyday life. Sontag, Peteu, and Lee (1999) indicate that this is especially true among adolescents and young adults, for whom clothing, personal image, and identity tend to be inextricably bound.

Impressions of other people can be classified into two categories: stereotypes and individuating information. Stereotypes focus on social categories, while individuating information is the focus of other factors, including personality, actions of the individual, and so forth (Kunda & Thagard, 1996). The stereotype effect, as defined by researcher Monica Biernat (2003), is "a finding that individual members (comparable in all ways except their category membership) are judged in a direction consistent with group-level expectations or stereotypes" (p. 1019). Under such circumstances, people are judged more by the category in which one can group them than by their qualities or skills as individuals. However, according to Kunda and Thagard (1996), the division of these types of judgment is not always clear. This was the influence for their impression-formation theory in which stereotypes, traits, and behaviors are all constrained by positive and negative associations. In their research, they found that appearance was crucial in this process.

The influential power of stereotypes is particularly interesting when gender boundaries are crossed. In a 2003 study, researchers Vescio, Snyder, and Butz found that while membership in a socioeconomic class or "power position" (p. 1062) tended to give participants a biased or predetermined opinion about the beliefs and behaviors (such as work ethic) by which a person in another category lived, gender exerted at least as great an influence on the manner in which people were categorized. Mansfield (2006) demonstrated that males in power positions were likely to be viewed differently than females in the same positions.

Text: Double-spaced

Signal phrase with parenthetical citation for date; the word *and* used before last author's name

Introduction: DeGroot provides background, definitions, hypothesis.

Signal phrase with parenthetical citation for date, page number included with quotation

Date of publication in text, so not in parentheses following author names

Would these findings remain consistent if only one gender were used in the study? That is, can we identify intra-gender roles or stereotypes that similarly affect perception and beliefs about individuals? A study by G. H. Edwards (1992) found that beliefs regarding men and women transcend gender, with subtypes or categories (such as for men, businessman, athlete, or loser) emerging within each sex. Typically, such seeming variations represent varying degrees of a supposed normative "masculinity," rather than truly distinct expressions of a male gender role. Rudman and Fairchild (2004) write that "for men, a lifetime of experience observing one's peers being teased or ostracized for 'effeminate' behavior may evoke strong normative pressures toward highly masculine self-presentations" (p. 160). Plummer (2001) indicates that boys begin pressuring one another to conform in childhood, telling each other to toughen up or to stop acting like a baby.

Direct quotation from PDF; page number included

The purpose of this study is to observe whether male participants are likely to be influenced by a stereotypically "male" opinion. Are college-age males more swayed by the "jock" or "cool guy on campus" than by those with an "average Joe" or a "metrosexual" appearance? Hypothetically, male participants should be more likely to be swayed by the opinions of the stereotypical male than by those of the control group ("average Joe") or the experimental group (counterstereotypical).

Hypothesis

Methods

First-level heading (centered, boldface)

Participants

Second-level heading (left, boldface)

Twenty-six undergraduate males from a large southeastern university (mean age = 19) participated in this study to fill a course requirement in their general psychology classes.

Methods: DeGroot explains how study was conducted.

Procedure

The participants were randomly assigned to one of three conditions in the study: the stereotypically "male" proctor group, the counterstereotypical proctor group, and the control group. The proctor was the same person in each condition, but his appearance was different in each (Figure 1). In the stereotypically male

proctor condition, the proctor wore an outfit consisting of team sports apparel: a

baseball cap, a basketball jersey, shorts, and sneakers. In the counterstereotypical

condition, he wore a long-sleeved, light pink button-down shirt (tucked in), creased

khaki pants, and dress shoes. In the control condition, the proctor wore a short-

sleeved blue polo shirt (not tucked in), khaki shorts, and sneakers.

The participants in each condition were told at the beginning of the experiment

that they were participating in a memory-recall task. They were to identify what

they could remember from a clip from the movie *Pretty Woman* (Milchan, Reuther,

& Marshall, 1990), a stereotypical "chick-flick." During the ten-minute film clip, which

was constant for each of the three conditions, the proctor read scripted lines such as

"Oh! I love this part!" and "I'm seriously such a sap, but this film is just so good!" The

script was a constant in each of the three conditions.

After the clip was viewed by all, the proctor handed out a questionnaire to

conduct the "memory-recall task." The questionnaire contained diversion questions

such as "What color is the dress that Vivian (Julia Roberts's character) wears in the

scene?" and "What game do Edward and Vivian play after the performance?" At the

end of the questionnaire, the participants rated the movie on an opinion scale from 1

to 10, with 10 being the highest overall liking.

After the experiment was over, participants in each condition were debriefed as

a group and were dismissed from the study.

Results

A one-way analysis of variance (ANOVA) was conducted on the data to

determine whether males are more influenced by a stereotypically "male" proctor

in comparison to the counterstereotypical and control-group proctors. The analysis

demonstrated that at least one group was significantly different from the others,

$F(2, 23) = 4.08$, $p < .05$. Tukey HSD post hoc tests were performed to measure

the difference between the groups individually. The Tukey HSD revealed that the

---

Projects for publication: Tables and figures follow reference list or endnotes. College projects: Ask your instructor—tables and figures may be included in the text, following the first reference to them. Figures for this project appear on p. 254.

Ampersand used in parenthetical citation

Results: DeGroot summarizes data and research findings; includes figures, p. 254.

participants were more likely to give a favorable movie rating under the influence

of the counterstereotypically masculine proctor (*M* = 8.67, *SD* = 1.53) than the

stereotypically masculine proctor (*M* = 5.31, *SD* = 1.97) or the control proctor (*M* =

5.20, *SD* = 1.99) (see Figure 2).

There were no significant differences in movie ratings between those in the

stereotypically masculine proctor's group and those in the control proctor's group.

These results were contrary to the study's initial hypothesis, and they suggest

that male participants are more likely to defy gender roles in the presence of a

counterstereotypical proctor than in the presence of a stereotypically masculine

proctor.

Discussion

The study elicited something beyond stereotypical responses from the

participants. In fact, the participants may have experienced gender role conflict

Instead of scoring the film favorably when the masculine male proctor said he

enjoyed the film, the participants scored it lower than initially expected. The

presence of a highly or moderately "masculine" male, though he made favorable

comments in each condition, may have caused the participants to adhere more

rigidly to socialized male gender roles and thus rate the movie lower than subjects

in the atypically "masculine" proctor group, who did not feel the pressure to assert

masculinity in their rating of *Pretty Woman*. (See McCreary et al., 1996.)

> Discussion: DeGroot interprets data, draws conclusions, expresses concerns, and raises questions for further study.

> Citations of six or more authors: First author plus *et al.*

Certain irregularities in the study provoked questions that might be

investigated in future research. Due to factors beyond the researcher's control,

each condition had a different number of participants. The counterstereotypical

condition, which had significant findings, had the smallest number of participants;

as a result, those scores are subject to greater statistical variation due to strong

individual opinion. However, one might also question whether the number of males

present influences a subject's tendency to admit to a counterstereotypical opinion

or value judgment. If the study were to be replicated to search for just stereotype

differences, it would be crucial for the number of participants in each condition to be the same. In contrast, a separate study might use multiple viewing groups of varying individual sizes to determine the effect of group size in gender-stereotype-determined valuations.

Another issue to consider is the effect of the fictional nature of the film to which the male viewers were asked to react. A study reported in *Business Week* suggests that men are more willing to show empathy when they know the stories eliciting their emotional response are fictional. Jennifer Argo, one of the authors of the study, is quoted as saying that fictional works provide "an excuse to relax gender stereotypes" (as cited in Coplan, 2008, p. 17). This factor was not considered in the study reported here.

References *Heading (centered), new page; entries alphabetized by author*

Biernat, M. (2003). Toward a broader view of social stereotyping. *American Psychologist,*
    58, 1019–1027. doi:10.1037/0003-066X.58.12.1019

Coplan, J. H. (2008, January 28). When it's all right for guys to cry. *Business Week,*
    4068, 17. Retrieved from http://www.businessweek.com

Edwards, G. H. (1992). The structure and content of the male gender role stereotype:
    An exploration of subtypes. *Sex Roles: A Journal of Research, 27,* 533–551.

Kunda, Z., & Thagard, P. (1996). Forming impressions from stereotypes, traits, and behaviors:
    A parallel-constraint-satisfaction theory. *Psychological Review, 103,* 284–308.

Mansfield, H. C. (2006). *Manliness.* New Haven, CT: Yale University Press.

McCreary, D. R., Wong, F. Y., Wiener, W., Carpenter, K. M., Engle, A., & Nelson, P.
    (1996). The relationship between masculine gender role stress and psychological
    adjustment: A question of construct validity? *Sex Roles: A Journal of Research, 34,*
    507–516.

Milchan, A. (Producer), Reuther, S. (Producer), & Marshall, G. (Director). (1990). *Pretty
    woman* [Motion picture]. USA: Touchstone Home Video.

Plummer, D. C. (2001). The quest for modern manhood: Masculine stereotypes, peer
    culture and the social significance of homophobia. *Journal of Adolescence, 24,*
    15–23.

Rudman, L. A., & Fairchild, K. (2004). Reactions to counterstereotypic behavior: The
    role of backlash in cultural stereotype maintenance. *Journal of Personality and
    Social Psychology, 87,* 157–176.

Sontag, M. S., Peteu, M., & Lee, J. (1999). *Clothing in the self-system of adolescents: Rela-
    tionships among values, proximity of clothing to self, clothing interest, anticipated
    outcomes and perceived quality of life.* Retrieved from Michigan State University
    Extension website: http://web1.msue.msu.edu/msue/imp/modrr/rr556098.html

Vescio, T. K., Snyder, M., & Butz, D. A. (2003). Power in stereotypically masculine
    domains: A social influence strategy X stereotype match model. *Journal of
    Personality and Social Psychology, 85,* 1062. doi:10.1037/0022-3514.85.6.1062

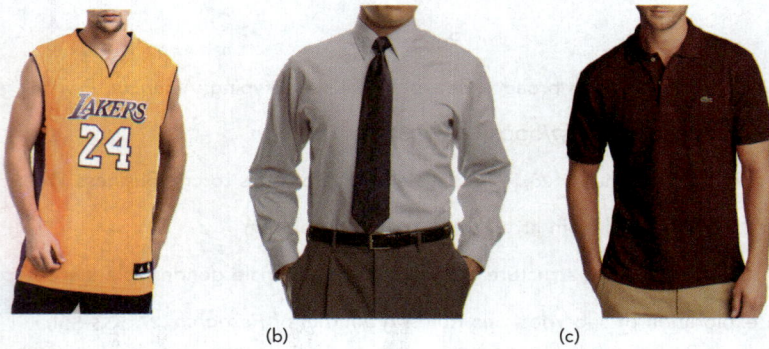

Figure caption: Label (*Figure*) and number in italics; caption below illustration

(a)   (b)   (c)

Figure 1. Male proctor in three conditions: (a) stereotypical, (b) counterstereotypical, and (c) control.

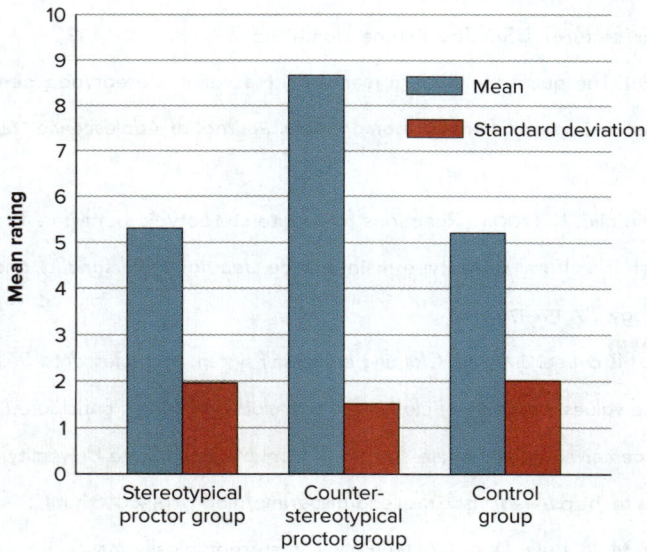

Figure 2. Tukey HSD post hoc test results for the three groups: Group with the stereotypical proctor, group with counterstereotypical proctor, and control group.

8

Documentation ❯❯

文献引用格式

Matters

Chicago and CSE Styles　文献引用格式：芝加哥格式和CSE格式

Use part 8 to learn, practice, and master these writer's responsibilities:

☐ **To Audience**

Cite and document sources so that readers can see where each use of sources begins and ends; format your research project using Chicago or CSE style, in keeping with readers' expectations.

☐ **To Topic**

Cite and document sources to demonstrate that you have explored your topic fully.

☐ **To Other Writers**

Provide citations for all borrowed ideas and information, whether quoted, para-phrased, or summarized; document all sources cited in the research project in notes and a bibliography or reference list at the end of the project.

☐ **To Yourself**

Use sources to build knowledge, and cite them to show readers where your ideas begin and end; to enhance your ethos, or credibility; and to present your ideas effectively.

27 Documenting Sources: *Chicago* Style
文献引注：芝加哥格式

Written by editors at the University of Chicago Press, the *Chicago Manual of Style* (17th ed.) provides advice to help writers and editors produce clear and consistent copy for their readers. Many writers in the humanities and social sciences (in history, economics, and philosophy, for example) follow the guidelines provided by the *Chicago Manual* for citing and documenting sources.

Editors at the University of Chicago Press recognize that readers from different disciplines may have different expectations about how in-text citations and bibliography entries should look, so the *Chicago Manual* provides an author-date system similar to that recommended by the American Psychological Association (APA) and the Council of Science Editors (CSE) for writers in the sciences. It also provides a note and bibliography system for writers in the humanities and social sciences. If your readers (including your instructor) expect you to use the author-date system, consult the *Chicago Manual* itself or follow the style detailed in the APA tab and CSE chapter in this book.

This chapter includes examples of the most common types of *Chicago*-style notes and bibliography entries. For more information or for examples of less common types of sources, consult the *Chicago Manual* itself. You can also subscribe to the *Chicago Manual* online.

> **More about**
> Popular academic documentation styles per discipline, 69
> MLA style, 157–211 (part 6)
> APA style, 213–54 (part 7)
> CSE style, 272–84 (ch. 28)

> **footnote** 脚注 Note that appears at the bottom of the page

> **endnote** 尾注 Note that appears in a list of notes at the end of the project

27a Creating *Chicago*-Style Notes and Bibliography Entries
注释和参考文献目录采用芝加哥格式

The note system offered by the *Chicago Manual* allows you to include full bibliographic information in a footnote or endnote or to use an abbreviated footnote or endnote with a bibliography. The University of Chicago Press recommends using abbreviated notes with a bibliography.

Writing Responsibly Citing and Documenting Sources

When you cite and document sources, you demonstrate how thoroughly you have researched your topic and how carefully you have thought about your sources, which encourages your audience to believe you are a credible researcher. In your citations and documentation, you acknowledge any material from which you have quoted, paraphrased, summarized, or drawn information, and you join the conversation on your topic by adding your own interpretation. Accurate entries in the body of your project and bibliography allow your audience to find and read your sources so that they can evaluate your interpretation and learn more about the subject themselves. Accurate entries also demonstrate the care with which you have written your research project, which further reinforces your credibility, or ethos.

to AUDIENCE

Examples of the *complete* form of notes and bibliography entries for different types of sources appear in the next section. An *abbreviated* note typically includes enough information for readers to recognize the work and find it in the bibliography. It usually includes the author's surname, a shortened version of the title that includes the title's key words in the same order as they appear on the title page, and the page number you are citing. Here is an example of an abbreviated note and a bibliography entry for the same book:

NOTE (ABBREVIATED)　　1. Vancouver, *Voyage of Discovery*, 283.

BIBLIOGRAPHY　　Vancouver, George. A *Voyage of Discovery* to the North
Pacific Ocean and Round the World, 1791–1795. Edited
by W. Kaye Lamb. London: Hakluyt Society, 1984.

A complete bibliographic note or bibliography entry includes three parts: the author's name, the title of the work, and the publication information (print, electronic, or both). The information you include in each of these parts will differ depending on the type of source you are citing. There are many models, but every variation cannot be covered, so be prepared to adapt a model to your special circumstances.

Books—Printed and Electronic 书籍——纸质版与电子版

In a printed book, the information you need to create a note and bibliography entry (with the exception of the page numbers) is on the title and copyright pages, at the beginning of the book. In an online or e-book, print and electronic publication information often appears at the top or bottom of the first screen or is available through a link.

1. One author

a. Printed The basic note for a printed book looks like this:

Ref. No. Author's first name Surname, *Title: Subtitle* (Place of Publication: Publisher, date of publication), page(s).

> Annotated visual of where to find author and publication information, tutorials in parts 6 and 7

Chicago Note & Bibliography Entries

1. One author
2. Two or three authors
3. More than three authors

> **More about**
Formatting notes (*Chicago* style), 271
Formatting bibliographies (*Chicago* style), 271

Tech　**Creating Footnotes and Endnotes**

Most word processing programs, including Microsoft Word and Google Docs, allow you to insert footnotes and endnotes easily. This automated system for inserting footnotes will automatically renumber all the notes in your project if you add or delete one. However, the software for managing notes may not provide many formatting options, so check with your instructor in advance to make sure the software's default format is acceptable.

Quick

Reference Examples of *Chicago*-Style Note and Bibliography Entries

Here is an example of an actual note:

> 1. Richard Wrangham, *Catching Fire: How Cooking Made Us Human* (New York: Basic Books, 2011), 96–98.

Chicago Note & Bibliography Entries

1. One author
2. Two or three authors
3. More than three authors

The basic bibliography entry for a printed book looks like this:

> Author's surname, First name. *Title: Subtitle*. Place of publication: Publisher, date of publication.

Here is an example of an actual bibliography entry:

> Wrangham, Richard. *Catching Fire: How Cooking Made Us Human*. New York: Basic Books, 2011.

The *Chicago Manual* allows for either full publishers' names (the name minus words like *Incorporated* or *Publishers*) or abbreviated versions (*Wiley* instead of *John Wiley & Sons,* for example). Be consistent within your research project. This chapter uses full names.

b. Database

2. W. E. B. Du Bois, *The Souls of Black Folk* (1903; Bartleby.com, 1999), chap. 1, www.bartleby.com/114/.

Du Bois, W. E. B. *The Souls of Black Folk.* Reprint of the 1903 edition, Bartleby.com, 1999. www.bartleby.com/114/.

> **Tech** Guidelines for Formatting URLs
>
> In *Chicago* style, if a URL will not fit on a single line, break it after a colon or a double slash (//), before or after an ampersand (&) or equals sign, and before a dot or other punctuation mark.

If the online book is *not* available in print or is not yet in final form and might change by the time your readers seek it out, provide your access date immediately before the DOI or URL. Separate the access date from the surrounding citation by commas in a note and by periods in a bibliography entry.

c. E-book

3. Charles C. Mann, *1491: New Revelations of the Americas before Columbus* (New York: Alfred A. Knopf, 2005), chap. 3, Adobe Reader.

Mann, Charles C. *1491: New Revelations of the Americas before Columbus.* New York: Alfred A. Knopf, 2005. Adobe Reader.

2. Two or three authors

4. David Gold and Catherine Hobbs, *Educating the New Southern Woman: Speech, Writing, and Race at the Public Women's Colleges, 1884–1945* (Carbondale, IL: Southern Illinois University Press, 2013).

5. William Rick Crandall, John A. Parnell, and John E. Spillan, *Crisis Management: Leading in the New Strategy Landscape* (Thousand Oaks, CA: Sage, 2012), 119.

Gold, David, and Catherine Hobbs. *Educating the New Southern Woman: Speech, Writing, and Race at the Public Women's Colleges, 1884–1945.* Carbondale, IL: Southern Illinois University Press, 2013.

Crandall, William Rick, John A. Parnell, and John E. Spillan. *Crisis Management: Leading in the New Strategy Landscape.* Thousand Oaks, CA: Sage, 2012.

Chicago Note & Bibliography Entries

1. One author
2. Two or three authors
3. More than three authors
4. Unnamed (anonymous) author

1st author only listed surname first

3. More than three authors

6. Lawrence Niles et al., *Life Along the Delaware Bay: Cape May Gateway to a Million Shorebirds* (Piscataway, NJ: Rutgers University Press, 2012), 87.

Niles, Lawrence, Joanna Burger, Amanda Dey, and Jan Van der Kam. *Life Along the Delaware Bay: Cape May Gateway to a Million Shorebirds.* Piscataway, NJ: Rutgers University Press, 2012.

1st author plus *et al.* ("and others" in Latin) in note

All authors in bibliography entry

Chicago Note & Bibliography Entries

4. Unnamed (anonymous) author If no author is listed, begin with the title.

7. *Terrorist Hunter: The Extraordinary Story of a Woman Who Went Undercover to Infiltrate the Radical Islamic Groups Operating in America* (New York: Ecco, 2003), 82.

Terrorist Hunter: The Extraordinary Story of a Woman Who Went Undercover to Infiltrate the Radical Islamic Groups Operating in America. New York: Ecco, 2003.

5. Two or more works by the same author Your note will be the same as for any book by one or more authors. In your bibliography, alphabetize the entries by the first important word in the title, and replace the author's name with three dashes in entries after the first.

Howard, Philip K. *Life Without Lawyers: Restoring Responsibility in America.* New York: Norton, 2011.

———. *Sacred Cows: How Dead Laws Drag Down Democracy.* New York: Norton, 2012.

6. Group or corporate author

group as author
8. Blackfoot Gallery Committee, *The Story of the Blackfoot People: Niitsitapiisinni* (Richmond Hill, ON: Firefly Books, 2002), 15.

group as author
Blackfoot Gallery Committee. *The Story of the Blackfoot People: Niitsitapiisinni.* Richmond Hill, ON: Firefly Books, 2002.

7. Editor (no author)

9. R. K. Ashdowne, ed., *Dictionary of Medieval Latin from British Sources, fascicule XVII, Syr-Z* (New York: Oxford University Press, 2013), 22.

Ashdowne, R. K., ed. *Dictionary of Medieval Latin from British Sources, fascicule XVII, Syr-Z.* New York: Oxford University Press, 2013.

Examples 1–3, 257–60

NOTE When the abbreviation *ed.* appears after a name, it means *editor*, so for more than one editor, change the abbreviation from *ed.* to *eds.*

8. Author and editor or translator

Edited by, Translated by, in bibliography

10. John Locke, *The Second Treatise of Government,* ed. Thomas P. Peardon (Indianapolis: Oxford University Press, 1990), 124.

11. Adania Shibli, *We Are All Equally Far from Love,* trans. Paul Starkey (Northhampton, MA: Interlink Books, 2012), 71.

Locke, John. *The Second Treatise of Government.* Edited by Thomas P. Peardon. Indianapolis: Oxford University Press, 1990.

Shibli, Adania. *We Are All Equally Far from Love.* Translated by Paul Starkey. Northhampton, MA: Interlink, 2012.

NOTE When the abbreviation *ed.* appears before a name, it means *edited by,* so do not add an *-s* when there is more than one editor.

9. Selection from an edited book or anthology

selection author / selection title / title of book in which selection appears

12. Rebecca Arnold, "Fashion," in *Feminist Visual Culture,* ed. Fiona Carson and Claire Pajaczkowska (New York: Routledge, 2001), 208.

Arnold, Rebecca. "Fashion." In *Feminist Visual Culture*, edited by Fiona Carson and Claire Pajaczkowska, 207–22. New York: Routledge, 2001.

selection pgs.

10. Edition other than the first

13. Patricia S. Daniels, Stephen G. Hyslop, and Douglas Brinkley, eds., *National Geographic Almanac of World History,* 3rd ed. (National Geographic, 2014), 72.

Daniels, Patricia S., Stephen G. Hyslop, and Douglas Brinkley, eds. *National Geographic Almanac of World History.* 3rd ed. Washington, DC: National Geographic, 2014.

11. Introduction, preface, foreword, or afterword by a different writer

14. Sister Helen Prejean, introduction to *Lead Me On, Let Me Stand: A Clergyman's Story in White and Black,* by William H. Barnwell (Columbia, SC: University of South Carolina Press, 2015), 7.

Prejean, Sister Helen. Introduction to *Lead Me On, Let Me Stand: A Clergy-man's Story in White and Black,* by William H. Barnwell, 3–12. Columbia, SC: University of South Carolina Press, 2015.

12. Entry in an encyclopedia or dictionary For a well-known reference work such as the *American Heritage Dictionary* or the *Encyclopedia Britannica,* a bibliography entry is not necessary.

a. Printed

15. *The American Heritage Dictionary,* 2nd college ed., s.v. "plagiarism."

> **s.v. 在该词下** Abbreviation of the Latin phrase *sub verbo,* "under the word"

b. Online Unless a "last updated" date appears on the site, include an access date before the URL.

16. *Dictionary.com,* s.v. "plagiarism," accessed July 14, 2010, http://dictionary.reference.com/browse/plagiarism.

13. Multivolume work

17. Robert Caro, *The Years of Lyndon Johnson,* vol. 3, *Master of the Senate* [vol. title] (New York: Alfred A. Knopf, 2002), 4.

> Vols. published in different years with different titles

18. George Brown Tindall and David E. Shi, *America: A Narrative History,* 8th ed. (New York: Norton, 2003), 2:123. [vol. pg.]

> Vols. published in same year with same title

Caro, Robert. *The Years of Lyndon Johnson.* Vol. 3, *The Master of the Senate.* New York: Alfred A. Knopf, 2002.

Tindall, George Brown, and David E. Shi. *America: A Narrative History.* 8th ed. 2 vols. New York: Norton, 2003.

14. Book in a series

19. Thomas Rickert, *Ambient Rhetoric: The Attunements of Rhetorical Being,* [book title] Pittsburgh Series in Composition, Literacy, and Culture [series title] (Pittsburgh, PA: University of Pittsburgh Press, 2013), 121.

Rickert, Thomas. *Ambient Rhetoric: The Attunements of Rhetorical Being.* [book title] Pittsburgh Series in Composition, Literacy, and Culture. [series title] Pittsburgh, PA: University of Pittsburgh Press, 2013.

15. Sacred text

book   lines   version

20. 1 Kings 3:23–26 (King James Version).

verse

21. Qur'an 17:1–2.

Generally, sacred texts are not included in the bibliography.

16. Dissertation or thesis For an unpublished dissertation or thesis, place the title in quotation marks; titles of published dissertations or theses are italicized. Include the type of document (*PhD diss., MA thesis*), the university where it was submitted, and the date of submission.

22. Jessica Davis Powers, "Patrons, Houses and Viewers in Pompeii: Reconsidering the House of the Gilded Cupids" (PhD diss., University of Michigan, 2006), 43–57, ProQuest (AAI 3208535).

Powers, Jessica Davis. "Patrons, Houses and Viewers in Pompeii: Reconsidering the House of the Gilded Cupids." PhD diss., University of Michigan, 2006. ProQuest (AAI 3208535).

Periodicals—Printed and Electronic 期刊——纸质版与电子版

A periodical is a publication issued at regular intervals—newspapers are generally published every day, magazines every week or month, and scholarly journals four times a year. For periodicals, include not only the title of the article (in quotation marks) but also the title of the periodical (in italics). The type of publication information you include depends on the type of periodical you are citing.

17. Article in a scholarly journal The information you need to create a note and bibliography entry for a printed journal article appears on the cover or title page of the journal and on the first and last pages of the article. For articles downloaded from a database, the information appears on the screen listing the articles that fit your search terms, on the full record of the article, or on the first and last pages of the file you download. For articles that appear in journals published solely online, you will find the publication information on the website's home page, in the journal's table of contents, or on the first page of the article.

a. Printed The basic note for an article in a printed journal looks like this:

Ref. No. Author's first name and Surname, "Title of Article," *Title of Journal* Vol. no., issue no. (Year of publication): Pages.

Chicago Note & Bibliography Entries

13. Multivolume work
14. Book in a series
15. Sacred text
16. Dissertation or thesis
17. Article in a scholarly journal
18. Article in a magazine
19. Article in a newspaper (signed)

Example 1, 257

Annotated visual of where to find author, title, and publication information, tutorials in parts 6 and 7

More about Formatting author information: Examples 1–6, 257–60

Months (May) or seasons (Winter) should be included before the year of publication. If a journal is paginated by volume—for example, if issue 1 ends on page 175 and issue 2 begins on page 176—the issue number may be omitted. Here are examples of notes and bibliography entries of journals with and without issue numbers.

Paginated by Issue (Issue Number Included)

23. Bishupal Limbu, "Democracy, Perhaps: Collectivity, Kinship, and the Politics of Friendship," *Comparative Literature* 63, no. 1 (2011): 92.

Limbu, Bishupal. "Democracy, Perhaps: Collectivity, Kinship, and the Politics of Friendship." *Comparative Literature* 63, no. 1 (2011): 92.

Paginated by Volume (No Issue Number)

24. Sarah Brown, "The Role of Elite Leadership in the Southern Defense of Segregation, 1954–1964," *Journal of Southern History* 77 (2011): 832.

Brown, Sarah. "The Role of Elite Leadership in the Southern Defense of Segregation, 1954–1964." *Journal of Southern History* 77 (2011): 827–64.

b. Accessed through a database Most researchers locate journal articles through subscription databases available through their college library. Frequently, articles indexed in such databases are also available in HTML or PDF format through the database. If the article you are citing is available in PDF format, include the page numbers you are citing in your note and the page range in your bibliography entry. If the article is available only in HTML format, add a subhead or paragraph number to your note if this will help readers locate the passage you are citing. To cite an article accessed through a subscription database, add the name of the database and reference number (if any) at the end of your entry, or include the URL if stable. More and more academic journals are also adding digital object identifiers (DOIs); if the article you are citing includes a DOI, add it in place of the database information.

HTML 超文本标记语言
Hypertext markup language, the coding system used to create websites and web pages

PDF 可携式文件格式
Portable document format, a method for sharing documents without losing formatting

DOI 数字对象识别码
Digital object identifier, a permanent identifier given to electronic sources

25. Kevin P. Dwyer et al., "Team Crisis: School Psychologists and Nurses Working Together," *Psychology in the Schools* 52, no. 7 (2015): 707, doi: 10.1002/pits.21850. Wylie Online Library.

Dwyer, Kevin P., et al. "Team Crisis: School Psychologists and Nurses Working Together." *Psychology in the Schools* 52, no. 7 (2015): 702–713. doi: 10.1002/pits.21850.

c. Online Online journals may not provide page numbers. Provide a subheading or paragraph number (if the article provides them), and include the DOI (if there is one) or the URL for the article (if there is no DOI).

> 26. Margaret F. Gibson, "Stressing Reproduction: Reading into Parents of Disabled Children," *Disability Studies Quarterly* 32, no. 1 (2012), http://www.dsq-sds.org/article/view/1654/3055.

> Gibson, Margaret F. "Stressing Reproduction: Reading into Parents of Disabled Children." *Disability Studies Quarterly* 32, no. 1 (2012). http://www.dsq-sds.org/article/view/1654/3055.

18. Article in a magazine Omit volume and issue numbers, and replace the parentheses around the publication date (month and year or month, day, and year) with commas. Page numbers may be omitted.

a. Printed

> 27. Marian Smith Holmes, "The Freedom Riders," *Smithsonian*, February 2009, 72.

> Holmes, Marian Smith. "The Freedom Riders." *Smithsonian*, February 2009, 70–75.

b. Accessed through a database

> 28. Lina Zeldovich, "Ancient Beer Recipes Lead to Modern Health Remedies," *Newsweek*, October 9, 2015. Access World News.
>
> *database*

> Zeldovich, Lina. "Ancient Beer Recipes Lead to Modern Health Remedies." *Newsweek*, October 9, 2015. Access World News.

c. Online

> 29. Alice Karekezi, "The Science of Warp," *Salon*, December 11, 2011, www.salon.com/2011/12/11/the_science_of_warp/.
>
> *article URL*

> Karekezi, Alice. "The Science of Warp." *Salon*, December 11, 2011. www.salon.com/2011/12/11/the_science_of_warp/.

19. Article in a newspaper (signed) Because page numbers may differ from edition to edition, use the edition name and section letter or number (if available) instead. A bibliography entry may be omitted.

a. Printed If the city in which the newspaper is published is not identified on the newspaper's masthead, add it in parentheses; if it might be
unfamiliar to readers, add the state, also.

30. Jim Kenneally, "When Brockton Was Home to a Marathon," *Enterprise*
<u>section no.</u>
(Brockton, MA), April 20, 2006, sec. 1.

Kenneally, Jim. "When Brockton Was Home to a Marathon." *Enterprise* (Brockton, MA), April 20, 2006, sec. 1.

For well-known national newspapers (such as *The Christian Science Monitor, USA Today,* and *The Wall Street Journal*), no city or state is needed.
If you are unsure whether the newspaper is well known, consult your
instructor or a reference librarian.

b. Accessed through a database

31. John M. Broder, "Geography Is Dividing Democrats over Energy,"
<u>database</u>
New York Times, January 26, 2009, late edition, sec. A, LexisNexis Academic.

Broder, John M. "Geography Is Dividing Democrats over Energy." *New York
Times,* January 26, 2009, late edition, sec. A, LexisNexis Academic.

c. Online

32. Victor Davis Hanson, "Oil-Rich America?," *Chicago Tribune,*
<u>article URL</u>
December 8, 2011, www.chicagotribune.com/news/politics/sns-201112070900-
-tms--vdhansonctnvh-a20111208dec08,0,6557873.column.

Hanson, Victor Davis. "Oil-Rich America?" *Chicago Tribune,* December 8, 2011.
www.chicagotribune.com/news/politics/sns-201112070900--tms--vdhan-
sonctnvh-a20111208dec08,0,6557873.column.

20. Article or editorial in a newspaper (unsigned) When no author is
named, place the newspaper's title in the author position in your bibliography entry. (*Chicago* style does not require a bibliography entry for
unsigned newspaper articles or editorials, but your instructor might.)

21. Review

33. Anthony Tommasini, review of *Siegfried,* by Richard Wagner, conducted
by Fabio Luisi, Metropolitan Opera, New York, *New York Times,* October 29, 2011,
sec. C.

Tommasini, Anthony. Review of *Siegfried,* by Richard Wagner, conducted by
Fabio Luisi, Metropolitan Opera, New York. *New York Times,* October 29,
2011, sec. C.

22. Letter to the editor Omit the letter's title, page numbers, and the edition name or number.

> 34. John A. Beck, letter to the editor, *Los Angeles Times*, March 16, 2010.

> Beck, John A. Letter to the editor. *Los Angeles Times*, March 16, 2010.

Other Electronic Sources 其他电子资源

Although it is usually easy to find citation information for books and articles in periodicals, websites can be a bit trickier. Most of the information you need will appear at the bottom or top of the web page or on the site's home page. Sometimes, however, you may need to look further. Click on links such as "About us" or "More information." Frequently, websites do not provide complete information, so provide as much information as you can. If no author is listed, place the site's sponsor in the "author" position. If key information is missing, include a phrase describing the site, in case the URL changes.

Annotated visual of where to find publication information, tutorials in parts 6 and 7

23. Website The basic note for a website looks like this:

> Ref. No. Website Title, Author, Sponsoring Organization, last update or access date if last update not provided, URL.

However, website titles that are the same as book titles or other types of publications should follow the styling for that publication. Here is an example of an actual note for a website that has the same title as a book:

> 35. *Victorian England: An Introduction,* Christine Roth, University of Wisconsin–Oshkosh, Department of English, accessed April 2, 2012, www.english.uwosh.edu/roth/VictorianEngland.htm.

The bibliography entry for the preceding note looks like this:

> Roth, Christine. *Victorian England: An Introduction.* University of Wisconsin–Oshkosh, Department of English. Accessed April 2, 2012. www.english.uwosh.edu/roth/VictorianEngland.htm.

Include an access date only when the publication date or last update is not indicated. *Chicago* style does not require an entry in the bibliography for web content, but if your instructor does, follow this example.

24. Web page or wiki article When referring to a specific page or article on a website or wiki, place that page's title in quotation marks. For a wiki article, begin with the article's title.

Chicago Note & Bibliography Entries

20. Article or editorial in a newspaper (unsigned)
21. Review
22. Letter to the editor
23. Website
24. Web page or wiki article
25. Discussion list or blog posting
26. CD-ROM

36. "Centennial Farm and Ranch Program," Montana History Wiki, Montana Historical Society, updated August 4, 2011, http://montanahistorywiki.pbworks.com/w/page/21639590/Centennial%20Farm%20and%20Ranch%20Program.

Montana Historical Society. "Centennial Farm and Ranch Program." Montana History Wiki. Updated August 4, 2011. http://montanahistorywiki.pbworks.com/w/page/21639590/Centennial%20Farm%20and%20Ranch%20Program.

25. Discussion list or blog posting A blog post need not be included in the bibliography.

26. CD-ROM If there is more than one version or edition of the CD-ROM, add that information after the title.

37. *History through Art: The 20th Century* (San Jose, CA: Fogware Publishing, 2000), chap. 1, CD-ROM.

History through Art: The 20th Century. San Jose, CA: Fogware Publishing, 2000. CD-ROM.

Audio and Visual Sources 视听资源

The information you need to create notes and bibliography entries for most audio and visual sources appears on the cover, label, or program or in the credits at the end of a film or a television show. Begin with the author, director, conductor, or performer, or begin your citation with the name of the work, depending on what your project emphasizes. The *Chicago Manual* provides few models of audiovisual sources. Those presented here are based on the principles explained in *Chicago*.

27. Motion picture (film, video, DVD)

38. *Juno*, directed by Jason Reitman, written by Diablo Cody (2007; Los Angeles: Fox Searchlight Home Entertainment, 2008), DVD.

Juno. Directed by Jason Reitman, written by Diablo Cody. 2007. Los Angeles: Fox Searchlight Home Entertainment, 2008. DVD.

28. Music or other audio recording

39. Johannes Brahms, *Piano Concerto no. 1 in D minor, op. 15*, Berliner Philharmoniker, conducted by Claudio Abbado, Philips Classics Productions BMG D153907, 1986, compact disc.

Brahms, Johannes. *Piano Concerto no. 1 in D minor, op. 15*. Berliner Philhar-

moniker. Claudio Abbado (conductor). Philips Classics Productions BMG

D153907, 1986, compact disc.

29. Podcast

40. Melvyn Bragg, "The Indian Mutiny," February 18, 2010, in *In Our Time*, BBC Radio 4, podcast, www.bbc.co.uk/programmes/b00qprnj.

Bragg, Melvyn. "The Indian Mutiny." *In Our Time*, BBC Radio 4, February 18, 2010. Podcast. www.bbc.co.uk/programmes/b00qprnj.

30. Performance

41. Jay O. Sanders, *Titus Andronicus*, dir. Michael Sexton, Anspacher The-ater, New York, NY, November 29, 2011.

Sanders, Jay O. *Titus Andronicus*. Directed by Michael Sexton. Anspacher The-ater, New York, NY, November 29, 2011.

31. Work of art If a reproduction of the work appears in your project, identify the work in a figure caption. If you discuss the work but do not show it, cite it in your notes but do not provide an entry in your bibliography. If the reproduction is taken from a book, follow the model for a selection from an edited book or anthology.

> **More about**
> Figure captions (*Chicago* style), 270

> Example 9, 261

42. Alexander Calder, *Two Acrobats*, 1929, wire sculpture, Menil Collec-tion, Houston.

Miscellaneous Sources—Printed and Electronic
其他来源——纸质版与电子版

32. Government publication For documents published by the US Gov-ernment Printing Office (or GPO), including the publisher is optional. If you omit the publisher, change the colon after the location to a comma.

33. Interview (published or broadcast)
a. Printed or broadcast

43. Barack Obama, interview by Maria Bartiromo, *Closing Bell*, CNBC, March 27, 2008.

Obama, Barack. Interview by Maria Bartiromo. *Closing Bell*, CNBC, March 27, 2008.

b. Online

> 44. Barack Obama, interview by Maria Bartiromo, *Closing Bell*, CNBC, March 27, 2008, www.cnbc.com/id/23832520.

> Obama, Barack. Interview by Maria Bartiromo. *Closing Bell*. CNBC, March 27, 2008. www.cnbc.com/id/23832520.

34. Personal communication Unless your instructor requires it, no bibliography entry is needed for a personal communication.

a. Letter

> 45. Theresa Dunn, letter to the author, August 13, 2016.

b. Email

> 46. Chris M. Anson, email message to the author, November 11, 2014.

35. Indirect source If you do not have access to the original source, mention the author you are citing in your text and include an entry in the bibliography that names both the original source and the source from which you borrowed the material.

27b Using *Chicago* Style for Tables and Figures
图表采用芝加哥格式

The *Chicago Manual* recommends that you number tables and figures in a separate sequence (*table 1, table 2, figure 1, figure 2*) both in the text and in the table title or figure caption. Tables and figures should be placed as close as possible after the text reference. For tables, provide a brief identifying title and place it above the table. For figures, provide a caption that includes any information about the figure that readers will need to identify it, such as the title of a work of art, the artist's name, the work's location, and a brief description. Place the caption below the figure. If the figure or table, or information used to create the figure or table, comes from another source, provide a source note. Source notes for tables generally appear below the table, while source information for figures appears at the end of the figure caption.

> *More about*
> MLA-style format-
>   ting, 198–11
> Formatting college
>   projects, 55

27c Formatting a *Chicago*-Style Research Project
研究项目版式采用芝加哥格式

The *Chicago Manual* provides detailed instructions about manuscript preparation for authors submitting their work for publication, but it does not offer formatting instructions for college projects. Follow the formatting instructions provided in chapter 8 or part 6, or consult your instructor.

Writing
Responsibly Of Deadlines and Paperclips

Instructors expect students to turn in thoughtful, carefully proofread, and neatly formatted projects on time—usually in class on the due date. They also expect writers to clip or staple the pages of the project *before* submitting it. Do justice to yourself by being fully prepared.

to SELF

1. Format notes The *Chicago Manual* recommends numbering bibliographic notes consecutively throughout the project, using superscript (above-the-line) numbers.

Mann, Charles C. *1491: New Revelations of the Americas before Columbus.* New York: Alfred A. Knopf, 2005. 173.

While acknowledging that not all scholars agree, Mann observes, "If Monte Verde is correct, as most believe, people were thriving from Alaska to Chile while much of northern Europe was still empty of mankind and its works."[8]

Type the heading "Notes" following the end of the text, and type the notes below the heading.

2. Format the bibliography To begin your list of works cited, type the heading "Bibliography," "References," or "Works Cited" at the top of a new page. (Ask your instructor which heading is preferred.) Entries should be formatted with a hanging indent: Position the first line of each entry flush with the left margin, and indent subsequent lines by one-half inch. Entries should be alphabetized by the author's surname.

More about
Hanging indent, 199, 244

Documenting Sources: CSE Style
文献引注：CSE格式

28

Writers in the sciences customarily use formatting and documentation guidelines from *Scientific Style and Format: The CSE Manual for Authors, Editors, and Publishers* (7th ed.) published by the Council of Science Editors (CSE). CSE style requires that sources be cited briefly in the text and documented in a reference list at the end of the project. The goal of providing in-text citations and a list of references is to allow readers to locate and read the sources for themselves and to distinguish the writer's ideas from those borrowed from sources.

28a Creating CSE-Style In-Text Citations 文内引用使用CSE格式

In-text citations, which appear in the body of your project, identify any material borrowed from a source, whether it is a quotation, paraphrase, summary, or idea. The CSE offers three formats for citing sources in the body of the project:

- Name-year
- Citation-sequence
- Citation-name

> *More about*
Popular academic documentation styles per discipline, 69
MLA style, 157–211 (part 6)
APA style, 213–54 (part 7)
Chicago style, 256–71 (ch. 27)

The *name-year system* requires you to include the last name of the author and the year of publication in parentheses whenever the source is cited:

> Advances have clarified the role of betalains and carotenoids in determining the color of flowers (Groteworld 2006).
>   *author*   *date*

If you use the author's name in your sentence, include just the year of publication in parentheses:

>   *author*
> Christoffel (2007) argues that public health officers adopted the strategies
> *date*
> they did because they were facing a crisis.

The name-year system tells readers immediately who wrote the source and how current it is, which is particularly crucial in the sciences. This system involves many rules for creating in-text citations (for example, how to create in-text citations for several authors, with organizations as authors, and so on), which can make it difficult to apply the rules consistently.

The *citation-sequence* and *citation-name systems* use a superscript number (the same number for a source each time it is cited) to refer the reader to a list of references at the end of the project.

Writing
Responsibly   **Citing and Documenting Sources**

When you cite and document sources, you acknowledge any material from which you have quoted, paraphrased, summarized, or drawn information, and you join the conversation on your topic by adding your own interpretation, data, methods, and results. Simultaneously, you give interested readers (including your instructor) a way to join the conversation. Accurate entries allow your audience to find and read your sources so that they can evaluate your research and learn more about the subject themselves. Accurate entries also demonstrate the care with which you have written your project, which reinforces your credibility, or ethos.

to AUDIENCE

Some testing of the River Invertebrate Prediction and Classification System (RIVPACS) had already been conducted[1]. Biologists in Great Britain then used environmental data to establish community type[2], and two studies developed predictive models for testing the effects of habitat-specific sampling[3,4]. These did not, however, account for the earlier RIVPACS research[1].

> Place reference numbers before punctuation marks. When drawing information from multiple sources, include multiple citations, separated by commas (no space between commas and reference numbers).

When using the citation-sequence system, arrange the sources in your reference list in order of first mention in your research report and then number them. (The first work cited is number 1, the second work cited is number 2, and so on.) When using the citation-name system, alphabetize sources and then number them. (The first work alphabetically is number 1, the second work alphabetically is number 2, and so on.)

The citation-sequence and citation-name systems need no rules about how to form in-text citations, but they do require readers to turn to the reference list to see the name of the author and the source's date of publication. Since the word processor's footnoting system cannot be used, numbering (and renumbering) of notes must be done by hand. To avoid the confusion that can arise during revision and editing, consider using a simplified author-date system while drafting the research project and inserting the numbers for the citation-sequence or citation-name system in the final draft.

Check with your instructor about which system to use, and use it consistently. If your instructor does not have a preference, consider the advantages and drawbacks of each system before making your choice.

Tech   **Creating Superscript Numbers**

The footnoting function in your word processing program will not work for inserting reference numbers for the citation-sequence or citation-name systems because it will insert the reference marks only in sequence (*1, 2, 3, . . .*), whereas the CSE system requires that you use the same superscript number for a source each time you cite it. Instead, insert superscript numbers manually, without using your word processing program's footnote function, and type your list of references separately. (Use the Help function of your word processor to learn about inserting superscript numbers.)

28b Preparing a CSE-Style Reference List
准备CSE格式的参考文献列表

A research report or project in CSE style ends with a list of cited references. How you format those references depends on the type of source and the system you use.

Books—Printed and Electronic 书籍——纸质版与电子版

In a printed book, you can find most or all of the information you need to create a reference list entry on the copyright and title pages at the beginning of the book. In an e-book, print and electronic publication information often appears at the top or bottom of the first page or is available through a link.

1. One author

a. Printed The basic format for a printed book looks like this:

Name-year system

> Author's surname First and Middle Initials. Date of publication. Title: subtitle. Place of publication: Publisher.

Citation-sequence and citation-name systems

> Ref. No. Author's surname First and Middle Initials. Title: subtitle. Place of publication: Publisher; date of publication.

NOTE Book titles are neither italicized nor underlined in CSE style.

Here are examples of actual reference list entries:

Name-year system

> Wedge M. 2012. Pills are not for preschoolers: a drug-free approach for troubled kids. New York (NY): Norton.

Citation-sequence and citation-name systems

> 1. Wedge M. Pills are not for preschoolers: a drug-free approach for troubled kids. New York (NY): Norton; 2012.

b. Online

Name-year system

> Stroup A. 1990. A company of scientists: botany, patronage, and community at the seventeenth-century Parisian Royal Academy of Sciences [Internet].
> *print publication information* *access date*
> Berkeley (CA): University of California Press [cited 2012 Mar 2]. Available from:
> *URL (permalink)*
> http://ark.cdlib.org/ark:/13030/ft587006gh/.

CSE Reference List Entries

1. One author
2. Two or more authors
3. Group or corporate author

No punctuation between surname and initials and no period or space between initials

---

Lines after the first align with the author's name, not the reference number.

> Annotated visual of where to find author, title, and publication information, tutorials in parts 6 and 7

Citation-sequence and citation-name systems

2. Stroup A. A company of scientists: botany, patronage, and community at the seventeenth-century Parisian Royal Academy of Sciences [Internet]. Berkeley (CA): University of California Press; 1990 [cited 2012 Mar 2]. Available from: http://ark.cdlib.org/ark:/13030/ft587006gh/.

> Period after citation only if it concludes in a forward slash

2. Two or more authors

Name-year system

Janzon L, Hallmen J. 2014. Bugs up close: a magnified look at the incredible world of insects. New York (NY): Skyhorse.

> Follow the order of authors on the title page. No *and* before last author.

Citation-sequence and citation-name systems

3. Janzon L, Hallmen J. 2014. Bugs up close: a magnified look at the incredible world of insects. New York (NY): Skyhorse.

If the source has more than ten authors, list the first ten; after the tenth author, insert the words *et al.*

CSE Reference List Entries

1. One author
2. Two or more authors
3. Group or corporate author
4. Edited book

3. Group or corporate author

Name-year system

Institute of Medicine Committee on the Use of Complementary and Alternative Medicine by the American Public. 2005. Complementary and alternative medicine in the United States. Washington (DC): National Academies Press.

Citation-sequence and citation-name systems

4. Institute of Medicine Committee on the Use of Complementary and Alternative Medicine by the American Public. Complementary and alternative medicine in the United States. Washington (DC): National Academies Press; 2005.

4. Edited book

Name-year system

Vogt T, Dhamen W, Binev P, editors. 2012. Modeling nanoscale imaging in electron microscopy. New York (NY): Springer.

Citation-sequence and citation-name systems

5. Vogt T, Dhamen W, Binev P, editors. Modeling nanoscale imaging in electron microscopy. New York (NY): Springer; 2012.

5. Selection from an edited book or conference proceedings

Name-year system

selection author / selection title
Berkenkotter C. 2000. Scientific writing and scientific thinking: writing the scientific habit of mind. In: Goggin MD, editor. book title — Inventing a discipline: rhetoric scholarship in honor of Richard E. Young. Urbana (IL): National Council of Teachers of English. selection pages p. 270–284.

Citation-sequence and citation-name systems

6. Berkenkotter C. Scientific writing and scientific thinking: writing the scientific habit of mind. In: Goggin MD, editor. Inventing a discipline: rhetoric scholarship in honor of Richard E. Young. Urbana (IL): National Council of Teachers of English; 2000. p. 270–284.

To cite a paper published in the proceedings of a conference, add the number and name of the conference, the date of the conference, and the location of the conference (separated by semicolons and ending with a period) after the title of the book and before the publication information.

presenter   title of presentation

Hazen RM. Mineral evolution, mineral ecology, and the coevolution of life and

                                date of   location of
           name of conference   presentation   conference

rocks. American Society for Cell Biology Conference; 2014 Dec 6; Philadelphia

(PA).

6. Dissertation For dissertations published by University Microfilms International (UMI), include the access number.

Name-year system

Song LZ. 2003. Relations between optimism, stress and health in

Chinese and American students [dissertation]. Tucson: University of Arizona.

access information   location   access no.
Available from: UMI, Ann Arbor, MI; AAI3107041.

Citation-sequence and citation-name systems

7. Song LZ. Relations between optimism, stress and health in Chinese and

American students [dissertation]. Tucson: University of Arizona; 2003. Avail-

able from: UMI, Ann Arbor, MI; AAI3107041.

If the location of the college is not listed on the title page of the dissertation, place square brackets around this information: [Tucson].

Periodicals—Printed and Electronic 期刊——纸质版与电子版

The information needed to document a printed journal article appears on the cover or table of contents of the journal and the first and last pages of the article. For articles downloaded from a database, the information you need appears on the screen listing the articles that fit your search terms, on the full record of the article, or on the first (and last) page of the file you download. For journal articles published online, the information you need appears on the website's home page, on that issue's web page, or on the first screen of the article.

7. Article in a scholarly journal

a. Printed The basic citation for an article in a scholarly journal looks like this:

Name-year system

Author's surname First and Middle Initials. Year of publication. Title: subtitle.

Abbreviated Journal Title. Vol. number(Issue number):page numbers.

CSE Reference List Entries

4. Edited book
5. **Selection from an edited book or conference proceedings**
6. **Dissertation**
7. **Article in a scholarly journal**
8. Article in a magazine

More about Formatting author information: Examples 1–5, 274–76

Annotated visual of where to find author and publication information, tutorials in parts 6 and 7

Citation-sequence and citation-name systems

> Ref. No. Author's surname First and Middle Initials. Title: subtitle. Abbreviated Journal Title. Year of publication; Vol. number(Issue number):page numbers.

Here is an actual citation of each type:

Name-year system

> Cox L. 2007. The community health center perspective. Behav Healthc. 27(3):20–21.

Citation-sequence and citation-name systems

> 8. Cox L. The community health center perspective. Behav Healthc. 2007; 27(3):20–21.

b. Accessed through a database Most researchers locate journal articles through subscription databases available through their college library. Frequently, articles indexed in such databases are available in HTML or PDF format through a link from the database. As yet, the CSE does not provide a model for an article accessed through an online database, but since most library databases are by subscription, readers will probably find the URL of the database's home page more useful than a direct link to the article itself. If a DOI is available, include it.

Name-year system

> Yuan F, Mayer B. 2012. Chemical and isotopic evaluation of sulfur
>
> sources and cycling in the Pecos River, New Mexico, USA. Chem Geol
>
> medium   access date   database
> [Internet]. [cited 2016 Aug 7];291(1–2):13–22. In: Science Direct. Available
> URL (database home page)   DOI
> from: www.sciencedirect.com doi:10.1016/j.chemgeo.2011.11.014

Citation-sequence and citation-name systems

> 9. Yuan F, Mayer B. Chemical and isotopic evaluation of sulfur sources and cycling in the Pecos River, New Mexico, USA. Chem Geol [Internet]. 2012 [cited 2016 Aug 7];291(1–2):13–22. Available from: www.sciencedirect.com doi:10.1016/j.chem geo.2011.11.014

c. Online Omit page numbers for online articles. When a subscription is not required to access the article, provide a direct permalink URL to the article; otherwise, provide the URL to the journal's home page. If a DOI is provided, include it.

Journal titles: Omit punctuation, articles (*an, the*), and prepositions (*of, on, in*), and abbreviate most words longer than five letters (except one-word titles like *Science* and *Nature*).

DOI 数字对象识别码 Digital object identifier, a permanent identifier assigned to electronic articles

No period after URL (unless it concludes with a forward slash) or DOI

CSE Reference List Entries

6. Dissertation
7. **Article in a scholarly journal**
8. Article in a magazine

Name-year system

Patten SB, Williams HVA, Lavorato DH, Eliasziw M. 2009. Allergies and major depression: a longitudinal community study. Biopsychosoc Med [Internet]. [cited 2016 Feb 5];3(3). Available from: www.bpsmedicine.com/content/3/1/3 doi:10.1186/1751-0759-3-3

URL (permalink)

DOI

No period after URL or DOI

Citation-sequence and citation-name systems

10. Patten SB, Williams HVA, Lavorato DH, Eliasziw M. Allergies and major depression: a longitudinal community study. Biopsychosoc Med [Internet]. 2009 [cited 2016 Feb 5];3(3). Available from: www.bpsmedicine.com/content/3/1/3 doi:10.1186/1751-0759-3-3

8. Article in a magazine

a. Printed
Name-year system

Schulz K. 2015 Oct 19. Pond scum. New Yorker. 40–45.

Citation-sequence and citation-name systems

11. Schulz K. Pond scum. New Yorker. 2015 Oct 19; 40–45.

b. Accessed through a database
Name-year system

Schulz K. 2015 Oct 19 [cited 2016 Apr 23]. Pond scum. New Yorker [Internet]: 138–149. Available from: www.newsbank.com

Citation-sequence and citation-name systems

12. Schulz K. Pond scum. New Yorker [Internet]. 2015 Oct 19 [cited 2016 Apr 23]: 138–149. Available from: www.newsbank.com

c. Online
Name-year system

Coghlan A. 2007 May 16 [cited 2016 May 19]. Bipolar children: is the US overdiagnosing? NewScientist.com [Internet] Available from: www.newscientist.com/channel/health/mg19426043.900-bipolar-children--is-the-us-overdiagnosing.html/.

URL (permalink)

CSE Reference List Entries

5. Selection from an edited book or conference proceedings
6. Dissertation
7. Article in a scholarly journal
8. Article in a magazine
9. Article in a newspaper
10. Website

Citation-sequence and citation-name systems

13. Coghlan A. Bipolar children: is the US overdiagnosing? NewScientist.com [Internet]. 2007 May 16 [cited 2016 May 19]. Available from: www.newscientist.com/channel/health/mg19426043.900-bipolar-children--is-the-us-overdiagnosing.html/.

9. Article in a newspaper

a. Printed

Name-year system

Stern J. 2015 Dec 5. How terror hardens us. New York Times (Late Ed.). Sun. Rev.:1.

Citation-sequence and citation-name systems

14. Stern J. How terror hardens us. New York Times (Late Ed.). 2015 Dec 5; Sun. Rev.:1.

b. Accessed through a database

Name-year system

Stern J. 2015 Dec 5 [cited 2016 Feb 7]. How terror hardens us. New York Times [Internet]. Sun. Rev.:1. Available from: www.lexisnexis.com/.

Citation-sequence and citation-name systems

15. Stern J. How terror hardens us. New York Times [Internet]. 2015 Dec 5 [cited 2016 Feb 7];Sun. Rev.:1. Available from: www.lexisnexis.com/.

c. Online

Name-year system

LaFee S. 2006 May 17. Light can hold fatal attraction for many nocturnal animals. San Diego Union-Tribune [Internet] [cited 2016 May 20] [about 11 paragraphs]. Available from: www.signonsandiego.com/news/science/.

Citation-sequence and citation-name systems

Include permalink URL if available; if not, use URL of home page.

16. LaFee S. Light can hold fatal attraction for many nocturnal animals. San Diego Union-Tribune [Internet]. 2006 May 17 [cited 2016 May 20] [about 11 paragraphs]. Available from: www.signonsandiego.com/news/science/.

Miscellaneous Sources—Printed and Electronic
其他资源——纸质版与电子版

The information needed to document a website or web page usually appears at the top or bottom of the home page or web page. You may also need to look for a link to a page labeled "About us" or "Contact us." Frequently, information needed for a complete reference list entry is missing, in which case you should provide as much information as you can.

> Annotated visual of where to find author, title, and publication information, tutorials in parts 6 and 7

10. Website

Name-year system

In the name-year system, a sample reference entry for a website looks like this:

Author. Title of website [Medium (Internet)]. Publication date [Access date]. Available from: URL (home page)

Here is an example of an actual entry:

MIT news [Internet]. 2009 Feb 9 [cited 2016 Mar 10]. Available from: http://web.mit.edu/newsoffice/index.html/.

The site has no author, so the reference-list entry begins with the name of the site's sponsor.

Citation-sequence and citation-name systems

When referencing an entire website, the only difference between the name-year system and the citation-sequence and citation-name systems is that the citation-sequence and citation-name entries add a reference number at the beginning of the entry.

11. Web page When documenting a web page or a document on a website, provide the URL for the web page, not the site's home page.

Name-year system

article author
Schorow S. 2009 Feb 5. Aliens at sea: anthropologist Helmreich studies article title
researchers studying ocean microbes. MIT news [Internet]. [cited 2015 Mar 10]. website
Available from: http://web.mit.edu/newsoffice/2009/alien-ocean-0205.html URL (web page)

Citation-sequence and citation-name systems

17. Schorow S. Aliens at sea: anthropologist Helmreich studies researchers studying ocean microbes. MIT news [Internet]. 2009 Feb 5 [cited 2015 Mar 10]. Available from: http://web.mit.edu/newsoffice/2009/alien-ocean-0205.html

CSE Reference List Entries

8. Article in a magazine
9. Article in a newspaper
10. Website
11. Web page
12. Discussion list or blog posting
13. Email message

12. Discussion list or blog posting

Name-year system

date/time posted

Bolden C. 2015 Jul 17, 10:47 am [cited 2015 Aug 27]. Request for observa-

disc. list   medium

tions of parasites in fisheries. In: FISH-SCI [Internet discussion list]. [Lulea (Swe-

den): National Higher Research and Education Network]. [about 2 paragraphs].

Available from: http://segate.sunet.se/cgi-bin/wa?A0=FISH-SCI

Citation-sequence and citation-name systems

18. Bolden C. Request for observations of parasites in fisheries. In: FISH-SCI

[Internet discussion list]. [Lulea (Sweden): National Higher Research and

Education Network]; 2015 Jul 17, 10:47 am [cited 2015 Aug 27]. [about 2

paragraphs]. Available from: http://segate.sunet.se/cgi-bin/wa?A0=FISH-SCI

13. Email message

Name-year system

email author   date/time sent   subject line

Martin SP. 2012 Nov 18, 3:31 pm. Revised results [Email]. Message to:

email recipient   length

Lydia Jimenez [cited 2012 Nov 20]. [about 2 screens].

Citation-sequence and citation-name systems

19. Martin SP. Revised results [Email]. Message to: Lydia Jimenez. 2012 Nov

18, 3:31pm [cited 2012 Nov 20]. [about 2 screens].

14. Technical report or government document If no author is listed, use the name of the governing nation and the government agency that produced the document, and include any identifying number.

Name-year system

Department of Health and Human Services (US). 1985 May. Women's health.

Report of the Public Health Service Task Force on Women's Health Issues.

[publisher unknown]. PHS:85-50206.

Citation-sequence and citation-name systems

20. Department of Health and Human Services (US). Women's health. Report

of the Public Health Service Task Force on Women's Health Issues. [pub-

lisher unknown]; 1985 May. PHS:85-50206.

More about
Writing an
  abstract, 245
Formatting college
  papers, 55
Formatting a
  paper in APA
  style, 243–54

Writing **Responsibly** | Of Deadlines and Paperclips

Instructors expect students to turn in thoughtful, carefully proofread, and neatly formatted projects on time—usually in class on the due date. They also expect writers to clip or staple the pages of the paper *before* the project is submitted. Do justice to yourself by being fully prepared.

to SELF

28c Formatting a CSE-Style Research Project
研究项目版式采用CSE格式

The CSE does not specify a format for the body of a college research report, but most scientific reports include the following sections:

- Abstract
- Introduction
- Methods
- Results
- Discussion
- References

Ask your instructor for formatting guidelines, refer to the general formatting guidelines provided in chapter 8, or follow the formatting guidelines for APA style in part 7.

Start a new page for your reference list, and title it "References."

Name-year system List entries in alphabetical order by author's surname. If no author is listed, alphabetize by the first main word of the title (omitting articles such as *the, a,* and *an*). Do not number the entries.

Citation-sequence system Number your entries in order of their appearance in your project. Each work should appear in your reference list only once, even if it is cited more than once in your project. Double-check to make sure that the numbers in your reference list match the numbers in your text.

Citation-name system Alphabetize the entries in your reference list first (by the author's surname or the first main word of the title if no author is listed). Then number them. Each work should appear in your reference list only once, even if it is cited more than once in your project. Double-check to make sure that the numbers in your reference list match the numbers in your text.

Student Model 学生范文 Research Project: CSE-Style Reference List

The sample reference list on the next page is taken from a laboratory report by Alicia Keefe, University of Maryland. Keefe fulfilled her responsibility to the writers from whom she borrowed information and ideas by supplying a complete citation for each source. She fulfilled her responsibility to her reader by formatting the entries using the name-year system in CSE style, in keeping with her reader's expectations.

References

Web page: Date cited and URL of web page provided

FlyBase: phylogeny. 2015 May 13. FlyBase [Internet] [cited 2015 7 Dec]. Available from: http://flybase.org/wiki/FlyBase:Phylogeny

Journal article: Accessed through a database, no DOI; URL of database home page provided

Hoikkala A, Aspi J. 1993 [cited 2016 Apr 28]. Criteria of female mate choice in *Drosophila littoralis, D. montana,* and *D. ezoana.* Evolution [Internet]. 47(3):768–778. Available from: http://web.ebscohost.com

Journal article: Printed, title of journal abbreviated

Ives JD. 1921. Cross-over values in the fruit fly, *Drosophila ampelophila,* when the linked factors enter in different ways. Am Naturalist. 6:571–573.

Mader S. 2005. Lab manual. 9th ed. New York (NY): McGraw-Hill.

Journal article: Accessed through a database, with DOI

Marcillac F, Bousquet F, Alabouvette J, Savarit F, Ferveur JF. 2005 [cited 2016 Apr 28]. A mutation with major effects on *Drosophila melanogaster* sex pheromones. Genetics [Internet]. 171(4):1617–1628. Available from: http://web.ebscohost.com doi:10.1534/genetics.104.033159

Journal article: Printed, one-word journal title not abbreviated

Service PM. 1991. Laboratory evolution of longevity and reproductive fitness components in male fruit flies: mating ability. Evolution. 47:387–399.

284

9

Style 关注语言风格

Matters

Writing Engagingly 体贴地写作

Use part 9 to learn, practice, and master these
writer's responsibilities:

❑ **To Audience**

Use parallelism to present ideas forcefully to your readers, use sentence openings and closings to highlight important information, choose language appropriate to your context, and hold your readers' attention with compelling words and figures.

❑ **To Topic**

Address your topic concisely but with substance, use coordination and subordination to distinguish primary from secondary information, choose words appropriately for both their meaning and their associations, and choose accurate synonyms.

❑ **To Other Writers**

Use responsible language to avoid misrepresenting others.

❑ **To Yourself**

Write concisely for increased clarity and effectiveness, choose the active voice whenever possible to energize your writing, and convey your thoughts forthrightly, avoiding euphemism and doublespeak.

29 Writing Concisely 简洁写作

Wordy writing is like young children's soccer: The point gets made haltingly, if at all. Concise writing, in contrast, is like the play of a World Cup team. Each word, like each player, counts; every point is made forcefully and without duplication of effort.

Conciseness What one culture considers wordy, another may consider elegant. Not only culture but also context affect what readers expect: In literary contexts and even in some personal writing, US readers sometimes appreciate rich, expansive sentences. In academic and business contexts, however, US readers usually prefer writing that is concise and to the point.

29a Eliminating Wordy Expressions 删除冗长的表达

First-draft writing sometimes contains common but wordy expressions that pad and clutter sentences. As you revise, prune these away.

Empty expressions like *to all intents and purposes, in fact, the fact is,* and *in the process of* carry no information, so you should delete them.

> ▸ My roommate was ~~in the process of~~ applying for the job, but ~~in fact~~ it had already been filled.

Similarly, intensifiers like *absolutely, actually, definitely, really,* and *totally* add little meaning to the words they modify.

> ▸ The tourists were ~~absolutely~~ thrilled. None of them had ~~actually~~ seen a polar bear before.

Phrases built around words like *aspect, character, kind, manner,* and *type* are also often mere filler.

> ▸ They ~~are the kind of people who~~ have always ~~behaved in a generous manner.~~ *been generous.*

Quick Reference **Strategies for Writing Concisely**

- ■ Cut wordy expressions. (286)
- ■ Cut ineffective or unnecessary repetition. (288)
- ■ Avoid wordy sentence patterns. (288–89)
- ■ Consolidate phrases, clauses, and sentences. (289)

Writing Responsibly

Conciseness versus the Too-Short Paper

Effective writing should be concise but not necessarily brief. Concise writing provides readers with all the information they need without distractions, but it does not skimp on essential detail. It may take a long sentence to express a complex thought. Do not shortchange your readers—or your ideas—by omitting necessary detail.

In contrast, a too-short paper may tempt you to pad, but that may make your writing hard (and boring) to read. Instead of adding words, try developing your ideas and searching for facts, statistics, expert testimony, and examples that will bring your paper to life.

to AUDIENCE

> **More about**
> Sentence length
>   and variety,
>   293–303
> Crafting a thesis,
>   23–24
> Developing para-
>   graphs, 32–35,
>   40–41

Some expressions say in many words what is better said with one.

Wordy Expression	Concise Alternative
at the present time	now (or delete entirely)
at this point in time	now (or delete entirely)
at that point in time	then (or delete entirely)
until such time as	until
at all times	always
at no time	never
most of the time	usually
in this day and age	today
due to the fact that	because
in spite of the fact that	although, even though
has the ability to	can
in the event that	if
in the neighborhood of	around

▸ ~~Due to the fact that~~ *Because* the housing market is ~~weak at this point in time,~~ *weak,* many homeowners are waiting to sell until ~~such time as~~ conditions improve.

Tech Style Checkers and Wordiness

Although they might occasionally flag an inappropriate wordy construction, computer style checkers are generally unreliable judges of wordiness. Rely on readers—yourself, your instructor, writing center tutors, your friends—to help you determine what is and is not acceptable.

29b Eliminating Ineffective Repetition 删除无效重复

As you revise your writing, look for words repeated unnecessarily, whether exactly or in a different form.

DRAFT	Robert Caro's ~~informative~~ overview provides particularly revealing ~~information~~ about the Johnson administration.
REVISION	Robert Caro's overview provides particularly revealing information about the Johnson administration.

Also watch for *redundancy*, unnecessary repetition.

> - The candidate's mistakes during the campaign were ~~few in number,~~ *few,* but they cost her the election, and she plans ~~for the future~~ never to repeat them ~~again.~~

More about
Transitions,
30–32
Repetition for
emphasis, 302
Parallelism,
290–93
Avoiding ambigu-
ity, 385–86

29c Avoiding Wordy Sentence Patterns 避免句式冗余

Certain sentence patterns tend toward wordiness. These include *expletive constructions*, sentences in the *passive voice*, and sentences built around weak verbs.

1. Sentences that begin with *There are…*, *It is…*
以 "There are…" "It is…" 开头的句子

More about
Expletive construc-
tions, 407

Expletive constructions are sentences that begin with expressions like *there are, there is,* or *it is.* (Do not confuse *expletive* in this sense with its other sense of *swear word* or *curse.*) Revising to eliminate expletives will often make a sentence more direct and concise.

DRAFT	There are several measures that institutions can take to curb plagiarism.
REVISION	Institutions can take several measures to curb plagiarism.

2. Passive voice 被动语态

More about
Passive versus
active voice,
302–03,
396–97

In an *active-voice* sentence, the subject performs the action. In a passive-voice sentence, the subject receives the action.

	subj. verb
ACTIVE	Jared photographed the bear.

	subj. verb
PASSIVE	The bear was photographed by Jared.

Rewriting to use the active voice usually makes sentences more concise and direct.

DRAFT (PASSIVE)	A motion was proposed by Andrew that concert planning be delayed until the cost of the party could be accurately determined by the treasurer.
REVISION (ACTIVE)	Andrew proposed delaying concert planning until the treasurer could accurately determine the party's cost.

3. Sentences built around weak verbs 围绕弱势动词构建的句子

If the sentence is built around a weak verb such as *is, are, were,* or *was* (all forms of the verb *to be*), sometimes replacing the verb can produce a more concise and vivid result.

DRAFT	The destruction of the town by the tornado was^{verb} complete.
REVISION	The tornado destroyed^{verb} the town.

29d Consolidating Phrases, Clauses, and Sentences
合并短语、从句和句子

You can often make your writing more concise by reducing *clauses* to *phrases* and clauses or phrases to single words.

DRAFT	Scientists cite glaciers, which have been retreating, and the polar ice caps, which have been shrinking, as evidence of global climate change.
REVISION	Scientists cite retreating glaciers and shrinking polar ice caps as evidence of global climate change.

> **clause** 从句 A word group with a subject and a predicate
> **phrase** 短语 A group of related words that lacks a subject, a predicate, or both

Sometimes you can also combine two or more sentences into one more concise, effective sentence.

DRAFT	Scientists note that glaciers have been retreating and the polar ice caps have been shrinking. Most of them now agree that these phenomena are evidence of global climate change.
REVISION	Most scientists now agree that retreating glaciers and the shrinking polar ice caps are evidence of global climate change.

30 Using Parallelism 使用平行结构

Piero di Cosimo (Florentine, 1462–1521), *Portraits of Giuliano and Francesco Giamberti da Sangallo*, 1482–1485.

The two portraits in this diptych show father and son Giuliano and Francesco Giamberti da Sangallo. Though they are clearly different from each other, the portraits show their connectedness: Both the foreground and the background of each portrait are strikingly similar. The artist uses visual parallelism to convey his subjects' connectedness despite their individuality. Similarly, writers use grammatical *parallelism*—the expression of equally important ideas in similar grammatical form—to increase the clarity of their writing and to emphasize important points. Here are some examples, with the parallel structures highlighted:

> Greed, for lack of a better word, is good. Greed is right. Greed works. Greed clarifies, cuts through, and captures, the essence of the evolutionary spirit.
>
> —speech by Gordon Gekko in the movie *Wall Street*

> I don't want to achieve immortality through my work; I want to achieve immortality by not dying.
>
> —Woody Allen

More about
Coordinating conjunctions, 336–37, 433–34

30a Expressing Paired Items and Items in a Series in Parallel Form 以并列形式表示成对项和串联项

Readers expect paired ideas and items in a series to be parallel.

1. Items paired with a conjunction such as *and* or *but*
与and或but等连词并行出现的词或表达

Make paired items linked by coordinating conjunctions (*and, but, for, nor, or, so,* and *yet*) parallel.

▸ Girls learn at a young age to be passive and ~~that they should be~~ deferential.

The original uses *and* to pair an infinitive phrase (*to be passive*) with a subordinate clause (*that they should be deferential*); the revision uses *and* to join a pair of adjectives (*passive and deferential*).

▸ The course always covers the twentieth century through World War II but sometimes *also touches* ~~touching~~ on the beginning of the Cold War ~~is possible also~~.

In the revision, the verbs *covers* and *touches on* are in parallel form.

Deceptive Parallelism Parallel structure is found in most languages, so you are probably familiar with the concept. Use caution, however, to ensure that items that seem parallel are all grammatically equivalent. For example, in "He spoke only positively and friendly about his previous professor," *positively* and *friendly* appear parallel, but *positively* is an adverb, whereas *friendly* is an adjective. To be parallel, the sentence requires revision along these lines: "He had only positive and friendly things to say about his previous professor."

2. Items paired with a correlative conjunction such as *bothe... and* or *neithere... nor*
与 "both... and" "neither... or" 等关联连词并行出现的词或表达

Conjunctions such as *both . . . and, either . . . or, neither . . . nor,* and *not only . . . but also* are **correlative conjunctions**. They come in pairs, and they link ideas of equal importance. Readers expect items linked by a correlative conjunction to be parallel. To be parallel, however, the items linked by the correlative conjunctions must have the same grammatical form.

FAULTY PARALLELISM	The defense attorney convinced the jury not only that her client had no motive for committing the crime, but also was nowhere near the scene of the crime when it occurred.

> **More about**
> Correlative
> conjunctions,
> 336–37

A clause beginning with *that* follows *not only,* so a clause beginning with *that* should follow *but also.*

REVISED	The defense attorney convinced the jury not only that her client had no motive for committing the crime but also that he was nowhere near the scene of the crime when it occurred.

FAULTY PARALLELISM	According to the prosecutor, the accused both had the opportunity and a motive.

In the original, a verb (*had*) follows *both,* but a noun (*motive*) follows *and.* In the revision, nouns follow both parts of the conjunction.

REVISED	According to the prosecutor, the accused had both the opportunity and a motive.

3. Items in a series 连续出现的词或表达

Like paired items, three or more equivalent items in a series should be in parallel form.

FAULTY PARALLELISM	The detectives secured the crime scene, examined it for clues, and the witnesses were then called in for questioning.

REVISED	The detectives secured the crime scene, examined it for clues, and then called in the witnesses for questioning.

> **Tech** **Parallelism and Computer Style Checkers**
>
> A computer style checker cannot identify ideas that merit parallel treatment in an otherwise grammatical sentence.

More about
Clear compari-
sons, 390–91,
404
Including function
words, 402–03

30b Maintaining Parallelism in Comparisons
做比较时要用平行结构

When you compare two items with *than* or *as,* the items should be in the same grammatical form.

▸ Getting into debt is unfortunately much easier than ~~to get~~ out of it.
getting

30c Including All Words Needed to Maintain Parallelism 保持平行结构所需的词

Words such as articles (*a, an, the*), conjunctions (*and, but, or*), and prepositions (*on, in, under*) indicate the relationships among other words in a sentence. They should be included or repeated as needed in linked items for clarity and grammar as well as for parallelism.

▸ The trail leads over high mountain passes and dense forests.
through

Trails lead *over* passes but *through* forests.

More about
Parallelism and
emphasis, 302

30d Using Parallelism for Emphasis 使用平行结构，表示强调

Placing ideas in parallel form highlights their differences and similarities.

▸ In Andy Warhol's painting *Marilyn Diptych,* all the images are copies of the same original, the same size, and ~~they have equal space between them~~ within a grid of rows and columns.
all are *all are equally spaced*

As the following passage from a speech by former President Barack Obama shows, parallelism can be a forceful tool for emphasizing import-

**Writing
Responsibly** **Using Parallelism to Clarify Relationships among Ideas**

An important component of the writing process is figuring out the *relationships* among your ideas and making those relationships clear to your readers. As you revise, ask yourself questions like these: What is the cause and what is the effect? Which items are truly a part of the group and which items are not? Which ideas are important and which ideas provide supporting information? Using parallelism can help you emphasize for your reader that ideas are of equal importance. (Coordination and subordination, discussed in the next chapter, can also help you emphasize that ideas or information are of equal or unequal importance.) Experimenting with some of the techniques you are learning in this chapter, and in other chapters in this part, can lead to new insights about your topic.

to AUDIENCE

ant ideas. Notice how Obama's parallelisms (and the parallelisms from the Declaration of Independence that he quotes) generate an almost musical rhythm that drive home the president's point.

> Two hundred and thirty-four years later, the words are just as bold, just as revolutionary, as they were when they were first pronounced: "We hold these truths to be self-evident, that all men are created equal, that they are endowed by their Creator with certain inalienable rights; that among these are life, liberty, and the pursuit of happiness." These are not simply words on aging parchment. They are the principles that define us as a nation, the values we cherish as a people, and the ideals we strive for as a society, even as we know that we constantly have to work in order to perfect our union, and that work is never truly done.
>
> —Former President Barack Obama,
> Remarks at an Independence
> Day Celebration, July 4, 2010

31 Engaging Readers with Variety and Emphasis 以多样性和强调吸引读者

In this painting, *At the Opera,* artist Mary Cassatt captures our interest with a variety of visual elements, among them the figure of the woman in the foreground; the more sketchily rendered figures in the background; the curving form of the balconies; the bright points of red and white; and the contrasting large, dark areas. Cassatt also structures the painting to emphasize certain elements over others and to direct our attention to a story unfolding within the scene. Our eyes go first to the woman in the foreground; then we follow her gaze through her opera glasses and let the curve of the balcony railing draw our attention to the upper left, where a male figure also is looking through opera glasses—not toward the stage, however, but directly at the woman in the foreground.

Writers also use variety and emphasis. They vary sentence length, sentence structure, and sentence openers to capture and hold their readers' attention, and they use coordination and subordination, strategic repetition, emphatic verbs, and the active voice to highlight key ideas.

31a Varying Sentence Length and Structure 句子长度和结构的变化

Confronting readers with page after page of sentences of uniform length—short, medium, or long—can make it hard for them to pick out important details. To hold readers' attention and direct it to the points you want

Quick

Reference **Achieving Variety and Emphasis**

- Vary sentence length and structure. (293)
- Use coordination to link or contrast equally important sentence elements. (294)
- Use subordination to distinguish main ideas from supporting ideas. (296)
- Vary sentence openings. (299)
- Use rhythm for emphasis. (300)
- Use strategic repetition. (302)
- Use emphatic verbs and favor the active voice. (302)

simple sentence 简单句 One independent clause and no subordinate clauses
compound sentence 并列句 Two or more independent clauses and no subordinate clauses
complex sentence 复合句 One independent clause with at least one subordinate clause
compound-complex sentence 并列复合句 Two or more independent clauses with one or more subordinate clauses

to emphasize, vary the length of your sentences and include a mix of sentence types: *simple*, *compound*, *complex*, and *compound-complex*.

Short sentences deliver information concisely and dramatically. They are most emphatic, however, when they are mixed with longer sentences. In the following passage, too many short sentences in a row create a choppy effect, leaving the reader with the impression that each point is equally important. The revision combines most of the short sentences into longer sentences that clarify the relationship among the ideas the writer wants to convey. The writer's main point is now dramatically isolated in the one short sentence that remains.

DRAFT   The whole planet is at risk. We need to put a stop to the wild spread of this disease. The key is education. First, we should educate those living with the virus. Then we should let them educate the world. They can help us win this war against HIV. They can help other people understand that everyone is vulnerable.

REVISION   With the whole planet at risk, we need to put a stop to the wild spread of this disease. The key is education. First, we should educate those living with the virus; then we should let them educate the world. They can help us win this war against HIV by helping other people understand that everyone is vulnerable.

phrase 短语 A group of related words that lacks a subject, a predicate, or both
clause 从句 A word group with a subject and a predicate. An *independent clause* can stand alone as a sentence; a *subordinate clause* cannot

31b **Using Coordination to Link or Contrast Equally Important Ideas** 使用并列结构连接或对比同等重要的概念

Coordination is the joining of elements of equal importance in a sentence. When you coordinate parts of a sentence—whether words, phrases, or clauses—you give them equal emphasis.

To coordinate terms and phrases use either a coordinating conjunction (*and, but, for, nor, or, so,* or *yet*) or a correlative conjunction (*both... and, either... or,* or *neither... nor*). Usually no punctuation separates a pair of coordinated words or phrases.

- Both <u>Steven Spielberg</u> and <u>George Romero</u> attended the New York Film Academy.
- London's Theatre Royal in Drury Lane has staged performances <u>by the Shakespearean actor Edmund Kean</u> and <u>by the Monty Python comedy troupe</u>.

Use commas to separate more than two terms or phrases in a coordinated series.

- My roommate's favorite directors are <u>Steven Spielberg</u>, <u>the Coen brothers</u>, and <u>James Cameron</u>.

Use a comma and a coordinating conjunction, a semicolon, or a semicolon and a conjunctive adverb such as *for example, however, in addition,* or *therefore* to coordinate a pair of independent clauses (clauses that can stand alone as a sentence).

- <u>Today we consider Shakespeare to be the greatest English playwright</u>, but <u>his contemporaries regarded him as just one among many</u>.
- <u>Adele's debut CD was a huge success</u>; <u>it sold millions of copies</u>.
- <u>The play received glowing reviews and won a Tony award</u>; however, <u>it closed after only a short run</u>.

1. Conjunctions and their meaning 连词及其含义

Conjunctions differ in meaning. The coordinating conjunction *and,* for example, suggests addition (*Jack <u>and</u> Jill went up the hill*), *or* suggests choice (*Jack <u>or</u> Jill fetched a pail of water*), and *but* suggests contrast (*Jack fell down, <u>but</u> Jill managed to keep her balance*). Make sure the meaning of the conjunction matches the relationship between the coordinated elements. In the following sentence, for example, changing *and* to *but* emphasizes the contrast between Spain's accomplishment and Paraguay's.

- Paraguay played well, ~~and~~ *but* Spain won and advanced to the semifinals.

2. Inappropriate coordination 并列结构使用不当

Coordination is inappropriate when it combines elements that are not of equal importance. The following sentence, for example, puts a minor bit of information—Spielberg's year of birth—on an equal footing with a statement about his early accomplishments. The revision subordinates the minor information.

INAPPROPRIATE COORDINATION	Steven Spielberg was born in 1946, and by 1975 he had achieved box office success with *Jaws*.
REVISED	Steven Spielberg, born in 1946, achieved box office success in 1975 with *Jaws*.

More about
Coordinating and correlative conjunctions, 336–37

More about
Commas with series, 435–36

More about
Punctuating coordinated independent clauses, 353–57
Semicolons, 442–44

> **Tech** | **Style Checkers and Coordination and Subordination**
>
> Using coordination and subordination requires you to figure out the logical relationships among the ideas you want to express and to decide on their relative importance, so that you can make these relationships clear to your audience. A computer style checker cannot do that for you.

3. Excessive coordination 过度使用并列结构

In everyday speech, people often coordinate long strings of sentences with *and* and other conjunctions. What is acceptable in speech, however, quickly becomes tedious, even confusing, in writing. As you edit, look for such *excessive coordination*.

EXCESSIVE COORDINATION
Steven Spielberg graduated from Saratoga High School, in Saratoga, California, in 1965, and he applied to the University of Southern California's film school three times, but he was rejected each time, so he finally decided to attend California State University at Long Beach, and while he was at Cal State he started an unpaid internship at Universal Studios, and an executive was impressed by his talent, so in 1969 he was allowed to direct a television episode there, and by 1975 he was directing films like *Jaws*, and that was his first big hit as a movie director, so perhaps in the end he was lucky to have been rejected by USC.

REVISED
Steven Spielberg, who graduated in 1965 from Saratoga High School in Saratoga, California, applied to the University of Southern California's film school three times and was rejected each time. Finally, he decided to attend California State University at Long Beach. While he was at Cal State, he started an unpaid internship at Universal Studios. An executive there was impressed by his talent, so in 1969 he was allowed to direct a television episode there. By 1975, he was directing films like *Jaws*, his first big hit as a movie director. Perhaps, in the end, he was lucky to have been rejected by USC.

31c Distinguishing Main Ideas from Supporting Ideas with Subordination 从属结构——区分主要观点和次要观点

Coordination allows you to link equally important ideas. Subordination, in contrast, allows you to emphasize main ideas and de-emphasize supporting examples, explanations, and details.

$\vdash$——— main idea ———$\dashv$ $\vdash$——— main idea ———$\dashv$
▶ The evidence is conclusive; my client is innocent.

Coordination gives each idea equal weight.

├────── subordinated idea ──────┤ ├───── main idea ─────┤

▸ As the evidence proves conclusively, my client is innocent.

The emphasis is on the client.

├───── main idea ─────┤ ├──── subordinated idea ────┤

▸ The evidence proves conclusively that my client is innocent.

The emphasis is on the evidence.

Subordination can also clarify the relationship among a series of ideas. The revised version of the following passage clarifies the chronological relationships and emphasizes that comic books did not become widely popular until 1938.

DRAFT   The first comic books appeared in the early 1920s. Nearly four decades earlier, comic strips had begun appearing in the major newspapers. Comic books did not gain widespread popularity until June 1938. Writer Jerry Siegel and artist Joe Shuster debuted their character Superman in June 1938.

REVISED   Although comic books first appeared in the 1920s, which was nearly four decades after comic strips had begun to appear in the major newspapers, they did not gain widespread popularity until June 1938, when writer Jerry Siegel and artist Joe Shuster debuted their character Superman.

1. Subordinating terms and their meaning 从属结构的术语及其含义

Subordinating terms include subordinating conjunctions such as *after, although, as, because, before, since, so that, unless, whereas,* and *while* and relative pronouns such as *that, where, which,* and *who.* As with coordinating terms, be sure the meaning of the subordinating term you use matches the relationship you intend to convey. The following sentence uses a term referring to cause in a context that calls for a term referring to purpose. Revising requires either changing the term or rewording the clause.

> **More about**
> Subordinating
> conjunctions,
> 336–37
> Relative pronouns,
> 334

DRAFT   He ran for mayor because he could bring the town's budget under control.

REVISED   He ran for mayor so that he could bring the town's budget under control.

or

He ran for mayor because he wanted to bring the town's budget under control.

Be particularly careful with the subordinating conjunctions *as* and *since,* which can refer ambiguously to both cause and time.

DRAFT   As she was applying the last coat of varnish, Leena declared the restoration complete.

REVISED   While she was applying the last coat of varnish, Leena declared the restoration complete.

or

Because she was applying the last coat of varnish, Leena declared the restoration complete.

2. Illogical subordination 不合逻辑的从属关系

State key ideas in an independent clause, and put illustrations, examples, explanations, and details in subordinate structures. Illogically subordinating a main idea to a supporting idea can confuse readers.

ILLOGICAL
SUBORDINATION   Jodie Foster was only fourteen, although she was already a movie star.

REVISED   Although she was only fourteen, Jodie Foster was already a movie star.

3. Excessive subordination 过度使用从属结构

Excessive subordination—stringing together too many subordinate structures—can make a sentence hard to read.

EXCESSIVE
SUBORDINATION   San Francisco, although generally an ideal habitat for peregrine falcons, is not entirely so, as became clear recently when rescuers had to remove falcon eggs from a nest on the Bay Bridge, despite the parents' protests, because once hatched, the fledglings would probably have drowned while learning to fly.

REVISED   San Francisco, although generally an ideal habitat for peregrine falcons, is not entirely so. Rescuers had to remove falcon eggs from a nest on the Bay Bridge recently, despite the parents' protests, because once hatched, the fledglings would probably have drowned while learning to fly.

Coordination and Subordination Mastery of subordination is considered a sign of sophistication in American academic writing, but this is not true of all languages or cultures. If academic style in your native language or your style in other contexts favors coordination over subordination, you may need to make a conscious effort to use more subordination in your writing. If academic style in your native language or your native style favors subordination over coordination, you may tend to oversubordinate your sentences in academic English. Your goal should be to strike a balance between coordination and subordination.

31d Varying Sentence Openings 句子开头的变化

In the default structure of an English sentence, the subject comes first, then the verb, and then the direct object if there is one. Reflecting this structure, most sentences start with the subject. However, a long string of subject-first sentences can make your text monotonous. Use modifying clauses and phrases to vary your sentence openings and to emphasize important information.

Adverbs and adverbial phrases and clauses Where you place an **adverb**, and the phrases and clauses that function as adverbs, affects the rhythm of a sentence and the information it emphasizes.

ADVERBIAL SUBORDINATE CLAUSE

Stocks can be a risky investment because they can lose value.

Because they can lose value, stocks can be a risky investment.

Stocks, because they can lose value, can be a risky investment.

ADVERBIAL PREPOSITIONAL PHRASES

We were in the same lab for physics class last semester.

Last semester, we were in the same lab for physics class.

For physics class, we were in the same lab last semester.

NOTE Moving an adverb can sometimes alter the meaning of a sentence. Consider these two examples:

- The test was surprisingly hard.
- Surprisingly, the test was hard.

In the first, *surprisingly* modifies *hard,* suggesting that the writer found the test harder than expected; in the second, *surprisingly* modifies the whole clause that follows it, suggesting that the writer expected the test to be easy.

Adjectival phrases The placement of **adjectives** and most adjectival phrases and clauses is less flexible than the placement of adverbs. However, participles and *participial phrases*, which act as adjectives, can often come at the beginning of a sentence as well as after the terms they modify.

- New York City's subway system, flooded by torrential rains, shut down at the height of the morning rush hour.
- Flooded by torrential rains, New York City's subway system shut down at the height of the morning rush hour.

An adjective phrase that functions as a *subject complement* can also sometimes be repositioned at the beginning of a sentence.

More about
Sentence structure, 337–46, 406–07

adverb 副词 A word that modifies a verb, adjective, other adverb, or entire phrase or clause and that specifies how, where, when, and to what extent or degree

adjective 形容词 A word that modifies a noun or pronoun with descriptive or limiting information

participial phrase 分词短语 A phrase in which the present or past participle acts as an adjective

subject complement 主语补足语 An adjective, a pronoun, or a noun phrase that follows a linking verb and describes or refers to the subject of the sentence

- The Mariana Trench is almost seven miles deep, making it the lowest place on the surface of the earth.

- Almost seven miles deep, the Mariana Trench is the lowest place on the surface of the earth.

More about
Placement of adjectives, 423

Appositives and absolute phrases An ***appositive*** is a noun or noun phrase that renames another noun or noun phrase. Because they designate the same thing, the appositive and the original term can switch positions.

- The governor, New York's highest official, ordered an investigation into the subway system's failure.

- New York's highest official, the governor, ordered an investigation into the subway system's failure.

An ***absolute phrase***, consisting of a noun or pronoun with a participle, modifies an entire independent clause. It can often fall either before or after the clause it modifies.

- The task finally completed, the workers headed for the parking lot.

- The workers headed for the parking lot, the task finally completed.

More about
Transitional expressions, 30–32

Transitional expressions A ***transitional expression*** relates the information in one sentence to material that precedes or follows. Its placement affects the emphasis that falls on other parts of the sentence. The second passage here, for example, calls more attention to Superman's distinctiveness than the first does.

- Most comic book characters from the 1930s quickly fell into obscurity. However, Superman was not one of them.

- Most comic book characters from the 1930s quickly fell into obscurity. Superman, however, was not one of them.

31e Using Sentence Rhythm to Emphasize Important Information 使用句子节奏强调重要信息

Sentences, like music, have rhythm, and within that rhythm, some beats get more stress than others. Readers readily notice the beginning of a sentence, where they usually find the subject, and they notice the end, where everything wraps up. Take advantage of readers' habits by slotting important or striking information into those positions. In the following example, the writer changed the subject of the sentence from *ready availability* to the more significant *free news* and moved *financial ruin* to the end, dramatically underscoring the seriousness of the challenge newspapers face.

DRAFT   The ready availability of free news on the Internet threatens financial ruin for traditional newspapers.

REVISED   Free news, readily available on the Internet, threatens traditional newspapers with financial ruin.

A common way to organize information in longer sentences is with a cumulative or loose structure. A *cumulative sentence* begins with the subject and verb of an independent clause and accumulates additional information in subsequent modifying phrases and clauses.

> That's the news from Lake Wobegon, where all the women are strong, all the men are good-looking, and all the children are above average.
>
> —Garrison Keillor, tag line from the radio show
> *A Prairie Home Companion*

A *periodic sentence*, in contrast, reserves the independent clause for the end, preceded by modifying details. The effect is to build suspense that highlights key information when it finally arrives.

> Through the center of town, up the strip, past the housing developments and shopping malls, street lights giving way to the thin streaming illumination of the headlights, trees crowding the asphalt in a black unbroken wall: that was the way to Greasy Lake.
>
> —T. Coraghessan Boyle, "Greasy Lake"

An interrupted periodic sentence begins with the subject of the independent clause but leaves the conclusion of the clause to the end, separating the two parts with modifying details. In the following example, the subject of the sentence is highlighted in yellow, and the predicate is highlighted in blue.

> The archaeologist Howard Carter, peering through the small opening to the main chamber of Tutankhamen's tomb at treasures hidden from view for more than three millennia, when asked what he saw, replied "wonderful things."

An *inversion* is a sentence in which, contrary to normal English word order, the verb precedes the subject. Inverted sentences call attention to themselves. Used sparingly, they can help you emphasize a point or create a sense of dramatic tension.

▸ Into the middle of town rode the stranger.
     verb   *subj.*

Developing an Ear for Sentence Variety Many of the sentence structures that add variety to written English are uncommon in conversation and as a result may not come naturally to you even if you are fluent in conversational English. To develop an ear for sentence variety in your academic writing, try imitating some of the structures in this chapter. Ask an instructor or another skilled writer of English to check your work to see if you have produced effective sentences.

31f Using Strategic Repetition 善用策略性重复

Redundancy and other forms of unnecessary repetition clutter writing and distract readers. Repetition is sometimes necessary, however, for clarity and to maintain parallelism. Repetition for emphasis works especially well within parallel structures, as in this sentence from a student project.

> Some children are never told that they are adopted, never given the opportunity to search for their biological parents.
>
> —Jessica Toro, Syracuse University

More about
Parallelism, 290–93

Toro could have used *or* instead of the second *never*, but the repetition dramatically underscores her concern about the consequences for adopted children of not telling them that they are adopted.

31g Creating Emphasis with Emphatic Verbs 善用强调动词表示强调

More about
Weak verbs and wordiness, 289

Verbs that describe an action directly are often more emphatic than verbs like *be, have,* or *cause* that combine with nouns or adjectives to describe an action indirectly.

> ▸ Many economists ~~have a belief~~ believe that higher gasoline taxes would ~~be beneficial~~ benefit to the economy in the long run. The increased costs would ~~have a stimulating effect on~~ stimulate research into alternative energy sources and eventually ~~cause a reduction in~~ reduce both carbon emissions and our dependence on oil.

More about
Passive voice and wordiness, 288–89

31h Distinguishing the Active from the Passive Voice 区分主动语态和被动语态

In an active-voice sentence, the subject performs the action of the verb; in a passive-voice sentence, the subject receives the action of the verb. Sentences in the active voice are usually more emphatic, direct, and concise than sentences in the passive voice.

ACTIVE VOICE: EMPHATIC

Rising oil prices stimulate research into alternative energy sources.

PASSIVE VOICE: UNEMPHATIC

Research into alternative energy sources is stimulated by rising oil prices.

If the performer of the action is unknown or unimportant, however, the passive voice can be appropriate.

> ▸ According to the coroner, the victim had been murdered between 3 and 4 in the morning.
>
> The identity of the murderer is unknown.

Writing Responsibly | Voice and Responsibility

Because the passive voice allows the agent of an action to remain unnamed, it lends itself to misuse by people avoiding responsibility for their mistakes and misdeeds. Consider, for example, the classic dodge of the cornered politician or bureaucrat: "Mistakes were made."

Be on the lookout for this evasive use of the passive voice in your own writing and the writing of others. It is a usage that comes all too readily when we need to convey unflattering or damaging information about ourselves or those we represent.

to TOPIC

▸ *The Second Sex*, a major work in feminist philosophy, was first published in 1949.

The focus is on the date of publication, not the identity of the author.

Similarly, in science writing, the passive voice allows the description of procedures without constant reference to the individuals who carried them out.

▸ The effects of human activities on seagrasses were studied at Sandy Neck and Centerville beaches from 31 March 2014 to 30 March 2016.

Text Credit

p. 301 *Greasy Lake and Other Stories*, Penguin Books, 1986.

32 Choosing Appropriate Language
选择合适的语言

During a job interview, both the applicant and the interviewer need to dress appropriately, behave appropriately, and use language appropriately. Neither would be likely to show up in a bathing suit, jump up and down on a couch, or use language that might offend the other. Such issues of appropriateness apply to your writing as well. In every document you write, use language that is appropriate to the context and avoids bias.

32a Matching Your Language to the Context 语言要符合语境

We all adjust our language to suit our audience and purpose. No form of the language is intrinsically better or more correct than another, but certain forms have become standard for addressing an academic or a business audience. In business and academic writing, using appropriate language usually means the following:

- Avoiding nonstandard dialects
- Avoiding regionalisms, colloquialisms, and slang
- Avoiding overly technical terminology (neologisms and jargon)
- Adopting a straightforward tone, one that is neither overly formal nor informal

1. Nonstandard dialects 不规范的方言

A *dialect* is a variant of a language with its own distinctive pronunciation, vocabulary, and grammar. A linguist once quipped that the only difference between the standard form of a language and its other dialects is that the standard form has an army and a navy. The standard form, in other words, became standard because it is the dialect of the elite and powerful.

> **More about**
> Standard
> American English
> grammar, 331–46

Nonstandard dialects of English are not "bad" English, as many mistakenly believe. If you speak a dialect like Appalachian English or African American Vernacular English and you are addressing an audience of peers from your community, then your home dialect *is* appropriate. If you are addressing a broader audience or writing in an academic or a workplace context, however, the dialect known as Standard American English, or Edited English, is usually the appropriate choice.

2. Regionalisms, colloquialisms, and slang 地方语言、口语体和俚语

Regionalisms are expressions that are characteristic of particular areas. Saying the car "needs washed" might be acceptable in Pittsburgh but not in Boston. The expression "I might could do it" might be acceptable in Pikeville, Kentucky, but not in Des Moines, Iowa. Regionalisms can be appropriate in conversation or informal writing but are usually out of place in formal academic writing.

- Many scientists believe that we might ~~could~~ *be able to* slow global warming if we can reduce carbon emissions.

Colloquialisms are informal expressions common in speech but usually out of place in formal writing.

- An R rating designates a movie that is not appropriate for ~~kids~~ *children* under seventeen who are not accompanied by a ~~grown-up~~ *an adult*.

Used judiciously, however, the occasional colloquialism can add spice to your writing.

- The musicians were only kids, none of them more than ten years old, but they played like seasoned professionals.

Writing **Responsibly** | **Online Shortcuts**

Users of text messaging, instant messaging, and social networking sites have developed a host of acronyms and abbreviations—like *BTW* for "by the way" and *IMO* for "in my opinion"—that save typing time and space on the tiny screens of mobile phones. With the possible exception of informal email, these expressions are almost never appropriate in other contexts, particularly not in academic or business writing. The same applies to emoticons and emojis like :-) and 👍 as well as other shortcuts such as writing entirely in lowercase without punctuation, as in *i saw her this am.*

to SELF

Slang is the extremely informal, inventive, often colorful (and sometimes off-color) vocabulary of a particular group. In general, slang is inappropriate in formal writing, but as with colloquial language, when used sparingly and judiciously, it can enliven a sentence and help emphasize an important point.

3. Neologisms and jargon 新词和行话

The world changes. Technology advances, new cultural trends emerge, and new research alters our understanding of ourselves and gives rise to new fields of study. As these changes occur, people necessarily invent new words and expressions—*neologisms*. Some neologisms become widely used and establish themselves as acceptable vocabulary for formal writing. Other neologisms, however, soon disappear or never move from informal to formal usage. When you consider using a neologism, ask yourself whether a more familiar synonym might serve as well. If the neologism is necessary but you are not sure your audience will be familiar with it, define it.

> , websites that allow a group of users to create and edit content collectively,
- Some instructors use wikis as tools for teaching collaborative writing.

The term *jargon* refers to the specialized vocabulary of a particular profession or discipline. Doctors speak of *adenomas* and *electroencephalograms*. Automobile mechanics speak of *camber angles* and *ring-and-pinion gears*. Lawyers speak of *effluxions of time* and *words of procreation*. For an audience of specialists, this kind of insider vocabulary can efficiently communicate complex ideas that might otherwise take several sentences, even paragraphs, to explain. If you are addressing other specialists, jargon may be appropriate. If you are addressing a general audience, however, it is usually inappropriate. In most cases, avoid it. When a specialized term is needed, define it.

> when their lease expired.
- The tenants lost the apartment ~~due to the effluxion of time on their lease.~~

4. Appropriate formality 适当的语言正式性

When you speak or write to close friends from your own age group, your language will probably—and appropriately—be relaxed and informal, sprinkled with dialect, slang, and colloquial expressions. Writing for most

More about
Using a thesaurus,
316

college courses or in the workplace, however, calls for a formal tone and clear, straightforward language free of slang and colloquialisms. Clear and straightforward, however, should not mean simpleminded or condescending. Use challenging vocabulary if it aptly expresses your meaning, but do not try to impress your readers by inflating your writing with fancy words mined from a thesaurus.

INAPPROPRIATELY INFORMAL	Tarantino is always ripping scenes from earlier flicks to use in his own.
INFLATED	It is a characteristic stylistic mannerism of the auteur Quentin Tarantino to allusively amalgamate scenic quotations from the repertory of his cinematic forebears in his own oeuvre.
APPROPRIATE	In his movies, the director Quentin Tarantino routinely alludes to scenes from earlier movies.

32b Avoiding Biased or Hurtful Language
避免有偏见或伤害性的语言

Biased language unfairly or offensively characterizes a particular group and its members. It can be as blatant as a slur that targets a specific group, such as *wetback,* for people of Mexican descent, or *guido,* for Italian American men. It can also be subtle and unintentional, as in thoughtless stereotyping or an inappropriately applied label.

More about
Stereotyping, 79

A *stereotype* is a simplified, uncritical, and often negative generalization about an entire group of people: *Blondes are ditzy; athletes are weak students; lawyers are unscrupulous; politicians are dishonest.* Even when they seem positive, stereotypes lump people together in ways that offensively ignore their individuality. In an article in *The New York Times,* for example, Chinese American writer Vivian S. Toy remembers among her "painful experiences of being different" that a college adviser once recommended that she switch her major to biology "since Chinese are better suited for the sciences."

Writing
Responsibly   Euphemisms and Doublespeak

We use *euphemisms* in place of words that might be offensive or emotionally painful. We speak to mourners about a relative who has *passed away,* and we excuse ourselves saying we have to go *to the bathroom* without referring to specific bodily functions.

The polite or respectful use of euphemisms, however, can easily shade into an evasive reluctance to address harsh realities. Why use *correctional institution,* for example, when what you mean is *prison*? Why use *ill-advised* when what you mean is *foolish* or *rash*?

Euphemisms that are deliberately deceptive, used to obscure bad news or sanitize an ugly truth, are called *doublespeak*. A company that announces that it is *downsizing,* not that it is about to lay off half of its workforce, is using doublespeak.

When reading, ask yourself: Does this word obscure or downplay the truth? When writing, think carefully about your motives: Are you using a euphemism (or doublespeak) to avoid hurting someone's feelings or to avoid confronting an uncomfortable truth?

to AUDIENCE

We label people whenever we call attention to a particular characteristic about them. *Labeling* is appropriate when it is relevant.

▸ Laura Grimm was the first female athletic director in the Western Pennsylvania Interscholastic Athletic League.

It is inappropriate, and usually offensive, when it is irrelevant.

▸ Muhammad Ali, an African American, was a famous boxer.

To appreciate how irrelevant the label "African American" is in that last sentence, consider the following:

▸ Babe Ruth, a man, was a famous baseball player.

1. Gender bias 性别偏见

English has no third-person pronouns that designate an individual person without also designating that person's gender (*she, he, her, him, hers, his, herself, himself*). This lack creates problems when a writer uses the singular to refer to people in general.

▸ The sensible student is careful what [*he? she?*] posts about [*himself? herself?*] on social networking sites such as Instagram or Twitter.

Until about the 1970s, the conventional solution to this problem was to use the masculine pronoun as the generic pronoun. In other words, depending on context, *he* referred either to a particular male human or to any human. Conversely, *she* always meant "female." Similarly, the terms *man* and *mankind* could refer generically to humanity as a whole, but *woman* and *womankind* only to women. Since the 1970s, writers have been replacing this usage—together with other vocabulary that reinforces gender stereotypes—with gender-neutral alternatives.

Avoid the generic **he** One way to avoid the generic *he*—and often the most graceful way—is to rewrite the sentence using plural nouns, pronouns, and verbs.

▸ ~~The~~ *Sensible students are* ~~sensible student is~~ careful what ~~he posts~~ *they post* about ~~himself~~ *themselves* on social networking sites such as Instagram or Twitter.

Another alternative is to use *he or she* (or *she or he*).

▸ The sensible student is careful what he or she posts on social networking sites.

Be sparing with *he or she* (*she or he*), however; used many times in quick succession, it becomes awkward.

AWKWARD   The sensible student is careful what <u>he or she</u> posts about <u>himself or herself</u> on the social networking sites <u>he or she</u> frequents.

More about
Pronoun-anteced-
ent agreement,
365–68

NOTE The use of *they* as a generic pronoun for singular antecedents is common in speech, and publications such as *The Washington Post* have endorsed it. Many readers consider this usage ungrammatical, however; when in doubt, avoid it.

> *Sensible students are*
> ~~The sensible student is~~ careful what they post about themselves.

Avoid generic man Replace terms like *man, men,* and *mankind* used to represent all human beings with gender-neutral equivalents such as *humanity, humankind,* or *humans.*

> *Humans are the only animals*
> ~~Man is the only animal~~ to have ventured into space.

Replace occupational names that include the term *man* with gender-neutral alternatives.

> *Members of Congress*
> ~~Congressmen~~ have excellent health insurance.

Avoid gender stereotypes and inappropriate gender labeling Some occupations with gender-neutral names are stereotypically associated with either men or women. Avoid perpetuating those stereotypes with inappropriate gender labeling.

> Nursing is an ancient, honorable profession. *People*
> ~~Women~~ who choose it can expect a rewarding career.

2. Cultural labels 文化标签

Use cultural labels with care. Racial and ethnic labels are appropriate only when race or ethnicity is relevant to the topic under discussion. The same is true for references to disabilities, sexual orientation, or other personal characteristics. When you do use labels, avoid terms that may give offense; instead, call people what they want to be called. When referring to a transgender person, use whichever pronoun that person prefers. And be aware that terms can become dated: A label that used to be acceptable may take on negative connotations over time. People from Asia are *Asians,* not *Orientals* (a term many find disparaging). The term *African American* is now widely accepted as a designation for Americans of African descent. The words *gay* and *lesbian* are preferable to *homosexual.* Be as specific as context permits. If what you mean is *Vietnamese,* or *Japanese,* or *Inuit,* or *Lakota,* or *Catalan,* or *Sicilian,* then use those terms, not the more general *Asian,* or *Native American,* or *European.*

33 Choosing Effective Words 选择有效的措辞

Words have both a literal meaning and emotional associations. **Diction**, or the choice of words to best convey an idea, requires attention to both.

33a Denotation and Connotation: Finding the Right Word
外延与内涵：找到合适的单词

The literal meaning of a word, its dictionary definition, is its **denotation**. When you use a word, be sure its denotation matches your intended meaning. Be particularly careful, for example, not to misuse words that are similar in pronunciation or spelling.

> ▶ Calling someone a Scrooge ~~eludes~~ *alludes* to a Charles Dickens story about a selfish man.

> To *elude* is to evade or escape; to *allude* is to make an indirect reference.

Be careful, too, with words that differ in meaning even though they are otherwise closely related.

> ▶ Many people owe their lives to the ~~heroics~~ *heroism* of volunteer firefighters.

> *Heroics* are melodramatic, excessive acts; *heroism* is courageous, potentially self-sacrificing behavior.

The secondary meanings of a word—the psychological or emotional associations it evokes—are its **connotations**. The word *walk,* for example, has many synonyms, including *amble, saunter, stride,* and *march.* Each of these, however, has distinctive connotations, as their effect in the following sentence suggests:

> ▶ The candidate ~~walked~~ *ambled / sauntered / strode / marched* to the podium to address her supporters.

> The verb *walk* in this context is emotionally neutral, but the others all have connotations that suggest something about the candidate's state of mind. *Amble* suggests a relaxed aimlessness, whereas *saunter* suggests a jaunty

▶ **More about**
Commonly
confused words,
318–23

Tech   Word Choice and Grammar and Style Checkers

The grammar and style checkers in most word processing programs offer little help with effective word choice. They often cannot distinguish an incorrectly used word from a correctly used one—*affect* from *effect*, for example—nor can they differentiate between the emotional associations of words whose literal meaning is similar.

Writing Responsibly

Word Choice and Credibility

The denotation and connotation of the words you choose can powerfully influence the tone of your writing, the effect you have on your readers, and what your readers conclude about you. Highly charged vocabulary, as in the following examples, might lead readers to question the writer's objectivity:

Hippie tree huggers are threatening the jobs of thousands of hard-working loggers.

Conscientious activists are trying to protect endangered forests from rapacious, tree-murdering logging companies.

In academic writing, you will enhance your credibility if you describe conflicting positions in even-toned language:

Environmentalists discuss their conflict with the logging industry in terms of the threat industry practices pose to a critical resource; the logging companies, contending that they are responsible forest stewards, describe the conflict in terms of their contribution to local economies.

Once you have looked at the issue fairly, nothing prevents you from then supporting one of these positions and challenging the other.

to AUDIENCE

self-confidence. *Stride* and *march* both suggest purposefulness, but *march*, with its military associations, also carries a hint of aggressiveness.

A word's connotations can vary from reader to reader. To some people, for example, the word *wilderness* evokes a place of great danger; to others, a place of excitement; and to still others, a treasure to be preserved.

33b Choosing Compelling Words and Figures
选择有说服力的单词和修辞

Some words are general, some specific, and others fall between:

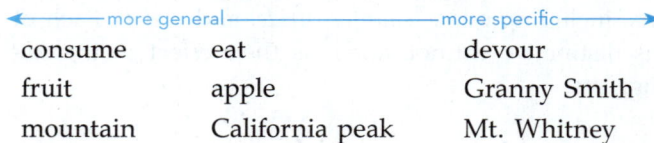

← more general		more specific →
consume	eat	devour
fruit	apple	Granny Smith
mountain	California peak	Mt. Whitney

In addition, some words are concrete, designating things or qualities that can be seen, heard, tasted, smelled, or touched; others are abstract, designating concepts like *justice*, *capitalism*, or *democracy*.

1. Compelling words 有说服力的单词

Bring your writing to life by combining general and abstract language with the specific and concrete. Use general and abstract language to frame broad issues, and specific, concrete language to capture readers' attention and help them see things through your eyes. Using general language without specifics leaves readers to fill in the blanks on their own, and using specific language without the general and abstract leaves readers wondering what the point is.

The first of the two following descriptions of the Badwater ultramarathon lacks specific language that can tell us how long the race is, why it is challenging, or exactly where it takes place. The second fills in those details with concrete words—like "hottest spot in America," "135 miles," "stinking water hole," "Death Valley," "piney oasis," "8,300 feet up the side of Mt. Whitney," and "asphalt and road gravel." With these specifics, the writer David Ferrell evokes the challenges of the race without recourse to the abstract word "challenging."

GENERAL AND ABSTRACT	Badwater is a long, physically challenging race over a partially paved course that begins in a geological depression and ends partway up a mountain.
CONCRETE AND SPECIFIC	Badwater is a madman's march, a footrace through the summer heat of the hottest spot in America. It extends 135 miles from a stinking water hole on the floor of Death Valley to a piney oasis 8,300 feet up the side of Mt. Whitney. The course is nothing but asphalt and road gravel. Feet and knees and shins ache like they are being whacked with tire irons. Faces turn into shrink-wrap.

—David Ferrell, "Far Beyond a Mere Marathon"

2. Figures of speech 修辞手法

In the preceding example, notice how Ferrell, in addition to providing concrete specifics, uses striking comparisons and juxtapositions to paint a vivid picture of the rigors of the race and to suggest the mind-set required to compete in it. He calls the race "a madman's march," for example, and conjures up a beating with a tire iron and an image of a shrink-wrapped face to convey the physical punishment contestants endure. These are examples of *figurative language*, or *figures of speech*, the imaginative use of language to convey meaning in ways that reach beyond the literal meaning of the words involved.

Among the most common figures of speech are similes and metaphors. A *simile* is an explicit comparison between two unlike things, usually expressed with *like* or *as:* "Feet and knees and shins ache like they are being whacked with tire irons." A *metaphor* is an implied comparison between two unlike things stated without *like, as,* or other comparative expressions: "Faces turn into shrink-wrap." (A list of common figures of speech appears in the Quick Reference box on the next page.)

3. Inappropriate figures of speech and mixed metaphors 修辞不当和混杂隐喻

Used well, figures of speech can spice up your writing. Used in the wrong context, they can be jarring, even silly.

► The new high-speed train, like a champion ~~pole vaulter~~, *thoroughbred,* made it from Boston to Washington in record time.

Mixed metaphors—which combine multiple, conflicting images for the same concept—confuse readers.

Quick **Reference** | **Figures of Speech**

Figure and Definition	Examples
simile: An explicit comparison between two unlike things, usually expressed with *like* or *as*	Feet and knees and shins ache like they are being whacked with tire irons. —*David Ferrell* Only final exams, like the last lap of a long race, lay between the members of the senior class and their diplomas.
metaphor: An implied comparison between unlike things stated without *like, as,* or other comparative expressions	Faces turn into shrink-wrap. —*David Ferrell* After crossing the finish line of their last exams, seniors looked forward to that moment on the victory stand when the president of the college would bestow a diploma on them.
analogy: An extended simile or metaphor, often comparing something familiar to something unfamiliar (well-constructed analogies can be particularly effective for explaining difficult concepts)	What that means [that the universe is expanding] is that we're not at the center of the universe, after all; instead, we're like a single raisin in a vast lump of dough that is rising in an oven where all the other raisins are moving away from each other, faster and faster as the oven gets hotter and hotter. —*David Perlman, "At 12 Billion Years Old, Universe Still Growing Fast"*
personification: The attribution of human qualities to nonhuman creatures, objects, ideas, or phenomena	The plague that rampaged through Europe in the fourteenth century selected its victims indiscriminately, murdering rich and poor in equal proportion.
hyperbole: Deliberate exaggeration for emphasis	That little restaurant on Main Street makes the best pizza on the planet.
understatement: The deliberate use of less forceful language than a subject warrants	The report of my death was an exaggeration. —*Mark Twain, clearly alive and well, responding to an obituary about him in a London paper*
irony: The use of language to suggest the opposite of its literal meaning or to express an incongruity between what is expected and what occurs	I come to bury Caesar, not to praise him. —*Mark Antony, in Shakespeare's play* Julius Caesar, *in a speech that praises the murdered leader effusively*

MIXED METAPHOR　Confronted with the <mark>tsunami of data</mark> available on the Internet, researchers, <mark>like travelers caught in a blinding desert sandstorm</mark>, may have trouble finding the <mark>nuggets of valuable information buried in a mountain</mark> of otherwise worthless ore.

This sentence confusingly invokes tsunamis, sandstorms, mountains, and mining. The revision here works with a single metaphor that compares finding useful information online to mining for precious minerals.

REVISED　As they <mark>mine the mountain of data</mark> available on the Internet, researchers may have trouble identifying the <mark>nuggets of valuable information buried with the otherwise worthless ore they dig up.</mark>

33c Mastering Idioms 掌握习语

Idioms are expressions whose meaning does not depend on the meanings of the words that compose them. Each idiom is a unified package of meaning with its own denotations and connotations. The following sentence, for example, would make no sense if you tried to interpret it based on the literal meaning of the words *call, on,* and *carpet:*

- ▸ The directors called the CEO on the carpet for the company's poor sales in 2016.

Of course, the expression *call on the carpet* has nothing to do with calls or carpets. It is an idiom that, understood as a whole, means *to reprimand* or *scold.*

Most dictionaries list idiomatic uses of particular words. The entry for the word *call* in the *Merriam-Webster Online Dictionary,* for example, provides definitions for the idioms *call for, call forth, call into question, call it a day,* and *call it quits,* among others. For more detailed information on the history and meaning of particular idioms, consult a specialized dictionary such as the *American Heritage Dictionary of Idioms.*

> *More about*
> Specialized
> dictionaries,
> 105–06, 315–18

Idioms, Prepositions, and Phrasal Verbs Non-native speakers of English have to learn idioms just as they must learn an unfamiliar word. If you are an English language learner, pay particular attention to the way prepositions combine with other words in idiomatic ways. A **phrasal verb**, for example, is a combination of a verb with one or more prepositions that has a different meaning than the verb alone.

> *More about*
> Prepositions, 336,
> 426–31
> Phrasal verbs, 373,
> 417–18

Raisa *saw* the flat tire on her car. [She looked at it.]

Raisa *saw to* the flat tire on her car. [She had it repaired.]

33d Avoiding Clichés 避免陈词滥调

A *cliché* is a figure of speech, idiom, or other expression that has grown stale from overuse (see the Quick Reference box below for some examples). Clichés come quickly to mind because they express common wisdom in widely recognized phrases. For the same reason, they provide an easy substitute for fresh expression. They may help you frame a subject in the early drafts of a project, but they can also make your writing sound trite and unimaginative. As the following example indicates, writing that is loaded with clichés is often also loaded with mixed metaphors.

CLICHÉ LADEN   As the campaign pulled into the home stretch and the cold, hard fact of the increasingly nip-and-tuck polls sank in, the candidates threw their promises to stay on their best behavior to the wind and wallowed in the mire of down-and-dirty attack ads.

REVISED   As Election Day neared and the polls showed the race tightening, the candidates abandoned their promises of civility and released a barrage of unscrupulous attack ads.

What Is the Difference between an Idiom and a Cliché? The only thing that separates an idiom from a cliché is the frequency with which it is used. If you are a native English speaker, be alert to idioms that appear often in popular sources and in conversation, and try to avoid those in academic and professional writing. If you are not a native English speaker, you may not recognize an idiom as a cliché if you have not encountered it often in your reading. If you have questions about clichés and idioms, ask your instructor or consult a dictionary of idioms, such as *McGraw-Hill's Dictionary of American Idioms and Phrasal Verbs* or the *Longman American Idioms Dictionary*.

Quick

Reference   Dodging Deadly Clichés

When you encounter clichés like these in your writing, delete them or replace them with fresher images of your own.

best thing since sliced bread	hit the nail on the head	smart as a whip
beyond a shadow of a doubt	a hundred and one percent	straight and narrow
cold, hard fact	in the prime of life	think outside the box
cool as a cucumber	just desserts	throw [something] to the wind
down and dirty	nip and tuck	
down the home stretch	no way, shape, or form	tried and true
easier said than done	one foot out the door	wallow in the mire
face the music	on their best behavior	without a moment's hesitation
faster than greased lightning	plain as the nose on your face	
green with envy	slow as molasses	zero tolerance

Text Credit

p. 312 SFGate, *May 26, 1999.*

34

Using the Dictionary and Thesaurus
使用词典和同义词词库

Samuel Johnson's *Dictionary of the English Language* (1755) established many of the conventions still found in dictionaries today. Johnson identified a core vocabulary of some 43,500 words, labeled each word's part of speech, briefly traced its origins, provided a concise, elegant (and sometimes humorous) definition of the word in all its senses, and accompanied each definition with an illustrative quotation. Johnson hoped to define and fix a standard of proper spelling and usage, but his dictionary, like those that have followed it, also reflects the state of the language in the time and place in which it was created.

34a Choosing a General-Purpose or a Specialized Dictionary
选择通用词典还是专用词典

Dictionaries today come in a variety of forms, both printed and electronic, large and small, general purpose and specialized. Abridged dictionaries, sometimes referred to as "desk dictionaries," contain information on approximately 200,000 words. Examples include the following:

The American Heritage College Dictionary (available online at Yahoo! Education)

Merriam-Webster's Collegiate Dictionary (available online as the *Merriam-Webster Online Dictionary*)

Random House Webster's College Dictionary

Most word processing programs also include a built-in dictionary with many features of an abridged dictionary.

Unabridged dictionaries contain detailed entries for most English words, some half a million in total. The most comprehensive unabridged dictionary is the twenty-volume *Oxford English Dictionary* (known as the *OED*). Others include *Random House Webster's Unabridged Dictionary* and *Webster's Third New International Dictionary, Unabridged.*

Writing Responsibly | Choosing Accurate Synonyms

When you consult a thesaurus, be sure to check both the meanings (*denotations*) and the associations (*connotations*) of the words you find there. A carelessly chosen synonym can distort the information you intend to convey. Suppose, for example, that you wanted to replace *intimidate* in the sentence "The professor's brilliance intimidated her students." Looking in a thesaurus, you might find both *overawe* and *bludgeon* listed as synonyms. *Overawe* is an appropriate substitute, probably more precisely reflecting the effect of the professor on her students than *intimidate*. *Bludgeon*, in contrast, inappropriately conjures visions of a bloody crime scene.

to TOPIC

> **More about**
> Denotation and
> connotation,
> 17–18, 309–10

315

Both the *OED* and *Webster's Third New International* are available online for a fee. You should be able to find an unabridged dictionary in the reference section of any library, however, and many libraries provide free access to online versions.

Dictionaries for Second-Language Learners In addition to translation dictionaries and standard abridged and unabridged dictionaries, you may want to consult an all-English dictionary tailored for the second-language learner, such as *Heinle's Newbury House Dictionary of American English,* the *Longman Dictionary of American English,* or the *Oxford Dictionary of American English.* To understand American slang and idioms, consult a dictionary such as *McGraw-Hill's Dictionary of American Slang and Colloquial Expressions.* Since slang and idioms change rapidly, you should also consult native-speaking and/or American peers.

Specialized dictionaries focus on a particular aspect of English vocabulary.

- Dictionaries of usage provide guidance about the use of particular words or phrases. Examples include the *American Heritage Book of English Usage* (available online at Bartleby.com) and *Right, Wrong, and Risky: A Dictionary of Today's American English Usage.* The *New Fowler's Modern English Usage* provides guidance on British and American usage.

- Subject-specific dictionaries explain the specialized terminology of particular fields and professions. Examples include *The Dictionary of Anthropology, Black's Law Dictionary,* and *A Dictionary of Business and Management.* For links to subject-specific dictionaries and glossaries available online, try Glossarist and YourDictionary.com.

> **More about**
> Finding subject-specific dictionaries, 105–06

34b Consulting a Thesaurus 查阅分类词典

Thesauruses and synonym dictionaries provide lists of words that are equivalent to or that overlap in meaning with one another (**synonyms**), as well as words that have contrasting meanings (**antonyms**). They can help you find just the right word for a particular context or an alternative to a word you have overused. Examples include *Merriam-Webster's Dictionary of Synonyms* and *The New American Roget's College Thesaurus.* Note also that most word processing programs have a built-in thesaurus.

34c Learning to Read a Dictionary Entry 学会查阅词典词条

Figure 34.1 shows the entry for the word *respect* in the *Merriam-Webster Online Dictionary,* Although most online and printed abridged dictionaries present the same kinds of information, each has its own format and system of abbreviations.

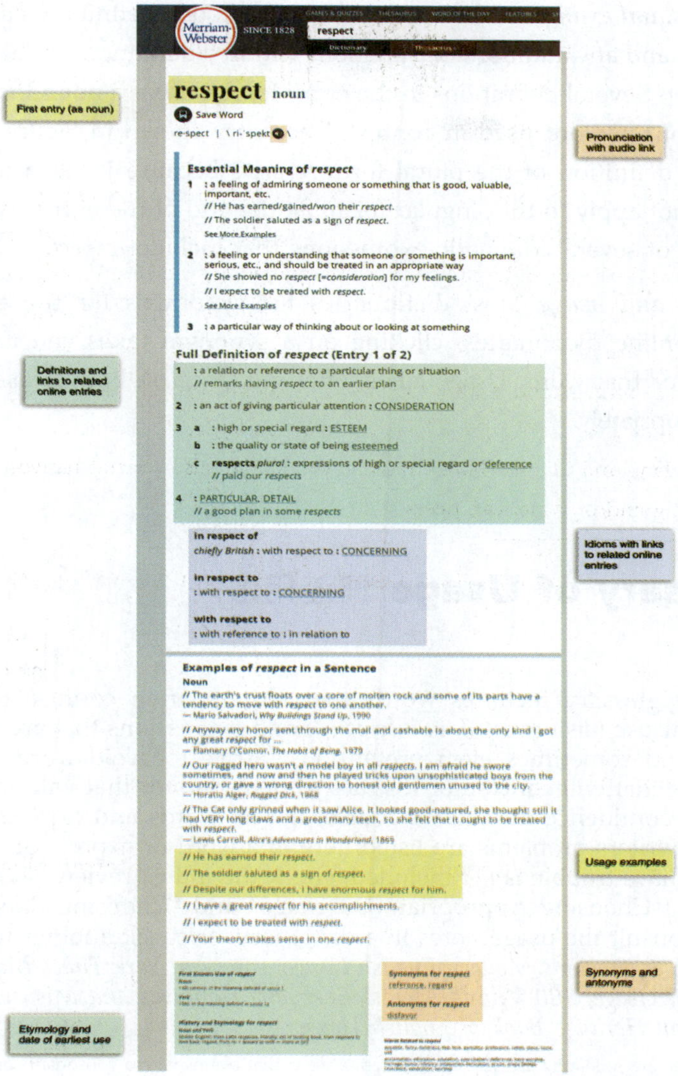

First entry (as a noun)

Pronunciation with audio link

Definitions and links to related online entries

Idioms with links to related online entries

Usage examples

Synonyms and antonyms

Etymology and date of earliest use

FIGURE 34.1 The entry for respect in the *Merriam-Webster Online Dictionary*

Spelling, word division, and pronunciation The main entry begins with the word correctly spelled, followed by acceptable variant spellings, if any. Dots show the division of the word into syllables, indicating where to put a hyphen if you must break the word between lines of text. Next, the pronunciation of the word is given. The print version has a key to pronunciation symbols; the online version has a link to this key, but it also gives the pronunciation in an audio link.

Grammatical functions and forms Labels indicate the part of speech and other grammatical aspects of a word. Most dictionaries specify the forms of irregular verbs (*draw, drew, drawn*) but not of regular verbs like *respect*, and they provide irregular plurals (*woman, women*) but not regular plurals (*dogs*).

> *More about*
> Hyphenation,
> 478–80

> *More about*
> Regular and irreg-
> ular verbs, 358–
> 59, 370–71
> Regular and
> irregular plurals,
> 476–77

Definitions and examples If a word has more than one definition, each is numbered, and any additional distinctions within a definition are labeled with a letter. Several definitions in the entry for *respect* as a noun include examples of the word used in context. The entry shown in Figure 34.1 includes a definition of the plural form *respects* because it has a usage that does not apply to the singular form. At the end of the entry are the definitions of several idiomatic expressions that include *respect*.

> **More about**
> Idiomatic expressions, 313

> **More about**
> Usage, 318–23

Synonyms and usage Most dictionaries list synonyms for the entry word; in online dictionaries, clicking on a synonym takes you to the full entry for that word. Usage labels offer guidance on how to use the word appropriately.

35 Glossary of Usage 词汇用法表

This usage glossary includes words that writers often confuse (*infer, imply*) or misuse (*disinterested, uninterested*) and expressions that are non-standard and sometimes even pretentious. Strive to avoid words and expressions that will confuse or distract your readers or that will undermine their confidence in you. Of course, not all words and expressions that cause writers problems are listed here; if a word or expression with which you have trouble is *not* included, check the index, review chapters 32 and 33 ("Choosing Appropriate Language" and "Choosing Effective Words"), consult the usage notes in a dictionary, or check another usage guide, such as *Fowler's Modern English Usage,* the *New York Times Manual of Style and Usage, 100 Words Almost Everyone Confuses and Misuses,* or the *American Heritage Book of English Usage.*

a, an　*A* and *an* are indefinite articles. Use *a* before a word that begins with a consonant sound: *a car, a hill, a one-way street.* Use *an* before a word that begins with a vowel sound: *an appointment, an hour, an X-ray.*

accept, except　*Accept* is a verb meaning "agree to receive": *I accept the nomination. Except* is a preposition that means "but": *Everyone voted for me except Paul.*

adapt, adopt　*Adapt* means "to adjust": *Instead of migrating, the park's ducks adapt to the changing climate. Adopt* means "to take as one's own": *I adopted a cat from the shelter.*

adverse, averse　*Adverse* means "unfavorable" or "hostile"; *averse* means "opposed": *She was averse to buying a ticket to a play that had received such adverse criticism.*

advice, advise　The noun *advice* means "guidance"; the verb *advise* means "to suggest": *I advised her to get some sleep. She took my advice and went to bed early.*

affect, effect　As a verb, *affect* means "to influence" or "to cause a change": *Study habits affect one's grades.* As a noun, *affect* means "feeling or emotion": *The defendant responded without affect to the guilty verdict.* As a noun, *effect* means "result": *The decreased financial aid budget is an effect of the recession.* As a verb, *effect* means "to bring about or accomplish": *Submitting the petition effected a change in the school's policy.*

aggravate, irritate　*Aggravate* means "to intensify" or "worsen": *Dancing until dawn aggravated Giorgio's bad back. Irritate* means "to annoy": *He was irritated that his chiropractor could not see him until Tuesday.* Colloquially, *aggravate* is often used to mean *annoy,* but this colloquial usage is inappropriate in formal contexts.

agree to, agree with　*Agree to* means "to consent to": *Chris agreed to host the party. Agree with* means "to be in accord with": *Anne agreed with Chris that a party was just what everyone needed.*

ain't　*Ain't* is a nonstandard contraction for *am not, are not,* or *is not* and should not be used in formal writing.

all ready, already　*All ready* means "completely prepared"; *already* means "previously": *They were all ready to catch the bus, but it had already left.*

all right, alright　*All right* is the standard spelling; *alright* is nonstandard.

all together, altogether　*All together* means "as a group": *When Noah's family gathered for his graduation, it was the first time they had been all together in years. Altogether* means "completely": *Noah was altogether overwhelmed by the attention.*

allude, elude, refer to　*Allude* means "to refer to indirectly"; *elude* means "to avoid" or "to escape": *He eluded further questioning by alluding to his troubled past.* Do not use *allude* to mean "refer directly"; use *refer to* instead: *The speaker referred to* [not *alluded to*] *slide six of her PowerPoint presentation.*

allusion, illusion　An *allusion* is an indirect reference: *I almost missed the author's allusion to* Macbeth. An *illusion* is a false appearance or belief: *The many literary quotations he drops into his speeches give the illusion that he is well read.*

almost, most　*Almost* means "nearly"; *most* means "the majority of": *My roommate will tell me almost anything, but I talk to my sister about most of my own problems.*

a lot, alot　*Alot* is nonstandard; always spell *a lot* as two words.

among, amongst　*Amongst* is a British alternative to *among*; in American English, *among* is preferred.

among, between　Use *among* with three or more nouns or with words that stand for a group composed of three or more members; use *between* with two or more nouns: *I'm double majoring because I could not decide between biology and English. Italian, art history, and calculus are among my other favorites.*

amoral, immoral　*Amoral* means "neither moral nor immoral" or "indifferent to moral standards"; *immoral* means "violating moral standards": *While secularists believe that nature is amoral, religionists often view natural disasters as punishments for immoral behavior.*

amount, number　Use *amount* with items that cannot be counted (noncount or mass nouns); use *number* with items that can be counted (count nouns): *The dining hall prepares the right amount of food based on the number of people who eat there.*

an　See *a, an.*

and/or　*And/or* is shorthand for "one or the other or both." It is acceptable in technical and business writing, but it should be avoided in most academic writing.

ante-, anti-　The prefix *ante-* means "before," as in *antebellum*, or "before the war"; the prefix *anti-* means "against," as in *antibiotic* ("against bacteria").

anxious, eager　*Anxious* means "uneasy": *Dan was anxious about writing his first twenty-page paper. Eager* indicates strong interest or enthusiasm: *He was eager to finish his first draft before spring break.*

anybody, any body; anyone, any one　*Anybody* and *anyone* are singular indefinite pronouns: *Does anybody* [or *anyone*] *have an extra pen? Any body* and *any one* are a noun and pronoun (respectively) modified by the adjective *any*: *She was not fired for making any one mistake but, rather, for making many mistakes over a number of years.*

anymore, any more　*Anymore* means "from now on": *She does not write letters anymore. Any more* means "additional": *I do not need any more stamps.* Both are used only in negative contexts—for example, with *not* or other negative terms such as *hardly* or *scarcely.*

anyplace　*Anyplace* is an informal way of saying *anywhere. Anywhere* is preferable in formal writing.

anyways, anywheres　*Anyways* and *anywheres* are nonstandard; use *anyway* and *anywhere* instead.

as　*As* should not be used in place of *because, since,* or *when* if ambiguity will result: *As people were lining up to use the elliptical machine, the management posted a waiting list.* Does this sentence mean that management posted the sign *while* people were lining up, or does it mean that management posted the sign *because* there was such demand for the machine?

as, as if, like　Use *as*, or *as if*, not *like*, as a conjunction in formal writing: *The president spoke as if* [not *like*] *he were possessed by the spirit of Martin Luther King, Jr. Like* is acceptable, however, as a preposition that introduces a comparison: *The president spoke like a true leader.*

at　*At* is not necessary to complete *where* questions: *Where is Waldo?* not *Where is Waldo at?*

averse, adverse　See *adverse, averse.*

awful, awfully　In formal writing, use *awful* and *awfully* to suggest the emotion of fear or wonder, not as a synonym for *bad* or to mean *very. The high priest gave forth an awful cry before casting the captive from the top of the pyramid toward the crowd below.*

awhile, a while　*Awhile* is an adverb: *They talked awhile before going to dinner. A while* is an article and a noun, and should always follow a preposition: *Rest for a while between eating and exercising.*

bad, badly　In formal writing, use the adjective *bad* to modify nouns and pronouns and after linking verbs (as a subject complement): *Because I had a bad day, my husband feels bad.* Use the adverb *badly* to modify verbs, adjectives, and adverbs: *Todd's day went badly from start to finish.*

being as, being that　*Being as* and *being that* are nonstandard substitutes for *because*: *Because* [not *being as*] *Marcus did well as a teaching assistant, he was asked to teach a class of his own the next year.* Avoid them.

beside, besides　*Beside* is a preposition that means "next to" or "along side of": *You will always find my glasses beside the bed. Besides* is an adverb meaning "furthermore" or a preposition meaning "in addition to": *Besides, it will soon be finals. Besides chemistry, I have exams in art history and statistics.*

between, among　See *among, between.*

bring, take　Use *bring* when something is coming toward the speaker and *take* when it is moving away: *When the waiter brought our entrees, he took our bread.*

burst, bursted; bust, busted　*Burst* is a verb meaning "to break apart violently"; the past tense of *burst* is also *burst*, not *bursted. Bust* is slang for *to burst* or *to break* and should be avoided in formal writing: *The boiler burst* [not *bursted* or *busted*] *in a deadly explosion.*

can, may Use *can* when discussing ability: *I know she can quit smoking.* Use *may* when discussing permission: *The server told her that she may not smoke anywhere in the restaurant.*

capital, capitol *Capital,* a noun, can mean "funds," or it can mean "the city that is the seat of government": *The student council did not have enough capital to travel to Harrisburg, Pennsylvania's capital.* The word *capitol* means "the building where lawmakers meet": *The state's capitol is adorned with a golden dome.* When capitalized, *Capitol* refers to the building in Washington, DC, where the US Congress meets.

censor, censure *Censor* means both "to delete objectionable material" (a verb) and "one who deletes objectionable material" (a noun): *The bedroom scenes, but not the battle scenes, were heavily censored. Clearly, the censors object more to sex than to violence. Censure* means both "to reprimand officially" (verb) and "an official reprimand" (noun): *The ethics committee censured the governor for lying under oath. Members of his party were relieved that a censure was all he suffered.*

cite, sight, site *Cite,* a verb, means "to quote" or "mention": *Cite your sources following MLA format. Sight,* a noun, means "view" or "scene": *The sight of a field of daffodils makes me think of Wordsworth. Site,* a noun, means "location" or "place" (even online): *That site has the best recipes on the Internet.*

climactic, climatic *Climactic* is an adjective derived from the noun *climax* and means "culminating" or "most intense"; *climatic* is an adjective derived from the noun *climate: The climactic moment of a thunderstorm occurs when the center of the storm is overhead. Tornados are violent climatic phenomena associated with thunderstorms.*

complement, compliment *Complement* is a noun meaning "that which completes or perfects something else"; it can also be used as a verb meaning "the process of completing or making perfect." *Compliment* means either "a flattering comment" or "the act of paying a compliment": *My husband complements me and makes me whole; still, it annoys me that he rarely compliments me on my appearance.*

conscience, conscious *Conscience* is a noun meaning "sense of right and wrong": *Skipping class weighed heavily on Sunil's conscience. Conscious* is an adjective that means "aware" or "awake": *Maria made a conscious decision to skip class.*

continual(ly), continuous(ly) *Continual* means "repeated frequently": *The continual request for contributions undermined her resolve to be more charitable. Continuous* means "uninterrupted": *The continuous stream of bad news forced her to shut off the television.*

could care less *Could care less* is an illogical, and nonstandard, substitute for *could not care less:* If one *could* care less, then one must care, at least a little, and yet this is not the intended meaning.

could of, must of, should of, would of These are misspellings of *could have, must have, should have,* and *would have.*

criteria, criterion *Criteria* is the plural form of the noun *criterion,* Latin for "standard": *His criteria for grading may be vague, but I know I fulfilled at least one criterion by submitting my paper on time.*

data, media, phenomena *Data, media,* and *phenomena* are plural nouns (*datum, medium,* and *phenomenon* are their singular forms): *The data suggest that the economy will rebound by the time you graduate. The news media raise the alarm about public corruption, but it is the voters who must take action. The aurora borealis is one of many amazing natural phenomena.* (Data is increasingly used as a singular noun, but continuing to use it as a plural is never wrong.)

differ from, differ with *Differ from* means "to lack similarity": *Renaissance art differs greatly from art of the Middle Ages. Differ with* means "to disagree": *Martin Luther's forty-nine articles spelled out the ways in which he differed with the Catholic Church.*

discreet, discrete *Discreet,* an adjective, means "tactful" or "judicious": *Please be discreet—don't announce that you saw Ada crying in the bathroom. Discrete* means "distinct" or "separate": *The study revealed two discrete groups, those who can keep a secret and those who cannot.*

disinterested, uninterested *Disinterested* means "impartial": *A judge who cannot be disinterested should recuse himself or herself from the case. Uninterested* means "indifferent": *The book seems well written, but I am uninterested in the topic.*

don't, doesn't *Don't* is a contraction of *do not;* it is used with *I, you, we, they,* and plural nouns: *I don't want to drive, but the trains don't run very often. Doesn't* is a contraction of *does not;* it is used with *he, she, it,* and singular nouns: *It doesn't matter whether you're a little late; Fred doesn't mind waiting.*

each and every *Each and every* is a wordy substitute for *each* or *every;* use one or the other but not both.

eager, anxious See *anxious, eager.*

effect, affect See *affect, effect.*

e.g., i.e. *E.g.* is an abbreviation of a Latin phrase meaning "for example" or "for instance"; *i.e.* is an abbreviation of a Latin phrase meaning "that is." In formal writing, use the English equivalents rather than the Latin abbreviations; the Latin abbreviations are acceptable in tables, footnotes, and other places where space is at a premium.

elicit, illicit *Elicit,* a verb, means "to draw out": *Every week,* American Idol *contestants try to elicit enough support to avoid elimination. Illicit,* an adjective, means "illegal" or "impermissible": *In 2003,* American Idol *contestant Frenchie Davis was disqualified for posing in illicit photos.*

elude, allude, refer to See *allude, elude, refer to.*

emigrate from, immigrate to *Emigrate from* means "to leave one's country and settle in another": *Jake's grandmother emigrated from Poland in 1919. Immigrate to* means "to move to and settle in a new country": *Jake's grandmother immigrated to the United States in 1919.*

eminent, imminent, immanent *Eminent* means "renowned": *The university hosts lectures by many eminent scientists. Imminent* means "about to happen" or "looming": *By January 2008, many felt that a recession was imminent. Immanent* means "inherent" or "pervasive throughout the world": *Many religions teach that God's presence is immanent.*

enthused *Enthused* is a colloquial adjective meaning "enthusiastic." In formal writing, use *enthusiastic: Because of the team's excellent record, Eric was enthusiastic* [not *enthused*] *about joining.*

etc. *Etc.* is an abbreviation of the Latin phrase *et cetera,* meaning "and others." Because *et* means "and," adding the word *and* before *etc.* is redundant. In a series, include a comma before *etc.: A great deal of online media are used in classes today: blogs, wikis, Blackboard, Facebook, etc.* In most formal writing, concluding with a final example or *and so on* (the English equivalet of *etc.*) is preferable.

everybody, everyone; every body, every one *Everybody* and *everyone* are interchangeable singular indefinite pronouns: *Everybody* [or *everyone*] *who went to the concert got a free T-shirt. Every body* and *every one* are a noun and a pronoun (respectively) modified by the adjective *every: Coroners must treat every body they examine with respect.*

except, accept See *accept, except.*

expect, suppose *Expect* means "to anticipate": *I expect to be home when she arrives. Suppose* means "to presume": *I suppose she should have a key just in case.*

explicit, implicit *Explicit,* an adjective, means "overt" or "stated outright": *The rules are explicit: "No running." Implicit* is an adjective that means "implied": *Implicit in the rules is a prohibition against skipping.*

farther, further Use *farther* with distances: *I'd like to drive a hundred miles farther before we pull over for dinner.* Use *further* to mean "more" or "in addition": *I have nothing further to add.*

fewer, less Use *fewer* with items that can be counted (count nouns). Use *less* with items that cannot be counted (noncount or mass nouns): *This semester, I am taking three fewer classes than I took in the fall, but because I have a job now, I have less time to study.*

first, firstly *Firstly* is used in Britain, but it sounds overly formal in the United States. *First* (and *second* and *third*) is the standard form in the United States.

flaunt, flout *Flaunt* means "to parade" or "show off"; *Ivan flaunted his muscular torso on the quad. Flout* means "to disobey" or "ignore": *He flouted school policy by parading about without his shirt on.*

further, farther See *farther, further.*

get Many colloquial expressions with *get* should not be used in formal writing. Avoid expressions such as *get with the program, get your act together, get lost,* and so on.

good, well *Good* is an adjective; *well* is an adverb: *Playing well in the tournament made Lee feel good.* In references to health, however, *well* is an adjective: *She had a cold, but now she is well and back at work.*

hanged, hung Use the past-tense verb *hanged* only to describe a person executed by hanging. Use the past-tense verb *hung* to describe anything else (pictures, clothing) that can be suspended.

hardly Use *can hardly* instead of *can't hardly,* a double negative: *I can hardly keep my eyes open.*

he, she; he/she; s/he Historically, the pronoun *he* was used generically to mean *he or she;* in informal contexts, writers avoid bias by writing *he/she* or *s/he.* In formal writing, however, revise your sentence to avoid a gendered pronoun: *Sensible students are careful what they post about themselves on social networking sites* [not *The sensible student is careful what he posts about himself on social networking sites*].

hisself *Hisself* is a nonstandard substitute for *himself.* Avoid it.

i.e., e.g. See *e.g., i.e.*

if, whether Use *whether,* not *if,* when alternatives are offered: *If I must go out, I insist that we go to a decent restaurant. I do not care whether we eat Chinese food or Italian, but I refuse to eat at Joe's.*

illicit, elicit See *elicit, illicit.*

illusion, allusion See *allusion, illusion.*

immigrate to, emigrate from See *emigrate from, immigrate to.*

imminent, eminent, immanent See *eminent, imminent, immanent.*

immoral, amoral See *amoral, immoral.*

implicit, explicit See *explicit, implicit.*

imply, infer *Imply* means "to suggest indirectly": *The circles under Phillip's eyes implied that he had not slept much. Infer* means "to conclude": *From the way he devoured his dinner, I inferred that Raymond was famished.*

incredible, incredulous *Incredible* means "unbelievable": *Debbie told an incredible story about meeting the Dalai Lama. Incredulous* means "unbelieving": *I am incredulous of everything that the tabloids print.*

infer, imply See *imply, infer.*

in regards to *In regards to* is nonstandard. Use *in regard to, as regards,* or *regarding* instead.

irregardless *Irregardless* is nonstandard; use *regardless* instead.

irritate, aggravate See *aggravate, irritate.*

is when, is where Avoid these phrases in definitions: *An oligarchy is a system of government in which the many are ruled by a few,* or *Oligarchy is government of the many by the few* [not *An oligarchy is when the many are ruled by a few*].

it's, its *It's* is a contraction of "it is" or "it has," and *its* is a possessive pronoun: *It's been a long time since the ailing pigeon flapped its wings in flight.* One trick for distinguishing the two is to recall that contractions such as *it's* are often avoided in formal writing, while possessive pronouns like *its* are perfectly acceptable.

kind, kinds *Kind* is a singular noun: *This kind of weather is bad for asthmatics. Kinds* (a plural noun) is used only to denote more than one kind: *Many kinds of pollen can adversely affect breathing.*

kind of, sort of *Kind of* and *sort of* are colloquial; in formal writing, use "somewhat" or "a little" instead: *Julia was somewhat [not kind of] pleased to be going back to school.* Use *kind of* and *sort of* in formal writing only to mean "type of": *The poetry of e. e. cummings creates a new kind of grammar.*

lay, lie *Lay* means "to place"; it requires a direct object. Its main forms are *lay, laid,* and *laid*: *She laid her paper on the professor's desk. Lie* means "to recline"; it does not take a direct object. Its main forms are *lie, lay,* and *lain*: *She fell asleep as soon as she lay down.*

leave, let *Leave* means "to go away"; *let* means "to allow." *If I leave early, will you let me know what happens?*

less, fewer See *fewer, less.*

like, as, as if See *as, as if, like.*

loose, lose The adjective *loose* means "baggy" or "not securely attached": *I have to be careful with my glasses because one of the screws is loose.* The verb *lose* means "to misplace": *I am afraid I will lose the screw and have to attach the earpiece with duct tape.*

lots, lots of *Lots* and *lots of* are colloquial and should be avoided in academic writing; use terms like *much, many,* and *very* instead.

may, can See *can, may.*

maybe, may be The adverb *maybe* means "possibly" or "perhaps"; the verb phrase *may be* means "have the possibility to be": *Maybe I'll apply for an internship next semester, but if I wait too long, all of the positions may be filled.*

may of, might of *May of* and *might of* are misspellings of *may have* and *might have.*

media See *data, media, phenomena.*

moral, morale *Moral* means "ethical lesson": *Aesop's fables each have a moral, such as "don't judge others by their appearance." Morale* means "attitude" or "spirits": *April's warm weather significantly raised student morale.*

most, almost See *almost, most.*

must of See *could of, must of, should of, would of.*

myself, himself, herself, etc. Use pronouns that end with *-self* to refer to or intensify other words: *Obama himself made an appearance.* Do not use them when you are unsure whether to use a pronoun in the nominative case (*I, she, he, we, they*) or the objective case (*me, her, him, us, them*): *This conversation is between him and me [not himself and myself].*

nohow, nowheres *Nohow* and *nowheres* are nonstandard forms of *anyway, in any way, in any place, in no place,* and *nowhere.* Avoid them.

number, amount See *amount, number.*

off of Omit *of*: *Sarah took the pin off [not off of] her coat.*

OK, O.K., okay These are all acceptable spellings, but the term is inappropriate in formal writing. Choose a more specific word instead: *Food served in the dining hall is mediocre [not okay].*

phenomena See *data, media, phenomena.*

plus Avoid using *plus* as a substitute for the coordinating conjunction *and* or the transition *moreover.*

precede, proceed *Precede* means "come before"; *proceed* means "continue": *Despite warnings from those who preceded me, I proceeded to take six classes in one semester.*

principal, principle *Principal,* a noun, refers to the leader of an organization. *Principal,* used as an adjective, means "main." *Principle,* used as a noun, means "belief" or "standard": *The school principal's principal concern is the well-being of her students. She runs the school on the principle that fairness is essential.*

proceed, precede See *precede, proceed.*

raise, rise The verb *raise* means "lift up" or "move up" and takes a direct object: *Joseph raised the blinds.* The verb *rise* means "to go upward" and does not take a direct object: *We could see the steam rise as the solution started to boil.*

real, really Do not use *real* or *really* as a synonym for *very*: *Spring break went very [not real or really] fast.*

reason is because, reason why To avoid redundancy and faulty predication, choose either *the reason is that* or *because*: *The reason Chris fell is that he is uncoordinated. It is not because his shoe was untied.*

refer to, allude, elude See *allude, elude, refer to.*

relation, relationship Use *relation* to refer to a connection between things: *There is a relation between the amount one sleeps and one's overall health.* Use *relationship* to refer to a connection between people: *Tony has always had a close relationship with his grandfather.*

respectfully, respectively *Respectfully* means "with respect": *Ben treats his parents respectfully. Respectively* means "in the given order": *My mother and father are 54 and 56, respectively.*

rise, raise See *raise, rise.*

set, sit The verb *set* means "to place" or "to establish," and it takes a direct object. *The professor set the book on the desk.* The verb *sit* means "to assume a sitting position," and it does not take a direct object: *You can sit in the waiting room until the doctor is ready.*

shall, will In the past, *shall* was used as a helping verb with *I* and *we,* and *will* was used with *he, she, it,* and *they*: *I shall go on dancing,* and *they will go home.* Now *will* is generally used with all persons: *I will go on singing, and they will all cover their ears. Shall* is used mainly with polite questions (*Shall we invite your mother?*) and in rules and regulations (*No person shall enter these premises after dusk.*).

should of See *could of, must of, should of, would of.*

since *Since* can mean "because" or "from that time," so use it only when there is no chance that readers will infer the wrong meaning. In the sentence that follows, either meaning makes sense: *Since I moved to the country, I have had no trouble sleeping.* Revise to make your meaning clear: *Since January, when I moved to the country ...* or *Because I moved to the country, ...*

sit, set See *set, sit.*

site, sight, cite See *cite, sight, site.*

somebody, someone *Somebody* and *someone* are interchangeable singular indefinite pronouns: *Someone* [or *somebody*] *is at the door.*

sometime, sometimes *Sometime* is an adverb meaning "at an indefinite time"; *sometimes* is an adverb meaning "on occasion," "now and then": *Sometimes I wish my future would come sometime soon.*

somewheres *Somewheres* is nonstandard; use *somewhere* instead.

stationary, stationery *Stationary* means "not moving"; *stationery* means "writing paper." (Thinking of the *e* in "stationery" as standing for *envelope* may help.)

supposed to, used to *Supposed to* means "should"; *used to* means "did regularly in the past." In speech, the final *-d* is often dropped, but in writing, it is required: *I was supposed* [not *suppose*] *to practice piano daily; instead, I used* [not *use*] *to play hockey.*

sure and, sure to; try and, try to *Sure to* and *try to* are standard; *sure and* and *try and* are not.

take, bring See *bring, take.*

than, then *Than* is a conjunction used in comparisons; *then* is an adverb of time: *If Betsy is already taller than I, then I will be impressed.*

that, which In formal writing, *that* is generally used with essential (or restrictive) clauses and *which* with nonessential (nonrestrictive) clauses: *The project that I am working on now is due on Monday, which is why I really have to finish it this weekend.*

that, who In formal writing, use *who* or *whom*, not *that*, to refer to people: *I. M. Pei is the architect who* [not *that*] *designed this building.*

their, there, they're *Their* is a possessive pronoun, *there* is an adverb of place, and *they're* is a contraction of "they are": *They're always leaving their dishes in the sink. Why must they leave them there instead of putting them in the dishwasher?*

theirself, theirselves, themself *Theirself, theirselves,* and *themself* are nonstandard. Use *themselves* instead.

them In colloquial speech, the pronoun *them* is sometimes used in place of the demonstrative adjective *those*; avoid this nonstandard usage: *Those* [not *them*] *are the books I need for class.*

then, than See *than, then.*

this here, these here, that there, them there *This here, these here, that there,* and *them there* are nonstandard for *this, these, that,* and *them.*

to, too, two *To* is a preposition, *too* is an adverb, and *two* is a number: *To send two dozen roses to your girlfriend for Valentine's Day is too expensive.*

try and, try to See *sure and, sure to; try and, try to.*

uninterested, disinterested See *disinterested, uninterested.*

unique *Unique* means "the one and only thing of its kind," so it is illogical to modify it with words like *somewhat* or *very* that suggest degrees: *Your approach to the issue is unique* [not *somewhat unique*].

usage, use The noun *usage*, which means a "customary manner, approach," should not be used in place of the noun *use*: *The use* [not *usage*] *of cell phones in this restaurant will not be tolerated.*

use, utilize The verb *utilize*, which means "to use purposefully," should not be used in place of *use*: *Students must use* [not *utilize*] *parking lots D, E, and F, not those parking lots reserved for faculty and staff.*

wait for, wait on Although *wait on* is sometimes used colloquially as a substitute for "wait for," it is nonstandard. Use *wait on* to mean "serve" and *wait for* to mean "await": *I am waiting for* [not *waiting on*] *my mother, who is always late.*

ways *Ways* is sometimes used colloquially as a substitute for "distance." Avoid this usage in formal writing: *We still have quite a distance* [not *ways*] *to go before we get to a rest area.*

weather, whether *Weather*, a noun, means "the state of the atmosphere"; *whether*, a conjunction, indicates a choice between alternatives: *It does not matter whether you prefer rain or snow; the weather will be what it will be.*

well, good See *good, well.*

whether, if See *if, whether.*

which, that See *that, which.*

who, that See *that, who.*

who, whom Use *who* for the subject of clauses; use *whom* for the object of clauses: *Who will be coming to the party? Whom did you ask to bring the cake?*

who's, whose *Who's* is a contraction of "who is" or "who has"; *whose* is a possessive pronoun: *Who's at the door? Whose coat is this?*

will, shall See *shall, will.*

would of See *could of, must of, should of, would of.*

you *You* (the second-person singular pronoun) should be used only to refer to the reader, not to refer to people in an indefinite sense (to replace *one*): *In medieval society, subjects* [not *you*] *had to swear an oath of allegiance to the king.*

your, you're *Your* is a possessive pronoun; *you're* is a contraction of "you are": *You're as stubborn as your brother.*

10 Grammar 关注语法
Matters

Grammar Guidance 语法指南

Use part 10 to learn, practice, and master these writer's responsibilities:

❏ **To Audience**

Choose language your readers regard as grammatically correct, keep sentence boundaries clear, and keep your writing intelligible by avoiding inappropriate grammatical shifts and hard-to-decipher mixed constructions.

❏ **To Topic**

Choose pronouns for grammatical correctness, clear reference, and, when appropriate, gender neutrality.

❏ **To Other Writers**

Use direct quotation to reproduce someone's exact words, and use indirect quotation to report what someone said but not in that person's exact words.

❏ **To Yourself**

Project your authority in clear, complete sentences with no confusingly placed or dangling modifiers.

Recognizing and Correcting Fragments (347–52)

A fragment is an incomplete sentence punctuated as if it were complete.

frag   The system of American higher ~~education. It is~~ founded on principles of _education is_

honesty and academic integrity.

Reducing the incidence of plagiarism among college students will be difficult,

~~however. Without~~ an understanding of its causes that goes beyond simplistic explanations. _however, without_

Maintaining Subject-Verb Agreement (358–65)

A verb and its subject agree when they match each other in person (first, second, or third) and

number (singular or plural).

sv agr For this reason, nearly everyone invested in this system—students, instructors, and

administrators—~~recognize~~ that plagiarism cannot be tolerated. _recognizes_

That plagiarism and related misconduct ~~has~~ become all too common is beyond dispute. _have_

Maintaining Pronoun-Antecedent Agreement (365–68)

A pronoun agrees with its antecedent (the word the pronoun replaces) when they match each

other in person (first, second, or third), number (singular or plural), and gender (masculine,

feminine, or neutral).

pn ag   In this myth, the ~~student is~~ too apathetic and slothful to finish their assignments on their _students are_

own; instead, they cheat.

Such students may treat the attainment of impressive marks as a necessity and will betray

the very academic system ~~he or she reveres~~ in order to sustain ~~his or her~~ average. _they revere_   _their_

Why Students Cheat:

The Complexities and Oversimplifications of Plagiarism (Draft 1)

frag
sv agr

The system of American higher education. It is founded on principles of honesty and academic integrity. For this reason, nearly everyone invested in this system—students, instructors, and administrators—recognize that plagiarism cannot be tolerated. People also agree that a lot of plagiarism is occurring. Reducing the incidence of plagiarism among college students will be difficult, however. Without an understanding of its causes that goes beyond simplistic explanations.

frag

sv agr

That plagiarism and related misconduct has become all too common is beyond dispute. A survey published in *Who's Who among American High School Students* (reported by Newberger) indicated that 15 percent of top-ranked high schoolers plagiarize. Practices among higher education students are not much better according to research by Donald L. McCabe, a professor at Rutgers University who has done extensive work on cheating, 38% of college students admitted to committing forms of plagiarism in the previous year (Rimer 7). A recent study by Hand, Conway, and Moran showed that plagiarism was common among the 411 students who participated in their research.

fs

There is a commonly held myth about how most plagiarism occurs. It is late at night, a student sits staring at a computer. A paper is due the following morning, and research needs to be done, notes need to be took, and, in the end, an essay needs to be wrote and edited. The student, overwhelmed, succumbs to the temptations of plagiarism—"cutting and pasting" from sources, downloading an essay from the Internet, or simply buying a paper from another student. In this myth, the student is too apathetic and slothful to finish their assignments on their own; instead, they cheat.

cs

vb

pn agr

Undeniably, some of it occurs because students find it easier than simply doing the work required. The argument that laziness is its main cause, however, is at best incomplete and seems, moreover, to be fed by unfair stereotypes of them as bored by academic rigor, more interested in video games or their Facebook pages than the hard work of learning.

ref

ref

ref

In fact, some plagiarism grows from the opposite of these characteristics. High-achieving students, for example, fear what a bad grade will do to their otherwise stellar GPA. Such students may treat the attainment of impressive marks as a necessity and will betray the very academic system he or she reveres in order to sustain his or her average.

pn agr

For the final draft of this paper, see pp. 82–86.

Recognizing and Correcting Fused (Run-On) Sentences (353–57)

In a fused (or run-on) sentence, one independent clause incorrectly follows another with no punctuation or joining words between them.

fs   Practices among higher education students are not much ~~better according to~~ *better. According to* research by Donald

L. McCabe, a professor at Rutgers University who has done extensive work on cheating, 38% of

college students admitted to committing forms of plagiarism in the previous year (Rimer 7).

Recognizing and Correcting Comma Splices (353–57)

In a comma splice, two independent clauses are incorrectly joined by a comma alone, without a coordinating conjunction such as *and* or *but*.

cs   It is late at night, *and* a student sits staring at a computer.

Using Irregular Verb Forms Correctly (369–74)

Regular verbs form the past tense and past participle by adding -ed to the base form; irregular verbs do not.

vb   A paper is due the following morning, and research needs to be done, notes need to be ~~took~~ *taken,*

and, in the end, an essay needs to be ~~wrote~~ *written* and edited.

Avoiding Unclear Pronoun Reference (385–87)

Pronoun reference is clear when readers can effortlessly identify a pronoun's antecedent (the word the pronoun replaces).

ref   Undeniably, some ~~of it~~ *plagiarism* occurs because students find ~~it~~ *plagiarizing* easier than simply doing the work required.
The argument that laziness is ~~its main cause, however, is~~ *the main cause of plagiarism, however, is* at best incomplete and seems,

moreover, to be fed by unfair stereotypes of ~~them~~ *students* as bored by academic rigor, more interested in video

games or their Facebook pages than the hard work of learning.

Avoiding Confusing Shifts in Tense and Voice (396–99)

Shifts from one tense to another or from the active to the passive voice are confusing when they occur for no clear reason.

shift   Students who view writing papers as hoops they must jump through to graduate, for

instance, ~~were~~ *are* more likely simply to ~~have downloaded~~ *download* a paper from an online "paper

mill" than to write one themselves.

Students draw a distinction between their interests and their academic assignments,

and ~~plagiarism is rationalized by them~~ *they rationalize plagiarism* as a way to escape an "unfair" academic obligation.

Avoiding Incomplete Constructions (402–04)

A phrase or clause is incomplete if it is missing any words required for idiomatic and grammatical clarity.

inc   Websites such as *essaytown.com*, which will write a paper to order, cater *to* students like

these, who consider at least some aspects of academia essentially useless.

Avoiding Mixed Constructions (399–402)

A mixed construction is a sentence with parts that do not fit together grammatically or logically.

mix   Even ~~recognizing~~ *students who recognize* the importance of citation may not know how to cite their sources

correctly.

Distinguishing Adjectives and Adverbs (387–91)

Adjectives modify nouns or pronouns; adverbs modify verbs, adjectives, other adverbs, and entire phrases and clauses.

ad   The Internet is a place of free exchange and information *the rapid movement of* ~~movement rapidly~~ from

computer to computer.

Draft of student paper with sentence problems

shift   Other students plagiarize more from lack of interest in a particular course than general idleness. Students who view writing papers as hoops they must jump through to graduate, for instance, were more likely simply to have downloaded a paper from an online "paper mill" than to write one themselves. For them, a college writing class is something to be endured rather than an opportunity for learning.

shift   Students draw a distinction between their interests and their academic assignments, and plagiarism is rationalized by them as a way to escape an "unfair" academic obligation.
inc   Websites such as *essaytown.com*, which will write a paper to order, cater students like these, who consider at least some aspects of academia essentially useless.

Many other instances of plagiarism are committed by students whom it turns   *case*
out have honest intentions but are ignorant of citation methods. Michael Gunn, a British student, copied quotations from Internet sources in numerous papers over several years and was shocked to learn that this qualified as plagiarism (Baty).
mix   Even recognizing the importance of citation may not know how to cite their sources correctly.
A student who omits the source of a paraphrase in a paper would probably be surprised to learn that him or her is often considered as guilty of plagiarism as the student who downloads   *case*
an essay.

The Internet has compounded confusion with regard to citation. The Internet is a place
ad   of free exchange and information movement rapidly from computer to computer. In this environment, ownership and citation become hazy. As John Leland, a reporter for the *New York Times*, writes, "Culture's heat now lies with the ability to cut, paste, clip, sample, quote, recycle, customize, and re-circulate." Many students—for example by highlighting it, copying   *mm*
it, and pasting it into a word processing document—find it easy and "natural" to take text from an online source. Having trouble keeping track of everything they have read, however,   *dm*
the chances increase of students accidentally plagiarizing by forgetting to cite a copied text.
So, too, does the likelihood of "patchwriting," the substitution of synonyms or the shuffing of sentences in a borrowed text without putting the information fully into the writer's own words (Howard 233). Finally, some students will also be tempted to commit intentional plagiarism, choosing to leave a block of copied text uncited.

For the final draft of this paper, see pp. 82–86.

He, She, Who or Him, Her, Whom? Matching Pronoun Case to Function (380–85)

A case problem occurs when the form of a pronoun—subjective, objective, or possessive—does not correspond to its grammatical role in a sentence.

case Many other instances of plagiarism are committed by students ~~whom it turns out~~ *who, it turns out,* have honest

intentions but are ignorant of citation methods.

A student who omits the source of a paraphrase in a paper would probably be surprised to learn

that ~~him or her~~ *he or she* is often considered as guilty of plagiarism as the student who downloads an essay.

Avoiding Misplaced Modifiers (391–94)

A misplaced modifer is an ambiguously, confusingly, or disruptively placed modifying word, phrase, or clause.

mm Many students—~~for~~ *find it easy and "natural" to take text from an online source—for* example by highlighting it, copying it, and pasting it into a word processing

document—~~find it easy and "natural" to take text from an online source.~~

Avoiding Dangling Modifiers (394–96)

A dangling modifier does not clearly modify the subject or any other part of a sentence, leaving it to the reader to infer the intended meaning.

dm ~~Having~~ *Because students can have* trouble keeping track of everything they have read, however,

the chances increase ~~of students' accidentally plagiarizing~~ *that they will plagiarize accidentally* by

forgetting to cite a copied text.

36 **Understanding Grammar** 理解语法

The rules of baseball, which give the game meaning and structure, have become second nature to proficient players. Most of these rules are inflexible: A player who ran around the bases carrying the ball would not be playing baseball. Some rules vary, however: In the American League but not in the National League, teams can designate another player to bat instead of the pitcher.

Languages, too, have rules—*grammars*—that structure words so that they can convey meaning. Just as baseball players have internalized the rules of the game, so have we all internalized the grammar of our native language. Most rules of grammar are inflexible. Any English speaker, for example, would recognize a statement like *throw Maria ball the base first to* as ungrammatical. Some aspects of grammar, however, can vary over time, from region to region, and from group to group.

The form of English accepted today in academic settings and in the workplace in the United States is known as *Standard American English*. Although it is not better or more correct than other varieties, Standard American English is what readers expect to encounter in academic and business writing in the United States. This chapter reviews the rules of Standard American English grammar, and the chapters that follow it in part 10 focus on aspects of grammar and usage that many writers find troublesome.

PARTS OF SPEECH 词性

The term *parts of speech* refers to the roles words play in a sentence. English has eight parts of speech:

- nouns
- pronouns
- adverbs
- prepositions
- verbs
- conjunctions
- adjectives
- interjections

Writing Responsibly | Why Grammar Matters

Sometimes a writer uses nonstandard grammar as a way of drawing attention to issues of culture and power, or as a way of asserting the legitimacy of nonstandard dialects. In most cases, though, writers have a responsibility to use language their readers regard as grammatically correct. A shared standard of grammar eases communication and demonstrates your respect for your readers.

to AUDIENCE

The same word can have more than one role, depending on the context in which it appears.

- ▸ Many students work to help pay for college. [*Work* is a verb.]
- ▸ Mastering calculus requires hard work. [*Work* is a noun.]

36a Nouns 名词

Nouns name ideas (*justice*), things (*chair*), qualities (*neatness*), actions (*judgment*), people (*Steven Spielberg*), and places (*Tokyo*). They fall into a variety of overlapping categories:

- *Proper nouns* name specific places, people, or things and are usually capitalized: *Nairobi, Hudson Bay, Hillary Rodham Clinton, the Taj Mahal.* All other nouns are *common nouns*, which name members of a class or group: *turtle, sophomore, skyscraper.*
- *Collective nouns* name a collection that can function as a single unit: *committee, administration, family.*
- *Concrete nouns* name things that can be seen, touched, heard, smelled, or tasted: *planet, liquid, symphony, skunk, pepper.* *Abstract nouns* name qualities or ideas that cannot be perceived by the senses: *mercy, wisdom.*
- *Countable* (or *count*) *nouns* name things or ideas that can be counted. They can be either *singular* or *plural*: *cat/cats, assignment/assignments, idea/ideas.*
- *Uncountable* (or *noncount*) *nouns* name ideas or things that cannot be counted and do not have a plural form: *homework, knowledge, pollution.*

> *More about*
> Count and noncount nouns, 411–16

Countable and Uncountable Nouns In many languages, the classification of nouns as countable or uncountable affects the way they combine with articles (*a, an, the*) and other determiners (*my, your, some, many, this, those*). Awareness of the effect of this aspect of nouns on sentence grammar will help you avoid errors.

> *More about*
> Noun plurals, 476–77

> *More about*
> Apostrophes and possession, 444–47

noun phrase 名词短语
A noun and its modifiers

> *More about*
> Pronouns, 361–62, 364, 365–68, 380–87

Most nouns form the plural with the addition of a final *-s* or *-es*: *book/books, beach/beaches, country/countries.* A few have irregular plurals: *woman/women, life/lives, mouse/mice.* For some nouns, the singular and the plural forms are the same: *deer/deer, fish/fish.*

Nouns indicate possession with a final *s* sound, marked in writing with an apostrophe: *Rosa's idea, the students' plan.*

36b Pronouns 代词

Pronouns rename or take the place of nouns or *noun phrases*. The noun that a pronoun replaces is called its *antecedent*. The Quick Reference box on page 334 summarizes pronoun types and their functions.

36c Verbs 动词

Verbs express action (*The quarterback* <u>throws</u> *a pass*), occurrence (*The play* <u>happened</u> *in the second half*), or state of being (*The fans* <u>are</u> *happy*).

Two kinds of verbs combine to make up a *verb phrase*: *main verbs* and *helping* (or *auxiliary*) *verbs*. Main verbs carry the principal meaning of a verb phrase. Almost all verb forms other than the present and past tenses, however, require a combination of one or more helping verbs with a form of the main verb. Some helping verbs (forms of *be*, *have*, and *do*) also function as main verbs. Others, called *modal verbs* (*can, could, may, might, must, shall, should, will, would,* and *ought to*), function only as helping verbs.

More about
Verb forms,
369–79

Modal Auxiliaries Modal auxiliaries can pose special challenges for multilingual students because other languages use very different grammatical strategies to express intention, possibility, or expectation. For more on their meaning and use, see pages 420–22.

Helping verbs always precede the main verb in a verb phrase.

|— verb phrase —|
main
verb

▶ The studio produced a successful movie.

helping   main
verbs   verb
▶ The movie may have broken a box office record.

NOTE Do not confuse *verbals* with complete verbs. Verbals are verb forms that act as nouns, adjectives, or adverbs, not as verbs.

More about
Verbals, 343, 350

- ▶ The potters *fired* the vessels in their kiln. [*Fired* is a verb.]
- ▶ The *fired* clay is rock hard. [*Fired* is a verbal, in this case an adjective modifying *clay*.]

36d Adjectives 形容词

Adjectives modify nouns or pronouns with descriptive or limiting information. They answer questions such as *What kind? Which one?* or *How many?*

More about
Adjectives,
387–91

	adj. noun
WHAT KIND?	a warm day
WHICH ONE?	the next speaker
HOW MANY?	twelve roses

Quick

Reference　**Pronouns and Their Functions**

Type and Function	Forms	Examples
Personal pronouns take the place of specific nouns or noun phrases.	**Singular:** *I, me, you, he, him, she, her, it* **Plural:** *we, us, you, they, them*	Yue bought the tickets for Adam, and she gave them to him before the concert.
Possessive pronouns are personal pronouns that indicate possession.	**Singular:** *my, mine, your, yours, his, her, hers, its* **Plural:** *our, ours, your, yours, their, theirs*	Adam gave one of the tickets to his roommate.
Reflexive pronouns refer back to the subject of a sentence.	**Singular:** *myself, yourself, himself, herself, itself, oneself* **Plural:** *ourselves, yourselves, themselves*	Laetitia reminded herself to return the books to the library.
Intensive pronouns rename and emphasize their antecedents.	Same as reflexive pronouns	Dr. Collins herself performed the operation.
Demonstrative pronouns rename and point to nouns or noun phrases. They can function as adjectives as well as nouns.	**Singular:** *this, that* **Plural:** *these, those*	Yameng visited the Forbidden City. That was his favorite place in China. That place was his favorite.
Relative pronouns introduce subordinate clauses that describe the pronoun's antecedent.	*who, whom, whoever, whomever, what, whose, whatever, whichever, that, which*	I. M. Pei is the architect who designed the East Wing of the National Gallery.
Interrogative pronouns introduce questions.	*who, whoever, whom, whomever, what, whatever, which, whichever, whose*	Who designed the East Wing of the National Gallery?
Indefinite pronouns do not refer to specific people or things.	**Singular:** *anybody, anyone, anything, each, either, everybody, everyone, everything, much, neither, nobody, no one, nothing, one, somebody, someone, something* **Singular or plural:** *all, any, more, most, some* **Plural:** *both, few, many, several*	Everybody talks about the weather, but nobody does anything about it. *—Attributed to Mark Twain*
Reciprocal pronouns refer to the individual parts of a plural antecedent.	*each other, one another*	The candidates debated one another many times before the primary.

Adjectives most commonly fall before nouns in a noun phrase and after *linking verbs* as *subject complements*.

linking verb 系动词
A verb that conveys a state of being linking a subject to its complement
subject complement 主语补足语 An adjective, pronoun, or noun phrase that follows a linking verb and describes or refers to the sentence subject

▸ The young musicians played a rousing concert.

     adj.   noun   adj.   noun

▸ They were enthusiastic.

  pro-   link.   adj.
  noun verb

Possessive, demonstrative, and indefinite pronouns that act as adjectives—as well as the articles *a, an,* and *the*—are known as *determiners* because they point to or indicate the amount of the nouns they modify. Determiners always come before other adjectives in a noun phrase. Some, like *all* and *both,* also come before any other determiners.

   det. adj. noun   det.   noun   dets.   adj. noun

▸ The new gym is in that building with all those solar panels on

   det. noun

the roof.

The Ordering of Adjectives The ordering of adjectives in noun phrases and the use of articles and other determiners in English can be challenging for multilingual writers. English sentences tend to place adjectives before nouns, while adjective placement in other languages varies and some languages do not use articles at all. For more on these topics, see pages 412–16 and 423.

36e Adverbs 副词

Adverbs modify verbs, adjectives, and other adverbs, as well as entire phrases and clauses. They answer such questions as *How? Where? When?* and *To what extent or degree?*

More about
Adverbs, 387–91

HOW?   adverb   verb adv.

                  Embarrassingly, my cell phone rang loudly.

                  The adverb *loudly* modifies the verb *rang.* The adverb *embarrassingly* modifies the whole sentence.

WHEN?   adv.   adj.

                  Dinner is finally ready.

                  The adverb *finally* modifies the adjective *ready.*

Quick Reference   Common Conjunctive Adverbs

accordingly	finally	instead	nonetheless	subsequently
also	for example	likewise	now	suddenly
anyway	furthermore	meanwhile	otherwise	then
as a result	hence	moreover	similarly	therefore
besides	however	nevertheless	specifically	thus
certainly	indeed	next	still	

verb   adv.   adv.

WHERE?   Stop right there!

EXTENT?

The adverb *right* modifies the adverb *there,* which modifies the verb *stop.*

More about
Adjective and
   adverb phrases,
   342–44
Adjective and
   adverb clauses,
   344–46

A *conjunctive adverb* is a transitional expression that links one independent clause to another and indicates how the two clauses relate to each other. A period or semicolon, not a comma, should separate independent clauses linked with a conjunctive adverb.

▶ Writers have several options for joining independent clauses; however, a comma alone is not one of them.

36f Prepositions 介词

Prepositions relate nouns or pronouns to other words in a sentence in terms of time, space, cause, and other attributes.

▶ The lecture begins at noon in the auditorium.

More about
Prepositions,
   426–31

As the Quick Reference box below indicates, prepositions can consist of more than one word.

36g Conjunctions 连词

Conjunctions join words, phrases, and clauses to other words, phrases, or clauses and indicate how the joined elements relate to each other. *Coordinating conjunctions* (*and, but, or, for, nor, yet,* and *so*) join similar elements, giving them each equal significance.

Quick Reference | **Common One-Word and Multiword Prepositions**

about	at	far from	near	past
above	because of	for	near to	since
according to	before	from	next to	through
across	behind	in	of	to
after	below	in addition to	off	toward
against	beneath	in case of	on	under
ahead of	beside	in front of	on account of	underneath
along	between	in place of	on behalf of	until
among	by	inside	onto	up
around	by means of	inside of	on top of	upon
as far as	close to	in spite of	out of	with
aside from	down	instead of	outside	within
as to	during	into	outside of	without
as well as	except	like	over	

> **More about**
> Independent and
> subordinate
> clauses, 344–45

_{Quick} **Reference** | **Common Subordinating Conjunctions**

after	before	since	when
although	even if	so that	where
as	even though	though	while
as if	if	unless	
because	once	until	

▶ Ingenious **and** energetic entrepreneurs can generate effective **but** inexpensive publicity. [The conjunction **and** pairs two adjectives; the conjunction **but** contrasts two adjectives.]

Correlative conjunctions are pairs of terms that, like coordinating conjunctions, join similar elements. Common correlative conjunctions include *either . . . or, neither . . . nor, both . . . and, not only . . . but also,* and *whether . . . or.*

▶ Fred Thompson was **both** an actor **and** a presidential candidate.

Subordinating conjunctions link subordinate clauses to the independent clauses they modify.

▶ The party could not begin **until** the guest of honor had arrived.

36h Interjections 插入语

Interjections are words like *alas, bah, oh, ouch,* and *ugh* that express strong feeling—of regret, contempt, surprise, pain, or disgust, for example—but otherwise serve no grammatical function.

▶ **Ugh!** That's the worst coffee I ever tasted.

SENTENCE STRUCTURE 句子结构

All sentences have two basic parts: a subject and a predicate. The *subject* is the thing the sentence is about. The *predicate* states something about the subject.

|——— subject ———| |——————— predicate ———————|

▶ Digital technology transformed the music industry.

Sentences fall into one of four categories:

- *Declarative sentences* (the most common type) make a statement.
  ▶ Digital technology transformed the music industry.
- *Imperative sentences* give a command.
  ▶ Join the digital bandwagon to survive in today's competitive media marketplace.
- *Interrogative sentences* ask a question.
  ▶ Will digital technology make printed books obsolete?

- *Exclamatory sentences* express strong or sudden emotion.

　▶ How I hate updating apps on my phone!

36i Subjects 主语

The *simple subject* of a sentence is a noun or pronoun. The *complete subject* consists of the simple subject plus any modifying words or phrases.

```
├── complete subject ──┤
                simple
                subject
```
▶ *Two robotic vehicles* began exploring Mars in January 2004.

A *compound subject* contains two or more simple subjects joined by a conjunction.

```
├─────────────────────── compound subject ───────────────────────┤
                    ss      conj                    ss
```
▶ *The six-wheeled, solar-powered* Spirit *and the identical* Opportunity landed within three weeks of each other.

In imperative sentences (commands), the subject, *you,* is unstated.

▶ [*You*] Learn about space exploration at www.nasa.gov.

In interrogative sentences (questions), the subject falls between a helping verb and the main verb or, if the main verb is a form of *be* alone, after the verb.

```
 helping                    main
 verb      ├─subject─┤      verb
```
▶ Did　the rovers　find evidence of water on Mars?

```
       verb    ├────── subject ──────┤
```
▶ Were *Spirit* and *Opportunity* more durable than expected?

Quick

Reference　Finding the Subject

The complete subject of a sentence is the answer to the question "Who or what did the action or was in the state defined by the verb?"

```
├── complete subject ──┤   verb
```
▶ Two robotic vehicles landed safely on Mars in January 2004.

What landed on Mars in January 2004? Two robotic vehicles did. The subject is *two robotic vehicles.*

```
├──────────── complete subject ────────────┤   verb
```
▶ The scientists and engineers who designed the rovers cheered.

Who cheered? The scientists and engineers who designed the rovers did. The subject is *the scientists and engineers who designed the rovers.*
　　The subject usually precedes the verb, but it is not always the first element in a sentence. In the following sentence, for example, the phrase *in July 2007* modifies the rest of the sentence but is not part of the subject.

```
├──── subject ────┤   verb
```
▶ In July 2007, Martian dust storms restricted the activity of the rovers.

Writers occasionally invert normal word order and place the subject after the verb for emphasis.

More about
Word order and emphasis, 293–301

 verb ┠─────── subject ───────┨
▶ Out of the swirling dust emerged the hardy Mars rover.

The subject also follows the verb in sentences that begin with *there* followed by a form of *be.* In these **expletive constructions**, the word *there* functions as a placeholder for the delayed subject.

 v ┠─subject─┨
▶ There are two vehicles roaming the surface of Mars.

English Word Order In English, word order is less flexible than in many other languages, and the position of a word often affects its grammatical role and meaning. English sentences tend to place subjects before verbs and verbs before their objects. English readers expect this order, so using other word orders can cause confusion.

More about
English word order, 406–10

36j Predicates 谓语

The **simple predicate** of a sentence is the main verb and any helping verbs. The **complete predicate** is the simple predicate together with any objects, complements, and modifiers.

 ┠─────complete predicate ─────┨
 simple
 pred.
▶ Polynesian mariners *settled the Hawaiian Islands.*

 ┠───────complete predicate ───────┨
 simple pred.
▶ The first settlers *may have arrived as early as the fourth century CE.*

A **compound predicate** is a complete predicate containing two or more simple predicates joined by a conjunction.

 ┠────────────────── complete
 simple pred.
▶ Polynesian mariners *navigated thousands of miles of open ocean and*

 predicate ─────────────────┨
 sp
settled the islands of the South Pacific.

36k Verb Types and Sentence Patterns 动词类型和句型

There are three kinds of verbs—*intransitive, linking,* and *transitive*—and they combine with other elements in the predicate in five basic sentence patterns.

Reference   Five Sentence Patterns

1. subject → intransitive verb
   - The lights dimmed.
     (s) (iv)
2. subject → linking verb → subject complement
   - The audience fell silent.
     (s) (lv) (sc)
3. subject → transitive verb → direct object
   - The orchestra played the overture.
     (s) (tv) (do)
4. subject → transitive verb → indirect object → direct object
   - The show gave the audience a thrill.
     (s) (tv) (io) (do)
5. subject → transitive verb → direct object → object complement
   - The applause made the actors happy.
     (s) (tv) (do) (oc)

1. Subject → intransitive verb 主语→不及物动词

Intransitive verbs require no object and can stand alone as the only element in a predicate. They are often modified, however, by adverbs and adverbial phrases and clauses.

├─ subj. ─┤   intrans. verb
- The volcano *erupted*.

├─ subj. ─┤   intrans. verb ├──────── adverbial modifiers ────────┤
- The volcano *erupted suddenly in a powerful blast of ash and steam.*

2. Subject → linking verb → subject complement
主语→系动词→主语补足语

A *subject complement* is an adjective, a pronoun, or a noun phrase that describes or refers to the subject of a sentence. A *linking verb* connects the subject to its complement. Linking verbs express states of being rather than actions. The verb *be,* when used as a main verb, is always a linking verb. Other verbs that can function as linking verbs include *appear, become, fall, feel, grow, look, make, prove, remain, seem, smell, sound,* and *taste.*

├─ subj. ─┤   link. vb.   ├─ subj. comp. ─┤
- The Oscar   is   a coveted award.

- The patient felt   better.

3. Subject → transitive verb → direct object
主语→及物动词→直接宾语

> **More about**
> Voice and style
> choices, 302–03

Transitive verbs have two *voices*: active and passive. *Transitive verbs* in the *active voice* require a *direct object*—a pronoun or noun phrase that receives the action of the verb.

active
├──────── subject ────────┤ trans. vb. ├──── do ────┤
▶ The undersea volcano created a new island.

The *passive voice* reverses the role of the subject, making it the recipient of the action of the verb. An active-voice sentence can usually be changed into a passive-voice sentence of the same meaning. The subject of the passive-voice version is the direct object of the active-voice version.

passive
├── subject ──┤ trans. verb
▶ A new island *was created* by the undersea volcano.

In the passive voice, the agent of the action can be left unstated.

▶ A new island *was created*.

NOTE Many verbs can be either transitive or intransitive.

		├────────do ────────┤
TRANSITIVE	My sister *won* the Scrabble game.	
INTRANSITIVE	My sister always *wins*.	

When in doubt about the usage of a verb, check a dictionary.

---

4. Subject → transitive verb → indirect object → direct object
主语→及物动词→间接宾语→直接宾语

Some transitive verbs can take an *indirect object* as well as a direct object. The indirect object, which comes before the direct object, identifies who or what benefits from the action of the verb.

├── s ──┤	├── tv ──┤	├── io ──┤	├──────── do ────────┤
▶ Juan	lent	Ileana	his notes.
▶ The donor	bought	the library	a new computer center.

Often, the indirect object can also be stated as a prepositional phrase that usually begins with *to* and follows the direct object.

▶ Juan lent his notes *to Ileana*.

Verbs that can take an indirect object include *ask, bring, buy, call, find, get, give, hand, leave, lend, offer, pass, pay, promise, read, send, show, teach, tell, throw,* and *write*.

Indirect Objects The use of indirect objects is highly idiomatic in English. The verbs that take them are similar to others that do not. Likewise, in some situations an indirect object before the direct object is interchangeable with a prepositional phrase after it, but in others only one or the other is acceptable. Learning how to use indirect objects effectively, then, requires exposure to a broad variety of English-language situations and texts.

❯ *More about*
Indirect objects, 408–09

5. Subject → transitive verb → direct object → object complement
主语→及物动词→直接宾语→宾语补足语

An *object complement* is an adjective or a noun phrase that follows the direct object and describes the condition of the object or a change that the subject has caused it to undergo.

|— s —| |— tv —| |— do —| |— oc —|

▶ The fans   considered   the umpire's call   mistaken.

▶ The manager named   David Ortiz   designated hitter.

361 Phrases 短语

A *phrase* is a group of related words that lacks a subject, a predicate, or both. Phrases function in various ways within sentences but cannot function as sentences by themselves. A phrase by itself is a *fragment*, not a sentence.

> **fragment** 片段 An incomplete sentence punctuated as if it were complete

1. Noun phrases 名词短语

A *noun phrase* consists of a noun together with any modifiers. Noun phrases function as subjects, objects, and complements within sentences.

|——— noun phrase/subject ———|

▶ *Sam's mouth-watering apple pie* emerged piping hot from the oven.

|——— noun phrase/direct object ———|

▶ The guests devoured *Sam's mouth-watering apple pie.*

|——— noun phrase subj. comp. ———|

▶ The high point of the meal was *Sam's mouth-watering apple pie.*

An *appositive phrase* is a noun or noun phrase that renames a noun or noun phrase and is grammatically equivalent to it.

|——— appositive ———|

▶ The high point of the meal, *Sam's mouth-watering apple pie,* emerged piping hot from the oven.

2. Verb phrases 动词短语

A *verb phrase* consists of a main verb and all its helping verbs. Verb phrases act as the simple predicates of sentences and clauses.

|——— verb phrase ———|

▶ By Election Day, the candidates *will have been campaigning* for almost two years.

3. Prepositional phrases 介词短语

A *prepositional phrase* is a preposition followed by the *object of the preposition*: a pronoun or noun and its modifiers. Prepositional phrases function as adjectives and adverbs.

▶ The train arrives in an hour. [The prepositional phrase *in an hour* functions as an adverb modifying the verb *arrives.*]

▶ She recommended the article about Spielberg. [The prepositional phrase *about Spielberg* acts as an adjective modifying the noun *article.*]

4. Verbal phrases 动词短语

Verbals are verb forms that function as nouns, adjectives, or adverbs. Although they may have objects and complements, verbals lack all the information required of a complete verb. A *verbal phrase* consists of a verbal and any modifiers, objects, or complements. There are three kinds of verbal phrases: gerund phrases, infinitive phrases, and participial phrases.

Gerunds A *gerund* is the present participle (or *-ing* form) of a verb used as a noun. Like nouns, gerunds and gerund phrases can act as subjects, objects, and complements.

> ├────── gerund phrase/subject ──────┤
> ▶ *Increasing automobile fuel efficiency* will reduce carbon emissions.

> ├────── gerund phrase/dir. obj.──────┤
> ▶ The mayor recommends *improving the city's mass transit system.*

Infinitives An *infinitive* is the *to* form of the verb (*to decide, to eat, to study*). Infinitives and infinitive phrases can act as adjectives and adverbs as well as nouns.

> ├── noun phrase/subj. comp. ──┤
> ▶ The goal of the law is *to increase fuel efficiency.*

> ├──── adjective phrase ────┤
> ▶ Congress passed a law *to increase fuel efficiency.*

> ├──── adverb phrase ────┤
> ▶ *To reduce traffic congestion,* the city improved its mass transit system.

Infinitive versus Gerund after the Verb Some verbs can be followed by a gerund but not an infinitive, others by an infinitive but not a gerund, and still others by either a gerund or an infinitive. Lists of verbs and what can follow them do exist, but learning specific examples is a matter of experience with a broad variety of English-language situations and texts.

> **More about**
> Infinitive versus gerund after verbs, 418–20

Participial phrases In a *participial phrase*, the present participle or past participle of a verb acts as an adjective. The present participle ends in *-ing*. The past participle of regular verbs ends in *-ed*, but some verbs have irregular past participles.

> **More about**
> Irregular past participles, 369–72

> ▶ *Surveying the disheveled apartment,* Grace wondered whether it would be possible to room with Maritza.

> ▶ *Deeply <u>concerned</u>,* she asked, "How long have you lived alone?"

5. Absolute phrases 独立短语

Absolute phrases modify entire sentences rather than particular words within sentences. They usually consist of a pronoun or noun phrase followed by a participle. Set off by commas, they can often fall flexibly before, after, or within the rest of the sentence.

▶ *All our quarrels forgotten,* we sat before the fire and talked quietly.

36m Clauses 从句

A *clause* is a word group with a subject and a predicate. An *independent* (or *main*) *clause* can stand alone as a sentence.

|————— independent clause —————|

▶ Sam's pie won first prize.

A *subordinate* (or *dependent*) clause is a clause within a clause.

|——————— independent clause ———————|

|——— sub. clause ———|

▶ Sam baked the pie that won first prize.

That is, a subordinate clause functions inside an independent clause (or another subordinate clause) as a noun, an adjective, or an adverb but cannot stand alone as a sentence. A subordinate clause by itself is a *fragment*. A subordinating word—either a *subordinating conjunction* (see the Quick Reference box on p. 337) or a *relative pronoun* (see the Quick Reference box on p. 334)—usually signals the beginning of a subordinate clause.

> **More about**
> Subordinate
>   clause fragments,
>   351–52
> Punctuating sub-
>   ordinate clauses,
>   434, 436–39

1. Adjective clauses 定语从句

Like adjectives, *adjective clauses* (also called *relative clauses*) modify nouns or pronouns. They usually begin with a relative pronoun that immediately follows the word the clause modifies and refers back to it.

▶ Sam baked the pie *that won first prize.*

▶ The donor *who paid for the library's new computer center* is a recent graduate.

In both these examples, the relative pronoun is the subject of the subordinate clause, and the clause follows normal word order, with the subject before the verb. When the relative pronoun is the direct object, however, it still comes at the beginning of the clause, reversing normal word order.

> **More about**
> *Who* versus
>   *whom,* 384–85

▶ The candidate *whom we supported* lost the election.

Adjective clauses can also begin with the subordinating conjunctions *when* and *where*.

▶ Tupelo, Mississippi, is the **town** *where Elvis Presley was born.*

It is sometimes acceptable to omit the relative pronoun that introduces an adjective clause when the meaning of the clause is clear without it.

▶ The candidate [*whom*] *we supported* lost the election.

2. Adverb clauses 状语从句

Adverb clauses usually begin with a subordinating conjunction, which specifies the relation of a clause to the term it modifies. Like adverbs, adverb clauses can modify verbs, adjectives, and adverbs as well as whole phrases and clauses.

▶ The baby boom **began** *as World War II ended.*
  The adverb clause modifies the verb *began.*

▶ The 1990s were an affluent decade, *although the general prosperity did not benefit everyone.*
  The adverb clause modifies the preceding independent clause.

> **More about**
> The meaning of subordinating conjunctions, 297–98

3. Noun clauses 名词性从句

Noun clauses replace noun phrases as subjects, objects, or complements within an independent clause. Noun clauses can begin with a relative pronoun as well as with certain subordinating conjunctions, including *how, if, when, whenever, where, wherever, whether,* and *why.*

├──────── subject ────────┤
▶ *Whoever crosses the finish line first* wins the race.

├── subject comp. ──┤
▶ Home is *where the heart is.*

├──────── direct object ────────┤
▶ The evidence proves *that the defendant is not guilty.*

36n Sentence Types 句型

Sentences fall into four types depending on the combination of independent and subordinate clauses they contain.

1. Simple sentences 简单句

A *simple sentence* has only one independent clause and no subordinate clauses.

├──────────────── independent clause ────────────────┤
▶ Lance Armstrong won the Tour de France seven times.

A simple sentence need not be short or even uncomplicated. A sentence with a compound subject, a compound predicate, or both is still a simple sentence as long as it has a single complete subject, a single complete predicate, and no subordinate clauses.

2. Compound sentences 并列句

A *compound sentence* has two or more independent clauses but no subordinate clauses. A comma and a coordinating conjunction, a semicolon, or a semicolon and a conjunctive adverb usually join the clauses in a compound sentence.

More about
Punctuating
compound sen-
tences, 353–57

├──────────── independent clause ────────────┤
▶ Lance Armstrong won the Tour de France seven times, and
├──────────── independent clause ────────────┤
in 2002, *Sports Illustrated* named him Sportsman of the Year.

3. Complex sentences 复合句

A *complex sentence* consists of a single independent clause with at least one subordinate clause.

├──────────────────────────────── independent
├──────────── subordinate clause ────────────┤
▶ The Tour de France, which is the world's longest cycling race, covers
clause ────────────────┤
nearly 2,000 miles in 22 days.

4. Compound-complex sentences 并列复合句

A *compound-complex sentence* has two or more independent clauses with one or more subordinate clauses.

├──────────── independent clause ────────────┤
▶ The Tour has long been plagued by allegations of doping among
──────────────┤ ├──────────────────── independent
├──────────── subordinate
contestants, but the 2007 race, which saw three riders disqualified
clause ────────────────────┤
clause ────────────┤
for doping-related offenses, was particularly scandal ridden.

37 Avoiding Sentence Fragments 避免残缺句

An open drawbridge is not a complete bridge; it is two bridge fragments, neither of which, by itself, will get travelers all the way across a river. Similarly, a *sentence fragment* is not a complete sentence. It may begin with a capital letter and end with a period (or a question mark or an exclamation point), but it lacks all the elements of a complete sentence. It takes readers only partway through the writer's thought, leaving them searching for the missing pieces. Although writers may use them intentionally in certain contexts, fragments are almost always out of place in academic and business writing.

37a Recognizing Fragments 辨别残缺句

A sentence must have at least one *independent clause*, which is a group of related words that has a *complete verb* and a *subject* but does not start with a subordinating term such as *although, because, who,* or *that.* If a word group does not satisfy these conditions but is punctuated like a sentence, it is a fragment, not a sentence.

No verb A *complete verb* consists of a main verb together with any helping verbs needed to express tense, mood, and voice. If a word group lacks a complete verb, it is a *phrase*, and if that phrase is punctuated like a sentence, it is a phrase fragment.

FRAGMENT **(NO VERB)**	Her beautiful new sports car.

	subj. complete verb
SENTENCE	Her beautiful new sports car was smashed beyond repair.

> subject 主语 A noun or pronoun that names the topic of a sentence
> complete verb 完整的动词 A main verb together with any helping verbs needed to indicate tense, voice, and mood

> **More about**
> Verbs, 369–79

Self Assessment — Identifying Fragments

To determine whether a word group is a fragment or a sentence, ask yourself the following questions, then make any necessary corrections to your work.

☐ Does it have a complete verb?
  ► If the answer is no, it is a fragment.

☐ Does it have a subject?
  ► If the answer is no, it is a fragment.

☐ Does it begin with a subordinating word but otherwise stand alone?
  ► If the answer is yes, it is a fragment.

No subject The subject of a sentence is the answer to the question "Who or what did the action defined by the verb?" If a word group lacks a subject, it is a phrase. If the phrase is punctuated like a sentence, it is a phrase fragment.

verb

FRAGMENT　Serves no purpose.

subject　　　　　　　　　verb

SENTENCE　The breadmaker in my cupboard serves no purpose.

Including a Stated Subject Unlike in most other languages, all sentences in formal English except commands always require an explicitly stated subject. See chapter 46, "Understanding English Word Order and Sentence Structure," page 406.

> **More about**
> Subordinate
> clauses, 344–45

Begins with a subordinating term A subordinate clause, like a sentence, has a subject and a predicate. However, a subordinate clause begins with a subordinating term that links it to another clause. Subordinating terms include subordinating conjunctions and relative pronouns (see the Quick Reference box on this page). A subordinate clause cannot be a sentence on its own. If it is punctuated like a sentence, it is a subordinate clause fragment.

subordinator

FRAGMENT　When the drawbridge closes.

subordinator

SENTENCE　We will cross the river when the drawbridge closes.

subordinator

FRAGMENT　Which made driving hazardous.

subordinator

SENTENCE　The storm left a foot of snow, which made driving hazardous.

Quick Reference　**Subordinating Terms**

Subordinating Conjunctions

after	before	since	unless	whereas
although	even if	so that	until	while
as	even though	than	when	why
as if	if	that	whenever	
because	once	though	where	

Relative Pronouns

that	whatever	whichever	whoever	whomever
what	which	who	whom	whose

Note that many relative pronouns can also act as interrogative pronouns to introduce questions. Questions beginning this way are complete sentences.

More about
Different types of
pronouns, 334

FRAGMENT   relative pronoun
    Who will be attending.

SENTENCE   interrogative pronoun
    Who will be attending?

37b Editing Fragments 修改殘缺句

When you identify a fragment, you have two options for correcting it:

1. Connect the fragment to a related independent clause.

   ▶ The first mission to Pluto was launched in 2006. ~~Arrived~~ *and arrived*
   in 2015.

   ▶ Archaeologists sift through the dust slowly. ~~Looking~~ *, looking* for
   personal belongings buried with the deceased.

2. Convert the fragment into an independent clause.

   ▶ The first mission to Pluto was launched in 2006. ~~Arrived~~ *It arrived* in 2015.

   ▶ Archaeologists sift through the dust slowly. ~~Looking~~ *; they are looking* for

   personal belongings buried with the deceased.

Writing Responsibly

Sentence Fragments and Context

Although writers sometimes use them deliberately in certain contexts (see 37c), for a variety of reasons you should avoid sentence fragments in your academic or business writing. One reason is that fragments can create ambiguities, as in the following example:

   ▶ Our small town has seen many changes. Some long-time stores went out of business. Because the new mall opened. There are now more options for family entertainment.

Did the new mall put stores out of business, provide new entertainment options, or both? To clarify this ambiguity, the writer would need to attach the fragment to the preceding or the following sentence or rewrite these sentences in some other way.

Another reason to avoid fragments is that readers may interpret them as the result of carelessness or a lack of competence, which would undermine your efforts to present yourself authoritatively.

to TOPIC

These options apply to both phrase fragments and subordinate clause fragments. Either option can fix a fragment; deciding on the best one is a stylistic choice that depends on the context in which the fragment occurs.

1. Phrase fragments 短语残缺

As you edit your writing, watch in particular for fragments based on certain kinds of phrases, including prepositional phrases, verbal phrases, appositive phrases, the separate parts of compound predicates, and items in lists and examples. A *prepositional phrase* consists of a preposition (such as *as, at, for, from, in addition to, to,* or *until*) followed by a pronoun or noun and its modifiers. You can usually correct a prepositional phrase fragment by attaching it to an adjacent sentence.

> More about
> Prepositions and prepositional phrases, 336, 342, 426–31

▶ The Kenyon College women won the NCAA Division III title

                for

~~again that year. For~~ the seventeenth consecutive year.

> More about
> Verbals, 333, 343

Verbals are words that look like verbs—they are derived from verbs—but they lack the information about tense required of a complete verb. *Verbal phrases* can function as adjectives, adverbs, or nouns within a sentence but not as sentences on their own. In the following example, *stranding* is a verbal.

                gas, stranding

▶ The car had run out of ~~gas. Stranding~~ us in the middle of nowhere.

> More about
> Appositives, 342

An *appositive phrase* renames a preceding noun or noun phrase. Appositives become fragments when they are separated by a period from the phrases they rename.

| noun phrase 名词短语 A noun together with any modifiers |

▶ In her acceptance speech, the Academy Award winner thanked her

              fan, her

biggest ~~fan. Her~~ mother.

> More about
> Compound predicates, 339

A *compound predicate* consists of two or more complete verbs, together with their objects and modifiers, that are joined by a coordinating conjunction (such as *or, and,* or *but*) and that share the same subject. A fragment results when the last part of a compound predicate is punctuated as a separate sentence.

Tech **Grammar Checkers and Sentence Fragments**

The grammar checkers in word processing programs may miss some fragments and, in some cases, may incorrectly flag imperatives (commands) as fragments. Although your grammar checker can help you, you will still need to edit your prose carefully for fragments.

▶ By the end of May, the band members hated one another. ~~But~~ *but* still had six weeks left on the tour.

Lists become fragments when they are separated from the sentence to which they belong. To correct list fragments, link them to the sentence by rephrasing the passage or replacing the period with a colon or a dash.

FRAGMENT Three authors are most commonly associated with the Beat movement. Allen Ginsberg, Jack Kerouac, and William Burroughs.

REVISED The three authors most commonly associated with the Beat movement are Allen Ginsberg, Jack Kerouac, and William Burroughs.

or

Three authors are most commonly associated with the Beat movement: Allen Ginsberg, Jack Kerouac, and William Burroughs.

> **More about**
> Punctuation for
> lists, 456–59

Examples or explanations that begin with transitional words such as *for example, in contrast,* and *in addition* can be sentences. They are fragments, however, if they are punctuated like a sentence but lack a subject or a complete verb or otherwise consist of only a subordinate clause. In the following example, the writer corrected a phrase fragment by rephrasing and attaching it to the preceding sentence.

▶ People today have access to many sources of news and ~~opinion. For~~ *opinion, including, for* example, the Internet and cable television as well as broadcast television and print newspapers and magazines.

The writer of the next example corrected a subordinate clause fragment by deleting the subordinating word *that*, which turns the fragment into a sentence.

▶ Certain facts underscore the rapid growth of the Internet. For *example,* ~~example that~~ web browsers did not become widely available until the mid-1990s.

2. Subordinate clause fragments 从句残缺

When you correct a subordinate clause fragment, be sure to consider the relationships among the ideas you are expressing before deciding whether to transform the subordinate clause into an independent clause or to connect it to a related independent clause. Subordinating conjunctions,

> **More about**
> Subordination and
> subordinating
> conjunctions,
> 296–98

for example, specify the relationship between the information in a subordinate clause and the clause it modifies. If that relationship is important, you will probably want to correct the fragment by connecting it to the independent clause to which it relates.

▶ Twitter continues to gain popularity as a source of information. ~~Because~~ *because* it can publish late-breaking news as soon as it occurs.

The correction retains the subordinating conjunction *because* and with it important information about the cause-and-effect relationship between the two parts of the sentence.

In other cases, revising a subordinate clause fragment into a separate sentence by deleting the subordinating word can produce a clearer, less awkward result than would attaching it to another sentence.

▶ Horses and camels have something in common. ~~That the~~ *The* ancestors of both originated in the Western Hemisphere and migrated to the Eastern Hemisphere.

37c Thinking Carefully before Using an Intentional Fragment
在有意使用残缺句之前要考虑周全

Writers sometimes use fragments not in error but intentionally for emphasis or to reflect how people actually speak. Exclamations and the answers to questions often fall into this category.

▶ Another loss! Ouch!

▶ What caused this disaster? The collapse of our running game.

Intentional fragments are also common in advertising copy, and many writers use them for effect when the context makes their full meaning clear.

▶ All science. No fiction.

—Toyota advertisement

▶ Man is the only animal that blushes. Or needs to.

—Mark Twain, *Following the Equator*

Consider your writing situation, your context and genre, and especially your audience before deliberately deciding to use a sentence fragment. In academic or business writing, where clarity of expression is highly prized, fragments are frowned upon and can undermine your authority. In contrast, if your purpose is expressive or if you are writing in an informal context or genre (for example, in a blog or a text message), the occasional intentional fragment can be highly effective.

38 Avoiding Comma Splices and Fused Sentences 避免粘连句和融合句

How things are joined together is important, whether those "things" are pipes or sentences. If they are not correctly connected, they will work poorly—or they may not work at all. A blowtorch is a good tool for reconnecting leaky pipes; correct punctuation is a good tool for repairing the comma splices and run-ons in "leaky" sentences. If clauses are incorrectly joined with a comma alone (a **comma splice**), the comma is too weak to show the connection between the two thoughts. If the clauses crash into one another with no separating punctuation (a **fused**, or **run-on**, **sentence**), readers will not know where one thought ends and the other begins.

38a Joining Independent Clauses Correctly 正确连接独立分句

An **independent clause** can stand on its own as a sentence. Related independent clauses can follow one another as separate sentences, each ending in a period.

> *More about*
> Clauses, 344–45

▶ |————————— independent clause —————————|
The blues singer Alberta Hunter retired in the 1950s.
|————————— independent clause —————————|
She made a successful comeback in the 1970s.

Alternatively, you can join (or *coordinate*) independent clauses in a compound sentence with a variety of coupling mechanisms that let readers know one clause is ending and another beginning. Of these, two are the most common:

> *More about*
> Coordination,
> 294–96

- A comma and a coordinating conjunction (*and, but, or, nor, for, so, yet*)

  ▶ The blues singer Alberta Hunter retired in the 1950s, but she made a successful comeback in the 1970s.

- A semicolon

  ▶ The blues singer Alberta Hunter retired in the 1950s; she made a successful comeback in the 1970s.

You can also use a colon or a dash between independent clauses when the first clause introduces the second or the second elaborates on the first. (The colon is usually more appropriate in formal writing.)

▶ The blues singer Alberta Hunter retired in the 1950s: She made a successful comeback in the 1970s.

38b Recognizing Comma Splices and Fused Sentences as Improperly Joined Independent Clauses
辨别逗号粘连句和融合句——连接不当的独立分句

When a writer improperly joins two independent clauses with a comma alone, the result is a *comma splice*.

COMMA SPLICE   Ronald Reagan was originally an actor, he turned
to politics in the 1960s.

When a writer runs two independent clauses together with no punctuation between them, the result is a *fused sentence* (also called a *run-on sentence*).

FUSED SENTENCE   Politics and acting have something in common they
both require a willingness to perform in public.

38c Recognizing When Comma Splices and Fused Sentences Tend to Occur 辨别容易出现逗号粘连句和融合句的情况

To avoid comma splices and fused sentences in your own work, pay attention to situations in which they are particularly likely to occur:

1. When the second clause begins with a conjunctive adverb (such as *for example, however,* or *therefore*) or other transitional expression

COMMA SPLICE   The blues singer Alberta Hunter retired in the 1950s, however, she made a successful comeback in the 1970s.

REVISED   The blues singer Alberta Hunter retired in the 1950s; however, she made a successful comeback in the 1970s.

Writing Responsibly   Clarifying Boundaries

Comma splices and fused sentences obscure the boundaries between linked ideas. If you leave these errors uncorrected in your writing, you burden readers with tasks that should be yours: identifying where one idea ends and another begins and specifying how those ideas relate to each other.
to AUDIENCE

Quick Reference   Identifying Comma Splices and Fused Sentences

When two independent clauses are joined by . . .	The result is . . .
A comma and coordinating conjunction	**Not** a comma splice or fused sentence
A semicolon	**Not** a comma splice or fused sentence
A colon or dash	**Not** a comma splice or fused sentence
A comma alone	A **comma splice—revise**
No punctuation at all	A **fused sentence—revise**

Quick

Reference   **Ways to Correct Comma Splices and Fused Sentences**

1. Use a period to divide the clauses into separate sentences. (355)
2. Join the clauses correctly with a comma and a coordinating conjunction. (356)
3. Join the clauses correctly with a semicolon. (356)
4. Join the clauses, when appropriate, with a colon or dash. (357)
5. Change one independent clause into a subordinate clause or modifying phrase. (357)

2. When the subject of the second clause is a pronoun that refers to the subject of the first clause

COMMA SPLICE   Ronald Reagan was originally an actor, he turned to politics in the 1960s.

REVISED   Ronald Reagan was originally an actor, but he turned to politics in the 1960s.

3. When the first clause introduces the second or the second explains or elaborates on the first

FUSED SENTENCE   Politics and acting have something in common both require a willingness to perform in public.

REVISED   Politics and acting have something in common: Both require a willingness to perform in public.

4. When one clause is positive and the other negative

COMMA SPLICE   We were not upset that the exam was postponed, we were relieved.

REVISED   We were not upset that the exam was postponed; we were relieved.

38d Editing Comma Splices and Fused Sentences
修改逗号粘连句和融合句

The Quick Reference box on this page lists five strategies for correcting comma splices and fused sentences. The strategy you choose should depend on the logical relationship between the clauses and the meaning you intend to convey.

1. Separate sentences 独立句子

Correcting a comma splice or fused sentence by dividing the independent clauses into separate sentences makes sense when one or both of the clauses are long or when the two clauses do not have a close logical relationship.

▶ My friends and I began our long-anticipated trip to Peru in early

. We

July we arrived in Lima on Saturday morning and flew to Cuzco

that same day.

Writing Responsibly

Is a Comma Splice Ever Acceptable?

Comma splices often show up in compound sentences composed of two short independent clauses in parallel form, particularly when one is negative and the other positive or when both are commands. This usage is common, for example, in advertising:

Buy one, get one free.

It can appear, too, in the work of experienced writers, who may use it deliberately because they feel a period, semicolon, or comma and coordinating conjunction would be too disruptive a separation in sentences like these:

You're not a man, you're a machine.

— George Bernard Shaw, *Arms and the Man*

Go ahead, make my day.

— Joseph C. Stinson, screenplay to *Sudden Impact*

However, this usage is best avoided in academic writing.

to TOPIC

Tech **Comma Splices, Fused Sentences, and Grammar Checkers**

Grammar checkers in word processing programs do not reliably identify comma splices or fused sentences. They catch some, but they miss many more. One word processor, for example, failed to identify this fused sentence: *We had not had lunch we were hungry.*

Also use a period when the second clause is a new sentence that continues a quotation that begins in the first clause.

▶ "We must not be enemies," Abraham Lincoln implored the South in

his first inaugural address, "Though passion may have strained, it
   ∧

must not break our bonds of affection."

2. Coordinating conjunction 并列连词

More about
The meaning of coordinating conjunctions, 295

When you join independent clauses with a comma and a coordinating conjunction (*and, but, or, nor, for, so,* or *yet*), choose the conjunction that best fits the logical relationship between the clauses.

▶ We needed to adjust to the altitude before we began hiking in the

                              , so
Andes we spent three days sightseeing in Cuzco.
        ∧

3. Semicolon 分号

More about
Coordinating with a semicolon, 295

Join two independent clauses with a semicolon when they have a clear logical relationship of contrast, example, or explanation.

▶ More than sixty people have won two or more Academy Awards in a single year, only one person, Walt Disney, has won four in the same year.

Using a semicolon in combination with a conjunctive adverb or other transitional expression can clarify the relationship between the clauses.

▶ More than sixty people have won two or more Academy Awards in a
; however,
single year, only one person, Walt Disney, has won four in the

same year.

4. Colon or dash 冒号或破折号

You can use a colon or, less commonly, a dash to join independent clauses when the first clause introduces the second or the second explains or elaborates on the first. This usage can create a more emphatic separation between the clauses than would a semicolon.

▶ The message is clear, smoking kills.

▶ Don't get kicked out of school, learn to study effectively.

More about
Colons, 458–60
Dashes, 456

5. Subordinate clause or modifying phrase 从句或修饰语

You can correct a comma splice or fused sentence by turning one of the independent clauses into a subordinate clause or a modifying phrase. Note, however, that putting information in subordinate clauses and phrases usually de-emphasizes it in relation to the information in the independent clause it modifies.

More about
Subordination
and emphasis,
296–98

COMMA SPLICE	Spanish, like French and Italian, is a Romance language, it derives from Latin, the language of the Romans.
REVISED: SUBORDINATE CLAUSE	Spanish, like French and Italian, is a Romance language ├─────── subordinate clause ───────┤ because it derives from Latin, the language of the Romans.
REVISED: MODIFYING	├─────── modifying phrase ───────┤ Spanish, a Romance language like French and Italian, derives from Latin, the language of the Romans.

Text Credit
p. 356 Warner Bros., 1983.

39

Maintaining Agreement 保持语法一致性

In many languages, the grammatical form of some words in a sentence must match the form of other words. When the forms match, the reader can easily understand the sentence; when they do not, the effect can be like trying to force a square peg into a round hole, leaving the reader distracted or confused. In English, subjects and verbs require this kind of matchup, or *agreement*, as do pronouns and the words to which they refer.

SUBJECT-VERB AGREEMENT 主谓一致

> **More about**
> Identifying sentence subjects, 338–39

A verb and its subject have to agree, or match each other, in person and number. *Person* refers to the form of a word that indicates whether it corresponds to the speaker or writer (*I, we*), the person addressed (*you*), or the people or things spoken or written about (*he, she, it, they, Alice, milkshakes*). *Number* refers to the form of a word that indicates whether it is singular, referring to one thing (*a student*), or plural, referring to more than one (*two students*).

39a Understanding How Subjects and Verbs Agree
了解主语和谓语动词如何保持一致

1. Agreement in the present tense with third-person subjects
现在时与第三人称主语保持一致

With just a few exceptions, it is only in the present tense that verbs change form to indicate person and number. Even in the present tense, they have only two forms. One form, which ends in *-s*, is for third-person singular subjects; the other is for all other subjects.

> **More about**
> The forms of regular and irregular verbs, 369–71

	Singular		Plural	
	subject	verb	subject	verb
First Person	*I*	vote	*we*	vote
Second Person	*you*	vote	*you*	vote
Third Person	*he, she, it,*	vote<u>s</u>	*they, the*	vote
	the student		*students*	

Tech Grammar Checkers and Subject-Verb Agreement

Grammar checkers in word processing programs can alert you to many subject-verb agreement problems, but they can also miss errors and can flag some constructions as errors that are not. Make your own informed judgment about any changes the computer might recommend.

Quick

Reference	Avoiding Subject-Verb Agreement Pitfalls

1. Ignore words that intervene between the subject and the verb. (359)
2. Distinguish plural from singular compound subjects. (360)
3. Distinguish singular from plural indefinite pronouns. (361)
4. Find agreement with collective-noun and numerical subjects. (362)
5. Recognize that some nouns that end in -s are singular. (363)
6. Treat titles, words as words, and gerund phrases as singular. (363)
7. Match the number of a relative pronoun subject (*who, which, that*) to its antecedent. (364)
8. Match the verb to the subject when the subject follows the verb. (364)
9. Match a linking verb with its subject, not its subject complement. (365)

Most nouns form the plural with the addition of an -s (*dog, dogs*) or -es (*coach, coaches*). In other words, an -s on a noun makes the noun plural; an -s on a present-tense verb makes the verb singular.

> **More about**
> Regular and irregular plural nouns, 476–77

	Noun	**Verb**
Singular	The dog	bark**s**
Plural	The dog**s**	bark

2. Agreement with *be* and with helping verbs
与be动词和助动词保持一致

Unlike any other English verb, *be* has three present-tense forms (*am, are, is*) and two past-tense forms (*was, were*). In **verb phrases** that begin with a form of *be*, *have*, or *do* as a helping verb, the subject agrees with the helping verb.

> **verb phrase** 动词短语
> A **main verb** together with any **auxiliary** (or **helping**) **verbs**. The main verb carries the principal meaning of the phrase; the auxiliaries provide information about tense, voice, and mood.

	┌── subject ──┐	┌── verb phrase ──┐
SINGULAR	The *price* of oil	*has* been fluctuating.
PLURAL	Commodity *prices*	*have* been fluctuating.
SINGULAR	The *price*	*was* fluctuating.
PLURAL	*Prices*	*were* fluctuating.

The modal helping verbs—*can, could, may, might, must, shall, should, will, would,* and *ought to*—have only a single form; they do not take an -s ending for third-person singular subjects.

> **More about**
> Forms of *be*, *have*, and *do*, 370–72

> **More about**
> Modal auxiliaries, 422

	├ subject ┤	├verb phrase ┤
SINGULAR	The *price*	*can* change.
PLURAL	*Prices*	*can* change.

39b Ignoring Words That Intervene between the Subject and the Verb 忽略主语和动词之间的词

In English, the subject of a sentence is usually found near the verb. As a result, writers sometimes mistakenly treat words that fall between the subject and the verb as if they were the subject. The writer of the following sentence mistook the singular noun phrase *Order of the Phoenix*

Writing
Responsibly | **Dialect Variation in Subject-Verb Agreement**

> The rules of subject-verb agreement are not the same in all dialects of English. In various communities in the English-speaking world, you might hear people say things like *"The cats is hungry,"* *"We was at the store,"* *"That coat needs washed,"* or *"She be walking to school."* In the contexts in which they occur, these variations are not mistakes; they reflect rules that are different from those of Standard American English. Still, the subject-verb agreement rules of Standard American English are what most readers in the United States expect to encounter in academic and business writing.
>
> to AUDIENCE

for the true subject, the plural noun *members.* The revision corrects the agreement error.

FAULTY   The members of the Order of the Phoenix is dedicated to thwarting Voldemort.

REVISED   The members of the Order of the Phoenix are dedicated to thwarting Voldemort.

NOTE When a singular subject is followed by a phrase that begins with *as well as, in addition to, together with,* or some similar expression, the verb is singular, not plural.

> ► Harry Potter, together with the other members of the Order of
>
> the Phoenix, ~~are~~ determined to thwart Voldemort.
>   is

> **conjunction** 连词 Part of speech that joins words, phrases, or clauses to other words, phrases, or clauses and specifies the way the joined elements relate to each other

39c Distinguishing Plural from Singular Compound Subjects
区分复合主语的单复数

A *compound subject* consists of two or more subjects joined by a *conjunction* (*Jack* <u>and</u> *Jill, one* <u>or</u> *another*).

1. Compounds joined by *and* or *both... and*
由and或both... and连接的复合主语

Most compound subjects joined by *and* or *both . . . and* are plural.

> ► Pinterest *and* Instagram <u>*are*</u> two popular social networking websites.

> ► *Both* Pinterest *and* Instagram <u>*allow*</u> users to include photos and videos in their profiles.

A compound subject joined by *and* is singular, however, if the items in the compound refer to the same person or thing.

▶ Under the current system, the winner *and* next president *is* the candidate with the most electoral votes.

A compound subject joined by *and* is also singular if it begins with *each* or *every*.

▶ *Each* paper *and* exam *contributes* to your final grade.

However, if it is followed by *each,* a compound joined by *and* is plural.

▶ The research paper *and* the final exam *each* *contribute* 25 percent toward your final grade.

2. Compounds joined by *or, nor, either... or, neither... nor*
由or、nor、either... or、neither... nor连接的复合主语

When a compound subject is joined by *or, nor, either . . . or,* or *neither . . . nor,* the verb agrees with the part of the compound that is closest to the verb.

▶ *Neither* the coach *nor* the players *were* worried by the other team's early lead.

> The second part of the compound is plural, so the verb is plural.

Applying this rule can produce an awkward result when the first item in a compound is plural and the second is singular. Reversing the order often resolves the problem. Sometimes the rule produces a result so awkward, however, that the only solution is to reword the sentence. This happens particularly when the subject includes the pronoun *I, we,* or *you* and the verb is a form of *be.*

AWKWARD   *Neither* Carla *nor* I *am leaving* until the job is finished.

REVISED   Carla *and* I *are not leaving* until the job is finished.

or

Neither Carla *nor* I *will leave* until the job is finished.

39d Distinguishing Singular and Plural Indefinite Pronouns
区分不定代词的单复数

Indefinite pronouns refer to unknown or unspecified people, quantities, or things. Most indefinite pronouns always take a singular verb. These include *anybody, anyone, anything, each, either, everybody, everyone, everything, much, neither, no one, nothing, one, somebody, someone,* and *something.*

▶ *Everybody* *talks* about the weather, but *nobody* *does* anything about it.
— Attributed to Mark Twain

Some indefinite pronouns (*both, few, many, others, several*) always take a plural verb.

▶ *Many* of us *make* New Year's resolutions, but *few* of us *keep* them.

Some indefinite pronouns (*all, any, more, most, none, some*) are either singular or plural, depending on context.

▶ *Some* of these questions *are* hard.

▶ *Some* of this test *is* hard.

> In the first sentence, *some* takes a plural verb because it refers to the plural noun *questions;* in the second sentence, *some* takes a singular verb because it refers to the singular noun *test.*

39e Finding Agreement When the Subject Is a Collective Noun or a Number 主谓一致：当主语是集合名词或数字时

A *collective noun* designates a collection, or group, of individuals: *audience, chorus, committee, faculty, family, government.* In US English, a collective noun is singular when it refers to the group acting as a whole.

▶ The *faculty is* revising the general education requirements.

> The group acts as a whole.

A collective noun is plural when it refers to the members of the group acting individually.

▶ The *faculty are* unable to agree on the new requirements.

> The individual members of the group disagree among themselves.

If this usage sounds odd to you, however, you can reword the sentence with a clearly plural subject.

▶ The *members* of the faculty *are* unable to agree on the new requirements.

Numbers, fractions, and units of measure take a singular verb when they refer to an undifferentiated mass or a quantity.

▶ *One-fourth* of the world's oil *is* consumed in the United States.

Numbers, fractions, and units of measure take a plural verb when they refer to a collection of individual people or things.

▶ *About a third* of the citizens naturalized in 2007 *were* immigrants from Asia.

The word *number* is plural when it appears with *a* but singular when it appears with *the*.

▶ *A number* of voters *are* in favor of the transportation bond.

▶ *The number* of voters in favor of the transportation bond *is* low.

39f Recognizing Nouns That Are Singular Even Though They End in -s 辨别以-s结尾的单数名词

Some nouns that end in *-s* are singular. Examples include diseases like *diabetes* and *measles*.

▶ *Measles is* a contagious disease.

Words like *economics, mathematics,* and *physics* are singular when they refer to an entire field of study or body of knowledge but plural when they refer to a set of individual traits related to the field of study.

▶ *Economics is* a popular major at many schools.

▶ *The economics* of the music industry *are* changing rapidly.

39g Treating Titles, Words as Words, and Gerund Phrases as Singular 标题和作为复数形式的单词以及动名词短语按单数处理

The titles of books, articles, movies, and other works; the names of companies and institutions; and words treated as words are all singular even if they are plural in form.

▶ *Harry Potter and the Order of the Phoenix was* the fifth book in J. K. Rowling's popular series.

▶ *The Centers for Disease Control and Prevention helps* protect the nation's health.

▸ *Fungi is* one of two acceptable plural forms of the word *fungus; funguses is* the other.

The *-ing* form of a verb used as a noun (a *gerund*) is also always singular.

gerund 动名词 The present participle (*-ing* form) of a verb used as a noun

▸ *Conducting excavations is* just one part of an archaeologist's job.

39h Matching a Relative Pronoun (*Who, Which,* or *That*) to Its Antecedent When the Pronoun Is the Subject of a Subordinate Clause 当关系代词（Who、Which或That）在从句中作主语时，与先行词保持一致

More about Pronouns and their antecedents, 365–68, 384–87

A relative pronoun (*who, which,* or *that*) that functions as the subject of a subordinate clause is singular if its *antecedent* (the word it refers to) is singular, but it is plural if its antecedent is plural.

▸ People *who live* in glass houses should not throw stones.

▸ The cactus is a plant *that thrives* in a hot, dry environment.

Be careful with antecedent phrases that include the expressions *one of* or *only one of. One of* usually signals a plural antecedent; *only one of* signals a singular antecedent.

▸ Barack Obama is *one of several presidents* of the United States *who were elected* to two terms.

Several presidents were elected to two terms, and one of them was Obama. The pronoun *who* refers to the plural noun *presidents.*

▸ Franklin D. Roosevelt is *the only one* of those presidents *who was elected* to more than two terms.

Only one president, Roosevelt, was elected to more than two terms. The pronoun *who* refers to that particular one and is singular.

39i Finding Agreement When the Subject Follows the Verb 主谓一致：主语位于谓语动词后面

More about Inverted word order, 301

If you reverse normal order and put the subject after the verb for emphasis or dramatic effect, be sure the verb agrees with the actual subject, not a different word that precedes the verb.

▸ Onto the tennis court *stride the defending champion and her challenger.*

The subject is the plural compound *the defending champion and her challenger,* not the singular term *tennis court.*

The subject also follows the verb in sentences that begin with *there* followed by a form of *be* (*there is, there are, there was, there were*).

▶ *There are*
~~There's~~ more people registered to vote than actually vote on
^
Election Day.

The subject, *people,* is plural, so the verb should be plural.

39j Matching a Linking Verb with Its Subject, Not Its Subject Complement 系动词与主语（而非主语补足语）保持一致

A *linking verb* (such as *was* or *were*) connects the subject of a sentence to a *subject complement*, which describes or refers to the subject. When either the subject or the subject complement is singular but the other is plural, make sure the verb agrees with the subject.

> **More about**
> Linking verbs and
> subject comple-
> ments, 340

▶ One influential voting bloc in the election *was*
                                        ~~were~~ young voters.
                                          ^

The subject is the singular noun *bloc,* not the plural noun *voters.*

PRONOUN-ANTECEDENT AGREEMENT 代词与先行词保持一致

Pronouns rename or take the place of nouns, noun phrases, or other pronouns. The word or phrase that a pronoun replaces is its *antecedent*. Pronouns and their antecedents must agree in person (first, second, or third), number (singular or plural), and gender (neutral, feminine, or masculine). The antecedent usually appears before the pronoun but sometimes follows it. The two pronouns in the following example have the same antecedent—*Emma*—which follows the first pronoun and precedes the second.

▶ In *her* haste, *Emma* shut down the computer without saving *her* work.

A Possessive Pronoun Agrees with Its Antecedent, Not the Word It Modifies In English, a possessive pronoun (such as *his, hers,* or *its*) agrees with its antecedent, not the word it modifies. In the following example, *father* is the antecedent, so the pronoun should be masculine.

▶ The father beamed joyfully at *his*
                            ~~her~~ newborn daughter.
                              ^

_____

Tech Grammar Checkers and Pronoun-Antecedent Agreement

Grammar checkers in word processing programs cannot identify pronoun-antecedent agreement errors.

More about
Singular and
plural indefi-
nite pronouns,
361–62

39k Matching Pronouns Appropriately with Indefinite Pronoun and Generic Noun Antecedents
代词与先行词保持一致：当先行词是不定代词和类名词时

Antecedents that are singular but have a plural sense are among the most common sources of pronoun-antecedent confusion. These include the following:

- *Indefinite pronouns* such as *each, everybody,* and *everyone* that are singular even though they refer to groups.

- *Generic nouns*—that is, singular nouns used to designate a whole class of people or things rather than a specific individual: *the typical student, the aspiring doctor.*

1. Singular indefinite pronoun or generic noun antecedents
先行词为单数意义的不定代词或类名词

A pronoun with a singular indefinite pronoun or generic noun antecedent should be singular. Do not let the plural sense of the antecedent distract you.

> The dog is a domesticated animal, unlike ~~their~~ *its* cousins the wolf and coyote.

> The antecedent is the singular generic noun *dog,* so the pronoun should also be singular.

More about
Avoiding gender
bias, 306–08,
398

This rule creates a problem, however, when the indefinite antecedent refers to both women and men. Correct agreement requires a singular pronoun, but using *he* as a substitute for either *man* or *woman* results in gender bias.

GRAMMATICALLY CORRECT BUT GENDER-BIASED AGREEMENT

In past downturns, *the affluent consumer* continued to spend, but now even *he* is cutting back.

Writers often try to avoid this conflict with a gender-neutral plural pronoun such as *they,* resulting in faulty pronoun-antecedent agreement.

UNBIASED BUT GRAMMATICALLY INCORRECT AGREEMENT

In past downturns, *the affluent consumer* continued to spend, but now even *they* are cutting back.

Quick **Reference** **Avoiding Pronoun-Antecedent Agreement Pitfalls**

1. Match pronouns appropriately with indefinite pronoun and generic noun antecedents. (366)
2. Match pronouns appropriately with collective-noun antecedents. (368)
3. Match pronouns appropriately with compound antecedents. (368)

Writing Responsibly | Using a Plural Pronoun with a Singular Antecedent

The use of a plural pronoun with singular indefinite antecedents is common in everyday speech, and many language experts maintain that it should be acceptable in formal writing, too. It is a usage, after all, that some of the finest writers in the English language have seen fit to employ:

God send everyone their heart's desire!

—Shakespeare, *Much Ado About Nothing*, 3.4

Everybody who comes to Southampton finds it either their duty or pleasure to call upon us. . . .

—Jane Austen, from a letter to Cassandra Austen, October 1, 1808

Nonetheless, many find the usage grating, so it is best to avoid it when you are writing for a general audience in an academic or business context.

to AUDIENCE

This usage is common in everyday speech, but it is inappropriate for formal writing (although, as the Writing Responsibly box on this page suggests, some language experts think differently).

You can avoid both gender bias and faulty agreement by rephrasing according to one of these strategies:

1. Make both the antecedent and the pronoun plural.

   ▶ In past downturns, ~~the affluent consumer~~ *affluent consumers* continued to spend, but now even ~~he is~~ *they are* cutting back.

2. Rephrase the sentence without the pronoun.

   ▶ ~~In past downturns, the~~ *Even the* affluent consumer *, who* continued to spend ~~but now even he~~ *in past downturns,* is *now* cutting back.

3. Use *he or she* or the appropriate variant (for example, *him or her* or *her or him*), but sparingly.

   ▶ In past downturns, the affluent consumer continued to spend, but even *she or* he is now cutting back.

CAUTION Avoid overusing the phrases *he or she* and *his or her*. They can make your text sound stuffy and strained.

---

2. Plural or variable indefinite pronoun antecedents
先行词为复数意义或可变的不定代词

Although most indefinite pronouns are singular, some (*both, few, many, others, several*) are always plural.

   ▶ *Both* of the writers submitted *their* drafts on schedule.

Others (*all, any, more, most, some*) are singular or plural depending on the context.

▶ When the teacher surprised the *students* with a pop quiz, she

discovered that *most* had not been doing *their* homework.

▶ Although some of the river's *water* is diverted for irrigation, *most*

still makes *its* way to the sea.

39l Matching Pronouns with Collective Noun Antecedents
代词与集合名词的先行词保持一致

Collective nouns (for example, *audience, chorus, committee, faculty, family, government*) are singular when they refer to a group acting as a whole.

▶ *My family* traces *its* roots to West Africa.

Collective nouns are plural when they refer to the members of a group acting individually.

▶ *The billionaire's family* fought over *their* inheritance.

39m Matching Pronouns with Compound Antecedents
代词与复合先行词保持一致

Compound antecedents joined by *and* are usually plural and take a plural pronoun.

▶ Back in 2008, *Clinton and Obama* were the leading candidates for *their* party's nomination.

Pronouns with compound antecedents joined by *or, nor, either . . . or,* or *neither . . . nor* agree with the nearest antecedent. To avoid awkwardness when one of the antecedents is plural and the other is singular, put the plural antecedent second. When the antecedents differ in gender or person, however, the results of the "nearest antecedent" rule can be so awkward that the only solution is to reword the sentence.

AWKWARD   It was clear after the New Hampshire primary that either Barack Obama or Hillary Clinton would find herself the Democratic Party's nominee for president.

REVISED   It was clear after the New Hampshire primary that either Barack Obama or Hillary Clinton would be the Democratic Party's nominee for president.

40 **Using Verbs** 使用动词

Verbs are the driving force in a sentence. They specify the action (*Sylvia won the race*), occurrence (*She became a runner in high school*), or state of being (*She was tired after the track meet*) that affects the subject.

VERB FORMS 动词形式

40a **Understanding the Basic Forms of Verbs**
理解动词的基本形式

With the exception of the verb *be*, all verbs have five forms: base, -s form, past tense, past participle, and present participle.

	Base Form	-s Form	Past Tense	Past Participle	Present Participle
Regular Verb	campaign	campaigns	campaigned	campaigned	campaigning
Irregular Verb	choose	chooses	chose	chosen	choosing

- The *base form* is what you find when you look up a verb in the dictionary.

  ▶ Presidential candidates *campaign* every four years.

  ▶ I usually *choose* candidates based on their policies.

- The *-s form* is the base form plus *-s* or *-es*.

  ▶ My favorite senator always *campaigns* in our town.

  ▶ She *chooses* positive messages instead of negative ones.

- The past-tense form of regular verbs such as *campaign* is the base form plus *-d* or *-ed*, but the past-tense forms of irregular verbs such as *choose* vary.

  ▶ The mayor *campaigned* downtown yesterday.

  ▶ Some people *chose* to protest his appearance.

- The past participle is the same as the past tense in most verbs but varies in some irregular verbs.

  ▶ The candidate *has <u>campaigned</u>* nonstop.

  ▶ The candidate *has <u>chosen</u>* our town for his last campaign stop.

- The present participle of all verbs, regular and irregular, is formed by adding *-ing* to the base form.

  ▶ Senator Brown *is <u>campaigning</u>* here today.

  ▶ They *are <u>choosing</u>* a running mate.

> **More about**
> Verb tenses, 374–78
> Voice, 288–89, 302–03

> **More about**
> Voice, 288–89, 302–03

40b **Using Regular and Irregular Verb Forms Correctly** 正确使
用规则动词和不规则动词

The vast majority of English verbs are *regular*, meaning that their past-
tense and past-participle forms end in *-d* or *-ed*.

Base	Past Tense	Past Participle
climb	climb**ed**	climb**ed**
analyze	analyze**d**	analyze**d**
copy	copi**ed**	copi**ed**

However, about two hundred English verbs are *irregular*, with past-tense
and past-participle forms that do not follow one set pattern and are easy
to confuse.

> ▶ My wool shirt ~~shrunk~~ *shrank* when I washed it in hot water.

If you are unsure whether a verb is regular or irregular or which form
you should use in a particular situation, consult a dictionary or the list
on the next page. In the dictionary, you will find any irregular forms
listed in the entry for the base form of a verb.

40c **Combining Main Verbs with Helping Verbs to Form
Complete Verbs** 主动词与助动词结合构成完整动词

Almost all verb constructions other than the present and past tenses
require the combination of a *main verb* with one or more *helping verbs*
(or *auxiliary verbs*) in a *verb phrase*. The most common helping verbs
are *be, have,* and *do,* all three of which can also function as main verbs
(*they* <u>are</u> *hungry; she* <u>had</u> *lunch; they* <u>did</u> *the dishes*). *Be,* unlike any other
English verb, has eight forms.

FORMS OF *BE*

Base		be
Present Tense	I	am
	we, you, they	are
	he, she, it	is
Past Tense	I, he, she, it	was
	we, you, they	were
Past Participle		been
Present Participle		being

Tech **Grammar Checkers and Verb Problems**

Grammar checkers in word processing programs will spot some
errors that involve irregular or
missing verbs, verb endings, and
the subjunctive mood, but they will
miss other errors and may suggest
incorrect solutions. You must look
for verb errors yourself and carefully
evaluate any suggestions from a
grammar checker.

Quick Reference | Common Irregular Verbs

Base Form	Past Tense	Past Participle	Base Form	Past Tense	Past Participle
arise	arose	arisen	leave	left	left
be	was/were	been	lend	lent	lent
bear	bore	borne, born	let	let	let
beat	beat	beaten	lie (recline)†	lay	lain
become	became	become	lose	lost	lost
begin	began	begun	make	made	made
bid	bid	bid	mean	meant	meant
bite	bit	bitten, bit	pay	paid	paid
blow	blew	blown	prove	proved	proved, proven
break	broke	broken	quit	quit	quit
bring	brought	brought	read	read	read
build	built	built	ride	rode	ridden
burst	burst	burst	ring	rang	rung
buy	bought	bought	rise	rose	risen
catch	caught	caught	run	ran	run
choose	chose	chosen	say	said	said
come	came	come	see	saw	seen
cost	cost	cost	send	sent	sent
cut	cut	cut	set	set	set
dig	dug	dug	shake	shook	shaken
dive	dived, dove	dived	shoot	shot	shot
do	did	done	shrink	shrank	shrunk
draw	drew	drawn	sing	sang	sung
drink	drank	drunk	sink	sank	sunk
drive	drove	driven	sit	sat	sat
eat	ate	eaten	sleep	slept	slept
fall	fell	fallen	slid	slid	slid
feel	felt	felt	speak	spoke	spoken
fight	fought	fought	spend	spent	spent
find	found	found	spread	spread	spread
flee	fled	fled	spring	sprang, sprung	sprung
fly	flew	flown	stand	stood	stood
forget	forgot	forgotten, forgot	steal	stole	stolen
freeze	froze	frozen	strike	struck	struck, stricken
get	got	gotten, got	swim	swam	swum
give	gave	given	swing	swung	swung
go	went	gone	take	took	taken
grow	grew	grown	teach	taught	taught
hang (suspend)*	hung	hung	tear	tore	torn
have	had	had	tell	told	told
hear	heard	heard	think	thought	thought
hold	held	held	throw	threw	thrown
hide	hid	hidden	wake	woke, waked	waked, woken
hit	hit	hit	wear	wore	worn
keep	kept	kept	win	won	won
know	knew	known	wind	wound	wound
lay	laid	laid	write	wrote	written
lead	led	led			

*Hang is regular—hang, hanged, hanged—when used to mean "kill by hanging."

†Lie is regular—lie, lied, lied—when used to mean "to be untruthful."

FORMS OF *HAVE* AND *DO*

Present Tense (Base	I, you, we, they	*have*	*do*
and -s *Form*)	he, she, it	*has*	*does*
Past Tense		*had*	*did*
Past Participle		*had*	*done*
Present Participle		*having*	*doing*

The ***modal verbs**—can, could, may, might, must, shall, should, will, would,* and *ought to*—function only as helping verbs. Modals indicate ability, intention, permission, possibility, desire, and suggestion. They do not change form to indicate number or tense.

More about
Modals, 422

Modal Verbs English modal verbs have a range of meanings and unusual grammatical characteristics that you may find challenging. For example, they do not change form to indicate number or tense.

▶ In a close election, one vote ~~cans~~ *can* make a difference.
_____

The main verb carries the principal meaning of the verb phrase; the helping verbs, if any, carry information about tense and voice. A ***complete verb*** is a verb phrase with all the elements needed to determine tense, voice, and mood. Main verbs can stand alone as complete verbs only in their present-tense and past-tense forms.

```
          |——— complete verb ———|
             main verb
```
▶ The candidates   campaigned   until Election Day.

Main verbs in other forms (past or present participles) require helping verbs.

```
          |——— complete verb ———|
          helping
          verbs        main verb
```
▶ The candidates   have been campaigning   for almost two years.

Sometimes in informal speech you can drop needed helping verbs, and some dialects allow certain constructions as complete verbs that Standard English does not allow. Helping verbs can sometimes be contracted (*they've voted already, we'll register tomorrow*) but in formal writing should never be omitted entirely.

▶ The candidates *have* been campaigning for almost two years.

CAUTION Do not use *of* for *have* in a verb phrase with a modal. When you use informal contractions like *could've* or *might've* in speech, remember that they mean *could have* and *might have*.
_____

40d Including *-s* or *-es*, *-d* or *-ed* Endings When Required
必要时词尾保留-s/-es和-d/-ed

Sometimes when speaking informally, you can omit the verb endings *-s*, *-es*, *-d*, or *-ed* or blend the sound of an ending inaudibly with the initial sound of the following word. Some dialects do not always require these endings. In formal writing, include them, or not, as standard usage requires.

More about
Subject-verb agreement, 358–65

▶ My dad *say* I am *suppose* to mow the lawn. I also *needs* to trim
        says   *supposed*   *need*

  the hedges. Before he *move* to Phoenix, my brother *use* to do
                   moved   *used*

  the mowing.

Phrasal Verbs Phrasal verbs, such as *ask out* and *give in*, combine a verb with one or more prepositions or adverbs known as *particles*. The verb and particle combination of a phrasal verb has a distinct meaning, one that is different from the stand-alone words that form it. Because phrasal verbs are idiomatic, native English speakers are usually comfortable using them spontaneously. But that does not mean they can explain why one "gets on" a plane but "gets in" a boat.

More about
Phrasal verbs, 417–18

40e Distinguishing *Rise* from *Raise*, *Sit* from *Set*, *Lie* from *Lay* 区分Rise与Raise、Sit与Set、Lie与Lay

The forms of *rise* and *raise*, *sit* and *set*, and *lie* and *lay* are easily confused. One verb in each pair (*rise*, *sit*, and *lie*) is **intransitive**, meaning that it does not take a direct object. The other verb in each pair (*raise*, *set*, and *lay*) is **transitive**, meaning that it does take a direct object (underlined in the following examples).

More about
Transitive and intransitive verbs, 339–42

■ *Rise* means "to move or stand up." *Raise* means "to cause something (the direct object) to rise."

  ▶ The plane *rises* into the air. The pilot *raises* <u>the landing gear</u>.

■ *Sit* means "to be seated." *Set* means "to place or put something (the direct object) on a surface."

  The passengers in coach *sit* in cramped seats. The attendants *set* <u>drinks</u> on their trays.

Reference	Distinguishing *Rise* from *Raise*, *Sit* from *Set*, and *Lie* from *Lay*			
Base Form	**-s Form**	**Past Tense**	**Past Participle**	**Present Participle**
rise (to get up)	*rises*	*rose*	*risen*	*rising*
raise (to lift)	*raises*	*raised*	*raised*	*raising*
sit (to be seated)	*sits*	*sat*	*sat*	*sitting*
set (to place)	*sets*	*set*	*set*	*setting*
lie (to recline)	*lies*	*lay*	*lain*	*lying*
lay (to place)	*lays*	*laid*	*laid*	*laying*

Quick

- *Lie* means "to recline." *Lay* means "to place or put something (the direct object) on a surface."

  ▶ The passengers in first class *lie* in fully reclining seats. During the landing, the pilot *lays* <u>the plane</u> gently on the runway.

A further difficulty with *lie* and *lay* is their confusing overlap of forms: The past tense of *lie* is *lay*, whereas the past tense of *lay* is *laid*. Changing the previous example to the past tense illustrates the issue.

  ▶ The passengers in first class ~~laid~~ *lay* in fully reclining seats. During the landing, the pilot lay ^*laid*^ the plane gently on the runway.

TENSE 时态

40f Using Appropriate Verb Tenses 使用适当的动词时态

Verb *tenses* provide information about the time in which an action or event occurs—past, present, or future—about whether the action is ongoing or completed, and about the time of one action relative to another.

1. Simple tenses 一般时

Use the *simple present tense* for current or habitual actions or events and to state general truths. Accompanied by a reference to a future event, the simple present can also indicate a future occurrence (also see *section 40h*, pp. 377–78).

CURRENT ACTION	Hernando *opens* the door to his classroom.
HABITUAL ACTION	He *enjoys* teaching second-graders.
GENERAL TRUTH	Earth *is* the third planet from the sun.
FUTURE OCCURRENCE	Winter *ends* in two weeks.

Use the *simple past tense* for completed actions or occurrences.

  ▶ The bell *rang.* Hernando *asked* his students to be quiet.

Use the *simple future tense* for actions that have not yet occurred.

  ▶ He *will give* them a spelling test this afternoon.

2. Perfect tenses 完成时

The perfect tenses generally indicate the completion of an action before a particular time. Use the *present perfect tense* for an action that started in the past but is now completed or for an action that started in the past but is ongoing.

COMPLETED ACTION	I *have read* all the Harry Potter books.
ONGOING ACTION	I *have read* books all my life.

Use the *past perfect tense* for actions completed by a specific time in the past or before another past action.

▶ Because the students *had studied* hard for their test, they knew most of the spelling words.

The studying—*had studied* (past perfect)—came before the knowing—*knew* (simple past).

Use the *future perfect tense* for an action that will be completed by a definite time in the future.

▶ By the time the semester ends, Hernando's students *will have improved* their spelling grades.

3. Progressive tenses 进行时

The progressive tenses indicate ongoing action. Use the ***present progressive tense*** for an action that is ongoing in the present.

▶ Matilda *is learning* Spanish.

Use the *past progressive tense* for an action that was ongoing in the past.

▶ Last night, Yue *was practicing* for her recital.

Use the *future progressive tense* for an ongoing action that will occur in the future.

▶ Elena *will be working* as a publishing company intern next summer.

Use the *present perfect progressive tense* for an ongoing action that began in the past.

▶ Hernando *has been working* on his master's degree in education since 2015.

Use the *past perfect progressive tense* for an ongoing past action that is now completed.

▶ Until this semester, he *had been taking* education courses at night.

Use the *future perfect progressive tense* for an ongoing action that will be finished at a definite time in the future.

▶ By the end of August, Hernando *will have been studying* education for more than six years.

Do Not Use the Progressive Tenses with All Verbs Certain verbs, typically those that convey a mental process or a state of being, are not used in the progressive tenses. Examples include *appreciate, belong, contain, envy, fear, know, like, need, owe, own, remember, resemble, seem,* and *want.*

▶ She is ~~seeming~~ *seems* angry with her boyfriend. He was ~~owing~~ *owed* her an apology.

Quick

Reference	**An Overview of Verb Tenses and Their Forms**	
Simple Tenses		
Simple present	base or *-s* form	I *learn* something new every day.
Simple past	*past-tense* form	I *learned* Spanish many years ago.
Simple future	*will* + base form	I *will learn* to ski next winter.
Perfect Tenses		
Present perfect	*has/have* + past participle	I *have learned* to water ski already.
Past perfect	*had* + past participle	I *had learned* to water ski by the time I was nine.
Future perfect	*will have* + past participle	I *will have learned* how to skydive by September.
Progressive Tenses		
Present progressive	*am/is/are* + present participle	I *am learning* about Japanese food.
Past progressive	*was/were* + present participle	I *was learning* to make sushi yesterday.
Future progressive	*will be* + present participle	I *will be learning* new skills next week.
Present perfect progressive	*have/has been* + present participle	I *have been cooking* seriously since I was a teenager.
Past perfect progressive	*had been* + present participle	I *had been preparing* simple dishes even before then.
Future perfect progressive	*will have been* + present participle	I *will have been enjoying* this hobby for two decades by the end of the year.

40g Following Conventions for Use of the Present Tense
遵循现在时用法的惯例

The present tense is conventionally used for describing works of art, for describing events in literary works, and for stating scientific facts.

▶ In the series *Sylvia Plath: Girl Detective*, producers Mike Simses
    and Kate Simses ~~brought~~ bring us a cheerful character who ~~was~~ is not at
    all depressed.

▶ Watson and Crick discovered that DNA ~~had~~ has a double helix structure.

    Although the discovery was in the past, it remains true.

In most cases, use the present tense to introduce a quotation, paraphrase, or summary.

▶ As Harriet Lerner ~~noted,~~ notes, "Anger is neither legitimate nor illegitimate, meaningful nor pointless. Anger simply is."

EXCEPTION The APA documentation style calls for the use of the past tense or the past perfect tense for reporting findings or introducing cited material.

More about
APA documen-
tation style,
217–54

▶ Chodoff (2002) <s>claims</s> *claimed* that in their efforts to put a diagnostic label on "all varieties and vagaries of human feelings," psychiatrists <s>risk</s> *risked* medicalizing "the human condition itself."

40h Using Tense Sequence to Clarify Time Relationships
用时态序列阐明时间关系

More about
Inappropriate
shifts in tense,
396

When a sentence contains two separate actions, readers need a clear idea of the time relationship between them, which writers communicate by their choice of tenses, or *sequence of tenses*. Do not shift tenses unnecessarily.

In a sentence with two past actions, for example, use the simple past tense for both verbs if the actions occurred simultaneously.

▶ When he *arrived* at the station, the train *departed*.

He arrived and the train departed at the same time.

If the actions happened at different times, use the past perfect tense for the action that occurred first.

▶ By the time he *arrived* at the station, the train *had departed*.

The train departed before he arrived.

1. Infinitives and tense sequence 不定式和时态顺序

An *infinitive* consists of *to* followed by the base form of the verb (*to listen, to go*). Use this form, the *present infinitive,* for an action that occurs after or simultaneously with the action of the main verb.

▶ Ivan is known to be a good student.

The knowing and the being happen together.

▶ Everyone expects Ivan to get an *A* on the exam.

The expectation is about Ivan's future performance on the exam.

Use the *perfect infinitive—to have* plus the past participle (*to have listened, to have gone*)—for an action that happened before the action of the main verb.

▶ Ivan is said to have studied all weekend.

The studying took place before the talk about it.

2. Participles and tense sequence 分词和时态顺序

Use the present participle (*listening, going*) to express action that happens simultaneously with the action of the main verb, regardless of the tense of the main verb.

▶ *Handing* her son Robbie a cup of coffee, Mona offered him some brownies.

Use the past participle (*listened, gone*) or the present perfect participle (*having listened, having gone*) to express action that happens before the action of the main verb.

> ▶ *Discouraged* by her daughter's aloofness, Mona asked her son to help.
>
> Mona was discouraged before she asked.

> ▶ *Having mediated* their disagreements for years, Robbie refused to intervene.
>
> Robbie mediated before he refused.

MOOD 语气

40i Understanding Verb Mood 理解动词的语气

The *mood* of a verb indicates whether a speaker or writer views what is said as a fact, a command, or a possibility. Most English sentences are in the *indicative mood*, which states facts or opinions and asks questions.

> ▶ Our research papers *are* due tomorrow morning.
> ▶ *Did* you *say* the deadline had changed?

The *imperative mood* issues commands, gives instructions, or makes requests. The subject of an imperative sentence (*you*) is usually left unstated.

> ▶ *Hand in* your papers by Friday afternoon.
> ▶ *Turn* left at the third stoplight.
> ▶ Please *pass* the salt.

The *subjunctive mood* expresses possibility (or impossibility), as in hypothetical situations, conditions known to be untrue, wishes, suggestions, and requirements.

> ▶ If I *were* finished, I could go to bed.
> ▶ The doctor suggests that he *get* more exercise.

40j Using the Subjunctive Mood Correctly 正确使用虚拟语气

The subjunctive has three tenses: present, past, and past perfect. The present subjunctive is always the base form of the verb, regardless of the person or number of the subject: *Ramon asks that his teacher give* (not *gives*) *him an extension.* The past subjunctive of *be* is *were: I wish I were* (not *was*) *finished.* For all other verbs, the past subjunctive is identical to the past tense. Similarly, the past perfect subjunctive is identical to the past perfect indicative.

Writing Responsibly — Using the Subjunctive in Formal Writing

Because the subjunctive has been fading from everyday usage, the indicative may seem more acceptable to you. Most readers, however, still expect to find the subjunctive used in formal writing.

▶ I wish that I ~~was~~ *were* finished.

to AUDIENCE

Clauses with verbs in the subjunctive are always subordinate clauses. They include **conditional clauses** that begin with *if, as if,* or *as though* and describe a condition known to be untrue. Conditional clauses put forward a set of circumstances and modify a main clause that states what follows from those circumstances.

▶ If I *were* taller, I would try out for basketball.

▶ The candidate acts as though he *were* already the winner.

When the main clause includes a modal auxiliary such as *would, could,* or *should,* do not use a similar construction instead of the subjunctive in the *if* clause.

▶ If I ~~would have been~~ *were* taller, I would try out for basketball.

Verbs in the main clause that express a wish, request, recommendation, or demand also require the subjunctive in the subordinate clause.

▶ The hikers wished their campground ~~was~~ *were* not so far away.

▶ Citizens are demanding that the government ~~fixes~~ *fix* the economy.

▶ Senators have requested that the president ~~is~~ *be* more responsive to the middle class.

▶ Alicia's adviser recommended that she ~~takes~~ *take* calculus.

NOTE When an *if* clause states something that is factual or probable, use the indicative mood, not the subjunctive.

If Susan *is* at the convention, she won't know about the accident.

Her brother hasn't heard about the accident if he *is* on his way to Atlanta.

The indicative mood is called for in these examples because the writer knows that Susan is at a convention and that her brother is traveling to Atlanta.

41 Understanding Pronoun Case and Reference 理解代词的格与指代

In an online multiplayer game like World of Warcraft, Dota 2, or Halo, you may be interacting with dozens of other players who could be located almost anywhere in the world. Instead of being physically present in the game, all players have virtual stand-ins—avatars. Your avatar acts on your orders and may even change form—from human to animal or from student to soldier, for example—depending on the way in which you want it to function in a particular environment.

Like avatars, pronouns are stand-ins. They represent other words—their **antecedents**—from one place to another in speech or writing. Also like avatars, pronouns sometimes change form depending on the role you want them to play within a sentence.

PRONOUN CASE 代词的格

Nouns and pronouns can play various roles within a sentence. They can be subjects.

> **More about**
> Subjects and objects, 338–42

		subject	
NOUN		**The Steelers**	lost.
PRONOUN		**They**	lost.

They can be objects (including direct objects, indirect objects, and objects of prepositions).

	subject		direct object
NOUN	The Bears	beat	**the Steelers**.
PRONOUN	We	beat	**them**.

They can indicate possession.

> **More about**
> Indicating possession with apostrophes, 444–47

	possessive			possessive	
NOUN	**Chicago's**	team	beat	**Pittsburgh's**	team.
PRONOUN	**Our**	team	beat	**their**	team.

Case refers to the different forms a noun or pronoun takes—*subjective, objective,* or *possessive*—depending on which of these roles it serves. Nouns have the same form as subjects that they do as objects, and they indicate possession with an *s* sound that is marked in writing with an apostrophe (*Chicago's team*). In contrast, most *personal pronouns* and some *relative* and *interrogative pronouns* have distinct forms for each of their roles.

		Subjective Case	Objective Case	Possessive Case
Personal Pronouns				
Singular	1st person	*I*	*me*	*my, mine*
	2nd person	*you*	*you*	*your, yours*
	3rd person	*he*	*him*	*his*
		she	*her*	*her, hers*
		it	*it*	*its*
Plural	1st person	*we*	*us*	*our, ours*
	2nd person	*you*	*you*	*your, yours*
	3rd person	*they*	*them*	*their, theirs*
Case-Variant Relative and		*who*	*whom*	*whose*
Interrogative Pronouns		*whoever*	*whomever*	

> **personal pronouns**
> 人称代词 Pronouns that take the place of nouns or noun phrases
> **relative pronouns**
> 关系代词 Pronouns that introduce subordinate clauses that describe the pronoun's antecedent
> **interrogative pronouns** 疑问代词 Pronouns that introduce questions

For native speakers of English, some case errors are easy to detect because they sound wrong.

▶ Hermione is one of Harry's best friends, and ~~her~~ *she* often gives ~~he~~ *him* sound advice.

However, in situations like those discussed in the following sections, the ear can be an unreliable guide to proper case usage.

41a Using the Subjective Case for Subject Complements
主语补足语用主格

A pronoun that functions as a *subject complement* should be in the subjective case, not the objective case.

▶ Asked who spilled the milk, my sister confessed that the guilty one was ~~her.~~ *she.*

If this usage sounds overly formal, try reversing the subject and subject complement.

> **subject complement**
> 主语补足语 An adjective, a pronoun, or a noun phrase that follows a linking verb and describes or refers to the sentence subject

▶ Asked who spilled the milk, my sister confessed that the guilty one was her. *she was* ~~one.~~

41b *She and I* or *Her and Me*? Keeping Track of Case in Compounds
用 "She and I" 还是 "Her and Me"？注意复合结构中的格

Pronouns that are part of compound subjects or subject complements should be in the subjective case.

compound subject

I
▶ My friends and ~~me~~ chat online while we play computer games.
⌃

Pronouns that are part of compound objects should be in the objective case.

compound dir. obj.

me
▶ My parents call my brothers and ~~I~~ every weekend.
⌃

Pronouns that are part of compound possessives should be in the possessive case.

compound possessive

my
▶ My father often gets ~~me~~ and my brother's names confused.
⌃

41c Keeping Track of Pronoun Case in Appositives
注意同位语中代词的格

appositive phrase 同位语短语 A noun or noun phrase that renames a preceding noun or noun phrase and is grammatically equivalent to it

The case of a pronoun in an ***appositive phrase*** should reflect the role of the phrase the appositive renames: subjective for a subject or subject complement, as in the first of the following examples; objective for an object, as in the second example.

she,
▶ The two most talented actors in our school, Valentino and ~~her,~~
⌃

always get the best roles in school productions.

her *me,*
▶ The director always wants the best artists, ~~she~~ and ~~I,~~ to work on
⌃ ⌃

the scenery.

Quick

Reference **Editing for Case in Compounds**

To determine the correct case of a pronoun in a compound, isolate the pronoun from the rest of the compound; then read the result aloud to yourself. If the pronoun is clearly wrong, replace it with the correct one.

Faulty   [~~My friends and~~] me chat online while we play computer games.
Revised   My friends and I chat online while we play computer games.

Me chat online is clearly wrong. Replacing the objective pronoun *me* with the subjective pronoun *I* corrects the problem.

Faulty   My parents call [~~my siblings and~~] I every weekend.
Revised   My parents call my siblings and me every weekend.

My parents call I is clearly wrong. Replacing the subjective pronoun *I* with the objective pronoun *me* corrects the problem.

Faulty   My father often gets me [~~and my brother's~~] names confused.
Revised   My father often gets my and my brother's names confused.

My father gets me names confused is clearly wrong. Replacing the objective pronoun *me* with the possessive pronoun *my* corrects the problem.

41d Deciding between *We* and *Us* before Nouns
确定名词前用We还是Us

In expressions that combine *we* or *us* with a noun, use *we* with nouns that are subjects or subject complements and *us* with nouns that are objects. To decide which is which, say the sentence to yourself with the pronoun alone.

▶ ~~Us~~ *We* gamers live vicariously in the game world through our avatars.

> *Us live vicariously* is clearly wrong.

▶ Our avatars act vicariously in the game world on behalf of ~~we~~ *us* gamers.

> *Avatars act on behalf of we* is clearly wrong.

41e Using the Objective Case Both before and after an Infinitive 不定式前后用宾格

Use the objective case for both the subject and the object of an ***infinitive***.

▶ I asked *her* to recommend *me* for the job.

> Both *her,* the subject of the infinitive *to recommend,* and *me,* its direct object, are in the objective case.

> **infinitive** 不定式 The *to* form of a verb (*to decide, to eat, to study*)

41f Deciding on Case with *-ing* Words 确定动名词的格

In most cases, use the possessive form of a noun or pronoun with a ***gerund*** (the *-ing* form of a verb used as a noun).

▶ Professor Nolan, I appreciate ~~you~~ *your* taking time to advise me.

Use the objective form of a noun or pronoun, however, when the *-ing* word functions as a modifier rather than a noun.

> **More about**
> Gerunds, 343

| PRONOUN IS THE MODIFIER | Debbie is an Albert Pujols fan. She admires *his* playing. |
| PRONOUN IS MODIFIED | Debbie saw *him* playing in the World Series. |

41g Clarifying Case in Comparisons with *Than* or *As*
厘清含Than或As的比较结构中的格

In comparisons with *than* or *as,* changing a pronoun's case can significantly change the meaning of a sentence.

▶ Amy likes her new car more than <u>I</u>.

▶ Amy likes her new car more than <u>me</u>.

In the first sentence, the subjective case (*I*) signals a comparison between Amy's and the writer's fondness for Amy's car (she likes it more than the writer does). In the second sentence, the objective case (*me*) signals a comparison between Amy's fondness for her car and her fondness for the writer (she likes her car more than she likes the writer). To avoid confusing readers in situations like this, supply any words needed to make the comparison explicit.

▶ Amy likes her new car more than I *do.*

▶ Amy likes her new car more than *she likes* me.

41h **Using *Who, Whom, Whoever,* and *Whomever***
使用Who、Whom、Whoever和Whomever

subordinate clause 从句 A word group with a subject and predicate that cannot stand alone as a sentence but instead functions within a sentence as a noun, adjective, or adverb

The pronouns *who, whom, whoever,* and *whomever* have two jobs. As *relative pronouns* they introduce *subordinate clauses*. As *interrogative pronouns* they introduce questions.

■ Use *who* or *whoever* for the subject of a subordinate clause or question.

⊢——————— subordinate clause ———————⊣
subj.
▶ Jackie Robinson, *who* integrated major league baseball, played for the Brooklyn Dodgers.

⊢——————— question ———————⊣
subj.
▶ *Who* integrated major league baseball?

■ Use *whom* or *whomever* for the object of a subordinate clause or question. Notice, however, that contrary to normal word order, in which direct objects follow verbs, *whom* and *whomever* usually come at the beginning of a clause or question.

⊢——————— subordinate clause ———————⊣
dir. obj.
▶ Robinson, *whom* the Dodgers hired in 1947, retired in 1956.

⊢——————— question ———————⊣
dir. obj.
▶ *Whom* did the Dodgers hire in 1947?

■ The case of a relative pronoun is determined by its role in a clause, not the role of the clause in the sentence. The relative pronoun in the following example is the subject of its clause and so should be in the subjective case—*whoever*—even though the clause as a whole is the object of the preposition *to.*

whoever
▶ In professional golf, the winner's prize goes to ~~whomever~~ completes the course in the fewest strokes.

Writing
Responsibly | **Case and Tone**

Many people now ignore the distinction between *who* and *whom*, using only *who*. In academic and business writing, however, many readers will assume that you do not understand correct usage if you use *who* when *whom* is called for.

So, even if *whom* and *whomever* sound inappropriately formal, even old-fashioned, to your ear, consider what your reader's expectations are and adjust your usage accordingly.

to AUDIENCE

- Match the pronoun to its verb, not to the verb of an intervening clause. In the following example, the pronoun should be the subjective case *who* because it is the subject of *was,* not the object of *know.*

  ▶ Thomas Edison, ~~whom~~ *who* many people know was the inventor of the lightbulb, was also the inventor of the phonograph.

CLEAR PRONOUN REFERENCE 指代清晰

Pronoun reference is clear when readers can easily identify a pronoun's antecedent.

▶ Mario talked to his sister Roberta about her career plans.

The pronoun *his* clearly refers to Mario; the pronoun *her* clearly refers to Mario's sister.

Pronoun reference is unclear when readers cannot be certain what a pronoun's antecedent is.

▶ Mario talked to Paul about his career plans.

Did Mario and Paul talk about Mario's career plans or Paul's? Without more information, readers will be uncertain.

41i Revising for Clear Reference 修改以明晰指代

The reference of a pronoun is ambiguous when it has two or more equally plausible antecedents.

▶ Mario talked to Paul about his career plans.

One way to resolve ambiguous reference is to replace the pronoun with the appropriate noun.

▶ Mario talked to Paul about Paul's career plans.

To avoid repeating the noun, rephrase the sentence in a way that eliminates the ambiguity.

▶ Paul talked about his career plans with Mario.

The position of the pronoun *his* associates the plans clearly and unambiguously with Paul, not Mario.

41j Revising for Specific Reference with *It, This, That,* and *Which* 修改以明晰含It、This、That和Which的特殊指代

When pronouns such as *it, this, that,* and *which* refer broadly to an entire clause, sentence, or series of sentences, readers may be uncertain about what specific information the pronouns cover.

▶ Who owns Antarctica? Several countries, including Argentina, Australia, Chile, France, New Zealand, Norway, the United Kingdom, and the United States, all claim or reserve the right to claim all or part of the continent.
These competing claims make the question of ownership
~~This makes it~~ difficult to answer.

The revision specifies which information the writer meant by *this* and *it*.

41k Avoiding Implied Reference 避免模糊指代

A pronoun should have a clearly identifiable antecedent—not, as with *they* in the following example, an unstated, or implied, antecedent.

DRAFT   From her stories of her small-town childhood, they seem like great places to grow up.

REVISED   Her stories of her childhood make small towns seem like great places to grow up.

Similarly, in the next example, the antecedent to *they—the researchers—*is implied, confusingly, in the possessive form *researchers'*.

More about
Citing sources, 161–211

▶ According to the researchers' study, ~~they found that~~ access to high speed Internet connections at home might reduce students' test scores (Vigdor and Ladd 1).

41l Avoiding the Indefinite Use of *They, It,* and *You* 避免在不确定的情况下使用They、It和You

In formal writing, the pronouns *they* and *it* need specific antecedents. Avoid using these pronouns to refer to unnamed people or things.

▶ At Hogwarts School of Witchcraft and Wizardry, *students* ~~they~~ use owls, not texting, for sending messages.

▶ *The* ~~In the~~ beginning of the chapter, ~~it~~ compares pronouns to computer-game avatars.

Likewise in formal writing, reserve the pronoun *you* (and the implied *you* of commands) to address the reader directly, as in "you, the reader." Do not use *you* as a substitute for indefinite words such as *anybody, everybody,* or *people.*

▶ Before computers and the Internet, ~~you~~ got ~~your~~ news mostly
  people   *their*

  from newspapers, radio, and television.

42 Using Adjectives and Adverbs
使用形容词和副词

The clothing, jewelry, and hairstyles we choose—our modifiers—send a message to others about how we want them to perceive us. A flamboyant dress, a tattoo, eye-catching jewelry, and flowing hair send one impression; a tailored business suit sends another. Similarly, we send readers a message about how we want them to understand our words by our choice of adjectives and adverbs to modify them.

42a Learning the Difference between Adjectives and Adverbs
掌握形容词与副词的区别

Adjectives modify (or describe) nouns and pronouns, answering questions such as *What kind? Which one?* or *How many? Adverbs* modify verbs, adjectives, other adverbs, and entire phrases, clauses, and sentences; they answer questions such as *How? Where?* or *When?*

Although many adverbs end in the suffix *-ly,* many do not (*later, often, quite, seldom*), and dozens of adjectives do (*elderly, lowly, scholarly*). The only reliable way to distinguish an adjective from an adverb is not from its form but from its function.

> **More about**
> Modifier placement, 391–96

42b Using Adjectives, Not Adverbs, as Subject Complements after Linking Verbs
系动词后用形容词作主语补足语，不用副词

Linking verbs express a state of being rather than an action or occurrence. They link the subject to a *subject complement*, which describes or refers to the subject. The subject complement, in other words, modifies the subject, not the verb; it can be an adjective or a noun, but not an adverb.

The verb *be*, when used as a main verb, is always a linking verb.

▶ The *solution* is <u>simple</u>.

The adjective *simple* modifies the subject, *solution.*

More about
Linking verbs and
subject comple-
ments, 340

Other verbs, such as *appear, become, feel, look, prove, sound,* and *taste,* may function as linking verbs in one context and action verbs in another. A word following one of these verbs should be an adjective if it modifies the subject and an adverb if it modifies the verb.

▶ *Maria* looked *anxious* to the dentist.

   Looked is a linking verb, and the adjective *anxious* is a subject complement that describes Maria's state of mind as the dentist perceived it.

▶ Maria *looked anxiously* at the dentist.

   Looked is an action verb modified by the adverb *anxiously,* which describes how Maria did the looking.

42c Is It *Bad* or *Badly, Good* or *Well*?
Bad与Badly、Good与Well的用法区分

In casual speech, we commonly confuse adjectives and adverbs. In writing, however, you should use adjectives to modify nouns and pronouns and adverbs to modify verbs, adjectives, or other adverbs. Do not confuse *bad* with *badly, good* with *well,* or adverbs that end in *-ly* with adjectives that do not.

■ *Bad* is an adjective; *badly* is an adverb.

▶ The Patriots played bad in the fourth quarter.
                      badly

   Badly modifies the action verb *played.*

▶ The quarterback feels badly about the loss.
                       bad

   Feels is a linking verb; *bad* modifies *quarterback.*

■ *Good* is an adjective, and *well* is its adverb counterpart. *Well* is an adjective, however, when it is used to mean "healthy."

▶ Leah did good on her final exams.
              well

   The adverb *well* modifies the verb *did.*

▶ Jalil looks well in his tuxedo.
              good

   Looks is a linking verb; the adjective *good* modifies *Jalil.*

Tech   **Grammar Checkers and Adjective-Adverb Problems**

Grammar checkers in word processing programs catch some adjective and adverb errors but miss many others. A grammar checker, for example, missed errors such as *The Patriots played bad, the boat rocked gentle,* and *Tomás looked well in his tuxedo.*

Quick

Reference | Forming Comparatives and Superlatives

Regular Forms

	Positive	Comparative	Superlative
Adjectives	*bold*	*bolder/less bold*	*boldest/least bold*
	helpful	*more/less helpful*	*most/least helpful*
Adverbs	*far*	*farther*	*farthest*
	realistically	*more/less realistically*	*most/least realistically*

Irregular Forms

	Positive	Comparative	Superlative
Adjectives	*bad*	*worse*	*worst*
	good	*better*	*best*
	little	*less* (quantity)/*littler* (size)	*least* (quantity)/*littlest* (size)
	many/much/some	*more*	*most*
Adverbs	*badly*	*worse*	*worst*
	well	*better*	*best*

▶ After a late-night graduation party, Leah is not feeling g̶o̶o̶d̶. *well.*

> *Well* is used as an adjective because it refers to health.

■ Do not confuse adverbs that end in *-ly* with their adjective counterparts that do not.

▶ You should play g̶e̶n̶t̶l̶e̶ *gently* with small children.

> The adverb *gently* modifies the verb *play.*

Order of Adjectives in a Series When more than one adjective modifies a noun, the adjectives usually need to follow a specific order.

▶ a ~~European~~ stunning *European* racehorse

For guidance on ordering multiple adjectives, see page 423.

42d Using Negatives Correctly 正确使用否定词

In Standard American English, when two negative modifiers describe the same word, they cancel each other out and the message becomes positive. The sentence *It is not unlikely that the volcano will erupt soon,* for example, means that the volcano is likely to erupt soon. Although some dialects allow the use of double (and more) negatives to emphasize a negative meaning, and many people use them that way in casual speech, you should avoid using them that way in formal writing.

Remember that contractions such as *couldn't* and *shouldn't* include the negative word *not,* and that words like *barely, hardly,* and *scarcely* have a negative meaning.

▶ Students ~~shouldn't~~ never park in a faculty-only lot.
   should ^

▶ I ~~can't~~ hardly argue with facts like those.
   can ^

42e Using Comparative and Superlative Adjectives and Adverbs Correctly 正确使用形容词和副词的比较级和最高级

Most adjectives and adverbs have three forms for indicating the relative degree of the quality or manner they specify: positive, comparative, and superlative. The ***positive form*** is the base form—the form you find when you look the word up in the dictionary.

POSITIVE   Daryl is *tall.*

The ***comparative form*** indicates a relatively greater or lesser degree of a quality.

COMPARATIVE   Daryl is *taller* than Ivan.

The ***superlative form*** indicates the greatest or least degree of a quality.

SUPERLATIVE   Daryl is the *tallest* player on the team.

Regular adjectives and adverbs form the comparative and the superlative with either the suffixes *-er* and *-est* or the addition of the words *more* and *most* or *less* and *least.* A few adjectives and adverbs have irregular comparative and superlative forms (see the Quick Reference box on page 389). If you are not sure whether to use *-er/-est* or *more/most* for a particular adjective or adverb, look it up in a dictionary. If the entry shows *-er* and *-est* forms, use them. If no such forms are listed, use *more* or *most.*

1. Comparative or superlative 比较级或最高级

Use the comparative form to compare two things, and the superlative to compare three or more.

▶ Between John Oliver and Margaret Cho, I think Cho is the ~~funniest.~~
   funnier. ^

▶ Of all comedians ever, I think Wanda Sykes is the ~~funnier.~~
   funniest. ^

2. Redundant comparisons 比较结构累赘

Do not combine the comparative words *more/most* with adjectives or adverbs that are already in comparative form with an *-er* or *-est* ending.

▶ Trains in Europe and Japan are ~~more~~ faster than trains in the United States.

3. Complete comparisons 完整的比较结构

More about
Complete
comparisons,404

Make sure your comparisons are logical and that readers have all the information they need to understand what is being compared to what.

▶ The nurses' test scores were higher*than those of the pre-med students.*

The first draft makes us ask, "Higher than what?" The revision clarifies the comparison.

4. Absolute terms 含最高级意义的词

Expressions like *more unique* or *most perfect* are common in everyday speech, but if you think about them, they make no sense. *Unique, perfect,* and other words such as *equal, essential, final, full, impossible, infinite,* and *unanimous* are absolutes, and absolutes are beyond compare. If something is unique, it is by definition one of a kind. If something is perfect, it cannot be improved upon. In formal writing, then, avoid using absolute terms comparatively.

▶ Last night's performance of the play was the ~~most perfect~~ *best* yet.

43 Avoiding Misplaced and Dangling Modifiers 避免错位和垂悬的修饰语

Since 1886 the Statue of Liberty has dominated New York harbor, holding aloft a torch in the hand of her outstretched right arm. In 1876, however, while work on the rest of the statue continued in France, the arm and torch stood incongruously at the Philadelphia Centennial Exhibition, displayed there, and later in New York's Madison Square Park, to help raise funds for the construction of the statue's pedestal. This photograph of the display may strike you as strange because this huge sculpture is supposed to be attached appropriately to the rest of the statue. Similarly, when you misplace modifiers in your sentences, you may inadvertently confuse or surprise your readers.

A modifying word, phrase, or clause is misplaced if readers have to puzzle out what it modifies or if they stumble over it while trying to get from one part of a sentence to the next. Look for such *misplaced modifiers* as you revise your drafts.

> **Tech** **Misplaced Modifiers and Grammar and Style Checkers**
>
> The grammar and style checkers in word processing programs usually cannot tell what a modifier is supposed to modify, so they rarely flag those that are confusingly or ambiguously placed. They do flag most split infinitives and some other disruptive modifiers.

43a Placing Modifiers Close to the Words They Modify
修饰语靠近所修饰的词

A modifier positioned far from its intended target might appear to modify some other part of the sentence instead.

> *because they needed more space*
> ► The couple moved to a bigger apartment after their first child was born ~~because they needed more space~~.

The couple's need for space did not cause the birth of their child.

> *that landed in January 2004*
> ► For more than four years, the two rovers had been exploring the surface of Mars ~~that landed in January 2004~~.

The rovers landed, not the surface of Mars.

43b Avoiding Squinting Modifiers and Ambiguously Placed Limiting Modifiers
避免歧形修饰语，限制修饰语位置产生歧义

A *squinting modifier* confuses readers by appearing to modify both what precedes it and what follows it.

> **DRAFT** People who study hard <u>usually</u> will get the best grades.

Do people who make a practice of studying hard get the best grades, or do the best grades usually (but not always) go to people who study hard? The sentence can be clarified in two different ways.

> **REVISION** People who <u>usually</u> study hard will get the best grades.

> **REVISION** People who study hard will <u>usually</u> get the best grades.

Limiting modifiers include qualifying words such as *almost, even, exactly, hardly, just, merely, only, scarcely,* and *simply.* In the following example, the ambiguous placement of the limiter *just* leaves the reader with a variety of possible interpretations.

> **AMBIGUOUS** The math department just offers Calculus III at night on Thursdays.

REVISED   At night on Thursdays, the math department offers just Calculus III. [That is the only math course you can take on Thursday nights.]

REVISED   On Thursdays, the math department offers Calculus III just at night. [That is the only time you can take the class on Thursdays.]

REVISED   The math department offers Calculus III at night just on Thursdays. [That is the only day you can take the class at night.]

43c Moving Disruptively Placed Modifiers
移动位置中断的修饰语

A modifier is disruptive when it awkwardly breaks the flow among grammatically connected parts of a sentence. Long adverbial phrases and clauses tend to be disruptive when they fall between subjects and verbs (as in the first example below), within verb phrases (as in the second example), or between verbs and their objects (as in the third example).

▸ *True Blood*, ~~well after its last episode aired in August 2014,~~ continued to elicit admiring commentary and analysis. *well after its last episode aired in August 2014.*

▸ *If it maintains a large following, the* The show might, ~~if it maintains a large following,~~ dominate streaming video for years to come.

▸ The show often jarringly contrasts~~, leaving the viewer torn between desire and revulsion,~~ the physical attractiveness of vampires with their violent nature. *, leaving the viewer torn between desire and revulsion.*

43d Avoiding Awkwardly Split Infinitives
避免不定式被不恰当地分隔开

An infinitive consists of *to* and the base form of a verb (*to share, to jump, to remember*). An infinitive splits when a modifier is inserted between the *to* and the verb. Although many authorities now consider them acceptable, split infinitives can be awkward and often should be revised, particularly in formal writing.

▸ Grant's strategy was *to* ~~relentlessly~~ *attack* Lee's army *relentlessly* despite the heavy losses the Union army suffered as a result.

Writing **Responsibly**

Misplaced Modifiers in the Real World

Misplaced modifiers can sometimes cause real distress. A confusing instruction like the one below from the website of the Federal Emergency Management Agency (FEMA) might bewilder a homeowner struggling to recover from a natural disaster.

> You will need your social security number, current and pre-disaster address, phone numbers, type of insurance coverage, total household annual income, and a routing and account number from your bank *if you want to have disaster assistance funds transferred directly into your bank account.* [Emphasis added.]

As written, this statement suggests that an applicant for relief needs all of the listed items to have disaster assistance deposited directly into a bank account. Here is what the writer meant to say:

> You will need your social security number, current and pre-disaster address, phone numbers, type of insurance coverage, total household annual income, and, *if you want to have disaster assistance funds transferred directly into your bank account,* a routing and account number from your bank.

to TOPIC

Sometimes, however, a modifier is less awkward when splitting an infinitive than in any other spot in a sentence. If the adverb *relentlessly* were placed anywhere else in the following sentence, for example, it would not clearly and unambiguously modify only the word *attack*.

▶ Lincoln urged his generals to *relentlessly* attack retreating enemy forces.

43e Identifying and Correcting Dangling Modifiers
辨别并纠正垂悬修饰语

Consider the following sentence:

▶ While paddling the canoe toward shore, our poodle swam alongside.

Who or what is paddling the canoe? Surely not the poodle, yet that is what the sentence seems, absurdly, to suggest. The problem here is that the phrase *while paddling the canoe toward shore* does not actually modify the subject, *poodle,* or anything else in the sentence. It dangles, unattached, leaving it to the reader to infer the existence of some unnamed human paddler. Correcting this **dangling modifier** requires either making the paddler the subject of the sentence (as in the first revision that follows) or identifying the paddler in the modifier (as in the second revision).

▶ While paddling the canoe toward shore, ~~our poodle~~ *I saw* our poodle ~~swam~~ *swimming* alongside.

▶ While ~~paddling~~ *I paddled* the canoe toward shore, our poodle swam alongside.

Dangling modifiers have the following characteristics:

- They are most often phrases that include a **verbal** (a gerund, infinitive, or participle) that has an implied but unstated actor.

verbal 动词的 Verb form that functions as a noun, an adjective, or an adverb

- They occur most often at the beginnings of sentences.
- They appear to modify the subject of the sentence, so readers expect the implied actor and the subject to be the same.
- They dangle because the implied actor and the actual subject of the sentence are different.

> **More about**
> Phrases and
> clauses,
> 342–45

DANGLING INFINITIVE PHRASE

To learn about new products, the company's sales meeting occurs annually in August. [Meetings do not learn.]

DANGLING PARTICIPIAL PHRASE

Hoping to boost morale, an attractive resort hotel is usually selected for the meeting. [Hotels cannot hope.]

DANGLING PREPOSITIONAL PHRASE WITH GERUND OBJECT

After traveling all day, the hotel's hot tub beckoned to the arriving sales reps. [The sales reps traveled, not the hot tub.]

Simply moving a dangling modifier will not correct it.

DANGLING   To learn more about new products, the company's sales meeting occurs annually in August.

STILL   The company's sales meeting occurs annually in August to
DANGLING   learn more about new products.

To correct a dangling modifier, first determine the identity of the modifier's unstated actor. You then have two options:

1. Rephrase to make the implied actor the subject of the sentence.
2. Rephrase to include the implied actor in the modifier.

Use the approach that works best given the purpose of the sentence in your draft.

MAKING THE IMPLIED ACTOR THE SUBJECT

sales reps attend   *annual*
To learn about new products, the company's sales meeting ~~occurs annually~~ in
August.

management usually selects
Hoping to boost morale, an attractive resort hotel ~~is usually selected~~ for the meeting.

In both of these cases, the implied actor—*sales reps* in the first, *management* in the second—was missing entirely from the original sentence.

INCLUDING THE IMPLIED ACTOR IN THE MODIFIER

As the sales reps arrived after

~~After~~ traveling all day, the hotel's hot tub beckoned to ~~the arriving sales reps.~~ *them.*

In this case, the implied actor, *sales reps,* appeared in the original sentence but needed to be repositioned.

44
Avoiding Confusing Shifts
避免易于混淆的转换

When NASCAR drivers round the curves or head into the straightaway, they need to shift gears, but an expert driver shifts only when doing so will provide a clear advantage. Similarly, good writers try not to jar their readers with unnecessary shifts in style or grammar.

44a Avoiding Awkward Shifts in Tense 避免时态转换不当

Verb tenses reveal when events in a sentence happen. Without a corresponding shift in time, shifts from one tense to another confuse readers. Avoid such inappropriate shifts, particularly when you are telling a story or describing a sequence of events.

> ▸ The guide waited until we had all reached the top of the pass; then
> *led* *made* *was*
> she ~~leads~~ the way down to the river and ~~makes~~ sure everybody ~~is~~
> safe in camp.

> **More about**
> Verb tenses,
> 374–78

It is customary to use the present tense when writing about literary events and characters as well as about films, plays, and other similar works.

> ▸ In his movie *Avatar,* director James Cameron ~~presented~~ a fantas-
> *presents*
> tic fictional world in rich, convincing detail.

44b Avoiding Awkward Shifts in Mood and Voice
避免语气和语态转换不当

Most sentences are consistently in the indicative mood, which is used to state or question facts and beliefs. It is, however, easy to shift inappropriately between the imperative mood—used for commands, directions, and entreaties—and the indicative mood when explaining a process or giving directions.

> **Tech** **Catching Confusing Shifts**
>
> The grammar and style checkers in word processing programs do not reliably identify confusing shifts. One style checker, for example, had no objection to this absurd statement: "Yesterday it will rain; tomorrow it snowed two feet." In contrast, the same style checker flagged every occurrence of the passive voice, regardless of whether it was appropriate to the passage in which it appeared.

▶ Dig a narrow hole about six inches deep, place the tulip bulb firmly at the bottom of the hole, and then ~~you can~~ fill the hole with dirt.

The subjunctive mood is used in certain situations to express a wish or demand or to make a statement contrary to fact. Although many of us often replace it with the indicative in everyday speech, readers expect to encounter the subjunctive in formal writing.

> **More about**
> Mood, 378–79

▶ If the presidential primary *were* ~~was~~ held earlier in the year, our state's voters would have a greater voice in the outcome of the race.

Avoid shifting needlessly between the active voice, in which the subject performs the action of the verb (*I wrote the paper*) and the passive voice, in which the subject receives the action (*The paper was written by me*).

> **More about**
> Voice, 92–93,
> 288–89,
> 302–03, 340–41

▶ During the eighteenth century, the British consumed most of their carbohydrates in the form of processed sugar. The Italians favored pasta, whereas sourdough bread *the French preferred* ~~was preferred by the French.~~

44c Avoiding Awkward Shifts in Person and Number
避免人称和数转换不当

Person refers to the identity of the subject of a sentence and the point of view of the writer. In the first person (*I, we*), the writer and subject are the same. In the second person (*you*), the reader and subject are the same. In the third person (*he, she, it, they, Marie Curie, electrons*), the subject is the writer's topic of discussion, what the writer is informing the reader about. *Number* refers to the quantity (singular or plural) of a noun or pronoun.

> **More about**
> Person and number, 358

Arbitrary shifts in person are distracting to readers. The revision to the following passage establishes a consistent first-person point of view.

▶ When I get together with my friends in the tech club, we usually discuss the latest apps. *We* ~~You~~ tend to forget, though, that a garden spade and a ballpoint pen are also technological tools and that thousands of nonelectronic items become part of *our* ~~your~~ technological world every year.

Most academic writing is in the third person. The second person, including commands, is best reserved for addressing readers directly, telling them how to do something or giving them advice. (You have probably noticed that this handbook often addresses you, the reader, in just this way.) Be consistent, however, and avoid shifting arbitrarily between second and third person.

▶ To train your dog properly, ~~people~~ *you* need plenty of time, patience, and dog biscuits. You should start with simple commands like "sit" and "stay."

More about
Avoiding gender bias, 306—08 366—67

Most inappropriate shifts in number are errors in agreement between a pronoun and its antecedent; they are often the result of the writer's desire to avoid gender bias. These kinds of errors can easily happen when the antecedent is a singular generic noun (*person, doctor*) or an indefinite pronoun (*anyone, everyone*).

FAULTY   When a <u>person</u> witnesses a crime, <u>they</u> should report it to the police.

The antecedent of the plural pronoun *they* is the singular generic noun *person*.

Such shifts can be revised in several ways. One is to use the plural throughout. Another is to replace the plural pronoun with *he or she* (although this expression becomes tedious when overused). A third is to rephrase the sentence to avoid the problem entirely.

REVISED:
PLURAL THROUGHOUT   When people witness a crime, they should report it to the police.

REVISED:
HE OR SHE   When a person witnesses a crime, he or she should report it to the police.

REVISED:
REPHRASED   Anybody who witnesses a crime should report it to the police.

44d Avoiding Awkward Shifts from Direct to Indirect Quotations and Questions
避免直接引语与间接引语和问题之间的转换不当

More about
Punctuating direct and indirect quotations 448—50
Quoting sources, 136—39

Direct quotations reproduce someone's exact words and must always be enclosed in quotation marks: *My roommate announced, "The party will start at 8 p.m."* **Indirect quotations** report what someone has said but not in that person's exact words: *My roommate announced that the party would start at 8 p.m.*

Abrupt shifts between direct and indirect quotations, like the one in the following example, are awkward and confusing.

AWKWARD SHIFT	Yogi Berra said that you should go to other people's funerals or "otherwise, they won't come to yours."
REVISED: DIRECT QUOTATION	As Yogi Berra said, "You should always go to other people's funerals. Otherwise, they won't come to yours."
REVISED: INDIRECT QUOTATION	Yogi Berra said that you should go to other people's funerals because if you don't, they won't come to yours.

Abrupt shifts between direct and indirect questions are also confusing. A **direct question** is stated in question (interrogative) form and ends with a question mark: *When does the library open?* An **indirect question** reports a question in declarative form and ends with a period: *I wonder when the library opens.*

> *More about*
Punctuating direct and indirect questions, 454

AWKWARD SHIFT	The author asks how much longer can the world depend on fossil fuels and whether alternative sources of energy will be ready in time.
REVISED: DIRECT QUESTION	The author asks two questions: How much longer can the world depend on fossil fuels, and will alternative sources of energy be ready in time?
REVISED: INDIRECT QUESTION	The author asks how much longer the world can depend on fossil fuels and whether alternative sources of energy will be ready in time.

45 Avoiding Mixed and Incomplete Constructions 避免混杂又不完整的结构

The year after Wassily (Vasily) Kandinsky painted this visually bewildering piece, he published a book that called for art that, instead of reproducing "reality," created "vibrations in the soul."[1] That seems to be his purpose in this painting. In today's academic writing, in contrast, writers work for clarity, not confusion. As you edit your writing, look for sentences that similarly start in one direction but turn disorientingly in another, leaving readers unsure where you have taken them. Look, too, for sentences that omit words that readers need to fully grasp your intended meaning.

[1]Kandinsky, Wassily. *Concerning the Spiritual in Art*. Dover, 1977.

45a Recognizing and Correcting Mixed Constructions
混杂结构的辨别与纠正

When a sentence begins one way and then takes an unexpected turn—in grammar or logic—the result is a *mixed construction*. To find and correct mixed constructions in your drafts, make sure every predicate has a grammatically and logically appropriate subject.

Grammatically mixed constructions can occur when a writer uses an introductory phrase or clause—which cannot function as the subject of a sentence—as if it were the subject. The following example starts with a long prepositional phrase (underlined) that the writer erroneously uses as the subject of the sentence. A prepositional phrase, although it can modify the subject or other parts of a sentence, cannot be the subject. The result is a *sentence fragment*, not a sentence.

> **sentence fragment** 残缺句 An incomplete sentence punctuated as if it were complete

MIXED   As a justification by American leaders for dropping atomic bombs on Hiroshima and Nagasaki maintained that doing so persuaded the Japanese to surrender without the need for an invasion that might have cost hundreds of thousands of casualties.

Fixing a sentence like this requires identifying a grammatical subject and isolating it from the introductory phrase. Here is one possible revision (with the subject underlined):

REVISED   As a justification for dropping atomic bombs on Hiroshima and Nagasaki, American leaders maintained that doing so persuaded the Japanese to surrender without the need for an invasion that might have cost hundreds of thousands of casualties.

Here is a more concise revision that eliminates the introductory phrase altogether:

REVISED   American leaders maintained that dropping atomic bombs on Hiroshima and Nagasaki persuaded the Japanese to surrender without the need for an invasion that might have cost hundreds of thousands of casualties.

> **More about**
> Clauses, 344–45
> Relating ideas with subordination, 296–98

In the next example, the writer follows a subordinate clause (*Because the bombings had devastating effects*) with the verb *provoked*, which has no subject. The editing changes the first part of the sentence into a noun phrase subject for *provoked.*

▸ ~~Because the bombings had devastating effects~~ *The devastating effects of the bombings* provoked intense debate over the morality of the military decision.

Mixed constructions also occur when a writer treats a modifying phrase or clause as if it were the predicate of a sentence. Look for this kind of mixed construction, especially in sentences that begin with the phrase *the fact that.* The following example begins with a subject, *the fact,* followed by a long adjective *that* clause that modifies the subject but cannot at the same time be the predicate of the sentence.

> MIXED   The fact that Hiroshima and Nagasaki, which were devastated by the bomb, are once again thriving cities.

One way to revise this sentence is to add the verb *is*, making the *that* clause into a **subject complement**.

> REVISED   The fact is that Hiroshima and Nagasaki, which were devastated by the bomb, are once again thriving cities.

An even better approach is simply to eliminate the phrase *the fact that,* a wordy expression that adds no information to the sentence.

> REVISED   Hiroshima and Nagasaki, which were devastated by the bomb, are once again thriving cities.

> **subject complement** 主语补足语 An adjective, pronoun, noun, or noun phrase that follows a linking verb and refers to the subject of the sentence

> ❯ **More about**
> Eliminating wordy expressions, 286–87

45b Recognizing and Correcting Mismatched Subjects and Predicates 主谓不匹配的辨别与纠正

The error of *faulty predication* occurs when a subject and a predicate are mismatched—when they do not fit together logically. For example, the original subject of the following sentence, *recommendation,* does not work with the verb *insisted.* Recommendations cannot insist; doctors can.

> ▶ The ~~doctor's recommendation~~ ^doctor^ insisted that Joe visit a chiropractor immediately.

Many instances of faulty predication involve a mismatch between the subject and the subject complement in sentences in which the verb is a form of *be* or other **linking verb**.

> MISMATCHED   Only <u>students</u> who are absent because of illness or a
>
> family emergency will be <u>grounds</u> for a makeup exam.

> REVISED   Only students who are absent because of illness or a family emergency will be permitted to take a makeup exam.

> **linking verb** 连系动词 A verb that connects a subject to a subject complement

Two forms of expression involving the verb *be* that have become commonplace in everyday speech are examples of faulty predication and should be avoided in formal writing. These are the use of *is where* or *is when* in definitions and the use of *the reason . . . is because* in explanations.

1. *Is where, is when* "is where" 与 "is when" 用法辨析

Using the expressions *is when* and *is where* creates illogical definitions if the terms defined do not involve a place (*where*) or a time (*when*).

> ▶ A tornado is ~~where~~ high winds swirl around in a funnel-shaped cloud.

a violent storm in which

> Because a tornado is a storm, not a place, use "which" instead of "where."

> ▶ A friend is ~~when~~ someone cares about you and has fun with you.

who

> A friend is a person, not a time.

The expressions result in grammatical mismatches, too, because *where* and *when* introduce adverb clauses, which cannot function as subject complements.

2. *The reason... is because* "The reason... is because..." 用法纠正

Explanations using the expression *the reason... is because* are similarly mismatched both logically (*the reason* and *because* are redundant) and grammatically (*because* introduces an adverb clause, which cannot function as a subject complement). The following example shows two simple ways to fix this kind of faulty predication.

> ▶ ~~The reason~~ I wrote this paper ~~is~~ because my instructor required it.

> ▶ The reason I wrote this paper is ~~because~~ my instructor required it.

that

45c Adding Essential Words to Compound and Other Constructions 在复合结构和其他结构中添加关键词

More about
Writing concisely, 286–89

As you draft sentences, you may unintentionally leave out grammatically or logically essential words. Sometimes these omissions result in sentence fragments. Often, however, they create seemingly minor but nonetheless distracting grammatical or idiomatic bumps. As you proofread and edit your drafts, be especially alert for such missing words in compound and other constructions.

In compound constructions, the omission of *nonessential* repetitions can often help tighten prose.

> ▶ Investigators wondered about the causes of the fire and [about] who might have been involved. They questioned six officials and then [they] arrested two.

elliptical construction
省略结构 A construction in which otherwise grammatically necessary words can be omitted because their meaning is understood from the surrounding context

Such *elliptical constructions* work, however, only when the stated words in one part of a compound match the omitted words in other parts. When grammar or idiom requires different words—different verb forms, different prepositions, or different articles, for example—those words should be included.

▶ The candidate claimed that she always had and always would
supported

support universal health care coverage.

The word *supported* is needed because *had support* would be ungrammatical.

▶ On the campaign trail and debates, her opponent for the nomi-
in

nation insisted that his plan was better than hers.

In this situation, the word *debates* requires the preposition *in,* not *on.*

Obligatory Words and Unacceptable Repetitions in English On the one
hand, unlike some languages, formal written English requires a stated subject
in all sentences except commands.

It rained
▶ ~~Rained~~ all day yesterday.

On the other hand, formal written English does not permit the use of a
pronoun to emphasize an already stated subject or direct object.

▶ Maria~~, she~~ forgot to take her umbrella.

_____

an *the*
▶ A yearning for change, unsettled economy, and character of the

candidates themselves combined to sustain high voter turnout

during the primary season.

The word *unsettled* requires a different form of the indefinite article (*a, an*)
than *yearning,* and in this situation the word *character* requires the definite
article (*the*) rather than the indefinite article.

Occasionally, you may need to repeat a modifier for clarity.

their
▶ The candidates asked their loyal backers and opponents to sup-

port the winner, whoever that might be.

The repeated *their* makes clear that the adjective *loyal* applies only to *backers*
and not to *opponents.*

Although you can often omit the word *that* without obscuring the
meaning of a subordinate clause, sometimes you need to include it to
avoid confusion.

that
▶ I know Sheila, who is a sympathetic person, will not be terribly

upset about the stains on the silk shirt ~~that~~ I borrowed from her.

In the original, without the first *that, Sheila* could be understood as the
object of *know* rather than the subject of the long subordinate clause that
follows. In contrast, the *that* at the end of the sentence can be eliminated
because no such ambiguity affects the subject (*I*) of the clause it introduces.

> **More about**
> Including a stated
> subject and elim-
> inating redun-
> dant subject and
> object pronouns,
> 406–08

45d Avoiding Incomplete or Ambiguous Comparisons
避免不完整或有歧义的比较结构

More about
Comparisons,
390–91

Comparisons show how two items are alike or different. For comparisons to be clear, the items they juxtapose must be logically equivalent. The original version of the following sentence confusingly compares a group of people, children, to a process, growing up.

▶ Children who grow up on farms are more active than ~~growing~~ up *those who grow* in big cities.

To be complete, comparisons must fully specify what is being compared to what.

▶ Lemon eucalyptus is better at deterring ticks. *than tea tree oil.*

Be careful how you use the terms *any* and *any other* when you compare one item to others that belong to the same category.

▶ Mount Everest is higher than any *other* mountain in the world.

Mount Everest is a mountain in the world, so without the modifier *other,* the sentence suggests that Mount Everest is higher than itself.

▶ Aconcagua, the highest mountain in South America, is higher than any ~~other~~ mountain in North America.

The sentence compares a mountain in South America to mountains in North America, not to other mountains in South America.

Be sure, also, to include any information you need to avoid ambiguity in your comparisons. In its draft form, the following comparison has two possible interpretations, as the revisions make clear.

DRAFT   Yvette is more concerned about me than my brother.

REVISED   Yvette is more concerned about me than <u>she is about</u> my brother.

REVISED   Yvette is more concerned about me than my brother <u>is</u>.

When you use the word *as* in a comparison, be sure to use it twice.

▶ Stephen King's horror stories are *as* scary as Edgar Allan Poe's.

11 **Language** 关注语言

Matters

Guidance for Multilingual Writers 多语种写作者指南

Use part 11 to learn, practice, and master these writer's responsibilities:

❏ **To Audience**

Address your readers in idiomatic Standard English.

❏ **To Topic**

Communicate your ideas in clear language that follows the conventions of American academic and business writing.

❏ **To Other Writers**

Share your knowledge and experience.

❏ **To Yourself**

Present yourself with confidence.

46 Understanding English Word Order and Sentence Structure
by Ted E. Johnston and M. E. Sokolik

理解英语语序和句子结构

（作者:特德·E. 约翰斯顿和M. E. 索科利克）

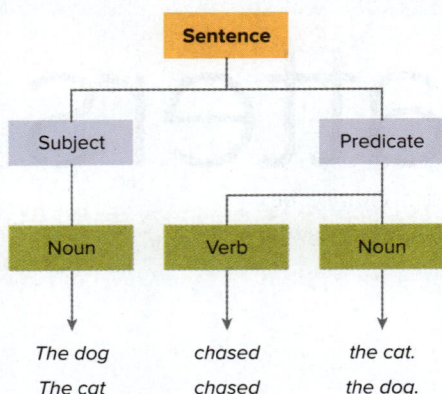

English is a word-order language, which means that the position of a word in a sentence often determines its grammatical function. As a result, *The dog chased the cat* means something different from *The cat chased the dog*. This chapter describes and explains word order and related aspects of English sentence structure.

Sentence

Subject — Predicate

Noun — Verb — Noun

The dog — chased — the cat.
The cat — chased — the dog.

46a Observing Normal Word Order
遵守规范的语序

In English, normal word order is subject–verb–object (or S–V–O). That is, the subject comes first, then the verb, and then the direct object, if there is one, or any other words that make up the predicate.

More about
Sentence types, 337–38
Word order in questions, 409–10

	v ? ?
FAULTY WORD ORDER	Chased the cat the dog.
	s v o
NORMAL WORD ORDER	The dog chased the cat.

46b Including a Stated Subject 包含明确的主语

Except for commands, English sentences and *clauses* require a subject to be stated, even if the identity of the subject is clear from a previous sentence or clause. In the following example, the pronoun *he*, referring to the subject of the first sentence, can serve as the subject of both clauses of the second sentence.

> **clause 从句** A word group with a subject and a predicate. An *independent clause* can stand alone as a sentence; a *subordinate clause* cannot.

He is .... *he*

▸ Nico has a hard life for a ten-year-old. Is just a boy, but is expected to work like a man.

Similarly, a subordinate clause requires a stated subject even if its subject is a pronoun or another noun phrase that obviously refers to the subject of the clause that comes before it.

— sub. clause —

she

▸ Lucy asked for directions because was lost.

In commands, the subject is unstated but is understood to be "you."

▸ [you] Leave now!

406

46c Managing *There* and *It* Sentences
掌握There be句型和It作形式主语的句型

Expletives are words that are empty of content; that is, they do not refer to anything. In English, the words *there* and *it* are often used as expletives.

There expletives begin with *there* followed by a form of *be*, but *there* is not the subject. Instead, the subject follows the verb, which is singular if the subject is singular or plural if the subject is plural. The expletive *it*, however, is the subject of the verb and is always singular. *It* expletives often describe an environmental condition (the weather, for example) or some aspect of time. The verb in expletive *it* constructions is often a form of *be*, but can include others, especially those related to process (for example, *start, continue, end*). The expletives *there* and *it* cannot be omitted from these sentences, even though they do not refer to anything.

> *There are*
> ▸ ~~Are~~ not enough reasons to support your argument.

> *there*
> ▸ Waiter, I am not pleased that is a fly in my soup.

> *it*   *it*
> ▸ When was almost 3:00 p.m., started hailing really hard.

In a similar construction, the pronoun *it* is not empty, but refers to content that follows the verb. In the following sentence, for example, *it* refers to *to drive during a snowstorm*. In either case, empty or meaningful, *it* is the subject and cannot be omitted.

> *It is*
> ~~Is~~ dangerous to drive during a snowstorm.

46d Eliminating Redundant Subject and Object Pronouns
删除多余的主格和宾格代词

Although English requires a stated subject in all clauses except commands, the use of a pronoun to reemphasize an already stated subject is not acceptable in writing, even though it often occurs in informal speech.

> subj.   redundant subject
> ▸ Rosalinda, ~~she~~ left early for the airport.

Similarly, when *which* or *that* begins a clause and serves as the clause's subject or direct object, do not also add *it* to serve as the subject or direct object. In the following sentences, for example, both *which* and *it* refer redundantly to the movie *The Big Short*; to correct the sentences, eliminate one pronoun or the other.

subj.

redundant subject

► Last night I saw *The Big Short*, **which** it impressed me very much.

or

;

► Last night I saw *The Big Short*, ~~which~~ it impressed me very much.

^

dir. obj.

redundant object

► I liked *The Big Short*, **which** many of my friends liked it too.

or

;

► I liked *The Big Short*, ~~which~~ many of my friends liked it too.

^

46e **Observing Standard Word Order with Direct Objects, Indirect Objects, and Object Complements**
区分直接宾语、间接宾语和宾语补足语，遵循标准语序

Direct objects, indirect objects, and object complements can follow a transitive verb.

> **More about**
> Transitive verbs and direct and indirect objects, 339–42

1. Direct and indirect objects 直接宾语和间接宾语

A *direct object* receives or carries the action of a transitive verb. Certain transitive verbs—such as *ask, find, give, order, send, show, teach, tell,* and *write*—can also take an *indirect object*, which identifies who or what benefits from the action of the verb. The indirect object falls between the verb and the direct object.

s   v   io   do

► She sent Michiko a **book** on Scandinavian cuisine.

Alternatively, the indirect object can be identified in a phrase beginning with a preposition, usually *to*, that follows the direct object.

s   v   do   alternative phrase

► She sent a **book** on Scandinavian cuisine to Michiko.

When the direct object is a personal pronoun, the pronoun follows the verb and is itself followed by a prepositional phrase containing the indirect object.

to Michiko.

She sent ~~Michiko~~ it. ✓

Several common verbs do not take indirect objects that fall between the verb and the direct object, even though the actions they refer to are similar to those of verbs that do. These verbs include *answer, carry, change, close, complete, deliver, describe, explain, keep, mention, open, propose, put, recommend, repair* (or *fix* when it means *repair*), and *say*. With these verbs, the indirect object can only come after the direct object in a prepositional phrase beginning with *to* (or sometimes *for*).

to my father.
- The doctor explained ~~my father~~ the dangers of secondhand smoke. ʌ

for us.
- The professor opened ~~us~~ the door to understanding. ʌ

2. Object complements 宾语补足语

An *object complement* follows a direct object and describes the condition of the object or a change that the subject has caused the object to undergo.

- Some workers here make my *job* *impossible*.
  (do) (obj. comp.)

Placing an object complement before the direct object will either make a sentence ungrammatical or change its meaning. The following sentence, as originally written, was ungrammatical.

their team captain.
- The players have just elected ~~their team captain~~ Paul. ʌ

In contrast, both of the following sentences are grammatical, but they have different meanings.

- We need to keep all the <u>happy</u> workers.
- We need to keep all the workers <u>happy</u>.

The first sentence, with the adjective *happy* before the direct object, recommends retaining the workers who are already happy, but not necessarily those who are not. The second, with *happy* in the object complement position after the direct object, recommends taking action to make sure that not one of the workers feels unhappy.

46f Observing Word-Order Patterns in Questions
遵循疑问句中的语序模式

In questions, unlike in other sentences, a verb nearly always precedes the subject.

- To form a question with one-word forms of the verb *be*, simply invert subject and verb.

  <u>The grapes</u> are ripe.   <u>Are</u> the grapes ripe?
  (s) (v)   (v) (s)

- In all other cases, a question requires a helping verb as well as a main verb. The subject goes after the first helping verb in a verb phrase and before the rest of the verb phrase.

  > **verb phrase** 动词短语 A main verb and all its helping verbs

  <u>They</u> have left for New York.   Have <u>they</u> left for New York?
  (s) (hv) (mv)   (hv) (s) (mv)

  <u>The children</u> can go with us.   Can <u>the children</u> go with us?
  (s) (hv) (mv)   (hv) (s) (mv)

  <u>The painters</u> should have finished.   Should <u>the painters</u> have finished?
  (s) (hv) (hv) (mv)   (hv) (s) (hv) (mv)

- To form a question with one-word verbs other than forms of *be*, use the appropriate form of *do* as the helper.

s   v
The prisoner escaped.

hv   s   mv
Did the prisoner escape?

- Questions that begin with question words like *what, who,* and *why* normally follow the same word order as other questions.

      hv   s   mv
What is the engineer saying about the project?

- If the question word is the subject, however, the question follows subject-before-verb word order.

s   v   do
Who is saying these things about the project?

46g Observing Inverted Word Order When Certain Conjunctions or Adverbs Begin a Clause
当某些连词或副词位于分句句首时，遵循倒装语序

When certain words and phrases appear at the beginning of a sentence, they require inverted word order similar to that used in questions. These include certain adverbs, adverb phrases, correlative conjunctions (such as *neither ... nor* and *not only ... but also*), and the conjunction *nor* by itself.

                  the parents   *they*
- *Neither* ~~the parents~~ have called the principal, *nor* ~~they~~ have informed the school board.

                    do
- The twins don't bowl, *nor* they play tennis.

Negating or limiting adverbs such as *rarely, seldom, no sooner,* and *no longer* also require inverted word order when they start a sentence or clause. Such sentences have a formal tone.

                  the dancers
- *Seldom* ~~the dancers~~ have had the opportunity to perform in public.

Moving the adverb to the interior of the sentence cancels the inversion.

- The dancers have *seldom* had the opportunity to perform in public.

Usually, this less formal, noninverted version is preferable to the inverted version.

> **More about**
> Adverbs, 387–91, 424–26

47

Using Nouns and Noun Determiners
by Ted E. Johnston and M. E. Sokolik

使用名词和名词限定词

（作者：特德·E. 约翰斯顿和M. E. 索科利克）

English nouns rarely appear by themselves. Most of the time they are paired with words such as *a, an, the, my, that, each, one, ten, several, more, less,* and *fewer*. These words are known as **determiners** because they help us figure out—or determine—how a noun works and what it means when we encounter it in a sentence. As this cartoon suggests, learning to use nouns and determiners appropriately can sometimes challenge native speakers as much as it does multilingual students.

"What can I say? I was an English major."

© J.C. Duffy/The New Yorker Collection/The Cartoon Bank

47a Identifying Different Types of Nouns
辨别不同类型的名词

To use a noun correctly, you need to know whether it is a *proper noun* or a *common noun*, and, if it is a common noun, whether it is *count* or *noncount*. A **common noun** identifies a general category and is usually not capitalized: *woman, era, bridge, corporation, mountain, war.* A **proper noun** identifies someone or something specific and is usually capitalized: *Sister Miriam Joseph, Middle Ages, Golden Gate Bridge, Burger King, Himalayas, World War II.*

Count nouns name discrete, countable things. **Noncount nouns** (also called **noncountable nouns** or **mass nouns**) usually name things made of a continuous substance or of small, indistinguishable particles, or they refer to a general quality. A *drop*, a *grain*, and a *suggestion*, for example, are count nouns, but *water, sand,* and *advice* are noncount nouns.

> **More about**
> Types of nouns, 332

- Count nouns can be singular (*drop*) or plural (*drops*). Most noncount nouns are singular, even those that end in *-s*, and thus should be matched with singular verbs. Noncount nouns cannot be preceded by a number or any other term that would imply countability (such as *a, an, several, another,* or *many*), nor can they be made plural if they are singular.

> **More about**
> Forming noun plurals, 476–77

▸ Aerobics ~~help~~ *helps* me to relax.

Here are some examples of contrasting count and noncount nouns:

Count	Noncount
car/cars	traffic
dollar/dollars	money
noodle/noodles	spaghetti
pebble/pebbles	gravel
spoon/spoons	silverware

Quick

Reference **Some Common Noncount Nouns**

Although there is no hard-and-fast way to distinguish noncount from count nouns, most noncount nouns do fall into a few general categories.

Abstractions and emotions	advice, courage, happiness, hate, jealousy, information, knowledge, love, luck, maturity, patriotism, warmth
Mass substances	air, blood, dirt, gasoline, glue, sand, shampoo, water
Food items	beef, bread, corn, flour, gravy, pork, rice, salt, sugar
Collections of related items	cash, clothing, equipment, furniture, graffiti, information, jewelry, luggage, mail, news, traffic
Games and other activities	aerobics, baseball, checkers, homework, news, poker, pool, soccer, tennis, volleyball, yoga
Weather-related phenomena	cold, drizzle, frost, hail, heat, humidity, lightning, rain, sleet, snow, sunshine, thunder
Diseases	arthritis, chickenpox, diabetes, influenza, measles
Fields of study	botany, chemistry, mathematics, physics, sociology

- Many nouns can be noncount in one context and count in another.

  ▸ While speaking of *love* [noncount], my grandmother recalled the three *loves* [count] of her life.

    In the opening phrase, *love* is an abstraction. In the main clause, *loves* refers to the people the grandmother has loved.

- All languages have count and noncount nouns, but a noun that is count in one language may be noncount in another.

47b **Using Nouns with Articles (*a, an, the*) and Other Determiners** 名词与冠词（a、an、the）及其他限定词连用

The *articles* *a*, *an*, and *the* are the most common determiners. Other determiners include possessives (*my, your, Ivan's*), numbers (*one, five, a hundred*), and other words that quantify (*some, many, a few*) or specify (*this, those*).

1. Articles with common nouns 冠词+普通名词

The main function of the *indefinite articles*, *a* and *an*, is to introduce nouns that are new to the reader. The *definite article*, *the*, usually precedes nouns that have already been introduced or whose identity is known or clear from the context. Noncount nouns and plural count nouns also sometimes appear with no article (or the *zero article*).

- Use *a* before a consonant sound (*a cat*) and *an* before a vowel sound (*an elephant*). Do not be misled by written vowels that are pronounced as consonants (*a European tour*) or written consonants that are pronounced as vowels (*an hour early*). Be especially careful with words that begin with *h* (*a hot stove*, *an honorary degree*) and *u* (*a uniform*, *an upheaval*).

- Use *a* or *an* only with singular count nouns. A singular count noun must be preceded by an article or some other determiner even if other modifiers come between the determiner and the noun.

  ▸ <u>A</u> friend of mine bought <u>an</u> antique car on eBay.

- Never use *a* or *an* with a noncount noun.

  ▸ <s>A</s> *Good* good advice is hard to find.

- Use *a* or *an* when you first introduce a singular count noun if the specific identity of the noun is not yet known to the reader or is not otherwise clear from the context. Use *the* for later references to the same noun.

  ▸ A friend of mine bought <u>an</u> antique car on eBay. She restored <u>the</u> car and sold it for <u>a</u> tidy profit. <u>The</u> profit came in handy when she took <u>a</u> vacation.

    The is appropriate for *car* in the second sentence because it refers to the same car introduced in the first sentence. The word *profit* in the second sentence takes *a* because it is making its first appearance there. The third sentence continues the process.

- Use *the* with both count and noncount nouns whose specific identity has been previously established or is clear from the context.

  ▸ We admired <u>the</u> antique car that my friend bought on eBay.

    The description *that my friend bought on eBay* identifies a specific car.

  ▸ She sold it for <u>a</u> tidy profit and used <u>the</u> money for <u>a</u> vacation.

    The context clearly identifies the money with the profit.

  ▸ My friend is traveling around <u>the</u> world for three months.

    The noun *world* logically refers to the planet we live on—not, say, Mars or Venus.

  ▸ Vicky is <u>the</u> fastest runner on her team.

    The superlative *fastest* refers specifically to one person.

- No article is used to introduce noncount nouns or plural count nouns used generically—that is, to make generalizations.

  ▸ Good advice is hard to find.
  ▸ Good teachers can change lives.

> **More about**
> Superlatives,
> 389–91

- Both the definite and indefinite articles can introduce singular nouns used generically. Sometimes either is appropriate.

  ▸ <u>The</u> good teacher can change lives.
  ▸ <u>A</u> good teacher can change lives.

Sometimes the generic meaning is clear with only one or the other.

  ▸ Thomas Alva Edison invented <s>a</s> *the* lightbulb.

2. Articles with proper nouns 冠词+专有名词

Proper nouns in English almost never occur with the indefinite article (*a, an*), and most occur with no article.

> ▸ Ruby grew up in Lima, Peru, but now lives in Wichita, Kansas.

There are many exceptions, however:

- Certain place names always occur with *the: the Bronx, the Philippines, the Northeast, the Pacific Ocean.*
- The names of ships (including airships) conventionally occur with *the: the Queen Mary, the Challenger.*
- Many product names can be used with *a* or *the* or sometimes both: *the Cheerios, an/the iPad, a/the Honda.*
- Many multiword proper nouns occur with *the: the United States, the Brooklyn Bridge, the Department of State, the War of 1812.* Others do not, however. The city of Chicago, for example, is home to both *the Wrigley Building* (with article) and *Wrigley Field* (no article).
- Most plural proper nouns occur with *the: the Bartons, the Chicago Cubs.*

3. Nouns and other determiners 名词和其他限定词

More about
Order of adjectives, 423

As with articles, the use of other determiners with nouns depends on the kind of noun in question, particularly whether it is singular or plural, count or noncount. In all cases, determiners precede any other adjectives that modify a noun.

Possessive nouns or pronouns Use possessive nouns (*Julio's*) and possessive pronouns (*my, our, your, his, her, its, their, whose*) with any count or noncount noun.

sing. count	plural count	noncount
Ann's book	*Ann's* books	*Ann's* information
her book	*her* books	*her* information

This, that, these, those The demonstrative pronouns *this, that, these,* and *those* specify, or single out, particular instances of a noun. Use *this* and *that* only with noncount nouns and singular count nouns. Use *these* and *those* only with plural count nouns.

sing. count	plural count	noncount
this book	*these* books	*this* information
that book	*those* books	*that* information

Quantifying words or phrases Use numbers only with count nouns: *one shirt, two shirts.* See the Quick Reference box on the next page for a list of other quantifying words and how they work with different kinds of nouns in most contexts.

Few *versus* a few *and* little *versus* a little The determiners *few* and *a few* (for count nouns) and *little* and *a little* (for noncount nouns) all indicate a small quantity, but they have significant differences in meaning. *Few*

Quick Reference Matching Nouns with Quantifying Words and Phrases

Quantifying Word or Phrase	Singular Count Nouns	Plural Count Nouns	Noncount Nouns	Examples
any, no	✓	✓	✓	You can read <mark>any</mark> book on the list. Have you read <mark>any</mark> books this summer? Do you have <mark>any</mark> information about the reading list?
another, each, every, either, neither	✓	no	no	I read <mark>another</mark> book last week.
the other	✓	✓	✓	The other <mark>book</mark> is a murder mystery. I haven't finished <u>the other</u> <mark>books</mark> on the reading list. The other <mark>information</mark> is the most reliable.
a couple of, a number of, both, few, a few, fewer, fewest, many, several	no	✓	no	The professor assigned <u>fewer</u> <mark>books</mark> last term.
a lot of, lots of, all, enough, more, most, other, some	no	✓	✓	Some <mark>books</mark> are inspiring. Some <mark>information</mark> is unreliable.
little, a little, much, a great deal of, less, least	no	no	✓	I need a little <mark>information</mark> about the course requirements.

means a negligible amount, whereas *a few* means a small but significant number. Likewise, *little* means *almost none*, whereas *a little* means *some*.

▸ Rhoda has *few* good friends.

　She is almost friendless.

▸ Rhoda has *a few* good friends.

　She has significant companionship.

▸ Pete provided *little* help before the party.

　He didn't do his share.

▸ Pete gave me *a little* help after everyone left.

　He made himself useful.

Indicating extent or amount with noncount nouns Because a noncount noun is always singular, do not make it plural or add a determiner that implies a plural form. For example, do not use a determiner such as *a large number of, many,* or *several* immediately before a noncount noun. Instead, use

Writing
Responsibly *Less* versus *Fewer*, or "Do as I Say, Not as I Do"

> The quantifier *less* is properly used only with noncount nouns, not count nouns.
>
> *fewer*
> ▸ The automobile industry sold less cars this year than last year.
> ^
>
> As the cartoon that opens this chapter suggests, however, many native English speakers violate this rule, particularly in everyday speech. (*Items* is a count noun.) Try not to follow their example, particularly when writing for an academic audience.
>
> to AUDIENCE

a determiner such as *a great deal of, less, little, much,* or *some*—or revise the sentence another way.

some
▸ The city is doing researches on the proposal.
^

> The modifier *some* is appropriate for the noncount noun *research* because it does not imply plurality.

loaves of
▸ Gina bought two breads at the store.
^

> In the edited version, *two* modifies the count noun *loaves.*

incidents of violence
▸ We do not have many violences in our neighborhood.
^

great deal
▸ A large number of information is available on your topic.
^

> *A large number of,* which suggests plurality, cannot be used with *information,* a noncount noun.

48

Managing English Verbs
by Ted E. Johnston and M. E. Sokolik
掌握英语动词
（作者：特德·E. 约翰斯顿和M. E. 索科利克）

Verbs can express an action or occurrence (*The dog jumps for the Frisbee*) or indicate a state of being (*The dog is frisky*). In many languages, verbs can have several forms. For example, they may change to indicate the identity of a subject or an object or the time frame in which an event happens. English verbs, in contrast, have only a few forms, but these combine with other words to accomplish the same functions.

48a **Understanding Phrasal Verbs** 理解短语动词

Phrasal verbs—sometimes called multiword verbs—consist of a verb and one or two *particles*. The particle takes the form of a preposition or an adverb, and it combines with the verb to create a new verb with a new meaning. For example, the verb *throw* means to project something through the air. The phrasal verb *throw out* consists of the verb *throw* and the particle *out*; it means to dispose of something.

> **More about**
> Verbs and verb phrases, 333, 343, 370–72

        phrasal vb. ———— particle
- Segundo threw out his old notebook.

        verb
- Segundo threw his old notebook on his bed.

The meaning of a verb-and-particle combination differs from the meaning of the same words in a verb-and-preposition combination. The phrasal verb *look up*, for example, means to consult or find something in a reference work, which is different from the meaning of *look* followed by a phrase that happens to begin with the preposition *up*.

PHRASAL VERB	phrasal vb. Svetlana looked up the word in the dictionary.
VERB WITH PREPOSITION	verb prep. Svetlana looked up the steep trail and began to hike.

A transitive phrasal verb is *separable* if its direct object can fall either between the verb and the particle (separating them) or after the particle.

            dir. obj.
- She looked up the address online.

            dir. obj.
- She looked the address up online.

If the direct object of a separable phrasal verb is a pronoun, it must come between the verb and the particle.

             it in.
- I decided to hand in it.

A phrasal verb is *inseparable* if no words can fall between the verb and the particle.

FAULTY	I came an old photo across in the drawer.
REVISED	I came across an old photo in the drawer.

The meaning of a phrasal verb changes when the particle changes (see the Quick Reference box on the next page). The phrasal verb *take on*, for example, means "to assume responsibility for."

Quick Reference — Some Common Phrasal Verbs and Their Meanings

SEPARABLE		INSEPARABLE	
ask out	invite for a date	*add up to*	total
calm down	make calm, become calm	*barge in on*	interrupt unannounced
give up	surrender	*call on*	visit, or ask for a response directly
hand in	submit		
hand out	distribute	*come across*	find accidentally
look up	find something in a reference work	*drop in*	visit unannounced
		get out of	evade an obligation, exit
put back	return to original position	*give in*	surrender
put down	criticize meanly; suppress	*grow up*	mature
		hint at	suggest
take back	return; retract	*look down on*	disdain
take off	remove	*look up to*	admire
take on	assume responsibility for	*put up with*	tolerate
		run into	encounter; collide
take up	begin a hobby or activity	*stand in for*	substitute for
throw out	dispose of	*turn up*	show up, arrive

▸ She took on the editing of the newsletter.

The phrasal verb *take back*, in contrast, means "return" or "retract."

▸ She took all her overdue books back to the library.

48b Learning When to Use Gerunds and Infinitives after Verbs and Prepositions
学会何时在动词和介词后使用动名词和不定式

A *gerund* is the *-ing* form of a verb used as a noun (*listening, eating*). An *infinitive* is the base form of a verb preceded by *to* (*to listen, to eat*).

1. Gerunds and infinitives after verbs 动名词和不定式位于动词之后

■ Only gerunds can follow some verbs, and only infinitives can follow others.

▸ The committee recommended ~~to submit~~ the proposal for a vote.
submitting

▸ Rosa Parks refused ~~leaving~~ her seat on the bus.
to leave

Quick

Reference Gerund or Infinitive after Selected Verbs

Some verbs that can be directly followed by a gerund but not an infinitive

admit	discuss	imagine	practice	risk
avoid	enjoy	mind	quit	suggest
consider	escape	miss	recall	tolerate
deny	finish	postpone	resist	understand

Some verbs that can be directly followed by an infinitive but not a gerund

agree	claim	hope	offer	refuse
appear	decide	manage	plan	wait
ask	expect	mean	pretend	want
beg	have	need	promise	wish

Some verbs that can be directly followed by a gerund or an infinitive with little effect on meaning

begin	hate	love		start
continue	like	prefer		

Some verbs for which choice of gerund or infinitive affects meaning

forget	remember	stop		try

Some verbs that take an infinitive only after an intervening noun or pronoun

advise	command	force	persuade	tell
allow	convince	instruct	remind	urge
cause	encourage	order	require	warn

- Some verbs can be followed by either gerunds or infinitives. For some of these verbs, the choice of gerund or infinitive has little effect on meaning, but for a few the difference is significant.

SAME   The economy *continued* to grow.
MEANING   The economy *continued* growing.

DIFFERENT   Juan *remembered* to email his paper to his professor.
MEANINGS   [He didn't forget to do it.]

               Juan *remembered* emailing his paper to his professor.
               [He recalled having done it already.]

- Some verbs that can be followed by an infinitive can also be followed by an infinitive after an intervening noun or pronoun.

‣ Yue *wanted* <u>to study</u> the violin.

‣ Yue's parents *wanted <u>her</u> to study* the violin.

Certain verbs, however, take an infinitive only after an object noun or pronoun.

‣ The candidate *urged <u>citizens</u> to vote* on Election Day.

A few verbs (for example, *feel, have, hear, let, look at,* and *see*) require an **unmarked infinitive**—the base verb alone, without *to*—after an intervening noun or pronoun.

‣ Paolo let his children t~~o g~~o to the movies.
go

‣ Jen heard a dog t~~o bark~~ late at night.
bark

2. Gerunds after prepositions 动名词位于介词之后

Only a gerund, not an infinitive, can be the object of a preposition.

‣ The article is about t~~o travel~~ in South America.
traveling

48c Understanding the Use of Participles as Adjectives 理解分词作形容词的用法

Both the present participle and the past participle of a verb can act as adjectives, but they convey different meanings, especially if the verb refers to an emotion or state of mind such as anger or boredom. The *present participle* (or *-ing* form) usually describes the cause or agent of a state of affairs. The *past participle* (the *-ed* form in regular verbs) usually describes the result of the state of affairs.

> **More about**
> Regular and irregular verb forms, 370–74

State of Affairs	Cause	Result
Physics class <u>bored</u> me today. *(verb)*	The class was bor<u>*ing*</u>. *(adj.)*	I was <u>bored</u>. *(adj.)*
Dr. Sung's lecture <u>interested</u> me. *(verb)*	The lecture was interes<u>*ting*</u>. *(adj.)*	I was <u>interested</u>. *(adj.)*

48d Using Helping Verbs for Verb Formation 助动词构成动词结构

> **More about**
> Verb forms, 369–79
> Subject-verb agreement, 358–65

Most complete English verbs, other than the present and past tenses, consist of a main verb with one or more helping (auxiliary) verbs. The main verb carries the principal meaning, and the helping verbs carry information about time, mood, and voice. There are two kinds of helping verbs: simple and modal.

■ The simple helping verbs—*have, do,* and *be*—also function as main verbs, and like other main verbs, they change form to indicate person and tense.

- The modal helping verbs—including *can, could, may, might, must, ought to, shall, should, will,* and *would*—carry information about attributes of the main verb such as ability, intention, permission, possibility, desire, and suggestion (see the Quick Reference box on the next page). Unlike the simple auxiliaries, the modal auxiliaries do not change form to indicate person and tense.

  ▸ All the contestants at the Olympics can swim fast, but Michael Phelps ~~cans~~ swim faster than any of the others.
  can

  ▸ William should work all day today, and he ~~shoulded work~~ yesterday too.
  should have worked

NOTE When you hear such contractions as *should've* or *could've* in speech (or similar contractions with other modals), remember that the contracted word is *have* (*should have, could have*), not *of*.

- In a verb phrase, auxiliaries almost always precede the main verb, and modals precede any other auxiliaries.

  ▸ In June, Chen will   have been   living in Seattle for ten years.
  modal *simple* — auxiliaries — *main verb*

- When forming verbs, include needed auxiliaries.

  ▸ Demetrio taking four courses this term.
  is

  ▸ My grandparents been visiting Scotland every year.
  have

- In general, never follow a modal with another modal, and always follow a modal with the base form of a simple auxiliary or main verb.

  ▸ Tomás should ~~can~~ finish his calculus homework before the movie starts.
  be able to

  ▸ Yuki must ~~to~~ take three more courses to graduate.

Quick

Reference | Modals and Meaning

Modals	Meaning	Examples
can, could	Used to indicate ability, possibility, and willingness and to request or grant permission	Sam can paint wonderful watercolors. [ability] You can leave class early today. [grant permission] Could we meet at the library? [request permission] I'm so tired I could fall asleep standing up. [possibility] I could work your shift if you need me to. [willingness]
may, might	Used to request and grant permission and to offer suggestions. For requests, *might* has a more hesitant and polite connotation than *may*, but they are otherwise usually interchangeable.	May I see the comments you wrote? [request permission] Might I borrow your car this afternoon? [more polite request for permission] It may/might rain this afternoon. [possibility] You may/might want to bring an umbrella. [suggestion]
must	Expresses necessity, prohibition (in the negative), and logical probability	Passengers must pass through airport security before boarding. [necessity] Passengers must not leave their seats while the seatbelt sign is illuminated. [prohibition] We must be on our final approach. [logical probability]
shall, should, ought to	*Should* and *ought to* express advisability and expectation, usually interchangeably. *Shall* expresses intention as well as advisability, but in American English it usually appears only in questions.	Shall/Should we eat in or go out for dinner tonight? [advisability] We should/ought to eat out less to save money. [advisability] The pizza should/ought to arrive in 20 minutes or so. [expectation]
will, would	*Will* expresses intention, willingness, and expectation. *Would* expresses intention, willingness, typical or repeated action, and logical assumption, and it is also used for polite requests.	I will finish the laundry if you want. [willingness] I will apply to graduate school next year. [intention] The bus will arrive soon. [expectation] Would you mind opening the window? [request] Amalia decided she would apply to graduate school. [intention] When preparing dinner, he would always clean up as he cooked. [repeated action] That alarm you're hearing would be the monthly test of the emergency system. [logical probability]

49 Managing Adjectives and Adverbs
by Ted E. Johnston and M. E. Sokolik

掌握形容词和副词

（作者：特德・E. 约翰斯顿和M. E. 索科利克）

Just as a coat of paint can change our perception of the surface it covers, adjectives and adverbs color our understanding of the words they modify. *Adjectives* modify nouns and pronouns. *Adverbs* modify verbs, adjectives, other adverbs, and entire phrases, clauses, and sentences. This chapter will help you use adjectives and adverbs correctly and place them appropriately in your sentences.

49a Placing Adjectives in the Proper Order
将形容词按适当的顺序排列

- Most English adjectives have only one form, regardless of whether the noun they modify is singular or plural.

  ▸ Serena wants a <u>white</u> dress, but many of these <u>white</u> dresses are not to her liking.

- English adjectives usually come before a noun (*Serena has a white dress*) or after a **linking verb** (*Serena's dress is <u>white</u>*).

- When multiple adjectives cumulatively modify the same noun, the kind of information they convey determines their proper order (see the Quick Reference box below).

> **linking verbs** 连系动词 *Be* and other verbs that express a state of being rather than an action and connect a subject to its subject complement

49b Choosing the Correct Prepositions with Adjectives
选择正确的介词与形容词搭配

On a particular day, you might be excited *by* a lecture, mad *at* a friend, or happy *about* the election in Pakistan. As these phrases reveal, you need to be careful when combining adjectives and prepositions. When

Quick Reference | Putting Cumulative Adjectives in Standard Order

Article or Other Determiner	Overall Evaluation or Opinion	Size	Shape or Other Intrinsic Aspect	Age	Color	Essence: Nationality, Material, or Purpose	Noun
two		big			red	rubber	balls
an	exciting			new		mystery	novel
my		tiny	helpless	newborn			kitten
those	funny			old	black-and-white		sitcoms
the	delicious		round			French	pastry

More about
Articles and other
  determiners,
  412–14
Cumulative versus
  coordinate adjec-
  tives, 436–37

More about
Prepositions,
  426–31

in doubt, consult a dictionary to make sure you are using the proper idiom. The editing in the following paragraph gives additional examples of idiomatic usage.

Aisha is delighted *with* in her midterm grades. She had been nervous *about* of flunking biochemistry. Aisha is grateful *to* at her instructors. When she struggled, they were not disappointed *in* at her, and they were proud *of* about her when she succeeded. She is dedicated *to* with completing her nursing degree.

49c Placing Adverbs Correctly 副词的正确位置

- An adverb cannot be located between a verb and its object.

  ▸ Susan plays ~~beautifully~~ the piano. *beautifully.*

  In this sentence, *beautifully* fits correctly only at the end, after *piano*, the direct object.

- Many adverbs, primarily those related to time (such as *often* and *frequently*), may be placed either before the subject or verb or after the direct object.

  ▸ *Recently,* Susan learned ~~recently~~ a new concerto.

  ▸ Susan learned *recently* ~~recently~~ a new concerto.

  ▸ Susan learned ~~recently~~ a new concerto. *recently.*

- When a main verb has no helping verbs, the adverb should precede it. When the main verb has helping verbs, the adverb should usually be placed between the first helper and the main verb.

  ▸ Carla <u>carelessly</u> *wasted* gas by leaving the motor running.

  ▸ Carla ~~carelessly~~ *has been* *carelessly* *wasting* gas by leaving the motor running.

  Some adverbs (but not all) can be placed between the second helper and the main verb.

  ▸ Carla ~~carelessly~~ has been *carelessly* wasting gas by leaving the motor running.

Writing Responsibly — Too Many Adjectives before a Noun

More than three adjectives in a row can be awkward. Instead, vary your sentences to distribute the adjectives without confusing your readers.

TOO MANY ADJECTIVES I love to ride my exciting, shiny, new, eighteen-speed bicycle.

REVISED I love my new eighteen-speed bicycle. It's shiny and exciting to ride.

to AUDIENCE

- In most instances, place an adverb first if it modifies the entire sentence.

  ▸ <u>Surprisingly</u>, she has decided to change her major to psychology.

- When certain negative adverbs or adverb phrases begin a sentence, they require a change in the standard subject-verb order. Included in this group are *at no time, never, not only, rarely,* and *seldom.*

  ▸ Seldom I *have* been so proud of my brother.

49d Distinguishing between Confusing Adverbs 易混淆的副词辨析

Certain English adverbs seem similar but actually have significantly different connotations and functions. Often-confused words include *too* with *so, too* with *either, not* with *no, hard* with *hardly,* and *such* with *so.*

1. Too and so too和so

To give an adjective a negative or more negative meaning, use *too* in most instances. To emphasize any adjective, use *so* or *very* or a similar adverb.

▸ The professor realized her first test had been *so* ~~so~~ difficult and was surprised to find us still ~~too~~ *too* excited about the class.

2. Too and either too和either

When following up a statement about one subject's action with a statement about another subject's doing likewise, use *either* after a verb that is grammatically negative (as with *not* or *never* or *won't* or *hasn't*), and use *too* after a verb that is grammatically positive. Remember that unless verbs such as *avoided* or *refused* are used with a negative adverb (such as *not*), they are grammatically positive, even though by themselves they have negative meanings.

▸ Floyd <u>didn't join</u> the fraternity, and I <u>didn't, either</u>.
  Neither one joined.

> **More about**
> Inverted word order when certain negative adverbs start a sentence, 410

> ‣ Floyd <u>joined</u> the fraternity, and I <u>did, too</u>.
>   Both joined.

> ‣ Floyd <u>refused to join</u>, and I <u>did, too</u>.
>   Neither one joined.

> ‣ Floyd <u>didn't refuse to join</u>, and I <u>didn't, either</u>.
>   Both were willing to join.

3. *Not* and *no* not和no

Because *no* is an adjective, it can modify only a noun. The adverb *not*, however, can modify an adjective, a verb, or another adverb. The expression *not a (an)* can replace the adjective *no* in front of a noun.

> ‣ Keith is <u>no</u> friendly. Because he will <u>no</u> talk to me, he is <u>not</u> friend of mine.

(*not* / *not* / *no (or: not a)*)

4. *Hard* and *hardly* hard和hardly

The word *hard* can be either an adjective or an adverb. As an adverb, it means *intensely* or *with great effort*. The adverb *hardly* means *just a little* or *almost not at all*.

> ‣ Juan got an *A* after he studied <u>hard</u> for the exam. Laura got a *D* because she <u>hardly</u> looked at her notes.

5. *Such* and *so* such和so

Such a (an), *such*, or *so* can emphasize a type or a quality. Use *such a (an)* before an adjective that precedes a concrete noun: *She is <u>such a</u> wise person*. Use *such* by itself directly in front of an abstract noun: *<u>Such</u> wisdom is rare*. To intensify any freestanding adjective, as in the case of a subject complement, use *so*: *She is <u>so</u> wise*.

50

Using Prepositions
by Ted E. Johnston and M. E. Sokolik

使用介词（作者：特德·E.约翰斯顿和M.E.索科利克）

Prepositions are words that specify a relationship between other words or phrases. They are seemingly insignificant words (*for, at, with, under, over*) that serve an important function. Like the thin line that indicates where the sky ends and the ocean begins, they provide important information about relationships between other words and phrases: "The mayor worked *against* the proposal"; "the laptop is *inside* my backpack."

To help you learn to use prepositions correctly, this chapter explains how to identify prepositions (*section 50a*), how to determine the function they serve (*50b*), and how to use them correctly (*50c* and *d*).

50a Recognizing Prepositions 辨别介词

Although there are fewer than one hundred single-word prepositions in use in English, many additional multiword prepositions function in similar ways. The Quick Reference box on the next page lists some of the most common of both.

50b Learning the Functions of Prepositions 掌握介词的功能

Every preposition has multiple possible functions depending on the context in which it occurs. As a result, it is often easier to understand prepositions in terms of their function than to try to memorize what each one means.

The most basic use for a preposition is to indicate *location*. Other important functions are to indicate *time*; to indicate *condition* or *degree*; to specify *cause* or *reason*; and to designate *possession, attribute,* or *origin*.

1. Location 表示地点

The most basic prepositions for indicating the location of things are *at*, *on*, and *in*.

- *At* specifies a general point of orientation.

  ‣ Meet me at the station.

- *On* specifies contact between two things.

  ‣ The book is on the table.
  ‣ The clipboard hangs on the wall.

- *In* specifies that one thing is contained within another.

  ‣ The solution is in the beaker.
  ‣ Liz is in San Francisco.

NOTE Many locations operate like *surfaces* or *containers*. Generally, use *in* for locations that seem like containers and *on* for locations that seem like surfaces.

CONTAINER　He sat in his car. [**Not:** *He sat on his car*, which would mean he was on top of it.]

SURFACE　He sat on the bus. [Buses, trains, and airplanes are usually considered surfaces because people can walk around on them.]

CONTAINER　We walked in the hallway.

SURFACE　We walked on the sidewalk.

Quick

Reference   Common Single-Word and Multiword Prepositions

Single-Word Prepositions

about	beneath	like	to
above	beside	near	toward
across	between	of	under
after	by	off	underneath
against	down	on	until
along	during	onto	up
among	except	out	upon
around	for	outside	with
at	from	over	within
before	in	past	without
behind	inside	since	
below	into	through	

Multiword Prepositions

according to	by means of	in front of	on account of
ahead of	close to	in place of	on behalf of
as far as	due to	inside of	on top of
aside from	far from	in spite of	out of
as to	in accordance with	instead of	outside of
as well as	in addition to	near to	
because of	in case of	next to	

Quick

Reference   Learning the Functions of Prepositions

Common functions of prepositions include the following:

1. To indicate *location* (427)
2. To indicate *time* (428)
3. To indicate *condition* or *degree* (429)
4. To specify *cause* or *reason* (429)
5. To designate *possession, attribute*, or *origin* (430)

2. Time 表示时间

The most commonly used prepositions for relating things to a moment in or period of time are *at, in, on*, and *by*.

- *At* designates a particular point in time.
  - ‣ Let's meet at 4:00.
  - ‣ The party ended at midnight.

- *In* can designate either a future time or a particular period.
  - ‣ I'll leave in 10 minutes.
  - ‣ We'll finish the job in April.

- *On* designates a particular day or date.
  - ‣ His birthday is on Friday.
  - ‣ Her birthday is on the twelfth.

- *By* indicates *no later than*.
  - ‣ Turn in your essay by 3:00 p.m.
  - ‣ They decided to leave by 5:00 a.m. to avoid rush hour.

3. Condition/Degree 表示条件/程度

Prepositions of condition or degree indicate the state of the object. Some common prepositions in this category are *in, on, of, around,* and *about.*

- *In* or *on* can specify a condition. These uses are often idiomatic.
  - ‣ The house is on fire.
  - ‣ She is on vacation.
  - ‣ Charlie is not in trouble.
  - ‣ Darlene left her desk in perfect order.

- *Of* is used in phrases indicating fractions or portions.
  - ‣ Three of the books are required for the course.
  - ‣ One of those coats is mine.

- *Around* or *about* can indicate approximation.
  - ‣ That book costs around twenty dollars.
  - ‣ I walked about ten miles.

4. Cause/Reason 表示原因/理由

Prepositions showing cause include *from, for, of,* and *because of.*

- *From* indicates cause or explains a condition.
  - ‣ We were wet from the rain.
  - ‣ We were tired from walking all day.

- *For* often indicates a cause and answers the question *Why?*
  - ‣ Oregon is famous for its forests.
  - ‣ She got an award for selling more cars than anyone else.

- *Of* and *because of* both show a reason.
  - ‣ The patient died of pneumonia.
  - ‣ I sneezed because of my cold.

5. Possession/Attribute/Origin 表示拥有/属性/起源

The most commonly used prepositions showing possession, attribute, or origin are *of*, *with*, and *from*.

- Possession is typically shown with *of*.

  ‣ That song is one *of* Wilco's.
  ‣ The composer *of* the song is Jay Bennett.

- An attribute can be indicated by *with*.

  ‣ He was a man *with* real talent.
  ‣ He is the one *with* the red beard.

- *From* can show origin.

  ‣ Bennett was *from* Illinois.
  ‣ The CD came *from* a website.

NOTE Indicating possession with *of* instead of *'s* or *s'* is often awkward.

AWKWARD   the bike of Maria

PREFERRED   Maria's bike

50c Using Prepositions Correctly 正确使用介词

Certain verbs or nouns suggest the use of particular prepositions. It may help to memorize these phrases:

- ‣ *give* something *to* someone
- ‣ *take* something *from* someone
- ‣ *sell* something *to* someone
- ‣ *buy* something *from* someone
- ‣ *lend* something *to* someone
- ‣ *borrow* something *from* someone
- ‣ get *married* or *engaged to* someone
- ‣ *fill* something *with* something
- ‣ *shout to* someone (in greeting)
- ‣ *shout at* someone (in anger)

In addition, some prepositions serve a particular grammatical function. For example, in the passive voice, the preposition *by* identifies who or what did something.

> **More about**
> Passive voice,
> 288–89, 302–
> 03, 341
> Direct and indirect
> objects, 340–42,
> 408–09

‣ The car was repaired *by* Pat.

Similarly, indirect objects, when placed after rather than before a direct object, are usually preceded by *to*.

‣ Theo gave the present *to* his father.

50d **Learning When Prepositions Are Needed** 学习介词的用法

Unfortunately, there is no rule of grammar to tell when a preposition is needed. Consider these examples:

- ▶ I like to listen ^*to* music.

- ▶ She was looking ^*at* the book.

Similarly, there is no rule to tell when one is not needed.

- ▶ ~~In~~ *One* ~~one~~ block from the school, there is a coffee shop.

- ▶ We were discussing ~~about~~ climate change in class.

To make things more complicated, sometimes a phrase is acceptable with or without a preposition.

- ▶ I've lived here for six years.

- ▶ I've lived here six years.

One strategy for mastering these usages, some of them idiomatic, is to notice in your reading when you encounter unfamiliar constructions involving prepositions. Some students keep a grammar log or other notebook to help them remember these constructions.

12 Detail 关注细节

Matters

Punctuation and Mechanics 标点符号与技术性细节

Use part 12 to learn, practice, and master these writer's responsibilities:

❑ **To Audience**

Convey your meaning clearly with the appropriate use of commas and other punctuation, avoid contractions in formal writing, confine online abbreviations and other shortcuts to informal communication, and choose italics only sparingly for emphasis.

❑ **To Other Writers**

Use *[sic]* with sensitivity when identifying another writer's error.

❑ **To Topic**

Use quotation marks when you borrow language from a source.

❑ **To Yourself**

Check your punctuation and spelling carefully to demonstrate careful attention to detail.

51 Using Commas 使用逗号

Commas function as dividers within—but not between—sentences. Think of each sentence as a room. If the periods are walls between these rooms, the commas are screens used to make subdivisions within a room. Just as a screen might set off a dressing area from a larger bedroom, a comma sets off information inside the main sentence. Problems with commas can be caused not only by omitting them but also by inserting them where they are *not* needed: Imagine having a screen in your kitchen between your stove and refrigerator.

51a Using Commas with *And, But, Or, Nor, For, So, or Yet* in Compound Sentences
逗号与And、But、Or、Nor、For、So或Yet一起用于复合句中

In a *compound sentence* a comma and a *coordinating conjunction* (*and, but, or, nor, for, so,* or *yet*) work together: The comma marks the break between the two *independent clauses*, and the coordinating conjunction joins them into a single sentence. When a coordinating conjunction combines two independent clauses, place a comma *before* it (not *after* it).

▶ My heart is in San Francisco, but my body is in New York.
(independent clause) (coord. conj.) (independent clause)

NOTE Unless readers will be confused, the comma can be omitted when the two independent clauses are very short.

▶ I sing in Italian but I speak only English.

> **compound sentence** 并列句 Two or more independent clauses linked by a comma and a coordinating conjunction or a semicolon

> **independent (or main) clause** 独立分句 A clause that can stand alone as a sentence

Writing Responsibly — Commas and Clarity

Incorrect comma use can distort the meaning of a sentence. Consider this example, with and without commas:

This sentence . . .	means . . .
Writing to my mother is a terrible chore.	I find writing to my mother a real pain!
Writing, to my mother, is a terrible chore.	My mother finds writing a real pain!

You have a responsibility to your reader to look carefully at your use of commas when editing a document. Ask yourself, "Does this say what I intended?" If the answer is no, correct your use of commas.

to AUDIENCE

Do not use a comma before the conjunction if each of the joined parts is not a complete sentence.

> independent clause   verb phrase
> ▸ My accountant left the country, **and** took my bank balance
>
> with him.

> pairs
> ▸ Both **my purse,** and my bank account are empty.

When the clauses are long and already contain commas, the sentence will be clearer if you use a semicolon instead of a comma before the coordinating conjunction.

> ▸ Comic books are gradually becoming more respectable as works of serious fiction, with graphic novels such as *Maus* and *Watchmen* earning tremendous critical acclaim; **yet** some people still refuse to take them seriously.

More about
Semicolons,
442–44
Comma splices,
353–57

NOTE Without a coordinating conjunction, a comma between two independent clauses creates a ***comma splice.***

51b Using Commas after Introductory Elements
逗号用于介绍性表达之后

A word, phrase, or subordinate clause introducing an independent clause is usually followed by a comma.

> introductory phrase   independent clause
> ▸ In an unguarded moment, the politician muttered an unprintable phrase into the live microphone.

> introductory subordinate clause   ind. clause
> ▸ Although Boythorn prided himself on his gruff demeanor, he doted on his pet bird.

subordinate clause
从句 A word group with a subject and predicate that acts as a noun or modifier within a sentence but that cannot stand alone as a sentence

phrase 短语 A group of related words that lacks a subject, predicate, or both; it cannot stand alone as a sentence, but it can function *in* a sentence as a noun, a verb, or a modifier

When an introductory element is very brief, some writers omit the comma. If readers might be confused, even for a moment, include it.

> ▸ Before eating the missionaries said grace.

EXCEPTIONS No comma follows an introductory word group that precedes the verb in an inverted sentence (one in which the subject follows the verb). Likewise, no comma follows an introductory word group that is the subject of the sentence.

> introductory word group   verb   subject
> ▸ Into the forbidding jungle marched Dr. Livingston.

> subject   verb
> ▸ Exploring forbidding jungles is what he does.

51c Using Commas to Set Off Conjunctive Adverbs and Most Transitional Phrases
连接副词和大多数过渡性短语用逗号隔开

Transitional expressions and *conjunctive adverbs* are usually set off by commas.

> The basking shark, in fact, consumes only zooplankton and small fish. It may end up as dinner for an orca or tiger shark, however.

When the transitional expression or conjunctive adverb is used to link independent clauses, place a semicolon before it.

> The whale shark is the largest fish in today's oceans; nevertheless, it presents no threat to humans.

> **transitional expressions** 过渡性短语 Words and phrases that link ideas within and between sentences

> **conjunctive adverb** 连接副词 A transitional expression that can link one independent clause to another

51d Inserting Commas to Set Off Interjections, Contrasting Information, Expressions of Direct Address, Parenthetical and Conversational Expressions, and Tag Questions
插入逗号：将感叹词、对比信息、直接称呼语表达、插入语、对话和附加疑问句隔开

> Wow, that wind farm is gorgeous!

> Some people, alas, think the industrial look of a wind farm is ugly.

> The current energy situation requires us to revise, not cling to, traditional notions of beauty.

> Professor Kinney, how much do you know about offshore wind farming?

> The first US offshore wind farm, it turns out, was on Nantucket Sound.

> No, wind farming alone isn't the solution to our energy problems.

> Wind farms will nevertheless make a big contribution, won't they?

51e Using Commas to Separate Items in a Series
连续项用逗号隔开

Place a comma between items in a series of three or more.

> Our new house will feature solar panels, a hilltop windmill, and rainwater conversion.

Some writers (particularly British writers) and many publications in the United States omit the comma before the coordinating conjunction (in this case *and*) that precedes the last element in a series. Readers, however, may find the final comma helpful in distinguishing paired and unpaired elements. The managing editor of the *Chicago Manual of Style* likes to quote this hypothetical dedication, which highlights the potential problems that can be caused by omitting the serial comma.

▸ I dedicate this book to my parents, Mother Teresa and the Pope.

▸ **More about**
Using semicolons
in a series, 443

When the items in the series are long or contain internal commas, substituting semicolons for commas can make the sentence easier to read.

▸ Phillis Wheatley was born in Senegal in 1753, was sold into slavery to a Boston, Massachusetts, family, studied Greek, Latin, and English, and became the first published African American writer.

51f Using Commas to Separate Coordinate, Not Cumulative, Adjectives 并列形容词用逗号隔开，累加形容词不用逗号隔开

Coordinate adjectives separately modify the noun or pronoun they precede and are of equal weight; *cumulative adjectives* modify not only the noun or pronoun they precede but also the next adjective in the series. Hence, changing the order of coordinate adjectives does not change their sense, but changing the order of cumulative adjectives usually results in nonsense.

Consider the following examples:

coordinate adjectives

▸ South Korea is a hot, humid country in the summer.
Hot and *humid* each equally modifies *country*. Changing their order (*humid, hot country*) or putting *and* between them (*hot and humid country*) does not change their sense.

Quick Reference   **Testing for Coordinate and Cumulative Adjectives**

To determine whether two or more adjectives should be separated by a comma, try these two tests:

1. **Place the word *and* between the two adjectives.** If the phrase still makes sense, then the adjectives are coordinate, and you should put a comma between them.

   Yes: sexy and exciting boyfriend
   No: enormous and shoulder bag

2. **Reverse the order.** If the meaning remains the same no matter what order they appear in, then the adjectives are coordinate, and you should insert a comma between them.

   Yes: sexy, exciting boyfriend = exciting, sexy boyfriend
   No: enormous shoulder bag ≠ shoulder enormous bag

cumulative adjectives

* His mother is a powerful corporate executive.
Powerful modifies *corporate*, and both modify *executive* together. It makes no sense to say *corporate powerful executive.*

coordinate adjectives

* The girl struggled to hide her brooding, moody nature from the

More about
Adjective order, 423

coordinate adjectives

sympathetic, insightful child psychologist she visited weekly.

cumulative adjectives

While you could reverse *brooding* and *moody* or *insightful* and *sympathetic*, you could not reverse *insightful* and *child*: A *child insightful psychologist* does not make sense.

51g Using Commas to Set Off Nonessential Appositives, Phrases, and Clauses
不重要的同位语、短语和从句用逗号隔开

Words, phrases, or clauses that add information to a sentence but do not identify the person, place, or thing being described are **nonessential** (or *nonrestrictive*) **elements** and should be set off by commas from the rest of the sentence. Words, phrases, or clauses that identify the person, place, or thing being described are **essential** (or *restrictive*) and should *not* be set off by commas.

essential nonessential

* My coworker Philip, whom I had never seen without a tie, arrived at the office this morning wearing yoga pants.

Philip picks out one coworker from among the rest, so that element is essential. *Whom I had never seen without a tie* provides important information about Philip but does not identify him from among the writer's colleagues, so it is nonessential.

Compare the sentence above to this sentence:

nonessential

* My coworker, Philip, showed up at work this morning wearing yoga pants.

In this sentence, *Philip* is set off by commas, suggesting that the writer has only one colleague, so identifying him by name is not essential.

1. Commas with nonessential appositives and other phrases
逗号与不重要的同位语及其他短语一起使用

An *appositive* renames a preceding noun phrase. When the appositive identifies, or specifies, the noun phrase, it is essential and is not set off by commas.

noun phrase essential appositive

* The Roman emperor Claudius suffered from an ailment that caused him to limp and to stammer uncontrollably.

appositive 同位语 A noun or noun phrase that renames the noun, pronoun, or noun phrase that precedes it

In this case, *Claudius* distinguishes this Roman emperor from all the other Roman emperors, so it is essential and should not be set off by commas.

When the appositive adds information but does not identify, it is nonessential and is set off by commas.

> noun phrase　　　nonessential appositive
> ▸ The fourth Roman emperor, Claudius, suffered from an ailment that caused him to limp and to stammer uncontrollably.

Because there was only one *fourth Roman emperor,* the name *Claudius* is nonessential.

A phrase that acts like an adjective, modifying a noun, pronoun, or noun phrase, can also be essential or nonessential. If it identifies what it is describing, then it is essential and should *not* be set off by commas; if it does not identify this item, then it is nonessential and *should* be set off by commas.

> noun　　　nonessential phrase
> ▸ The girl, asked by her father to behave, said, "I am behaving."

> noun　　　essential phrase
> ▸ The girl asked by her father to behave is my niece.

2. Commas with nonessential clauses 逗号与不重要的从句一起使用

A subordinate (or dependent) clause can also act like an adjective, modifying a noun, pronoun, or noun phrase. When it identifies the noun, pronoun, or noun phrase, the clause is essential and is *not* set off by commas; when it does not, it is nonessential and *is* set off by commas.

That *clauses versus* **which** *clauses* Subordinate clauses beginning with the word *that* are always essential and thus never set off by commas.

> essential clause
> ▸ Produce that has been genetically modified differs from its non-GM counterpart by a human-made alteration to its DNA.

The word *which,* by comparison, is used today to introduce both essential and nonessential clauses.

> nonessential clause
> ▸ Genetically modified produce, which is sold in grocery stores throughout the United States, is still looked on with suspicion by many consumers.

NOTE Some writers (and instructors), especially in the United States, believe *which* should be used exclusively with nonessential clauses.

Adverb clauses If an adverb clause appears at the beginning of a sentence, it is usually set off by a comma. Most adverb clauses are essential and are not set off by a comma when they fall at the end of a sentence.

nonessential adv. clause

▸ Because he found the politics required to win an Academy Award
demeaning, George C. Scott refused to accept an Oscar for his
performance in the movie *Patton*.

▸ George C. Scott refused to accept an Academy Award for his
performance in the movie *Patton* because he found the politics
required to win an Oscar demeaning.

Adverb clauses beginning with words like *although* and *whereas* that present contrasting information are usually nonessential and are set off by a
comma when they fall at the end of a sentence.

51h Using Commas with Quotations 逗号与引语一起使用

In most cases, separate a *direct quotation* from a *signal phrase* with a
comma.

▸ After learning that he had been appointed poet laureate, Charles
Simic exclaimed, "I'm almost frightened to get out of bed—too
much good luck in one week."

Exceptions

■ When the quotation begins the sentence and ends with a question mark or exclamation point, no comma should be added.

▸ "When shall we three meet again, in thunder, lightning, or in
rain?" asks the first witch in Shakespeare's *Macbeth* (1.1.1–2).

■ When the quotation is integrated into your own sentence, omit
the comma.

▸ Friar Lawrence warns Romeo that "these violent delights have
violent ends" *Romeo and Juliet* (2.6.9).

■ When the signal phrase is incorporated into a complete sentence
that makes sense without the quotation, use a colon before the
quotation.

▸ Hamlet exits the graveyard scene with a veiled threat: "The
cat will mew, and dog will have his day" *Hamlet* (5.1.298).

Indirect quotations should *not* be set off by commas.

■ New poet laureate Charles Simic confessed that having so much
good luck worried him.

---

direct quotation 直接
引语 The exact words
someone has used;
direct quotations must
be placed in quota-
tion marks to avoid
plagiarism

signal phrase 信号短
语 A noun or pronoun
plus an appropriate
verb identifying the
writer from whom you
are borrowing words
or ideas

indirect quotation 间接
引语 A quotation that
has been paraphrased
(put into the writer's
own words), instead of
taken word-for-word
from the source

51i Using Commas with Numbers, Names and Titles, Place Names and Addresses, and Dates
逗号与数字、姓名和头衔、地名和地址以及日期一起使用

Numbers, names and titles, place names and addresses, and dates are each punctuated according to specialized conventions, some of which vary from one community or discipline to another.

> **More about**
> Numbers, 472–73

1. In numbers 在数字中

The following conventions are standard in most American English usage.

- In four-digit numbers, using a comma to mark divisions of hundreds is optional, except with years, when no comma should be included.
  - ▸ The company paid $9347 for those supplies in 2016.
  - ▸ The company paid $9,347 for those supplies in 2016.
- In numbers of five digits or more, a comma is used to mark divisions of hundreds.
  - ▸ Workers have filed 93,471 unemployment claims since January.

2. Between personal names and titles 在个人姓名与头衔之间

Use a comma to separate a personal name from a title that follows it.

- ▸ Send the request to Janet Woodcock, director of the Center for Drug Evaluation and Research.

Use no comma when a title precedes the name or when the "title" consists of Roman numerals.

- ▸ Send the request to Doctor Janet Woodcock.
- ▸ My son will be named Albert Farnsworth IV.

The titles Jr. and Sr. may appear with or without commas.

- ▸ Ken Griffey, Jr., appears in the *Simpsons* episode "Homer at the Bat."
- ▸ Ken Griffey Jr. appears in the *Simpsons* episode "Homer at the Bat."

3. In place names and addresses 在地名与地址之间

Use a comma to separate names of cities from states, provinces, regions, or countries.

- ▸ Boston, Massachusetts, was the birthplace of Benjamin Franklin. Franklin also lived for several years in London, England, and Paris, France. He died at age eighty-four in Philadelphia, Pennsylvania.

Do *not* place a comma between the name of a state and the zip code.

- ▸ The Franklin Institute, founded to honor Benjamin Franklin, is located at 222 North 20th Street, Philadelphia, Pennsylvania 19103.

4. In dates 在日期中

Use commas to set off dates in which the day follows the month and when dates include the time of day or the day of the week.

▸ I will never forget that my son was born at 5:17 a.m.ˌ Tuesdayˌ March 17ˌ 2009.

No comma is needed in dates when only the month and year are used or when the day *precedes* the month.

▸ My niece was born in Februaryˌ2015.

▸ Her exact birth date is 13 February 2015.

51j Using Commas to Avoid Ambiguity 使用逗号，避免歧义

A comma can separate ideas that might otherwise be misinterpreted, and it can also mark places where words have been deleted.

1. To separate ideas 分隔概念

When two ideas could be misread as a single unit, add a comma to separate the two.

▸ My friends who can afford toˌtake taxis frequently.
⌃

2. To replace omitted words and avoid repetition 替换省略的词，避免重复

Replace a repeated word with a comma after its first use:

▸ I vacationed in the Adirondacks and my brotherˌ ~~vacationed~~ in British Columbia.
⌃

51k Avoiding Commas between Subjects and Verbs, Verbs and Objects 避免在主语和谓语动词、谓语动词和宾语之间使用逗号

A single comma should not separate a subject from its verb or a verb from its object unless another rule calls for it.

▸ The Senate Finance Committeeˌ is the focus of much attention.
  [subject]   [verb]

▸ The committee must explainˌ its decision to a nervous public.
              [verb] [object]

Text Credit

p. 439 Simic, Charles, quoted in "Simic Reflects on Poet Laureate Honor," *NPR Weekend Edition Sunday*, August 5, 2007.

52 Using Semicolons 使用分号

"I think Lassie is trying to tell us something, ma."

© Gerard Whyman/CartoonStock

Although it has other uses, the semicolon's main function is to link two independent clauses into a single sentence. The semicolon, however, is seldom the only option for this job. You can also usually combine independent clauses with a comma and a coordinating conjunction, you can divide them into separate sentences with a period, or you can revise to make one clause subordinate to the other. What makes the semicolon useful is the signal it sends. It tells the reader that the linked clauses are of equal importance and have a close, logical relationship.

52a Using a Semicolon to Link Closely Related Independent Clauses 用分号连接密切相关的独立分句

> **independent (or main) clause** 独立分句 A clause that can stand alone as a sentence

A semicolon is a good choice for linking two *independent clauses* when both are of equal weight and the second relates closely to the first. For example, the second clause might give a reason for the first, restate its meaning, or introduce a contrast to it.

GIVING A REASON

————— independent clause 1 —————

My grandparents' grandparents immigrated to this country in 1895;

————— independent clause 2 —————

they were seeking a better life for themselves and their children.

RESTATING MEANING

————— independent clause 1 —————

In the more than one hundred years since our immigrant ancestors

————— independent clause 2 —————

arrived, our family has grown and dispersed; I have dozens of cousins

who live in almost every region of the country.

INTRODUCING CONTRAST

————— independent clause 1 —————

My ancestors took months to journey from the land of their birth to

————— independent clause 2 —————

their new home; we can make the return journey in hours.

> **More about**
> Parallelism, 290–93
> Commas, 433–41
> End punctuation, 453–55
> Coordinating conjunctions, 295, 356

Writing Responsibly Sending a Signal with Semicolons

Randomly using the semicolon to connect independent clauses can lead readers to see a connection between ideas that the writer did not intend. Consider this sentence: *Angelina is working in New York; Brad has a headache.* The semicolon here suggests that there is a logical relationship between the two clauses, that one is the cause or effect of the other, when in fact the two may reflect mere coincidence. Avoid conveying more than you mean; use the semicolon with care.

to TOPIC

52b Using a Semicolon with a Conjunctive Adverb or a Transitional Phrase to Link Two Independent Clauses 分号与连接副词或过渡性短语一起使用，连接两个独立分句

More about
Conjunctive adverbs (list), 335
Transitional words and phrases (list), 31

A semicolon can also join two independent clauses when the second clause begins with or includes a conjunctive adverb (such as *therefore, however,* and *furthermore*) or a transitional phrase such as *in addition* or *for example.* A comma should follow the conjunctive adverb or transitional phrase when it begins the clause and should set it off on both sides when it falls within the clause.

▶ *Shakespeare in Love* introduced the playwright to a new
generation of moviegoers; **moreover,** it was an entertaining film.
semi. + conj. adv. + comma

▶ Film is a popular form of entertainment; it can be, **in addition,**
a means of exploring literature's classic themes in contemporary contexts.
semi.　　comma + trans. + comma

52c Using a Semicolon to Separate Items in a Series When the Items Have Internal Punctuation 当项目内部有标点符号时，使用分号分隔连续项

Ordinarily, commas separate items in a series. Use semicolons, however, when the items are especially long or complex or when one or more of the items in the series has internal punctuation.

▶ The architectural firm of Hanover, Harvey, and Witkins recommends

creating an off-grid home by building with straw bales; packing them
①

tightly, which makes them flame-resistant; utilizing solar power; and
②　　　　　　　　　　　　　　　　　③

generating additional energy through windmills on the property.
④

52d Using a Semicolon to Repair a Comma Splice or a Fused Sentence 使用分号纠正逗号粘连句和融合句

A semicolon can repair a *comma splice* (two independent clauses improperly joined with a comma alone) or a *fused sentence* (two independent clauses joined without any punctuation).

More about
Comma splices
and fused sen-
tences, 353–57

- Reporters Without Borders fights restrictions placed on journalists; the group also raises awareness about this increasingly important issue.

52e Avoiding Misusing Semicolons 避免误用分号

Do not use a semicolon to link an independent clause to a phrase, subordinate clause, or anything except another, related independent clause.

independent clause   phrase
- That new Harry Potter film proved successful; grossing $22 million in the first night.

Use a colon, not a semicolon, to introduce a list.

list
- On our vacation we visited the following national parks; Yosemite, Grand Teton, and Glen Canyon.

53

Using Apostrophes 使用所有格符号

Apostrophes, like patches on torn clothing, replace something that is missing: Patches replace missing fabric; apostrophes replace letters in contractions (*can't, ma'am*). Apostrophes also make nouns and indefinite pronouns possessive (*Edward's* or *somebody's horse*).

53a Using Apostrophes to Indicate Possession
使用所有格符号表示所属

The possessive form of a noun or pronoun indicates ownership. In spoken English, the possessive form of most nouns and indefinite pronouns ends with an *s* sound. Written English marks the possessive form with an apostrophe plus an *-s: Yue's violin, someone's book.*

noun 名词 A word that names ideas, things, qualities, actions, people, and places

1. With singular nouns and indefinite pronouns (but not personal pronouns) 用于单数名词和不定代词（而非人称代词）

Singular *nouns* and *indefinite pronouns* add an apostrophe and an *-s* to indicate possession.

indefinite pronouns
不定代词 Pronouns that do not refer to specific people or things, such as *all, anybody, either, everybody, few, many, neither, no one, someone*

- The factory's smokestacks belched thick, black smoke.

- No one's health was unaffected.

Even for most singular nouns that already end in *-s*, add an *-'s.*

- Dolores's asthma was particularly aggravated.

Writing Responsibly | Contractions in Formal Writing

Contractions and other abbreviations provide useful shortcuts in speech and in informal writing, and they are finding their way into more formal academic and business writing. They are still not fully accepted, however. To determine whether contractions will be acceptable to your audience or undermine your authoritative tone, check with your instructor, look for contractions in academic journals in your field, or consult reports or business letters written by other company employees. If you have any doubt about whether a contraction is appropriate, spell the words out.

to SELF

Add an apostrophe alone to a singular noun or pronoun only when adding an *-'s* would make the word difficult to pronounce.

▸ Socrates꞉ pneumonia became so serious he had to be hospitalized.

Never use an apostrophe to make a ***personal pronoun*** possessive. The personal pronouns all have their own possessive forms: *my, mine, your, yours, her, hers, his, its, our, ours, their, theirs.*

> ▸ We regret that ~~you're~~ *your* new power plant will have to close, but ~~they're~~ *their* health is more important.

personal pronouns 人称代词 Pronouns that replace specific nouns or noun phrases, such as *I, me, he, him, she, her, it, we, us, you, they, them*

Be especially careful with *its.*

- *It's* (*it is*) is a contraction like *don't* (*do not*) and *can't* (*cannot*).

- *Its* is a ***possessive pronoun*** like *his* and *hers.*

If you tend to confuse *it's* and *its,* remember that the contraction always takes an apostrophe, but the personal pronoun never does.

> ▸ The restaurant serves Italian cuisine at *its* best, so *it's* a good idea to call ahead for reservations.

possessive *contraction*

possessive pronouns 物主代词 Pronouns that indicate ownership, such as *my, his, hers, yours, mine, theirs*

2. With plural nouns 用于复数名词

To make plural nouns possessive, first form the plural and then form the possessive. When the plural form ends in *-s,* just add an apostrophe; when it does not end in *-s,* add an apostrophe and *-s.*

Tech | Apostrophes and Spelling or Grammar Checkers

Be wary of apostrophe-related "errors" identified by your device's spelling or grammar checker. These programs usually do a good job of automatically inserting apostrophes in contractions such as *don't,* but too often they erroneously change *its* to *it's,* and they do not automatically insert apostrophes for possessive proper nouns such as *Matthew's.* Pay attention to the program's suggestions, but always double-check them for accuracy.

Singular	Plural	Possessive
lady	ladies	ladies'
person	people	people's

- By midnight, the ladies' maids were exhausted.

- I'm often amazed by people's consideration for the well-being of others.

This rule applies to family names that end in -s, too: Make the name plural and then possessive.

- *Williamses'*
  The ~~Williams~~ parties always ended at dawn.

NOTE Just because a word ends with an -s does not mean that it needs an apostrophe. Delete apostrophes from plural nouns and singular verbs.

- noun (plu.)   verb (sing.)
  Your dog's bark wildly, but my cat remain's placid.)

---

3. To indicate joint or individual ownership or possession 表示共同或个人拥有或占有

First, decide whether the apostrophe indicates *joint* or *individual ownership*. When the nouns share possession, make only the last noun possessive.

- We all enjoy Mikel and Laetitia's parties.

  They give the parties collaboratively.

When the nouns each possess the same object, quality, or event, make each noun possessive.

- Mikel's and Laetitia's jobs don't leave them much free time.

  They have different jobs.

4. With compound nouns 用于复合名词

Although in a compound noun, number (singular or plural) is usually attached to the core noun, the possessive is attached to the last noun.

- core (plural)
  Jeremiah is driving his sisters-in-law crazy.

  Jeremiah has more than one sister-in-law, and he is driving them all crazy. Attach number to the core noun, *sister*.

- last (possessive)
  Jeremiah is driving his sister-in-law's car.

  Jeremiah is using the car belonging to his sister-in-law; attach possession to the last noun, *law*.

- core (plural) last (possessive)
  Jeremiah has his sisters-in-law's unwavering support.

Jeremiah has more than one sister-in-law, and he has their unwavering support; attach the plural to the core noun (*sisters*) and possession to the last noun (*law's*).

53b Using Apostrophes in Contractions and Abbreviated Years 在缩略词和缩写年份中使用所有格符号

An apostrophe can stand in place of missing letters or numbers in a contraction or in an abbreviated year.

▸ I am	I'm	▸ Cannot	Can't
▸ He is, she is	He's, she's	▸ Could not Would not	Couldn't Wouldn't
▸ It is/has	It's	▸ Let us	Let's
▸ They are	They're	▸ Who is	Who's
▸ You are	You're	▸ 2012	'12

53c Avoiding, in General, Using Apostrophes to Form Plurals of Abbreviations, Dates, Numbers, and Words or Letters Used as Words 一般应避免使用所有格符号来构成缩写、日期、数字以及以词的形式出现的单词或字母的复数形式

Until recently, adding -'*s* was an accepted way to form the plural for abbreviations, dates, and words or characters used as words, but this practice seems to be falling out of fashion. Unless the style guide you use instructs otherwise, do not use apostrophes to form these plurals.

▸ My brother has stayed in more YMCA's than anyone else I know.

▸ Van Gogh's paintings were first exhibited in the late 1880's.

▸ Now he minds the *p*'s and *q*'s of students in composition classes.

▸ His students give him 5's on his evaluations.

You can, however, use an apostrophe to form a plural letter if its absence might cause confusion.

may be misread as *is*

CONFUSING You've dotted your *is* and crossed your *ts*.

CLEAR　　You've dotted your *i*'s and crossed your *t*'s.

Add the apostrophe to *t*'s for consistency's sake.

NOTE The Modern Language Association (MLA) still recommends the use of an apostrophe with the plurals of letters.

Now he minds the *p*'s and *q*'s of students in composition classes.

———————————

54 Using Quotation Marks 使用引号

Indicating who said what is an important use of quotation marks. Failing to indicate—whether accidentally or on purpose—that words were spoken or written by others leaves a writer open to charges of plagiarism. Misusing quotation marks can also confuse or annoy readers. Learning when to use—and when *not* to use—quotation marks is an important part of a writer's responsibilities.

...IS IT BECAUSE I'M NOT "HANDSOME", "RICH", OR "WELL-DRESSED"?

IF ONLY YOU DIDN'T PUT QUOTATION MARKS AROUND EVERYTHING...

©2003 Stivers
©2003 Stivers. November 20, 2003
www.markstivers.com

54a Setting Off Direct Quotations with Quotation Marks 用引号标注直接引用

1. Direct versus indirect quotations 直接引用和间接引用

Double quotation marks ("") indicate the beginning and end of direct quotations (someone's exact words, whether written or spoken).

▸ Of grappling with the unknown, Albert Einstein wrote this: "The most beautiful thing we can experience is the mysterious. It is the source of all true art and all science."

Single quotation marks ('') indicate quotations within quotations.

▸ Barbara Jordan, the first African American woman to represent a southern state in Congress, felt that when the Constitution was written, she "was not included in that 'We, the people.'"

> **More about**
> Paraphrasing,
> 124–26

Indirect quotations, which paraphrase someone's words, do *not* use quotation marks.

▸ Albert Einstein said that "the unknown inspires scientists as well as artists."

2. Dialog 对话

When quoting dialog, start a new paragraph each time the speaker changes, and put all spoken words in quotation marks.

▸ "Have you brought women here before?" He smiled and kept chewing, so I said, "Do you always use the same tricks?"

"What tricks?" He looked at me like he didn't understand.
—Leslie Marmon Silko, "Yellow Woman"

If one speaker continues for more than a paragraph, use quotation marks at the beginning of each paragraph, but omit closing quotation marks until the end of the speech.

3. Long quotations 大段引文

For lengthy quotations, omit quotation marks, and indent quotations in a block from the left margin.

▶ Lucio Guerrero examines how local Goths feel about their lifestyle's mass-market appeal:

> For some, that suburbanization of Goth may be what saves the subculture. "If someone who identifies as Goth doesn't have easy access to the fashion or accouterments that they feel drawn to, but they do have access to a store like Hot Topic, then it's a positive thing," said Scary Lady Sarah, a local DJ and supporter of Chicago's Goth community.
>
> —Lucio Guerrero, "Like a GOTH," *Chicago Sun-Times*, September 16, 2005

> Generally, introduce block quotations with a complete sentence plus a colon.

> In block quotations, use double quotation marks for quotations within a quotation.

Quotation Marks in American English Use of quotation marks varies from place to place and from culture to culture. In contemporary American English, double quotation marks signal a quotation, and single quotation marks signal a quotation within a quotation:

▶ John complained, "For the third time this month, Mary said, 'I need a few bucks to tide me over until payday.' And it's only June 15!"

Quick Reference **Common Quotation Mark Do's and Don'ts**

Do use quotation marks . . .

. . . **to set off direct quotations. (448)**
▶ Eisenhower once said that any person "who wants to be president is either an egomaniac or crazy."

. . . **to indicate irony (use sparingly). (451)**
▶ After an unsuccessful stint as president of Columbia University, Eisenhower let himself be "persuaded" to run for the US presidency.

. . . **to refer to words as words. (451)**
▶ "Popular" is an adjective often attached to Eisenhower's presidency.

(Italics are also widely used for this purpose.)

Do not use quotation marks . . .

. . . **to set off indirect quotations (paraphrases). (448)**
▶ Eisenhower once said that "lunatics or narcissists are the only people who would desire the presidency."

. . . **for emphasis. (451)**
▶ Eisenhower was a five-star general and "Supreme" Commander of Allied forces in Europe during World War II.

. . . **with slang or clichés. (451)**
▶ "Snafus" occur regularly in the army, but Eisenhower generally avoided them through careful planning.

In formal contexts, consider recasting to avoid slang. Clichés are rarely appropriate; rewrite to avoid them.

British usage is the opposite and would be considered wrong in the United States:

> John complained, "For the third time this month, Mary said, "I need a few bucks to tide me over until payday." And it's only June 15!"

4. Quotations from poetry 引用诗句

More about
Formatting block quotations, 165, 200 (MLA style), 243 (APA style)

When quoting one to three lines of poetry, use quotation marks and run the lines into your text. Indicate the end of each line by inserting a slash with a space on each side.

> Shelley sets the tone right away. The violence in lines 3–4 ("Millions to fight compell'd, to fight or die / In mangled heaps on War's red altar lie") is a clear criticism of the ruling class into which he was born.

When quoting four or more lines, omit quotation marks, set the poetry as a block, and retain the original line breaks.

> Shakespeare's "Sonnet 147" begins with evocative imagery:
>
> My love is a fever, longing still
>
> For that which longer nurseth the disease,
>
> Feeding on that which doth preserve the ill,
>
> Th' uncertain sickly appetite to please. (lines 1–4)

54b Indicating the Titles of Short Works with Quotation Marks
用引号标明短篇作品的标题

More about
Italicizing titles of longer works, 466

Most American style guides suggest placing titles of short works in quotation marks and titles of long works in italics.

> Lahiri's short story "Year's End" appeared in the collection *Unaccustomed Earth.*

> "Front Lines," a poem by Gary Snyder, is from his book *No Nature.*

> Ben Brantley's review of *Romeo and Juliet,* "Rash and Unadvis'd Seeks Same," ran in *The New York Times.*

> *Outlander* is my guilty pleasure; "The Wedding" is my favorite episode.

More about
Citing and documenting sources 157–211 (MLA style, part 6), 213–54 (APA style, part 7), 256–71 (*Chicago* style, ch. 27), 272–84 (CSE style, ch. 28)

> The podcast "Of Two Minds, One Consciousness" from the *Scientific American* website uses results from split-brain studies to explore thought.

> "Good for You," from Selena Gomez's album *Revival,* reached the top of the Billboard charts.

In APA, CSE, and *The Chicago Manual of Style* parenthetical style, omit quotation marks from the titles of short works in bibliographic entries.

54c Using Quotation Marks to Indicate Words Used in a Special Sense 用引号表示具有特殊意义的词

Quotation marks can call attention to words used in a special sense. When talking *about* a word, enclose it in quotation marks to avoid confusion.

> ▸ Many people confuse "lay" and "lie."

Italics can also be used for this purpose.

To signal that you are using a word ironically or sarcastically, place it in quotation marks.

> ▸ I didn't know that the Indian "problem" on the plains began in the 1860s. . . .
>
> —James Welch, *Killing Custer*

Overusing quotation marks in this way, however, can annoy readers. Your words should usually be able to convey irony on their own.

Set a term to be defined in italics and the definition in quotation marks.

> ▸ Many writers don't realize that *e.g.* stands for "for example" in Latin.

54d Avoiding the Misuse of Quotation Marks 避免误用引号

- Do not use quotation marks for emphasis.
  - ▸ Beyoncé's debut album was ~~"amazing,"~~ hitting number 1 on the *Billboard* charts in its first week.

More about
Using italics for emphasis, 467

- Do not use quotation marks for slang. If slang is acceptable in a particular context, use it without the apology that quotation marks represent; if not, replace it with a more appropriate word or phrase.
  - ▸ "Writing's on the Wall" won the Academy Award for best original song in 2016, ~~"beating out"~~ ^besting^ several strong contenders.
- Do not justify the use of a cliché by enclosing it in quotation marks. Instead, avoid the cliché.
  - ▸ I left the party before ~~the "sun was over the yardarm."~~ ^drinks were served.^

54e Positioning Quotation Marks Correctly with Punctuation 引号与其他标点符号的位置

More about
Periods, 453–54
Commas, 433–41
Question marks, 454
Exclamation points, 455
Dashes, 456

Whether punctuation appears before or after the closing quotation mark depends on the punctuation mark.

1. With periods and commas 与句点和逗号一起使用

In American English, commas and periods go *inside* the closing quotation mark, except when a citation follows the quotation.

More about
Citing indirect
sources, 172
(MLA), 225 (APA)

▸ "Sacred cows," said the sixties radical Abbie Hoffman, "make the tastiest hamburger."

▸ According to sixties radical Abbie Hoffman, "Sacred cows make the tastiest hamburger" (qtd. in Albert 43).

Commas and Periods with Quotation Marks In many countries that use the roman alphabet, commas and periods follow rather than precede the closing quotation mark. Since American English requires that commas and periods come before the closing quotation mark, be sure to adjust your usage to meet readers' expectations.

2. With question marks, exclamation points, and dashes
与问号、感叹号和破折号一起使用

Question marks, exclamation points, and dashes go *inside* the closing quotation mark when they are part of the quotation.

▸ In Megan Mayhew Bergman's short story "The Siege at Whale Cay," Marlene asks, "You like girls with guns, don't you, Joe?"

They go *outside* the closing quotation mark when they are not:

▸ Why does Robert Duvall's character in *Apocalypse Now* (1979) say "I love the smell of napalm in the morning"? He explains that "it smells like victory"!

3. With colons and semicolons 与冒号和分号一起使用

Colons and semicolons go outside the closing quotation mark.

▸ "I was not going to ask for mercy"; so wrote Cheryl Strayed in *Wild*.

▸ "Lions and tigers and bears": These are the only problems Dorothy does not encounter on her yellow-brick road to self-knowledge.

54f **Introducing and Identifying Quotations**
引出引文并确定引文位置

More about
Clauses, 344–45

Use a colon to introduce a quotation if the clause preceding the quotation could stand on its own as a sentence and could make sense without the quotation.

▸ Darwin's own words clarify the issue: "It is not the strongest of the species that survive . . . but the ones most responsive to change."

Writing Responsibly   Using Quotations Fairly

More about
Plagiarism, 121–30
Patchwriting,
124–28

You have a responsibility to your reader and to other writers to supply quotation marks whenever you borrow language from a source. Omitting quotation marks when they are needed can mislead your readers and undermine your reputation as a writer to be trusted.

to OTHER WRITERS

Use a comma with signal phrases such as "Darwin said" or "she wrote."

signal phrase
▸ Charles Darwin said, "It is not the strongest of the species that survive . . . but the ones most responsive to change."

More about
Using signal phrases, 137–38, 218

Use no punctuation if the quotation is needed to complete the sentence (as when the word *that* precedes it), and do not capitalize the first word in the quotation.

▸ Darwin asserts that "[i]t is not the strongest of the species that survive . . . but the ones most responsive to change."

If a signal phrase interrupts the quotation, insert a comma before the closing quotation mark and after the signal phrase.

signal phrase
▸ "It is not the strongest of the species that survive," Darwin asserts, ". . . but the ones most responsive to change."

Text Credits

p. 448 *Storyteller.* New York: Seaver Books, 1981. **p. 451** Welch, James, with Paul Stekler, *Killing Custer: The Battle of Little Bighorn and the Fate of the Plains Indians.* New York: W.W. Norton, 1994. **p. 452** Bergman, Megan Mayhew, "The Siege at Whale Cay," *The Kenyon Review,* Fall 2014, Volume XXXVI, Number 4; Strayed, Cheryl, *Wild: From Lost to Found on the Pacific Crest Trail.* New York: Alfred A. Knopf, 2013.

55 Using End Punctuation
Periods, Question Marks, and Exclamation Points
使用句末标点
句点、问号和感叹号

Imagine that each of the people in these photographs has just uttered the words "you're here." Just by looking at their faces, can you guess who was perplexed, thrilled, or neutral? In face-to-face encounters, sight and sound play a huge role in how we interpret tone and meaning, but in a written text, we depend on words and punctuation—especially the punctuation ending the sentence—to signal mood. Think of the question mark as a raised eyebrow, the exclamation point as wide eyes and an open mouth, and the period as the neutral expression we usually wear.

55a Using Periods to End Statements and Mild Commands
使用句点结束陈述和语气温和的命令

Periods end most sentences, including statements (or *declarative sentences*), mild commands, and *indirect* (or reported) *questions.*

STATEMENT	Our library has survived a flood and two fires.
MILD COMMAND/ INSTRUCTION	Please urge the council to situate the new library building on higher ground.
INDIRECT QUESTION	She wondered whether the water had ever risen so fast before.

More about
Using periods with abbreviations, 469

Periods are also used with some, but not all, abbreviations.

55b Using Question Marks to End Direct (Not Indirect) Questions 使用问号结束直接（非间接）问句

Use a question mark to end a *direct question.*

> ▶ Which country has the highest life expectancy in the world?

> ▶ Did you know that life expectancy at birth in Japan is 82.17 years?

Use a period, not a question mark, to punctuate *indirect* questions—that is, questions that are reported, not asked directly.

> ▶ Dr. Wilson asked why life expectancy in Japan is so high.

Use a period, not a question mark, in requests phrased as questions.

> ▶ Would you please find out the life expectancy in the United States.

A question mark in parentheses can also suggest doubt about a date, number, or word.

> ▶ Life expectancy at birth in the United States is 78.24 years (?).

Note that capital letters are optional if each question is not a complete sentence.

You may also punctuate a series of questions with question marks, even when they are part of the same sentence.

> ▶ Which country has the fastest-growing economy? the highest average income? the lowest inflation rate?

Tech Using Exclamation Points in Email Messages

Because warmth can be difficult to convey in email, writers sometimes use an exclamation point to soften the tone. Compare:

- We look forward to seeing you next week.
- We look forward to seeing you next week!

Use exclamation points sparingly; otherwise, they lose their effectiveness.

Writing
Responsibly Question Marks and Exclamation Points

In an email to a friend, you might use a series of question marks or exclamation points to convey surprise or lend emphasis:

▶ Isn't it about time Joey got rid of the soul patch???!

But such techniques are not appropriate in more formal contexts, such as an email to an instructor:

▶ I look forward to studying American history with you next term.!!!!
                                                                      ∧

Overusing exclamation points or other punctuation may undermine your credibility with readers. Your responsibility to yourself as an authoritative writer is to use restraint.

to SELF

55c Using Exclamation Points with Strong Commands or to Express Excitement or Surprise
使用感叹号表示语气强烈的命令或表达兴奋或惊讶

When giving an emphatic command or expressing sudden excitement or surprise, use an exclamation point to end the sentence.

▶ Don't go there!

▶ "Mom is coming!"

The same sentence, when ended with a period, conveys much less urgency.

▶ Don't go there.

▶ "Mom is coming."

NOTE Overusing exclamation points, especially in more formal contexts, may undermine your credibility with readers.

56 Using Other Punctuation
Dashes, Parentheses, Brackets, Colons, Ellipses, and Slashes
使用其他标点符号
破折号、圆括号、方括号、冒号、省略号和斜杠

Writers thinking about punctuation typically focus on the comma, the semicolon, the period, and maybe the quotation mark—the star players on the punctuation team. But dashes, parentheses, brackets, colons, ellipses, and slashes also play key roles. Think of these other marks as the supporting players of punctuation: While you may call on them in only a limited number of situations, when needed, there is no better punctuation mark for the job.

56a Using Dashes to Set Off and Emphasize Information
用破折号引出和强调信息

Dashes lend emphasis to examples, explanations, and appositives. Use them singly when the information to be set off falls at the end of a sentence or in pairs when it falls in the middle.

▸ In almost every era of Western culture, women's clothing has been decidedly restrictive and uncomfortable—and the garments of the mid–nineteenth century are a prime example. *(example)*

▸ To be fashionable, women had to wear clothing that hampered their mobility—cumbersome petticoats and long dresses dragged in puddles and snagged on stairways, turning even a short walk into a navigational challenge. *(explanation)*

▸ In the 1870s another torture device—the bustle—was introduced. *(appositive)*

Dashes also emphasize contrasts, definitions, and items in a list.

More about
Apostrophes,
444–47

▸ The bustle, which emphasized a woman's backside, was considered erotic in its day—but from a modern perspective, it is quite modest. *(contrast)*

▸ For both daytime and evening wear, women were strapped into corsets—close-fitting undergarments that laced tightly around the torso. *(definition)*

▸ The trappings of mid-nineteenth-century dress—six petticoats, a long hem, a bulky bustle, and a tight corset—guaranteed women's discomfort. *(list)*

Dashes can also indicate a break in thought, speech, or tone.

▸ Women's dress today ranges from the restrained to the risqué—anything goes! *(break (tone))*

CAUTION If you use dashes more than once or twice over several pages, consider replacing one or more with commas: Overuse of dashes undermines their effectiveness.

Tech   Typing a Dash

The built-in keyboards on many phones and tablets do not have a single key for dashes, but you can type two hyphens (--) to represent the dash.

56b Enclosing Supplementary Information in Parentheses
在括号内附上补充信息

Use parentheses to set off supplementary information (such as examples, dates, abbreviations, or citations) to avoid distracting readers from the main point. Parentheses also enclose letters or numbers delineating items in a list.

▸ The English word for a trifling flaw or offense, *peccadillo,* comes from the Spanish word for a small sin, but many other borrowings

   from Spanish (*barbecue, chocolate, hammock, potato, tomato*)   examples actually originated in languages of the peoples whom the Spanish conquered in the Caribbean, Mexico, and South America.

▸ In 1991, the Spanish government founded the Instituto Cervantes (IC), named for Miguel de Cervantes (1547–1616), the author of *Don Quixote* (1605, 1615).   abbrev.   dates   dates

▸ The goals of the IC are (1) to promote the study of Spanish worldwide, (2) to improve the methods of teaching Spanish as a second language, and (3) to advance understanding of Spanish and Latin American cultures.   list item 1   list item 2   list item 3

▸ The proverb "Make hay while the sun shines" first appeared in *Don Quixote* (vol. 1, ch. 11).   citation

> Unless a complete sentence is enclosed, punctuation goes outside the closing parenthesis.

56c Using Brackets in Quotations and within Parentheses
在引文和圆括号内使用方括号

Square brackets have two primary uses—to indicate additions or changes to a quotation and to replace parentheses within parentheses.

▸ Ramo and Burke explain that "[i]n 1456, when the first Bible rolled off [Gutenberg's] press, there were fewer than 30,000 books in Europe."

▸ Only four years after Gutenberg printed his first book, the Spanish explorer Vincente Yanez Pinzón reached the mouth of the Amazon, which he called Río Santa María de la Mar Dulce ("River St. Mary of the Sweet [Freshwater] Sea").

Square brackets are also used to enclose the Latin word *sic,* which means *thus* or *so.* [*Sic*] is inserted into a quotation following an error to make clear that it was the original writer, not the person using the quotation, who made the mistake.

> **More about**
> Altering quotations with ellipses and brackets, 457, 460–61

> Capital replaced to fit quotation into writer's sentence.

> *Gutenberg's* replaces *his* in source for clarity.

> *Freshwater* added to explain an antiquated meaning of "sweet."

Writer uses *[sic]* to point out subject-verb agreement error (*are* should be *is*).

▸ The most compelling review noted that "each of these blockbusters are [sic] flawed in a different, and interesting, way."

NOTE The Modern Language Association (MLA) and the Council of Science Editors (CSE), on the one hand, do not recommend underlining or italicizing *sic*; *The Chicago Manual of Style* and the American Psychological Association (APA), on the other hand, do recommend italicizing this Latin word.

▶ **More about**
Independent clauses, 344–45, 353–54

56d Using Colons to Introduce Elaborating Material and Quotations 用冒号引出解释性信息和引文

A colon usually follows an independent clause to introduce and call attention to what follows. Colons are also used to separate titles from subtitles and in other conventional ways.

1. To introduce an example, explanation, appositive, or list 引出例子、解释、同位语和列举项

Use a colon following an independent (or main) clause to introduce an example, an explanation, an appositive, or a list.

▸ Cervantes was unlucky: At the battle of Lepanto, he lost the use of his left hand, and on the return journey, he was captured by Algerian pirates.
examples

When the colon introduces a second independent clause, as here, you can start the second clause with either a capital or a lowercase letter, but whichever you choose, be consistent in other similar situations.

▸ Writing *Don Quixote* gave its impoverished author something more than just satisfaction: the opportunity to make some money.
appositive

▸ A number of important writers died on April 23: Rupert Brooke, William Wordsworth, Miguel de Cervantes, and William Shakespeare.
list

A dash can substitute for a colon in these cases, but a colon is more appropriate in formal writing.

Writing Responsibly   Using *[sic]*

Use *[sic]* cautiously: Calling attention to an error simply to point out another writer's mistake can make you look impolite or even condescending and might undermine your reputation (or ethos) as a respectful writer. When you come across a simple typographical error in a passage you want to quote (the writer typed *teh* instead of *the*, for example), either paraphrase or correct the error.

to SELF

Colons are also used to introduce a list that is preceded by the phrases *as follows* or *the following*.

> list
> • The following writers all died on April 23: Rupert Brooke, William Wordsworth, Miguel de Cervantes, and William Shakespeare.

Do not introduce a list with a colon when the introductory clause concludes with *like, such as,* or *including*.

> • A number of important writers all died on April 23, including: Rupert Brooke, William Wordsworth, Miguel de Cervantes, and William Shakespeare.

▸ **More about**
Using commas in quotations, 439

2. To introduce a quotation 引出引文

Use a colon to introduce a quotation only when it is preceded by an independent clause that would make sense without it, but not when the quotation is introduced by a signal phrase such as *she said* or *Hughes asks*.

> ind. clause makes sense without quotation
> **COLON** In 1918, William Strunk, Jr., gave writers a piece of time-
>
> less advice: "Omit needless words."

> signal phrase needs quotation to make sense
> **COMMA** In 1918, William Strunk, Jr., said, "Omit needless words."

3. Other conventional uses 其他常规用法

■ Between title and subtitle and between publication date and page numbers (for periodicals) and location and publisher (for books) in bibliographic citations for some documentation styles

> title   subtitle
> DelRosso, Jeana. "De-tangling Motherhood: Adoption Narratives in Disney's *Tangled*."
>
> *The Journal of Popular Culture*.

> title   subtitle   publisher
> Satrapi, Marjane. *Persepolis 2: The Story of a Return*. Pantheon, 2004.

▸ **More about**
MLA style, 157–211 (part 6),
APA style, 213–54 (part 7),
Chicago style, 256–71 (ch. 27),
CSE style, 272–84 (ch. 28)

■ Following the salutation and following *cc* in formal business correspondence

> • Dear Professor Howard:
> • cc: June Carter

■ Between chapter and verse in scripture; between hours, minutes, and seconds; in ratios

> • Song of Solomon 3:1–11
> • 4:30 p.m.
> • Women outnumber men in college 2:1.

▸ **More about**
Business letter formats, 55–58

4. Common mistakes with colons 冒号的常见用法错误

- Do not insert a colon between a verb and its complement or object.

  ▸ Young readers awaited: the next volume in Stephenie Meyer's

    vampire love saga.

    (verb: awaited / object: the next volume...)

- Do not insert a colon between a preposition and its object.

  ▸ *Vogue* announced a return to: hippie-style clothing.

    (prep.: to / object: hippie-style clothing)

56e Using Ellipses to Indicate Deletions in Quotations and Dramatic Pauses in Dialog
用省略号表示引文中的删除和对话中的戏剧性停顿

An *ellipsis* is a deliberate omission of a portion of a quotation. The word *ellipsis* (plural: *ellipses*) also refers to the punctuation used to mark an omission: a set of three periods—or *ellipsis points*—with a space between each. Ellipses are also sometimes used to indicate a dramatic pause or to suggest that the writer is unable or unwilling to say something.

1. To indicate deletions from quotations 表示引文中的删除

Although it is not acceptable to alter the meaning of a quotation, writers can and do omit words from quotations as needed to delete irrelevant information or to make a quotation fit into their own sentence. The ellipsis alerts readers that a change has been made.

> Use four dots—a period plus the ellipsis—if a deletion occurs at the end of the sentence.

- ▸ *Don Quixote* begins like a fable: "In a village of La Mancha, . . .
  (comma + ellipsis)
  there lived not long since one of those gentlemen that keep a lance, . . .
  (comma + ellipsis)
  a lean hack, . . . and an old greyhound for coursing. . . ."
  (comma + ellipsis) *(period + ellipsis)*

With a parenthetical citation, insert the ellipsis before the closing quotation marks and the period after the citation.

- ▸ "They will have it his surname was Quixada . . ." (1).
  (ellipsis + closing quote) *(citation + period)*

> **More about**
> Altering quotations, 144–45, 457–58, 460–61

Quotations of only a few words or that begin with a lowercase letter are obviously taken from a longer original and do not require ellipses.

Writing Responsibly — Altering Quotations

Exercise care when changing quotations with brackets or ellipses: Never make a change that might distort the original or that might mislead readers, and always use ellipses and brackets to indicate alterations.

to OTHER WRITERS

Similarly, a quotation of an entire sentence does not need ellipses to indicate that it comes from within a longer passage.

When quoting poetry, use not a single ellipsis mark (three dots) but a whole line of dots to replace one or more missing lines.

> One of the most famous lines in Robert Frost's poem "Mending Wall" is "Good fences make good neighbors," but the speaker's meaning is lost when this line is taken out of context:
>
> There where it is we do not need the wall:
> ....
> My apple trees will never get across
> And eat the cones under his pines, I tell him.
> He only says, "Good fences make good neighbors." (lines 23–27)

2. To indicate a dramatic pause or interruption in dialog
表示对话中的戏剧性停顿或中断

An ellipsis can indicate an incomplete thought, a dramatic pause, or an interruption in speech.

> The disgruntled writer muttered, "The only word to describe my editor is . . . unprintable."

56f Using Slashes in Verse, Fractions, and URLs
在诗歌、分数和网址中使用斜杠

The slash (or *virgule*) is used to mark the ends of lines in poetry when the poetry is run into a sentence. Insert a space on either side of the slash.

> *Don Quixote* opens with some "commendatory verses" that warn the writer "Whoso indites frivolities, / Will but by simpletons be sought" (lines 62–63).

Slashes are also used in fractions and URLs. For these uses, do not insert a space around the slash.

> 1/2   1/3   3/4
> www.unh.edu/writing/cwc/handouts

In informal contexts, the slash is sometimes used to indicate that either of two terms is applicable.

> I've got so many courses this semester that I decided to take Spanish pass/fail.

In more formal contexts (such as academic or business writing), replace the slash with the word *or*, or rewrite the sentence.

> The test consisted entirely of ~~true/false~~ *true or false* questions.

Text Credit
p. 461 Frost, Robert, "Mending Wall," *North of Boston* (1914).

57 Capitalizing 大写

Like a spire soaring over surrounding rooftops, a capital letter beckons the reader, calling attention to the word it adorns. But just as architecture varies from place to place, so the rules of capitalization vary from language to language. This chapter summarizes the most important rules of capitalization in English.

Capitalization English capitalization can be confusing to people for whom English is a foreign language. In Spanish, French, and German, the first-person singular pronoun is lowercased (*yo, je, ich*), but in English it is capitalized (*I*), although the other personal pronouns (*she, he, it, they*) are not. In Spanish and French, the names of months and days of the week are lowercased, but not in English. In German, all nouns are capitalized, but in English only proper nouns are. Languages such as Arabic and Korean have no capital letters at all. Proofread your work carefully to adhere to the conventions of English capitalization, referring to this chapter and a good college dictionary as needed.

Quick Reference   Common Capitalization Do's and Don'ts

***Do* capitalize ...**

. . . the first word of a sentence. (463)
▶ The day broke gray and dull. —Somerset Maugham, *Of Human Bondage*

. . . proper nouns and proper adjectives. (465)
▶ Aunt Julia, Beijing, Dad (used as a name), Band-Aid, Shakespearean, Texan

. . . the first, last, and important words in titles and subtitles. (465)
▶ *Avengers: Age of Ultron*

. . . the first-person pronoun *I*. (465)
▶ I think; therefore, I am. —René Descartes

. . . abbreviations and acronyms. (465)
▶ Eng. Dept., UCLA, NYPD

Do *not* capitalize . . .

. . . common nouns and common adjectives. (464)
▶ dog, cat, aunt, city, my dad, bandage

. . . compass directions. (464)
▶ north, south, northwest, southeast

. . . seasons or academic years and terms. (464)
▶ spring, freshman, intersession

57a Capitalizing the First Word of a Sentence 大写句子的第一个单词

Capitalize the first letter of the first word of every sentence.

▸ In response to Franklin Roosevelt's long tenure, the US Congress passed an amendment limiting a president to two terms.

This rule applies even to sentences in parentheses, unless they are incorporated into another sentence.

▸ His vice president, Harry S. Truman, decided not to run for reelection, although the amendment did not apply to him. (The sitting president was exempted.)

▸ Although the amendment did not apply to him (the sitting president was exempted), Truman decided not to run for reelection.

> **More about**
> Parentheses, 457

Capitalize the first word of a sentence you are quoting, even when it is incorporated into your own sentence.

▸ In response to a question about the amendment, President Eisenhower said, "By and large, the United States ought to be able to choose for its president anybody that it wants, regardless of the number of terms he has served."

Do not capitalize the first word when you are quoting only a phrase.

▸ President Eisenhower's "faith in the long-term common sense of the American people" made him feel the amendment was unnecessary.

When interrupting a quoted sentence, do not capitalize the first word of the second part.

▸ "By and large," Eisenhower said, "the United States ought to be able to choose for its president anybody that it wants, regardless of the number of terms he has served."

NOTE In MLA style, if you must change a capital to a lowercase letter (or vice versa) to incorporate a quotation into your sentence, place brackets around the letter to alert readers to the change.

> **More about**
> Brackets, 457–58
> Altering quotations, 144–45, 457–58, 460–61

If a colon links two *independent clauses*, the second clause can begin with a capital letter or not. Whichever option you choose, apply it consistently.

▸ Our company is at a crossroads: We must adapt to new conditions.

or

▸ Our company is at a crossroads: we must adapt to new conditions.

> **independent (or main) clause** 独立分句 A clause that can stand alone as a sentence

Reference   Capitalizing Proper Nouns and Proper Adjectives

	Proper Nouns and Proper Adjectives	Common Nouns and Common Adjectives
Departments and Disciplines	Political Science Department	political science
Historical Events, Eras, and Documents	Korean War, Roaring Twenties, the Emancipation Proclamation	the war, the twenties, the proclamation
Nations, Ethnic Groups, Races, and Languages	Pakistan, Pakistani, African American, Swahili	her country, his nationality, their language
Organizations, Offices, and Companies	National Wildlife Federation, Government Accountability Office, National Broadcasting Corporation	a conservation group, the legislative branch, the network, the corporation
People and Titles	Lewis and Clark, Senator Bob Corker, Dickens, Dickensian	the expedition leaders, the senator, the author, satirical
Places, Compass Directions	Central Park, Neptune, the Northwest	the park, an outer planet, northwest
Religions, Sacred Texts, and Religious Terms	Buddhism, Presbyterian, Vedas, Bible, God	your religion, denominational, a sacred text, biblical, the gods
Time Periods and Holidays	Tuesday, June, Memorial Day	a weekday, this summer, spring break
Trade Names and Products	Coke, Kleenex, Google	a soda, a tissue, a search engine
Vessels, Vehicles, and Modes of Transportation	U.S.S. *Constitution*, Greyhound, Amtrak	this battleship, a bus, the train

Writing
Responsibly   Capitalizing in Email and IM

The rules of capitalization are usually the same online as they are in print. But while in print a writer may sometimes type a word in all capital letters for emphasis, in email or other online contexts, words typed in all capital letters are interpreted as shouting. When formatting is available, use italics (or boldface type) for emphasis in online writing; when such formatting is unavailable, place an asterisk before and after the word you want to emphasize. Also, although omitting capital letters in email and instant messages may be acceptable in informal contexts, to maintain a professional tone you should follow the rules of capitalization when texting or emailing in business or academic settings.

to SELF

57b Capitalizing Proper Nouns and Proper Adjectives
大写专有名词和专有形容词

Capitalize the first letter of *proper nouns* (the names of specific people, places, and things) and the adjectives derived from them. Do not capitalize common nouns (names for general groups of people, places, and things) or common adjectives. The Quick Reference guide on previous page provides examples of words in each group.

57c Capitalizing Titles and Subtitles 大写标题和副标题

In most cases, capitalize the first and last words of titles and subtitles, as well as any other important words: nouns (*Pride, Persuasion*), verbs (*Is, Ran*), pronouns (*It, Their*), adjectives (*Green, Starry*), and adverbs (*Slow, Extremely*). Do not capitalize prepositions (*in, at, to, by*), coordinating conjunctions (*and, but, for, nor, or, so, yet*), *to* in infinitive verbs, or articles (*a, an, the*) unless they begin or end the title or subtitle or are part of the title of a periodical (*The New Yorker, The New York Times*).

Go Set a Watchman: A Novel (novel)	"Uptown Funk" (song)
"In the Basement of the Ivory Tower" (article)	*The Dark Knight* (movie)
Pokémon XD: Gale of Darkness (game)	Flying Popcorn (software)

NOTE Style guides may recommend different capitalization for titles and subtitles in reference lists and bibliographies. Check the style guide you are using and follow the rules described there.

> **More about**
> MLA style, 157–211 (part 6)
> APA style, 213–54 (part 7)
> *Chicago* style, 256–71 (ch. 27)
> CSE style, 272–84 (ch. 28)

57d Capitalizing the First-Person Pronoun *I*
大写第一人称代词 "I"

In all formal contexts, capitalize the first-person singular pronoun *I*.

▸ I wish I could meet myself in twenty years.

57e Capitalizing Abbreviations and Acronyms 大写缩略词和首字母缩略词

Abbreviations of proper nouns should be capitalized, and acronyms should be typed in all capital letters.

ABBREVIATIONS	U. of Mich., Anthro. Dept.
ACRONYMS	RADAR, NASA, OPEC

> **More about**
> Abbreviations, 469–71

> **acronym** 首字母缩略词
> Word formed from the first letter of each major word in a name

58 Italics and Underlining 斜体和下画线

Before the computer, writers typed on typewriters and used underlining to emphasize words; to set off the titles of longer works; to distinguish words, letters, and numbers used as words; to set off unfamiliar non-English words; and to call out the names of ships, airplanes, spacecraft, and other vehicles. Now writers type on computers and use italics for these purposes.

58a Italicizing Titles of Long Works 长篇作品的标题用斜体

More about
Using quotation marks with titles of shorter works, 450

Use italics (or underlining) for titles of long works such as books, periodicals (magazines, journals, and newspapers), films, CDs, television series, and websites; use quotation marks for short works, such as stories, articles, songs, television episodes, and web pages.

> Annie Proulx's collection *Close Range: Wyoming Stories* includes the story "Brokeback Mountain," which originally appeared in *The New Yorker* magazine. Kenneth Turan, critic for *The Los Angeles Times,* called the 2005 film *Brokeback Mountain* "groundbreaking," and Roger Ebert of *The Chicago Sun-Times* gave it two thumbs up. The *Brokeback Mountain* soundtrack includes songs like "He Was a Friend of Mine" by Willie Nelson and "The Devil's Right Hand" by Steve Earle.

In addition, the titles of stand-alone items like court cases and works of art (paintings and sculptures) are italicized.

- *Bowers v. Hardwick*
- *Mona Lisa*
- *The Bronco Buster*

In contrast, the titles of major historical documents and religious works are not italicized.

- Magna Carta, Mayflower Compact, Kyoto Protocol
- Bible, Qur'an, Vedas

Writing Responsibly | Using Italics for Emphasis

When using italics for emphasis, consider your reader. Sometimes italics can help convey the writer's feelings, but will readers be interested? In a personal context, the following use of italics might be acceptable:

- Should *I* call *him*, or should I wait for *him* to call *me*?

In contrast, such emphasis on the writer's emotions is usually inappropriate in a business or academic context.

to AUDIENCE

58b Italicizing for Emphasis Sparingly 适当使用斜体，表示强调

Italics are sometimes used for emphasis.

> ▸ Rowling wants readers to *identify* with Harry, not merely to *sympathize* with him.

In this sentence, the italics heighten attention to the contrast. To be effective, italics must be used sparingly for emphasis. Using italics haphazardly or overusing them can annoy or even confuse readers.

58c Italicizing Names of Vehicles 交通工具名称用斜体

The names of individual trains, ships, aircraft, and spacecraft are all italicized.

> ▸ *Titanic, Spirit of St. Louis, Challenger*

However, vehicles referred to by company, brand, or model names are not.

> ▸ Corvette, Boeing 747

Quick

Reference　**Common Italics Do's and Don'ts**

Do use italics . . .

. . . with titles of long works. (466)

> ▸ We will be discussing the novel *Wuthering Heights* for the next two weeks. By the way, the novel's main character has nothing to do with the comic strip *Heathcliff.*

. . . for emphasis. (467)

> ▸ I ask you *not* to read beyond the first chapter until we have discussed it in class.

(Use italics for emphasis sparingly in academic prose.)

. . . with words, letters, or numbers used as words. (468)

> ▸ You will notice that several of the characters' names begin with the letter *h;* this can be confusing.

Do *not* use italics . . .

. . . with titles of short works. (466)

> ▸ Jamaica Kincaid's story ~~*Girl*~~ "Girl" is only one page long.

. . . with historical documents and religious works. (466)

> ▸ The ~~*Declaration of Independence*~~ Declaration of Independence and the ~~*Bible*~~ Bible take pride of place on my grandmother's bookshelf.

. . . with links to websites and web pages (underline if a hyperlink). (468)

> ▸ If you do not want to buy the book discussed in Salon.com, you can download it from Project Gutenberg <www.gutenberg.org/etext/768>.

58d Italicizing Words, Letters, or Numbers Used as Words
具有单词意义的单词、字母或数字用斜体

When referring to words, letters, or numbers used as words, set them off from the rest of the sentence with italics.

More about
Plurals of letters, 447

▸ My chemistry instructor used the word *interesting* to describe the results I got on my last lab. He told me to be more careful next time to dot all my *i*'s and cross all my *t*'s.

58e Italicizing Unfamiliar Non-English Words and Latin Genus and Species Names
不熟悉的非英语词与拉丁属和物种的名称用斜体

English is an opportunistic language: When encountering new things or ideas, English speakers often adopt words already used in other languages. The word *raccoon,* for example, comes from Algonquian and the word *sushi* from Japanese. Once they are fully absorbed, borrowed words are typed with no special formatting. Until then, borrowings should be italicized.

▸ The review provides a good example of *diegesis* in that it describes the film without making a judgment about it.

To determine whether a non-English word warrants italics, check your dictionary: Words familiar enough to be found in a college dictionary should not be italicized.

Latin genus and species names are also italicized.

▸ The Latin term *Acer saccharum* identifies the genus and species of the sugar maple.

58f Underlining Hyperlinks 超链接用下画线

In recent years, underlining has taken on a new, specialized meaning: It is used (along with color) to indicate hyperlinks in both printed and online documents. Because many documents today will ultimately appear online, writers are increasingly reserving underlining for hyperlinks and are using italics for all the other purposes outlined in this chapter.

▸ The Library of Congress website (www.loc.gov) has a wealth of digital resources.

59 Using Abbreviations 使用缩写

When you see this familiar symbol, you know at a glance that the object it adorns was made from recyclable materials. When they are familiar to an audience, icons like this one communicate information briefly and quickly. Abbreviations accomplish a similar goal in writing: They convey information rapidly but only when readers know what they stand for. Although they are used frequently in business, scientific, and technical contexts, abbreviations are used sparingly in writing in the humanities and for a general audience, except in tables (where space is at a premium) and in bibliographic citations.

When you do abbreviate, use a period with a person's initials and with most abbreviations that end in lowercase letters:

‣ J. K. Rowling   Perry Mason, Esq.   Blvd.   Ave.

Use a period after each letter with abbreviations of more than one word:

‣ i.e.   e.g.   a.m.   p.m.

Most abbreviations made up of all capital letters no longer use periods:

‣ BS   MA   DVD   UN

59a Abbreviating Titles before and after Names
人名前后的头衔用缩写

‣ Mr. Mike Moore   Christopher Aviles, PhD

‣ Ms. Aoife Shaughnessy   Namazi Hamid, DDS

‣ Dr. Jonnelle Price   Robert Min, MD

‣ Rev. Jane Genung   Frederick C. Copelston, SJ

In most cases, avoid abbreviating titles when they are not used with a proper name.

‣ I'm hoping my English prof. *professor* will write me a letter of recommendation.

Academic degrees are an exception.

‣ My auto mechanic comes from a highly educated family: His father has an MS, his mother has an MLS, and his sister has a PhD.

Never use a title both before and after a name: Change *Dr. Hazel L. Cunningham, PhD* to either *Dr. Hazel L. Cunningham* or *Hazel L. Cunningham, PhD*.

59b Using Acronyms and Initialisms Appropriately 适当使用首字母缩略词（分别按单词拼读和按字母读音读两种）

Acronyms and *initialisms* are abbreviations made of all capital letters formed from the first letters of a series of words. Acronyms are pronounced as words (*AIDS, CARE, NASA, NATO, OPEC*), while initialisms are pronounced as a series of letters (*DNA, HBO, JFK, USA*). Familiar acronyms and initialisms are acceptable in any context.

> ▸ The UN Security Council met to discuss a response to North Korea's nuclear tests.

However, if the abbreviation is likely to be unfamiliar to readers, spell out the term on first use and follow it with the abbreviation in parentheses. Subsequently, just use the abbreviation.

> ▸ The International Olympic Committee (IOC) failed to take action following the arrest of two elderly Chinese women who had applied for permission to protest in the designated protest areas during the Beijing Olympics. A spokesperson claimed that the IOC has no control over the protest areas.

59c Using Abbreviations with Specific Years (BC, BCE, AD, CE), Hours (a.m., p.m.), Numbers (no.), and Dollars ($) 使用特殊年份（BC、BCE、AD、CE）、钟点（a.m.、p.m.）、编号（no.）和货币单位的缩略式（$）

AD precedes the year; BC, BCE, and CE follow the year.

> ▸ The emperor Augustus ruled Rome from 27 BCE until his death in 14 CE.

> ▸ The Roman historian Titus Livius (known as Livy) lived from 59 BC until AD 17.

Writing Responsibly | Using Online Abbreviations Appropriately

A new breed of initialism has emerged in online discourse. Here are some examples:

BFN (bye for now)	OIC (oh, I see!)
IDK (I don't know)	OTOH (on the other hand)
IMO (in my opinion)	ROTFL (rolling on the floor, laughing)
LOL (laughing out loud)	TMI (too much information!)

The irreverence of some of these initialisms corresponds with the casual tone of online discourse. Use them in text messages or on informal networking sites, but avoid them in college and professional writing, including emails. While they might establish your online savvy or serve as a handy shorthand, they might also annoy readers in more formal contexts, undermining your credibility.

to SELF

▸ I didn't get home until 11:45 p.m. because the no. 27 bus was
so late.

▸ I owe my sister $27.32, and she won't let me forget it.

NOTE The abbreviations BCE (for *before the common era*) and CE (for
common era) are now generally preferred over BC (*before Christ*) and AD
(*anno domini*, "the year of the Lord" in Latin).

59d **Avoiding, in Prose, Abbreviating Names, Words, Courses,
Parts of Books, States and Countries, Days and Months,
Holidays, and Units of Measurement** 避免在散文中使用人
名、单词、课程、书的章节、国家、日期、假期和度量单位的
缩写

▸ In *France,* Fr., people receive gifts not on *Christmas* Xmas but on *January* Jan. 6.

▸ On *Monday* Mon. mornings, *Psychology* Psych. 121 meets in a tiny classroom: It is
only ten *feet* ft. wide.

▸ My *English* Eng. teacher, *Elizabeth* Eliz. Santos, recommends that we always read
the *introduction* intro. first.

An exception is the names of businesses, when the abbreviation is part
of the official name:

▸ Dun & Bradstreet, Inc., was *incorporated* inc. in New York *and* & is still located
there.

59e **Replacing Latin Abbreviations with English Equivalents in
Formal Prose** 在正式的散文中，用英语缩写代替拉丁文缩写

Generally, avoid Latin abbreviations, like those below, in formal writing
(except in bibliographies).

▸ e.g.　for example　　　▸ cf.　compare

▸ i.e.　in other words　　▸ et al.　and others

▸ etc.　and so forth　　　▸ N.B.　note especially

NOTE Both *etc.* and *and so forth* are best avoided in formal prose.
Instead, include all the items or precede a partial list with *such as* or *for
example*. Follow *e.g.* and *i.e.* with a comma if you use them in tables or
parenthetical material. Common Latin abbreviations are not italicized
or underlined.

60

Using Numbers 使用数字

Are we "number one" or "#1"? It depends on the context. Rules for deciding whether to use numerals or to spell out numbers vary widely according to context. In business and the news, single-digit numbers are usually spelled out, while numerals are used for numbers over ten. The rules in this chapter are appropriate to an academic audience in the humanities.

60a Spelling Out Numbers When They Can Be Expressed in One or Two Words 当数字可以用一个或两个单词来表达时，拼写出完整的单词

Spell out numbers under one hundred and round numbers—numbers that can be expressed in one or two words.

▸ Satchel Paige pitched sixty-four scoreless innings and won twenty-one games in a row.

If your text uses a combination of numbers—some that can be expressed in one or two words and others that cannot—use numerals throughout for consistency's sake.

▸ Satchel Paige pitched an estimated ~~two thousand~~ *2,000* baseball games during his career. At his first game, 78,383 fans were in attendance, and at his first game as a starter, 72,434 spectators looked on.

Avoid beginning a sentence with numerals. Instead, spell out the number or revise your sentence.

▸ *Seventy-eight thousand* ~~78,000~~ people attended Satchel Paige's first game as a pitcher.

▸ Satchel Paige's first game as a pitcher drew 78,000 fans.

Writing Responsibly | Ethos and Convention

Using numbers and symbols in conventional ways does not normally affect meaning. Yet conventional usage is important, especially in formal contexts like school or the workplace, because it lends support to your ethos, or credibility. The way you use numbers and symbols can subtly affect the way your audience perceives you and, in turn, how seriously they take what you say.

to SELF

> **More about**
> Appropriate language, 303–08
> Ethos, 75

Numbers over a million are often best expressed as a combination of words and numerals.

▸ More than 10 million fans attended Negro League baseball games in 1930.

60b **Following Conventions for Dates, Times, Addresses, Specific Amounts of Money and Other Quantitative Information, and Divisions of Literary Works**
遵循日期、时间、地址、具体金额和其他定量信息以及文学作品划分的惯例

- **Dates:** May 4, 2017   the fourth of May   429 BCE   1066 CE   AD 1066

- **Times, years:** 4:15 p.m.   seven o'clock   1990s   the nineties   1999–2017   from 1999 to 2017

- **Phone numbers, addresses:** (800) 555-5789
  26 Peachtree Lane   221 W. 34th Street
  Atlanta, GA 30303   New York, NY 10001

- **Exact sums of money:** $10.95 $579.89 $24 million

- **Decimals and fractions:** half   ½   three-quarters   ¾   4⅝   3.95

NOTE MLA style generally recommends using the percent symbol (%) with numerals. *The Chicago Manual of Style* recommends using the word *percent* with numerals in writing for the humanities and the symbol % with numerals in writing for the sciences.

- **Scores, statistics, and percentages:** 5 to 4   42–28   13.3 percent (or 13.3%)   3 out of 10

- **Measurements:** 55 mph   90–100 rpm   135 pounds   5 feet   9 liters   41°F

- **Divisions of books, plays, poems:** part 3   book 7   chapter 15   page 419 or p. 419   act 1   scene 3   lines 4–19

Punctuating Numbers in American English Conventions for punctuating numbers differ across cultures. In many European countries, for instance, commas separate whole numbers from decimal fractions, where periods mark divisions of thousands. In the United States, the convention is reversed:

▸ 2,541   94.7

61

Mastering Spelling and Hyphenation
掌握拼写和连字符

RED

GREEN

BLUE

In a well-known experiment, psychologists found that people have little difficulty when asked simply to read the words in the box shown here, yet they have a lot of trouble when asked to identify the color of ink each word is printed in. We absorb the meaning of each word alone automatically, but when we try to identify the ink color, we get confused because the color conflicts with the word's meaning. Readers similarly process most correctly spelled words automatically but get distracted or confused by misspelled words. If you want readers to pay attention to your ideas rather than to struggle to decipher your meaning word by word, you should check your spelling carefully.

61a Distinguishing Homonyms and Other Problem Words
区分同音异义词和其他问题词

Many spelling errors result from confusion over homonyms and near-homonyms.

> *Homonyms* are groups of words that sound exactly alike but have different spellings and meanings, such as *to/too/two* and *cite/sight/site*.

> *Near-homonyms* are groups of words such as *personal/personnel* and *conscience/conscious* that are close but not the same in pronunciation. Near-homonyms also include different forms of the same word, such as *breath/breathe* and *advice/advise*.

> **More about**
> Confusing words and phrases in "Glossary of Usage," 318–23

There is no easy formula for mastering these words. If any of them give you trouble, try to memorize their spellings and meanings, and always check for them as you proofread your writing.

Use American Rather Than British Spelling Multilingual writers who began their study of English outside the United States may be accustomed to British spelling, which is often different from American. For example, Americans fly in *airplanes* (not in *aeroplanes*), and they pay bills with *checks* (not *cheques*). Some writers striving for formality mistakenly believe that British spellings are preferable. If you are writing for a US audience, be sure to follow American spelling. When in doubt, consult an American dictionary, which will give the preferred American spelling before any alternatives.

61b Remembering Spelling Rules 牢记拼写规则

Mastering a few key rules—and noting their exceptions—can improve the accuracy of your spelling.

1. The *ie/ei* rule ie/ei的拼写规则

The traditional rule—"*i* before *e* except after *c* or when sounded like *ay* as in *neighbor* and *weigh*"—will help you spell words like *believe, receive,* and *sleigh* correctly.

I BEFORE *E*   diesel, piece, pier, retrieve, shield, siege

E BEFORE *I* / AFTER *C* ceiling, conceit, conceive, deceit, perceive, receipt

EI SOUNDS LIKE *AY*   beige, deign, eighteen, reindeer, sleigh, veil

Some exceptions: *feisty, forfeit, heifer, height, heir, neither, protein, sovereign, seize, their, weird.*

2. Suffixes 后缀

Suffixes attach to the end of a root word to change its meaning and grammatical form.

Words that end with a silent e In most instances, drop the silent *e* if the suffix starts with a vowel.

observe → observant   response → responsible   revoke → revoked

Retain the silent *e* if the suffix starts with a consonant.

hope → hopeful   love →lovely   polite → politeness

Some exceptions: *advantageous, argument, judgment, serviceable.*

Words that end in y For most words that end in a consonant and *y*, change the *y* to an *i* when you add a suffix.

apology → apologize   deny → denies
heavy → heavier   merry → merriment

Writing Responsibly   Spelling Errors

A misspelled word is not an important issue when you are texting friends, but in other situations it may signal that you are careless about details. If you misspell *accountant* in a job-application letter to a financial firm, for example, the recipient may wonder how accurate you are about numbers. If you misspell a name, people may interpret it as a sign of indifference or disrespect.

to SELF

Retain the *y* if the suffix is *-ing,* if a vowel precedes the *y,* or if the word ending in *y* is a proper name.

spy → spy<u>ing</u>	play → play<u>ful</u>	McCoy → McCoy<u>s</u>

Suffixes *-ally* versus *-ly* and *-efy* versus *-ify* When a word ends in *ic,* use the suffix *-ally.* In all other instances, use *-ly.*

basi<u>c</u> → basic<u>ally</u>	magi<u>c</u> → magic<u>ally</u>
brisk → brisk<u>ly</u>	confident → confident<u>ly</u>

Only four words use the suffix *-efy: liquefy, putrefy, rarefy, stupefy.* All other such words use the suffix *-ify: beautify, certify, justify, purify.*

Words that end with a consonant Do not double a final consonant if the suffix begins with a consonant (*commitment, fearless, kinship, poorly*). For suffixes that begin with a vowel, follow these guidelines:

- **One-syllable root words.** Double the final consonant if only one vowel precedes it; otherwise, do not double the consonant.

bit → bit<u>t</u>en	chat → chat<u>t</u>y	skip → skip<u>p</u>ing
chart → char<u>t</u>ed	droop → droo<u>p</u>ing	speak → spea<u>k</u>er

- **Multisyllable words.** Double the final consonant if only one vowel precedes it and if the final syllable of the root is accented in the new word containing the suffix.

admit → ad**mit**tance	concur → con**cur**rent

For multisyllable words that do not meet these criteria, do not double the final consonant.

devil → devi<u>l</u>ish	proclaim → proclai<u>m</u>ing

61c **Forming Plurals Correctly** 复数的正确拼法

To form the plural of most English nouns, add an *-s.*

letter → letter<u>s</u>	shoe → shoe<u>s</u>	Erickson → the Erickson<u>s</u>

To form the plural of nouns that end in *s, sh, ch, x,* or *z,* add *-es.*

miss → miss<u>es</u>	dish → dish<u>es</u>	latch → latch<u>es</u>
box → box<u>es</u>	quartz → quartz<u>es</u>	Davis → the Davis<u>es</u>

To form the plural of some nouns that end in *f* or *fe,* change the *f* to a *v* and add *-s* or *-es.*

knife → kni<u>ves</u>	loaf → loa<u>ves</u>

However, words that end in *ff* or *ffe* and some words that end in *f* or *fe* form the plural just with the addition of an *-s.*

bluff → bluff<u>s</u>	giraffe → giraffe<u>s</u>	safe → safe<u>s</u>

To form the plural of nouns that end in *o*, add *-s* if the *o* is preceded by a vowel or if the word is a proper noun. Add *-es* if the *o* is preceded by a consonant.

duo → duos	ratio → ratios	video → videos
echo → echoes	potato → potatoes	veto → vetoes

Some exceptions: *autos, ponchos, sopranos, tacos.*

To form the plural of words that end in *y*, add *-s* if the *y* is preceded by a vowel or if the word is a proper noun.

decoy → decoys	essay → essays	Hagarty → the Hagartys

Change the *y* to *i* and add *-es* if the *y* is preceded by a consonant.

berry → berries	enemy → enemies	family → families

Irregular plurals The only way to learn irregular plurals is to memorize them. Many nouns have irregular plurals that have survived from earlier forms of English.

woman → women	child → children	deer → deer

Other nouns with irregular plurals were borrowed into English from languages such as Greek, Latin, and French and retain the plural form of the original language.

alumna → alumnae	analysis → analyses	criterion → criteria

Plurals of compound nouns To form the plural of compound nouns composed of separate or hyphenated words, add *-s* or *-es* to the main noun in the compound.

brigadier generals	chiefs of staff	runners-up

An exception: *passersby.*

Tech Use Spelling Checkers Cautiously

Most of today's word processing programs correct some misspelled words while you type, identify other words that may be misspelled, and let you run a manual spelling check whenever you wish. Although these features are helpful, you cannot depend on them alone to guarantee error-free spelling. Spelling checkers, for example, do not differentiate homonyms and commonly confused words such as *descent, dissent* or *too, two*. If you type a correctly spelled word that happens not to be correct for the context, a spelling checker will not mark it wrong.

Spelling checkers, then, are a useful tool but not a replacement for a dictionary and careful proofreading. Check the spelling checker.

61d Using Hyphens to Form Compounds 使用连字符构成复合词

1. Hyphenate compound adjectives. 用连字符连接复合形容词。

Hyphenate compound adjectives when they precede the noun but not when they follow it.

- The well-intentioned *efforts* [noun] by the International Olympic Committee (IOC) to allow peaceful protests were blocked by some countries.
- The *efforts* [noun] of the IOC to allow peaceful protests were well-intentioned but ill-conceived.

When an adverb ending in *-ly* is part of a compound adjective, no hyphen is necessary.

- In some countries, politically-sensitive websites are blocked by the government.

When two or more parallel compound adjectives share the same base word, avoid repetition by putting a space after the first hyphen and stating the base word only once.

- Class- and race-based analyses of *To Kill a Mockingbird* show that Harper Lee was not completely able to rise above her social background.

2. Link prefixes and suffixes to root words. 词根加上前缀和后缀。

In general, hyphens are not needed to attach prefixes and suffixes to the root word.

*de*compress	*pre*test	*re*define	*sub*category

But the prefixes *all-*, *ex-*, and *self-* and the suffix *-elect* are always attached to the root word with a hyphen.

- *all*-star   *ex*-boyfriend   *self*-absorbed   president-*elect*

In most cases, to avoid double- or triple-letter combinations, add a hyphen.

- *anti*-inflationary   *multi*-institutional   *re*-education   ball-*like*

Some exceptions: *override, cooperate.*

If the prefix will be attached to a numeral or to a root that begins with a capital letter, insert a hyphen.

- post-1914   pre-1945   anti-Semite   un-American

Finally, if the prefix-plus-root combination could be misread as another word, add a hyphen to avoid confusion.

- He finally recovered from a bout of the flu.
- We re-covered the sofa with a floral fabric.

3. Use hyphens in numbers, number ranges, and scores.
连字符在数字、数值范围和得分中的用法。

Numbers over twenty and under one hundred are hyphenated when written out.

- Workaholics would work twenty-four hours a day, seven days a week, fifty-two weeks a year if their bodies would cooperate.

A hyphen can replace the words *from* and *to* with dates.

- The years from 1919 to 1938 offered a brief respite between the two world wars.

  or

- The years 1919–1938 offered a brief respite between the two world wars.

But do not combine methods.

- from 1919–1938   or   ~~from~~ 1919–1938

In sports scores, use a hyphen between numbers instead of *to*.

- The Vikings lost to the Bengals 23-17.

61e Using Hyphens to Break Words at the Ends of Lines
行尾使用连字符，方便单词跨行

Most word processing programs automatically move a too-long word from the end of one line to the beginning of the next or break the word between lines with a hyphen. To break words manually or to check words you think your word processor may have broken incorrectly, follow these rules:

- Break words between syllables. (Check your dictionary for syllable breaks.)

  - CIA operatives in the Middle East have found it impossible to infiltrate al Qaeda.

Tech   Breaking URLs and Email Addresses

Most word processing programs offer automatic hyphenation of words. However, you must break URLs or email addresses manually. If you are following MLA or CSE style guidelines, break URLs after a slash but before other punctuation. If you are following APA guidelines, break URLs before most punctuation (except the *://* following *http*). If you are following *Chicago Manual* guidelines, break a URL or email address before a period or other punctuation, or after the @ symbol, a single or double slash, or a colon. Do *not* insert a hyphen when a URL breaks to the next line.

■ Break compound words between parts or after hyphens.

> ▸ Washington, DC's long-standing handgun ban was ~~overturn~~*over-* ~~ed~~*turned* in 2008 by the Supreme Court.

■ Do not break one-syllable words or contractions.

> ▸ To determine surface area, multiply the ~~wid~~*width* ~~th~~ of a room by its length.

■ Break words so that at least two letters remain at the end of a line and at least three letters move down to the beginning of the next line.

> ▸ Increases in the cost of gas and food have ~~reduc~~*re-* ~~ed~~*duced* discretionary spending.